D0138779

Great Lives from History

Notorious Lives

Great Lives from History

Notorious Lives

Volume 1

Sani Abacha - Gary Gilmore

Editor
Carl L. Bankston III
Tulane University

SALEM PRESS
Pasadena, California   Hackensack, New Jersey

Editor in Chief: Dawn P. Dawson

Editorial Director: Christina J. Moose
Acquisitions Editor: Mark Rehn
Research Supervisor: Jeffry Jensen
Manuscript Editors: Sarah M. Hilbert
Elizabeth Ferry Slocum

Production Editor: Joyce I. Buchea
Graphics and Design: James Hutson
Layout: William Zimmerman
Photo Editor: Cynthia Breslin Beres
Editorial Assistant: Dana Garey

Cover photos (pictured clockwise, from top left): Richard Nixon (Dennis Brack/Landov); Lizzie Borden (The Granger Collection, New York); Saddam Hussein (Hulton Archive/Getty Images); Adolf Hitler (Hulton Archive/ Getty Images); Timothy McVeigh (Jim Bourg/Reuters/Landov); Rasputin (The Granger Collection, New York)

∞ The paper used in these volumes conforms to the American National Standard for Permanence of Paper for Printed Library Materials, Z39.48-1992 (R1997).

Library of Congress Cataloging-in-Publication Data

Great lives from history. Notorious lives / editor, Carl L. Bankston III.
v. cm.
Includes bibliographical references and index.
ISBN-13: 978-1-58765-320-9 (set : alk. paper)
ISBN-13: 978-1-58765-321-6 (vol. 1 : alk. paper)
ISBN-13: 978-1-58765-322-3 (vol. 2 : alk. paper)
ISBN-13: 978-1-58765-323-0 (vol. 3 : alk. paper)
1. Criminals—Biography. 2. Terrorists—Biography. 3. War criminals—Biography. 4. Dictators—Biography.
5. Political corruption.
I. Bankston, Carl L. (Carl Leon), 1952- II. Title: Notorious lives.

HV6245.G687 2007
364.1092′2—dc22
[B]

2006032935

First Printing

PRINTED IN THE UNITED STATES OF AMERICA

Contents

Publisher's Note

Great Lives from History: Notorious Lives expands Salem's *Great Lives* series by adding 637 biographies in 3 volumes to *The Ancient World, Prehistory-476 C.E.* (2004), *The Middle Ages, 477-1453* (2005), *The Renaissance and Early Modern Era, 1454-1600* (2005), *The Seventeenth Century, 1601-1700* (2006), *The Eighteenth Century, 1701-1800* (2006), *The Nineteenth Century, 1801-1900* (2007), and *The Twentieth Century* (to appear in 2008). The entire set when completed will comprise more than 4,300 essays and offer biographies of approximately 4,400 historic figures.

The focus of *Notorious Lives* is not to glorify the individuals covered or their deeds but, rather, to document their vital data, offenses, and sociohistorical impact for students of history, politics, criminal law, sociology, psychology, and related disciplines. The editors had several criteria for inclusion of an individual in this list:

- We wished to fill a niche in the biographical reference literature by documenting the basic biographical data, offenses, and outcomes of those whose lives, although considered negative in the main, nevertheless had historical impact: on politics, society, forensics, criminology, law enforcement, social reform, or daily life and popular culture.

- We wished to include a broad range of individuals, from assassins to dictators, con artists to serial killers, politicians to cult leaders. We also wished to include individuals from all eras, from Attila the Hun to Osama Bin Laden.

- We have avoided including those individuals who (a) have yet to be fully judged by history, or (b) had scandalous episodes in their lives but are not remembered (or, in our judgment, will not be remembered) primarily for that negative episode. We have avoided the young and still-living who might be considered victims of circumstance as well as poor judgment.

- Similarly, we have avoided those individuals whose notoriety stems primarily from an intellectual stance (ideas vs. actions) or from merely scandalous celebrity. We have not, for example, included Martin Heidegger or Knut Hamsun. We have not included notorious sports stars, rappers, musicians, actors, or other much-publicized celebrities whose historical impact is questionable.

- Nevertheless, we have included some individuals whose place here may be considered controversial, and we are well aware that many will take issue with some of our inclusions. One notable individual who falls into this category may be President Richard M. Nixon, whose legacy can be seen as both positive and negative. Our judgment is that his criminal action in the White House and its far-reaching aftereffects on the Presidency justify his inclusion here. Another individual, O. J. Simpson, may be considered by some as questionable in historic significance; moreover, our justice system has acquitted him of the crime of murder in the Brown case. However, we see his trial and its outcome as significant beyond the Brown case itself.

- We are well aware that many individuals could be included in a set of this sort but were deliberately omitted simply to avoid dominating the set with serial killers, murderers, and other felons. We deliberately confined this group to the most notorious—those cases that have had some significant impact on society and criminal justice.

Scope of Coverage

The editors have sought to provide coverage that is broad thematically as well, addressing many parts of the curriculum, from American and World History to Criminology. Figures fall into the following categories: Assassins (40), Biblical Villains (7), Con Artists, Cheats, and Frauds (41), Corrupt Politicians (96), Cult Leaders (13), Dictators, Tyrants, and Bad Rulers (100), Gangsters and Associates (44), Military Figures (27), Murderers and Accused Murderers (75), Nazis and Fascists (27), Notorious Popes (5), Outlaws and Gunslingers (30), Pirates (20), Political Rebels and Revolutionaries (20), Racists and Hatemongers (36), Scientists and Doctors (8), Serial Killers (30), Sexual Predators and Accused Predators (14), Terrorists (20), Thieves and Bank Robbers (18), Traitors and Spies (42), War Criminals (15), White-Collar Criminals (10), and Witches and Occultists (13).

The geographic scope of the individuals covered in *Great Lives from History: Notorious Lives* is equally broad, with a view to including influential individuals worldwide. The figures covered in these volumes are identified with one or more of the following countries or regions: Afghanistan (2), Albania (1), Algeria (1), Argentina (5), Atlantic Coast (1), Australia (2), Barbados (1), Belgium (3), Bolivia (1), Bosnia-Herzegovina (2), Brazil (2), Burma (2), Byzantine Empire (2), Cambodia (3), Canada (8), Caribbean (4), Central African Republic (1), Chile (1), China (9), Colombia (1), Congo (1), Croatia (1), Cuba (3), Denmark (1), Dominican Republic (1), Egypt (2), England (58), Ethiopia (1), France (37), Galilee (1), Germany (35), Greece (5), Guatemala (2), Guyana (1), Haiti (2), Hungary (4), India (7), Indonesia (1), Iran (3), Iraq (4), Ireland (8), Israel (7), Italy (19), Jamaica (1), Japan (6), Jordan (1), Judaea (2), Korea (North and South) (4), Kuwait (1), Liberia (2), Libya (1), Madagascar (1), Mexico (7), Mongolia (1), Netherlands (3), Newfoundland (1), Nicaragua (2), Nigeria (1), Norway (2), Pakistan (1), Palestine (1), Panama (3), Paraguay (1), Peru (1), Philippines (2), Poland (4), Portugal (2), Romania (2), Rome or Roman Empire (12), Russia (19), Saudi Arabia (1), Scotland (6), Serbia (3), Siberia (1), Sicily (1), Somalia (1), South Africa (3), Soviet Union (18), Spain (11), Sri Lanka (1), Sudan (1), Sweden (2), Switzerland (1), Tahiti (1), The Bahamas (1), Transylvania (2), Turkey (1), Turkmenistan (1), Uganda (1), Ukraine (1), United States (302), Venezuela (2), Vietnam (2), Wales (1), Yugoslavia (1), Zaire (2), and Zimbabwe (1).

Essay Length and Format

Each essay ranges from 700 to 1,200 words (roughly 1 to 3 pages) and displays standard ready-reference top matter offering easy access to biographical information:

- The **name** of the individual as it is best known (monikers and epithets are not used here but appear in the "Also known as" line below).

- The individual's **identity** follows in the second line, including reign dates or terms of office where appropriate.

- The **"Born"** and **"Died"** lines list the most complete dates of birth and death available, followed by the most precise locations available, as well as an indication of when these are unknown, only probable, or only approximate; both contemporary and modern place-names (where different) are listed. A question mark (?) is appended to a date or place if the information is considered likely to be the precise date or place but remains in question. A "c." denotes circa and indicates that historians have only enough information to place the date of birth or death in a more general period. When a range of dates is provided for birth or death, historians are relatively certain that it could not have occurred prior to or after the range.

- **"Also known as"** lists all known versions of the individual's name, including full names, birth names, aliases, monikers, and alternative spellings.

- **"Cause of notoriety"** (or, for convicted criminals, **"Major offenses"**) summarizes the reasons for the person's infamy.

- **"Active"** lists the date or range of years when the individual gained notoriety.

- **"Locale"** identifies the place or places where the individual was most active.

- **"Sentence"** appears where legal action led to a conviction and sentencing; the sentence and, where applicable, time served are listed here.

The body of each essay is divided into the following parts:

- **"Early Life"** provides facts about the individual's upbringing and the environment in which he or she was reared, as well as the pronunciation of his or her name. Where little is known about the individual's early life, historical context is provided.

- The **"Career"** section—e.g., "Criminal Career," "Political Career," "Military Career," or whatever most accurately describes the individual's activity—forms the heart of each essay, consisting of a straightforward account of the period during which the individual committed those acts that led to infamy.

- **"Legal Action and Outcome"** appears where applicable and summarizes the roles played by law enforcement and the criminal justice system (whether domestic or international).

- **"Impact"** assesses the historical impact and significance of the individual's actions: on law and law enforcement, criminal justice, public attitudes, social reform, history, even legend and the arts.

- **"Further Reading,"** an annotated bibliography, lists approximately three to six books or articles that form a starting point for further research.

- **"See also"** cross-references other essays in the set covering personages who are related or may also be of interest (e.g., the essays on Clyde Barrow and Bonnie Parker are cross-referenced to each other).

Special Features

Several features distinguish this series as a whole from other biographical reference works:

- **200+ sidebars** have been added to enhance and supplement the text throughout, often bringing the notorious personage to life in his or her own words.

- **Complete List of Contents:** This alphabetical list of contents appears in all three volumes.

- **Key to Pronunciation:** A key to in-text pronunciation appears in all volumes.

- **List of Sidebars:** Lists sidebars by keyword.

The back matter to Volume 3 includes several appendixes and indexes:

- **Chronological List of Entries:** Individuals covered by birth year.

- **General Bibliography**

- **Electronic Resources**

- **Category Index:** Lists biographies by area of notoriety, from assassins to white-collar criminals.

- **Geographical Index:** Lists biographies by country, from Albania to Zimbabwe.

- **Personages Index:** An index of all persons, both those who are subjects of essays and those discussed within the text.

Usage Notes

The worldwide scope of the set results in the inclusion of names and words transliterated from languages that do not use the Roman alphabet. In some cases, there is more than one transliterated form in use. In many cases, transliterated words in this set follow the American Library Association and Library of Congress (ALA-LC) transliteration format for that language. However, if another form of a name or word has been judged to be more familiar to the general audience, it is used instead. The variants for names of essay subjects are listed in ready-reference top matter and are cross-referenced in the personages index. The Pinyin transliteration was used for Chinese topics, with Wade-Giles variants provided for major names and dynasties. In a few cases, a common name that is not Pinyin has been used. Sanskrit and other South Asian names generally follow the ALA-LC transliteration rules, although again, the more familiar form of a word is used when deemed appropriate for the general reader.

Titles of books and other literature appear, upon first mention in the essay, with their full publication and translation data as known: an indication of the first date of publication or appearance, followed by the English title in translation and its first date of appearance in English; if no translation has been published in English, and if the context of the discussion does not make the meaning of the title obvious, a "literal translation" appears in roman type.

Throughout, readers will find a limited number of abbreviations used in both top matter and text, including "r." for "reigned" or "ruled" and occasionally "b." for "born," "d." for "died," and "fl." for flourished. Where a date range appears appended to a name without one of these designators, the reader may assume it signifies birth and death dates.

Acknowledgments

Salem Press would like to extend its appreciation to all who have been involved in the development and production of this work. Special thanks go to Carl L. Bankston III, Professor of Sociology at Tulane University, who developed the contents list and coverage notes for contributing writers to ensure the set's relevance to the high school and undergraduate curricula. The essays were written and signed by sociologists, psychologists, criminologists, and historians, as well as independent scholars. Without their expert contributions, a project of this nature would not be possible. A full list of their names and affiliations appears in the front matter of this volume.

CONTRIBUTORS

Patrick Adcock
Henderson State University

Bland Addison
Worcester Polytechnic Institute

Olutayo C. Adesina
University of Ibadan

Emily Alward
Henderson, NV District Libraries

Carolyn Anderson
University of Massachusetts

Mike Ashley
Independent Scholar

Charles Avinger
Washtenaw Community College

Thomas E. Baker
University of Scranton

Rachel Kate Bandy
University of Colorado at Boulder

Carl L. Bankston III
Tulane University

John W. Barker
University of Wisconsin—Madison

David Barratt
Independent Scholar

Rozmeri Basic
University of Oklahoma

Frederic J. Baumgartner
Virginia Polytechnic Institute & State University

Albert A. Bell, Jr.
Hope College

Alvin K. Benson
Utah Valley State College

Donna Berliner
University of Texas at Dallas

Milton Berman
University of Rochester

Nicholas Birns
New School University

Devon Boan
Belmont University

Olivia Boler
Independent Scholar

Jackie R. Booker
Claflin University

Denise Paquette Boots
University of Texas at Dallas

Bernadette Lynn Bosky
Independent Scholar

William Bourns
California State University, Stanislaus

Frank La Brasca
University of Tours

Howard Bromberg
Ave Maria School of Law

Kendall W. Brown
Brigham Young University

Thomas W. Buchanan
Ancilla Domini College

Kevin G. Buckler
Georgia Southern University

Michael A. Buratovich
Spring Arbor University

Michael H. Burchett
Limestone College

Alison S. Burke
Indiana University of Pennsylvania

Joseph P. Byrne
Belmont University

Avelina Carrera
Universidad de Valladolid

Diane S. Carter
Independent Scholar

Elisabeth Cawthon
University of Texas, Arlington

David R. Champion
Slippery Rock University

Frederick B. Chary
Indiana University Northwest

Carol A. Cheek
Independent Scholar

Dennis W. Cheek
Pennsylvania State University Great Valley

Michael W. Cheek
Independent Scholar

Lindsay M. Christopher
University of Denver

S. E. Costanza
Salem State College

John K. Cox
Wheeling Jesuit University

Tyler T. Crogg
Southern Illinois University, Carbondale

Richard A. Crooker
Kutztown University

Frank Day
Clemson University

Robert E. Dewhirst
Northwest Missouri State University

Kim Díaz
Texas A&M University

Margaret A. Dodson
Independent Scholar

Cecilia Donohue
Madonna University

Thomas Drucker
University of Wisconsin—Whitewater

Margaret Duggan
South Dakota State University

John P. Dunn
Valdosta State University

Víctor Manuel Durán
University of South Carolina, Aiken

Christine Ivie Edge
Georgia Southern University

K Edgington
Towson University

Mark R. Ellis
University of Nebraska at Kearney

William E. Engel
University of the South

Patricia E. Erickson
Canisius College

Thomas L. Erskine
Salisbury University

Todd W. Ewing
William Baptist College

K. Thomas Finley
SUNY—College at Brockport

Annette Finley-Croswhite
Old Dominion University

Gerald P. Fisher
Georgia College and State University

Dale L. Flesher
University of Mississippi

Charles H. Ford
Norfolk State University

Timothy C. Frazer
Western Illinois University

Gennifer Furst
The College of New Jersey

Francesca Gamber
Southern Illinois University, Carbondale

John F. Gamber, Jr.
Southern Illinois University, Carbondale

Gayle Gaskill
College of St. Catherine

Gilbert Geis
University of California, Irvine

Jennifer C. Gibbs
University of Maryland

C. Herbert Gilliland
U.S. Naval Academy

Sheldon Goldfarb
University of British Columbia

Johnpeter Horst Grill
Mississippi State University

Scot M. Guenter
San José State University

Michael Haas
College of the Canyons

Irwin Halfond
McKendree College

Gavin R. G. Hambly
University of Texas at Dallas

Richard D. Hartley
Texas A&M International University

Karen L. Hayslett-McCall
University of Texas at Dallas

Peter B. Heller
Manhattan College

Patricia K. Hendrickson
Tarleton State University

Mark C. Herman
Edison College

Steve Hewitt
University of Birmingham

Carly M. Hilinski
Indiana University of Pennsylvania

Carl W. Hoagstrom
Ohio Northern University

Samuel B. Hoff
Delaware State University

David B. Hollander
Iowa State University

Jerry W. Hollingsworth
McMurry University

Kimberley M. Holloway
King College

Lisa Hopkins
Sheffield Hallam University

Leslie J. Hoppe
Catholic Theological Union

Gregory D. Horn
Southwest Virginia Community College

Sheryl L. Van Horne
Rutgers University

Nancy A. Horton
University of Maryland Eastern Shore

Charles C. Howard
Tarleton State University

J. Donald Hughes
University of Denver

Alex Hunnicutt
University of Texas, Arlington

Patrick Norman Hunt
Stanford University

Raymond Pierre Hylton
Virginia Union University

Bryan Jack
Winston-Salem State University

Cathy M. Jackson
Norfolk State University

Robert Jacobs
Central Washington University

Jenephyr James
Indiana University of Pennsylvania

Elizabeth Jarnagin
Drew University

Barbara E. Johnson
University of South Carolina, Aiken

Edward Johnson
University of New Orleans

Scott P. Johnson
Frostburg State University

Sheila Golburgh Johnson
Independent Scholar

Yvonne Johnson
Central Missouri State University

David M. Jones
University of Wisconsin—Oshkosh

Mathew J. Kanjirathinkal
Park University

Tracie L. Keesee
University of Denver

Mara Kelly-Zukowski
Felician College

John C. Kilburn, Jr.
Texas A&M International University

Leigh Husband Kimmel
Independent Scholar

William B. King
Coastal Carolina University

Paul M. Klenowski
Wheeling Jesuit University

Gayla Koerting
University of South Dakota

Grove Koger
Boise Public Library, Idaho

David B. Kopel
Independence Institute

Paul E. Kuhl
Winston-Salem State University

Karen F. Lahm
Capital University

Philip E. Lampe
University of the Incarnate Word

David H. J. Larmour
Texas Tech University

Eugene Larson
Los Angeles Pierce College

Sally A. Lasko
University of Colorado

Linda Ledford-Miller
University of Scranton

Ann M. Legreid
Central Missouri State University

Margaret E. Leigey
University of Delaware

John Lewis
Ashland University

Thomas Tandy Lewis
St. Cloud State University

Ellen B. Lindsay
Independent Scholar

Scott Lingenfelter
Roosevelt University

Roger D. Long
Eastern Michigan University

Pietro Lorenzini
Elgin Community College

Martha Oehmke Loustaunau
New Mexico State University

Eric v.d. Luft
SUNY, Upstate Medical University

Anthony J. Luongo III
Temple University

R. C. Lutz
CII

Marion S. McAvey
Becker College

Michael McCaskey
Georgetown University

Jennie MacDonald
University of Colorado at Denver

John L. McLean
Missouri Valley College

Edward W. Maine
California State University, Fullerton

Michael T. Martin
Fort Lewis College

Laurence W. Mazzeno
Alvernia College

Beth A. Messner
Ball State University

Eric Metchik
Salem State College

J. Mitchell Miller
University of South Carolina

Randall L. Milstein
Oregon State University

Damon Mitchell
Central Connecticut State University

R. Scott Moore
Indiana University of Pennsylvania

William V. Moore
College of Charleston

Caitlin L. Moriarity
University of Missouri—Columbia

Alice Myers
Simon's Rock College of Bard

Jerome L. Neapolitan
Tennessee Technological University

Holly Faith Nelson
Trinity Western University

Corinne Noirot-Maguire
Goucher College

Ayodeji Olukoju
University of Lagos

Douglas A. Orr
Independent Scholar

Robert J. Paradowski
Rochester Institute of Technology

Jim Pauff
Tarleton State University

Tinaz Pavri
Spelman College

Jan Pendergrass
University of Georgia

Matthew Penney
University of Auckland

Gerhard Petersmann
University of Salzburg

Sara Elise Phang
Independent Scholar

Erika E. Pilver
Westfield State College

Julio Pino
Kent State University

Wayne J. Pitts
University of Memphis

Marguerite R. Plummer
Louisiana State University in Shreveport

Clifton W. Potter, Jr.
Lynchburg College

Luke Powers
Tennessee State University

Victoria Price
Lamar University

Maureen Puffer-Rothenberg
Valdosta State University

Cat Rambo
Independent Scholar

Steven J. Ramold
Eastern Michigan University

Kevin B. Reid
Henderson Community College

Cassandra L. Reyes
Indiana University of Pennsylvania

Betty Richardson
Southern Illinois University, Edwardsville

Janice G. Rienerth
Appalachian State University

Cliff Roberson
Washburn University

James C. Roberts
Independent Scholar

John Jacob Rodriguez
Prairie View A&M University

Stephen F. Rohde
Rohde & Victoroff

Thomas E. Rotnem
Southern Polytechnic State University

Joseph R. Rudolph, Jr.
Towson University

Concepción Sáenz-Cambra
University of California, Santa Barbara

Sean J. Savage
Saint Mary's College

Jean Owens Schaefer
University of Wyoming

Elizabeth D. Schafer
Independent Scholar

Giuseppe Di Scipio
Hunter College

Rebecca Lovell Scott
Northeastern University

Brion Sever
Monmouth University

Manoj Sharma
University of Cincinnati

Taylor Shaw
ADVANCE Education & Development Center

Martha A. Sherwood
University of Oregon

Ted Shields
Charleston Southern University

R. Baird Shuman
University of Illinois at Urbana-Champaign

Jeffrey M. Shumway
Brigham Young University

Patricia J. Siegel
SUNY—College at Brockport

Jules Simon
University of Texas at El Paso

Paul P. Sipiera
William Rainey Harper College

Shumet Sishagne
Christopher Newport University

Emilie B. Sizemore
Pepperdine University

Cary Stacy Smith
Mississippi State University

Stefan Halikowski Smith
University of Wales, Swansea

Brian Stableford
Independent Scholar

David Stefancic
Saint Mary's College

Barry M. Stentiford
Grambling State University

Stephen A. Stertz
Seton Hall University

Grant T. Stewart
Independent Scholar

Robert Stewart
California Maritime Academy

Toby Stewart
Independent Scholar

Fred Strickert
Wartburg College

Taylor Stults
Muskingum College

Randall D. Swain
Morehead State University

Glenn L. Swygart
Tennessee Temple University

G. Thomas Taylor
University of Maine

Jonathan L. Thorndike
Belmont University

Anh Tran
Wichita State University

Marcella Bush Trevino
Barry University

Larry W. Usilton
University of North Carolina at Wilmington

Theodore M. Vestal
Oklahoma State University

Sara Vidar
Independent Scholar

Kathryn Vincent
University of Maryland

Jennifer Cripps Vinsky
California State University, Chico

Linda Volonino
Canisius College

Mary C. Ware
SUNY—College at Cortland

Robert P. Watson
Florida Atlantic University

Donald A. Watt
Dakota Wesleyan University

Shawncey Webb
Taylor University

Jack H. Westbrook
Brookline Technologies

Winifred Whelan
St. Bonaventure University

Lisa A. Williams-Taylor
CUNY Graduate Center

Raymond Wilson
Fort Hays State University

Richard L. Wilson
University of Tennessee at Chattanooga

Sharon Wilson
Fort Hays State University

Shelley Wolbrink
Drury University

Susan J. Wurtzburg
University of Utah

Robert B. Youngblood
Washington & Lee University

Robert Zaller
Drexel University

Lilian H. Zirpolo
Aurora, The Journal of the History of Art

Key to Pronunciation

Many of the names of personages covered in *Great Lives from History: Notorious Lives* may be unfamiliar to students and general readers. For all names, guidelines to pronunciation have been provided upon first mention of the name in each essay. These guidelines do not purport to achieve the subtleties of all languages but will offer readers a rough equivalent of how English speakers may approximate the proper pronunciation.

Vowel Sounds

Symbol	**Spelled (Pronounced)**
a	answer (AN-suhr), laugh (laf), sample (SAM-puhl), that (that)
ah	father (FAH-thur), hospital (HAHS-pih-tuhl)
aw	awful (AW-fuhl), caught (kawt)
ay	blaze (blayz), fade (fayd), waiter (WAYT-ur), weigh (way)
eh	bed (behd), head (hehd), said (sehd)
ee	believe (bee-LEEV), cedar (SEE-dur), leader (LEED-ur), liter (LEE-tur)
ew	boot (bewt), lose (lewz)
i	buy (bi), height (hit), lie (li), surprise (sur-PRIZ)
ih	bitter (BIH-tur), pill (pihl)
o	cotton (KO-tuhn), hot (hot)
oh	below (bee-LOH), coat (koht), note (noht), wholesome (HOHL-suhm)
oo	good (good), look (look)
ow	couch (kowch), how (how)
oy	boy (boy), coin (koyn)
uh	about (uh-BOWT), butter (BUH-tuhr), enough (ee-NUHF), other (UH-thur)

Consonant Sounds

Symbol	**Spelled (Pronounced)**
ch	beach (beech), chimp (chihmp)
g	beg (behg), disguise (dihs-GIZ), get (geht)
j	digit (DIH-juht), edge (ehj), jet (jeht)
k	cat (kat), kitten (KIH-tuhn), hex (hehks)
s	cellar (SEHL-ur), save (sayv), scent (sehnt)
sh	champagne (sham-PAYN), issue (IH-shew), shop (shop)
ur	birth (burth), disturb (dihs-TURB), earth (urth), letter (LEH-tur)
y	useful (YEWS-fuhl), young (yuhng)
z	business (BIHZ-nehs), zest (zehst)
zh	vision (VIH-zhuhn)

Complete List of Contents

Volume I

Volume 2

Volume 3

Appendixes

Indexes

List of Sidebars

Volume I

Volume 2

Volume 3

Great Lives from History

Notorious Lives

Sani Abacha

Nigerian military dictator (1993-1998)

Born: September 20, 1943; Kano, Nigeria
Died: June 8, 1998; Abuja, Nigeria
Cause of notoriety: During his repressive regime, Abacha hanged environmental and oil minority rights activist Ken Saro-Wiwa and eight Ogoni compatriots, killed or jailed political opponents, and siphoned billions of dollars of state funds into foreign banks.
Active: November, 1993-June, 1998
Locale: Nigeria, West Africa

Early Life

Born of Kanuri parentage in Kano, Northern Nigeria, Sani Abacha (SAWN-ee AH-bah-chah) attended elementary school before commencing a career in the army. Though limited in intellect, he had natural cunning. For two decades, between the early 1960's and the early 1980's, Abacha polished his military knowledge by attending a series of military academies and courses in Nigeria, England, and the United States: the Nigerian Military Training College in Kaduna, Northern Nigeria; the Mons Defence Cadet College in Aldershot, England; the School of Infantry in Warminster, England; the Command and Staff College in Jaji, Nigeria; the National Institute for Policy and Strategic Studies in Kuru, Nigeria; and an international defense course in the United States.

Military Career

Abacha served as a lieutenant at the outbreak of the Nigerian Civil War (1967-1970). He then became a colonel in 1975 and a brigadier in 1982. On December 31, 1983, Abacha was involved in the successful military coup against the civilian regime of Alhaji Shehu Shagari; Major-General Muhammadu Buhari took control of the country. Abacha was a member of the Supreme Military Council and served as the general officer commanding the second infantry division of the Nigerian Army.

After a palace coup that overthrew General Buhari in August, 1985, Abacha became the chief of army staff and de facto deputy to General Ibrahim Babangida, the self-styled military president. Under Babangida, Abacha, already a major-general, was promoted to the ranks of lieutenant-general and general and was appointed defense minister in 1990.

Following the annulment of the June, 1993, presidential election, which was won by the Yoruba businessman Moshood K. O. Abiola, protesters rioted, and President Babangida was forced to step aside and give power to an interim national government, headed by Abiola's kinsman Ernest Shonekan. Shonekan was supposed to rule until new elections could be held in February, 1994. However, Abacha, who was retained as defense minister and the de facto second-in-command in the Shonekan government, overthrew the interim government on November 17, 1993.

Reign of Terror

Abacha immediately abolished the democratic structures at the state and local government levels and reestablished full-blown military rule. He then proceeded to decimate all forms of opposition to his rule. Abiola, the winner of the June, 1993, presidential election, was put into prison, where he remained for five years and then died a month after Abacha's death in 1998. Abacha also eliminated well-known opposition figures who formed the National

Sani Abacha. (AP/Wide World Photos)

Democratic Coalition (NADECO): Anthony Enahoro, a leading figure in the anticolonial movement of the 1940's and 1950's, fled into exile together with scores of other NADECO activists. Alfred Rewane, another septuagenarian nationalist, and Abiola's wife, Kudirat, were assassinated by persons who were later unmasked as members of Abacha's killer squad. Abacha's paramilitary organization also caused panic by exploding bombs in cities and then ascribing such acts to the opposition.

Abacha also contrived coup plots in which he implicated opponents of his regime and journalists. Former military head of state Olusegun Obasanjo and his deputy, Major-General Shehu Musa Yar'Adua, were detained and tried under inhumane conditions and jailed for treason in 1995. Yar'Adua died in prison, allegedly by poisoning from an agent of the Abacha regime.

While Abacha was suppressing internal opposition, he rarely ventured out of the country. At home, he relied on a security apparatus coordinated by his chief security officer. He also amassed incredible wealth for his family and friends by siphoning billions of dollars of state funds into foreign banks.

Abacha perhaps gained greatest criticism by ruthlessly crushing the nonviolent resistance movement of the Ogoni people in the oil-rich region of the Niger Delta. The Movement for the Survival of the Ogoni People (MOSOP) was led by Ken Saro-Wiwa, an environmental activist who called attention to the ways in which international oil companies, especially Shell Oil, were extracting large oil profits from Ogoni lands. MOSOP demanded a portion of the proceeds of oil extraction and remediation of environmental damage to Ogoni lands. In May, 1994, Saro-Wiwa was arrested and accused of incitement to murder following the deaths of four Ogoni elders believed to be sympathetic to the military. Saro-Wiwa denied the charges but was imprisoned for more than a year before being found guilty. In a move that attracted intense international criticism, Saro-Wiwa was sentenced to death by a specially convened tribunal. The hasty execution of the Ogoni activists in November, 1995, despite appeals from world leaders such as the Roman Catholic pope and South Africa's Nelson Mandela, sealed Abacha's reputation as a bloodthirsty tyrant.

Impact

Sani Abacha died suddenly in 1998. News of his death was received with relief and spontaneous jubilation across Nigeria. He was buried in Kano without the military honors typical of his position.

Four billion dollars stolen by him and his fronts were traced to Middle Eastern and Western banks, only a small fraction of which was then repatriated to the country. His children and business associates profited from the importation of fuel into Nigeria.

Abacha is remembered for his intransigence, despotism, and corruption. His disdain for world opinion and his repressive tactics toward political opponents, nonviolent resistance movements, and the press made Nigeria a pariah worldwide. However, Abacha's informal division of Nigeria's thirty-six states into six geopolitical zones outlived him, and the Obasanjo administration militarized the oil-rich territory of Izon in the Niger Delta, much like what occurred in the Ogani region under Abacha.

Further Reading

Kukah, Matthew Hassan. *Democracy and Civil Society in Nigeria.* London: Spectrum, 1999. An authoritative study of the role of civil society in the tumultuous history of democratic struggles in Nigeria.

Maier, Karl. *This House Has Fallen: Nigeria in Crisis.* London: Penguin, 2000. A foreign journalist gives a graphic account of Nigeria's political crisis, especially following the 1990's.

Osaghae, Eghosa. *Crippled Giant: Nigeria Since Independence.* London: Hurst, 1998. A scholarly analysis of Nigeria's postindependence political developments.

—*Ayodeji Olukoju*

See also: Samuel K. Doe; Mobutu Sese Seko; Muhammad Siad Barre.

Frank W. Abagnale, Jr.

American forger and con artist

Born: April 27, 1948; Bronxville, New York
Also known as: Frank William Abagnale, Jr. (full name); Frank Williams; Frank Adams; Robert Conrad; Robert Monjo; and other aliases
Major offenses: Fraud, forgery, and embezzlement
Active: 1963-1969
Locale: France, Sweden, and the United States
Sentence: One year in prison in France, served six months; six months in prison in Sweden; twelve years in prison in the United States, served five years

Early Life

Frank W. Abagnale, Jr. (A-buhg-nayl), appears to have led an uneventful childhood in the suburbs of New York. At a young age, he exhibited unusual intelligence and maturity, absorbing the language and mannerisms of the business world from his father, a Manhattan shopkeeper. While Abagnale was in his mid-teens, his parents divorced, and he moved in with his father. He soon turned to petty crime and, after charging thousands of dollars to his father's credit card, was returned to his mother's custody in 1963 and placed in a reformatory. He left home the following year for New York City.

Criminal Career

In New York City Abagnale attempted to earn a legitimate living but was hampered by his youth and lack of a high school diploma. To compensate, he falsified his age and educational background but soon became frustrated with his modest standard of living. He concocted a scheme to pose as an airline pilot in order to cash fraudulent checks. Through intensive research and elaborate deception, he managed to acquire the uniform of a Pan-American Airlines pilot and to falsify identification and credentials. Under the name Frank Williams, Abagnale lived the fast-paced life of an airline pilot, traveling internationally as he opened bank accounts in various cities and countries under a number of assumed names, overdrew them by thousands of dollars, and stored the cash in safe-deposit boxes.

Abagnale's activities soon attracted the attention of law enforcement authorities, forcing him to relocate. He moved to Atlanta, where he posed as a physician and secured a job supervising interns in a hospital emergency room. By delegating direct patient care to his subordinates, Abagnale was able to cover up his lack of a medical education. He resigned within a year, as maintaining this persona proved increasingly difficult.

He then moved to Louisiana and posed as an attorney, using a forged Harvard University diploma and passing the state's bar examination on his third attempt. Abagnale briefly worked as a legal assistant in the state attorney general's office but abandoned the job after a Harvard alumnus working in the office nearly uncovered his ruse. Abagnale returned to impersonating an airline pilot in 1966, resuming his international forgery and check-kiting practices. Nearly captured on several occasions, Abagnale assumed a variety of alternative personas when necessary, including a brief stint as a university professor.

Legal Action and Outcome

In 1969, Abagnale was arrested in France, where he was posing as an expatriate writer, on fraud charges. He

Frank W. Abagnale, Jr. (AP/Wide World Photos)

served six months in the notorious Perpignan prison, nearly dying of malnutrition and pneumonia. Extradited to Sweden, he served an additional year under less harsh conditions, after which he was extradited to the United States. After serving five years of a twelve-year sentence for forgery and check fraud, Abagnale was released with the understanding that he would assist federal authorities by sharing his knowledge of check forgery and other crimes. His work as an unpaid consultant eventually led to paid jobs, allowing Abagnale to build a successful practice as a security consultant for banks and other businesses.

Impact

By the end of the twentieth century, Frank W. Abagnale, Jr., was known as one of the world's foremost authorities on financial crimes, was an author of several books, and was the designer of secure check technology created to combat the crimes that he had successfully perpetrated in the past. He continued to volunteer as a consultant to the Federal Bureau of Investigation, assisting in the resolution of numerous fraud and forgery cases. In 2002, a feature film based on his autobiography, *Catch Me if You Can* (1980), became a box-office success.

Further Reading

Abagnale, Frank W. *The Art of the Steal: How to Protect Yourself and Your Business from Fraud.* New York: Broadway Books, 2001. Abagnale draws upon his experience as a security consultant for this educational text, which uses case studies of financial crimes and identity theft.

Abagnale, Frank W., and Stan Redding. *Catch Me if You Can.* 1980. Reprint. New York: Broadway Books, 2000. This autobiography emphasizes the sensational nature of Abagnale's exploits yet provides detailed information about the machinations of financial crime in the late twentieth century.

Waldie, Paul. "The World's Greatest Con Artist Switches Sides." *The Financial Post* (October 1, 1994): 5. A brief discussion of Abagnale, his consulting business, and his motives for assisting businesses and authorities in fighting financial crimes.

—*Michael H. Burchett*

See also: Billy Cannon; Susanna Mildred Hill; Megan Louise Ireland; Victor Lustig; Alexandre Stavisky; Joseph Weil.

Abu Nidal

Palestinian terrorist

Born: May, 1937; Jaffa, Palestine (now in Israel)
Died: August 16, 2002; Baghdad, Iraq
Also known as: Amin al-Sirr; Sabri Khalil Abd Al Qadir; Sabri Khalil al-Banna (birth name)
Cause of notoriety: Abu Nidal is considered responsible for terrorist acts in twenty countries and the deaths or injuries of more than nine hundred people.
Active: 1973-1991
Locale: Iraq, Syria, Libya, and Egypt

Early Life

Abu Nidal (AH-bew nee-DAHL) was the twelfth child in his family (eleven were born to his stepmother; he was the child of a sixteen-year-old maid). His father was a prosperous Palestinian merchant specializing in citrus fruit. When his father died in 1945, the rest of the family turned against Abu Nidal, and his mother was thrown out of the family home. He dropped out of third grade, and his childhood pain may have sown the seeds for his later cruelty.

Abu Nidal grew up during the tumultuous period of the birth of Israel, and his family moved to Nablus on the West Bank, then ruled by Jordan. There he became involved in the radical Ba'th Party, which nurtured Arab nationalist aspirations. After this party was crushed in Jordan by King Hussein, Abu Nidal moved to Riyadh, Saudi Arabia, where he went into business and founded a small terrorist cell. He became heavily involved in Yasir Arafat's Fatah movement. Following the June, 1967, war, he was expelled by Saudi Arabia as a subversive and went to Amman, Jordan. There he aligned himself with Palestinian guerrillas planning violent attacks against the Israelis.

Criminal Career

Abu Nidal gained notoriety for establishing a terrorist network that carried out a series of attacks starting in 1973, after a split with Arafat and the Palestine Liberation Organization (PLO). These included embassy attacks in Europe, airplane hijackings, and assassinations

The Abu Nidal Organization

In its "Country Reports on Terrorism" for 2004, the U.S. Department of State described the Abu Nidal Organization (ANO) as follows:

Other Names
- Fatah Revolutionary Council
- Arab Revolutionary Brigades
- Black September
- Revolutionary Organization of Socialist Muslims

Description
- The ANO international terrorist organization was founded by Sabri al-Banna (*a.k.a.* Abu Nidal) after splitting from the PLO [Palestine Liberation Organization] in 1974. The group's previous known structure consisted of various functional committees, including political, military, and financial. In November 2002 Abu Nidal died in Baghdad; the new leadership of the organization remains unclear.

Activities
- The ANO has carried out terrorist attacks in 20 countries, killing or injuring almost 900 persons. Targets include the United States, the United Kingdom, France, Israel, moderate Palestinians, the PLO, and various Arab countries. Major attacks included the Rome and Vienna airports in 1985, the Neve Shalom synagogue in Istanbul, the hijacking of Pan Am Flight 73 in Karachi in 1986, and the City of Poros day-excursion ship attack in Greece in 1988. The ANO is suspected of assassinating PLO deputy chief Abu Iyad and PLO security chief Abu Hul in Tunis in 1991. The ANO assassinated a Jordanian diplomat in Lebanon in 1994 and has been linked to the killing of the PLO representative there. The group has not staged a major attack against Western targets since the late 1980's.

Strength
- Few hundred plus limited overseas support structure.

Location/Area of Operation
- Al-Banna relocated to Iraq in December 1998, where the group maintained a presence until Operation Iraqi Freedom, but its current status in country is unknown. Known members have an operational presence in Lebanon, including in several Palestinian refugee camps. Authorities shut down the ANO's operations in Libya and Egypt in 1999. The group has demonstrated the ability to operate over a wide area, including the Middle East, Asia, and Europe. However, financial problems and internal disorganization have greatly reduced the group's activities and its ability to maintain cohesive terrorist capability.

External Aid
- The ANO received considerable support, including safe haven, training, logistical assistance, and financial aid from Iraq, Libya, and Syria (until 1987), in addition to close support for selected operations.

of Arab political figures seen as hostile to the Palestinian national cause.

The first incident, an attack on the Saudi embassy in Paris on September 5, 1973, set the tone for many that followed. Thirteen hostages were taken, and the terrorists threatened to bomb the building unless Jordan would agree to release prisoner Abu Dawud, one of the masterminds of the 1972 "Black September" kidnappings and murders of eleven Israeli Olympic athletes in Munich. The standoff ended with a surrender after three days, but in the interim Kuwait agreed to pay King Hussein twelve million dollars for his release of Dawud.

Following this incident, PLO officials tried to reason with Abu Nidal that these types of attacks did not further the Palestinian cause, and in fact set it back. Iraq claimed credit for ordering the embassy attack and said that Abu Nidal's group had been contracted to put the plan into action. Any reputation as a visionary that Abu Nidal might have enjoyed waned, and he came to be viewed as simply a "terrorist for sale" to the highest bidder.

One especially high-profile incident served to confirm this assessment. On December 27, 1985, the El Al (Israeli national airline) ticket counters in Rome and Vienna were attacked by Abu Nidal operatives, who threw grenades and fired at random in an attempt to kill as many people as possible. Eighteen victims died in these attacks; scores of others were wounded.

The random cruelty of this act marked Abu Nidal as sadistic and psychopathic, tendencies that came to bear on the treatment even of those within his organization. No one was allowed to leave the group, and most members were suspected of disloyalty, even of serving as double agents. The most primitive forms of torture were used to interrogate them, and large groups were killed and buried in mass graves in the late 1980's.

Abu Nidal died on August 16, 2002, in a luxury villa in Baghdad. Iraqi forces surrounded the house, allegedly on the orders of Iraqi dictator Saddam Hussein, who felt threatened by him. There were conflicting reports as to whether Abu Nidal shot himself to death or was killed by the Iraqi gunmen.

Impact

Abu Nidal's acts of terrorism served to weaken Arafat's Fatah organization. They also promoted radicalization of Arab terrorist groups, inspiring them to commit acts in foreign countries on a scale that had not been previously envisaged. Abu Nidal's resistance to advice from more moderate Arabs concerning the futility of his approach in furthering the cause of a Palestinian state served as a model to others who succeeded him and continued with similar tactics. Much about Abu Nidal remains unclear, even after his death. One scenario concerns possible Israeli infiltration of his organization and its effects on the trajectory of the terrorist activities.

Further Reading

Melman, Yossi. *The Master Terrorist: The True Story of Abu-Nidal*. New York: Adama Books, 1986. A detailed analysis of Abu Nidal's methodology, including an accounting of each terrorist act perpetrated by his group.

Post, Jerrold M. "When Hatred Is Bred in the Bone: Psycho-cultural Foundations of Contemporary Terrorism." *Political Psychology* 26, no. 4 (2005): 615-636. A psychological analysis of terrorism in the Abu Nidal organization.

Seale, Patrick. *Abu Nidal: A Gun for Hire*. New York: Random House, 1992. A comparative analysis of all aspects of Abu Nidal's terrorist activities, including their historical and political development. The author is considered to be the official biographer of Abu Nidal.

—*Eric Metchik*

See also: Mohammed Atta al-Sayed; Osama Bin Laden; Khalid Shaikh Mohammed; Zacarias Moussaoui; Ilich Ramírez Sánchez.

Joe Adonis

American gangster

Born: November 22, 1902; Montemarano, Italy
Died: November 26, 1972; Naples, Italy
Also known as: Giuseppe Antonio Doto (birth name); Joey A.; Joe Adone; Joe Arosa; James Arosa; Joe DeMio
Major offenses: Bootlegging, gambling, pimping, and murder
Active: 1920's-1950's
Locale: Primarily New York and New Jersey
Sentence: Deportation

Early Life

Joe Adonis (ah-DAH-nihs) was born Giuseppe Antonio Doto in Montemarano, Italy, a small town near Naples. In 1915, at the age of thirteen, Doto illegally stowed away on an ocean liner headed for New York. Upon his arrival in the United States, Doto moved to Brooklyn, where he began a career of petty crime. He supported himself as a teenager by picking pockets and stealing all that he could.

It was during this time that Doto met another young street thug, Charles "Lucky" Luciano. The two quickly became loyal friends and began participating in petty crime rackets, including prostitution and organized gambling rings. Shortly after meeting Luciano in the early 1920's, Doto changed his name to Joe Adonis.

Adonis chose the moniker because of his extreme vanity. The name allowed Adonis to see himself as an irresistible Mediterranean god, which was the image he strove to project. Adonis was known as being sexually promiscuous and served time in jail on rape charges after a woman refused his advances.

Criminal Career

By the late 1920's Adonis had acquired a strong reputation in the underground crime world and went to work as an enforcer for crime boss Frankie Yale. While employed by Yale, Adonis came into contact with key figures in organized crime, including Al Capone.

Luciano at this time was working for New York crime kingpin Joe Masseria. When Luciano organized a plot to murder Masseria, his loyal friend Adonis was one of the four gunmen (along with Bugsy Siegel, Vito Genovese, and Albert Anastasia) to carry out the job on April 15, 1931.

Adonis and Luciano went on to murder another underground crime lord, Salvatore Maranzano (Masseria's archrival). With two of the biggest New York Mafia bosses dead, Luciano created the National Crime Syndicate, which united the top Mafia gangs across the United States and placed Adonis on its board of directors. In his new position Adonis became extremely powerful, with politicians and members of the police force on his payroll. With his newfound power and influence, Adonis found himself ruling Broadway and midtown Manhattan but kept his headquarters in his Brooklyn restaurant, Joe's Italian Kitchen. Adonis continued to build his multimillion-dollar empire through illegal alcohol sales, prostitution, and cigarette sales. He bought several car dealerships across New Jersey, where his customers were coerced into buying ten-thousand-dollar insurance policies.

After World War II, Luciano was deported to Italy, never to set foot in the United States again. With Luciano out of the picture, Adonis took over the National Crime Syndicate, keeping a low profile and remaining unknown to the federal authorities. When his connections and control in underground crime became apparent and it was discovered that Adonis had never become a naturalized U.S. citizen, he agreed to be deported back to Italy in 1953 to avoid jail time. Adonis sailed home in luxury, with millions of dollars, to a villa awaiting him outside Naples.

In 1972 Italy began a crackdown on organized crime and set out to arrest all known members of the Mafia. Adonis was pulled from his villa on November 26, 1972, and taken to an undisclosed location to be questioned. It was during the excruciating interrogation that Adonis suffered a fatal heart attack. He received a small funeral attended by immediate family and was buried in Madonna Cemetery, Fort Lee, New Jersey.

Legal Action and Outcome

In 1946, former mobster Abe Reles became a federal informant and told the government about Adonis and his power across the United States in underground crime. Realizing the mounting problem organized crime was presenting, the United States organized the Kefauver Committee, which sat from 1950 through 1951, composed of senators who were responsible for examining the underground crime epidemic. Adonis was brought before the committee and questioned extensively. Although he pleaded the Fifth Amendment to all questions and avoided jail time, he was suddenly closely monitored by the Federal Bureau of Investigation, culminating in his deportation in 1953.

Impact

The growing difficulty presented by Joe Adonis and organized crime forced the U.S. government to take action. Through the Kefauver Committee, senators were able to explore the world of organized crime, uncover and interrogate its key criminals, and develop strategies to handle the existing dangers and prevent further issues from arising. As a result of the hearings, the government gained a deep understanding of the power and danger organized crime possessed, and Joe Adonis and many principal criminals were identified and monitored. The Kefauver Committee put Adonis in the spotlight, letting him know that his movements were watched and that actions against him and his activities were being taken.

Court hearings and the press placed Adonis, as well as other mob bosses and key Mafia figures, in the spotlight and also romanticized them in popular culture. They became recurring subjects in literature and films throughout the first half of the twentieth century, as did their slang and dress styles. Adonis and the Mafia embodied the image of toughness during this time and were elevated to celebrity status.

Further Reading

Davis, John H. *Mafia Dynasty: The Rise and Fall of the Gambino Crime Family*. New York: HarperCollins, 1993. Davis provides a good foundation that traces and explains the beginnings of the Sicilian Mafia in New York.

Downey, Patrick. *Gangster City: The History of the New York Underworld, 1900-1935*. Fort Lee, N.J.: Barricade Books, 2004. A thorough and concise history of early Mafia bosses and kingpins. Offers the reader a well-researched chronology of the New York Mafia.

Reppetto, Thomas. *American Mafia: A History of Its Rise to Power*. New York: Henry Holt, 2004. Provides a clear time line, showing the mob's humble beginnings in the boroughs of New York to the national Kefauver Committee trials in the 1950's.

Turkus, Burton B., and Sid Feder. *Murder Inc.: The Story of the "Syndicate."* Cambridge, Mass.: Da Capo Press, 2003. A comprehensive history of Mafia dealings and also a thoroughly researched book which explores, explains, and clears up myths about the mob.

—*Sara Vidar*

See also: Albert Anastasia; Vincent Coll; Joe Colombo; Carmine Galante; Carlo Gambino; Sam Giancana; Vincent Gigante; John Gotti; Sammy Gravano; Henry Hill; Richard Kuklinski; Meyer Lansky; Salvatore Maranzano; Carlos Marcello; Joseph Profaci.

Mehmet Ali Ağca

Turkish nationalist and assassin

Born: January 9, 1958; Yesiltepe, Turkey
Also known as: Faruk Ozgun; Mehmet Őzbay
Major offenses: Murder of Abdi İpekçi, a newspaper editor, and the attempted assassination of Pope John Paul II
Active: February 1, 1978, and May 13, 1981
Locale: Istanbul, Turkey, and Rome, Italy
Sentence: Life imprisonment for the murder (served five months, then escaped); life imprisonment in Italy for the assassination attempt (pardoned and extradited to Turkey in 2000; released briefly in 2006 only to be reimprisoned)

Early Life

Mehmet Ali Ağca (MEH-meht AH-lee AH-juh) was born into a Muslim family in a village of the Malatya Province, about three hundred miles east of Ankara, Turkey. He was eight years old when his father died, and he later joined a street gang. As an adolescent, he began to commit minor crimes, and within a few years he had become a successful smuggler of cigarettes, drugs, and arms between Turkey and Bulgaria. Although he claimed that these youthful transgressions were rooted in his need for money, his trip to Syria—during which he was trained in terrorist tactics—and his membership in the Gray Wolves, a fascist organization, indicate that he had political commitments, even though they were inchoate and confused.

Criminal Career

Ağca became a notorious criminal in 1979 when, in Istanbul, he murdered Abdi İpekçi, the editor of *Milliyet*, a liberal newspaper. Because of information provided by an informant, Ağca was eventually arrested, tried, convicted, and sentenced to life imprisonment. However, several months later, sympathizers of the Gray Wolves smuggled him out of his military prison. Shortly after his escape, Ağca sent a letter to the *Milliyet* in which he threatened to kill John Paul II during the pope's upcoming trip to Turkey, explaining that this task was his sole motive in escaping from prison.

During the eighteen months between Ağca's threat and his actual attack on the pope, he traveled to various countries, including Bulgaria, Spain, France, Switzerland, and Austria, occasionally committing thefts to provide money for his expenses. According to some sources, Abdullah Çatli, Ağca's Gray Wolves mentor, provided him with a passport and forged identity papers.

On May 11, 1981, in Milan, Italy, an agent of the Gray Wolves furnished Ağca with a Browning pistol, and Ağca traveled by train to Rome. There, on May 13, 1981, he used the pistol to shoot Pope John Paul II, who was greeting the crowd around Saint Peter's Square in his touring vehicle dubbed the "popemobile." The pope was severely wounded in the abdomen and was rushed to a hospital, where emergency surgery and a blood transfusion saved his life. Ağca was grabbed by a Franciscan nun and other members of the crowd, who handed him over to security guards.

Legal Action and Outcome

Ağca was tried, convicted, and, in July of 1981, sentenced to a life term in Rebibbia Prison. Within days of the crime, the pope forgave Ağca, who initially claimed to have acted alone; however, he soon began to tell another story that implicated Bulgarians and Turks in a

Pope John Paul II in an early version of the "popemobile." (Library of Congress)

conspiracy to assassinate the pope. Largely based on Ağca's testimony, Italian authorities eventually charged three Bulgarians and several Turks with conspiracy. The trial of these alleged conspirators began in June of 1985 and lasted ten months. Ağca was caught in several lies and behaved bizarrely in court, claiming at one point that he was Jesus Christ. In 1986, all the defendants, with the exception of Ağca, were released for lack of evidence.

On June 13, 2000, in accord with the pope's wishes, Carlo Azeglio Ciampi, the president of Italy, pardoned Ağca, who was then extradited to Turkey to complete his sentence for the murder of İpekçi. When John Paul II died in 2005, Ağca's brother told the press that Ağca was in "deep sorrow" over the pope's passing. Less than a year later, on January 12, 2006, Ağca was released from prison as a result of a combination of amnesty and European-inspired reforms in Turkey's penal code. However, the Turkish Supreme Court ruled on January 20 that Ağca's prison time in Italy could not be used to lessen the sentence for his Turkish crimes, and he was taken into custody and reimprisoned.

Impact

Mehmet Ali Ağca's crime complicated the relationship between the Vatican and such countries as Turkey, Bulgaria, and the Soviet Union. The failed case against the alleged Bulgarian and Turkish conspirators exposed weaknesses not only in the Italian legal system but also in the Western press's handling of the case. After the collapse of the Soviet and Bulgarian Communist governments, scholars found little evidence for any KGB or Bulgarian conspiracy. Confused by his many self-contradictory statements, Ağca himself stated that even he was unsure of why he tried to kill the pope.

Further Reading

Herman, Edward S., and Frank Brodhead. *The Rise and Fall of the Bulgarian Connection.* New York: Sheridan Square, 1986. The authors not only attack the theory of a KGB-Bulgarian plot to kill Pope John Paul II as a hoax but also criticize American and European journalists for their gullibility.

John Paul II (Karol Jósef Wojtyła). *Memory and Identity: Conversations at the Dawn of a Millennium.* New York: Rizzoli, 2005. In chapter 26, "Someone Must Have Guided the Bullet," the pope answers the questions of his close friend, Stanisław Dziwisz, about Ağca's attempt to kill him. Notes but no index.

Weigel, George. *Witness to Hope: The Biography of Pope John Paul II, 1920-2005.* New York: HarperPerennial, 2005. This highly praised and comprehensive account of John Paul's life is updated with a preface to take into account the pope's final years. Many pages are devoted to Ağca's life, crimes, and his relationship to the pope. Extensive notes and a large thematic bibliography. Index.

—Robert J. Paradowski

See also: Said Akbar; Yigal Amir; Nathuram Vinayak Godse; John Hinckley, Jr.; Mijailo Mijailovic; Thenmuli Rajaratnam; Beant Singh; Satwant Singh; Volkert van der Graaf; Ramzi Yousef.

Said Akbar

Afghan assassin

Born: Date unknown; Afghanistan
Died: October 16, 1951; Rawalpindi, Pakistan
Also known as: Said Akbar Zadran; Saad Akbar; Seyed Akbar; Syed Akbar; Said Akber
Cause of notoriety: Akbar murdered Pakistan's prime minister Liaquat Ali Khan for reasons that were never fully determined.
Active: October 16, 1951
Locale: Company Gardens, Rawalpindi, Pakistan

Early Life

Said Akbar (sah-EED AK-bah) was one of the younger of the nine sons of Babrak, the leader of the Zadran tribe of Khost in southern Afghanistan. Babrak was killed fighting for the king of Afghanistan, and his eldest son, Mazarak, became a high official. Akbar claimed to have been a brigadier in the Afghan army. In 1944, Mazarak was suspected of being disloyal to the king, and he and Akbar fled across the border to India. Afghanistan protested to the British government, which induced the two brothers and their followers to surrender to the British authorities. On January 11, 1947, the two men did surrender and received political asylum and a monthly payment as political refugees in Britain. They had to inform the British government of their movements and to agree not to have any connections with Afghanistan without permission.

Activist Career

For several months, the two brothers and their families lived together at Miram Shah before they were moved by the British government to Abbottabad, a city in British India. On February 26, 1948, the central government of Pakistan issued a warrant that restricted him to his house at night and prohibited him from leaving the district without permission. He was also to be closely watched by the police.

On October 13, 1951, Akbar heard on the radio that Prime Minister Liaquat Ali Khan would be visiting Rawalpindi—a city approximately sixty miles from Abbottabad—on October 16 in order to give a speech. On the morning of October 14, Akbar informed the area officer that he was leaving for Rawalpindi and would be staying at the Grand Hotel for three days so he could do some shopping. He took his eldest son, Dilawar Khan, with him. At 8:00 a.m., the Rawalpindi police were informed that Akbar should be kept under strict surveillance. He was, and a daily report was kept of his activities by the police officers following him.

On October 16, Akbar left the hotel with his son and was followed to Company Gardens. At about 2:00 p.m., he sat down on the grass about eighteen feet away from the stage. Liaquat's speech was scheduled for 4:00 p.m. Sixteen police officers were assigned as security for the stage area, and more than one hundred police officers and the First Armed Reserve provided security. Akbar was surrounded by armed police.

Liaquat arrived and after a short introduction, he got up to speak. He said a few words before Akbar fired one shot into Liaquat's chest and another into his abdomen with a Mauser pistol. Liaquat died almost immediately. Akbar was tackled by those surrounding him, including four police officers; one of them fired five bullets into him, killing him instantly.

Legal Action and Outcome

An official commission was established to determine whether Akbar was part of a conspiracy. He inexplicably had the large sum of more than two thousand rupees in his pocket, and there were another seven thousand rupees at his house. The investigation concluded that there was no evidence of a conspiracy, although many people believed that there indeed had been. Detectives were also called in from London to investigate, but they could not expand on the commission's findings. The commission concluded that Akbar had acted alone out of a fanatical religious conviction that Liaquat had failed to wage war on India over Kashmir.

Impact

Prime Minister Liaquat was the principal architect of the partition of India and the creation of Pakistan in 1947. Pakistan lost perhaps its greatest leader—Mohammed Ali Jinnah—soon after the founding of the country, and the nation soon became ruled by a military dictatorship, opening the door to civil unrest of which Said Akbar seemed to have taken advantage.

Further Reading

Munir, M. *Assassination of Mr. Liaquat Ali Khan: Report of the Commission of Enquiry*. Karachi: Government of Pakistan, February 28, 1952. This 114-page report, known as the Munir Report, documents all the information unearthed by the commission about Said Akbar and the assassination. It is the most important source on the event and the assassin.

Talbot, Ian. *Pakistan: A Modern History*. New York: St. Martin's Press, 1998. Pages 131-132 and 136-139 consider the prime ministership of Liaquat and the criticism that he came under.

Ziring, Lawrence. *Pakistan in the Twentieth Century: A Political History*. New York: Oxford University Press, 1997. Pages 113 to 117 offer an account of the reasons behind Liaquat's visit to Rawalpindi, the assassination, and the consequences.

—Roger D. Long

See also: Reginald Dyer; Nathuram Vinayak Godse; Thenmuli Rajaratnam; Beant Singh; Satwant Singh; Ramzi Yousef.

Alcibiades of Athens

Athenian politician and general

Born: c. 450 B.C.E.; Athens, Greece
Died: 404 B.C.E.; Phrygia, Asia Minor (now in Turkey)
Also known as: Alkibiades; son of Cleinias; son of Kleinias
Cause of notoriety: Deserted and betrayed his city of Athens to the Spartans
Active: c. 432-404 B.C.E.
Locale: Athens, Greece

Early Life

In 448 B.C.E., when Alcibiades (al-sih-BI-uh-deez) was a child, his father, Cleinias, an Athenian war hero, was killed. His mother, Deinomache, was a cousin of Pericles, in whose household he was raised after his father's death. Alcibiades grew into a young man of athletic beauty and charm, which he deliberately accentuated. He was a friend of Socrates, who recognized Alcibiades' potential; that is, the worst man in Athens was the student and, as rumored, beloved of the best man in Athens. However, Alcibiades did not conform to Socrates' ideals. Once he tried (unsuccessfully) to seduce Socrates, who replied that accepting the young man's physical favors in return for knowledge of the good would be a poor trade.

Political Career

Alcibiades was cited as the bravest of soldiers in the Battle of Potidaea (432 B.C.E.), where Socrates saved his life. In the Battle of Delium (424 B.C.E.), Alcibiades returned the favor. A successful general, he inspired men with his own bravado.

His political rival was Nicias, a general and diplomat who arranged a truce during the Peloponnesian War with Sparta (431 B.C.E.). Six years later, Alcibiades, seeking further glory, won a bitter debate against Nicias, convincing the assembly to vote for a military expedition to Sicily. The Athenians created an armada and appointed three generals, including Alcibiades and Nicias. However, before they sailed, statues of the god Hermes were vandalized. Rumor accused Alcibiades and his friends of the deed. Alcibiades demanded a trial, but his enemies refused to act until after he and the fleet had left. They then recalled him.

Alcibiades escaped to the Spartans, whom he advised how to defeat the Athenian campaign. The Athenians condemned him to death in absentia, confiscated his property, and posted a reward for anyone who would kill him.

Adopting Spartan manners, Alcibiades made himself popular in Sparta. However, while on a mission, he found himself in trouble for seducing the wife of Agis, one of the two kings. He consequently deserted to the Persians and insinuated himself into the confidence of their governor, Tissaphernes, whom he advised to intervene. He sent word to the Athenians that if they would replace democracy with an aristocratic government, he would arrange Persian gold for them.

The Athenians put oligarchs in power, but they ignored Alcibiades and negotiated with Sparta. He again switched sides and, with the support of the Athenian navy, restored democracy in Athens. Alcibiades won battles against the enemy fleet, and his fame was never greater. The people reelected him general. Then the navy lost a crucial battle while Alcibiades was away engaging in useless diplomacy. The Athenians held him responsible and banished him.

Alcibiades retreated to a fortress above Aegospotami, where by chance the Athenian and Spartan navies had their final confrontation. The Athenians rejected his advice on how to win the battle, and their navy was destroyed. Fearing the victorious Spartans, Alcibiades sought shelter with the Persians. However, their well-founded mistrust was his undoing. One night, lying naked in the arms of a courtesan, Alcibiades discovered that Persian soldiers had surrounded the house and set it on fire. Wrapping a cloak around his arm, he grasped his sword and ran out to confront them. Fearing to get close to Alcibiades, the soldiers killed him with arrows.

Impact

More than any other individual, Alcibiades was responsible for the defeat of Athens in the Peloponnesian War. He represents the breakdown of loyalty to the city-state in Greek society, and he paved the way for the eclipse of

Alcibiades of Athens (standing center right). (F. R. Niglutsch)

Party Crasher

Alcibiades liked to be the center of attention, especially when his old teacher Socrates was around. In his *Symposion (Symposium,* 1701), Plato describes a hilarious but emotionally charged scene involving the two men. According to Plato, in 416 B.C.E., as Alcibiades was at the height of his popularity in Athens, Socrates and several prominent authors held a party for the poet Agathon, who had just won a drama award. They passed the evening discussing ideal love. Socrates had just finished a long speech, to everyone's admiration and approval, when Alcibiades arrived. Demanding to be included, he tumbled into the room, drunk and wearing a large, unraveling wreath on his head. At once, he squeezed his way onto the bench next to Agathon. He claimed he came to bestow the wreath upon Agathon in honor of his triumph.

Then Alcibiades noticed that Socrates was sitting on the other side of Agathon. What followed was a medley of jealousy, strained charm, and sardonic banter, with an underlying hint of Alcibiades' spite-tinged regret that he had disappointed Socrates in a basic way. Alcibiades pretended to be startled and then made a show of preparing a wreath for Socrates too. He called out for more wine, teasing Socrates. When another partygoer upbraided him for interrupting their conversation, Alcibiades launched into a long, rambling oration in praise of the old philosopher. First admitting that Socrates was the only person who had ever made him ashamed of himself, Alcibiades then raved about the old man's endurance and bravery in battle, his wisdom and eloquence, his indifference to time and weather, and his drinking capacity. However, he then complained, at length, that he could never succeed in seducing Socrates, no matter what he tried. "I really don't know what to do about him," he said.

Socrates was not fooled. He understood that his attention to Agathon had made Alcibiades jealous. Alcibiades was only pretending to be drunk, he warned Agathon, in order to grab attention. When Alcibiades threatened to move in between Agathon and Socrates, Agathon got up to prevent it. A scramble for seating on the bench nearly ensued when more merrymakers suddenly crowded into the room from the street and drowned out all further conversation. At that point, apparently, Alcibiades gave up and left.

Athens under the shadow of the Macedonian empire of Philip II and Alexander the Great.

Alcibiades has therefore been remembered as an archetypal traitor. The biographer Plutarch matched him with another famous traitor, Coriolanus, the general who fought against his own motherland, Rome. American writers have compared Alcibiades with Benedict Arnold, the American commander who betrayed the Americans during the Revolutionary War.

Further Reading

Ellis, Walter M. *Alcibiades*. London: Routledge, 1989. Scholarly and readable, this is the standard biography.

Plato. *The Symposium*. Translated by Christopher Gill. London: Penguin Books, 1999. The final speech by the drunken Alcibiades is among the finest pieces of Greek literature.

Plutarch. *The Rise and Fall of Athens*. Translated by Ian Scott-Kilvert. London: Penguin Books, 1960. *Life of Alcibiades*, the surviving ancient biography, is the eighth of nine lives covered in this collection.

Strassler, Robert B., ed. *The Landmark Thucydides*. New York: Free Press, 1996. An excellent edition of Thucydides' *Peloponnesian War*. Alcibiades' part in the conflict is covered in books 5-8.

—J. Donald Hughes

See also: Benedict Arnold.

Alexander VI

Roman Catholic pope (1492-1503)

Born: January 1, 1431; Játiva, near Valencia, Aragon (now in Spain)
Died: August 18, 1503; Rome, Papal States (now in Italy)
Also known as: Rodrigo Borgia; Rodrigo de Borja y Doms (birth name)
Cause of notoriety: As the 211th pope of the Catholic Church, Alexander VI earned a reputation for immorality and corruption.
Active: 1492-1503
Locale: Rome, Papal States (now in Italy)

Early Life

Born into a noble family that had long contributed prelates to the Catholic Church, Rodrigo de Borja y Doms—to be known as Pope Alexander VI (al-ihg-ZAN-uhr)—began a clerical career early in life. In 1449, he went to Italy, where his name was Italianized to Borgia, to study law at the University of Bologna. In 1454, his uncle became Pope Callistus III, who, in 1457, named Borgia the cardinal, papal vice-chancellor, and governor of the Papal States. These were major offices which provided Borgia the opportunity to amass wealth and power, and he made the most of it. His abilities enabled him to serve as vice-chancellor through the reigns of four more popes. Although a priest, he had as many as eight children. Fathering children was common for cardinals during the Renaissance, but few had so many. In 1473, Vannozza dei Catanei became his mistress and bore his famous children: Cesare, Giovanni, and Lucrezia.

Papal Career

In the papal election of 1492, Borgia was regarded as an unlikely choice because he was not Italian. However, when the cardinals deadlocked, they turned to him. Because he voted for himself, Borgia won the election. The new pope took the name Alexander VI, but his reason for this choice remains unknown. He made Cesare a cardinal at age eighteen and set to work to make Giovanni a prince. He also arranged marriages for his daughters, especially Lucrezia, whose bad reputation owes much to the fates of her first two husbands: Alexander forced her to have her first marriage annulled, and Lucrezia's second husband was murdered, probably by her brother Giovanni. It is unlikely that she was guilty of incest with her father, an accusation that was used to blacken the reputations of both.

As pope, Alexander had two more sons and took Julia Farnese, sister of the future Pope Paul III, as his mistress. After unknown murderers killed Giovanni in 1497, Alexander focused on establishing Cesare as the ruler of a region carved out of the Papal States. Cesare resigned his office of cardinal on the grounds that his father had coerced him into the clergy. Then, commanding a papal army, Cesare sieged several cities in the pope's name, badly damaging respect for the papacy across Europe. The pope then sent Cesare to France in 1498 to negotiate with Louis XII, who gave him a French duchy. In exchange, Alexander annulled Louis's first marriage.

Alexander's reign saw Christopher Columbus's first voyage in 1492, which opened a dispute between Portu-

Alexander VI.

gal and Spain over claims to the newly discovered lands. The countries took the matter to the pope, who mediated the Treaty of Tordesillas in 1494; it divided the new lands between the two realms. Also in 1494, Charles VIII of France, deciding to make good a French claim to the kingdom of Naples, led the first French invasion of Italy and ousted Ferdinand II from Naples. Aragon in turn intervened in support of his relative. Alexander helped Ferdinand establish control over Naples and put Spain in the position to dominate the papacy for the next one hundred years.

In 1503, Alexander became sick a day after he attended a dinner at which Cesare and several other persons also fell ill, and he died a week later. Since his corpse reputedly turned black immediately and Cesare was also ill, contemporary belief was that both had been poisoned. Modern experts argue that no known poison causes such a pattern of death and Alexander's death was probably from malaria.

Too Much for His Coffin

Rodrigo de Borja y Doms was a man of great appetites, which only increased after he entered the Church as a prelate. Although he was reportedly abstemious with food and drink, he so pursued society, money, power, and women that he scandalized an age used to rapacity and corruption. While he was a cardinal, Rodrigo earned a reprimand from Pope Pius II for his flagrantly unholy life. He accumulated wealth and power by acquiring benefices. He had mistresses, two of them long-term, and at least eight children. When he became Pope Alexander VI, his greed increased with his power. Besides appointing his children to lucrative church offices, he transferred benefices to them, sold indulgences with abandon, and bought and sold ecclesiastical posts—the forbidden practice of simony. In fact, he may have bribed his way into the papacy itself. When rivals appeared, he had them murdered. He has been accused of poisoning three cardinals himself.

Alexander VI earned a black reputation early, and it grew steadily darker; however, he seemed to have taken it all calmly. He laughed at the cleverness of the racy songs that circulated about his crimes, for instance, and did not shy away from socializing. Still, his death and its aftermath show that this reputation haunted him ever afterward and effaced anything of actual merit in his papacy: The account from Johannes Burchard, a contemporary papal official, seems to reflect a punishment as diabolical as his sins. Alexander's body decayed rapidly, emitting sulfurous fumes; the tongue swelled so much it jammed open the mouth; and the corpse looked inhuman when displayed to the public. Burchard claims that officials had to jump on the coffin lid in order to close it over the body.

Only four prelates attended the traditional requiem mass for the dead pope, after which his successor, Pope Pius III, prohibited further memorial masses. Pius III said, "It is blasphemous to pray for the damned." After the briefest mourning period, Alexander's body was buried in a minor church outside St. Peter's Basilica. Until well into the nineteenth century, no historian or Catholic writer made any attempt to revise Alexander's reputation. In 1860, Jacob Burckhardt credited Alexander with restoring the temporal power of the Church, and a few other writers expressed doubt that he had committed some of his most wicked crimes, such as incest with his daughter Lucrezia.

Source: Johannes Burchard, *Johannis Burchardi Argentinensis capelle pontificie sacrorum rituum magistri diarium, sive Rerum urbanarum commentarii (1483-1506)*, edited by L. Thuasne (Paris: E. Leroux, 1883-1885).

Impact

Alexander VI's reputation as a corrupt and immoral pope badly harmed the prestige of the papacy. The reign of Julius II (1503-1512), "the Warrior Pope," further damaged the papacy's reputation by the methods he used to recover the Papal States from Cesare Borgia shortly before the Protestant Reformation began. Nevertheless, actions effected or endorsed by Alexander, such as the implementation of the Tordesillas Line (which was officially in effect until at least 1560), had long-range impact on Europe and the world.

Further Reading

Cloulas, Ivan. *The Borgias*. Translated by Gilda Roberts. New York: Watts, 1998. Excellent study of the family by a prominent French historian of the Renaissance era, with a large section devoted to Alexander.

Ferrara, Orestes. *The Borgia Pope, Alexander the Sixth*. New York: Sheed, 1940. A dated but detailed biography, highly sympathetic to Alexander and eager to disprove most of the accusations against him.

Masson, Georgina. *The Borgias*. New York: Penguin, 2001. A popular account of the family, which draws on modern scholarship. It argues against the most lurid elements of Alexander's reputation.

—*Frederic J. Baumgartner*

See also: Cesare Borgia; Lucrezia Borgia.

Aldrich Ames

American spy

Born: June 16, 1941; River Falls, Wisconsin
Also known as: Aldrich Hazen Ames (full name); Rick Ames
Major offenses: Conspiracy to commit espionage and tax evasion
Active: April, 1985-February, 1994
Locale: United States, Europe, and Soviet Union
Sentence: Life in prison without possibility of parole

Early Life

Aldrich Ames (AWL-drihch aymz) was born to Carleton Cecil and Rachel Aldrich Ames in River Falls, Wisconsin, the eldest of three children. His father was a college professor and his mother a high school English teacher, both in River Falls. His father began a career with the Central Intelligence Agency's (CIA's) directorate of operations in 1952, but because of alcohol abuse, his career with the agency was somewhat troubled. The younger Ames worked as a CIA records analyst, marking classified documents during the summer of 1957, and returned to the same job the following two summers. He graduated from McLean (Virginia) High School and entered the University of Chicago in 1959, taking classes in drama; he dropped out because of failing grades. Ames returned to the CIA as a clerk typist in 1962 and later took a job as a document analyst for the agency while attending George Washington University, from which he received a bachelor's degree in history in 1967.

Espionage Career

Ames was accepted into the CIA's Career Trainee Program in 1967, where he was trained as an operations officer for the recruitment of foreign agents. He placed low in psychological evaluation for the job, but he finished his training with strong marks. His first overseas assignment was to Ankara, Turkey, which began in 1969. In the early 1970's, Ames received training in Russian language and was assigned to the Soviet-East European Division. From 1976 to 1981, he served as an agent in New York, and in 1982, he received his last promotion.

From April, 1985, to February, 1994, Ames led a double life as a mole for the KGB (the Soviet intelligence agency), providing it with an abundance of classified documents. He effectively shut down all CIA intelligence in the Soviet Union by revealing to the KGB the names of all Soviets employed as spies by the United

Spy vs. Spy

In 1999, George Washington University's National Security Archive published a declassified interview with Aldrich Ames. Asked if he had considered the effects of betraying the double agents of the Central Intelligence Agency (CIA), he replied:

I knew quite well, when I gave the names of our agents in the Soviet Union, that I was exposing them to the full machinery of counterespionage and the law, and then prosecution, and capital punishment, certainly, in the case of KGB and GRU [Soviet military intelligence] officers who would be tried in a military court, and certainly others, that they were almost all at least potentially liable to capital punishment. There's simply no question about this. Now . . . I believed that the KGB with the support of the political leadership, would want to keep it very much under wraps, and I felt at the time that not only for the overriding reason, practical reason of protecting me, they would also find it useful to cover up the fact, the embarrassing fact of who so many of these people were, and that this would all have a somewhat dampening effect on the results of the compromise. But of course you know, given time and circumstances, obviously these folks I knew would have to answer for what they'd done. And certainly I inured myself against, you know, a reaction to that. The only thing I ever withheld from the KGB . . . were the names of two agents whom I personally had known and handled and had a particular feeling for. So, obviously . . . obviously I was feeling something; I distinguished two agents from all the rest, on the basis of my personal feelings. Later, after the compromises, when I was in Rome, feeling that, for particular reasons, these folks would not be persecuted, much less prosecuted, I did give the KGB their names, but I felt confident when I did that, that the consequences to them would not be significant, and they have not been. But it is important to at least recognize in retrospect that while a number of the agents that I compromised were executed others were treated with relative leniency.

Later in the interview, Ames expressed surprise that the Soviets punished so many moles so swiftly. The disappearance of these agents eventually led to his own arrest.

Source: National Security Archive, "Cold War, Episode 21: Spies" (March 14, 1999).

States. In places such as Bogotá, Colombia; Caracas, Venezuela; Vienna, Austria; and Washington, D.C., Ames had numerous meetings with Soviet agents, sharing classified documents on sensitive security, defense, and foreign relations issues. The secrets included detailed information on double agent operations, security weaknesses, and the agency's mode of operation.

Ames would wrap classified documents in plastic bags in packets of five to seven pounds each and would carry them without suspicion from the agency. He became the highest paid spy in the world: His treasonous activities brought him $1.8 million in payoffs; an additional $900,000 was held for him in a Moscow bank. Ames lived a lavish lifestyle with Jaguar cars, expensive furniture, many charge cards, and a half-million-dollar home, yet these excesses did not raise suspicions within the CIA. After a long and often bungled investigation, in February, 1994, the fifty-two-year-old Ames was arrested at his home in Arlington, Virginia, and charged with espionage.

Legal Action and Outcome

Ames was charged with conspiracy to commit espionage and tax evasion. He pleaded guilty to these charges on April 28, 1994. His wife, Maria del Rosario Casas Ames, was arrested later at their home on the same charges. Ames and his wife cooperated fully with authorities and arranged plea bargains by which they forfeited their assets to the U.S. government. About one-half million dollars of those assets were given to the Justice Department's Victims Assistance Fund.

Ames was sentenced to life in prison without the possibility of parole, and Maria was given a sentence of sixty-three months. Based on interrogations and interviews after his arrest, it is clear that Ames's motive for spying changed markedly through the years, from a need to pay off modest debts to a desire to support a lavish lifestyle.

Impact

The information provided by Aldrich Ames led to the compromise of approximately one hundred U.S. intelligence operations and the execution of ten U.S. sources. Ames arguably inflicted more harm on U.S. security than any single person in American history. He also engaged in flagrant personal and professional misconduct, including inattention to detail, alcohol abuse, financial excesses, administrative carelessness, and an extramarital affair with a foreign national. His egregious acts against the country went undetected for nine years; during his thirty-one years in the agency, he received no reprimands. In the long term, however, his actions contributed to a growing public mistrust and cynicism toward government agencies.

Ames committed espionage for money and ego, with no philosophical allegiance to the Soviet Union. Psychologists have characterized him as grandiose, impulsive, and interested in short-term financial gain. Numerous articles and books have been written on the case, and Ames's life was portrayed by Timothy Hutton in the 1998 television film *Aldrich Ames: Traitor Within*.

Further Reading

Cherkashin, Victor. *Spy Handler: Memoir of a KGB Officer*. New York: Basic Books, 2005. A scholarly account of Cold War espionage by the retired KGB officer who recruited Ames for the Soviet Union.

Earley, Pete. *Confession of a Spy: The Real Story of Aldrich Ames*. New York: Putnam, 1997. Based on fifty hours of interviews with Ames and interviews with KGB handlers and the CIA agents who collected the evidence that ultimately led to Ames's arrest.

Richelson, Jeffrey T. *The U.S. Intelligence Community*. Boulder, Colo.: Westview Press, 1999. An overview of many dimensions of the intelligence community with numerous references to the Ames case.

—*Ann M. Legreid*

See also: Anthony Blunt; Christopher John Boyce; Guy Burgess; John Cairncross; Klaus Fuchs; Robert Philip Hanssen; Alger Hiss; Daulton Lee; Donald Duart Maclean; Kim Philby; Jonathan Pollard; Ethel Rosenberg; Julius Rosenberg.

Oakes Ames

American capitalist and railroad promoter

Born: January 10, 1804; Easton, Massachusetts
Died: May 8, 1873; North Easton, Massachusetts
Cause of notoriety: Ames was accused of bribing congressmen by offering them stock in the Union Pacific construction company at prices below true value
Active: 1865-1872
Locale: Washington, D.C.

Early Life

The son of Oliver Ames, a manufacturer, Oakes Ames (ohks aymz) attended district schools and spent a few months at a local academy before apprenticing, at age sixteen, at the family shovel factory. His father retired in 1844, turning over the business to Oakes and his younger brother, Oliver, Jr. The firm flourished, meeting growing demand for quality shovels created by westward expansion, the California gold rush, and the rise of railroads. By 1855 Oakes Ames began investing profits in Western land and railroads.

A strong Free Soil advocate, Ames contributed substantial sums to sustain the Emigrant Aid Society's active support of antislavery groups in Kansas. In 1862 he won election to Congress as a Republican and served ten years. Ames rarely spoke on the floor of the House but was active in committees, especially the Committee on the Pacific Railroad.

Crédit Mobilier

In 1865 Thomas Durant, chief promoter of the Union Pacific Railroad, convinced the Ames brothers to invest in his company. In August, Oakes Ames bought a major stake in the Crédit Mobilier construction company Durant established to actually build the Union Pacific. Durant followed a practice common in mid-nineteenth century railroad building, in which directors and other major investors in the road formed a separate corporation to construct the line. Inflating costs guaranteed insiders a profit on their investment, regardless of whether the railroad itself ever produced dividends for other stockholders. Ames helped Durant sell $2,500,000 in stock for the Crédit Mobilier, which would finance the building and be repaid by Union Pacific stock and bonds, including government bonds Congress authorized to subsidize constructing a transcontinental railroad through unprofitable uninhabited territory.

The Ames brothers soon entered into a struggle for control with Durant. Although unable to eliminate Durant from the enterprise, the Ames group made Oliver acting president of the Union Pacific in 1867, and Oakes effectively took over Crédit Mobilier.

After Congress resumed session in November, 1867, amid rumors that a major distribution of bonds and stock would soon occur, Ames sold 160 shares of Crédit Mobilier to nine representatives and two senators at par value of $100. Ames explained in letters, later published to his intense discomfort, that he wanted to engage the interests of congressmen on behalf of the Union Pacific and thus increase the railroad's influence. Ames permitted some congressmen to pay for their stock out of future

Oakes Ames. (Library of Congress)

dividends. In December, 1867, and January, 1868, Crédit Mobilier distributed bonds and stock salable for more than $99 for each $100 par share. Four more allotments quickly followed in 1868, making it an immediately profitable investment.

Political Disgrace

On September 4, 1872, in the midst of the presidential campaign, the *New York Sun* published Ames's letters along with allegations grossly exaggerating the amount of money involved. Ames was now central to the biggest political scandal of the century; among the recipients of his largesse were current vice president Schuyler Colfax and vice president-elect Henry Wilson.

In December, Congress appointed investigative committees that heard much contradictory evidence. A February committee report asserted that Ames tried to bribe congressmen by offering them Crédit Mobilier stock much below true value and had lied to the committee about his motives. The committee recommended that Ames be expelled from Congress, along with James Brooks of New York, the lone Democrat involved. However, the eleven implicated Republicans were absolved of accepting bribes and merely criticized for bad judgment in accepting stock. On February 28, 1873, the House rejected expulsion, instead voting to censure Ames and Brooks formally for their conduct.

Ames had not sought reelection; when the session ended on March 4 he went home, where he was welcomed by a brass band and a testimonial dinner. Ames refused to concede that he had done anything unethical, but the scandal destroyed his reputation for impeccable honesty, an outcome he and his descendants bitterly resented. On May 5, Ames suffered a paralytic stroke and died three days later.

Impact

The major impact of Oakes Ames's Crédit Mobilier scandal was on public opinion. Except for Ames and Brooks, no official suffered any consequence. No politician lost an election because of his Crédit Mobilier connection. Indeed, Representative James A. Garfield of Ohio, recipient of ten shares he expected to pay for out of future distributions, was elected president in 1880.

The sensational newspaper coverage and congressional hearings on the scandal validated cynical beliefs that all politicians were corrupt and all businessmen criminally greedy. Crédit Mobilier became the symbol of post-Civil War corruption, and every later reform movement could cite the scandal to justify its program. When the Union Pacific went bankrupt in 1893, long-defunct Crédit Mobilier was blamed, despite the fact that most nineteenth century railroads became bankrupt.

Grossly exaggerated estimates of Crédit Mobilier profits have become embedded in the historical record. *Americana* and *Encarta* encyclopedia articles assert that congressmen received $33 million in bribes from the company, ignoring a careful 1960 study by an outstanding economic historian who estimated total Crédit Mobilier profit on railroad building at between $13 million and $15.5 million (still a handsome return on a $2.5 million investment in five years). Although few people remember Oakes Ames, his scandal became a permanent part of American historical mythology.

Further Reading

Ambrose, Stephen E. *Nothing Like It in the World: The Men Who Built the Transcontinental Railroad, 1863-1869*. New York: Simon & Schuster, 2000. An anecdotal narrative of creating the transcontinental railroad, praising engineers, workers, and financiers involved.

Ames, Charles Edgar. *Pioneering the Union Pacific: A Reappraisal of the Builders of the Railroad*. New York: Appleton-Century-Crofts, 1969. The author, a direct descendant of Oakes Ames, uses an extended examination of Union Pacific financing to defend his ancestor against all accusations.

Bain, David Haward. *Empire Express: Building the First Transcontinental Railroad*. New York: Viking, 1999. A detailed history with extensive information on insider infighting that led to exposure of Oakes Ames's stock distributions to congressmen.

Fogel, Robert William. *The Union Pacific Railroad: A Case in Premature Enterprise*. Baltimore: The Johns Hopkins University Press, 1960. A future Nobel Prize winner in economics dispels myths concerning the financing of the Union Pacific.

—*Milton Berman*

See also: Schuyler Colfax; Jim Fisk.

Idi Amin

Dictator of Uganda (1971-1979)

Born: c. 1925; near Koboko, West Nile Province, British East Africa (now Uganda)
Died: August 16, 2003; Jiddah, Saudi Arabia
Also known as: Idi Amin Dada Oumee (full name); Big Daddy; Butcher of Africa; Conqueror of the British Empire; Lord of All the Beasts of the Earth and Fishes of the Sea
Cause of notoriety: While president of Uganda, Amin disregarded human rights, oppressed ethnic minorities, and orchestrated a reign of terror that resulted in the deaths of approximately 300,000 Ugandans.
Active: 1971-1979
Locale: Uganda

Early Life

Idi Amin (EE-dee ah-MEEN) was born in about 1925 to Muslim parents in northwest Uganda, which was then part of the British Empire. His father, a member of the Kakwa ethnic group, deserted the family when Amin was a young child. His mother, a member of the Lugbara ethnic group, was sometimes said to be a sorceress. She and her son lived in poverty, frequently moving in search of employment. Amin attended a missionary school through the fourth grade but was then forced to quit in order to work at odd jobs.

Idi Amin. (Hulton Archive/Getty Images)

Political Career

At the age of twenty-two, Amin enlisted as a private in the British army. While serving in Uganda, Somalia, and Kenya, he earned a reputation as a zealous, skillful, and ruthless soldier. In 1951, he further demonstrated his combative spirit by winning the title of Uganda's light heavyweight boxing champion, which he kept for nine years. When Uganda became independent in 1962, he was one of only two commissioned African officers in the armed forces.

Having established a close relationship with Milton Obote, Uganda's first prime minister, Amin was promoted to major general and named commander of the army in 1966. When both men were accused of involvement in gold smuggling, Obote suspended Uganda's constitution and declared himself president, relying on Amin's control of the army. Obote showed his gratitude by promoting Amin to chief of the general staff of the entire armed forces. Amin soon used this position to supply arms to Sudanese and Congolese rebels and to make contacts with British and Israeli agents. In 1970, after Obote barely survived an assassination attempt, he suspected Amin of involvement and ordered an investigation.

On January 25, 1971, when Obote was out of the country, Amin seized control of the Uganda government in a coup d'état. Although most Ugandans and foreign observers initially welcomed Obote's ouster, the new president quickly established a dictatorship based on terror and extreme violence. In addition to authorizing the military police to arrest and detain citizens indefinitely without judicial supervision, Amin secretly organized extermination squads to eliminate actual and potential enemies. His first targets were officers and solders of the Acholi and Lango ethnic groups (Obote's strongest supporters). Within a year, about six hundred soldiers and scores of leading civilians were dead at Amin's hands. Frequently, their bodies were thrown into the Nile River.

In 1972, Amin declared an "economic war" against the country's large minority group from India, who dominated much of Uganda's trade and manufacturing. After forcing about seventy thousand Indians to leave Uganda within three months, Amin transferred titles of some four thousand abandoned houses and businesses to his friends and supporters. When Britain protested and broke diplomatic ties with Uganda, Amin nationalized almost a hundred British-owned companies. Although such policies were popular among many poor Ugandans, they garnered fierce criticism from abroad and did great damage to the country's fragile economy.

Another of Amin's early goals was to make Uganda into an Islamic country. In 1972 he ordered Israelis to leave Uganda, then made an alliance with the anti-Israeli Palestinian Liberation Organization (PLO). When the PLO brought a highjacked jetliner carrying ninety-one hostages to Entebbe in 1976, Ugandan troops helped guard the hostages. With a rapid strike, however, Israeli paratroopers freed the hostages. Amin was so angry that he ordered the execution of two hundred army officers and government officials.

In 1977, following an attempt to assassinate him, Amin ordered the slaughter of tens of thousands of civilian dissidents, most of whom belonged to the Acholi and Langi groups. The victims included an Anglican archbishop and two cabinet members. The leaders of the British Commonwealth and other foreign observers condemned the killings. About this time, rebellions began to break out in various parts of Uganda. Observing Amin's increasing irrationality and emotional outbursts, some speculated that he was suffering from an undiagnosed mental disorder.

In 1978, despite his deteriorating situation, Amin invaded Tanzania with the goal of annexing the disputed Kagera region. Within a few months, however, Tanzanian troops successfully launched a counterattack against Uganda, and they captured the city of Kampala on April 10, 1979. Having arranged for such an emergency, Amin boarded a plane and fled to Libya with several of his wives and mistresses, as well as about twenty of his children. He eventually settled in Saudi Arabia, where he lived comfortably until dying of kidney failure in 2003.

Statements Attributed to Idi Amin

Many of Idi Amin's public statements reflected his egotism and arrogance:

- I myself consider myself the most powerful figure in the world.
- Sometimes people mistake the way I talk for what I am thinking.
- If we knew the meaning to everything that is happening to us, then there would be no meaning.
- In any country there must be people who have to die. They are the sacrifices any nation has to make to achieve law and order.
- You cannot run faster than a bullet.
- *To an adviser:* I want your heart. I want to eat your children.

Impact

More than a quarter of a million Ugandans died as a result of Idi Amin's despotic rule, and he left the country economically devastated and fractured into numerous warring fractions. The population of Uganda continued to suffer from the consequences of his inept and arbitrary rule long after his ouster. Tanzania's army occupied Uganda until 1981. This was followed by a succession of coups and unstable presidents, while rival groups conducted guerrilla campaigns until the achievement of a precarious peace in the late 1980's.

Further Reading

Allen, John. *Idi Amin*. Farmington Hills. Mich.: Thomson Gale, 2003. A brief account of the tyrant and his acts, written primarily for junior high and high school students.

Allen, Peter. *Interesting Times: Life in Uganda Under Idi Amin*. East Sussex, England: Book Guild, 2000. A fascinating book based on the diaries of a white Briton who lived and worked in Uganda for thirty-two years.

Decalo, Samuel. *Psychoses of Power: African Personal Dictatorships*. Gainesville: Florida Academic Press, 1998. From a political psychology perspective, the book focuses on Idi Amin and two other brutal leaders.

Gwyn, David. *Idi Amin: Death-Light of Africa*. Boston: Little, Brown, 1977. Gwyn, who lived for a time in Uganda, asserts that Amin suffered from "hypomania" and probably exaggerates his role in the country's tragedy.

Omara-Otunnu, Amii. *Politics and the Military in Uganda, 1890-1985*. New York: St. Martin's Press, 1987. A scholarly and readable survey of the role of military power in governing Uganda.

Smith, George Ivan. *Ghosts of Kampala: Rise and Fall of Idi Amin*. New York: St. Martin's Press, 1980. Dramatic account of the suffering of Uganda's people during Amin's regime.

Turyahikayo-Rugyema, Benomi. *Idi Amin Speaks: An Annotated Selection of His Speeches*. Madison: University of Wisconsin Press, 1998. A collection of primary source materials that gives insight into the way Amin perceived his own policies and goals.

—*Thomas Tandy Lewis*

See also: Sani Abacha; Omar al-Bashir; Jean-Bédel Bokassa; Samuel K. Doe; Mengistu Haile Mariam; Mobutu Sese Seko; Robert Mugabe; Muhammad Siad Barre; Charles Taylor.

Yigal Amir

Israeli assassin

Born: May 23, 1970; Herzliya, Israel
Major offense: Murder of Israeli prime minister Yitzhak Rabin
Active: November 4, 1995
Locale: Kings of Israel Square (now known as Rabin Square), Tel Aviv, Israel
Sentence: Life imprisonment plus fourteen years

Early Life

Yigal Amir (YEE-gol ah-MEER) was one of eight children born to a religious family of Jews who emigrated to Israel from Yemen. His mother taught kindergarten, and his father was a biblical scribe. Amir served in the Israel Defense Forces in the prestigious Golani Brigade unit and was a member of the Hesder program, which combined army service and religious study. Amir studied law at Bar Ilan University and was active in right-wing groups that held demonstrations to oppose Prime Minister Yitzhak Rabin's signing of the Oslo accords.

Criminal Career

Amir, who had no previous criminal record on November 4, 1995, went to a Tel Aviv peace rally held in support of the Oslo accords. He waited for Rabin by his limousine, then shot him twice. He also injured Yoram Rubin, a security guard. As part of a biblical justification for this act, he referred to Rabin as a *moser*, one who hands over fellow Jews to be killed. Amir said Rabin was a legitimate target for assassination because he authorized the transfer of land in the West Bank and Gaza to the Palestinians.

Legal Action and Outcome

Amir was apprehended at the scene and expressed satisfaction with Rabin's death. He was convicted and sentenced to life imprisonment plus six years for injuring the security guard and eight additional years for conspiring to commit the murder with one of his brothers, Hagai Amir, and a friend, Dror Adani. Amir expressed no remorse for his act.

Impact

Yigal Amir's crime was a shock to the collective Israeli psyche, as all previous assumptions (including those of personnel charged with protecting the prime minister) were that any serious threats came from hostile elements in the Arab population. Following Amir's arrest, the religious right—including its vast majority of nonextremist, nonviolent adherents—was vilified in the Israeli and world presses.

The case also generated legal challenges and innovations. In December, 2001, for example, the Israeli Knesset passed a law preventing presidential pardons or commutations for those convicted of murdering the prime minister. This act did not name Amir specifically, but he was clearly its impetus.

In January, 2004, the Israel Prison Authority rejected Amir's request to marry a Russian émigré who had been visiting him in prison on a regular basis. This request also met with great opposition across the Israeli political spectrum. The marriage was officially approved by the Jerusalem Rabbinical Court in 2005, but the Interior Ministry resisted registering the two as a couple. The Israel Prison Authority continued to deny the couple conjugal visiting rights. They, in turn, asked prison authorities for permission to have a child through artificial insemination.

Further Reading

Karpin, Michael, and Ina Friedman. *Murder in the Name of God: The Plot to Kill Yitzchak Rabin*. New York: Metropolitan Books, 1998. Detailed analysis of the religious and political framework in both Israel and the United States that led to the Rabin assassination.

Kiener, Ronald C. "Gushist and Qutbian Aapproaches to Government: A Comparative Analysis of Religious Assassination." *Numen* 44, no. 3 (1997): 229-241. An analysis of the contrasting ideological underpinnings involved in the murders of Anwar Sadat and Yitzhak Rabin.

Shahak, Israel, and Norton Mezvinsky. *Jewish Fundamentalism in Israel.* London: Pluto Press, 1999. Promotes the thesis that Jewish fundamentalist attitudes toward non-Jews and sovereignty over the land of Israel helped some to try to justify Yitzhak Rabin's assassination and Baruch Goldstein's attack at the Tomb of the Patriarchs in Hebron.

—*Eric Metchik*

See also: Said Akbar; Jean-Marie Bastien-Thiry; Nathuram Vinayak Godse; Mijailo Mijailovic; Thenmuli Rajaratnam; Beant Singh; Satwant Singh; Sirhan Sirhan; Ramzi Yousef.

Albert Anastasia

New York Mafia boss

Born: February 26, 1902; Tropea, Italy
Died: October 25, 1957; New York, New York
Also known as: Umberto Anastasio (birth name); Mad Hatter; High Executioner; Lord High Executioner
Cause of notoriety: Anastasia served as the homicide contract negotiator for the national crime syndicate.
Active: 1921-1957
Locale: New York, New York

Early Life

Albert Anastasia (AL-burt ah-nah-STAHSH-yah) was born Umberto Anastasio in 1902. He and his brother Anthony ("Tough Tony") immigrated to the United States during World War I. By young adulthood, both brothers were employed on the New York docks, where Albert was arrested for murder in 1921. There were several witnesses to his crime, and Albert was convicted and sentenced to death. However, he won a new trial after spending eighteen months on death row in Sing Sing prison. During the new trial, four witnesses disappeared. Others reversed their statements. The trial could not continue, and Albert was free. In 1922, he changed his name from Anastasio to Anastasia. It is speculated that he anticipated a life of crime and did not want to embarrass his family. Tony kept the family name and continued to gain influence around the docks.

Criminal Career

Anastasia began working as a bodyguard for Mafia boss Vincent Mangano during the 1920's. The Castellemmarese War—a conflict between two Prohibition-era crime bosses in New York, Joe Masseria and Salvatore Maranzano—raged from 1930 to 1931. In 1930, Charles "Lucky" Luciano approached Anastasia about overthrowing Masseria and Maranzano. Anastasia was enthusiastic and stated that he would "kill everybody" for the charismatic Luciano. Luciano successfully conspired with Meyer Lansky to gain the cooperation of many underbosses in overthrowing both Masseria and Maranzano. The coup left Luciano as the de facto "boss of bosses" in New York.

Luciano and Lansky then placed Anastasia, along with Louis Buchalter, in charge of a unit specially charged with carrying out syndicate-authorized murders. Crime historians have dubbed this unit Murder Incorporated. In 1944 Buchalter was executed, and Anastasia became the singular head of Murder Incorporated.

Anastasia achieved the title of "boss" in 1951, when Mangano disappeared. Both Anastasia and Frank Costello (who acted as syndicate boss during Luciano's exile) had reasons to want Mangano dead. Costello was facing a veiled threat from crime boss Vito Genovese. Mangano, never considered loyal to Luciano's upper echelon, could not provide Costello with "muscle." With Murder Incorporated at his disposal, Anastasia therefore seemed the logical replacement for Mangano.

Anastasia and Mangano had often squabbled about Anastasia's loyalty to Luciano, who in 1936 was sentenced to fifty years in prison for operating houses of prostitution. When an Allied troop ship caught fire during World War II, Luciano was tapped by the Navy to thwart pro-Nazi sabotage on the New York waterfront. Anastasia and his brother Tony were in a perfect position to "protect" the docks—and after the war, Luciano was pardoned.

Costello ensured that Anastasia, who named Carlo Gambino his underboss, was given the top seat in Mangano's former family. Unfortunately Anastasia (as Luciano had suspected) was better suited to killing than to acting as "godfather." Anastasia's lack of political savvy did little to thwart Genovese's plans to usurp Costello's leadership.

Genovese used an indirect approach, secretly undermining the authority of Costello. Genovese also gained a financial advantage by becoming one of the first Mafiosi to succeed in the narcotics market.

By 1957, Anastasia had lost favor with the syndicate. Some evidence suggests that Anastasia's psychopathic tendencies, which often disturbed other Mafia bosses, were the source of his undoing. Others have speculated that he was becoming too ambitious, attempting to interfere with Lansky's Cuban casino operations. On October 25, 1957, two assassins shot and killed Anastasia in the barbershop of a New York hotel.

Legal Action and Outcome

In 1954, Anastasia was tried on charges of tax evasion after building a lavish home that, according to his tax statements, he could not afford. The government called Charles Ferri as a witness. Ferri was a plumber whom Anastasia had paid for work done on his home. Ferri's statement was damaging. The government intended to call next upon Vincent Macri, a former Anastasia bodyguard. After Macri was found dead, a mistrial was declared. In 1955, the government tried Anastasia again, with the intention of using Ferri as a key witness. However, when federal agents tried to locate Ferri, he could not be found. As the trial was finally about to begin, Anastasia pleaded guilty to tax evasion. The terms of his plea bargain were a sentence of one year in jail and a twenty-thousand-dollar fine. It was the first time since 1921 that Anastasia was imprisoned.

Impact

Albert Anastasia was responsible for the prosperity of the New York crime syndicate after Prohibition. While he headed Murder Incorporated, the syndicate asserted influence over underworld operations in several major cities. Anastasia's manipulation of waterfront operations ensured that Luciano, perhaps the most important figure in the syndicate, could maintain power.

Anastasia's failures as a Mafia don also bore a legacy. Genovese took Anastasia's murder to mean that he himself was now the top boss in New York. However, the ascension of Genovese to the chief position in the syndicate was convenient for Gambino. In 1959, Gambino helped federal agents collar Genovese in a narcotics bust. Genovese was convicted on weak evidence and spent the last years of his life in prison. His demise paved the way for Gambino, and the Gambino family emerged from the 1950's at the head of the syndicate. Gambino's territory was inherited by John Gotti in 1985. Gotti had always been fond of the Anastasia legend.

Anastasia's demise also lends credibility to the claim that the syndicate may have had some "code of honor" regarding murder. One famous anecdote involves Anastasia's 1952 execution of a clothing salesman. The man had helped police identify a bank robber and was then rewarded; his story appeared on national television. The bank robber was not affiliated with the syndicate in any regard, but Anastasia issued a curt order to his own men: "Hit that guy! I can't stand squealers!"

Anastasia's small funeral did not truly befit a don. His wife, Elsa, moved to Canada after his death. Tony lost most of his clout when his brother was killed. Federal agents tried to convince Tony to be an informant; however, he died of natural causes before he could pursue such a career.

Further Reading

Abadinsky, Howard. *Organized Crime*. 6th ed. Belmont, Calif.: Wadsworth, 2000. An introductory text on the Mafia and organized crime.

Davis, John H. *Mafia Dynasty: The Rise and Fall of the Gambino Crime Family*. New York: Harper, 1994. Covers the history of the Gambino family.

Gosch, Martin A., and Richard Hammer. *The Last Testament of Lucky Luciano*. New York: Little, Brown, 1975. Luciano's account of Mafia activities in the United States.

Maas, Peter. *The Valachi Papers*. Rev. ed. New York: Pocket Books, 1986. Joseph Valachi's official testimony regarding the activities of the Mafia in the United States.

Raab, Selwyn. *Five Families: The Rise, Decline, and Resurgence of America's Most Powerful Mafia Empires*. New York: Thomas Dunne Books, 2005. A comprehensive analysis of the Mafia families in New York City.

Turkus, Burton B., and Sid Feder. *Murder, Inc.: The Story of "the Syndicate."* New York: Da Capo Press, 2003. Covers the syndicate before, during, and after Anastasia's rule.

—*S. E. Costanza*

See also: Joe Adonis; Paul Castellano; Vincent Coll; Joe Colombo; Carmine Galante; Carlo Gambino; Sam Giancana; Vincent Gigante; John Gotti; Sammy Gravano; Henry Hill; Richard Kuklinski; Meyer Lansky; Salvatore Maranzano; Carlos Marcello; Joe Masseria; Joseph Profaci; Dutch Schultz.

Ion Antonescu

Prime minister of Romania (1940-1944)

Born: June 15, 1882; Pitești, Romania
Died: June 1, 1946; near Jilava, Romania
Also known as: Conducător (leader); Câinele Roșu (the red dog); Ion Victor Antonescu (full name)
Major offenses: War crimes, specifically the murder of Jews
Active: 1940-1945
Locale: Romania
Sentence: Death by firing squad

Early Life

Ion Antonescu (I-on an-tohn-EHS-kyew) attended military schools in Craiova and Iaşi and graduated from the Cavalry school at the top of his class. As a lieutenant, Antonescu took part in the repression of the 1907 peasants' revolt in and around the city of Galaţi. In 1913, he won Romania's highest military decoration for his role in the Second Balkan War. During World War I, he served as chief of staff for Marshal Constantin Prezan (1916-1918). Antonescu was considered the primary reason for Romania's successful defense against the attempted invasion of Moldavia by Field Marshal Mackensen in the second half of 1917.

Military and Political Career

Between 1922 and 1926, Antonescu served as military attaché to Romania in France and Great Britain. Upon returning to Romania, he was made commander of the Scoala Superioara de Razboi (Upper School of War) between 1927 and 1930, chief of the Great Headquarters of the Army between 1933 and 1934, and defense minister between 1937 and 1938.

He was appointed prime minister by King Carol II in September, 1940, immediately after Romania had surrendered both Bessarabia and northern Bukovina to the Soviet Union on June 28, 1940. The northern half of Transylvania was ceded to Hungary on August 30. Forty-eight hours after his appointment, Antonescu forced King Carol to abdicate, with his son becoming the new king (though the post was devoid of power). Antonescu faced war on three separate fronts (the Soviet Union to the east, Germany to the west, and Bulgaria to the south). He finally decided to enter into an alliance with the Nazis. This partnership was welcomed by the Germans, who wanted open access to Romania's huge oil reserves.

Once he attained power, Antonescu formed an alliance with the Fascist Iron Guard, an ultranational, highly anti-Semitic group that sought political power. Like Adolf Hitler and the Schutzstaffel (SS) in Germany, Antonescu wanted the paramilitary guard under his direct control, as their activities undermined the state's authority. He offered them seats in the government. Once in office, the Iron Guard enacted anti-Semitic legislation: Soldiers (as well as common citizens) could initiate pogroms against Romania's Jews with impunity. Also, political assassination and blackmail of those in both financial and commercial sectors occurred commonly.

More than sixty former dignitaries or officials were executed in Jilava prison before ever being tried. Famed historian and former prime minister Nicolae Iorga and economist Virgil Madgearu, also a former government

Ion Antonescu. (AP/Wide World Photos)

official, were assassinated without even the pretense of an arrest.

The Iron Guard, like its German counterpart, was particularly adept at killing Jews. It was reported that in some situations the Germans restrained the Romanians; in other words, the Iron Guard was moving so fast it was commanded to slow its pace. Antonescu authorized special units, really death squads, to target the Jewish population. More than one hundred thousand massacres were staged for effect. During his tenure in office, Antonescu was responsible for the murders of some 280,000 to 380,000 Jews in Romania and the various territories occupied by the army.

In 1941, as the Romanian army advanced, rumors spread about how Jewish "resistance groups" attacked and killed Romanian soldiers. Antonescu ordered the "deportation" to Transnistria of the Bessarabian and Bukovinian Jews (approximately 80,000 to 150,000 individuals), who were considered "Communist agents." The term "deportation" was misleading, as the government's primary goal was not to move the people; rather, it was to eliminate as many Jews as possible. Only a small coterie of those deported ever made it back to Romania.

After the Romanian army suffered huge losses in the Battle of Stalingrad, Antonescu's influence declined sharply. In 1944, as the Germans also lost ground to the Soviets, King Michael was able to dismiss Antonescu and have him arrested.

Legal Action and Outcome

On May 17, 1946, after a ten-day trial in a Romanian court, Antonescu and twelve of his associates were convicted on charges of war crimes and sentenced to death. Both the supreme court and the king refused Antonescu's appeal for clemency. The former dictator was executed by firing squad.

Impact

After Ion Antonescu's execution, a leftist government won a rigged election in November, 1946. Many complained that the Communists took power because of Antonescu's barbaric behavior toward Jews (as well as his relationship with Hitler). On April, 13, 1948, two years after Antonescu's death, the government proclaimed itself the Romanian People's Republic and adopted a Stalinist constitution. Romania remained under Communist rule until December, 1989, when dictator Nicolae Ceauşescu was overthrown in a violent revolution. Ceauşescu stated that without Antonescu, Communism would not have gained power in Romania and, thus, a debt of gratitude was owed him.

Further Reading

Braham, R. L. *The Destruction of the Romanian and Ukrainian Jews During the Antonescu Period.* New York: Columbia University Press, 1997. Details the wanton destruction of the Jews in Romania and the Ukraine.

Ioanid, R. *The Holocaust in Romania: The Destruction of Jews and Gypsies Under the Antonescu Regime, 1940-1944.* New York: Ivan Dee, 2000. Shows that Jews were not the only ethnic minority who suffered during World War II; likewise, Hitler was not the only dictator who believed in genocide.

Watson, L. *Antonescu, Marshal of Romania: From the Great War to World War II.* London: Center for Romanian Studies, 2003. Excellent book, lucidly written; of interest to anyone studying World War II.

—*Cary Stacy Smith*

See also: Nicolae Ceauşescu; Adolf Hitler; Enver and Nexhmije Hoxha; Slobodan Milošević; Joseph Stalin; Tito.

Apache Kid

American Indian outlaw

Born: c. 1860; San Carlos Reservation, New Mexico Territory
Died: After 1894; place unknown
Also known as: Haskaybaynaynatyl (Apache for "Tall Man Who Dies Mysteriously"); Ski-be-nan-ted; the Kid
Cause of notoriety: A one-man crime wave in the 1880's and 1890's, the Apache Kid terrorized both the American Indian and Anglo-American communities in the Southwest near the Mexican border; crimes attributed to him include cattle rustling, kidnapping, rape, and murder.
Active: 1887-1894
Locale: San Carlos Reservation; New Mexico and Arizona Territories

Early Life

The Apache Kid (ah-PA-chee kihd) was born to the Pinal Apache band on the San Carlos Indian Reservation, located in the mountainous terrain of southern New Mexico. As a young man, he was known to the white settlers of nearby Globe, New Mexico, as simply the Apache Kid. He had assimilated enough into the Anglo-American community that famed U.S. Army scout Al Sieber recruited him into the corps of Native American Scouts, and the Kid participated in numerous military actions against renegade Apache bands, including that of Geronimo.

Criminal Career

The Apache Kid's criminal career began in June, 1887: Under the influence of tiswin, a powerful Native American corn liquor, he murdered a fellow Apache in accordance with a tribal vendetta code. The Kid's attempt to turn himself in to San Carlos authorities, including Sieber, exploded into a shoot-out, which maimed the latter. When the Kid turned himself in a month later, he was court-martialed for the attempted murder of Sieber and sentenced to death, though a sympathetic General Nelson Miles commuted the death sentence to ten years' imprisonment. This sentence, and the verdict, were overturned in 1889, when civil authorities in Arizona prosecuted and convicted the Kid for the attempted murder of Sieber and sentenced him to seven years in the Yuma penitentiary. Ironically, he was never arrested or prosecuted for the original murder of his fellow Apache.

On the way to Yuma, the Kid escaped custody and went into hiding in the southwestern mountains. From the likable "Kid," he transformed into a despised outlaw capable of unbridled ruthlessness. In addition to rustling cattle, he was rumored to have supported himself on the outlaw trail by killing lone whites and American Indians. He was also alleged to have been a sexual predator who kidnapped, raped, and then murdered a series of Apache women. In the 1890's he was enough of a threat to both American Indian and Anglo-American communities that territorial authorities in Arizona offered the significant sum of five thousand dollars for his capture. However, few definite facts are known of his actual criminal career—even basic information such as whether he operated with a small band or alone. Unlike the renegade Apache Geronimo, the Apache Kid made no attempt to broaden his cause into a political conflict against U.S. oppression.

Impact

Because he was never captured, the Apache Kid achieved mythic status. Although his criminal activities appear to have ceased in the mid-1890's, he became a romantic figure of the Old West in the following decades. Essentially forced into an outlaw existence, he was seen as a tragic victim, a man torn between two cultures—Apache and Anglo-American—who retreated from both into the vast spaces of the southwestern wilderness. According to one legend, the Kid retired from his life of crime to live into old age in the mountains of rural Mexico. A comic book published in the 1950's, titled *The Apache Kid*, was loosely based upon the Kid and featured an outlaw hero at odds with both the white and Indian communities.

Further Reading

Garza, Phyllis de la. *The Apache Kid*. Tucson, Ariz.: Westernlore Press, 1995. A thorough, dramatic retelling of the Kid's life, from a popular Western author.

Prassel, Frank Richard. *The Great American Outlaw: A Legacy of Fact and Fiction*. Norman: University of Oklahoma Press, 1993. Examines the social psychology of the enduring popularity of a number of Western "badmen," including the Apache Kid.

Thrapp, Dan. *Al Sieber: Chief of Scouts*. 1964. Reprint. Norman: University of Oklahoma Press, 1995. Classic biography of the Apache Kid's mentor-turned-antagonist. Provides rich background on the San Carlos Reservation and the U.S.-Apache Wars.

—*Luke Powers*

See also: Tom Bell; William H. Bonney; Curly Bill Brocius; Butch Cassidy; Bob Dalton; Emmett Dalton; Bill Doolin; John Wesley Hardin; Doc Holliday; Jesse James; Tom Ketchum; Harry Longabaugh; Bill Longley; Joaquín Murieta; Johnny Ringo; Belle Starr; Henry Starr; Hank Vaughan; Cole Younger.

Marshall Applewhite

American cult leader

Born: May 17, 1931; Spur, Texas
Died: c. March 26, 1997; Rancho Santa Fe, California
Also known as: Marshall Herff Applewhite, Jr. (full name); Bo; Do; the Mouthpiece
Cause of notoriety: Applewhite, the leader of the Heaven's Gate cult, committed suicide along with thirty-eight of his followers.
Active: c. March 26, 1997
Locale: Western United States

Early Life

Marshall Applewhite (A-puhl-wit) was the son of a Presbyterian minister in a small west Texas town. Intending to follow his father into the ministry, Applewhite entered a seminary after graduating from college in 1952. Soon he decided that his calling was music—his baritone voice had always won him praise—and he earned a master's degree from the University of Colorado. He was hired to direct choral groups at the University of Alabama. By that time he was married with two children, but in 1965, after he had a homosexual affair, his wife took the children and left. Shortly afterward, conflicts between Applewhite and university administration caused him to lose his job.

Applewhite moved to Houston, where he became the music director at St. Thomas University. He flourished there and even became engaged to a student. When he broke off the engagement, the student's father, a university trustee, used his influence to get Applewhite fired. Although Applewhite found work as choral director at a Houston theater, the loss of his job at St. Thomas and his ambivalence over his sexuality made him depressed. According to his account, it was while visiting a friend at a hospital in March, 1972, that he met Bonnie Nettles, who was working there as a nurse. Applewhite and Nettles would later recall that their meeting occurred on the propitious day of the spring equinox.

Marshall Applewhite. (AP/Wide World Photos)

Religious Career

Applewhite and Nettles immediately became inseparable. Although their relationship was reportedly platonic, Applewhite lost his job at the theater because he spent too much time with Nettles. She introduced him to theosophy, spiritualism, and channeling. The two founded the Christian Art Center in a Houston church, which taught astrology, theosophy, and mysticism. Only months later, lack of funds and rumors that they held séances in the church led to the center's closing. They both claimed to hear voices coming from unidentified flying objects (UFOs), persuading them that their destiny required them to leave behind their ordinary lives. Applewhite began to refer to himself as the "Mouthpiece" and Nettles as the "Battery."

They abruptly left Houston in 1973 and wandered about the western states. They eventually reached the Oregon coast, where after a month of meditation, their destiny was revealed to them: Like the two witnesses described in the biblical book of Revelation, they would be killed and resurrected; moreover, they believed they would be taken to Heaven in a spaceship. Others would be allowed to join them in their journey; those who wished to do so would have to undergo a metamorphosis, which required giving up human attachments and property and being celibate, as sex took energy away from the "Process," as they referred to the metamorphosis. The Process would be completed when they boarded the UFO. Meanwhile, their lack of money and hostility to convention led them to defraud motel keepers and credit card companies. Applewhite was arrested in August, 1974, for failing to return a rental car, and he spent four months in jail in St. Louis, where he was described as a model prisoner.

Still Crazy After All These Years

In 2006, the Heaven's Gate Web site was still accessible, spreading its dangerous message and glorifying the tragic suicides that occurred in conjunction with the sighting of the Hale-Bopp comet in 1997:

Whether Hale-Bopp has a "companion" or not is irrelevant from our perspective. However, its arrival is joyously very significant to us at "Heaven's Gate." The **joy** is that our Older Member in the Evolutionary Level Above Human (the "Kingdom of Heaven") has made it clear to us that Hale-Bopp's approach is the "marker" we've been waiting for—the time for the arrival of the spacecraft from the Level Above Human to take us home to "Their World"—in the literal Heavens. Our 22 years of classroom here on planet Earth is finally coming to conclusion—"graduation" from the Human Evolutionary Level. We are happily prepared to leave "this world" and go with Ti's crew. If you study the material on this website you will hopefully understand our joy and what our purpose here on Earth has been. You may even find your "boarding pass" to leave with us during this brief "window." We are so very thankful that we have been recipients of this opportunity to prepare for membership in Their Kingdom, and to experience Their boundless Caring and Nurturing.

Cult Leader

Once Applewhite was released from jail in early 1975, Nettles rejoined him. The two traveled to Los Angeles, where they won converts from a New Age group. They left the city within weeks, taking twenty-four followers with them. The believers were told that they could transform their human bodies into eternal, genderless, extraterrestrial bodies, and that UFOs would soon pick them up. They traveled widely, speaking in public—mostly to college students—and soon they had some two hundred followers. Applewhite and Nettles, considering themselves the shepherds of their flock, began to call themselves Bo and Peep.

Peep announced that a UFO would pick them up in Colorado; when it failed to appear, many left the group. After being heckled at a meeting in Kansas in April, 1976, Applewhite and Nettles, who now called themselves Do and Ti after notes in the celestial harmony, became secretive and stopped trying to win converts. Little is known about their lives during the following years except that they dashed from place to place across the western states, expecting to board a UFO. When Nettles died of cancer in 1985, Applewhite declared that she had originally come from another planet to teach him the Process, and that she had returned to the "level above human."

Suicide

After remaining out of sight for seventeen years, Applewhite reappeared in 1993 with his followers, appearing on a video, advertising in magazines, and creating a Web site in order to win converts. The Web site was called "Heaven's Gate," which became the popular name for the group. That year, eight male members, including Do, underwent castration in order to eliminate their sex drives. Do preached the message that weeds had taken over the earth, and the time had come for "spading." In 1996 the group rented a mansion in the San Diego suburb of Rancho Santa Fe, with money they had made by designing Web sites. By then Do was suffering from severe coronary arteriosclerosis.

When the comet Hale-Bopp came into view in 1997, rumors that a UFO had been sighted behind it led the Heaven's Gate members to conclude that Ti was coming to pick them up. Because it was necessary to leave their earthly vessels behind, Do and thirty-eight followers committed suicide in a meticulous fashion over a three-day period beginning on March 23, 1997.

IMPACT

News of the mass suicide and the castration of several male members of the Heaven's Gate cult astounded the United States and reinforced the image of the mad cult leader who brainwashed his followers into blind obedience.

FURTHER READING

Balch, Robert. "Bo and Peep: A Case Study of the Origins of Messianic Leadership." In *Millennialism and Charisma*, edited by Roy Wallis. Belfast: The Queen's University, 1982. Balch and another sociologist joined Bo and Peep's group as observer-participants for two months in 1975; this article provides information on Applewhite's background and early beliefs, drawing on interviews and letters written before the events of 1997.

_______. "The Evolution of a New Age Cult: From Total Overcomers Anonymous to Death at Heaven's Gate." In *Sects, Cults, and Spiritual Communities*, edited by William Zellner. Westport, Conn.: Praeger, 1998. This article by a sociologist of charismatic leadership follows the story of Heaven's Gate from 1975 to the suicides of 1997.

Wessinger, Catherine. *How the Millennium Comes Violently: From Jonestown to Heaven's Gate*. New York: Seven Bridges Press, 2000. Contains a lengthy section on Heaven's Gate with details about Applewhite's life and includes valuable insights into the process of group suicide.

—*Frederic J. Baumgartner*

SEE ALSO: Shoko Asahara; L. Ron Hubbard; Jim Jones; David Koresh; Charles Manson; Sun Myung Moon; Bonnie Nettles; Charles Sobraj.

EUGENE ARAM

English

BORN: 1704; Ramsgill, Netherdale, Yorkshire, England
DIED: August 6, 1759; York, England
MAJOR OFFENSE: Murder
ACTIVE: 1745
LOCALE: Knaresborough, Yorkshire, England
SENTENCE: Death by hanging

EARLY LIFE

The son of a gardener, Eugene Aram (YEW-jeen AY-ram) procured enough education on his own behalf to become a schoolmaster, initially in his native Ramsgill. In 1734, he and his wife, Anna, moved to Knaresborough, where he met and befriended a shoemaker, Daniel Clarke. Clarke disappeared mysteriously in February, 1745, after borrowing various items of silver, silver plate, and jewelry from his neighbors, all of which also vanished with him.

CRIMINAL CAREER

Local residents assumed that Clarke had fled with his booty, but several men were interrogated as possible accomplices, including Aram; Richard Houseman, a flax dresser; and Henry Terry, an innkeeper. Some of the missing property was found in Houseman's home and more in Aram's garden, but Aram was acquitted of theft for lack of proof that he had hidden it there. Aram left Knaresborough thereafter, abandoning his wife and followed a nomadic existence for some years. He made a living as a schoolmaster while doing research for a book he planned to write on the relationship between the Celtic and Indo-European languages.

When a skeleton was found in August, 1758, on Thistle Hill, near Knaresborough, Anna Aram declared that it must be that of Clarke and alleged that Aram, Houseman, and Clarke had come to Aram's house at 2:00 A.M. on February 8, 1845, and left together at 3:00 A.M.; they returned without Clarke at 5:00 A.M. and lit a fire. Anna claimed that she had overheard them planning to shoot her and had subsequently discovered pieces of cloth and a bloody handkerchief in the ashes of the fire. When questioned, Houseman denied that the skeleton was Clarke's but eventually elected to prove it by leading the authorities to the place where the body was actually buried, near St. Robert's Cave. Houseman claimed that he had seen Aram bludgeon Clarke to death.

LEGAL ACTION AND OUTCOME

Aram was found living in King's Lynn in Norfolk and was brought back to Yorkshire for trial. At first, he denied everything but then admitted to being in on the fraud with Clarke, Houseman, and Terry. However, he claimed that he had not gone into St. Robert's Cave when the three had returned to meet their co-conspirator and did not know that Clarke had been killed.

The trial was held at York on August 3, 1759. Anna could not testify against her husband, but Houseman gave evidence for the crown, this time telling a different story that was incompatible with his having known where the body was buried. Aram conducted his own defense, allegedly eloquently, but he failed to attack the inconsistency in Houseman's evidence and was convicted. Aram was said to have confessed to the crime thereafter, but that sort of claim was routine. He wrote a suicide note but failed in his attempt to anticipate the hangman by slashing his own wrists.

Impact

Eugene Aram's case attracted a great deal of publicity, by virtue of his having labored so long as a respected schoolmaster and his scholarly work. His story became the basis for several literary works, most notably a novel, *Eugene Aram*, penned by Edward Bulwer-Lytton in 1832 and a long poem by the younger Thomas Hood titled *The Dream of Eugene Aram: The Murderer* (1832). Bulwer-Lytton's dramatization assumes that Aram's conviction was just and attempts a proto-psychological explanation of how a man of learning and apparent good character might have committed a dreadful act. Subsequent historians, however, have wondered whether the conviction was correct, since the only evidence given against Aram was evidently perjured; it was offered by a man who was certainly involved in the murder. A much stronger case could have been made against Houseman, since Anna's evidence would have been admissible against him, and he knew where the body had been buried.

Further Reading

Bulwer-Lytton, Edward. *Eugene Aram: A Tale*. 3 vols. London: Henry Colburn and Richard Bentley, 1831-1832. Bulwer-Lytton's characterization of Aram purports to explain how an educated and seemingly respectable person might commit an ostensibly aberrant act.

Fryer, Michael, of Reeth. *The Trial and Life of Eugene Aram*. Richmond, England: M. Bell, 1832. An updated version of the 1765 account, striking a more obviously Victorian (that is, sternly disapproving) attitude to the protagonist's career.

The Genuine Account of the Trial of Eugene Aram for the Murder of Daniel Clark. York, England: Etherington, c. 1765. A typical and anonymous sensational eighteenth century pamphlet that recounts the case for the benefit of thrill-seeking readers.

Hood, Thomas. *The Dream of Eugene Aram: The Murderer*. London: Charles Tilt, 1832. A poem that attempts, less pretentiously than the Fryer account, to provide a speculative analysis of the psychological aftermath of Aram's presumed crime.

Watson, Eric R. *Eugene Aram: His Life and Trial*. Edinburgh: William Hodge, 1913. A further updating of the earlier accounts, this time adapted to twentieth century interests; it pays more attention to the actual legal proceedings and the dubious value of the evidence.

—*Brian Stableford*

See also: William Burke.

ROSCOE ARBUCKLE
Silent-film comedian

BORN: March 24, 1887; Smith Center, Kansas
DIED: June 29, 1933; New York, New York
ALSO KNOWN AS: Fatty Arbuckle; Will B. Good; William B. Goodrich; Roscoe Conkling Arbuckle (full name)
CAUSE OF NOTORIETY: At his third trial following the death of a young woman, Arbuckle was acquitted of manslaughter, but his name was forever tainted by the scandal.
ACTIVE: September, 1921
LOCALE: San Francisco, California

EARLY LIFE

Roscoe Arbuckle (AR-buh-kuhl) was born in 1887, the last of six children, to migrant parents who moved to Kansas to homestead government acreage. His birth weight, by some accounts a record-setting sixteen pounds, characterized him as an oddity. The following year the family moved to Southern California, where Arbuckle endured a difficult childhood, marked by the early death of his mother, abandonment by his father, and taunts of fellow students who labeled him "Fatty." Like many of the great silent-film comedians, Arbuckle began entertaining audiences as a child performer, first appearing on stage when he was only eight years old.

FILM CAREER

Arbuckle's film career began with the Selig Polyscope Company in 1909, but he continued stage work until 1913, when he joined the Keystone Film Company. At Mack Sennett's "fun factory," Arbuckle appeared in scores of one- and two-reel comedies, quickly becoming an audience favorite, especially with children. In the mid-teens, Arbuckle and Charles Chaplin were equally popular. Arbuckle loathed the screen name "Fatty," upon which Sennett insisted; however, the appellation that recognized Arbuckle's baby face and enormous body stuck. In 1914 Arbuckle began directing his own films, often costarring with Mabel Normand, herself a great physical comic. For a large man, Arbuckle was amazingly agile; he was an expert tumbler and a marvelous dancer. His best films were dazzling in their energy, timing, and invention; thus, he was one of a handful of comics who moved successfully from shorts to features.

In 1920 Adolph Zukor signed Arbuckle to a two-million-dollar contract that allowed the comedian complete creative control. Across more than a hundred films, Arbuckle had created a consistent screen persona of an overgrown bad boy, often pictured as a salacious flirt and a heavy drinker who misbehaved when drunk. The persona that delighted moviegoers came to haunt Arbuckle when, at a Labor Day party cohosted by Arbuckle at the St. Francis Hotel in San Francisco in 1921, a young woman became seriously ill and died several days later. Gossipmongers went into action and accused Arbuckle of raping and murdering the actress and model Virginia Rappe.

Roscoe ("Fatty") Arbuckle in 1919.

The Hays Code

In 1930, several years after the 1921 Arbuckle scandal, Will Hays devised the "Code to Govern the Making of Talking, Synchronized and Silent Motion Pictures. Formulated and Formally Adopted by the Association of Motion Picture Producers, Inc. and The Motion Picture Producers and Distributors of America, Inc. in March 1930." Known as the "Production Code" or simply the Hays Code, it was used by the film industry as an instrument to regulate material depicted in motion pictures and to stave off government-imposed censorship; it resulted, however, in self-censorship. Among its provisions were the following:

General Principles

1. No picture shall be produced that will lower the moral standards of those who see it. Hence the sympathy of the audience should never be thrown to the side of crime, wrongdoing, evil or sin.
2. Correct standards of life, subject only to the requirements of drama and entertainment, shall be presented.
3. Law, natural or human, shall not be ridiculed, nor shall sympathy be created for its violation.

Particular Applications

I. Crimes Against the Law

These shall never be presented in such a way as to throw sympathy with the crime as against law and justice or to inspire others with a desire for imitation. . . . The technique of murder must be presented in a way that will not inspire imitation. . . . Methods of Crime should not be explicitly presented. . . . Illegal drug traffic must never be presented. . . . The use of liquor in American life, when not required by the plot or for proper characterization, will not be shown.

II. Sex

The sanctity of the institution of marriage and the home shall be upheld. Pictures shall not infer that low forms of sex relationship are the accepted or common thing. . . . In general passion should so be treated that these scenes do not stimulate the lower and baser element. . . . Seduction or Rape . . . should never be more than suggested, and only when essential for the plot, and even then never shown by explicit method. . . . Sex perversion or any inference to it is forbidden. . . . Miscegenation (sex relationships between the white and black races) is forbidden. . . .

III. Vulgarity

The treatment of low, disgusting, unpleasant, though not necessarily evil, subjects should always be subject to the dictates of good taste and a regard for the sensibilities of the audience.

IV. Obscenity

Obscenity in word, gesture, reference, song, joke, or by suggestion (even when likely to be understood only by part of the audience) is forbidden.

V. Profanity

Pointed profanity (this includes the words, God, Lord, Jesus, Christ—unless used reverently—Hell, S.O.B., damn, Gawd), or every other profane or vulgar expression however used, is forbidden. . . .

Legal Action and Outcome

Arbuckle was initially charged with first-degree murder, which carried the death penalty in California. After a grand jury inquest, a judge reduced the charge to manslaughter. A district attorney with political ambitions, Matthew Brady, saw the Arbuckle case as a convenient platform for public attention and aggressively exploited the case, as did many newspapers, especially those published by William Randolph Hearst. Concerned citizens formed groups such as the Women's Vigilante Committee to decry the moral depravity of Hollywood stars.

Due to the unreliability and contradictory testimony of witnesses, the lack of circumstantial evidence, revelations of Rappe's medical and sexual history, and Arbuckle's persuasive testimony, the first trial ended in a hung jury, with a vote of ten to two for acquittal. A second trial went to fourteen ballots, with jurors voting ten to two for conviction. In April, 1922, a third jury deliberated for a single minute, then spent five minutes crafting a statement that began, "Acquittal is not enough for Roscoe Arbuckle. We feel that a great injustice has been done to him." Nevertheless, the rumor that a drunken Arbuckle had raped Rappe with a bottle persisted, and his name continues to be associated with Hollywood scandal.

Later Career

Such was the national revulsion toward Arbuckle that his return to movie work had to be behind the camera, and disguised at that. Using the pseudonyms Will B. Good and William B. Goodrich, Arbuckle directed two-reel comedies and a feature, ironically produced by Hearst. The comedian revived his old vaudeville act, which, despite protests, was successful in some American cities, including New York, and especially well received in Europe. A return to the legitimate theater was short-lived, as were other business endeavors. By 1931 a survey of *Motion Picture Magazine* readers indicated that moviegoers supported Arbuckle's desire to resume screen acting. In 1932, the former silent star returned to a drastically changed movie world, for talking pictures had become the norm. Under contract to Warner Bros. studios, Arbuckle acted in several comedy shorts, the first of which delighted preview audiences. Finally, the corner had been turned. Then, the night after shooting the last of his "comeback" comedies, Arbuckle experienced a heart seizure and died in his sleep.

IMPACT

The public outcry at Roscoe Arbuckle's arrest and several other Hollywood scandals in 1921 resulted in the introduction of dozens of legislative bills advocating censorship. The Hollywood industry responded by quickly forming the Motion Picture Producers and Directors Association (MPPDA). In an immediate, decisive, and well publicized move, the MPPDA appointed a Hollywood outsider, a well-respected midwestern Republican, as its director and spokesman: Will Hays. The former postmaster general functioned as a glorified public relations man for the film industry, demonstrating the movie colony's sincerity about cleaning its own house and thus arguing against the necessity of any outside control.

Hays at first banned Arbuckle's films, then changed his mind; several films were released, but resistance, sometimes organized by church groups, led to the withdrawal of Arbuckle's 1921 releases from exhibition. An energized scrutiny of the private lives of movie stars resulted in the introduction of "morality clauses" in players' contracts that would allow studios to fire contracters who misbehaved. Arbuckle became a scapegoat, and most movie people, with prominent exceptions such as Buster Keaton and Charles Chaplin, disassociated themselves from him and the taint of scandal that he carried.

FURTHER READING

Mast, Gerald. *The Comic Mind: Comedy and the Movies*. 2d ed. Chicago: University of Chicago Press, 1973. Arbuckle's achievements as a silent comedian are considered within various traditions of comic performance and popular American film.

Oderman, Stuart. *Roscoe "Fatty" Arbuckle: A Biography of the Silent Comedian, 1887-1993*. Jefferson, N.C.: McFarland, 1994. Written by a silent-film pianist, this sympathetic biography builds on interviews with the comedian's contemporaries, including his first wife. Includes dozens of archival photographs and an extensive bibliography.

Sklar, Robert. *Movie-Made America: A Cultural History of American Movies*. Rev. ed. New York: Vintage Books, 1994. A thoughtful history that situates Arbuckle's career and his scandalous trials within a larger context of American popular entertainment and political culture.

Young, Robert. *Roscoe "Fatty" Arbuckle: A Bio-Bibliography*. Westport, Conn.: Greenwood Press, 1994. This comprehensive resource contains a biography, an 1887-1993 chronology, interviews and essays published between 1916 and 1931, theater credits, an annotated filmography, a detailed videography, a listing of stage and film portrayals of Arbuckle, an extensive bibliography, and information on archival holdings.

—*Carolyn Anderson*

SEE ALSO: O. J. Simpson; Henry Starr.

Johnnie Armstrong

Scottish border reiver

Born: c. 1490's; Gilnockie, Ineskdale, Scotland
Died: 1530; Carlingrigg, Scotland
Major offenses: Rustling, robbery, murder, and arson
Active: c. 1505-1530
Locale: Scottish-English borderlands
Sentence: Death by hanging without trial

Early Life

John Armstrong (ARM-strong) of Gilnockie was born into the powerful Clan Armstrong of the marsh borderlands of Scotland and England. Armstrong's father was laird of Mangerton and chief of the clan; the Armstrongs were the greatest of the riding families known as border reivers. Armstrong forays and raids along the borderlands caused more carnage then any other two Scottish or English clans combined.

Reiving was a life-culture forced upon borderlands clans by the constant border wars between Scotland and England. Because armies were constantly crossing the frontier, raising livestock or crops was nearly impossible. Clans fed themselves by raiding and counterraiding one another's limited resources. This back and forth raiding was reiving, and it was the only possible lifestyle if one lived in the Anglo-Scottish borderlands between the fourteenth and late sixteenth centuries.

The effect of this constant raiding created a society that ignored centralized governance, and by the early sixteenth century had become a dangerous flashpoint between the Scottish and English crowns. It was under these circumstances that Armstrong became leader of the most powerful band of Scottish border reivers.

Criminal Career

Armstrong's reivers savaged the borderlands until young King James V of Scotland decided to put a stop to it. One of James's royal goals was to pacify the borderlands to keep peace with England's Henry VIII, who in 1528 had made specific demands of James to have Armstrong arrested. James ordered his royal household and a command of soldiers to engage in a royal hunt near Ettrick. The hunt was actually a cover for a punitive expedition to the borderlands. After hunting for a few days, the king invited Armstrong and leaders of other reiving clans for a royal audience. King James assured all that, as royal guests, they were safe. Armstrong and a troop of fifty reivers accepted the invitation, expecting royal pardons. The reivers arrived at James's encampment wearing their finest clothes and weapons.

Legal Action and Outcome

When Armstrong met the king, the royal was angered by Armstrong's self-confidence and finery and said, "What want you knave that a king should have?" He then ordered Armstrong and his men executed. Armstrong pleaded for his life and those of his men, saying they had never reived in Scotland or harmed a Scot and that they swore loyalty to the crown.

King James said Armstrong must die, and Armstrong is quoted as replying directly to the King's face: "I am but a fool to seek grace at a graceless face, but had I known you would have taken me this day, I would have lived in the Borders despite King Harry and you both." Armstrong and nearly fifty of his followers were hanged immediately, without trial. Several reivers were spared, and one was instead burned alive as punishment for burning a house in which a mother and her children perished.

Impact

The blood feud and reiving culture of the Anglo-Scottish borderlands lasted nearly three hundred years. Some seventy lawless clans engaged in continual raiding, rustling, arson, and blackmail, rendering the borderlands nearly ungovernable by either Scotland or England. With the execution of Johnnie Armstrong and his immediate followers, James V was gradually able to bring some order to the region. Armstrong's hanging alienated the western clans against the Scottish crown, the powerful Armstrong Clan in particular. Subsequently the Armstrongs would side militarily with the English in many future border disputes.

One outcome of the reiving culture still extant is a musical tradition called border ballads. These Scottish and English folk songs celebrate border reivers, outlaws, and historical events. The most famous of these songs is "The Ballad of Johnnie Armstrong," which recounts Armstrong's exploits and his betrayal and execution by King James.

Further Reading

Armstrong, William, A. *The Armstrong Borderland: A Reassessment of Certain Aspects of Border History*. Edinburgh: John McQueen, 1960. An Armstrong family biography and detailed overview of the Anglo-Scottish borderers.

Durham, Keith. *The Border Reivers*. Toronto, Ont.: Osprey, 1995. A well-illustrated book about the borderlands reiving and blood feud culture, with emphasis on weapons and raiding.

Fraser, George M. *The Steel Bonnets*. New York: Alfred A. Knopf, 1972. A scholarly history of the border reivers and how they operated their raiding and blackmail systems. Contains biographical information on prominent marsh clans and families.

Sadler, John. *Border Fury: England and Scotland at War, 1296-1568*. New York: Longman, 2005. A detailed overview of the Anglo-Scottish border wars and how the outcome still affects relations between both cultures.

—*Randall L. Milstein*

SEE ALSO: Rob Roy.

BENEDICT ARNOLD

American general

BORN: January 14, 1741; Norwich, Connecticut
DIED: June 14, 1801; London, England
CAUSE OF NOTORIETY: In the United States, the name of Benedict Arnold, who sought to surrender West Point to the British during the American Revolutionary War, is now synonymous with treason.
ACTIVE: 1779-1780
LOCALE: West Point, New York

EARLY LIFE

Benedict Arnold (BEHN-uh-dihkt AHR-nohld) was born on January 14, 1741, in Norwich, Connecticut. He was the son of Benedict Arnold, Sr., and Hannah Waterman King Arnold. He was one of six children, but only he and his sister Hannah survived into adulthood. Business setbacks led to financial struggles for the family, and young Benedict was forced to withdraw from school. He later served as an apprentice in the Norwich apothecary business of family cousins. He also briefly served in the Connecticut army during the French and Indian War (1754-1763). He moved to New Haven, Connecticut, in 1762 and became a druggist and bookseller there. He also acquired some property and became involved in the trading and shipping businesses. He married Margaret Mansfield on February 22, 1767; they had three sons before Margaret died in 1775.

MILITARY CAREER

Arnold achieved both fame and notoriety during the American Revolutionary War (1775-1783). He had become a captain in a Connecticut military company when he heard news of the battles at Lexington and Concord. The provincial Congress of Massachusetts commissioned him as a colonel, and the Massachusetts Committee of Safety approved his plan to capture Fort Ticonderoga on Lake Champlain. Arnold helped capture the fort as part of a larger force under the command of Ethan Allen and Allen's renowned Green Mountain Boys.

In 1775, Arnold and General Richard Montgomery led a two-pronged invasion of Canada. Arnold's men endured great hardships during their famous march through the wilderness to lay siege to Quebec. Montgomery cap-

Benedict Arnold. (Library of Congress)

tured Montreal and then joined Arnold to attack Quebec on December 30, 1775. During the fierce battle, Montgomery was killed and Arnold severely wounded in the leg. Arnold was promoted to the rank of brigadier general.

After the British drove the Americans from Canada, Arnold returned to New York to defend Lake Champlain. There he was involved in the Battle of Valcour Island. Despite Arnold's success in the naval battle, Congress passed over Arnold and promoted five brigadier generals with junior status to the rank of major general in February, 1777. Arnold finally received his promotion to major general later that year, after leading a successful attack on the British forces at Danbury, Connecticut. He was denied the restoration of his seniority, however, and he resigned in July, 1777, only to reconsider quickly.

Arnold fought in the New York wilderness under General Horatio Gates against British forces under the command of General John Burgoyne. Arnold's next major military accomplishment came in the Battle of Saratoga (September 19-October 7, 1777), the turning point of the Revolutionary War. Arnold had quarreled with Gates and had been ordered to the rear but valiantly fought without permission in the October 7 Battle of Bemis Heights. He suffered a severe wound in the same leg that he had injured earlier. The American victory helped cement a critical alliance with France.

The Continental Congress restored Arnold's military seniority in 1778 and gave him command of Philadelphia. It was there that the widower Arnold became engaged to his second wife, the teenage Margaret (Peggy) Shippen, daughter of Judge Edward Shippen. Arnold was in his mid-thirties. Money problems caused by a lavish lifestyle, quarrels with fellow commanders, and corruption charges led to Arnold's court-martial in 1780. He was exonerated of all but two minor corruption charges and received a mild reprimand from General George Washington; he soon resigned command of Philadelphia.

The Text of Treachery

On July 12, 1780, Benedict Arnold sent a letter, in cipher, to Major John André of the British Army:

I wrote to Captain Beckwith on the 7th of June, that a French fleet and army were expected to act in conjunction with the American army. At the same time I gave Mr. Stansbury a manifesto intended to be published in Canada, and have from time to time communicated to him such intelligence as I thought interesting, which he assures me he has transmitted to you. I have received no answer from my Letter, or any verbal Message. I expect soon to command West Point and most seriously wish an interview with some intelligent officer in whom a mutual confidence could be placed. The necessity is evident to arrange and to cooperate. An officer might be taken Prisoner near that Post and permitted to return on parole, or some officer on Parole sent out to effect an exchange.

General Washington expects on the arrival of the French Troops to collect 30,000 Troops to act in conjunction; if not disappointed, New York is fixed on as the first Object, if his numbers are not sufficient for that Object Canada is the second; of which I can inform you in time, as well as of every other design. I have accepted the command at West Point As a Post in which I can render the most essential Services, and which will be in my disposal. The mass of the People are heartily tired of the War, and wish to be on their former footing. They are promised great events from this year's exertion. If disappointed you have only to persevere and the contest will soon be at an end. The present Struggles are like the pangs of a dying man, violent but of a short duration.

As Life and fortune are risked by serving His Majesty, it is Necessary that the latter shall be secured as well as the emoluments I give up, and a compensation for Services agreed on and a Sum advanced for that purpose, which I have mentioned in a letter which accompanies this, which Sir Henry [Clinton] will not, I believe, think unreasonable. I am Sir, your humble Servant.

Source: From the Clinton Collection of the Clements Library, University of Michigan, Ann Arbor.

Traitorous Act

Arnold's next actions would change him from a patriot to a traitor. In May of 1779, Arnold began a secret correspondence with British general Henry Clinton through the agency of several American Loyalists and, most notably, British major John André. Arnold sought and received command of the strategic American fortress at West Point in 1780, significant for its location on the Hudson River. He then negotiated its surrender to the British in exchange for a British military commission and a monetary settlement. Arnold's traitorous scheme was revealed when the Americans captured Major André in September, 1780.

André was executed as a spy, but Arnold was able to escape to the British and received a commission as a brigadier general, among other compensations. He led British troops in Connecticut and Virginia but never received a major command. He was never captured and did not face punishment for his traitorous actions. After a brief London stay, Arnold moved in 1787 to Saint John, New Brunswick, Canada, and began a shipping business. He settled in London, England, in 1791 and died there on June 14, 1801.

Impact

Benedict Arnold's actions, while demoralizing to the Americans and his friend and supporter George Washington, did not adversely affect the war's outcome. The capture of André prevented Arnold's plan from being carried out and kept West Point in American hands. The name Benedict Arnold would become synonymous with the word "traitor" in the United States and remained in use in modern-day English as a term for someone who has betrayed another.

Further Reading

Brandt, Clare. *The Man in the Mirror: A Life of Benedict Arnold.* New York: Random House, 1994. Brandt utilizes a variety of sources to outline Arnold's complete life and offer psychological insights into the possible causes of his actions.

Flexner, James Thomas. *The Traitor and the Spy: Benedict Arnold and John André.* 1975. Reprint. Syracuse, N.Y.: Syracuse University Press, 1991. This recounting of Arnold's defection and relationship with his chief accomplice André is considered a well-written and entertaining classic.

Martin, James Kirby. *Benedict Arnold, Revolutionary Hero: An American Warrior Reconsidered.* New York: New York University Press, 2000. Outlines Arnold's significant contributions to the American Revolutionary War efforts that are often overlooked in light of his later treachery.

Sale, Richard T. *Traitors: The Worst Acts of Treason in American History, from Benedict Arnold to Robert Hanssen.* New York: Berkley, 2003. The section on Arnold offers a concise depiction of his treachery and places it within its historical context.

—Marcella Bush Trevino

See also: Charles Lee; James Wilkinson.

ʿAruj

Muslim pirate and governor of Algiers

Born: c. 1473; Lesbos, Greece
Died: 1518; Tlemcen (now in Algeria)
Also known as: Baba ʿAruj; Barbarossa I; Sultan of Algiers
Cause of notoriety: ʿAruj's maritime activities in the western Mediterranean Sea against Christians and on behalf of the Ottoman Turks earned him a fearsome reputation in Europe.
Active: 1505-1518
Locale: Tunis and Algeria

Early Life

ʿAruj (AH-roozh) was the eldest of four sons born to a Christian woman and a retired Janissary (taken as a child by the Ottomans and raised in the Muslim faith) on the Greek island of Lesbos around 1473. ʿAruj began his maritime career by working on his father's boat as a merchant and privateer. Early in his career, his ship was attacked and captured by the Knights of St. John, Christian raiders operating from their base on the island of Rhodes. In the attack, ʿAruj's brother Isaac was killed, and ʿAruj was forced into service as a galley slave. He eventually escaped (or was ransomed), obtained another ship, and began raiding in the Aegean Sea.

Naval Career

Operating out of Alexandria, Egypt, ʿAruj attacked Christian ships and Christian-controlled islands in the eastern Mediterranean. During this period he acquired the nickname Barbarossa, meaning "the red-bearded." In 1505 ʿAruj, now accompanied by his younger brother Khiḍr, began operating in the western Mediterranean along the coast of North Africa, mainly out of Tunis. They attacked shipping as well as towns along the Spanish and Italian coasts and in the Aegean Sea. ʿAruj was able to disrupt shipping in the western Mediterranean and capture many Christians, who were then sold into slavery. Within only a few years, ʿAruj accumulated a vast fortune and a fleet of eight ships. Wanting more freedom, in 1510 the brothers moved their fleet to the nearby island of Djerba (modern Jerba, off the coast of Tunisia), where they could operate without the interference of local North African rulers.

In 1512 ʿAruj led an attack on the Spanish-held

Prisoners of Barbarossa. (F. R. Niglutsch)

coastal town of Bougie (Bejaïa, in modern Algeria), an important North African trading center. In leading the assault on the city walls, ʿAruj was knocked down by a shot that severed his left arm. This injury caused ʿAruj's forces to abandon the attack and withdraw. After recuperating from his wound, ʿAruj worked to expand his control over the North African coastline.

In 1516, ʿAruj launched a series of attacks that resulted in the capture of Shershell (Cherchell) and Algiers, which allowed ʿAruj to become known as the sultan of Algiers. The following year, he continued his expansion by capturing the city of Tlemcen. His successes led the Ottoman sultan, Selim I "the Grim" (r. 1512-1520), to recognize him officially as the Ottoman ruler of the Algerian region.

The Spanish governor of Oran, fearing that ʿAruj would eventually attack his city, secured support from King Charles I of Spain and led an assault on Tlemcen in 1518. When reinforcements failed to reach ʿAruj, he withdrew from the city and attempted to reach Algiers overland. The Spanish cavalry was able to catch his forces before they reached the safety of the walls of Algiers, and in the ensuing battle ʿAruj was killed. With the death of ʿAruj, his brother Khiḍr (the future Turkish admiral Khair al-Dīn) dyed his beard red and took the name Barbarossa as his own.

Impact

The maritime activities of ʿAruj and his brother helped create the Barbary States (Algeria, Morocco, Tripoli, and Tunisia), which served as a haven for pirates in the western Mediterranean from the sixteenth to nineteenth centuries. The outposts also gave the Ottoman Empire a toehold in North Africa. After ʿAruj's brother Khair al-Dīn assumed the mantle of Barbarossa, he became one of the most famous naval commanders of his day, helping to extend the Ottomans' reach and solidifying their empire as a world power that would last well into the twentieth century.

Further Reading

Bradford, Ernle. *The Sultan's Admiral: The Life of Barbarossa*. New York: Harcourt, Brace, 1968. While this book focuses mainly on the life of Khair al-Dīn,

ʿAruj's youngest brother, it also includes many details about the life of ʿAruj.

Davis, Robert C. *Christian Slaves, Muslim Masters: White Slavery in the Mediterranean, the Barbary Coast, and Italy, 1500-1800.* New York: Palgrave Macmillan, 2004. An examination of the slave trade practiced by the Muslim corsairs of North Africa and its impact on Europe.

Heers, Jacques. *The Barbary Corsairs: Warfare in the Mediterranean, 1480-1580.* Translated by Jonathan North. London: Greenhill Books, 2003. An examination of the formation of the Barbary pirates and their early successes.

Soucek, S. "The Rise of the Barbarossas in North Africa." *Archivum Ottomanicum* 3 (1971): 238-250. A brief description of the rise to power of ʿAruj and Khiḍr Barbarossa.

—*R. Scott Moore*

See also: Genghis Khan.

Shoko Asahara

Japanese founder and leader of the Aum Shinrikyo religious sect

Born: May 2, 1955; Yatsushiro City, Kumamoto Prefecture, Kyushu, Japan
Also known as: Chizuo Matsumoto (birth name)
Major offenses: Leader of the 1995 Tokyo Subway gas attack; murder and attempted murder
Active: 1989-1995
Locale: Tokyo, Japan, and Kamikuishikimura, Nishiyatsushiro District, Yamanashi Prefecture
Sentence: Death

Early Life

Shoko Asahara was born as Chizuo Matsumoto and came from a family of modest means. His eyesight was so poor that he was classified as legally blind, and from the time that he was six, he lived in a boarding school for the blind, at public expense, where he was trained in acupuncture. Matsumoto graduated in March, 1973, but lived at the boarding school for two more years. After failing the entrance exams for nearby Kumamoto University, he moved to a preparatory school in Tokyo in April, 1977. He hoped to get into Tokyo University but never passed the entrance exams. He supported himself in Tokyo as an acupuncturist and herbal medicine seller.

Criminal Career

Matsumoto's early acupuncture training involved some acquaintance with traditional medicine, which contained elements from Sino-Japanese esoteric religions. Thus, Matsumoto had enough knowledge to develop a career as a faith healer. He was active in religious groups focused on healing but planned to create his own group. In 1978, he married a student whom he had met at preparatory school and started his own acupuncture clinic in Funabashi,

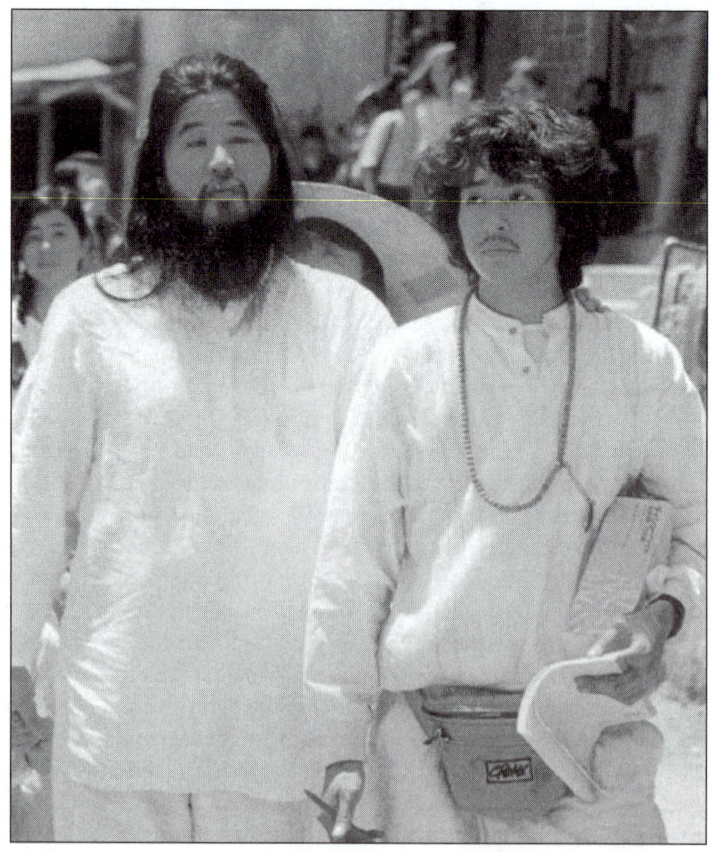

Shoko Asahara, left, with one of his disciples. (AP/Wide World Photos)

northeast of Tokyo. Matsumoto had a setback in 1982, when he was arrested and fined for selling medicine without a license. However, by 1984, he had gained a large enough following to establish the Om Spiritual Academy in downtown Tokyo.

Matsumoto focused on yoga and spiritual training, adopting the traditional Indian sound Om (thought to have spiritual power when chanted) as the name for his religious system but spelling it "um," following archaic religious usage. In 1987, he expanded the name to Aum Shinrikyo (Om Supreme Truth Religion) and changed his name to Shoko Asahara. In 1989, Aum Shinrikyo was recognized legally as a religion, claiming to have more than ten thousand members in Japan and overseas. In 1990, Asahara set up a new center at Kamikuishikimura on the slopes of Mount Fuji, where his followers practiced austerities under his direction. Asahara managed to persuade them that he had enormous spiritual powers and sold them vials of his bodily fluids at high prices, which they could consume to gain these powers themselves.

People outside the sect began to hear about these bizarre austerities and practices. A Yokohama lawyer, Sakamoto Tsutsumi, received complaints from concerned parents of Aum members and spearheaded an investigation in mid-1989. In November, 1989, Sakamoto disappeared, along with his wife and baby son. Though evidence implicating Asahara was found, the police did not follow up on these leads. It was later discovered that the Sakamotos were indeed murdered, but their bodies were never found. Asahara had others killed from time to time, but there was often no physical evidence left behind. It is known that at least one victim, public employee Kariya Kiyoshi, was killed by a barbiturate overdose and then cremated in an industrial-size microwave oven in Kamikuishikimura in February, 1995.

Asahara established a political party and planned to become a national political leader. In 1990, he fielded twenty-five Upper House candidates, including himself, but every one lost; Asahara received only 1,785 votes. Asahara was pessimistic about the future, predicting natural disasters that would bring destruction to Japan. He began to think about unleashing disasters himself, and in 1993, his inner circle began making sarin gas at Kamikuishikimura. People nearby complained about discharges of noxious gas, but police did not pursue the complaints.

On the night of June 27, 1994, Aum carried out an experimental sarin release in the Kita-Fukashi district of Matsumoto. Hundreds of people suffered disabilities, some long-term, and seven died. Police initially accused a local farmer, Kono Yoshiyuki, of mixing chemical fertilizer incorrectly. Kono remained under investigation until July, 1995, when Aum members confessed that they caused the Matsumoto disaster.

National newspapers began to link Aum-related dis-

Aum Shinrikyo

Variously translated as "Om Supreme Truth Religion" and "Aum Divine Wizard Association," Aum Shinrikyo began as a doomsday cult, but Shoko Asahara, unlike most end-of-the-world prophets, was unwilling simply to wait for it. He wanted to speed it along. After his spiritual revelation in the Himalayas in 1989, he returned to Japan with a plan. He introduced group religious training for his disciplines, preparing them for Armageddon. Asahara taught that nuclear war would inevitably break out in 1999 as a punishment for the evil of the world. Still, there remained one hope for humanity. If he could lead thirty thousand people to spiritual awakening, their holy energy would stave off the worst effects of the nuclear holocaust.

Proclaiming himself the reincarnation of the Hindu god Shiva, Asahara taught a mixture of Hindu, Buddhist, and yogic doctrines but took his basic doomsday scenario from the Book of Revelation and the teachings of the sixteenth century Christian monk Nostradamus. His training focused on four areas: the doctrine assembled from these sources, meditation, asceticism, and initiation to spiritual awakening. These his students practiced in three courses: a tantric yoga course, bodha course, and siddhi course. They could quicken their progress to spiritual awakening, salvation from Armageddon, and eternal happiness by drinking Asahara's bathwater or blood, for a small fee. As for their connection to society and their wealth, they did not need them. They were to give themselves and all their worldly goods to the Aum Shinrikyo.

To ensure that Armageddon happened according to schedule, sect members attempted to synthesize chemical weapons (the nerve agent sarin among them) and to acquire nuclear weapons. Even though their two nerve gas attacks in Japan failed to jump-start the war, even though the prophesied doomsday date of 1999 has come and gone, and even though their leader is in prison and eleven members have been sentenced to death, Aum Shinrikyo lives on. It has been renamed Aleph and retains well over one thousand members. However, Aleph has split into two groups, one still attached to Asahara, the other following one of his former lieutenants.

appearances and disasters, and by January, 1995, evidence pointed toward Asahara. Asahara sued one of the papers, the *Asahi Shimbun*, for libel, but it was becoming clear to him that the authorities might close in soon. Then, on March 20, 1995, the group coordinated five simultaneous attacks during the morning rush hour on the Tokyo subway system. Sarin gas was released into the subway, especially on routes serving government headquarters; twelve were killed and several thousand more were injured. This act of domestic terrorism served as a final curtain to Asahara's career.

Legal Action and Outcome

The police carried out raids, finding enough sarin to kill one million or more people. Aum leaders were arrested, but Asahara was not apprehended until May 16, 1995, almost two months later. Proceedings against Asahara began on April 24, 1996, when prosecutors read out the names of more than three thousand victims of the sarin attack. Trial proceedings continued until February 27, 2004, when Asahara was sentenced to death by the Tokyo District Court. Asahara lawyers appealed the sentence, but on March 27, 2006, the Tokyo High Court ruled that the time limit for appeals had expired, although one final appeal to the Supreme Court of Japan remained possible.

Impact

Shoko Asahara attracted highly educated followers, including computer programmers, scientists, government officials, and police officers. By the 1990's, the radical politics and social idealism that were prevalent among young intellectuals in Japan during the 1960's and 1970's had declined as a result of attractive career opportunities and societal pressures to conform. Some successful people sought to recapture youthful idealism through cults. Asahara promised them a higher level of spiritual existence, and many were ready to believe and follow him.

The Aum-related murders and disasters, however, caused many Japanese to distrust spiritualist religions. People also wondered why authorities had not intervened much earlier. Asahara's actions created among Japanese citizens a lack of confidence in the ability of the authorities to provide protection.

Further Reading

Daly, Sara A. *Aum Shinrikyo, al Qaeda, and the Kinshasa Reactor: Implications of Three Case Studies for Combating Nuclear Terrorism*. Santa Monica, Calif.: Rand, 2005. Discusses three terrorist situations and their implications for the future.

Lifton, Robert Jay. *Destroying the World to Save It: Aum Shinrikyo, Apocalyptic Violence, and the New Global Terrorism*. New York: Henry Holt, 1999. Analysis of the psychology of terrorism.

Murakami, Haruki. *Underground: The Tokyo Gas Attack and the Japanese Psyche*. New York: Vintage International, 2001. Subjective analysis by a leading Japanese writer.

Reader, Ian. *Religious Violence in Contemporary Japan: The Case of Aum Shinrikyo*. Honolulu: University of Hawaii Press, 2000. A well-researched and well-documented case study of the sarin attacks.

Tu, Anthony T. *Chemical Terrorism: Horrors in the Tokyo Subway and Matsumoto City*. Fort Collins, Colo.: Alaken, 2002. Focuses on the technical aspects of the attacks.

—*Michael McCaskey*

See also: Andreas Baader; Osama Bin Laden; Theodore Kaczynski; Timothy McVeigh; Zacarias Moussaoui; Terry Nichols; Ilich Ramírez Sánchez; Eric Rudolph; Fusako Shigenobu; Abu Musab al-Zarqawi.

Mohammed Atta al-Sayed

Egyptian al-Qaeda terrorist

Born: September 1, 1968; Kafr el-Sheikh, Egypt
Died: September 11, 2001; New York, New York
Also known as: Mehan Atta; Mohammed Atta; Mohammad El Amir; Mohamed El Sayed; Muhammad Muhammad Al Amir Awag Al Sayyid Atta; Muhammad Muhammad Al-Amir Awad Al Sayad; Mohamed el-Amir; Mohamed Mohamed el-Amir Awad el-Sayed Atta
Cause of notoriety: Atta, the tactical leader of the September 11, 2001, terrorist plot against the United States, was also the lead hijacker of American Airlines Flight 11, which was one of the planes that crashed into the World Trade Center in New York City.
Active: c. 1995-September 11, 2001
Locale: New York, New York

Early Life

Mohammed Atta al-Sayed was born to an ambitious lawyer and the daughter of a prominent family. He was the third of three children and the only son. Atta's father demanded that his children succeed academically above all; Atta had to attend to his studies prior to playing with friends, which isolated him from children his own age. Atta's mother coddled and pampered him, which some believe led him to develop a virginal, effeminate quality.

Atta attended Cairo University and received a degree in architectural engineering in 1990. Atta's father wanted him to earn a Ph.D. like his sisters, so Atta made preparations to study in Germany. He arrived in Hamburg but was refused entrance to the Hamburg University of Applied Science. His father threatened the university with racial discrimination charges. Atta instead attended the Technical University of Hamburg-Harburg. He began graduate course work in architecture but determined it was too similar to his undergraduate courses and switched his concentration to urban planning.

Atta was noted for being shy, intelligent, and disapproving of liberal Western behaviors and notions. During his time in Hamburg, Atta made several trips back to the Middle East. In 1994, Atta met a Palestinian woman on a trip to Syria. The two admired each other, but she could not meet the standards for marriage of Atta and his family.

Atta made a pilgrimage to Mecca in 1995. This trip proved to be a turning point in his life and was probably where he first established contact with al-Qaeda, a fundamentalist Islamic terrorist organization. Atta began to perceive injustices in the treatment of Muslims and their culture and historical sites at the hands of Westerners. In his mind, Western influence had made Egypt unfriendly to fundamentalist Muslims. Atta wanted to live and work in Egypt to help his people, but he felt that his appearance and practices would mark him as a criminal.

Terrorist Career

Feeling lost in secular Germany, Atta became a regular at the fundamentalist Al Quds mosque in Hamburg. German and American officials believe that this mosque is where Atta was recruited into the al-Qaeda network. He became associated with Ziad Samir Jarrah and Marwan Yousef al-Shehhi. These men, together with Atta, would become the nucleus of the operational force of the September 11, 2001, attacks on the World Trade Center in New York City. The men began building a terrorist cell at

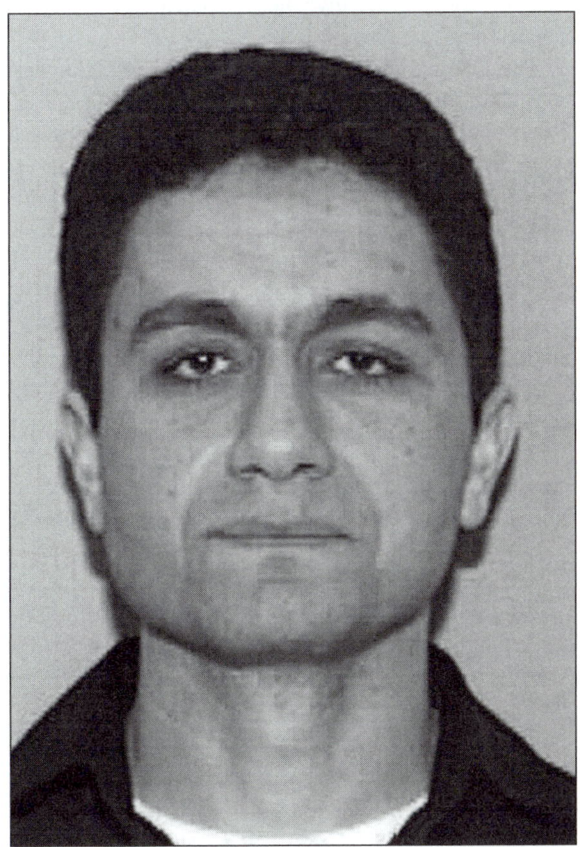

Mohammed Atta al-Sayed. (AP/Wide World Photos)

an apartment at 54 Marienstrasse in Hamburg. It was at this apartment that the cell began planning and solidifying logistical support for their upcoming terrorist attacks against the United States.

In the summer of 2000, Atta, Jarrah, and al-Shehhi moved the cell's operations to Venice, Florida. They were able to begin flight lessons at Florida schools, even though they had tourist visas instead of the required student visas. At his school, Atta was noted for having attitude problems and difficulties associating with women. Regardless of any red flags that might have arisen, the three future hijackers received pilot's licenses by the end of 2000.

Atta returned to Europe several times during 2001. During these trips, he handed over 54 Marienstrasse to associates in the terror network and met with other members of al-Qaeda in Spain. On his first return trip to the United States in 2001, Atta reentered the country on an expired tourist visa by convincing Immigration and Naturalization Service (INS) agents that he was waiting for a student visa to arrive. During his final months in the United States, Atta is believed to have visited a naval base in Virginia and a town near a nuclear power plant in Tennessee.

The planning and training for the 9/11 attacks were completed in late summer, 2001. A fourth pilot, Hani Saleh Hanjour, and fifteen so-called muscle terrorists were added to the hijacking teams. On September 10, 2001, Atta used his credit card in Manhattan and was believed to have visited the World Trade Center's observation deck. Atta then drove to Portland, Maine, with fellow hijacker Abdulaziz al-Omari.

On September 11, 2001, Atta and al-Omari left Portland to catch American Airlines Flight 11 from Boston's Logan Airport. Atta and four other hijackers sat in business and first class as the plane lifted off at 8:02 A.M. When the seat belt lights went out and drink service began, the hijackers started their assault. At 8:21 A.M., flight attendant Betty Ong called the airline to report that Flight 11 had been hijacked. The hijackers used utility knives and debilitating sprays to gain control of the plane. Atta altered the flight path south, toward his intended target in Manhattan. The North Tower of the World Trade Center was hit between floors 93 and 99 by the jet at 8:46 A.M. Atta and the other hijackers died as a result of the impact, along with nearly three thousand innocent men, women, and children from many nations, who were beginning their workday at the World Trade Center.

IMPACT

The 9/11 attacks propelled Western countries into a response that perhaps would not have occurred had the effects not been so obvious and close to home. The United States and others declared war on Afghanistan because of the evidence of the Taliban leadership aiding and harboring al-Qaeda operations. Many new laws and guidelines, notably those in the Patriot Act (passed by Congress in 2002), were enacted in the United States with the purpose of closing the gaps that Atta and his associates had exploited. The Bush administration upheld the necessity of a "war on terror" that required a preemptive response to potential threats, as opposed to the defensive responses that followed the al-Qaeda attacks on the USS *Cole*, the Khobar Towers in Saudi Arabia, and the 1993 attack on the World Trade Center.

FURTHER READING

Corbin, Jane. *Al-Qaeda: In Search of the Terror Network That Threatens the World*. New York: Thunder's Mouth Press/Nation Books, 2002. Corbin investigates the al-Qaeda network and provides excellent background information about it.

Kean, Thomas H., et al. *The 9/11 Commission Report: Final Report of the National Commission on Terrorist Attacks upon the United States*. New York: W. W. Norton, 2004. The official report of the bipartisan 9/11 commission. Contains highly specific data regarding the lead-up and response to the 9/11 attacks.

McDermott, Terry. *Perfect Soldiers—The Hijackers: Who They Were, Why They Did It*. New York: HarperCollins, 2005. An informative source about the hijackers. Includes biographical information and statements from relevant parties.

—*Grant T. Stewart*

SEE ALSO: Abu Nidal; Osama Bin Laden; Khalid Shaikh Mohammed; Zacarias Moussaoui.

Attila

King of the Huns (r. 433-453 c.e.)

Born: c. 406 c.e.; probably Pannonia (now primarily in Hungary)
Died: 453 c.e.; probably Jazberin (now in Hungary)
Also known as: Atli; Attila the Hun; Etzel; Flagellum Dei (Scourge of God)
Cause of notoriety: In his military campaigns against the Roman Empire, Attila engaged in invasion, conquest, and devastation involving mass murder, rape, and other atrocities.
Active: 433-453 c.e.
Locale: Southern and Central Europe

Early Life

Attila was the son of Mundiuch, king of the Huns, but little is known of his youth. In 433 c.e., with his brother Bleda, Attila became coruler of the Huns, succeeding his uncle, Rua, who had united the Huns. At the beginning of their reign, the corulers negotiated with representatives of the Eastern Roman emperor Theodosius II about the return of several tribes, who, opposed to the new rulers, had fled into Roman (Byzantine) territory. The following year, the Hunnic kings, satisfied with the return of the tribes and a large tribute from the Romans, moved east in an attempt to conquer Persia.

Military Career

By 440, Attila and Bleda, accusing the Romans of breaking the agreement, invaded the Roman Balkans (approximately modern Croatia and Serbia). In 443, after Theodosius had refused the Huns' demands, the kings invaded Roman territory farther south, in modern Bulgaria, and ransacked cities; they were unable to breach the walls of Constantinople (modern Istanbul). The result was peace bought by the Romans for a much larger tribute. Attila murdered Bleda in 445 and became the sole Hunnish ruler. He attacked the Balkans again, demanding a larger tribute and Roman withdrawal from a large area in modern Serbia and Bulgaria.

In 447, another Hunnish attack on Constantinople was defeated because the city's walls had been restored and in places rebuilt following destructive earthquakes. As a condition of peace, Attila demanded a still larger tribute together with Roman withdrawal from a vast area south of the Danube, in modern Serbia and Bulgaria. Negotiations continued for three years; the Roman embassy to Attila's camp included the historian Priscus, who later gave an elaborate description of Attila, Attila's entourage, and events occurring during this period.

Around 449, Attila turned his interests westward and planned to attack the Western Roman Empire. Attila was allied with the Western Roman emperor Valentinian III, who had given him the honorary title of "military commander." Valentinian's sister, Princess Justa Grata Honoria, was caught in an illicit love affair and sent to Constantinople. She sent Attila a ring and appealed to him for help. Attila, interpreting this gesture as a proposal of marriage, asked for half of the Western Roman Empire as a dowry. A struggle ensued between Valentinian III and Attila, who, convinced that there was little left to plunder in the Eastern Empire, went west with an immense army, including many Germanic allies. Numerous cities in modern Belgium and northern France were plundered. However, after a battle near modern Châlons, France, Attila was defeated by Roman armies under his former ally Aetius, a Roman general. The Gothic king, Theodoric, temporarily allied with the Romans, died in the battle.

In 452, Attila invaded and plundered the Alps region of Italy but was persuaded not to attack Rome by a delegation headed by Pope Leo I, who reportedly told Attila that almost everything of value had been taken from the city during the invasion of Alaric I forty-two years earlier. Turning eastward to his palace near modern Budapest, conceivably because of an epidemic that may have broken out among his troops, Attila died there early in 453, either of disease or at the hand of his wife, Ildico, who, according to a later Roman historian, had married him earlier that day. After Attila's death, his three sons fought one another and were defeated by other tribes; the Huns lost their empire and were disbursed among other ethnic groups.

Impact

The impact of Attila's depredations arguably helped usher in the Dark Ages. It has been said that if Europe had had steppes such as those in Central Asia, the Huns and other Turkic and Mongol groups would have permanently destroyed Western civilization. In literature, Attila and the Huns figure prominently in the *Nibelungenlied* and other Germanic epics, including early Viking sagas. Some Turkish and Hungarian nationalists regard Attila as a national hero, but among many Europeans, his name is synonymous with "barbarian" and "boor."

Men of an Ugly Pattern

This description of Hun warriors comes from Ammianus Marcellinus, a fourth century Roman historian:

And though they do just bear the likeness of men (of a very ugly pattern), they are so little advanced in civilization that they make no use of fire, nor any kind of relish, in the preparation of their food, but feed upon the roots which they find in the fields, and the half-raw flesh of any sort of animal.

When attacked, they will sometimes engage in regular battle. Then, going into the fight in order of columns, they fill the air with varied and discordant cries. More often, however, they fight in no regular order of battle, but by being extremely swift and sudden in their movements, they disperse, and then rapidly come together again in loose array, spread havoc over vast plains, and flying over the rampart, they pillage the camp of their enemy almost before he has become aware of their approach.

When in close combat with swords, they fight without regard to their own safety, and while their enemy is intent upon parrying the thrust of the swords, they throw a net over him and so entangle his limbs that he loses all power of walking or riding.

In 448 another Roman historian, Priscius, attended a banquet as a member of an embassy from the emperor Theodosius II to Attila. The after-dinner entertainment showed him that Huns had grown a little more cultured and sentimental in the interim, but not much.

As twilight came on torches were lit, and two barbarians entered before Attila to sing some songs they had composed, telling of his victories and his valor in war. The guests paid close attention to them, and some were delighted with the songs, others excited at being reminded of the wars, but others broke down and wept if their bodies were weakened by age and their warrior spirits forced to remain inactive.

Source: Ammianus Marcellinus translation from Edward Gibbon, *The History of the Decline and Fall of the Roman Empire* (1776-1788). Priscius translation from J. H. Robinson, *Readings in European History* (Boston: Ginn, 1905).

Further Reading

Gordon, C. D. *The Age of Attila: Fifth-Century Byzantium and the Barbarians*. Ann Arbor: University of Michigan Press, 1960. A collection of translated original sources, with notes and commentary.

Maenchen-Helfen, Otto. *The World of the Huns: Studies in Their History and Culture*. Berkeley: University of California Press, 1973. Continental Europe's leading expert on the Huns thoroughly surveys the topic.

Man, John. *Attila: The Barbarian King Who Challenged Rome*. London: Bantam, 2005. Although intended primarily for a popular audience, this work covers the facts thoroughly and includes biblographical references.

Thompson, E. A. *The Huns*. Rev. ed. Oxford: Basil Blackwell, 1999. A revised edition of *A History of Attila and the Huns*, originally published by Oxford University Press in 1948. One of the standard works in English on the subject. The author attributes Attila's victories to the weakness and disorganization of opposing forces.

—Stephen A. Stertz

See also: Caligula; Charles II; Christian VII; Clement VII; Commodus; Cypselus of Corinth; Domitian; Elagabalus; Fulvia; Galerius; Genghis Khan; al-Ḥākim; Ivan the Terrible; Justin II; Nero; Nicholas I; Peter the Cruel; Phalaris; Polycrates of Samos; Robespierre; Shi Huangdi; Lucius Cornelius Sulla; Theodora.

Andreas Baader

German terrorist

Born: May 6, 1943; Munich, Germany
Died: October 18, 1977; Stammheim Prison, Stuttgart, West Germany (now Germany)
Major offenses: Arson, murder, attempted murder, and forming a criminal association
Active: 1964-1972
Locale: West Germany (now Germany)
Sentence: Three years' imprisonment for arson of a department store; life sentence for four murders, twenty-seven attempted murders, and for forming a criminal association

Early Life

The father of Andreas Baader was a historian who was also in the army; he died on the Russian front in 1945. His mother did not remarry and became a typist in order to provide for her son. He was a very handsome child who was pampered by his mother and nearby neighbors, but he did not do well in school. He transferred public schools a number of times until his mother decided that a private education would suit him better.

Baader's grades did not improve, and he continued bullying and fighting other students as he had done in public school. He did not graduate from high school. Instead, when he was twenty, he traveled to Berlin, where he was exempt from national service. For three weeks, he worked for a newspaper owned by the Springer firm, the *Bild-Zeitung*. Penniless and without employment, Baader nonetheless had no trouble meeting women. He went to live with Ellinor Michel, a married artist, whose husband was also still living with her at the time. In 1965, she bore Baader a child, Suse. However, in 1967, Baader met Gudrun Ensslin, who fell in love with him. They both left their children behind to move to Frankfurt.

Criminal Career

Between 1964 and 1967, Baader was convicted of minor offenses such as traffic violations, driving without a license, license forgery, and theft of a motorbike. Following the death of a university student, Benno Ohnesorg, by police at a demonstration against a visit to Germany by the Shah of Iran, Mohammad Reza Shah Pahlavi, Baader and others formed a militant group, the Movement 2 June (in commemoration of the date when Ohnesorg was killed). The group ultimately became the basis of the Red Army Faction. Also known in this early incarnation as the Baader-Meinhof Gang, the group is thought to be one of the earliest to use violence and bombs for political purposes, although by all accounts, Baader cared little about politics. He stole cars, lived in hiding from the law for long periods of time, robbed banks, planted bombs, and ultimately killed people.

Legal Action and Outcome

On October 31, 1968, Baader, along with three of his comrades, was convicted of arson and endangering human life; he received a three-year sentence for placing bombs in a department store. While imprisoned and awaiting trial, he and two of his colleagues made three attempts to escape. On June 13, 1969, he and three gang members were released while awaiting an appeal. In November, 1969, Baader's appeal was denied, but rather than turning himself in, he and Ensslin hid in Paris for a time, went to Italy, and returned first to Stuttgart and then to Berlin.

While in Berlin, Baader was stopped by police while out driving. He had an identity card that said he was Peter C., but upon further questioning by police, Baader could not remember how many children Peter C. was supposed to have; the police arrested him. He was then sent to Tegel Prison to serve the remainder of his sentence. However, on May 14, 1970, Baader was freed by journalist and sympathizer Ulrike Meinhof. Meinhof had been given the opportunity to conduct research for a book about the organization of marginalized youth, and with the help of other supporters, including Baader's lawyer, Horst Mahler, she helped free Baader. However, in June, 1972, Baader was apprehended in a lengthy shoot-out in Frankfurt and was returned to prison.

While incarcerated at Stammheim Prison, Baader died on October 18, 1977, from a gunshot wound. There is considerable debate as to whether his death was a suicide or a government undertaking, especially since other Red Army Faction members incarcerated at Stammheim—namely Jan-Carl Raspe and Ensslin—also died that night.

Impact

The Red Army Faction was the first urban guerrilla group in West Germany, and Andreas Baader was its leader. Although his actions are thought to have been more criminally than politically motivated, Baader was instrumental in leading the violent uprisings against German politics, and without his influence on the formation of the Red Army Faction, the group would most likely not have been so infamous and would not have had such a great impact on the German community.

The Red Army Faction would continue to grow and transform itself for the next two decades. A second generation emerged in the mid-1970's at about the time when Baader, Meinhof, Ensslin, and Raspe were undergoing trial (1975-1977). During this period, the group perpetrated kidnappings and murders in the name of political protest, and it was associated with, if not directly responsible for, the October, 1977, hijacking of Lufthansa flight LH 181. It was shortly after this tragedy that Baader was found dead in his prison cell. The Red Army Faction (or an entity using that name) continued to promote car bombings, killings, and other so-called political acts of terrorism as late as 1993.

Further Reading

Aust, Stefan. *The Baader-Meinhof Group: The Inside Story of a Phenomenon*. London: Butler and Tanner, 1985. Provides a detailed account of the activities of numerous members of the Red Army Faction and the outcomes and legal consequences of such activities.

Becker, Jillian. *Hitler's Children: The Story of the Baader-Meinhof Terrorist Gang*. New York: J. B. Lippincott, 1977. Discusses events leading up to the formation of the Baader-Meinhof Gang and its changes in membership and leadership. Provides detailed accounts of its terrorist activities and encounters with the law.

Giles, Steve, and Maike Oergel. *Counter-Cultures in Germany and Central Europe: From Sturm und Drang to Baader-Meinhof*. New York: Peter Lang, 2004. A collection of papers presented in 2001 which include descriptions of various forms of counterculture and terrorism from the 1770's until the 1990's.

Varon, Jeremy. *Bringing the War Home: The Weather Underground, the Red Army Faction, and Revolutionary Violence in the Sixties and Seventies*. Berkeley: University of California Press, 2004. Focuses on political uprisings led by young, middle-class individuals and how they used violence, both successfully and unsuccessfully, to attempt to achieve their political goals.

—Sheryl L. Van Horne

See also: Horst Mahler; Ulrike Meinhof.

Bobby Baker

Aide and secretary to U.S. Senate Democrats

Born: 1928; Pickens, South Carolina
Also known as: Robert Gene Baker (full name); Little Lyndon; Lyndon Junior
Major offenses: Influence peddling and defrauding the government
Active: 1960's
Locale: Washington, D.C.
Sentence: Three years in prison; served sixteen months

Early Life

Bobby Baker, the son of a mailman, grew up in the small town of Pickens in northwest South Carolina. When he was eight years old, Baker began work in a drugstore. He was admired by his teachers as someone who could get things done. In 1942, at the age of fourteen, Baker, through the offices of U.S. Senator Burnet Maybank (Democrat from South Carolina), became a page in the Senate in Washington, D.C. As a page, Baker joined a corps of twenty-two teenage boys who wore dark blue knickers, attended a special school in the Capitol, and ran errands on the floor of the Senate, filling inkwells and snuffboxes in the chamber.

Through hard work and hustle, Baker earned the reputation of a reliable page, and senators asked for him by name. By frequently visiting with Senate parliamentarian Charles Watkins in his office, Baker learned the traditions and procedures of the upper house. Baker so ingratiated himself with the senators that, at sixteen, he was named chief page, and at eighteen he was given a title on the Senate staff so that he, unlike other pages, could remain on the Senate payroll even after Congress had adjourned for the year.

Political Career

The Senate became Baker's home. He graduated from high school there. Baker earned a degree from George Washington University and attended law school at night at American University. In 1948 he married a senator's secretary. His wedding reception was held in the Capitol and was attended by five senators. By the time he was twenty-one, Baker was one of the best-known Senate staffers, and many senators talked to him freely. He developed a shrewd knowledge of the personal and professional lives of individual senators.

In 1949, a newly elected senator from Texas, Lyndon B. Johnson, befriended Baker and sought his advice on where true power lay in the Senate. Baker flattered Johnson, who purportedly thought of him as a son and invited him to dinner parties attended by senators and journalists at the Johnson residence. Johnson referred to Baker as his strong right arm. The indefatigable Baker worked so hard for his mentor that he was given the nicknames Little Lyndon and Lyndon Junior. In 1951 Baker was appointed assistant of the Democratic cloakroom, a role that freed him from the status and duties of a page and gave him an opportunity to spend much of his time in the Senate cloakroom, where he learned even more about the members.

The information Baker gained gave him insights into how senators were likely to vote on a particular bill. Such knowledge was indispensable to Johnson, who had become assistant majority leader (Democratic whip). Johnson instructed Baker to know the whereabouts of every Democratic senator at all times and to have a phone number where each senator could be reached. Baker's job was to round up senators to vote for measures favored by the party leadership. The precision of Baker's preliminary head counts was remarkable. In addition, his doing favors for senators and others won him power and prestige in the Capitol. Baker's hard work was rewarded by his being made assistant secretary to the Democratic minority in 1953 and secretary to the Senate majority leader (who was Johnson) in 1955.

Johnson also used Baker to solicit money for the party by cajoling or subtly threatening donors and to deliver funds from Johnson to other senators. Baker called himself the "official bagman" for Senate Democrats. From 1957 to 1960, Baker furthered his influence by serving as secretary-treasurer of the Senate Democratic Campaign Committee.

In the mid-1950's, Baker helped the Intercontinental Hotels Corporation establish casinos in the Dominican Republic. This assignment brought him in contact with organized crime figures, and he subsequently worked with known mobsters in establishing the Serv-U Corporation, which provided vending machines for companies working on federally granted programs.

In 1960 Johnson was elected vice president, and Baker continued as his secretary and political adviser. In 1961

Bobby Baker. (AP/Wide World Photos)

Baker returned to the Senate to work for the new majority leader, Mike Mansfield (Democrat from Montana), but during the Kennedy administration, he was more closely associated with Robert Kerr (Democrat from Oklahoma). Most notably, Baker assisted Kerr in defeating the administration's medicare bill in July, 1962.

In 1963 rumors circulated that Baker had used his official position to enrich himself. His salary as Johnson's assistant was $19,600, yet his net worth was $1.7 million. Baker was investigated by Attorney General Robert Kennedy, who discovered Baker had links to Texas oil tycoon Clint Murchison and several Mafia bosses. Evidence also emerged that Baker had been involved in procuring "party girls" for a number of congressmen and even President John F. Kennedy. Other allegations about his "influence peddling" in the press and by Republicans forced Baker to leave his job on October 7, 1963.

Legal Action and Outcome

The Senate Rules Committee investigated the allegations against Baker in 1964 and 1965 and found that he had accepted payments for influencing legislation and had acquired vending contracts for his Serv-U Corporation from aerospace firms working for the government. The Rules Committee's report found Baker "guilty of many gross improprieties."

In January, 1967, a U.S. District Court found Baker guilty of seven counts of theft, income tax evasion, and fraud, including his accepting large sums of "campaign donations" intended to buy influence with various senators but which Baker had kept for himself. In January, 1971, he was sentenced to serve three years in prison, but he was paroled in June, 1972.

Impact

The Bobby Baker scandal was a major campaign issue in the 1964 presidential elections. The unsuccessful Republican candidate Barry Goldwater characterized the scandal as typical of the ethics of Johnson and his cronies. Goldwater maintained that the Baker affair hurt Johnson more than any other campaign issue.

Further Reading

Baker, Robert Gene, with Larry L. King. *Wheeling and Dealing: Confessions of a Capitol Hill Operator.* New York: Norton, 1978. Baker, assisted by a noted political writer, is surprisingly candid about his own actions and sincerely stands by his deals.

Caro, Robert A. *Lyndon Johnson: Master of the Senate.* New York: Knopf, 2002. The third volume of a biography of Johnson focuses on his Senate years, featuring Baker as his trusted assistant.

Rowe, Robert. *The Bobby Baker Story.* New York: Parallax, 1967. The public integrity scandals of the Johnson administration focused national attention on ethics in Washington, and Rowe provides a contemporary, pre-Watergate view of the Baker affair.

—*Theodore M. Vestal*

See also: Oakes Ames; Jim Folsom; Abe Fortas.

Jim Bakker

Televangelist and founder of Praise the Lord Ministries

Born: January 2, 1939; Muskegon, Michigan
Also known as: James Orson Bakker (full name)
Major offenses: Embezzlement and tax evasion
Active: 1980-1987
Locale: Charlotte, North Carolina, and Fort Mill, South Carolina
Sentence: Forty-five years in prison and $500,000 fine; reduced to eight years in prison and no fine; served five years

Early Life

Jim Bakker , a self-described wild youth, grew up in the greater Muskegon, Michigan, area. During his late teens, he decided that he needed to refocus his life on God and as a result became a minister. Some biographers contend that it was a revival meeting offered by evangelist Oral Roberts in 1960, which highlighted the relationship between show business and evangelizing, that inspired Bakker to enter the ministry. While attending North Central Bible College in Minneapolis, Minnesota, in 1961, Bakker fell in love and married his first wife, classmate and later cofounder of Praise the Lord (or People That Love) Ministries, Tammy Faye.

In 1964, after Jim was ordained a minister in the Assemblies of God Church, he and Tammy Faye began working with Pat Robertson at the Robertson Christian Broadcasting network. As time went on, Jim convinced Robertson to change the format of his nightly telethon to a daytime talk show in order to reach more Christian viewers; the show's success then increased dramatically.

Jim Bakker and his wife, Tammy Faye. (Hulton Archive/Getty Images)

Bakker's Prosperity Gospel

In his 1996 confessional book I Was Wrong, *Bakker described his original "prosperity gospel" and his revised thinking about it:*

For years I had embraced and espoused a gospel that some skeptics had branded a "prosperity gospel." I didn't mind the label; on the contrary, I was proud of it. "You're absolutely right!" I'd say to critics and friends alike. "I preach it and live it! I believe in a God who wants to bless His people. Look at all the rich saints in the Old Testament. And the New Testament clearly say that above all, God wants us to prosper even as our souls prosper. If your soul is prospering, you should be prospering materially as well!"

I even got to the point where I was teaching people at PTL, "Don't pray, 'God, Your will be done,' when you're praying for health or wealth. You already know it is God's will for you to have those things! To ask God to confirm His will when He has already told you what His will is in a matter is an insult to God. It is as though you don't really trust Him or believe that He is as good as His Word. Instead of praying 'Thy will be done' when you want a new car, just claim it. Pray specifically and tell God what kind you want. Be sure to specify which options and what color you want too."

Such arrogance! Such foolishness! Such sin! The Bible says we are not to presume upon God, but we should say, "If the Lord wills, we shall live and do this or that" (James 4:15).

Source: Jim Bakker with Ken Abraham, *I Was Wrong* (Nashville, Tenn.: Thomas Nelson, 1996).

In late 1972, Jim and Tammy decided to form their own Christian network. Initially, the two partnered with another minister, Paul Crouch, and created both Trinity Broadcasting and a daily talk show called *Praise the Lord*. After less than a year, the Bakkers and Crouch had a falling-out, and the Bakkers once again broke off to form their own network. They retained the legal rights to use the initials P.T.L. (for Praise the Lord) and began their own network in Charlotte, North Carolina, in early 1974. By 1976, their television show *The PTL Club*, running on their new PTL Network, was carried by more than seventy commercial stations and twenty cable services around the globe, reaching an estimated 13.5 million viewers per day.

During the late 1970's and early 1980's the Bakker ministry grew exponentially; estimated contributions raised from viewers exceeded one million dollars per week. Jim and Tammy also created the United States' first Christian-themed amusement park, Heritage USA, situated on twenty-three hundred acres in Fort Mill, South Carolina. The park generated more than $130 million a year. Both Jim and Tammy attributed their unprecedented success to the fact that PTL Ministries was nondenominational and never refused the opportunity to minister, regardless of a person's race, sexual orientation, ethnicity, creed, or criminal record.

Criminal Career

Jim Bakker's fall from glory began when the *Charlotte Observer* uncovered—with the assistance of rival televangelist Jimmy Swaggart—that a few years prior, Bakker had one of his associates offer former PTL secretary Jessica Hahn $265,000 for her silence regarding a sexual encounter between her and Bakker in 1980. However, this issue appeared to be only the tip of the proverbial iceberg: Federal authorities ascertained in 1987 that Bakker and his wife had been collecting some $158,000,000 in salaries and other perks—monies they had embezzled from their faithful followers.

Although the Bakkers explained that all the cash they raised went into PTL Ministries' coffers, the outlandish bonuses they gave themselves included luxury cars, a private jet, four lavish homes, a twentieth wedding anniversary party, numerous cosmetic surgeries, a houseboat, and thousands of dollars in gold and jewelry. More serious, it was proved that Bakker and his associates had coerced thousands of followers each to donate one thousand dollars, for which they were to receive a once-a-year, paid vacation at the Heritage USA theme park. Federal investigators uncovered not only that the facility Bakker was constructing could not accommodate all of the actual donors but also that Bakker purposely had been keeping two sets of accounting books, to conceal his fraudulent activities. Finally, in late 1989, Jim and Tammy Bakker and numerous members of PTL Ministries were indicted by a federal grand jury on various counts ranging from fraud to tax evasion.

Legal Action and Outcome

In October, 1989, a federal judge in North Carolina found Bakker guilty on twenty-four counts of fraud, conspiracy to commit fraud, mail fraud, Federal Communications Commission violations, wire fraud, and tax evasion. He was sentenced to forty-five years in prison and ordered to pay a $500,000 fine. This sentence was later reduced by a federal appeals court decision which eliminated the fine and reduced his prison sentence to eight years. He served five years before being released for his exemplary behavior as an inmate.

Impact

The PTL Ministries case became the first well-publicized criminal case regarding religious fraud in U.S. history. Jim Bakker's crimes opened the eyes of millions of Christians and other religious dominations throughout both the United States and the world to the potential for fraud cloaked in religious garb on a scale made possible by television.

Further Reading

Bakker, Jay. *Son of a Preacher Man: My Search for Grace in the Shadows.* San Francisco: Harper, 2002. Bakker's son gives his firsthand account of his father and mother's fraudulent careers inside the infamous PTL Ministries.

Richardson, Michael. *The Edge of Disaster: The Story of Jim and Tammy Bakker.* New York: St. Martin's Press, 1987. The author offers a detailed look at the trials and tribulations of PTL Ministries and the Bakkers. The book follows the beginnings of their rise to fame and continues to the time of Jim's conviction.

Shepard, C. E. *Forgiven: The Rise and Fall of Jim Bakker and the PTL Ministry.* New York: Atlantic Monthly Press, 1989. Gives a synopsis of the rise and fall of one of the United States' most notorious religious fraudsters.

Tidwell, Gary. *Anatomy of a Fraud: Inside the Finances of the PTL Ministries.* New York: John Wiley & Sons, 1993. Offers personal testimony by Bakker's followers who lost much more than just the money they donated.

—*Paul M. Klenowski*

See also: Father Divine; Aimee Semple McPherson.

Joe Ball

American serial killer

Born: January 7, 1896; Elmendorf, Texas
Died: September 24, 1938; Elmendorf, Texas
Also known as: Joseph D. Ball (full name); Alligator Man; Butcher of Elmendorf; Bluebeard of Texas
Cause of notoriety: A bootlegger-turned-tavern owner, Ball murdered several of his girlfriends as well as barmaids, then shot himself when confronted by authorities.
Active: Summer, 1937-September, 1938
Locale: Elmendorf, Texas

Early Life

Joseph D. Ball (bahl) was born on January 7, 1896, and was raised in the largely unsettled frontier of southern Texas by his parents, Frank Ball and Elizabeth Ball. Ball was the second of eight children and grew up in a very comfortable and stable household. His father was a successful businessman who owned a general store in the small town of Elmendorf. Ball spent much of his childhood involved in outdoor activities such as fishing and target shooting. In 1917, he enlisted in the U.S. Army, serving on the front lines in Europe during World War I. In 1919, he received an honorable discharge and returned to Elmendorf.

Criminal Career

After a brief stint working for his father's business, Ball began selling illegal whiskey to local customers. Ball's career as a bootlegger ended in 1933, when Prohibition ended after the Eighteenth Amendment. Shortly thereafter, he opened his own tavern, the Sociable Inn, just outside Elmendorf. Behind his tavern, Ball built a concrete pond, surrounded by a large wire fence and stocked with five alligators. As an attraction, Ball would entertain his intoxicated customers by feeding the reptiles live dogs, cats, and other animals. As another draw to his tavern, Ball would hire young, attractive barmaids and waitresses to work there.

Ball initiated romantic relationships with his women employees, often several at a time. In 1934 Ball met Minnie Gotthardt, and eventually she operated the tavern with him. Their relationship lasted three years, until Ball began courting a young waitress named Dolores Goodwin in 1937. That summer, Gotthardt disappeared. Ball began another relationship with a young barmaid named

Hazel Brown. In September, 1937, Ball married Goodwin, but she disappeared the following April.

While local law enforcement was increasingly suspicious of Ball after the disappearances of several barmaids, his two girlfriends, and his wife, there was no real evidence to refute Ball's claims that the women "just moved on." In addition, Ball's intimidating personality and unusual business practices made local residents reluctant to challenge or cross him.

Legal Action and Outcome

On September 23, 1938, Bexar County Deputy Sheriff John Gray was approached by a man who reported seeing a barrel covered in flies and smelling of human decomposition behind Ball's sister's barn. The next day, Deputy Sheriffs Gray and Klevenhagen went to the barn, but the barrel was gone. They questioned Ball, but he denied any wrongdoing. When they returned to the barn, Ball's sister confirmed the presence of the foul-smelling barrel. Deputies Gray and Klevenhagen returned to the Sociable Inn to transport Ball to San Antonio for interrogation. When confronted by the deputies, Ball opened the register and removed a .45-caliber revolver from the drawer. Ball turned the gun to his heart and shot himself dead.

With the magnitude of the crimes becoming clearer, Deputies Gray and Klevenhagen questioned Ball's handyman, Clifford Wheeler. Initially denying involvement, Wheeler then admitted to assisting Ball dispose of the bodies of two women. Minnie Gotthardt's body was found buried in sand near Corpus Christi, and Hazel Brown's dismembered body was found buried in a shallow grave near the San Antonio River. Wheeler claimed Ball had killed Gotthardt because she was pregnant and that Ball had killed Brown because she wanted to end their relationship. Wheeler was incarcerated for two years after pleading guilty. When investigators searched Ball's property, they found a scrapbook with dozens of pictures of women. Many speculated that Ball might have killed at least twenty women, and the alligators disposed of the physical evidence. No human remains were found near the alligator pond to support that assertion.

Impact

Joe Ball's criminal career was familiar in Texas folklore, but factual details of his life and crimes remained obscure until the twenty-first century. In 2002, newspaper editor Michael Hall published a detailed article in the July issue of *Texas Monthly* magazine. Ball's reputation also drew attention in Tobe Hooper's 1977 film *Eaten Alive*, inspired by Ball's crimes.

Further Reading

Hall, Michael. "Two Barmaids, Five Alligators, and the Butcher of Elmendorf." *Texas Monthly* (July, 2002): 114-126. A comprehensive account of Ball's life in words, interviews, and photos. Also examines the legends and folklore surrounding Ball's serial murders.

Lohr, David. *Joe Ball: The Butcher of Elmendorf.* Court TV, Crime Library. www.crimelibrary.com. A clear, detailed biography of Ball's upbringing, saloon, personal relationships, criminal career, and suicide.

Newton, Michael. *The Encyclopedia of Serial Killers.* New York: Checkmark Books, 2000. A brief, factual account of Ball's life and crimes.

—Anthony J. Luongo III

See also: David Berkowitz; Kenneth Bianchi; Ted Bundy; Angelo Buono, Jr.; Andrei Chikatilo; Andrew Cunanan; Jeffrey Dahmer; Albert DeSalvo; Albert Fish; John Wayne Gacy; Ed Gein; Karla Homolka; Leonard Lake; Charles Ng; Dennis Rader; Richard Speck; Aileen Carol Wuornos.

MARGITA BANGOVÁ
Romani-Czech panhandler

BORN: c. 1936; Czechoslovakia
ALSO KNOWN AS: Margita Horváthová
CAUSE OF NOTORIETY: Although Bangová was arrested and convicted for minor assault, she had already garnered widespread press both for allegedly being a con artist and for her indirect role in encouraging Romani émigrés to come to Canada.
ACTIVE: 1997-2004
LOCALE: Toronto, Ontario

EARLY LIFE

Little is known of the early life of Margita Bangová , a Romani (or Gypsy) born in the Slovakian section of the former Czechoslovakia; however, one can speculate, based on the severe treatment of the Romani by the Nazis during World War II, that her childhood would have been harsh, if not brutal. She and her family may have been among the small number of Slovakian Romani who escaped the horrors of Nazi work camps by hiding in remote rural areas.

Following the war, she was relocated to the northern portion of the newly established Czechoslovakia. In 1997, Bangová joined a growing number of Romani who emigrated to Canada, seeking refugee status on the basis of increasing violence and racial prejudice against Gypsies within the Czech Republic.

CON ARTIST CAREER

While applying for asylum, Bangová received government assistance, which she supplemented by panhandling in downtown Toronto. Within a few months of her arrival, she appeared well dressed and healthy in a documentary produced for the Czech television station Nova. Bangová described life in Canada as luxurious and carefree. The airing of the documentary in the Czech Republic in August, 1997, triggered a wave of Romani emigration. As a result of this surge, the Canadian government reinstated visa restrictions for travelers from the Czech Republic. The situation received international press coverage, and Bangová, who was identified by name in the documentary, was widely quoted.

For the next few years, Bangová continued to panhandle in Toronto, where she often displayed a cardboard sign claiming she was ill. Local residents began to refer to her as Shaky Lady because she sometimes trembled violently. However, at the end of each day, Bangová could be seen walking without apparent discomfort to a nearby corner, where she entered an automobile and was driven away.

In March, 2002, the *Toronto Sun* published a front-page story by reporter Mike Strobel that proclaimed Bangová a con artist who earned $2,500 (Canadian) a week and lived with family members in a comfortable, well-furnished apartment. Bangová responded by calling a press conference, at which her immigration lawyer, Leonard Hochberg, denounced the *Toronto Sun* reports; Hochberg maintained that Bangová suffered from medical problems that caused her tremors and for which she received a disability pension. The lawyer also disputed the reporter's statement of her earnings, which he estimated at forty to fifty dollars a day, an amount similar to that reported by other Toronto panhandlers. Panhandling is not a crime in Toronto, where, in 2002, there were an estimated one thousand homeless persons relying on begging for income. In July, 2002, Bangová was arrested for striking with her cane a woman who accused her of fakery. Bangová's single arrest and conviction were for minor assault, and although found guilty, she was released without further punishment.

In July, 2004, the *Toronto Sun* published another article, again by Strobel, which reported that Bangová was recognized in Montreal by a reader of Strobel who claimed she was panhandling in a wheelchair but fled when he tried to photograph her.

IMPACT

The *Toronto Sun* articles drew immediate criticism from those concerned both with the well-being of the poor andwith the perpetuation of negative stereotypes of Gypsies being criminals. Supporters of Margita Bangová attributed the press coverage to her unwitting role in the influx of Romani asylum seekers from Eastern Europe. Bangová, finding herself subject to harassment in Toronto, began traveling to nearby cities to ply her trade. Although she quickly faded from the headlines, her reputation as a con artist, whether justified or not, spread on the Internet.

FURTHER READING

Belton, Brian A. *Gypsy and Traveller Ethnicity: The Social Generation of an Ethnic Phenomenon*. London: Routledge, 2004. An examination of the impact of social conditions and ethnic narrative on the lives of Gypsies.

Hancock, Ian. *We Are the Romani People*. Hatfield, England: University of Hertfordshire Press, 2002. A cultural history of the Romani people that challenges negative stereotypes.

Lacková, Ilona. *A False Dawn: My Life as a Gypsy Woman in Slovakia*. Edited and translated by Milena Hübschmannová. Hatfield, England: University of Hertfordshire Press, 2000. This memoir recounts life in Slovakia from the prewar era through the early decades of communist rule.

—*K Edgington*

See also: Susanna Mildred Hill; Megan Louise Ireland.

Barabbas

Jewish rebel against Rome

Born: Early first century c.e.; Galilee (now in Israel)
Died: First century c.e.; place unknown
Also known as: Jesus bar-Abbas; Yeshua
Cause of notoriety: Barabbas was the leader in an insurrection against Rome and was labeled a robber and murderer by Roman officials.
Active: 30 c.e.
Locale: Jerusalem, Judea

Early Life

Nothing is known about the early life of Barabbas except possibly through his name. In first century Judaism, the patronymic name was regularly preceded by *Bar*, the Aramaic word for "son." Since "Abbas" is rarely attested as a name during this period, it may well designate Abba, a name of endearment for well-respected rabbis.

Barabbas is released.

GIVE US BARABBAS

The Barabbas described in the Gospels is a shadowy figure, lacking a distinct history, character, or destiny. He is also an intriguing figure. What happened to him after the Romans freed him? The Gospels are silent on that point, but the question proved irresistible to Pär Lagerkvist; the Swedish novelist wrote *Barabbas* (1950; English translation, 1951) to explore an imaginative answer. The book helped him win the 1951 Nobel Prize in Literature. It opens with Barabbas watching the crucifixion and not liking what he sees of the man who has taken his place:

> He did not know this man, had nothing to do with him. What was he doing at Golgotha, he who had been released?
>
> The crucified man's head hung down and he was breathing heavily; it would not be long now. There was nothing vigorous about the fellow. His body was lean and spindly, the arms slender as though they had never been put to any use. A queer man. The beard was sparse and the chest quite hairless, like a boy's. He did not like him.

Lagerkvist's story goes on to describe how Barabbas is not only skeptical about Jesus' claims to be the son of God but also fascinated. He meets Jesus' followers, observes Mary and the family, and learns a little about the radical religious views attributed to him. Still, a rough-and-ready man, Barabbas has little sympathy for the nascent Christianity. Eventually, he makes his way to Rome. When a great fire breaks out in the city, his muddled notions lead him to believe that the promised Kingdom of Heaven is at hand, and because of that he helps spread the flames. The Roman authorities arrest him and condemn him to death—by crucifixion. There is no way out this time. Lagerkvist leaves the ending ambiguous, yet one thing is clear: The dying Barabbas, whether understanding his fate or not, has remained tied to the dying Jesus:

> When he felt death approaching, that which he had always been so afraid of, he said out into the darkness, as though he were speaking to it:
>
> To thee I deliver up my soul.
>
> And then he gave up the ghost.

Source: Pär Lagerkvist, *Barabbas*, translated by Alan Blair (New York: Random House, 1951).

REBELLION

The account of Barabbas is recorded only in four ancient sources—the four Gospels—and in reference only to the period of his confinement in Jerusalem. The earliest Gospel, Mark, refers to Barabbas as "one of those among the rebels who had committed murder in the insurrection." Matthew adds that he was considered "a notorious prisoner," and John refers to him as a "robber."

Following 6 C.E., when Roman procurators were installed to provide direct rule over Judea, there was a long series of rebellions against Rome. Many of the acts of insurrection occurred in response to offensive actions of the procurators, especially under Pontius Pilate, who ruled from 26 to 36 C.E.

Because Pilate's offenses often showed a lack of sensitivity to Jewish religious custom, one can understand how someone from a religious background—if the view of Barabbas being the son of a rabbi is correct—would turn to violence against the ruling authorities. According to the ancient historian Flavius Josephus, many of these rebels sought refuge in the desert or in the mountains and supported themselves by highway robbery. This would fit the varied descriptions of Barabbas in the Gospels.

Shortly before the trial of Jesus Christ, Pilate had brought offensive images to Jerusalem, stolen from the temple treasury, and slaughtered several Galilean worshipers while they were sacrificing in the Jerusalem Temple. Subsequently, a number of rebellious acts occurred, including the riot that led to Barabbas's arrest. Since Pilate visited Jerusalem only several times a year, it is likely that Barabbas was held in prison in order to await Pilate to pass sentence on him officially. The two criminals who were executed with Jesus were likely fellow rebels of Barabbas.

LEGAL ACTION AND OUTCOME

Barabbas was released without charge by Pilate on April 7, 30 C.E., as part of a customary Passover festival prison release. While it is difficult to know what details were added by the evangelists for dramatic effect, it seems that the crowds requested the release of Barabbas rather than of Jesus. Thus, Jesus was condemned to death by crucifixion while Barabbas went free. It may be that the labels "murderer" and "robber" as used by the Gospel writers may reflect popular sentiment rather than legitimate charges of a lesser Roman judge. However, Pilate released Barabbas without charge. There is no information concerning the later life of Barabbas and whether he continued in further insurrection against Rome.

IMPACT

Theologically, the Barabbas episode played a critical part in the Gospels. While the innocent Jesus was condemned to death, the guilty Barabbas—representing humankind in general—went free. The Barabbas figure was meant to instill introspection and a penitent attitude. Instead, it served to facilitate the rise of anti-Semitism. Christians soon blamed the Jews because the crowds favored Barabbas. The term "Christ-killer" became an excuse for certain Christians to bring violence upon later generations of innocent Jews.

Further Reading

Brown, Raymond E. *The Death of the Messiah*. 2 vols. Garden City, N.Y.: Doubleday, 1999. Detailed exegetical study of the Gospel accounts of the death of Jesus.

Crossan, John Dominic. *Who Killed Jesus? Exposing the Roots of Anti-Semitism in the Gospel Story of the Death of Jesus*. San Francisco: Harper, 1996. New Testament scholar investigates the language of the Gospel accounts, including the story of Barabbas, that led to the growth of anti-Semitism.

Horsley, Richard A., and J. S. Hanson. *Bandits, Prophets, and Messiahs*. Minneapolis: Fortress, 1985. Studies the phenomenon of social banditry in first century Israel.

Merritt, R. L. "Jesus Barabbas and the Paschal Pardon." *Journal of Biblical Literature* 104 (1985): 57-68. Presents evidence for the custom of prisoner release in the ancient world.

Lagerkvist, Pär. *Barabbas*. Reprint. New York: Vintage Books, 1989. Originally published in 1949, this is a fictional psychological study that intertwines Barabbas's fate with Christian martyrs in Rome.

Rhoads, David M. *Israel in Revolution, 6-74 C.E.: A Political History Based on the Writings of Josephus*. Philadelphia: Fortress, 1976. Investigates first century Jewish revolts against Rome.

—Fred Strickert

See also: Herod Antipas; Herod the Great; Flavius Josephus; Judas Iscariot; Pontius Pilate.

Klaus Barbie

Nazi war criminal

Born: October 25, 1913; Bad Godesberg, Germany
Died: September 25, 1991; Lyon, France
Also known as: Butcher of Lyon; Klaus Altmann
Major offenses: Crimes against humanity, specifically torture, "deportation," and murder
Active: 1941-1945
Locale: Lyon, France, and Amsterdam, Holland
Sentence: Life imprisonment

Klaus Barbie. (Witschel/dpa/Landov)

Early Life

Three months following the illegitimate birth of Klaus Barbie, his parents married. His alcoholic father was first an office worker but later became a schoolteacher. In 1923, after Barbie moved away to the Friedrich-Wilhelm school in Trier, he was relieved finally to be free of his disciplinarian father. Two years later, however, his entire family moved to Trier, and Barbie moved back in with them. In 1933, the year Adolf Hitler became chancellor of Germany, both Barbie's father and younger brother died.

Barbie, with average marks, passed his final exams in 1934. He had an affinity for languages and was fluent in French, German, and Spanish. At the age of twenty, he joined the Hitler Youth and became an assistant to his lo-

Barbie's Barbarity

Klaus Barbie is infamous for two main reasons. One was his torture of resistance leaders. The other was a raid on a children's school, told here by the only surviving witness:

On April 6, 1944 . . . three vehicles, two of which were lorries, pulled up in front of the children's refuge in Izieu, a sleepy village nestled in the piedmont east of Lyon. The children, most of whom were Jewish, were hiding in Izieu in order to escape their hunter, the regional Gestapo, which was led by First Lieutenant Klaus Barbie. The lorries' arrival signaled the end of this hunt and as a witness later recalled, Barbie's Gestapo caught its quarry:

It was breakfast time. The children were in the refectory drinking hot chocolate. I was on my way down the stairs when I saw three trucks in the drive. My sister shouted to me: it's the Germans, save yourself! I jumped out the window. I hid myself in a bush in the garden. . . . I heard the cries of the children that were being kidnapped and I heard the shouts of the Nazis who were carrying them away. . . . They threw the children into the trucks like they were sacks of potatoes. Most of them were crying, terrorized.

Following the raid on their home in Izieu, the children were shipped directly to the "collection center" in Drancy by the Gestapo. Upon reaching Drancy, the children were put on the first available train "towards the East" and, of the forty-four children kidnapped by the Nazis in Izieu, not a single one returned. The most tragic aspect of the Izieu raid, however, was that Barbie would have never found the children had patriotic French citizens not volunteered to help him search for refugees.

When Klaus Barbie arrived in Lyon in November, 1942, he was assigned two tasks, to dismantle the Resistance and rid the city of Jews. . . . Barbie's job, however, was not nearly as difficult as it sounded. For every *résistant* he encountered, Barbie found that there were equal numbers of French willing to collaborate with him. Many of the French who collaborated with Barbie did so out of greed or a lust for power, but many more collaborated simply because they believed what they were doing was good for France.

Source: Serge Klarsfeld, *The Children of Izieu: A Human Tragedy* (New York: Abrams, 1984).

cal party leader. He also volunteered for a six-month stint at a work camp in Schleswig-Holstein.

On September 26, 1935, Barbie joined the Schutzstaffel (SS). He was then posted to Berlin as an assistant at the Sicherheitsdienst (SD) main office, then trained as an interrogator and investigator at police headquarters in Alexanderplatz. His next post was on a vice squad which carried out raids and arrested prostitutes, homosexuals, and Jews. In 1936, he was transferred to an SD squad in Düsseldorf. Barbie was automatically enrolled in the Nazi Party in 1937. He graduated from the SD school in Bernau and was sent to the leadership course in Charlottenburg, Berlin.

Beginning in September, 1938, Barbie served three months in the Thirty-ninth Infantry. On April 20, 1940, he graduated from the leadership course and was promoted to second lieutenant (SS Untersturmführer). Five days after graduating, he married Regine Willms, a twenty-three-year-old maid. Barbie was then assigned to the intelligence section within the SD (section VI). He was subsequently posted to Amsterdam, to the Central Bureau for Jewish Emigration.

Criminal Career

While in Amsterdam in 1941, Barbie was responsible for rounding up Freemasons, German émigrés, and Jews. For his hard work and dedication he was promoted to first lieutenant. Barbie was awarded the Iron Cross, second class, for his management of the Jewish resistance to relocation in Holland. Exemplary of his style, Barbie politely approached members of the local Jewish Council and asked for a list of three hundred Jewish boys who had been forced to leave their training camp by the German authorities. He said that the Germans had decided that the young apprentices should return to the camp, and that he needed to write to the boys to tell them. The Jewish leaders promptly handed over the list. They later discovered that all the boys had been arrested as a reprisal for a bomb attack on a German officers' club. All the boys were executed at Mathausen.

The following year, as Gestapo chief in Lyon, France, Barbie ordered the deportation of forty-four Jewish children. He was also involved in the capture and torture of some influential members of the French Resistance movement, including Jean Moulin, the highest-ranking member of the Resistance ever to be caught by German authorities. Barbie took part in a sting operation that resulted in capturing at least eighty-six Jews, who were then deported to Auschwitz. Barbie personally interrogated people at the École de Santé Militaire, which opened as a torture center in June, 1943. Many of his victims claimed that Barbie would often be smiling, quite enjoying the torture of others. Through either his actions or orders, he was responsible for deporting approximately 7,500 people to death camps, torturing 14,311 Resistance members, and killing a total of 4,342 people.

After World War II ended, the American Counter-Intelligence Corps hired Barbie to spy on German Communists and those who resisted American and British occupation in Western Europe. In 1955, Barbie assumed the name Klaus Altmann and moved to Bolivia. There he disappeared.

Legal Action and Outcome

In France, Barbie was twice tried and sentenced to death in absentia. His whereabouts in Bolivia were finally discovered by Serge and Beatte Klarfeld in 1971. Barbie was not extradited until 1983, thanks to the protection of the Bolivian military dictatorship. By this time, his two prior convictions were void under a statute of limitations; he was tried again in May, 1987. His lawyer, Jacques Vergès, argued that Barbie's actions were no worse than those undertaken by any colonizing nation, including France. Nonetheless, Barbie was convicted and sentenced to life imprisonment on July 4. He died of cancer in the prison hospital four years later.

Impact

Klaus Barbie's impact upon all the families of those murdered, tortured, and deported is impossible to quantify. However, his trial did raise interesting questions as to the policies of the French government in its colonies and the tactics employed as well as historic questions about French and American collaboration with the Nazis during and after the war.

Further Reading

Bower, Tom. *Klaus Barbie: The Butcher of Lyons.* New York: Bookmoat, 1984. An account of the life of Barbie, his exploits in the Nazi Party, his hiding and trial, and the possible reasons for his barbarity.

Finkielkraut, Alain. *Remembering in Vain: The Klaus Barbie Trial and Crimes Against Humanity.* New York: Columbia University Press, 1992. A complete account of the Klaus Barbie trial as well as some of the revelations that the trial brought to light.

Murphy, Brendan. *The Butcher of Lyon: The Story of Infamous Nazi Klaus Barbie.* New York: Empire Books, 1983. Accounts for Barbie's acts in Lyon and the events that occurred after World War II as well.

—Michael W. Cheek and Dennis W. Cheek

See also: Elisabeth Becker; Martin Bormann; Léon Degrelle; Karl Dönitz; Adolf Eichmann; Hans Michael Frank; Joseph Goebbels; Magda Goebbels; Hermann Göring; Rudolf Hess; Reinhard Heydrich; Heinrich Himmler; Adolf Hitler; Alfred Jodl; Josef Mengele; Joachim von Ribbentrop; Baldur von Schirach; Otto Skorzeny; Albert Speer; Julius Streicher.

Velma Margie Barfield

American "black widow" serial killer

Born: October 29, 1932; Cumberland County, North Carolina
Died: November 2, 1984; Central Prison, Raleigh, North Carolina
Also known as: Margie Bullard (birth name); Death Row Granny
Major offense: First-degree murder
Active: 1969-1978
Locale: North Carolina
Sentence: Death by lethal injection

Early Life

Velma Margie Barfield was born in rural North Carolina, the second child in a family of nine children. She claimed that her father beat and raped her and her sisters, although this claim was vehemently denied by her siblings. Velma dropped out of school at a young age, and by age nineteen she was married to Thomas Burke, with whom she had two children. Burke suffered severe head injuries in a car crash in 1966 and became unable to work. He became an alcoholic, and Velma began to take antidepressants and tranquilizers, to which she ultimately became addicted. Burke died in a house fire in 1969. Velma was remarried in 1970, to Jennings Barfield. Barfield was dead within six months of their marriage; physicians believed his death to have occurred from natural causes.

Criminal Career

In 1974, Velma Barfield's mother, Lillie Bullard, died unexpectedly from what were believed to be natural causes. At the time of her death, Barfield had forged her mother's name on a one-thousand-dollar loan application. Barfield also served a short amount of time in a correctional facility for writing bad checks. After the death of her mother, Barfield, who was by now completely dependent on prescription drugs, took a job as a live-in maid for Dollie Edwards. During her employment with Edwards, Barfield met Edwards's nephew Stuart Taylor, with whom she began a romantic relationship which would last for two years. Her employment ended when Edwards died unexpectedly in 1977 from acute gastroenteritis.

Barfield then took a job with John Lee and his wife and began forging checks against the Lees' bank account. In June, 1977, John Lee died after two months' suffering a severe stomach ailment. Barfield began forging checks against Stuart Taylor's bank account. Taylor took ill around the time he became suspicious concerning his checking account activity. In February, 1978, Taylor died after suffering intense abdominal pains. The cause of his death was determined to be acute gastroenteritis. Taylor's relatives disagreed with the diagnosis and demanded a full autopsy. The autopsy showed that the actual cause of his death was arsenic poisoning, and Barfield was arrested. Once in custody, Barfield confessed to spiking Taylor's beer with arsenic. She then confessed to murdering her mother, whom she had poisoned with insecticide, as well as Dollie Edwards and John Lee.

Legal Action and Outcome

Barfield was charged only with the death of Stuart Taylor. A jury found her guilty of first-degree murder and sentenced her to death. While in prison, Barfield came to be widely known as a deeply religious woman. She attempted to receive clemency from the governor of North Carolina but was denied and was executed by lethal injection on November 2, 1984, in Raleigh, North Carolina.

Impact

Known as the Death Row Granny, Velma Margie Barfield became the first woman to be executed in the United States in more than twenty years, and the first woman executed in the United States since the reinstatement of the death penalty in 1976. She was also the first woman to be executed by lethal injection.

Further Reading

Barfield, Velma. *Woman on Death Row*. Nashville: Oliver Nelson Books, 1985. Barfield's autobiography.

Bledsoe, Jerry, and Velma Barfield. *Death Sentence: The True Story of Velma Barfield's Life, Crimes, and Execution*. New York: E. P. Dutton, 1998. Based mainly on anecdotes from Barfield's two children, Kim and Ronnie, this book details Barfield's childhood, her married years, her crimes, and her trial.

Kelleher, Michael D., and C. L. Kelleher. *Murder Most Rare*. New York: Dell, 1998. Provides examples and detailed biographical information for a variety of women serial killers, including Barfield.

Newton, Michael. *Bad Girls Do It: An Encyclopedia of Female Murderers*. Port Townsend, Wash.: Loompanics Unlimited, 1993. An encyclopedia of women serial killers, this book provides biographical sketches of female murderers throughout the world, including Velma Barfield.

—*Carly M. Hilinski*

See also: Ruth Ellis; Linda Burfield Hazzard; Marie Hilley; Karla Homolka; Karla Faye Tucker; Aileen Carol Wuornos.

Ma Barker

American gangland figure

Born: c. 1871; Ash Grove, near Springfield, Missouri
Died: January 16, 1935; Lake Weir, near Oklawaha, Florida
Also known as: Arizona Donnie Clark (birth name); Bloody Mama; Kate Barker; Arizona Donnie Barker
Cause of notoriety: Barker, as the matriarch of an outlaw gang, was implicated in kidnappings and robberies.
Active: 1925-1935
Locale: American West, Midwest, and South

Early Life

Arizona Donnie Clark—to come down in legend as Ma Barker (BAHR-kuhr)—was born in Ash Grove, near Springfield, Missouri. She was raised in a religious family and believed in hard work and traditional values. She married George Barker at the age of twenty and had four boys: Herman, Lloyd, Arthur, and Fred. Her husband disappeared after the last son's birth and left her to raise the boys on her own. They lived in poverty, and the boys often got into trouble. She usually managed to get them out of jail by having emotional outbursts in police stations or with arresting officers.

Gangster Career

Differing opinions exist on whether Ma Barker did, in fact, have a criminal career with her sons and another famous gangster, Alvin Karpis. Some allege that she was simply a mother, traveling and protecting her sons, who were criminals. Others have portrayed her as a mastermind of the sons' crimes. She has been credited with planning a number of bank robberies. Several kidnappings of major public figures were also attributed to the Barker-Karpis gang. In 1927, her son Herman was killed by a federal agent during a robbery in which he had killed a police officer. Federal Bureau of Investigation (FBI) head J. Edgar Hoover, in accounts after Ma's death, said that the death of her son turned her into an even more dangerous criminal.

In 1935, another son, Fred (called Freddie by his mother), was out on parole and living with his mother at a cottage on Lake Weir. Although Ma was never arrested or tried for a crime, she was considered dangerous by the FBI, and this fact was used as justification for her killing at the hands of FBI agents during a raid of the cottage. The FBI has extensive files on her and her sons, which later became available through the Freedom of Information Act.

Impact

The life and death of Ma Barker gained much public attention and became the basis of numerous books and films. She was the main character portrayed in a 1970 film titled *Bloody Mama*, starring Shelley Winters. The 1996 film *Public Enemies* also included her life as part of its story. Much of the debate about her case stems from historical analysis of the actions of Hoover, who had described her as a dangerous criminal.

Near Lake Weir, Florida, a reenactment of the final shoot-out is held annually to commemorate the biggest gun battle in FBI history (three to four thousand rounds were used). The event includes vintage cars, gunfights, and actors representing the Barkers and the FBI.

Further Reading

Gentry, Curt. *J. Edgar Hoover: The Man and the Secrets*. New York: W. W. Norton, 2001. This book is based on more than two hundred interviews and access to previously classified FBI documents. Despite lengthy footnotes and an extensive list of source materials, it is very readable. Since Hoover labeled Barker as a dangerous criminal, accounts of his life provide background on his pursuit of her and her sons.

Hamilton, Sue, and John Hamilton. *Public Enemy Number One: The Barkers*. Bloomington, Minn.: Abdo and Daughters, 1989. A book written for young

Cop vs. Robber

To FBI chief J. Edgar Hoover, Ma Barker was a "veritable beast of prey":

Ma Barker and her sons, and Alvin Karpis and his cronies, constituted the toughest gang of hoodlums the FBI ever has been called upon to eliminate.... Looking over the record of these criminals, I was repeatedly impressed by the cruelty of their depredations . . . murder of a policeman . . . murder of two policemen. . . . machine gun murder of an innocent citizen who got in the way during a bank robbery . . . kidnapping and extortion . . . train robbery . . . mail robbery . . . the protection of high police officials bought with tainted money . . . paroles bought.

Source: Ken Jones, *The FBI in Action* (New York: Signet, 1957).

adults, it summarizes the lives of Ma Barker and her sons.

Karpis, Alvin, with Bill Livesey. *On the Rock: The Prison Story of Alvin Karpis*. Toronto, Ont.: Beaufort Books, 1980. Karpis was associated with Barker's sons and took part in several of their major escapades. He was captured in 1936 and told his story while in captivity. A description of his association with the Barkers is included.

Maccabee, Paul. *John Dillinger Slept Here: A Crook's Tour of Crime and Corruption in St. Paul, 1920-1936*. St. Paul: Minnesota Historical Society Press, 1995. The Barkers were instrumental in two kidnappings in St. Paul: those of William Hamm, Jr., and Edward Bremer. Both of these crimes are chronicled in this definitive work on crime in St. Paul.

Winter, Robert. *Mean Men: The Sons of Ma Barker*. Danbury, Conn.: Routledge Books, 2000. Traces the escapades of Barker and her sons.

—*Mary C. Ware*

See also: Clyde Barrow; John Dillinger; Pretty Boy Floyd; Alvin Karpis; Machine Gun Kelly; Baby Face Nelson; Bonnie Parker.

Clyde Barrow

American serial robber, murderer, and gang leader

Born: March 24, 1909; near Telico, Texas

Died: May 23, 1934; near Gibsland, Bienville Parish, Louisiana

Also known as: Clyde Chestnut Barrow (full name); Clyde "Champion" Barrow

Cause of notoriety: Although the bank robberies Barrow and his gang committed were typically small in monetary yield, the brutal murders that often accompanied them placed Barrow and his partner Bonnie Parker among the most notorious "public enemies" of the Depression era.

Active: 1931-1934

Locale: Southern and midwestern United States

Early Life

Born to a poor family on a farm south of Dallas, Texas, Clyde Barrow reportedly began his criminal career at a young age, collaborating with his brother Ivan "Buck" Barrow on numerous burglaries, armed robberies, and other crimes. After his first two arrests in 1926, Barrow briefly held several legitimate jobs in addition to his ongoing criminal pursuits, barely escaping another arrest in a high-speed police chase that resulted in the apprehension and imprisonment of his brother. Shortly afterward, Barrow met Bonnie Parker, an unemployed waitress married to a convicted murderer serving a ninety-nine-year prison sentence.

Criminal Career

Barrow and Parker immediately forged a relationship, reportedly cohabitating as Barrow made another brief, unsuccessful attempt to earn a legitimate living. Convicted of burglary and auto theft in 1930, Barrow was sentenced to two years in prison, and after a brief escape was sent to the Texas State Prison at Eastham Farm. The harsh, brutal conditions at Eastham transformed Barrow into a seasoned criminal; it was there that he reportedly committed his first homicide. Pardoned by the Texas governor in 1932 after serving twenty months at Eastham, Barrow allegedly vowed that he would rather die than return to prison.

Following his release from prison, Barrow committed a series of robberies in Texas, often accompanied by Parker, who was arrested following a botched auto theft and served three months in prison. She returned to Barrow upon her release, and the couple resumed their criminal activity, along with a rotating gang of accomplices. Barrow was the undisputed leader of the gang, his reputation as a skilled driver augmented by a growing penchant for violent confrontations that often resulted in the deaths of resisting victims and pursuing law enforcement officers. Although the robberies Barrow and his gang committed were typically small in monetary terms, the brutal murders that often accompanied them rendered Barrow and Parker dangerous fugitives, placing them among the most notorious "public enemies" of the Great Depression era.

As the gang expanded its crime spree into several midwestern states, news media nationwide began to report sensationalized accounts of their exploits, which frequently portrayed Barrow and Parker, known to the public simply as "Bonnie and Clyde," as romantic antiheroes. Barrow and Parker actively exploited their public image: Parker submitted autobiographical poems to nu-

Bonnie Parker and Clyde Barrow. (Library of Congress)

merous newspapers, often with photographs showing the couple smoking cigars and brandishing firearms. Barrow is reputed to have sent a letter to Henry Ford praising a stolen Ford coupe, although the authenticity of the letter was never confirmed.

By mid-1933, the authorities were closing in on Barrow and his gang. After shoot-outs with police in Missouri and Iowa left Buck Barrow dead and Parker injured, members of the gang began to desert. Barrow and Parker remained on the run, alternating among several hiding places. In January of 1934 Barrow conducted a raid upon the Eastham prison farm, freeing several of his associates. The Texas Department of Corrections, embarrassed by the raid and exasperated by the failure of authorities to capture the Barrow gang, hired Frank Hamer, a former Texas Ranger with a reputation for engaging in shoot-outs with alleged criminals, to track down Barrow and Parker. On a tip from a former Barrow associate, Hamer and his assembled posse of Texas and Louisiana officers lay in wait for Barrow and Parker along a stretch of highway near Gibsland, Louisiana, on May 21, 1934. On the morning of May 23, Barrow and Parker, in a car, approached the decoy vehicle set by the posse and occupied by the father of the associate who tipped the authorities.

LEGAL ACTION AND OUTCOME

What happened afterward is the source of controversy. As the car came to a stop, the officers apparently opened fire without attempting to apprehend the couple or ordering them to surrender. One officer later admitted to having fired the first shot into Barrow's head at close range. The officers riddled the car and its occupants with bullets, firing more than 130 rounds.

Following the deaths of Barrow and Parker, Hamer publicly admitted that the posse had lain in wait for Barrow and Parker with the intent of ambushing them with deadly force. Newspapers continued to sensationalize the couple in death, publishing lurid accounts of the ambush and photographs of their bullet-riddled automobile. Barrow was buried in the Western Heights Cemetery in Dallas, Texas, next to his brother, Buck, but away from Parker, who was buried in another Dallas cemetery.

IMPACT

The crimes and violent deaths of Clyde Barrow and his accomplices occurred during the final wave of the "public enemy" era, contemporaneous with the careers of other famous criminal gang leaders such as John Dillinger (1903-1934) and Kate "Ma" Barker (c. 1871-1935). Popular media trumpeted the killing of "Bonnie and Clyde" as a victory for law enforcement and evidence of the devastating and inevitable consequences of a life of crime. Yet the romantic legend of the couple survived, spawning a multitude of books, articles, feature films, and other popular culture references.

The criminal exploits of Barrow and other high-profile criminals of the Great Depression era prompted the U.S. government to consolidate its chief federal law enforcement agencies into the Federal Bureau of Investigation (FBI) in 1935, leading to an expansion of the role of the federal government in combating organized crime and inspiring the federalization of a number of crimes whose enforcement was previously the primary responsibility of the states.

Further Reading

Barrow, Blanche, and John Neal Phillips. *My Life with Bonnie and Clyde*. Norman: University of Oklahoma Press, 2004. Memoir by the sister-in-law of Clyde Barrow includes accounts of her experiences with the Barrow gang and previously unpublished photographs from the author's personal collection.

Bruns, Roger. *The Bandit Kings from Jesse James to Pretty Boy Floyd*. New York: Crown, 1995. An examination of the outlaw as folk hero through case studies of prominent American criminals between 1850 and 1940.

Knight, James, and Jonathan Davis. *Bonnie and Clyde: A Twenty-first-Century Update*. Austin, Tex.: Eakin Press, 2003. A detailed biography of Bonnie Parker and Clyde Barrow, containing previously unpublished information and photographs.

Phillips, John Neal. "The Raid on Eastham." *American History* 35, no. 4 (October 2000): 54. Recounts Barrow's orchestration of the prison raid that eventually led to his ambush by the Hamer posse.

—*Michael H. Burchett*

See also: Ma Barker; John Dillinger; Pretty Boy Floyd; Baby Face Nelson; Bonnie Parker.

Sydney Barrows

American procurer

Born: January 14, 1952; near Rumson, New Jersey
Also known as: Sydney Biddle Barrows (full name); Sheila Devin; Mayflower Madam
Major offense: Promoting prostitution
Active: 1979-1984
Locale: New York City
Sentence: Five-thousand-dollar fine

Early Life

When Sydney Barrows was four years old, her father left her mother, married a woman who worked at his office, and moved to New York. Sydney and her younger brother, Andrew, stayed with their mother in Hopewell, New Jersey, until 1961, when her mother moved in with her own parents, who lived on the Jersey shore in Rumson. There Sydney attended Rumson Country Day School and then enrolled in Stoneleigh, a private high school in Greenfield, Massachusetts. When she left to visit her boyfriend at Franklin and Marshall College in Lancaster, Pennsylvania, she was expelled from Stoneleigh just before she was to graduate. She then went to live with her father in Old Lyme, Connecticut, where she attended the local high school. Before she left Stoneleigh, she had been accepted at Elmira College in New York, but when her father declined to pay her tuition, she decided to wait a year, save some money, and then enroll in a two-year program at the Fashion Institute of Technology in New York City.

During the following year, Barrows worked for her father's company and was presented at the annual ball of the Mayflower Society, where she was introduced as a descendant of *Mayflower* pilgrim William Brewster. While Barrows attended the institute, she worked part-time at Macy's department store. At school, she finished first among the fashion buying and merchandizing majors and won the Bergdorf Goodman Award for having the highest grades in her graduating class. In 1973, after graduation, she and Steve Rozansky, a photography stu-

The Biddle Family

Sydney Biddle Barrows, the enterprising "Mayflower Madam," stemmed from an accomplished Pennsylvania family descended from English Quakers who first arrived in New Jersey in 1681. Among her ancestors were the following illustrious individuals:

- **Edward Biddle** (1738-1779), soldier, lawyer, and delegate to the Continental Congress
- **Nicholas Biddle** (1786-1844), financier and president of the Second Bank of the United States
- **Richard Biddle** (1796-July 7, 1847), author, politician, and Whig member of Congress
- **Charles John Biddle** (1819-1873), soldier
- **Francis Beverly Biddle** (1886-1968), lawyer and judge in the World War II Nuremberg trials
- **Nick Biddle,** lead singer of the band The Naturals

dent at the institute, toured Europe together, and in Amsterdam he took some revealing pictures of her which would resurface later when she was on trial.

Upon her return to the United States, Barrows was hired to work as a trainee and assistant buyer at Abraham & Straus at the Brooklyn store. After spending two years as an assistant buyer, she became a department manager at the Abraham & Straus store in Paramus, New Jersey. A year later she took a position with the May Company department store and in 1978 joined The Cutting Edge as a buyer for boutiques across the United States. After a dispute with her boss, she left that job.

While looking for another position, she worked part time answering telephones for Executive Escorts, and then she went to work full time for the escort agency. She learned from the mistakes of her employer, and when one of his employees mentioned starting a competitive firm, she decided to go into the business with her. After doing a great deal of research (interviewing and talking with call girls), Barrows and her partner decided on a name for their company: Cachet, a word they believed suggested elegance, a French aura, and sophistication. They drew up a partnership agreement, opened a corporate bank account, got business certificates, and described their company as a "temporary help agency." Cachet opened for business in May, 1979.

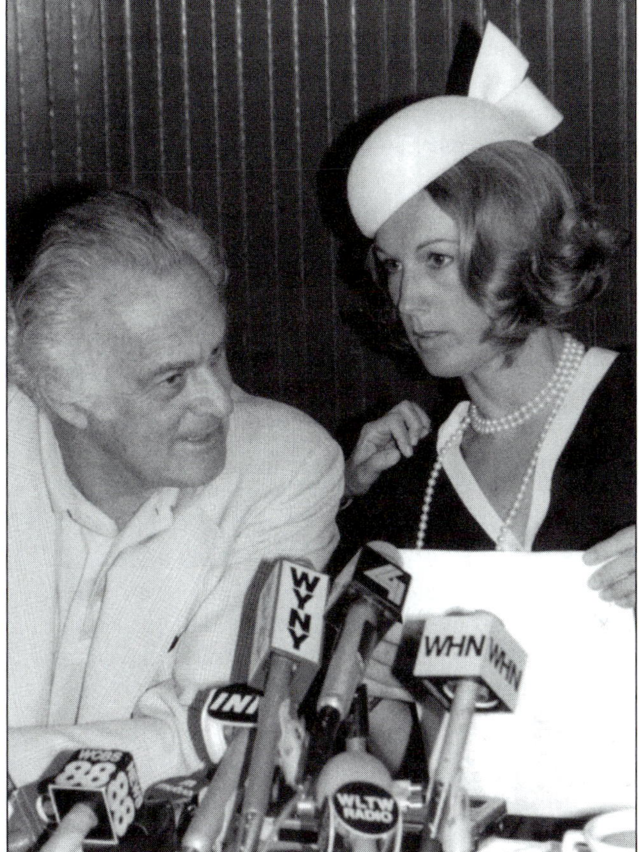

Sydney Barrows, right, with television producer Robert Halmi. (AP/ Wide World Photos)

Criminal Career

From 1979 until 1984, when the New York City Police closed it down, Cachet flourished, serving wealthy and powerful clients in New York, including dignitaries visiting from all over the world. In order to evade the laws against prostitution, Barrows's call girls charged by the hour, not by the service. To increase sales, Cachet advertised, first in *Screw*, the only magazine that would accept its ads, and then later in the *International Herald Tribune* and *New York* magazine. To recruit employees, Cachet advertised in *Show Business* and in the *Village Voice*. The company began showing a profit after only four months.

At the end of the first year, Barrows's partner opted to leave. Business was so good that Barrows soon opened another escort service, called Finesse. In 1984, however, a landlord tried to evict the company so he could raise the rent for the space, which was subject to rent control regulations. Then a former employee informed the police about Cachet and Finesse. Barrows told her employees to be careful, but three of them were arrested for prostitution that very night. The judge at their trials dismissed the charges, but an outbreak of gonorrhea threatened the operation. Thanks to the efforts of Elmo Smith, a New York police officer who was intent on stopping Barrows, three Cachet employees were arrested in a sting operation, widely covered by the news media.

Legal Action and Outcome

A warrant for promoting prostitution, a felony, was issued for Barrows. She turned herself in to authorities and was released on seventy-five hundred dollars' bail. The ensuing publicity included the release of nude photographs that her former friend Rozansky had taken in Amsterdam. The grand jury returned a one-count indictment, charging Barrows with promoting prostitution in the third degree. She did not want to plead guilty and appeared to be ready to go to trial, hoping that the possibility of having the names of her rich and famous clients exposed would result in the case being thrown out. Finally, the prosecution made her an offer she would not refuse: plead guilty to the misdemeanor of promoting prostitution and pay a five-thousand-dollar fine. On July 19, 1985, she entered her guilty plea.

Impact

After gaining her freedom, Sydney Barrows married Darney Hoffman in 1994, wrote her autobiography plus three other books, wrote an advice column for New York journals, was featured in an A&E (Arts and Entertainment) television biography, and became the subject of a television film starring Candice Bergen (1987).

Barrows's trial, which occurred at about the same time that New Yorkers were focusing on matters of police brutality, including the fatal shooting of an innocent woman, became a bit of an embarrassment to police officials, who had more important matters to consider and were eager to conclude the matter. The Barrows case, however, did result in law enforcement regarding prostitution becoming more lax, and impediments to advertising "escort services" disappeared. In fact, ads for sexual services became steadily more blatant after that time.

Financially, Barrows profited more from her conviction and its attendant publicity than she did from her two escort services. She went on to publish books, write columns, and have her life publicized by films about her career, trial, and conviction. All these activities were directly attributable to her trial and to the unique circumstances involving a descendant of a *Mayflower* passenger and prostitution.

Further Reading

Barrows, Sydney Biddle. *Getting a Little Work Done*. New York: HarperCollins, 2000. Barrows offers advice on balancing sex and a career.

_______. *Just Between Us Girls: Secrets About Men from the Mayflower Madam*. New York: St. Martin's Press, 1996. Advice to wives on keeping their husbands contented.

Barrows, Sydney Biddle, with William Novak. *Mayflower Madam*. New York: Arbor House, 1986. Autobiography of Barrows, focusing on her "career" as a madam and concluding with the aftermath of her trial.

Barrows, Sydney Biddle, with Ellis Weiner. *Mayflower Manners*. New York: Doubleday, 1991. Tongue-in-cheek book of sexual etiquette.

—Thomas L. Erskine

See also: Ada Everleigh; Heidi Fleiss.

Omar al-Bashir

Sudanese dictator (1989-)

Born: January 1, 1944; Hosh Bannaga, Shendi district, Sudan

Also known as: Omar Hasan Ahmad al-Bashir (full name)

Cause of notoriety: The deaths of some 200,000 people can be charged to Sudanese tyrant Bashir.

Active: Beginning in 1989

Locale: Sudan

Early Life

Born in the small town of Hosh Bannaga, Omar al-Bashir entered Sudan's military academy in 1960, only four years after his country obtained its independence from the British Empire. Six years later, he was an officer in the elite paratroop battalion, commanding the portion sent to fight with Egypt against Israel in 1973. Afterward, he directed military campaigns against rebels in Sudan's uneasy southern provinces.

Political Career

Southern Sudan comprised a mix of peoples who shared a widespread distrust of the central government. Animists and Christians who tended to have an "African" cultural background, they were excluded from power by the Muslim north and its "Arab" culture. North-south disputes began as soon as Sudan gained its independence and produced a series of devastating wars that plagued Sudan into the twenty-first century.

Bashir spent much of the 1970's and 1980's fighting his country's main southern rebel group, the Sudan People's Liberation Movement (SPLM). After more than a decade of conflict, he rose to high command and was noted for his commitment to total victory. Such dedication was not shared at the capital, Khartoum, where Prime Minister Sadiq al-Mahdi strove to end the struggle via compromise. Mahdi had already suspended legislation aimed at instituting the Sharia (Islamic law code) and was willing to grant a truce and consider power-sharing with the southern rebels.

Such concessions angered then-Brigadier-General al-Bashir and like-minded military officers. On June 30, 1989, Bashir staged a successful coup against Mahdi, "to save the nation from rotten political parties." Within months, thousands were arrested, while nearly one hundred military officers, politicians, and journalists were executed. This marked the start of a brutal dictatorship that significantly exacerbated Sudan's troubles.

Bashir quickly made himself chief of state, prime minister, minister of defense, and commander in chief of the armed forces. Simultaneously, he created the Public Order Police, a gendarmerie designed to maintain his power and aid in a drive to enforce "Islamic values." The latter was more than political posturing, for Bashir had supported fundamentalist political parties from his youth. A good example was the National Islamic Front, led by Hassan al-Turabi, who wanted all Sudanese converted into Muslims.

An important member of Bashir's government between 1990-1999, Turabi started the conversion process in 1991, when Sharia was reintroduced as the basis of Sudanese law. It continued with government slave-raiding, as military units kidnapped southern Sudanese children, bringing them to the north for indoctrination as Muslims and then conversion into soldiers to feed the never-ending civil war.

Turabi's influence ended in 1999, when Bashir declared a state of emergency and ousted his ally. This partially resulted from friction over how to handle another civil conflict, this one in Darfur. A western region of the Sudan, it was almost completely made up of Muslims, thus presenting a greater challenge for Bashir's claim to lead a "perfect" Islamic state. The struggle in Darfur was so important to Bashir that he agreed to peace talks with SPLM leaders (2001-2004) in order to concentrate his resources on crushing the new rebellion.

As with the south, Bashir could not quickly crush Darfur. His forces spread fire and sword throughout the region, however, bringing world attention to the Sudan. The human cost of Bashir's policies in Darfur were staggering. As of March, 2006, 180,000 of its people were dead and another 2 million displaced.

Impact

Omar al-Bashir, who obtained 86.5 percent of the vote in Sudan's 2000 presidential elections, appointed all members of parliament and maintained key government ministries under his direct authority. His policies were a major reason for the continuation of Sudan's horrific civil war. Although *Parade* magazine in May, 2006, declared Bashir the worst dictator on the planet, mainly for implementing "a colossal humanitarian tragedy in Darfur," he was accountable for much more. As of summer, 2006, his power remained undiminished, and Sudan's miseries continued.

Further Reading

Johnson, Douglas. *The Root Causes of Sudan's Civil Wars*. Oxford, England: International African Institute, 2004. A respected expert on Sudanese affairs provides both historical background and detailed analysis of Bashir's regime.

Prunier, Gérard. *Darfur: The Ambiguous Genocide*. Ithaca, N.Y.: Cornell University Press, 2005. Looks at why Bashir pressed the conflict with fellow Muslims; criticizes the failure by world leaders to intervene.

Rake, Alan. *African Leaders: Guiding the New Millennium*. London: Scarecrow Press, 2001. Noted journalist on African affairs places Bashir in context with his contemporaries.

—John P. Dunn

See also: Sani Abacha; Idi Amin; Jean-Bédel Bokassa; Samuel K. Doe; Mengistu Haile Mariam; Mobutu Sese Seko; Robert Mugabe; Muhammad Siad Barre; Charles Taylor.

Sam Bass

American highwayman

Born: July 21, 1851; near Mitchell, Indiana
Died: July 21, 1878; Round Rock, Texas
Also known as: Samuel Bass (full name)
Cause of notoriety: Bass was a frontier-era outlaw who robbed a Union Pacific train at Big Springs, Nebraska, and various stagecoaches.
Active: 1877-1878
Locale: Nebraska, Texas, and Dakota Territory

Early Life

Samuel Bass (bas) was born the sixth of ten children to Daniel and Elizabeth (Sheeks) Bass on a farm near Mitchell, Indiana, on July 21, 1851. Tragically, Bass was orphaned before his thirteenth birthday and went to live with an uncle. Not much is known about Bass's early life, but periodic disagreements with his uncle probably enticed him to leave Indiana in 1869. At the age of eighteen, Bass left home, and after brief layovers in Missouri and Mississippi, he found his way to Denton, Texas. For several years, the young man worked as a freighter, laborer, and liveryman. After acquiring a fleet-footed horse in 1874, Bass focused all his energy on horse racing. His horse won race after race, and the animal gained legendary notoriety in North Texas as the Denton Mare. By 1876, Bass apparently became acquainted with a small-time thief named Joel Collins. At the same time, the goldfields in the Black Hills offered riches for those who could provide food, supplies, and materials to the mining communities. Bass and Collins headed north to Deadwood, Dakota Territory, with a herd of Texas longhorns. The pair reportedly cleared more than eight thousand dollars in the Black Hills mining camps but soon squandered their earnings on gambling and failed freighting and saloon operations. Down on the their luck and low on finances, the pair eventually turned to the dangerous but lucrative field of highway robbery.

Outlaw Career

Bass's outlaw career began in earnest in 1877, when he and Collins recruited a handful of men to rob stagecoaches in and around the Black Hills mining towns. The gang reportedly robbed seven stagecoaches but eventually came down the Sidney-Deadwood Trail to Nebraska. After losing money in the gaming houses of Sidney and Ogallala, Nebraska, the gang turned to train robbery. On the evening of September 18, 1877, Bass and five accomplices held up a Union Pacific passenger train near Big Springs, Nebraska, a small whistle-stop on the transcontinental line close to the Nebraska-Colorado border. The bandits made off with more than sixty thousand dollars but were quickly pursued by posses—including the United States Army—hoping to collect the sizable reward offered by the Union Pacific Railroad.

Within two weeks, pursuing posses killed Collins and several other accomplices. With the law hot on his trail, Bass returned to Texas, where he resumed his occupation as a stagecoach and train robber. After forming another gang, Bass and his fellow highwaymen held up stagecoaches and trains around the vicinity of Dallas. Bass's criminal exploits sparked one of the largest manhunts in Texas history, a chase that was followed enthusiastically by the Texas press. With each escape, the elusive Bass gained more notoriety. After eluding escape for more than four months, Bass was finally betrayed by Jim Murphy, a fellow gang member who turned informant. With information provided by Murphy, the Texas Rangers and local posses surprised the Bass gang in Round Rock, Texas, on July 19 as they prepared to rob a bank. In the ensuing gunfight, Bass was mortally wounded. He succumbed to his wounds on July 21, 1878, his twenty-seventh birthday.

Impact

Sam Bass had a short and relatively unsuccessful criminal career. Other than his impressive haul during the Big Springs train robbery, Bass's earnings as a highwayman were insignificant. His outlaw career lasted barely more than a year, and it ended in a blazing gunfight with the Texas Rangers. Still, Bass's name and fame—particularly in Texas—reached legendary status. Shortly after his death, Bass, like Jesse James in Missouri, became immortalized as a Robin Hood-type figure who was forced into a life of crime because of the graft and malfeasance of those in power. Popular histories, songs, and Hollywood films have helped keep Bass's name and exploits alive. Less than a month after his death, for example, two books appeared that began building the Sam Bass myth, as did a song titled "The Ballad of Sam Bass," a tune sung by school-age children for more than a century. In 1949, the film *Calamity Jane and Sam Bass* portrayed Bass as a good-hearted cowboy who, through deceit, was forced into a life of crime in order to restore his good name. The Bass myth existed into the twenty-first century: Rumors of Bass gold, stashed in an undetected cave for more than one hundred years, abounded in north Texas and kept fortune seekers interested in sites where Bass was said to have visited. When entering Round Rock, Texas, from the north on Interstate 35, travelers see an exit sign pointing to "Sam Bass Road," a monument to a fallen cultural hero.

Further Reading

Gard, Wayne. *Sam Bass*. Boston: Houghton Mifflin, 1936. Written by a noted historian of the frontier American West, this book stood as the premier biography of Sam Bass for more than sixty years.

Hogg, Thomas E. *Authentic History of Sam Bass and His Gang*. 1878. Reprint. Bandera, Tex.: Frontier Times, 1926. The first biography of Sam Bass. Written and published within weeks of his death, this book began to mold Bass into a mythic Robin Hood figure.

Miller, Rick. *Sam Bass and Gang*. Austin, Tex.: State House Press, 1999. The definitive biography of Sam Bass. A thoroughly researched book that leaves few questions unanswered.

O'Neal, Bill. *Encyclopedia of Western Gunfighters*. Norman: University of Oklahoma Press, 1979. This valuable collection of 587 gunfighter biographies provides a biography of Bass along with short descriptions of his criminal exploits and three gunfights.

—*Mark R. Ellis*

See also: Apache Kid; Tom Bell; William H. Bonney; Curly Bill Brocius; Butch Cassidy; Bob Dalton; Emmett Dalton; Bill Doolin; John Wesley Hardin; Doc Holliday; Jesse James; Tom Ketchum; Harry Longabaugh; Bill Longley; Joaquín Murieta; Johnny Ringo; Belle Starr; Hank Vaughan; Cole Younger.

Jean-Marie Bastien-Thiry

French would-be assassin

Born: October 19, 1927; Luneville, France
Died: March 11, 1963; Fresnes Prison, Ivry-sur-Seine Val-de-Marne, France
Also known as: Germain; Didier
Major offense: Attempted assassination of President Charles de Gaulle
Active: August 22, 1962
Locale: Petit-Clamart, Paris, France
Sentence: Death by firing squad

Early Life

Jean-Marie Bastien-Thiry (zhahn-mah-ree bah-shteen tee-ree) was born into a family of Catholic military officers. From a young age, he evidenced an intense devotion to France and an extraordinary sense of patriotism. After completing his required military service, he spent two years at the École Polytechnique (1948-1950) and then studied for two more years at the École Supérieure de l'Aéronautique. He then entered the French Air Force as a design specialist of air-to-air missiles. While visiting his parents in Morocco, he met Geneviève Lamirand, the daughter of Georges Lamirand, former Vichy minister of youth. They married in 1955 and had three daughters. Bastien-Thiry continued to work in the missile program. In 1957, he received a promotion to principal air military engineer. He was instrumental in perfecting the French SS 10 and SS 11 ballistic missiles.

Criminal Career

During the early 1950's, Bastien-Thiry was a supporter of French president Charles de Gaulle, but he was also a staunch opponent of independence for Algeria. He believed that the loss of Algeria would be as crucial as losing Alsace-Lorraine. He was highly opposed to any discussion between the French government and the Front de Libération Nationale (FLN), the main Algerian political organization advocating independence. Bastien-Thiry considered the FLN to be little more than a terrorist group. Due to his strong opposition to Algerian independence, he joined the Organisation de l'Armée Secrète (OAS), whose membership was made up of military men and white French colonists living in Algeria. Bastien-Thiry soon became one of the principal operatives in the organization's efforts to thwart the movement for Algerian independence.

As de Gaulle moved closer to granting Algeria independence, Bastien-Thiry came to see de Gaulle as a traitor to France and to believe that his assassination was necessary and justifiable. The OAS made its first assassination attempt on September 5, 1961, but the plan failed because the assassin lost his courage and failed to detonate the planted bomb. In May, 1962, André Canal, leader of the OAS, was arrested. The leadership passed to a group referred to as "the old General Staff" under the command of Bastien-Thiry. On July 1, 1962, de Gaulle held a referendum in Algeria. The vote was overwhelmingly for independence. On July 3, 1962, de Gaulle proclaimed Algerian independence. On August 22, 1962, the assassination attempt which would result in Bastien-Thiry's arrest took place. Twelve men with automatic weapons opened fire on de Gaulle's car as it passed the Café Trianon on the avenue Petit-Clamart. De Gaulle's wife, his chauffeur, and de Gaulle himself, except for a cut on his finger, escaped without injury.

Legal Action and Outcome

Bastien-Thiry was arrested and charged with attempted assassination on September 17, 1962. His trial before a military tribunal began on January 28 and concluded on March 4, 1963. He readily admitted his role in the assassination attempt and, citing Saint Thomas Aquinas, insisted that it was a justifiable act of tyrannicide. Later, he changed his testimony, maintaining the conspirators were only trying to kidnap de Gaulle. On March 4, 1963, Bastien-Thiry received the sentence of death for the attempted assassination of de Gaulle. He was executed by a firing squad on March 11, 1963, at Ivry-sur-Seine.

Impact

Jean-Marie Bastien-Thiry's attempt to assassinate de Gaulle had no effect on the issue of Algerian independence, which had already been granted. De Gaulle remarked that by refusing clemency for Bastien-Thiry, he had given the French people a martyr. He also stated that Bastien-Thiry deserved to be one. The anti-Gaullists did view Bastien-Thiry as a martyr. His patriotism and lifelong devotion to France, the failure of the attempt, and his execution when the others were pardoned made him a martyr to others as well.

Further Reading

Daley, Robert. *Portraits of France*. New York: Back Bay Books, 1995. Chapter titled "Colombey les Deux Églises" presents a very detailed account of the assassination attempt.

Horn, Alistair. *Seven Ages of Paris*. New York: Knopf, 2002. The chapter "Age Seven, 1940-1969" places the de Gaulle period and Algerian conflict in the general course of French history and treats the assassination attempt in this light.

Williams, Charles. *The Last Great Frenchman: A Life of General de Gaulle*. New York: John Wiley and Sons, 1997. Comprehensive biography of de Gaulle explores his handling of the Algerian War; looks at opposition to his policies and why the assassination attempt occurred.

—*Shawncey Webb*

See also: Said Akbar; Yigal Amir; Nathuram Vinayak Godse; John Hinckley, Jr.; Mijailo Mijailovic; Lee Harvey Oswald; Thenmuli Rajaratnam; James Earl Ray; Beant Singh; Satwant Singh; Sirhan Sirhan; Ramzi Yousef.

Elizabeth Báthory

Hungarian countess and serial killer

Born: August 7, 1560; Ecsed Castle, Transylvania (now in Romania)

Died: August 21, 1614; Cséjthe Castle, Hungary (now Ćachtice Castle, Slovakia)

Also known as: Erzsébet Báthory; Elizabeth Nádasdy; Blood Countess

Cause of notoriety: Báthory, in her sadistic torture and murder of more than six hundred girls, became the most notorious female mass murderer in European history.

Active: 1575-1610

Locale: Hungary and Slovakia

Early Life

Elizabeth Báthory (BA-tohr-ee) belonged to one of the greatest families in early modern Hungary. At age eleven, she was betrothed to Count Ferenc Nádasdy and went to live in his ancestral castle at Sarvar near Szombathely. Around this time, a sadistic bisexual Báthory aunt initiated her into the torture of servant girls. Báthory and Ferenc were married in May, 1575. Ferenc was a born warrior and spent much of his time fighting the Turks during the Fifteen Years' War (1591-1606). Mostly absent from Sarvar, he left his wife to indulge her predilections. Whether he knew or cared about them is not recorded.

For ten years, the couple was childless, but starting around 1585, three daughters and a son, Pal, were born. Báthory informed Ferenc that all these births had been induced by witchcraft. She had become fascinated by the occult sciences and black magic, surrounding herself with an eccentric band of women who ministered to her

Elizabeth Báthory in the Movies

In addition to inspiring the protagonist of the novel The Blood Countess *(1996), by Andrei Codrescu (a descendant of Báthory), the countess has inspired several films:*

Released	*Title*	*Director*
1970	*Countess Dracula*	Peter Sasdy
1971	*Les Lèvres rouges (Daughters of Darkness)*	Harry Kummel
1973	*Ceremonia sangrienta (Blood Castle)*	Jorge Grau
1973	*El Retorno de Walpurgis (Curse of the Devil)*	Carlos Aured
1974	*Contes immoraux (Immoral Tales)*	Walerian Borowczyk
1975	*Al beta Hrozná alebo Krw sto ry (Elisabeth the Terrible)*	Stanislav Štepka
1980	*Krvavá pani (The Bloody Lady)*	Viktor Kubal
1980	*El Retorno del Hombre-Lobo (Night of the Werewolf)*	Jacinto Molina
1988	*The Mysterious Death of Nina Chereau*	Dennis Berry
2000	*Báthory*	Brian Topping
2002	*Killer Love*	Lloyd A. Simandl
2004	*Eternal*	Wilhelm Liebenberg
2004	*Tomb of the Werewolf*	Fred Olen Ray
2006	*Stay Alive*	William Brent Bell

obsessions. One witch, who might also have been her lover, Anna Davulia, persuaded Báthory that she could retain her far-famed beauty if she bathed in virgins' blood. To this end, young serf-girls were brought to the noblewoman, and no questions were asked; like all Hungarian aristocrats, Báthory wielded powers of life and death over her dependents.

Criminal Career

Ferenc died in January, 1604. By his will, Sarvar and other estates, as well as the education of his son, Pal, were entrusted to a man named Imre Megyery, who was perhaps an illegitimate son of Ferenc. Báthory feared and hated Megyery. She left Sarvar and moved to the Nádasdy Palace in Vienna on the Augustinerstrasse, but the monks across the street complained of inhuman shrieks issuing from the building at midnight and of blood running from the palace drains into the street. The abbot was told that the countess's health required the slaughter of fresh meat.

However, Vienna was too public for Báthory's lifestyle, and she withdrew to her castles of Beckov and Cséjthe. There, she kept iron cages in which girls were slashed to ribbons by movable steel blades, while the countess, standing underneath, bathed in their still-warm blood.

When Davulia died, Báthory replaced her with a new witch, Erzsi Marjorova. Báthory, despite her bloody bathing, saw herself aging, and Marjorova told her that it was a mistake to bathe in serfs' blood—she needed girls of a higher class. Báthory then grew reckless in seizing middle-class girls and even those from the gentry; rumors grew. The pastors at Cséjthe began asking questions, there were petitions about missing persons, and Báthory's servants had difficulties disposing of the bodies.

The palatine (regent) of Hungary, György Thurzó, distantly related to the Báthorys, finally intervened in order to prevent public humiliation for the family and the confiscation of Báthory's estates. On December 29, 1610, Thurzó, with a band of retainers, entered Cséjthe, confined the countess to her room, and carried off her servants to his castle at Bytca. There, torture soon provided lurid confessions, including the production by a servant girl of a list in the countess's handwriting naming 650 victims. A commission, meeting at Bytca on January 2 and 7, 1611, condemned Báthory's servants for

Elizabeth Báthory.

monstrous crimes and punished some with red-hot pincers, fire, and an ax. A few days later, Marjorova was captured, tried, and burnt.

Báthory never faced trial but was confined to her room, which was sealed up except for a grill to serve as a food-hatch. After her death, her body was taken to Ecsed for reinterment, and her estates passed intact to her son and sons-in-law. By coincidence, her death seemed to mark the end of the Báthorys' longtime ascendancy. The last Báthory prince of Transylvania, the mad Sigismund, died in exile in 1613. Báthory's Nádasdy grandson, another Ferenc, died on the scaffold in 1671.

IMPACT

Belief in witchcraft and the occult was widespread in Central Europe during the early Renaissance. What is unique about Elizabeth Báthory is the sheer number of her reported victims and the length of her grisly career, which was tolerated in the unjust social order of contemporary Hungary. There were surely criminal psychopaths in Jacobean England, but the social system most likely would have made it nearly impossible for a mass murderer to kill more than six hundred people. Some believe that Báthory may have been one of the influences on Bram Stoker's *Dracula* (1897). In the modern era, the gruesome stories surrounding Báthory have provided ample fodder for numerous B- and C-class horror films.

FURTHER READING

Elsberg, R. A. von. *Die Blutgrafin.* 2d ed. Breslau, Poland: Schlesiche Verlags-Anstalt v. S. Schottländer, 1904. Although more than one hundred years old, this remains the standard biography of Báthory. In German.

Evans, R. J. W. *Rudolf II and His World.* New York: Oxford University Press, 1973. A good account of the occultism embedded in contemporary intellectual life.

McNally, Raymond T. *Dracula Was a Woman.* New York: McGraw-Hill, 1984. A popular account for a nonspecialist readership.

Penrose, Valentine. *The Bloody Countess: The Atrocities of Erzsébet Báthory.* London: Creation, 2000. A modern biography.

Pocs, Eva. *Between the Living and the Dead.* Budapest, Hungary: Central European University Press, 1999. An authoritative study of witchcraft in early modern Hungary.

—*Gavin R. G. Hambly*

SEE ALSO: Ivan the Terrible; Vlad III the Impaler.

Fulgencio Batista y Zaldívar

Cuban president and dictator (1940-1944, 1952-1959)

Born: January 16, 1901; Banes, Cuba
Died: August 6, 1973; Guadalmina, Spain
Cause of notoriety: Batista, after leading a brutal military dictatorship, was overthrown by Fidel Castro in the Cuban Revolution.
Active: 1933-1959
Locale: Cuba, mostly Havana

Early Life

Born in a small town to an extremely poor family in the Oriente province of Cuba, close to the home of his future nemesis, Fidel Castro, Fulgencio Batista y Zaldívar (fuhl-HEN-see-oh bah-TEES-tah ee zahl-DEE-vahr) was of uncertain heritage; his family lineage possibly contained Caucasian, African, and Chinese ancestry, an important fact in a race-conscious society like Cuba. Orphaned at age eleven and having very little formal education, the young Batista toiled at numerous jobs, including sugarcane cutter, before joining the army, where he rose from private to sergeant and was assigned to stenography. From this position he was able to create a network of privates and noncommissioned officers (NCOs), who would later serve him well in his political career.

Political Career

The overthrow of President Gustavo Machado y Morales in 1933 by students and elements of the middle class put Cuba into political turmoil. Machado's successor, Ramón Grau y San Martín, was deemed too radical by the American ambassador in Havana, and the United States withheld diplomatic recognition from the new regime. Batista saw in this power vacuum a chance to seize control of the Cuban government. He organized the Sergeants' Coup of September 4, 1933, mobilizing NCOs throughout the island to bring him to power in Havana. Batista, a political unknown whose racial and class background made him a dubious candidate for the nation's highest office, lacked the legitimacy to capture the presidency for himself. However, during the next seven years, he ruled Cuba from behind the scenes, installing and unseating puppet presidents. By 1940, he felt secure enough to run for the presidential office, winning a bitterly contested election.

President Batista created a mixed record. He oversaw the writing of what came to be known as the Constitution of 1940, which forbade immediate presidential reelection; revamped the Cuban political system on the American model of separation of powers between three branches of government; and incorporated labor and education reform laws that were inspired by U.S. president Franklin D. Roosevelt's Depression-era New Deal program. In order to secure support from the Left, Batista asked members of the Cuban Communist Party to join his cabinet and personally appointed the leaders of some of Cuba's most important trade unions. At the same time, Batista helped himself to a large share of the public treasury, particularly the national lottery and lucrative government contracts, and used some of these funds to outfit the army with uniforms.

In 1944, because he was forbidden to run for reelection by law and because his handpicked successor lost the presidential election, Batista went into self-imposed exile in Miami. The former president was unable to alter the course of Cuban politics through flunkies, as in prior decades. In 1952, although Batista proclaimed himself a candidate for president, polls showed him trailing badly.

Fulgencio Batista y Zaldívar.

BOOKS BY BATISTA

Date	*Title*
1944	*Ideario de Batista*
1944	*Revolucion social o politica reformista*
1946	*Sombras de America: Problemas economicos y sociales*
1960	*Respuesta*
1961	*Piedras y leyes*
1962	*Cuba Betrayed*
1962	*To Rule Is to Foresee*
1963	*Paradojas*
1963	*Piedras y leyes: Balance sobre Cuba*
1964	*The Growth and Decline of the Cuban Republic*
1964	*Paradojismo: Cuba, victima de las contradicciones internacionales*
1973	*Dos fechas (aniversarios y testimonios)*
1976	*El pensamiento politico del presidente Batista a traves de su propia palabra*

However, returning to Cuba, he staged a coup in March of 1952 that made him president by force of arms. Many within the Cuban middle and working classes turned then to Castro, a young lawyer who had denounced Batista's unconstitutional capture of power and called on the Cuban people to take up armed struggle against the dictator.

At first, Batista felt little worry concerning Castro. The rebel's attempt to start a national uprising by taking control of the Moncada Barracks in Oriente had failed, and Castro and his followers were sent to prison. Batista gained new allies in the anticommunist administration of U.S. president Dwight D. Eisenhower and also among the American Mafia, particularly gangster Meyer Lansky. Mobster investment in Havana casinos earned the dictator millions in skimmed profits. However, a popular outcry forced Batista to grant amnesty to Castro and his partisans, who soon regrouped and fostered a guerrilla campaign in Oriente and urban insurrection in Havana. Batista's army was neither trained nor equipped to fight a counterinsurgency war. Moreover, the middle class and U.S. government distanced themselves from Batista once news of gross human rights violations against political prisoners surfaced. Therefore, completely isolated in the Cuban political scene and with his army retreating hastily before Castro's troops, Batista resigned from office and fled the country on January 1, 1959. The remainder of his life was spent in opulent exile, first in the Dominican Republic and then in Spain, where he died in 1973.

IMPACT

Fulgencio Batista y Zaldívar dominated Cuban politics for a quarter of a century, from 1933 to 1958, first as president and later by installing himself as military dictator. His shrewd political instincts helped him hold on to power by juggling allies ranging from the army to American gangsters. However, his personal corruption and his dismissal of Cubans' longing for clean government and democracy paved the way for Castro's revolution in 1959.

FURTHER READING

Argote-Freyre, Frank. *Fulgencio Batista: From Revolutionary to Strongman*. New Brunswick, N.J.: Rutgers University Press, 2004. Argote-Freyre affirms that Batista did not belong to the political Right, nor was he merely a pawn of the United States. Rather, Batista pursued his own agenda, which, during the 1930's, was indeed "revolutionary" in reinventing the Cuban republic after the downfall of President Machado.

Batista y Zaldívar, Fulgencio. *Cuba Betrayed*. New York: Vantage Press, 1962. Batista's memoirs are naturally self-serving, mostly a list of his achievements on behalf of the Cuban people. Significantly, he blames the Eisenhower administration for his downfall and for not having spotted Castro as a communist until it was too late for both Cuba and the United States.

Kapcia, Antoni. *Fulgencio Batista, 1933-1944: From Revolutionary to Populist*. Westport, Conn.: Greenwood Press, 1996. A revisionist study that casts Batista in the same mold of populist dictators such as Juan Perón of Argentina, rather than kleptocrats such as Anastasio Somoza García of Nicaragua.

Whitney, Robert. *State and Revolution in Cuba: Mass Mobilization and Political Change, 1920-1940*. Chapel Hill: University of North Carolina Press, 2001. The author argues that Batista was a political opportunist and the paladin of the political awakening of the Cuban middle and working classes during the turbulent two decades that preceded his presidency.

—*Julio Pino*

SEE ALSO: Fidel Castro; Che Guevara; Meyer Lansky.

Dave Beck

American union organizer

Born: June 16, 1894; Stockton, California
Died: December 26, 1993; Seattle, Washington
Major offenses: Federal income tax evasion and embezzlement
Active: 1950-1956
Locale: Seattle
Sentence: Served two years in prison; pardoned after his parole

Early Life

Born in Stockton, California, to a carpet cleaner and a laundress, Dave Beck (behk) relocated with his parents to Seattle when he was four. His family, who was poor, settled in Seattle's old Belltown area, and Beck delivered newspapers, sold Christmas trees, and caught rats, shellfish, and fish to support them. Although he dropped out of school because of his family's financial situation, he later attended night extension classes in law, economics, and business administration at the University of Washington. Beck enlisted in the Navy in 1917 and saw action as a gunner in patrols of the North Sea on anti-zeppelin missions. He married Dorothy E. Leschander while on shore leave.

Business Union Career

After returning from World War I and taking a job as a laundry truck driver, Beck became secretary-treasurer of the Laundry Drivers Union in 1924. In 1927, he became a full-time organizer for the West Coast Teamsters Union, which he would ultimately lead for more than forty years. Early in his career, he determined that regional organization was key to the success of the unions and organized the Western Conference of Teamsters, despite the objections of the Teamster general Dan Tobin. Within the decade, as a result of his successes, Beck led the union. His support of the Newspaper Guild Strike in 1936 was a major cause of the strike's success. By the 1940's, Beck was a popular Seattle figure and a member of the State Parole Board, the Seattle Civil Service Commission, and the University of Washington Board of Regents.

Within the labor movement, as a representative of the American Federation of Labor (AFL), Beck faced leftist Harry Bridges, who represented the longshoremen and the Congress of Industrial Organizations (CIO). Beck professed a business-union policy, opposing radicals and union democracy, and was therefore favored by conservative community elements such as regional chambers of commerce. The difference in philosophy led to a split between the CIO and AFL, the most intense struggle the two labor organizations had undergone. Beck did not believe the rank and file workers were capable of making informed decisions and once noted, "I'm paid $25,000 a year to run this outfit . . . why should truck drivers and bottle washers be allowed to make decisions affecting policy? No corporation would allow it."

Beck's successes in organizing unions in Seattle were often the result of strong-arm tactics and blackmail, including a Teamsters-level refusal to deliver supplies to any business that fought him. Some claimed the Teamster slogan had become "Vote no and go to the hospital." Nonetheless, his success was so marked that presidents Franklin D. Roosevelt, Harry S. Truman, and Dwight D. Eisenhower all offered him the position of secretary of labor, which he repeatedly turned down in order to remain part of the labor movement. In 1940, he was elected as an international vice president of the Teamsters and joined the Teamsters International Executive Board. In 1952, he became the general president of the International Brotherhood of Teamsters and continued to lead the organization in its rapid expansion, taking the membership from 78,000 to more than 1,580,000 members.

Legal Action and Outcome

In 1956, Robert F. Kennedy, working for the U.S. Senate Labor Committee (also known as the McClellan Committee for its chair, Senator John McClellan), began investigating graft within the Teamsters Union. He was surprised to find evidence of Beck's corruption, including interest-free loans for over $320,000 extended to Beck as well as a home that had been purchased for him by the Teamsters union, which bought it from him and then allowed him to live in it rent-free. Brought before the McClellan Committee hearing on March 26, 1957, to answer questions about misappropriation of funds, Beck invoked the Fifth Amendment and did not answer sixty-five of the questions put to him.

In May, 1957, Beck was heard before the AFL/CIO Ethical Practices Committee, led by AFL/CIO President George Meany. Because the committee could not guarantee that Beck would not be subpoenaed by the Senate Labor Committee if he answered questions, Beck refused to answer those questions. His membership on the

AFL/CIO Executive Council was withdrawn, and the Teamsters were expelled from the organization.

Beck faced indictments charging him with helping file a fraudulent 1950 tax return for the Joint Council 28 Building Association and pocketing proceeds from the sale of a 1952 Cadillac belonging to the Teamsters, as well as $240,000 in back income taxes. He was convicted in 1959 of income tax evasion and state embezzlement charges. In 1962 he went to prison, serving at McNeil Island in Washington. In 1964, after he was paroled, he returned to lead a quiet existence out of the public eye. Beck was pardoned by U.S. president Gerald Ford in 1975 and lived the rest of his life in Seattle. He died in 1993.

IMPACT

The Teamsters retained a reputation for corruption long after Dave Beck's departure. His conservative approach influenced the organization for years, perhaps because of his successor, Jimmy Hoffa. The Teamsters developed strong ties to organized crime under Beck's leadership, leading the U.S. government to sue the union in 1988 in order to impose federal supervision of the union's daily operations and its internal election process.

FURTHER READING

Hass, Eric. *Dave Beck, Labor Merchant: The Case History of a Labor Leader*. New York: New York Labor News, 1957. A brief overview of Beck's life, which focuses on his activity as a Teamsters leader.

Jacobs, James B. *Mobsters, Unions, and Feds: The Mafia and the American Labor Movement*. New York: New York University Press, 2006. This narrative of the ties between organized crime and unions includes a lengthy examination of the corruption in the Teamsters and Beck and Hoffa's connections.

McCallum, John. *Dave Beck*. Mercer Island, Wash.: Writing Works, 1978. Provides an in-depth look at Beck's life, including his criminal conviction, although it focuses mainly on his influence on and history with the Teamsters.

—*Cat Rambo*

SEE ALSO: Jimmy Hoffa.

ELISABETH BECKER

German-Polish war criminal

BORN: July 20, 1923; Neuteich, West Prussia, Germany (now Nowy Staw, Poland)

DIED: July 4, 1946; Biskupia Gorka Hill, Gdańsk, Poland

MAJOR OFFENSES: War crimes, specifically participating in mass murder

ACTIVE: September, 1944-May, 1945

LOCALE: Stutthof concentration camp, Poland

SENTENCE: Death by hanging

EARLY LIFE

Elisabeth Becker (BEHK-uhr) was the daughter of Germans who lived in Neuteich, Prussia (now Nowy Staw, Poland) at the time of her birth. Not much is known about Becker's early life or family. Some sources state that Becker was married in 1936 but do not clarify whether Becker was her maiden or married surname. Becker affiliated with the League of German Girls and the National Socialist German Workers Party.

After relocating in 1938 to nearby Danzig (later Gdańsk), Poland, by the Baltic Sea, Becker secured employment as a cook. When German troops invaded Danzig in early September, 1939, Becker's Germanic heritage assured her safety. She returned to her hometown the following year to take a position with a local company. By 1941, Becker had again relocated to Danzig for an agricultural job supporting the German war effort.

CRIMINAL CAREER

Becker accepted a guard assignment at the Stutthof (*Sztutowo*) concentration camp, approximately thirty-five kilometers (twenty-two miles) east of Danzig, in summer, 1944. Camp officials particularly sought women workers from local communities who, like Becker, had proven their loyalty to the Nazi Party. At Stutthof she supervised prisoners, mostly Poles of all religions, who had been deported to Stutthof in order to support Adolf Hitler's *Lebensraum*, the plan to move Germans onto lands seized from other ethnic groups.

Starting on September 5, 1944, Becker began preparing for Schutzstaffel (SS) Aufseherin (woman overseer) duties. Once assigned to area SK-III of Stutthof, Becker managed female internees and their children. Her primary task was to designate which women and young prisoners were murdered in Stutthof's gas chambers.

Legal Action and Outcome

Hearing news of Russian troops approaching to liberate Stutthof in spring, 1945, and fearing retaliation, Becker slipped away, seeking sanctuary among relatives and friends in Neuteich. After Russian troops arrived at Stutthof on May 9, 1945, officials collected information including the names of Stutthof workers and the atrocities they had committed. Police arrested Becker, who was suffering from typhoid, in a Danzig hospital.

Beginning on April 25, 1946, Becker was tried in Danzig's Polish Special Law Court. She was accused of being a murderess. Declaring themselves not guilty of war crimes, Becker, five other women personnel from Stutthof, several male workers, and the camp's commandant, Max Pauli, listened to eyewitness testimony. On May 31, the court found Becker and her associates guilty, declaring death sentences to be justifiable punishment for their wartime crimes at Stutthof.

Becker resisted being condemned. She wrote to Poland's president, Bolesław Bierut, insisting she had not treated prisoners cruelly, even though other female camp staffers had. Although court officials suggested that Becker serve fifteen years in prison instead of being executed, Bierut disagreed. Polish police delivered Becker to the gallows on Biskupia Gorka Hill on the early evening of July 4, 1946. They hanged her simultaneously with several other convicted Stutthof war criminals.

Impact

Although the trial of the Stutthof camp personnel was not as well known as the Nuremberg war crimes trials, Elisabeth Becker's case and other smaller tribunals represented Allied efforts to achieve justice for civilians by punishing identified war criminals, regardless of their status. Becker's public execution provided some vengeance for Poles enraged by German collaborators' abuses during World War II.

Becker's crimes exemplified the horrors Jews and marginalized people encountered during the Holocaust. One of approximately twenty-one women war criminals executed by Allied authorities after the war, Becker had participated in the murders of many of the sixty-five thousand people who died at Stutthof. Today, the museum at Stutthof preserves artifacts and prisoners' accounts of ordeals they suffered, inflicted by collaborators like Becker.

Further Reading

Harvey, Elizabeth. *Women and the Nazi East: Agents and Witnesses of Germanization*. New Haven, Conn.: Yale University Press, 2003. Includes a chapter examining occupied Poland and why Poles like Becker with German identities embraced the Nazi ideology and agenda.

Piotrowski, Tadeusz. *Poland's Holocaust: Ethnic Strife, Collaboration with Occupying Forces, and Genocide in the Second Republic, 1918-1947*. Jefferson, N.C.: McFarland, 1998. Discusses the diversity among Poles deported to Stutthoff. Text contains excerpts from liberated prisoners' depositions regarding the death camp.

Rabinovici, Schoschana. *Thanks to My Mother*. Translated by James Skofield. New York: Dial Books, 1998. Memoir of a woman who was interned in Stutthof as a child. Provides details about that camp and the maliciousness during the time Becker worked there.

—Elizabeth D. Schafer

See also: Adolf Eichmann; Reinhard Heydrich; Heinrich Himmler; Adolf Hitler.

BYRON DE LA BECKWITH

American white supremacist and Ku Klux Klan leader

BORN: November 9, 1920; Colusa, California
DIED: January 21, 2001; Jackson, Mississippi
ALSO KNOWN AS: Dee Lay
MAJOR OFFENSE: Murder
ACTIVE: June 12, 1963
LOCALE: Jackson, Mississippi
SENTENCE: Life imprisonment

EARLY LIFE

Byron De La Beckwith (BI-ruhn day lah BEHK-wihth) was born in Colusa, California, and moved to Mississippi with his widowed mother at the age of five. Upon entering adulthood, Beckwith joined the armed services and received the Purple Heart for his combat service during World War II. After returning to the United States, Beckwith became a fertilizer salesman in Mississippi.

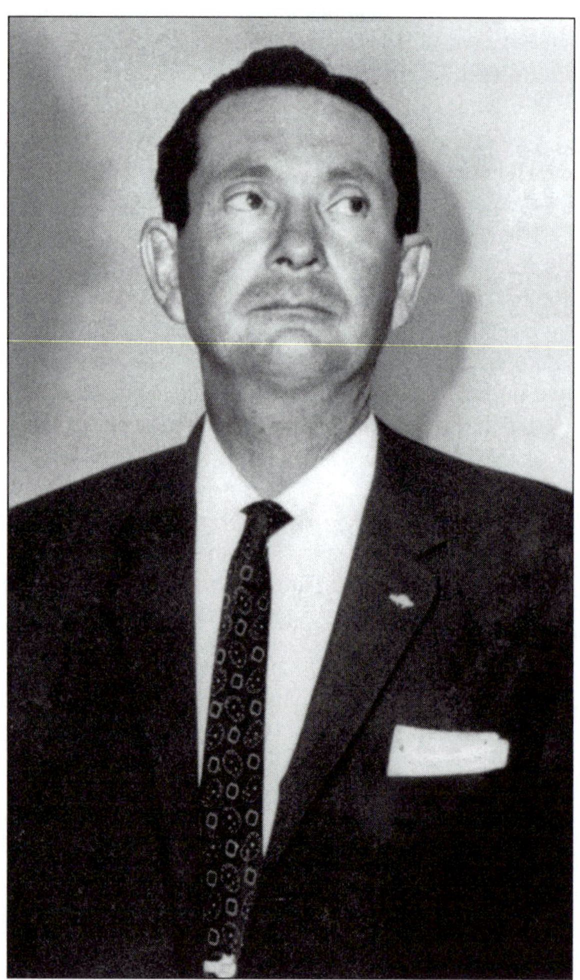

Byron De La Beckwith. (AP/Wide World Photos)

Beckwith's early life in Mississippi and his return to the state after his military services appears to have impacted his attitudes about race and ethnicity rather substantially. Many residents of Mississippi and other southern states had clear inclinations toward preserving past racial separation policies. However, the United States was in the midst of a desegregation movement. The U.S. Supreme Court ruling in *Brown v. Board of Education* in 1954 had overruled the prior "separate but equal" doctrine of *Plessy v. Ferguson* (1896). These changes in society were viewed by Beckwith and many southerners as an attack on their way of life forced upon them by the federal government and civil rights advocates. Upon returning to Mississippi, Beckwith became a member and leader of the white supremacist group known as the Ku Klux Klan (KKK). The organization had a history of engaging in violence against African Americans. In the 1960's, this violence escalated in the form of lynchings, church bombings, and assaults against African Americans.

CRIMINAL CAREER

Beckwith gained his notoriety in the mid-1960's when he was tried twice for the assassination of Medgar Evers, a popular civil rights leader in Jackson, Mississippi. Myrlie Evers, Evers's wife, and her three young children were watching President John F. Kennedy's address to the nation on civil rights when a rifle shot rang out. Medgar Evers was shot in the back while standing in the driveway of his home. He managed to drag himself to the doorway of his home, where he was met by his frantic wife and children. He died less than one hour later.

LEGAL ACTION AND OUTCOME

Beckwith was charged with the murder of Evers after his rifle was found at the scene of the crime and his fingerprints were found on the scope of the rifle. In addition, some witnesses came forward to make eyewitness identifications that placed Beckwith at the crime scene. Other witnesses reported seeing Beckwith's Plymouth Valiant in the vicinity of the Evers residence. Beckwith explained away the direct evidence against him by claiming that his rifle had been stolen. Moreover, Beckwith's attorney called two police officers from the town of Greenwood, Mississippi, to the witness stand; these two officers testified to seeing Beckwith there at a gas station. Greenwood is about eighty miles from Jackson, the scene of the crime; therefore, if the officer testimony was accurate, it would have been impossible for Beckwith to have committed the murder. On two different occasions, all-white male juries failed to convict Beckwith; instead, they returned hung verdicts, which led to mistrials.

During the civil rights era, it was traditionally very difficult to obtain a conviction in a Mississippi courtroom of a white offender charged with a crime against an African American victim. In many areas of Mississippi, the white-supremacist ideology was so entrenched that it frequently made its way into governmental offices, including local sheriff offices, police departments, and the courts. However, in one of Beckwith's trials, there was some indication that the powerful ideology of white supremacy had made its way all the way up to the governor's office. During the first trial, Mississippi governor Ross Barnett walked up to Beckwith and shook his hand in full view of the jury.

In the immediate aftermath of the trials, Beckwith remained in the public spotlight. In 1967, he ran for lieutenant governor of Mississippi, finishing fifth out of six candidates. In 1973, police stopped Beckwith in New Orleans, Louisiana, and found bombs inside his vehicle. He was convicted in state court of transporting explosives without a permit and was sentenced to five years in a Louisiana prison.

Beckwith was not held accountable for the murder of Evers until 1994. Myrlie Evers convinced Hinds County district attorney Bobby DeLaughter to bring Beckwith to court for a third trial in her husband's death. During his investigation, DeLaughter found several different witnesses to testify that Beckwith had, at various times, bragged both about his shooting death of Evers and about the fact that he had not been held accountable for the offense.

Beckwith had essentially believed that he would never be found guilty by a jury in Mississippi for killing an African American. He therefore apparently saw no harm in telling people about his involvement in the murder. During his third trial, Beckwith remained openly defiant and blatantly proud of is separatist views. He even wore a Confederate flag on his lapel during the trial. His incredible swagger would eventually lead to his downfall: After considering the new evidence, the jury—composed of eight black and four white jurors—convicted Beckwith of Evers's murder. Beckwith was sentenced to life imprisonment.

Impact

The Byron De La Beckwith case was important for a variety of reasons. Most important, the case served as a historical lens into the deep-seated racial biases and bigotry of the South that existed for most of the twentieth century. However, the case was also important because it served as a mechanism for change and clearly delineated a social shift toward white supremacist accountability for racist actions, even years after supremacist members committed their offenses.

Following Beckwith's conviction, several other cases of violent crimes committed against African Americans during the 1960's were reassessed and retried. In 1998, Sam Bowers was tried and convicted of the 1966 murder in Hattiesburg, Mississippi, of local National Association for the Advancement of Colored People (NAACP) president Vernon Dahmer. In 2000 and 2001, Thomas Blanton, Jr., and Bobby Frank Cherry were found guilty for their roles in the Birmingham church bombing that resulted in the deaths of four teenage African American girls in September, 1963.

Further Reading

DeLaughter, Bobby. *Never Too Late: A Prosecutor's Story of Justice in the Medgar Evers Case.* New York: Simon & Schuster, 2001. Written by the prosecuting attorney who was instrumental in bringing Beckwith to trial for the third time in 1994, the book highlights the evidence against Beckwith and the difficulties and triumphs in bringing a thirty-year-old case to trial.

Morris, W. *Ghosts of Medgar Evers: A Tale of Race, Murder, Mississippi, and Hollywood.* New York: Random House, 1998. An account that traces the development of the 1994 trial against Beckwith, as well as the development of the 1996 *Ghosts of Mississippi* film that chronicled the case.

Wilkie, C. *Dixie: A Personal Odyssey Through Events That Shaped the Modern South.* New York: Simon & Schuster, 2001. Presents a historical look at some of the important race-related events of the 1960's and their influence on modern issues in the South.

—Kevin G. Buckler

See also: J. B. Stoner.

Tom Bell

American outlaw

Born: 1825; Rome, Tennessee
Died: October 4, 1856; near Nevada City, California
Also known as: Thomas J. Hodges (birth name); Outlaw Doc
Cause of notoriety: Bell and his outlaw gang are credited with the first attempted stagecoach holdup in California.
Active: October 8, 1851-October 4, 1856
Locale: Auburn, Calaveras, Nevada City, Sacramento, San Francisco, and Stockton, California

Early Life

Thomas J. Hodges, also known as Tom Bell (behl), was born in 1825 just east of Nashville in Rome, Tennessee. Not much is known about his early life. At six feet, two inches tall, with long red hair and a striking beard, Bell was an imposing physical presence. Educated as a physician in Tennessee, Bell saw action in the Mexican-American War as an Army doctor. After his service in the military, he joined the gold rush to California, where he sought his fortune as a gambler.

Outlaw Career

Before long, Bell's troubles with the law began. On October 8, 1851, he was sentenced to five years in state prison for grand larceny committed in Sacramento County. At the time, California's prison system was new, and Bell was only the twenty-fourth person sentenced to prison. Initially he was held in a ship just off the coast of San Francisco, but he was later housed at the newly constructed Angel Island Prison at San Quentin. On May 12, 1855, Bell escaped from custody along with several other convicts, including Bill Gristy (alias Bill White). Within months, Bell was the leader of a well-organized gang of more than thirty outlaws.

On August 12, 1856, Bell and his gang attempted a feat never before tried in California: robbing a stagecoach. They chose a Camptonville-Marysville stage carrying $100,000 worth of gold bullion. One passenger, the wife of a local barber, was killed, and two male passengers were wounded before Bell's gang was chased away by the stagecoach guards. A short time later, a Jewish peddler named Rosenthal was robbed and murdered by Bell and several members of his gang. The murder occurred not far from his Bell's suspected hideout. The robberies, and especially the death of the woman on the Marysville stage, led to a massive manhunt, led most notably by Bell's nemesis Placer County Sheriff John C. Boggs.

By late September, Gristy and many other suspected gang members had been captured. Sheriff Boggs and his deputies interrogated Gristy, who eventually shared information about Bell's hideout near the Mountaineer House, a hotel and tavern located about eight miles outside Auburn. Another suspect interrogated by Boggs, named Charley Hamilton, also reported that he knew Bell. Hamilton agreed to infiltrate the Bell gang and try to arrange the outlaw's capture. Simultaneously, Deputy Sheriff Bob Paul of Calaveras County posed as an outlaw and attempted to obtain evidence against Jack Phillips, the owner of the Mountaineer House and a suspected collaborator and fence for Bell's gang. Boggs had previously raided the Mountaineer House several times but had never been able to locate Bell.

Legal Action and Outcome

On September 29, 1856, the hotelkeeper was arrested for harboring Bell, and the authorities began to close the net on the fugitive. Later that evening, Hamilton, the desperado who had gained Bell's trust, told Sheriff Boggs where Bell was camped. Sometime after midnight, while riding toward the suspected encampment, Boggs and his men intercepted Bell on the road, and a gunfight ensued. Outlaw Ned Conway was killed, but Bell and another outlaw known as Texas Jack escaped on foot, unharmed. Bell headed for another tavern and hotel about four miles away, known as the Pine Grove House, where he stole a horse and headed south toward the San Joaquin River. Four days later, on October 4, 1856, Bell was captured and lynched outside Nevada City by a posse from Stockton led by Judge George Belt.

Impact

Following his prison break, Tom Bell, who has also been referred to as the "Outlaw Doc," became the most infamous fugitive to hit the California gold rush fields since Joaquín Murieta. He will be remembered primarily for attempting the first stage holdup in California.

Further Reading

Boessenecker, John. *Badge and Buckshot: Lawlessness in Old California*. Norman: University of Oklahoma Press, 1988. An authoritative narrative on lawlessness in the Old West. Provides a candid account of the sometimes ragged past of this important period in American history.

Drago, Sinclair. *Road Agents and Train Robbers: Half a Century of Western Banditry*. New York: Dodd, 1973. Does an excellent job of dispelling common misconceptions about criminal activities of well-known outlaws in the last half of the nineteenth century.

Secrest, William B. *California Desperadoes: Stories of Early California Outlaws in Their Own Words*. Clovis, Calif.: Word Dancer Press, 2000. The author has compiled an amazing collection of rare photographs and first-person accounts of authentic Old West desperadoes.

—Wayne J. Pitts

See also: Apache Kid; William H. Bonney; Curly Bill Brocius; Butch Cassidy; Bob Dalton; Emmett Dalton; Bill Doolin; John Wesley Hardin; Doc Holliday; Jesse James; Tom Ketchum; Harry Longabaugh; Bill Longley; Joaquín Murieta; Johnny Ringo; Belle Starr; Henry Starr; Hank Vaughan; Cole Younger.

Samuel Bellamy

British pirate

Born: 1689; Devonshire, England

Died: April 26, 1717; near Wellfleet, Massachusetts, off the coast of Cape Cod

Also known as: Black Bellamy; Black Sam; Pirate Prince

Cause of notoriety: Bellamy, a pirate who plundered fifty ships in eighteen months, captured the British slave ship *Whydah*, earning a lifetime's fortune. However, the ship sank as Bellamy sailed for home, and he died.

Active: 1716-1717

Locale: North American Atlantic coast

Early Life

Samuel Bellamy (BEHL-ah-mee) was born into a poor family in Devonshire, England. His mother died at his birth. It is thought that Bellamy had to work starting at the age of ten and that he spent his early years as a sailor. In his early twenties, Bellamy went to Cape Cod, Massachusetts, to live with relatives while looking to make his fortune. Some sources say that Bellamy left a wife in England; other sources say he fell in love with a young girl named Maria Hallett in Cape Cod, and still other sources say he did both.

Bellamy became interested in searching for treasure from Spanish fleets that sank in Florida waters. Paulsgrave Williams became Bellamy's benefactor, lending him the money to buy a ship to sail to Florida. Williams also decided to become Bellamy's quartermaster, and with a crew of thirty they sailed to Florida. When they arrived there, they learned that most of the gold had been recovered and put into local storage. A group of pirates soon raided the

"This My Conscience Tells Me"

In A General History of the Robberies and Murders of the Most Notorious Pyrates, *believed to have been written by Daniel Defoe under the pseudonym Captain Charles Johnson (although some scholars dispute this authorship), Bellamy is said to have made the following speech to the captain of a merchant vessel he has just taken captive:*

I scorn to do any one a mischief, when it is not to my advantage; damn the sloop, we must sink her, and she might be of use to you. Though you are a sneaking puppy, and so are all those who will submit to be governed by laws which rich men have made for their own security; for the cowardly whelps have not the courage otherwise to defend what they get by knavery; but damn ye altogether: damn them for a pack of crafty rascals, and you, who serve them, for a parcel of hen-hearted numbskulls. They vilify us, the scoundrels do, when there is only this difference, they rob the poor under the cover of law, forsooth, and we plunder the rich under the protection of our own courage. . . . You are a devilish conscience rascal, I am a free prince, and I have as much authority to make war on the whole world, as he who has a hundred sail of ships at sea, and an army of 100,000 men in the field; and this my conscience tells me. . . .

Source: Captain Charles Johnson, *A General History of the Robberies and Murders of the Most Notorious Pyrates* (London: C. Rivington, 1724).

storage area and absconded with a quarter-million silver coins.

Pirating Career

Bellamy and his crew decided that pirating could be a lucrative career and signed on with Ben Hornigold on his ship, the *Mary Anne*. Bellamy became captain of the ship when Hornigold angered the crew by refusing to attack British ships.

Bellamy became quite successful in his short career as a pirate, looting more than fifty ships in just eighteen months. During the same period of time, he commanded a crew of two hundred men and five ships. He was known for his interesting habit of offering one of his own ships to the captain and crew that he attacked. He would also give the overthrown captain and crew the option to join his own crew as pirates. If they refused, he allowed them to leave safely.

One of Bellamy's most successful takeovers was of the English ship the *Whydah*. It took Bellamy three days to capture the *Whydah*, and when he did, he made it his flagship. After eighteen months of pirating, Bellamy and his crew had enough money to sail back to New England, divide their holdings, and enjoy their success.

On the trip back to New England, Bellamy decided to sail into Cape Cod, allegedly to inform Hallett of the fortune he had acquired. He was caught in a terrible storm with winds up to eighty miles per hour just off the coast of Cape Cod. The *Whydah* ran aground some two hundred yards from shore and was inundated with tons of water. Bellamy and most of his crew were killed in the storm; only two members of the crew survived the shipwreck. Most of the pirates' bodies washed to shore over time, but not that of Bellamy.

Impact

The *Whydah* is the only pirate ship ever to be salvaged. Its salvage in 1984 allowed the public to see at first hand the treasures, tools, and other artifacts from a real pirate ship. A museum dedicated to the *Whydah* and the history of Samuel Bellamy was created in Provincetown, Massachusetts. The salvage of the ship, its artifacts, and the museum have kept Bellamy's story and legend alive. One legend tells how the ghost of Maria Hallett still walks the hills near the beach of Cape Cod, looking for Bellamy. Another legend implies that Bellamy made it to shore alive and lived incognito in Cape Cod.

Further Reading

Clifford, Barry. *Expedition Whydah*. New York: Cliff Street Books, 1999. This book blends the true story of finding the pirate ship *Whydah* with the story and legend of Bellamy and his pirating career. Includes photographs and drawings of coins, pistols, dinnerware, and treasure from the *Whydah*.

Cordingly, David. *Under the Black Flag: The Romance and Reality of Life Among the Pirates*. New York: Random House, 1995. In addition to details of Bellamy's career, the book gives interesting descriptions of the storms that Bellamy and his crew encountered on the *Mary Anne* and the *Whydah*.

Cordingly, David, ed. *Pirates: Terror on the High Seas from the Caribbean to the South China Sea*. Atlanta: Turner, 1996. Explains some of Bellamy's motives for being a pirate and discusses his pirating career.

—*Toby Stewart*

See also: Stede Bonnet; Anne Bonny; William Kidd; John Rackham; Mary Read; Bartholomew Roberts; Dominique You.

John Bellingham

British businessman and murderer

Born: 1776; St. Neots, Huntingdonshire, England
Died: May 18, 1812; London, England
Major offense: Murder of British prime minister Spencer Perceval
Active: May 11, 1812
Locale: London, England
Sentence: Death by hanging

Early Life

John Bellingham (BEHL-ihng-ham) was born in 1776 at St. Neots, Huntingdonshire, England, the son of a land surveyor who died insane. Apprenticed to a jeweler at sixteen, Bellingham soon quit. A business attempt ended in bankruptcy. After drifting from one job to another, he found employment with a Liverpool shipping firm. He married Mary Neville, an Irish milliner; the couple had two children. Fortunately, her shop provided a steady income, for John's career consisted of an unbroken string of failures. However, with the exception of a single notorious murder, he committed no known crimes.

Criminal Career

The chain of events culminating in the murder of Spencer Perceval, the prime minister of England, began in Russia in 1804, when Bellingham was arrested there for incurring large debts and attempting to leave the country without paying. A mediation board ruled in favor of the creditor. Over the next three years, the British ambassador, Granville Leveson-Gower, received numerous petitions from Bellingham, but he could do little because the imprisonment was consistent with Anglo-Russian commercial treaties. When Britain and Russia severed diplomatic relations in 1807, Leveson-Gower returned to England while Bellingham remained in St. Petersburg. He was released in 1809.

Bellingham then deluged the government with claims for compensation for his imprisonment and the embassy's alleged mishandling of the affair. Denying these increasingly paranoid petitions fell to the Foreign Office and the prime minister. Perceval's shaky ministry governed a country that was at war with France and convulsed by urban unrest and industrial sabotage. Its lack of sympathy for a bankrupt businessman's dubious claims was understandable.

On May 5, Bellingham presented a last petition to the London police office at Bow Street, reiterating his story and concluding: "Should this reasonable request be denied . . . I shall then feel justified in executing justice myself." He purchased two small pistols and began haunting the visitor's gallery of the House of Commons. On the evening of May 11, 1812, as Perceval entered the lobby of the House of Commons, Bellingham shot him through the heart at point-blank range. He made no effort to escape, allowing himself to be disarmed by spectators. A disorganized attempt by the London mob to rescue him as he was being transferred to Newgate Gaol, and the cries of "Long live Bellingham" at his execution, were almost certainly expressions of hostility to Perceval's policies rather than sympathy for his murderer.

Legal Action and Outcome

Bellingham's trial took place at Old Bailey on Friday, May 15; he was hanged the following Monday. This rapid sequence of events was standard at the time for a murder with multiple witnesses, when the accused did not request additional time. Insanity was the only possible defense. The court refused to allow time to call witnesses from Liverpool. Bellingham's deliberate planning and his articulate stance while defending himself made a verdict of insanity very unlikely in 1812.

While awaiting execution, Bellingham told his jailers that he looked forward to being "freed." His calm demeanor on the scaffold also suggests that he wanted to be executed and that this may have been a motive for his crime.

Impact

Spencer Perceval was not an unlikely target for John Bellingham: The prime minister had many enemies. His assassination left a vacuum that took nearly two months to fill; during that time, Napoleon Bonaparte invaded Russia and the United States declared war. Irish Catholics hated Perceval for his adamant opposition to Catholic emancipation, and the Luddites blamed him for the hardships of the working class. Perceval's death thus had the potential to benefit both foreign powers and domestic opponents, including the Whigs and Radicals in Parliament. That it did not is one of the ironies of history. The Tory ministry that succeeded Perceval's defeated Napoleon, rode out a wave of domestic unrest that would probably have toppled a weaker government, and remained in power for a tempestuous fifteen years.

FURTHER READING

Goddard, Kathleen S. "A Case of Injustice? The Trial of John Bellingham." *American Journal of Legal History* 46, no. 1 (2004): 1-25. Examines the question of Bellingham's insanity.

Gray, Denis. *Spencer Perceval: The Evangelical Prime Minister, 1762-1812*. Manchester, England.: Manchester University Press, 1963. The last two chapters describe the political situation in 1812, the assassination, and the trial of Bellingham.

Mathew, H. C. G., and Brian Harrison, eds. *Oxford Dictionary of National Biography, from the Earliest Times to the Year 2000*. New York: Oxford University Press, 2004. Good entries on Bellingham, Perceval, and Leveson-Gower.

—Martha A. Sherwood

SEE ALSO: Jacques Clément; Charlotte Corday; Guy Fawkes; Balthasar Gérard; François Ravaillac; Miles Sindercombe.

BAMBI BEMBENEK

American murderer

BORN: August 15, 1958; Milwaukee, Wisconsin
ALSO KNOWN AS: Lawrencia Bembenek (full name); Laurie Bembenek (legal name as of 1994)
MAJOR OFFENSES: Murder and escape from prison
ACTIVE: May, 1981
LOCALE: Milwaukee, Wisconsin
SENTENCE: Life in prison

EARLY LIFE

Bambi Bembenek (BAM-bee behm-BEHN-ihk) grew up on south side of Milwaukee, Wisconsin. She entered the Milwaukee Police Academy when she turned twenty-one but was dismissed in 1980 on suspicion of smoking marijuana. Following her dismissal, she filed a sex discrimination lawsuit against the department. Faced with large debts, she became a Playboy club waitress and aerobics instructor to pay her bills. She married police officer Elfred Schulz, Jr., after a brief courtship.

CRIMINAL CAREER

In May, 1981, four months after Bembenek married Schulz, his former wife, Christine, was shot to death in her home with Elfred's revolver. Bembenek was accused of the murder. She consistently denied any involvement in the crime and alleged that the police had focused their investigations on her to keep her from testifying in her sex discrimination suit.

LEGAL ACTION AND OUTCOME

In a trial widely described as sensational, Bembenek was convicted of first-degree murder and was sentenced to life in prison at Taycheedah Correctional Institute. While in prison, she initiated class-action suits, charging inhumane conditions. She assisted other inmates in researching their appeals and started a prison newspaper. She exercised for long hours every day and read extensively. Eventually, she won the right to be admitted to a college extension program and earned a bachelor's degree in humanities, graduating with honors.

After ten years in prison, Bembenek became romantically involved with the brother of a fellow inmate. With his assistance, she escaped and fled to Canada, where she worked as a waitress for three months before a customer recognized her from the television show *America's Most Wanted* and notified police. She and her fiancé were arrested and returned to the United States, where he was sentenced for abetting her escape. She was placed in solitary confinement in a federal penitentiary.

Bembenek's lawyers appealed the case several times over the following years. The appeal filed after her escape from prison and recapture resulted in the vacating of her first-degree-murder life sentence because of evidence of sloppy police work at the time of the murder. Rather than face continued imprisonment, Bembenek decided not to fight for a new trial, instead pleading no contest to second-degree murder. In December, 1992, she was sentenced to twenty years in prison but was placed on parole, based on time already served.

The question of who murdered Christine Schultz may never be answered. Bembenek passed all lie-detector tests relating to the killing, but Elfred Schulz remained convinced that Bembenek murdered his wife. A case could be made against an acquaintance of theirs who was later convicted of armed robberies around the time of the murder and who bragged in prison of having killed Christine.

In 2002, Bembenek filed for DNA testing, but the results were equivocal. In 2003, she filed suit against Dr.

Phil McGraw, alleging that the staff of his television program had imprisoned her in an apartment while awaiting results of their own DNA testing. She escaped from a window and shattered her leg, which later required amputation.

Thereafter, Bembenek disappeared from public view. Depressed and suffering from panic attacks, she admitted that she was an alcoholic and was returned to jail briefly for use of marijuana and cocaine. She contracted hepatitis C and moved to the Pacific Northwest, where she lived in poverty.

Impact

Bambi Bembenek's case generated enormous publicity. She became a folk hero, with thousands of people following media accounts of the trials and her escape from prison and watching her appearances on celebrity television shows. The combination of her glamorous looks and the suggestions of a miscarriage of justice captured people's imagination and prompted sales of books, magazine articles, and two television movies that covered her story.

Further Reading

Radish, Kris. *Run, Bambi, Run: The Beautiful Ex-Cop and Convicted Murderer Who Escaped to Freedom and Won America's Heart.* New York: Carol, 1992. A detailed account of the case against Bembenek and its numerous shortcomings.

Roddick, Bill. *After the Verdict: A History of the Lawrencia Bembenek Case.* Milwaukee, Wisc.: Composition House, 1999. Questions the evidence against Bembenek.

—*Rebecca Lovell Scott*

See also: Antoinette Frank; Jean Harris; Sante Kimes; Sam Sheppard; Pamela Ann Smart; Madeleine Smith; Ruth Snyder; Harry Kendall Thaw; Carolyn Warmus.

Maurycy Beniowski

Hungarian nobleman and pirate

Born: September 20, 1746; Vrbové, near Trnava, Hungary (now in Slovakia)

Died: May 23, 1786; Madagascar

Also known as: Maurycy August Beniowski (full name); Maurice-Augustus de Benyowski; Maurice d'Aladar; Maurice Auguste Benyowsky; Móric Ágost Beňovszký

Cause of notoriety: Beniowski's irrepressible political scheming and delusions of grandeur led him to pirating activities; he and his crew pirated international shipping in the heavily trafficked waters off Madagascar.

Active: 1772-1786

Locale: Siberia and Madagascar

Early Life

As a young man, Maurycy Beniowski (mohr-REE-cee behn-YOV-skee) married a Polish noblewoman, Susanna Henska, and trained to become a military officer, though his devout Roman Catholicism and Polish nationalism in the partition era became an issue. In 1768, he joined the rebellion against Russian rule that became known as the Bar Confederation. Captured in a military encounter on the River Prut, he was exiled first to Kazan; however, after involvement in a plot against Catherine the Great, he was condemned to lifelong exile in Siberia. There, among other exiles, he stirred up a revolt and escaped to Kamchatka, where he seized a Russian galliot. After numerous adventures, Beniowski arrived at Mauritius with his entourage in two French ships and was welcomed by the French governor Julien François Dudresnay Desroches, although he was disliked by the intendant Pierre Poivre.

Pirating Career

In 1772, Beniowski persuaded the French king Louis XV to back an armed expedition to establish a trading post and colony in the southern part of Madagascar in return for the stolen archives of Kamchatka and the title Governor General of Madagascar. Stopping off at Mauritius in September, 1773, Beniowski was refused any help by the French governor and sailed on to Madagascar. Beniowski quickly set about establishing himself at a new settlement he christened Louisbourg, profiting from the production of rice and cattle, which he supplied to Mauritius. Embroiled in political conflict with the French-led Mauritians, who increasingly viewed him as an opportunist and impostor, and consequently stripped of his French commission, Beniowski turned first to the Habsburg monarch Joseph II and then to the American politician Benjamin Franklin. Beniowski proposed the fantastic idea that Madagascar provide a base for the American army in its struggle against England. Congress, not surprisingly, rejected Beniowski's proposal, though Beniowski himself was able to return to Madagascar after convincing European merchants settled in Baltimore to finance a voyage to that part of the world. Less than a year after his return, Beniowski was killed by French forces from Mauritius which were led by Captain Lacher de Vermond in May, 1786, and bent on destroying Louisbourg and razing Mauritiana.

Impact

Legends surrounding Maurycy Beniowski abound, many cultivated by Beniowski's own pen. One suggests that he mustered a force of twenty thousand local men to defeat the French and was subsequently named emperor by the native Madagascans. Other legends concentrate on how the incipient colony blossomed into a hub for pirates, who were both offered rich pickings from the major sea route that went on to India and could rely on a rich stock of fresh supplies on Madagascar (including native women, many of whom were captured and became part of the pirates' harems). The area became a marketplace for stolen goods, and lawlessness was an endemic problem.

Some time after his death, the island Mauritius was named after Beniowski, and he continued to be remembered there into the twenty-first century. The verdict of contemporary writers representative of the French establishment, however, was that Beniowski cost France millions and, to quote author Abbé Rochon (a contemporary of Beniowski who wrote about Madagascar), "brought calamities upon Madagascar."

Further Reading

Benyowski, M. A. *Memoirs and Travels*. London: G. G. J. & J. Robinson, 1791. Throughout his life, Beniowski kept a careful diary of his adventures, which were published posthumously as a best-selling book in English (1790), in French (1791), and in Polish (1797). In keeping with the character of the author, the work is a self-promotional work.

Dvoichenko-Markov, Eufrosina. "Benjamin Franklin and Count M.A. Benyowski." *Proceedings of the American Philosophical Society* 99, no. 6 (1955): 405-417. This article traces Beniowski and his wife's correspondence with Benjamin Franklin and Beniowski's proposals to place himself and his colony in Madagascar at the service of the American republic.

Kotzebue, August von. *Count Benyowski: Or, The Conspiracy of Kamchatka, a Tragi-Comedy in Five Acts*. In *The Beauties of Kotzebue, Containing the Most Interesting Scenes, Sentiments, Speeches and All His Admired Dramas*, edited by Walley C. Oulton. London: Crosby & Letterman, 1800. Benyowski became the subject of a number of late eighteenth and early nineteenth century dramas, including this one by August von Kotzebue. Kotzebue plays up the romantic interest and is specifically concerned with Beniowski's adventures in Siberia.

Rochon, Abbé Alexis. *A Voyage to Madagascar and the East Indies*. London: E. Jeffery, 1793. A critical, French-establishment interpretation of the governor general of Madagascar appears on pages 206-311, describing Beniowski as a liar, philanderer, and despot. Beniowski's death at the hands of French forces in 1786 is seen as an opportunity for a new beginning on Madagascar.

—Stefan Halikowski Smith

See also: ʿAruj; Bartholomew Roberts.

David Berg

American cult leader

Born: February 18, 1919; Oakland, California
Died: November, 1994; Costa de Caparica, Portugal
Also known as: David Brandt Berg (full name); Moses David; Mo; King David; Father David; Dad; Grandpa
Cause of notoriety: Berg, as the leader of various pseudoreligious cults, engaged in pedophilia and sexual abuse of the cult's members.
Active: 1940's-1994
Locale: Worldwide

Early Life

David Berg (buhrg) was born to Hjalmer Emmanuel Berg and the Reverend Virginia Lee Brandt. His mother was a Christian evangelist, and his father was a minister in the Christian and Missionary Alliance (CMA). Berg was the youngest of three children; two boys and one girl. He graduated from Monterey High School in northern California in 1935 and continued his studies at the Elliott School of Business Administration. On July 22, 1944, Berg married Jane Miller in Glendale, California. The couple had four children: Linda, Paul Brandt, Jonathan Emanuel, and Faith.

By 1948, Berg had joined the CMA and was relocated to Valley Farms, Arizona, to begin his ministry. However, he was expelled from the church because of significant differences in his interpretation of the church's teachings and the true mission of the organization. He was also alleged to have engaged in sexual misconduct with a church employee. After his dismissal, Berg worked as an independent evangelist and later worked with the Reverend Fred Jordan's Soul Clinic in locations across the United States.

Cult Career

In 1968, Berg and his children founded Teens for Christ in Huntington Beach, California. The group primarily preached to surfers and beachcombers, terrifying them with apocalyptic prophecies and urging them to renounce their lives of sin. It was during this period that Berg first adopted the alias Moses David and was affectionately referred to as "Mo" or "Dad" within the group. The group took on the name Children of God. Shortly after the group's founding, Berg separated from his first wife and married young follower Karen Zerby in August, 1969. Karen became known as Maria within the group, and Berg's first wife eventually left the movement.

The group quickly acquired followers by staging public demonstrations, stressing that America would soon experience God's wrath. The members would dress in sackcloth, smear their faces with ashes, and tie giant yokes around their necks. The group soon had an impressive following, and its momentum was growing. Berg saw himself as a prophet and relocated to England in 1971 in order to begin a worldwide mission. Berg also wanted to leave North America because of the growing anticult movements that began to surface in the early 1970's.

Berg encouraged an open sexual policy within the ministry, which was referred to as the Law of Liberty and included the practice of having multiple sexual partners and swapping partners. In the 1970's, Children of God introduced "flirty fishing" (also called "hooking for Jesus"), a practice in which women would engage in

Are the Children of God a Sect?

In a letter dated 1972, David Berg discussed the nature of the Children of God:

What church did the Children of God split off from? Is a new child a sect? No, he's a totally new birth!—An absolutely new creation!—Dropped out, yes, but a totally new creation! We are not a sect! We belonged to no religious denomination as a group. In order to be a sect, you must first be part of the whole to begin with. But we are not even a break with the Church System because we didn't break off from it, because we were never a part of it!

Every single sect or group that you can think of has been a split off or division of some former group. What religious body are we a split off from? They say we're separatists. We have separated ourselves from the churches. But most of us were never a part of any church. The word section itself means cut off. What church were we cut off of?—None! . . .

We are not Protestants or Catholics or Jews. We are not coming out of anything. . . . We were always the Children of God! He's just gathered us together. We are a new Nation, born in a day, this day, today! So we are God's seed & His Children & we were scattered abroad, but are now being gathered together by the Lord. We are no sect or cut-off of something else. We are His totally new creation!—Hallelujah!

sexual relationships with people to whom they were witnessing.

By the late 1970's, a paranoid Berg fired the managers of the Children of God and formed a new ministry, the Family of Love, and later, the Family. The Family promoted the same sexual freedoms but also focused on child rearing and children's sexuality. Berg's open stance regarding children and sex attracted pedophiles and other sex offenders to his organization. The Family's views on sex, especially involving minors, brought much criticism and investigations. Although Berg maintained that the Family's views on sexual relations with minors concerned teenagers and never young children, he was forced to change the movement's policies regarding the Law of Liberty, to end flirty fishing, and to denounce any type of sexual relationship with a minor.

Legal Action and Outcome

In the late 1970's and early 1980's, former cult members and concerned relatives began producing evidence to foreign governments about sexual abuse and pedophilia occurring within the group. Investigations were launched, which resulted in several lawsuits in Australia, Argentina, France, Great Britain, and Spain. However, there was never enough evidence to convict Berg or any Family member criminally, and all cases were resolved in the Family's favor.

During this period, further and more troubling accusations against Berg surfaced. At least six women, including Berg's two daughters, his daughter-in-law, and two granddaughters, alleged that Berg sexually molested them when they were children. As these women publicly accused Berg, others began to come forward in public interviews. With more accusations occurring and the anticult movement growing, Berg went into seclusion, moving frequently internationally with only the top members of the group knowing his location. As his health failed in the 1990's, Berg handed control of the organization over to his second wife, Karen "Maria" Zerby. Maria began drafting a new charter that addressed many of the complaints and concerns that the movement's critics voiced and granted its members new rights. In the twenty-first century, the Family continued to have more than nine thousand members across fifty countries.

Impact

With families losing their children to David Berg's cult, concerned parents formed the Parents' Committee to Free Our Sons and Daughters from the Children of God, later called Free the Children of God, in the 1970's. The group launched the investigations that drew considerable press and resulted in widespread criticism of the group. As a result of the organization's efforts, the New York attorney general published an anti-Children of God broadside. The group was instrumental in paving the way for the Cult Awareness Network, which began in the 1980's.

Further Reading

House, Wayne H. *Charts of Cults, Sects, and Religious Movements*. Grand Rapids, Mich.: Zondervan, 2000. A comprehensive resource listing the history and ideologies of cults and religious groups in an easy-to-read chart format.

Lewis, James R., and J. Gordon Melton, eds. *Sex, Slander, and Salvation: Investigating the Family/Children of God*. Stanford, Calif.: Center for Academic Publication, 1994. A thorough look into the history of the cult in its various incarnations, its members, and its leadership.

Pritchett, W. Douglas. *The Children of God, Family of Love: An Annotated Bibliography*. New York: Garland, 1985. Lists books and other sources about the Children of God and the Family movement.

Rhodes, Ron. *The Challenge of the Cults and New Religions*. Grand Rapids, Mich.: Zondervan, 2001. Rhodes examines cults and religious zealots, their doctrines, and their beliefs. The book reveals the way in which these groups stray from true Christianity and other organized religions.

Singer, Margaret Thaler. *Cults in Our Midst: The Continuing Fight Against Their Hidden Menace*. San Francisco: Jossey-Bass, 2003. An in-depth look at cult leaders and members. Singer reveals their techniques and warns of their dangers.

—Sara Vidar

See also: Marshall Applewhite; Jim Jones; David Koresh; Jeffrey Lundgren; Charles Manson; Bonnie Nettles.

LAVRENTY BERIA

Georgian-Russian politician and chief of Soviet secret police (1938-1953)

BORN: March 29, 1899; Merkheuli, Georgia, Russian Empire

DIED: December 23, 1953; Moscow, Soviet Union (now in Russia)

ALSO KNOWN AS: Lavrenty Pavlovich Beria (full name)

CAUSE OF NOTORIETY: As Joseph Stalin's right-hand man, Beria conducted purges in Transcaucasia, oversaw expansion of the Gulag system, and engineered mass relocation of ethnic minorities during World War II.

ACTIVE: 1917-1953

LOCALE: Soviet Union, mostly the Caucasus region and Russia

EARLY LIFE

Lavrenty Pavlovich Beria (lahv-REHN-tee PAV-loh-vihch BEH-ree-uh) was born to a peasant family in Georgia, part of the Russian Empire. The merchant for whom he worked while attending high school in Sukhumi paid for Beria to attend a technical college in Baku, from which he obtained an engineering degree in 1920. During the period between 1917 and 1920, Beria was active in the Georgian Communist Party, working closely both with its head, Grigoryi Ordzhonikidzhe, and with Joseph Stalin, to whom Beria owed his later advancement. After the short-lived Transcaucasian Republic merged with the Soviet Union in 1921, Beria became chief of secret police for Transcaucasia. He became first secretary to the Georgian Communist Party in 1931 and first secretary of the Transcaucasian Party in 1932. As an administrator, Beria was ruthlessly efficient, particularly at eliminating former associates who stood in the way of him and Stalin in their rise to power.

Lavrenty Beria. (Hulton Archive/Getty Images)

In 1935, Beria published *Kvoprosu ob istorii bolshevistskikh organizatsii v Zakavkaze* (*On the History of the Bolshevik Organizations in Transcaucasia*, 1939), which adulated Stalin and downplayed Ordzhonokidzhe's role within the party. With Stalin's sanction, Beria then eliminated any remaining Caucasian Bolsheviks who remembered a different version of history. The period between 1934 and 1938 witnessed the height of the purges, as Stalin systematically destroyed all potential political rivals and their supporters and removed former associates of Bolshevik revolutionary Leon Trotsky from the military.

SECRET POLICE CAREER

In July of 1938, Stalin summoned Beria to Moscow and appointed him deputy to Nikolay Ivanovich Yezhov, the chief of the People's Commissariat for Internal Affairs (NKVD), an organization that served as the Soviet Union's secret police force. In December, Yezhov was arrested and executed, and Beria took over his position. Because the purge had become so extensive and was taxing the Soviet infrastructure, Beria immediately set to work on "purging the purgers," that is, overseeing the release of thousands of people from custody. Beria also undertook the reform of the Gulag system of slave labor camps, making them more effective as instruments of economic development by reducing mortality and setting rational production goals. However, even with the reforms, Stalin's labor camps were scenes of appalling brutality and inhuman hardship. People were imprisoned in them for vague crimes against the state following trials that used evidence extracted under torture. Beria took an evil system that might have collapsed under the sheer weight of inefficiency and insanity and transformed it into an entrenched feature of Soviet society.

After Nazi Germany invaded Russia in 1941, Stalin transferred Beria to the State Defense Committee with responsibility for internal security and foreign intelligence. In this capacity, Beria ordered the mass transportation of Volga Germans, Crimean Tatars, and several other minority groups from their European homelands to Central Asia. Many died en route or under conditions of wartime privation in an unfamiliar region. Allegedly done in the name of national security, these deportations freed up some of Russia's most desirable territory and provided Central Asia with an educated, disciplined workforce. Stalin's and Beria's personal ethnic prejudices also may have played a part in the deportations.

> **BERIA'S STATURE AMONG THE COMMUNIST ELITE**
>
> *Milovan Djilas, a high-ranking Communist Party member in the former Yugoslavia, met Lavrenty Beria in 1944. In* Conversations with Stalin *(translated by Michael B. Petrovich, 1962), he drew this unflattering portrait of the Soviet Union's top secret policeman:*
>
> Beria was also a rather short man—in [Joseph] Stalin's Politburo there was hardly anyone taller than himself. He, too, was somewhat plump, greenish, and pale, and with soft damp hands. With his square-cut mouth and bulging eyes behind his pince-nez, he suddenly reminded me of Vujkovic, one of the chiefs of the Belgrade Royal Police who specialized in torturing Communists. It took an effort to dispel the unpleasant comparison, which was all the harder to forget because the similarity extended even to his expression—a certain self-satisfaction and irony mingled with a clerk's obsequiousness and solitude. Beria was a Georgian, like Stalin, but one could not tell this at all from the looks of him. Georgians are generally bony and dark. Even in this respect he was nondescript. He could have passed more easily for a Slav or a Lett, but mostly for a mixture of some sort.

In 1946, Beria was finally admitted as a full member of the Politburo and appointed head of the Soviet Union's Atomic Energy Program, which involved both a concerted mobilization of scientific resources in a war-devastated country and a nontrivial amount of espionage. To the rest of the world, this program appeared to pose a grave threat at the time; in retrospect, the overall specter of nuclear disaster during the Cold War Era was probably minor.

Beria fell from favor with Stalin in the early 1950's. At the beginning of 1953, the so-called Doctor's Plot—in which a number of the country's prominent Jewish doctors were accused of poisoning top Soviet leaders and were arrested—pointed to a breach in state security and may have presaged Beria's downfall.

DOWNFALL

Stalin died abruptly of a stroke on March 5, 1953, leaving Beria, Georgy Malenkov, and Nikita S. Khrushchev as the three leading members of the Communist Party. Initially, it appeared that the three might be able to share power. Beria acted swiftly to consolidate his position, denouncing the Doctor's Plot as fraud, proclaiming more autonomy for non-Russian nationalities, relaxing the collective farm system, and restoring many former Georgian associates to power. Other Politburo members viewed Beria's sudden turn to liberalism with deep distrust. All of them had been to some degree complicit in what were now being denounced as Stalin's crimes, and the evidence could be found easily in Beria's files.

On July 23, 1953, Beria walked into an elaborately laid trap. He was arrested both for antiparty and antistate activities and for espionage. He was kept in solitary confinement until December 23, when he was tried, convicted, and shot. The chief charge against him—that he used his position in newly acquired territories for personal aggrandizement—had some basis but was little more than an excuse for a preordained verdict.

IMPACT

For the following three years, the Soviet press ascribed responsibility for the horrors of Stalin's police state to Lavrenty Beria. Following Khrushchev's denunciation of Stalin at the 1956 Party Congress, Beria's name all but disappeared from official publications. However, with relaxation of censorship during perestroika (a period of reconstruction of Soviet politics, economy, and society) in the late 1980's, several reassessments of Beria's career appeared in Russia, and a complete account of his trial appeared for the first time.

Khrushchev described Beria as being "devoid of all human decency." Perhaps the only thing to be said in Beria's favor is that he was exceedingly capable, efficient, and diligent in everything he attempted, a dubious honor since nearly all of it was unequivocally bad. He willingly associated with Stalin and shares with his chief the responsibility for the death of several million innocent people in labor camps and through forced relocation, famines associated with collectivization, and lack of preparedness for the German onslaught in 1941. Beria is a prime example of a modern monster: the calculating facilitator who makes a career out of atrocity.

Further Reading

Beria, Sergio. *Beria, My Father: Inside Stalin's Kremlin*. Translated by Brian Pearce. London: Duckworth, 2001. Written by Beria's son, the book provides a wealth of insight into the inner workings of Stalinist-era politics and downplays Beria's role in Soviet atrocities.

Knight, Amy. *Beria, Stalin's First Lieutenant*. Princeton, N.J.: Princeton University Press, 1993. Comprehensive, balanced biography that makes use of archives unavailable before perestroika.

Kramer, Mark. "The Early Post-Stalin Succession Struggle and Upheavals in East-Central Europe: Internal-External Linkages in Soviet Policy Making. Part 2." *Journal of Cold War Studies* l, no. 2 (1999): 3-38. A detailed account of Beria's fall from power and his trial in 1953.

—Martha A. Sherwood

See also: Felix Dzerzhinsky; Lazar Kaganovich; Nikita S. Khrushchev; Vladimir Ilich Lenin; Vyacheslav Mikhailovich Molotov; Symon Petlyura; Joseph Stalin; Leon Trotsky; Vasili Vasilievich Ulrikh; Andrey Vyshinsky; Genrikh Yagoda; Nikolay Ivanovich Yezhov; Andrey Aleksandrovich Zhdanov; Grigory Yevseyevich Zinovyev.

David Berkowitz

American serial killer

Born: June 1, 1953; Brooklyn, New York
Also known as: Richard David Falco (birth name); David Falco Berkowitz (full name); Son of Sam; .44-Caliber Killer
Major offense: Murder
Active: 1976-1977
Locale: New York, New York
Sentence: 365 years in prison

Early Life

David Berkowitz (DAY-vihd BUR-koh-wihtz) was born to Betty (Broder) Falco, as a result of her extramarital affair with Joseph Kleinman. Because Kleinman threatened to end the relationship, Falco gave up her son. Berkowitz was adopted by a middle-class Jewish couple, Nathan and Pearl Berkowitz. Berkowitz was raised in the Bronx and had a relatively normal childhood. The only indicators of his future criminal behavior were his hyperactivity and his neighbors' characterization of him as a bully.

After his adopted mother died in 1967, Berkowitz began to exhibit marked changes, and his school performance was poor. Berkowitz lived with his adopted father until he remarried—his new wife did not relate well to David. The couple soon retired to Florida, leaving Berkowitz to drift. Berkowitz took a few classes at a community college and then spent three years in the Army. While in the Army, he contracted a venereal disease in Korea. He found his biological mother and sister, who were very welcoming, but Berkowitz ended contact with them soon afterward.

Criminal Career

After he left the Army in 1974, Berkowitz committed almost fifteen hundred acts of arson, recording each one in a journal. Around Christmas of 1975, he stabbed two women, claiming that demons in his head had instructed him to do so. He began a murderous spree on July 29, 1976. Six murders were attributed to him, and he was also responsible for critically wounding seven people. The media christened him the .44-Caliber Killer, for the weapon he used. Berkowitz targeted young couples, usually in parked cars. After one double homicide, Berkowitz left a note, calling himself the "Son of Sam," and was known by that moniker after that.

Berkowitz's first shooting victims were Donna Lauria and Jody Valenti, two teenage women sitting in a parked car outside Lauria's apartment building in the Bronx. Lauria died, and Valenti survived a shot to her thigh. Three months later, Berkowitz attacked Carl Denaro, whom he shot in the head, and Rosemary Keenan in Queens. In November, he attacked Donna DeMasi and Joanne Lomino, teenagers who were walking home from a bus stop after a late-night movie. Both girls survived, but Lomino was rendered a paraplegic. Two months later, Berkowitz fatally shot Christine Freund. In March, 1977, he killed Virginia Voskerichian, a Barnard College student. In April, he shot and killed Valentina Suriani and her boyfriend Alexander Esau while they were sitting in a parked car. It was there that Berkowitz left the "Son of Sam" letter.

The recipient of much media attention, Berkowitz

David Berkowitz. (AP/Wide World Photos)

also wrote letters to local newspapers. In late June, he shot Judy Placido, wounding her in the arm, as she sat in a parked car with Sal Lupo. Two days before the anniversary of the first murder, Berkowitz struck again, killing Stacy Moskowitz and wounding her boyfriend Bobby Violante while they were parked in his father's car.

Legal Action and Outcome

After Berkowitz killed his last two victims in Brooklyn, he drove away in his car—which had just been ticketed. The police investigated parking tickets in the area and were able to trace the murder to Berkowitz. He was arrested on August 10, 1977, outside his apartment in Yonkers, New York. There police found a collection of weapons in his trunk, apparently stored in anticipation of a suicide mission targeting a Long Island disco.

Berkowitz confessed right away. During interrogation, he revealed the origins of his nickname. He believed his neighbor, Sam, was a powerful demon who sent messages to his pet dog, a black Labrador retriever called Harvey. Berkowitz claimed to be following death orders from Sam's dog.

Although he was diagnosed with paranoid schizophrenia, Berkowitz was found competent to stand trial. He pleaded guilty and was sentenced on June 12, 1978, to 365 years' imprisonment. In prison, Berkowitz became a born-again Christian and also became a televangelist on public-access television. He requested the cancellation of his parole hearings, claiming that he did not want to be released from prison; the parole board denied his release in 2002 and 2004.

Impact

The year David Berkowitz was arrested, the "Son of Sam" law was enacted by the New York State Legislature. Written in the wake of speculation about large sums offered Berkowitz to tell his story, the law held that the state of New York can confiscate any money earned by convicted criminals as a result of selling their criminal stories. The money went to a fund for crime victims. The law, however, was declared unconstitutional by the Supreme Court in *Simon & Schuster, Inc. vs. New York Crime Victims Board* (1991). "Son of Sam" also became the name or theme of several songs by popular bands. A film about Berkowitz's crimes directed by Spike Lee, *Summer of Sam*, was released in 1999.

Further Reading

Fox, James Alan, and Jack Levin. *Extreme Killing: Understanding Serial and Mass Murder.* Thousand Oaks, Calif.: Sage, 2005. Explores the Son of Sam killings and other serial and mass murders through multiple theoretical approaches. Identifies factors related to such offenses.

Hickey, Eric W. *Serial Murderers and Their Victims.* Pacific Grove, Calif.: Brooks/Cole, 1991. Takes a sociological approach to understanding serial murder, identifying its causes and correlates. Hickey applies criminological theories to gain insight into offenders, examining the lives of more than two hundred serial killers, including David Berkowitz.

Klausner, Lawrence D. *Son of Sam: Based on the Authorized Transcription of the Tapes, Official Documents, and Diaries of David Berkowitz.* New York: McGraw-Hill, 1981. Biography of Berkowitz recounts the Son of Sam crimes.

—*Jennifer C. Gibbs*

See also: Joe Ball; Kenneth Bianchi; Ted Bundy; Angelo Buono, Jr.; Andrei Chikatilo; Andrew Cunanan; Jeffrey Dahmer; Albert DeSalvo; Albert Fish; John Wayne Gacy; Ed Gein; Karla Homolka; Leonard Lake; Charles Ng; Dennis Rader; Richard Speck; Aileen Carol Wuornos.

Paul Bernardo

Canadian serial rapist and murderer

Born: August 27, 1964; Scarborough, Ontario, Canada
Also known as: Scarborough Rapist; Ken
Major offenses: Rape, first-degree murder, aggravated assault, kidnapping, and performing an indignity on a human body
Active: May, 1987-April, 1992
Locale: Scarborough, Port Dalhousie, and St. Catharines, Ontario, Canada
Sentence: Convicted September 1, 1993, to serve a life sentence with no possibility of parole for twenty-five years and classified as a dangerous offender under Canadian law, permitting indeterminate incarceration

Early Life

Paul Bernardo (buhr-NAHR-doh) was born into a dysfunctional family. His father was abusive toward his wife and children, and his mother had serious psychological problems as well. As a boy, Bernardo showed signs of scoptophilia—looking in women's windows for sexual gratification (a "peeping tom"). Along with his friends, Bernardo began a series of scams, beginning with a backyard muscular dystrophy "charity" event whose proceeds they kept and ending with regular smuggling runs across the border with untaxed cigarettes concealed in the panels of cars with stolen license plates.

The two most significant events in the life of the young teenage Bernardo mirror occurrences in the life of American serial killer Ted Bundy: a traumatic breakup with a girlfriend, which Bernardo viewed as a betrayal, and the revelation that he was born out of wedlock. His friends noted that thereafter his attitude toward women became quite hostile and included violent sexual fantasies.

Criminal Career

Bernardo's career as the Scarborough Rapist lasted between May 4, 1987, and April 16, 1992, during which time he attacked at least eighteen women. On October 17, 1987, Bernardo met Karla Homolka; writer Nick Pron would later characterize their relationship as a "lethal marriage." While they were still dating, Bernardo expressed a sexual interest in Homolka's thirteen-year-old sister, Tammy Lyn Homolka. Deciding to "give" Tammy Lyn to her boyfriend as a Christmas present, Homolka stole sedative and anesthetic drugs from the veterinary clinic where she worked. Rendered unconscious by the sedatives, Tammy was raped by her own sister and Bernardo. However, the anesthetic used to keep her unconscious also caused her to vomit and choke to death. No one imagined the truth, and the case was closed as an accidental death.

In 1991, Bernardo and Homolka moved into a Cape Cod in St. Catherines, where they tortured, raped, and killed their second victim, fourteen-year-old Leslie Mahaffy. The girl's remains, encased in concrete, were discovered in a nearby waterway while the Bernardos celebrated a lavish wedding. The next victim, fifteen-year-old Kristen French, followed in the spring of 1992. The atrocities committed upon these teenage girls, as well as several others who survived the encounters, were videotaped by the Bernardos for what they thought would be their private collection; the videos eventually became court evidence.

Legal Action and Outcome

Bernardo was convicted in 1993 of thirteen crimes, including two counts of first-degree murder, two of aggravated assault, two of forcible rape, two of kidnapping, and one of "performing an indignity on a human body." He was sentenced to life in prison without possibility of parole for twenty-five years and was classified as a dangerous offender under Canadian law, permitting indeterminate incarceration.

Impact

Paul Bernardo and his wife were dubbed the Ken and Barbie Murderers: They projected fairytale beauty, upwardly mobile success, and marital bliss, hiding the darkness of psychopathic sexual sadism from the world. The house where the crimes occurred was torn down and a new one built in its place; however, the shadow of the case fell over the controversial 2005 film *Karla*, and Canadian citizens protested its release, claiming it exploited a sensitive case for financial gain without consideration for the victims' families.

A more serious influence of the case was on law enforcement: The previous lack of coordination between Canadian law enforcement agencies would forever change as law enforcement agencies, especially in separate jurisdictions, began to make an effort to work together and share knowledge and resources in these cases.

Further Reading

Burnside, Scott, and Alan Cairns. *Deadly Innocence*. New York: Warner Books, 1995. Thorough account of the case from various perspectives, with photographs.

Pron, Nick. *Lethal Marriage: The Unspeakable Crimes of Paul Bernardo and Karla Homolka*. New York: Seal, 1995. A *Toronto Star* crime reporter for more than thirty years, Pron investigates the reasons behind and outcomes of the Bernardo-Homolka murders.

Schechter, Harold. *The Serial Killer Files*. New York: Ballentine, 2003. Briefly examines the dynamics behind killer couples, including the Bernardos.

Williams, Stephen. *Invisible Darkness*. Toronto, Ont.: Bantam, 1996. Considered a leading authority on this case, Williams presents facts, intelligence, and insight—the product of in-depth scholarship.

_______. *Karla: A Pact with the Devil*. Toronto, Ont.: Random House of Canada, 2003. Although focusing on Homolka, this follow-up to Williams's previous book provides a different perspective on Bernardo's behavior.

—Charles Avinger

See also: Karla Homolka.

Charlotte de Berry

English pirate

Born: 1636; England

Died: Date and place unknown

Cause of notoriety: De Berry's legendary exploits include killing a British navy captain, taking charge of his ship, and converting the crew to piracy.

Active: Seventeenth century

Locale: Atlantic Ocean

Early Life

Charlotte de Berry (SHAHR-lot duh BEH-ree) was born in England in 1636. She came from a poor but respectable family. Her father had been a shipowner but lost a considerable amount of his money and retired from the shipping business. As he had considerable leisure time, he devoted himself to the education of Charlotte. Growing up in a seaport, de Berry developed an intense love for the sea and regretted not being a man so that she could go to sea. Dressed in men's clothing, she frequented the local pubs. She met an English sailor, fell deeply in love, and secretly married him. When he was ordered back to sea, she disguised herself as a man and joined the British navy.

Piracy Career

De Berry fought side by side with her husband, often saving his life and earning the respect of fellow sailors by her courage and expertise. Unfortunately, de Berry's husband angered a sadistic captain under whom they were serving. The captain sentenced him to be flogged, and he died. Once ashore, de Berry avenged his death by shooting and robbing the captain. De Berry remained filled with an unquenchable hatred for the British navy. Shortly thereafter, she was kidnapped by a sea captain. When his crew was ready to mutiny, she convinced them to become pirates, with her as captain. She killed the captain and took charge of the ship and crew. She plied her trade as a pirate for some time, remarried, was marooned without food, and saw her husband sacrificed as food for the hungry crew. She supposedly went mad with grief and lost command of her ship. When the pirates engaged a Dutch merchant ship, de Berry, wounded, fell overboard and shouted that she was joining her husband. The crew, realizing they were losing, blew their ship up to avoid cruel deaths at the hands of the Dutch.

Impact

Charlotte de Berry may have actually lived, or she may be a totally fictional character created by Edward Lloyd in *History of the Pirates*, published in 1836. Lloyd's history is the first written source to mention de Berry and did not appear until two hundred years after her birth; it appears odd that so much time would pass with no reference to her. Furthermore, the book contains many anachronisms and appears to have drawn stories from other fictions. Lloyd's book is the source for information about de Berry in later books.

Many of de Berry's exploits, as recounted above and all of which can be found in Lloyd's book, are scarcely believable. The death of de Berry and her entire crew leaves no one to recount the last events of her life. Scholarly investigation tends to disprove her actual existence. However, she continues to be part of the history of pirates. Whether de Berry was a real person or a fictional character, she is included in current lists of woman pirates. She is mentioned briefly in many books about pirates. Among pirate reenactors, there are a number of "krewes" of de Berry that are currently active; she remains a part of popular culture.

Further Reading

Cordingly, David. *Under the Black Flag: The Romance and Reality of Life Among the Pirates*. New York: Random House, 1996. Discusses the reality of pirate life: hardships, brutality, trials, executions. Chapter on women pirates. The afterword looks at romanticized pirates of fiction and film.

Konstam, Angus. *The History of Pirates*. Guilford, Conn.: The Lyons Press, 2002. Well-researched history of pirates and their activities. Detailed maps, color photos, illustrations.

Lloyd, Edward. *History of the Pirates of All Nations*. (1836). A "penny magazine" containing the first mention of Charlotte de Berry. Includes many statements and incidents that cannot be corroborated. Recounts incidents similar to ones in other well-known books published before this text. Also contains words and references belonging to later periods that would not have been used in the 1600's. For specific examples, see the Web site: www.bonaventure.org.uk/ed/lloyddscdb.htm

Meltzer, Milton. *Piracy and Plunder: A Murderous Business*. New York: Dutton Children's Books, 2001. Although published by the children's division of Penguin Putnam, the book actually targets young adult and adult readers as it invalidates the romanticized portrait of the swashbuckling, inept, often foppish pirate.

Platt, Richard. *Eyewitness: Pirate*. New York: DK, 2000. Treats all aspects of pirates and piracy. Explores reasons individuals became pirates, discusses women pirates and their reasons for disguising themselves as men. Well illustrated.

Rediker, Marcus. *Villains of All Nations: Atlantic Pirates in the Golden Age*. Boston: Beacon Press, 2004. Examines piracy and the reasons individuals became pirates.

—Shawncey Webb

See also: Anne Bonny; Grace O'Malley; Mary Read.

Kenneth Bianchi

American serial killer

Born: May 22, 1951; Rochester, New York

Also known as: Kenneth Alessio Bianchi (full name); Hillside Strangler

Major offenses: Kidnapping, rape, torture, strangulation, and murder

Active: October 16, 1977-October 22, 1979

Locale: Los Angeles, California, and Bellingham, Washington

Sentence: Life in prison without parole

Early Life

Kenneth Bianchi (bee-AHN-kee) was adopted at a very young age. His birth mother was an alcoholic teenage prostitute, and his adoptive mother was controlling and manipulative. From an early age, Bianchi repeatedly wet the bed, had insomnia and problems with authority figures, displayed no emotion, and lacked impulse control. He engaged in frequent temper tantrums and theft both as a child and as an adult. Bianchi attended a community college and received training as a police officer and security guard, but he bounced from job to job. He also had a series of bad relationships with women. As a result of these failures, he moved to California in 1977, where he joined his cousin Angelo Buono, Jr. There, Bianchi was rejected for several law enforcement positions and began to hire out prostitutes with Buono. Eventually, Bianchi married and had a son.

Criminal Career

Bianchi and Buono terrorized the city of Los Angeles for about four months during 1977 and 1978 with several murders; the bodies of the victims showed signs of rape and torture. Initially, their victims were mostly prostitutes: For Bianchi and Buono, the advantage of killing prostitutes was that no one would readily notice or care about the women's absence. The men would often rape the victims and then strangle them in some manner. They also tortured some of the victims with electrical burns, medical instruments, and asphyxiation. Bianchi and Buono then dumped the completely or partially nude victims' bodies on a hillside or in a heavily wooded area, thus earning the killers the nickname the Hillside Strangler.

Bianchi and Buono then moved from targeting prostitutes to victimizing young girls and middle-class women. In one particularly gruesome incident, they dumped two victims, both girls, in a rubbish dump. This change in targets made headlines in local newspapers and created panic among residents in Los Angeles. After this widespread publicity, the murders slowed a bit. Investigators later learned that during this time, Bianchi moved to Bellingham, Washington. Two murders then occurred in Bellingham in 1979; the bodies of the victims there showed similarities to those of the murdered women in Los Angeles, creating suspicion among authorities that they may have fallen to the same killer or killers. When police discovered that Bianchi had asked the two Bellingham women who were eventually murdered to house-sit for him, the police went to his residence, where they found jewelry belonging to some of the Los Angeles victims. Bianchi was then arrested. Police charged Bianchi with the murders of twelve victims who ranged from twelve to twenty-eight years old.

Legal Action and Outcome

Bianchi pleaded guilty by reason of insanity to the crimes. His trial antics became almost as well known as the crimes themselves. He claimed that he had multiple personalities and that his evil personality, Steve Walker, killed several victims in Los Angeles and the two women in Washington. This alter ego of Bianchi also implicated Buono in the California killings. Moreover, Bianchi tried to convince psychiatrists that he had three other personalities. Several experts examined Bianchi, and they ultimately decided that Bianchi was faking his mental illness. Bianchi eventually admitted to faking his multiple personalities in order to avoid the death penalty. (Some researchers later came to believe that Bianchi in fact did suffer from multiple personality disorder.) He eventually agreed on a plea bargain and testified against his cousin Buono in 1981. As a result of this testimony, Bianchi was given a sentence of life without parole rather than the death penalty. He was moved to Walla Walla State Prison in Washington State to carry out his sentence.

Impact

Bianchi's lengthy trial made headlines both for the gruesome crime details that emerged and for Bianchi's theatrics during his testimony. Bianchi's lies regarding multiple personality disorder forced criminal justice agents and experts to reexamine how mental illness is often used falsely as a defense tactic for offenders. Moreover, Bianchi's experience as an adopted child also shed light on experiences that can foster murderous tendencies in young people: As investigators were beginning to understand, isolation and feelings of abandonment during formative years, like those Bianchi had experienced, seemed to be a common factor in the histories of several serial killers who emerged during this period. The stories surrounding the Hillside Strangler outlived Bianchi's crime spree: The sheer brutality of the crimes provided ample fodder both for authors and for creators of television films.

Further Reading

Fox, James A., and Jack Levin. *Overkill: Mass Murder and Serial Killing Exposed.* New York: Plenum Press, 1994. A comprehensive examination of how and why serial killers and mass murderers operate. The authors especially focus on the motives of these killers and how they picked their victims.

Hickey, Eric W. *Serial Murderers and Their Victims.* California: Brooks/Cole, 1991. A thorough examination of all types of serial killers, including those who are male, female, or foreign or who work within a team. Also examines methods by which the killers are apprehended.

Schwartz, Ted. *The Hillside Strangler: A Murderer's Mind.* New York: Vivisphere, 2001. An in-depth examination of Bianchi's life and crimes. The author suggests that Bianchi may have suffered from multiple personality disorder.

—*Karen F. Lahm*

See also: Joe Ball; David Berkowitz; Ted Bundy; Angelo Buono, Jr.; Andrei Chikatilo; Andrew Cunanan; Albert DeSalvo; Albert Fish; John Wayne Gacy; Ed Gein; Karla Homolka; Leonard Lake; Charles Ng; Dennis Rader; Richard Speck; Aileen Carol Wuornos.

Bligh was one of the officers required to leave his ship, although there was no specific accusation made against him. Bligh was present at a few battles with the Danish fleet and served with distinction in 1801 at the Battle of Copenhagen, where he was under the direct command of British admiral Horatio Nelson. At the same time, he had to appear before a court-martial for insulting one of his subordinates. While the court-martial found him guilty of strong language, no penalty was exacted.

Bligh returned to the Pacific for one more command, as he was appointed governor of New South Wales in 1805. The army there was involved in various forms of illegal commerce, and Bligh's assignment was to stop all such activity. The forces arrayed against him proved too strong, however, and the army mutinied in 1808. Another round of trials in England ensued, and Bligh's reputation was the target of a campaign of innuendo by those who had been responsible for the mutiny. Nevertheless, his career did not suffer, and he was gazetted rear admiral in 1811. After his retirement from the British Navy, he lived in the country in the company of his wife Elizabeth. He died on a visit to London to see his doctor.

A Right Tartar

The name Bligh is now eponymous for a tyrannical, abusive commander—a "right tartar" in the terminology of the eighteenth century Royal Navy. However, by the standards of his times and profession, William Bligh was a progressive, philosophically minded officer. His care for his crew, in fact, stands out as atypical. Bligh first acquired a reputation as a navigator and cartographer on Captain Cook's third voyage (1776-1780). When he himself became a commander, he drew from Cook's ideas for maintaining crew health: regular exercise and bathing, clean laundry, and a diet that included sauerkraut and lime juice to ward off scurvy, the curse of long voyages. These measures, later officially adopted by the Royal Navy, were successful. The HMAV *Bounty* had a healthy crew. Some commentators, in fact, believe Bligh's sympathy for the sailors' lot went too far: He should not have let his men have a six-month furlough on Tahiti because it ruined their discipline.

Bligh's forty-two-day, 3,700-mile voyage in an open boat after the mutiny is famous, and he received the Society of Arts medal for the unequaled feat of navigation and leadership, but what is less known is the reason for his going to Tahiti in the first place. Sir Joseph Banks, president of the Royal Society, arranged for Bligh's trip there to acquire breadfruit trees. Bligh and his scientific assistants spent six months cultivating saplings from seeds in preparation for taking them to the West Indies. The *Bounty*'s mission failed because of the mutiny, but Bligh's next attempt, as commander of the HMS *Falcon*, succeeded, and he introduced breadfruit from Africa to Jamaica in 1793. Banks and others hoped that the breadfruit could be grown as inexpensive food for the slave population that served the sugar plantations in the West Indies. It was later planted in Brazil, too, where it became feral.

For his achievements in navigation and botany, Bligh himself was elected a fellow in the Royal Society in 1801, and he rose in rank to vice admiral in 1814. His scientific efforts in support of slavery have been eclipsed by his notorious volatile temper (biographers have suggested that he suffered from paranoia or from Tourette's syndrome) and the mutiny.

Impact

The mutiny on the *Bounty* was far from the most spectacular in the annals of the British Navy. It did not lead to any great reforms or interfere with Bligh's subsequent career. In general, Bligh's command on shipboard appears to have been well within the limits of acceptable behavior for naval officers, and he did not resort to flogging as often as many of his colleagues did. However, his well-known temper and choice of language probably help explain the reactions displayed by his subordinates.

Following the real-life events, the human drama of the mutiny interested literary fans and filmgoers of subsequent generations. A series of three books by Charles Nordhoff and James Norman Hall devoted to the mutiny became a best-seller in the 1930's, and actors such as Charles Laughton, Clark Gable, Marlon Brando, and Mel Gibson appeared in feature films either as Bligh or as Fletcher Christian. Bligh felt that his merits were never fully recognized, but, aside from Horatio Nelson and James Cook, he is remembered better than any sailor of his time.

Further Reading

Alexander, Caroline. *The Bounty: The True Story of the Mutiny on the Bounty*. New York: Viking, 2003. A well-documented account with an eighteen-page bibliography.

Dening, Greg. *Mr. Bligh's Bad Language: Passion, Power, and Theatre in the Bounty*. Cambridge, England: Cambridge University Press, 1992. Investigates the story as drama and its subsequent history in various dramatic embodiments.

Hough, Richard. *Captain Bligh and Mr. Christian: The Men and the Mutiny*. London: Hutchinson, 1972. Argues that Bligh suffered from a form of paranoia.

Kennedy, Gavin. *Bligh*. London: Duckworth, 1978. Tries to play down the spectacular aspects of the mutiny in favor of Bligh's career as naval officer.

Nordhoff, Charles, and James Norman Hall. *The Bounty Trilogy, Comprising the Three Volumes, "Mutiny on the Bounty," "Men Against the Sea," and "Pitcairn's Island."* Boston: Little, Brown, 1951. A collection of three well-known stories about Bligh's adventures; *Mutiny on the Bounty* was made into two popular film versions during the twentieth century.

Toohey, John. *Captain Bligh's Portable Nightmare*. New York: HarperCollins, 1998. Recounts Bligh's later attitudes about his earlier journey with Cook.

—*Thomas Drucker*

See also: William Kidd; John Rackham.

Tamsin Blight

Cornish witch

Born: 1798; Redruth, Cornwall, England
Died: October 6, 1856; place unknown
Also known as: Thomasina Blight; Tammy Blee (Cornish for "wolf")
Cause of notoriety: Blight was famous for her reputed magic charms and powers to heal.
Active: c. 1830-1856
Locale: Cornwall, England

Early Life

Almost nothing is known about the early life of Tamsin Blight (TAM-sihn BLIT), and her feats, if not her existence, may be merely legendary. She most likely came from a poor family, perhaps from parents who taught her how to use various methods of repelling harmful spells and charms. She began her practice as a "cunning woman" about 1830. By 1835, she was well known as a "peller," that is, as one who repels evil spirits.

Healing Career

Blight was a woman with great power to heal. In 1835 she married James (Jemmy) Thomas, a widower who also was believed to have magic powers. He and Blight moved to Helston, where they were known to have cured hundreds of people in the area. People would bring their loved ones on stretchers to visit them, and often after treatment the sick person would get up and walk away. Those who sought Blight and Thomas's healing powers came from as far away as the Scilly Isles, Hayle, St. Ives, and even Swansea. They would line up outside Blight and Thomas's door, often leaving with bags of earth, teeth, or bones taken from a grave. These were to be worn around the neck, to prevent or cure fits. Sometimes the afflicted received words written on parchment. Stones carved by the peller were also to be worn around the neck.

There was at that time a practice in the area known as ill-wishing. If someone ill-wished another, terrible things could happen to the object of the ill-wisher, and Blight and her husband were often called upon to undo an ill-wish. One legend has it that a miner scolded Blight because he thought she had taken some coals from his mine; the next day, things did not go well for the miner. He realized that he had been ill-wished and went to Blight to have the ill-wish undone. Blight was paid well for the undoing. Once a shoemaker refused to mend her shoes, saying she did not pay well. Blight ill-wished him, and eventually the shoemaker had to go out of business. People feared ill-wishing, and it was believed the practice could even cause death.

Later in life, Blight separated from her husband, apparently because of his bad reputation. There was a warrant for his arrest by the magistrates of St. Ives, but Thomas fled the area and did not return for two years. He was said to be a drunken, disgraceful, beastly fellow. His conduct was said to be outrageous, and he allegedly slept with male clients (a taboo practice that would have shocked and outraged this society). However, he was supposed to have been able to cure every human ailment as well as those of cows, pigs, and horses. He died in 1874, eighteen years later than Blight.

Impact

The story of Tamsin Blight reaffirms how strongly people in her time and locale feared unknown spirits, such as the evil eye, and ill-wishers. Blight lived at a time when very little was known about medicine, when people trusted in what would now be called magic. Blight is one in a long history of wise women who played an important part in the well-being of agricultural societies. Overall she was not an evil woman but rather one who helped people overcome their fear of evil magic.

Further Reading

Davies, Owen. *Cunning-Folk: Popular Magic in English History*. New York: Hambledon, 2003. An examination of the tradition of cunning folk and the key social roles they played in nineteenth century British life. The author estimates that there were thousands of such individuals across the British isles. Illustrated, with a detailed bibliography and an index.

Guiley, Rosemary Ellen. *The Encyclopedia of Witches and Witchcraft*. 2d ed. New York: Checkmark Books, 1999. Provides an alphabetical listing of spells, charms, and names of witches and various types of witchcraft from many parts of the world.

Jones, Kelvin I. *The Wise Woman*. Corpusty, Norwich, England: Oakmagic, 2004. Details the history of the cunning, or wise, woman throughout British social history. The author demonstrates how the wise woman was instrumental to the well-being of agricultural societies in an age when medicine was in its infancy. The work contains an exhaustive list of herbal and magical cures used by wise women and a compendium of their methods of divination.

Semmens, Jason. "'Whyler Pystry': A Breviate of the Life and Folklore-Collecting Practices of William Henry Paynter (1901-1976) of Callington, Cornwall." *Folklore* 116 (April, 2005): 75-94. Much of what is known about Blight comes from Paynter, who lived in Cornwall from 1901 to 1976. He was a member of Old Cornwall societies, a movement to collect and preserve stories or memories of the old practices of healing and of the lifting of spells.

_______. *Witch of the West*. Plymouth, England: Jason Semmens, 2005. The story of Blight (here known as Thomasina), greatest of the Cornish "cunning folk" in the nineteenth century, provides social history as well as a tale of witchcraft.

—*Winifred Whelan*

See also: Mary Butters; Margaret Jones; Lady Alice Kyteler; Florence Newton; Dolly Pentreath; Elizabeth Sawyer; Mother Shipton; Joan Wytte.

Lou Blonger

American swindler

Born: May 13, 1849; Swanton, Vermont
Died: April 20, 1924; Cañon City, Colorado
Also known as: Louis H. Belonger (birth name); the Fixer
Major offenses: Fraud and theft
Active: 1880's through 1922
Locale: Denver, Colorado
Sentence: Seven to ten years in prison

Early Life

Lou Blonger (BLAHN-guhr), who altered his surname's spelling, was the son of Simon Peter Belonger and Judith Kennedy Belonger. In 1853, Blonger moved from New England to Shullsburg, Wisconsin, with his family. Chores often disrupted his schooling. Blonger's mother died when he was ten. On May 10, 1864, Blonger enlisted as a musician for Company B of the 142nd Illinois Regiment, injuring his left leg during a march.

After being discharged, Blonger accompanied his older brother, Samuel Blonger, to several Western states. They established the Blonger Brothers partnership, operating saloons and billiard halls wherever they lived. In Albuquerque, New Mexico, Blonger assisted his brother, who was the town marshal. He submitted a disability pension application in 1887, claiming his wartime injury prevented him from working, before moving to Denver and investing in nearby mines.

Criminal Career

A skilled confidence man, Blonger began swindling people when he was a young man, stealing millions of dollars during his lifetime. He rigged gambling associated with his brother's racehorses, fixed elections, and cheated at poker. By the late 1890's, Blonger controlled most of Denver's politicians and law enforcement officials, who protected Blonger and his associates in exchange for money and favors. Blonger intimidated rival thieves unless they allied with him.

Blonger masterminded a scheme targeting tourists in Colorado, vacation areas along U.S. coasts, and Cuba. No longer directly scamming people, Blonger supervised approximately five hundred criminals who victimized wealthy tourists by befriending and convincing them to invest large amounts at Blonger's phony stock exchange. As the head swindler, Blonger received half of stolen monies.

Legal Action and Outcome

Denver district attorney Philip Van Cise, who had refused Blonger's campaign contribution, vowed to gather irrefutable evidence to prove Blonger's swindling crimes. Law-abiding citizens gave Van Cise funds to allow him to investigate Blonger independently of law officers the suspect had influenced.

Van Cise hired detectives to put recording devices in Blonger's office chandelier, secured records concerning telegrams and phone calls he received, and arranged for janitors to save his trash. After collecting sufficient proof, including Blonger's notebook filled with contact information, Van Cise directed state rangers to arrest Blonger and his cohorts.

On August 24, 1922, rangers apprehended Blonger and thirty-three of his men, holding them in a local church because Van Cise distrusted jail workers, whom Blonger might have bribed. Blonger paid his twenty-five-thousand-dollar bond and was released.

The trial for Blonger and nineteen associates charged with crimes began on February 5, 1923. After six weeks of testimony, Blonger was convicted of being a conspirator to fraud on March 28, 1923. Refusing Blonger's request for a new trial, Judge George F. Dunklee sentenced him to a seven- to ten-year prison term on June 1, 1923. Because Blonger's health had weakened, he stayed in the Denver County jail until October 18, 1923, when he was transferred to the Cañon City, Colorado, penitentiary.

Impact

Lou Blonger's criminal network affected people in the United States and internationally. Newspapers nationwide covered his trial, emphasizing Blonger's unique role as the mastermind of the largest gang of crooks in U.S. history at that time. Many of Blonger's supporters, including law enforcement personnel, were enraged by his conviction. Blonger became a popular character in local lore, which often romanticized his exploits and fabricated biographical information.

Denied both a pardon and parole, Blonger died within a year of being incarcerated. His will instructed his lawyers to continue demanding that the state supreme court contemplate an appeal to overturn Blonger's guilty verdict. Several victims, Van Cise, and the government successfully secured funds from Blonger's estate.

Further Reading

Hyde, Stephen, and Geno Zanetti, eds. *Players: Con Men, Hustlers, Gamblers, and Scam Artists*. New York: Thunder's Mouth Press, 2002. Anthology contains several nonfiction essays examining the mindset and strategies of swindlers.

Murphy, Jan. *Outlaw Tales of Colorado: True Stories of Colorado's Notorious Robbers, Rustlers, and Bandits*. Guilford, Conn.: The Globe Pequot Press, 2006. Includes a chapter featuring Blonger, detailing his confidence scheme involving a mock stock exchange and techniques his swindlers used.

Van Cise, Philip S. *Fighting the Underworld*. 1936. Reprint. New York: Greenwood Press, 1968. Written by the district attorney who prosecuted Blonger, with photos of people, sites, and evidence. Includes glossary and appendix of investigators, financial supporters, and Blonger's crooks.

—*Elizabeth D. Schafer*

See also: John R. Brinkley; Charles Ponzi; Alexandre Stavisky.

Anthony Blunt

British art historian and spy for the Russians

Born: September 26, 1907; Bournemouth, Hampshire, England

Died: March 26, 1983; London, England

Also known as: Anthony Frederick Blunt (full name)

Cause of notoriety: An admitted spy for the Soviets, Blunt later cooperated with British authorities and was granted immunity from prosecution.

Active: 1937-1983

Locale: London, England

Early Life

Anthony Frederick Blunt (bluhnt) was born at Holy Trinity Vicarage, Bournemouth, Hampshire, England. He was the third son of an Anglican clergyman, the Reverend Arthur Stanley Vaughan Blunt, and his mother was Hilda Violet, née Master, a distant relative of Queen Mary. He was educated at Marlborough College, a prestigious boarding school, but also spent time in Paris, France, where his father had become chaplain to the British embassy. It is there that he fell in love with French culture, especially French art. He won a scholarship to Trinity College, Cambridge, where he gained first-class honors in mathematics, French, and German.

While at Cambridge University, he became a member of the "Cambridge Apostles," a semisecret society, where he became attracted to Guy Burgess, who was gay, like Blunt, and an avid communist, later to become one of the most productive spies for the Soviets, alongside two other Cambridge graduates, Donald Duart Maclean and Kim Philby.

After graduation, Blunt taught French briefly before election as a fellow of Trinity College for a dissertation on the history of art theory. He was also becoming increasingly committed to Marxism, reflected in art reviews that were being published in the *The Spectator*. In spring, 1937, he was introduced to Theo Maly, a Hungarian communist, a former priest, and now an agent for the Narodnyi Komissariat Vnutrennikh Del (NKVD), a Soviet government department and the forerunner of the KGB. He was asked to become a "talent-spotter," which he agreed to do. Blunt recruited an American, Michael Straight, and several others before the London branch of the NKVD was withdrawn.

Espionage Career

In summer, 1937, Blunt obtained a post at the prestigious Warburg Institute in London, where he met a number of Jewish refugee art professors and historians who greatly influenced him. At the outbreak of war, he joined the military and was appointed to Military Intelligence in France. Following the withdrawal of British forces, he was recruited into MI5, a branch of British intelligence responsible for internal affairs, and assigned surveillance duties with foreign embassies in London. Shortly after, the NKVD cell was reestablished, and Blunt agreed to pass on to it all he knew about MI5. Blunt had access to Ultra, the German code-breaking operation at Bletchley Park and one of Britain's most sensitive secrets. He rose to become chief assistant to Guy Liddell, the chief of MI5, helping him restructure its surveillance system. In all, Blunt passed to the Soviets some one thousand documents (as compared with four thousand from Burgess), although KGB archives later revealed not all documents were even translated, let alone acted upon.

At the end of the war in 1945, Blunt left MI5 to resume his art career and could pass on only gossip to the KGB. In 1951, Burgess and Maclean had to flee to Moscow, and Blunt's minder, Yuri Modin, urged Blunt to leave with them, as it appears Blunt had helped to arrange their escape and certainly had been seen with them. Blunt, however, felt his cover was strong enough to resist discovery and refused. By this point, he had become director of the Courtauld Institute of Art and professor of art history at London University and was regularly publishing books, especially on the French painter Nicholas Poussin. In 1952, he was appointed Surveyor of the King's (later the Queen's) Pictures, an honorary post, and in 1956, he was knighted for his services to art.

During the 1950's, Blunt had been questioned some eleven times about Burgess and Maclean by the security services. The stress of such scrutiny led Blunt to heavy drinking. However, it was not until 1964 that Blunt's cover collapsed. Straight had gone to the U.S. Federal Bureau of Investigations (FBI) in 1963, told them of his espionage activities, and stated he was ready to testify against Blunt. MI5 went to Blunt and offered him immunity, with the authority of the attorney general, if he would tell them all he knew about the KGB. Blunt did so and named other spies he had recruited, such as John Cairncross.

Several former MI5 offices felt aggrieved that Blunt was not prosecuted and indeed, was living prestigiously. They leaked his story to Andrew Boyle, a writer with an intelligence background, and in 1979, he published a novel titled *The Climate of Treason*, in which a character called Maurice resembled Blunt. Questions were asked about a "fourth man" in the House of Commons of Prime Minister Margaret Thatcher; she acknowledged that Blunt was indeed the fourth man.

Initially, no legal action occurred. However, Blunt was immediately stripped of his knighthood, only the second person in British history to suffer this disgrace. He was also dismissed as Surveyor of the Queen's Pictures. By 1974, he had already retired from the Courtauld. His partner committed suicide, and three years later, Blunt himself died, shunned and alone. It seems the main guilt he had felt was in deceiving his friends.

Impact

One of the reasons for the cover-up of Blunt's spying had been to retain confidence in the British intelligence. With his exposure, the search for a "fifth man" of the Cambridge Five began. Intelligence secrets suddenly became much more public, leading to the notorious trial of Peter Wright, a former MI5 agent, for publishing a book, *Spycatcher* (1987). The fact that Blunt had been inside the royal household caused special alarm, though it was established that he had never had access to anything confidential there. Blunt's own considerable reputation as an art historian was sullied. Most people were unable to comprehend how such an established figure could have gone undetected for so long and why the intelligence service had not exposed him years before.

Further Reading

Boyle, Andrew. *The Climate of Treason*. London: Hutchinson, 1979. The novel that originally sparked the search for the fourth man, after the exposure of Burgess, Maclean, and Philby.

Carter, Miranda. *Anthony Blunt: His Lives*. London: Pan, 2001. A thorough biography of Blunt that seeks to understand the double life he led and the toll it took on him as a person.

Modin, Yuri, et al. *My Five Cambridge Friends: Blunt, MacLean, Philby, Burgess, and Cairncross, by Their KGB Controller*. New York: Farrar, Strauss and Giroux, 1995. An insider's view of the Cambridge Five.

Stafford, David, and Rhodri Jeffreys-Jones. *American-British-Canadian Intelligence Relationships, 1939-2000*. London: Routledge, 2000. A comprehensive survey of Western intelligence, putting the Blunt affair in its full context.

Straight, Michael. *After Long Silence*. London: Collins, 1983. The man who exposed Anthony Blunt tells the story of the Cambridge spy network from the inside.

—David Barratt

See also: Guy Burgess; John Cairncross; Donald Duart Maclean; Kim Philby.

Ivan Boesky

American investment banker

Born: March 6, 1937; Detroit, Michigan
Also known as: Ivan Frederick Boesky (full name)
Major offense: Insider trading
Active: 1980's
Locale: Manhattan, New York
Sentence: Three and a half years in prison; released after two years

Early Life

Ivan Boesky (BOH-skee) was born in Detroit. His father, William Boesky, was a Jewish immigrant from Russia who had arrived in the United States in 1912. The elder Boesky became prosperous through opening a chain of bars, known as the Brass Rails, in Detroit. After graduating from Mumford High in central Detroit, Ivan Boesky took classes at Wayne State University, the University of Michigan, and Eastern Michigan College. Without having earned a degree, he went to Iran; it is unclear what he did there.

After returning to the United States, Boesky was able to enroll at Detroit College of Law in 1959, despite his lack of a college degree. In 1964, after five years of off-and-on study, he obtained a law degree, but he was unable to find a job with a law firm. His father then made him a partner with the Brass Rails.

In 1960, while studying law, Boesky met Seema Silberstein, the daughter of Detroit real estate developer Ben Silberstein. After Boesky's graduation the two married, and the bride's father enabled the couple to move to New York and take an apartment on Park Avenue.

Boesky decided to try his hand at arbitrage, or trading in stock.

He worked for a number of firms as a stock trader and became known for reckless dealing. In 1975, he struck out on his own and opened Ivan F. Boesky Company with $700,000 borrowed from his in-laws. A difficult and demanding employer, he refused to give his employees days off and insisted on their dedication to his firm. He was also a hard worker, committed to making his firm a success and to earning the greatest possible profits for himself.

Criminal Career

In 1981, Boesky sold his interest in Ivan F. Boesky Company, which became Bedford Partners. He then organized the Ivan F. Boesky Corporation. The new arbitrage corporation came into existence at a time when corporate mergers and takeoffs were rapidly increasing. Stock prices for companies that were targeted for buyouts or takeovers by other companies would go up, as the effort to buy enough stock to take over a company increased the demand for the stock. Boesky's corporation specialized in purchasing stock in companies destined for leveraged buyouts (buyouts on borrowed money) and hostile takeovers (takeovers intended to sell off the assets of the intended company). He prospered at this activity and in 1985 published the book *Merger Mania*, which purported to tell readers how to know when a merger was approaching and how to profit from it.

According to Boesky's book, his success was a matter of legitimate analysis that made it possible to detect impending mergers. Investigators at the U.S. Securities and Exchange Commission (SEC) were suspicious, though. Boesky was repeatedly able to buy up shares of stock before mergers were officially announced, suggesting that he was not merely good at prediction but that he received information from people working at companies involved in takeovers. This is known as "insider trading," and it is illegal because it is manipulating and controlling the market and taking advantage of investors who are not insiders.

What Is "Insider Trading"?

According to the U.S. Securities Exchange Commission, the term "insider trading" is defined as follows:

"Insider trading" is a term that most investors have heard and usually associate with illegal conduct. But the term actually includes both legal and illegal conduct. The legal version is when corporate insiders—officers, directors, and employees—buy and sell stock in their own companies. When corporate insiders trade in their own securities, they must report their trades to the SEC. . . .

Illegal insider trading refers generally to buying or selling a security, in breach of a fiduciary duty or other relationship of trust and confidence, while in possession of material, nonpublic information about the security. Insider trading violations may also include "tipping" such information, securities trading by the person "tipped," and securities trading by those who misappropriate such information. . . .

Because insider trading undermines investor confidence in the fairness and integrity of the securities markets, the SEC has treated the detection and prosecution of insider trading violations as one of its enforcement priorities. The SEC adopted new Rules 10b5-1 and 10b5-2 to resolve two insider trading issues where the courts have disagreed.

- Rule 10b5-1 provides that a person trades on the basis of material nonpublic information if a trader is "aware" of the material nonpublic information when making the purchase or sale. The rule also sets forth several affirmative defenses or exceptions to liability. The rule permits persons to trade in certain specified circumstances where it is clear that the information they are aware of is not a factor in the decision to trade, such as pursuant to a pre-existing plan, contract, or instruction that was made in good faith.
- Rule 10b5-2 clarifies how the misappropriation theory applies to certain nonbusiness relationships. This rule provides that a person receiving confidential information under circumstances specified in the rule would owe a duty of trust or confidence and thus could be liable under the misappropriation theory.

Source: Securities Exchange Commission, http://www.sec.gov.

Legal Action and Outcome

Boesky's downfall began in May, 1985, when the SEC charged Dennis Levine of the company Drexel Burham Lambert with insider trading and learned that Boesky had been paying Levine for insider information. Boesky agreed to cooperate with the SEC and allowed it to tape his conversations with other insiders. This deal with the SEC enabled Boesky to sell off some of his assets before his legal problems became public. When he was officially charged, such sales made him even more notorious, because it appeared that he had managed to minimize penalties for his crimes. As the investigation deepened, it brought down some of Boesky's best-

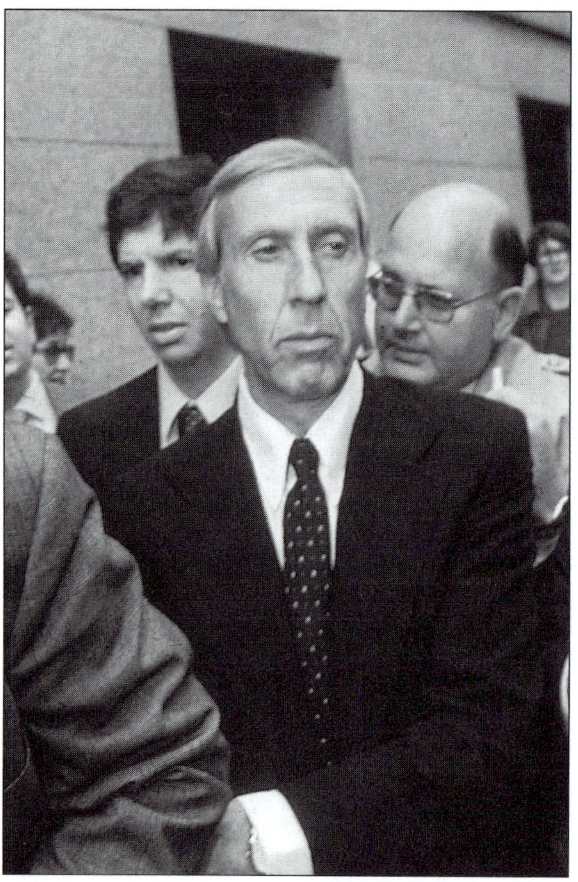

Ivan Boesky. (AP/Wide World Photos)

known associates, including Michael Milken, known as the junk bond king because he pioneered investments in relatively high-risk stocks.

On November 14, 1986, Boesky reached a settlement with federal prosecutors. He agreed to plead guilty in return for a fine of one hundred million dollars, a ban from future trading in securities, and a sentence to a minimum security prison. He served twenty-two months of his three-year prison term before being released. His wife Seema divorced him after his imprisonment.

Impact

Ivan Boesky's case rocked Wall Street. It brought down some of the most important and widely known figures in the investment world, and November 14 is still referred to as "Boesky Day" on Wall Street. Before the case, insider trading was illegal but rarely prosecuted. Afterward, it appeared that firms would be held to higher standards.

Boesky also had an impact on popular culture and on the popular perception of Wall Street. His success made him into a celebrity and a notorious figure. In 1986, he made headlines when he gave a speech at the University of California at Berkeley in which he declared that greed was healthy and a good thing. This speech helped to make him the model for the ruthless investor Gordon Gecko in the film *Wall Street* in 1987. In that film, the Boesky-like figure came to symbolize the moral emptiness and corruption of the profit-seeking 1980's.

Further Reading

Boesky, Ivan. *Merger Mania: Arbitrage: Wall Street's Best Kept Money-Making Secret.* New York: Holt, Rinehart, and Winston, 1985. Boesky's own story of his success before his downfall, written as a how-to book for investors.

Bruck, Connie. *Predators' Ball: The Inside Story of Drexel Burnham and the Rise of the Junk Bond Raiders.* New York: Simon & Schuster, 1988. Tells the story of the Drexel Burnham case, focusing on Michael Milken, and describes Milken's dealings with Boesky.

Levine, Dennis B., with William Hoffer. *Inside Out: An Insider's Account of Wall Street.* New York: Putnam, 1991. An account of the insider trading scandal by one of the Wall Street businessmen who gave Boesky information. Contains descriptions of Boesky's dealings and character.

Stewart, James B. *Den of Thieves.* New York: Simon & Schuster, 1992. A detailed but readable history of the investigation into the Wall Street insider trading ring of Ivan Boesky, Michael Milken, Dennis Levine, and others.

—*Carl L. Bankston III*

See also: Martin Frankel; Dennis Levine; Michael Milken.

Jean-Bédel Bokassa

President (1966-1976) and emperor (1976-1979) of the Central African Republic

Born: February 22, 1921; Bobangui, Oubangui-Chari, French Equatorial Africa (now in Central African Republic)

Died: November 3, 1996; Bangui, Central African Republic

Also known as: Bokassa I; Ogre of Bereng; the Apostle

Major offenses: Treason, murder, cannibalism, and embezzlement

Active: 1966-1979

Locale: Bangui, Central African Republic

Sentence: Death (later commuted to life imprisonment, then reduced to ten years with hard labor); granted amnesty in 1993

Early Life

Jean-Bédel Bokassa (zhahn beh-dehl boh-KAH-sah) was the son of a village chief. When he was six years old, his father was assassinated by the French, and his mother committed suicide a week later. Thus, after becoming an orphan, he became a ward of Christian missionaries. At the outbreak of World War II in 1939, Bokassa joined the French colonial army at the age of eighteen. He was among thousands of African troops who took active part in World War II on the side of the Free French. At the end of the war, he served with the French army in Indochina and Algeria, earning the Légion d'Honneur (legion of honor) and Croix de Guerre (war cross). He ended his career in the French army in 1961 with the rank of captain and returned to his newly independent country. In 1964, his cousin, President David Dacko, appointed him the army chief of staff. In December of 1965, however, Bokassa overthrew the government and assumed the role of president.

Political Career

Shortly after taking power, Bokassa adopted a populist policy when he promised to abolish the bourgeoisie. Soon after that, he began a career of erratic and dictatorial policies and actions. In 1972, he declared himself president for life and in 1974 marshal of the republic. On December 4, 1976, in a highly extravagant and colorful ceremony, he proclaimed a Central African Empire and a year later crowned himself Emperor Bokassa I. His cruel approach to rule soon became known worldwide. In 1979, international outcry followed his massacre of schoolchildren who protested being forced to wear uniforms (which were produced by Bokassa's factory and sold by his retail outlet). Bokassa was alleged to have eaten some of the victims of that massacre.

Bokassa sought further notoriety by associating himself with notable figures and enacting strange stunts for publicity. At one point, he claimed to have been made an apostle of the Roman Catholic Church by Pope John Paul II. He also briefly converted to Islam after fraternizing with Colonel Muammar al-Qaddafi of Libya. Furthermore, he gained attention for a lavish wedding he orchestrated. He had been married to a Vietnamese woman in 1953 whom he had abandoned along with their daughter to return to Europe. Years later, in his search for his long-lost daughter, two women claiming to be Martine Nguyen, the name of Bokassa's daughter, arrived in

Jean-Bédel Bokassa. (AP/Wide World Photos)

Bangui—one an impostor, the other the genuine daughter. However, rather than imprison the impostor, Bokassa adopted her. His two "daughters" were later auctioned off as brides at a colorful double marriage ceremony in the Bangui cathedral.

In 1979 and while he was on a state visit to Libya, Bokassa was removed from power in a coup, code-named Barracuda, which was engineered with French support. Dacko was reinstated as president. Bokassa then began an ignominious life in exile. He was initially refused entry into France after his fall from power and instead went to Côte d'Ivoire, where he resided for four years before being allowed back into France in order to take possession of his house at Haudricourt, west of Paris.

Legal Action and Outcome

In October, 1986, Bokassa unexpectedly returned to his country and was promptly arrested. He was tried for atrocities that he had committed during his fourteen years in power, including cannibalism and mass murder. French soldiers who had raided his villa following his overthrow had found cadavers of some of his political opponents in freezers near his kitchen and at the bottom of swimming pools. Bokassa also stood accused of participating in the murder of the schoolchildren in 1979. He was found guilty of treason, murder, cannibalism, and embezzlement and was sentenced to death. The sentence was later commuted to life imprisonment and then further reduced to ten years with hard labor. His palaces in the country were confiscated, and his châteaux in France was seized.

In 1993, he was granted amnesty by President Andre Kolingba and released from prison. He lived out the rest of his life in the ruins of his former palace in Bangui. He succumbed to a heart attack at the age of seventy-five, leaving behind a total of fifty-five children borne by seventeen wives.

Impact

Jean-Bédel Bokassa's extravagance ruined the economy of the Central African Republic and launched his country on the path of acute corruption, odium, ridicule, and disrepute. His reign would consistently be remembered for his bizarre cruelty and violence, as well as for the gruesome trail of blood in his alleged murders and cannibalism of political opponents. Association with Bokassa proved to be a liability for some foreign politicians. For example, the failure of French president Valéry Giscard d'Estaing in the 1981 presidential election was partly linked to his admission that he had accepted a gift of diamonds from the African dictator. He was also alleged to have enjoyed free elephant-hunting trips from Bokassa.

Further Reading

Decalo, Samuel. *Psychoses of Power: African Personal Dictatorships*. 2d ed. Gainesville: Florida Academic Press, 1998. A solid work about the aberrant and demented rule of some of Africa's dictators.

Riccardo, Orizio. *Talk of the Devil: Encounters with Seven Dictators*. London: Secker and Warburg, 2003. A profound and carefully crafted work on dictators whose careers ended in ignominy. The special focus on personalities accused of cannibalism is particularly fascinating.

Titley, E. Brian. *Dark Age: The Political Odyssey of Emperor Bokassa*. Montreal, Canada: McGill-Queen's University Press, 1997. An excellent political biography that details the stewardship of the Central African Republic dictator.

—*Olutayo C. Adesina*

See also: Sani Abacha; Idi Amin; Omar al-Bashir; Samuel K. Doe; Mengistu Haile Mariam; Mobutu Sese Seko; Robert Mugabe; Muammar al-Qaddafi; Muhammad Siad Barre; Charles Taylor.

Boniface VIII

Roman Catholic pope (r. 1294-1303)

Born: c. 1235; probably Anagni, Papal States (now in Italy)
Died: October 11, 1303; Rome, Papal States (now in Italy)
Also known as: Benedict Caetani (birth name)
Cause of notoriety: Boniface VIII was an assertive pope who advocated papal superiority. His dispute with the French king produced a posthumous show trial, where critics depicted him as greedy, heretical, and worthy of hell.
Active: 1294-1303
Locale: Rome, Papal States

Early Life

Benedict Caetani, the future Boniface VIII (BAHN-uh-fihs), was born around 1235, probably in Anagni, a hill town outside Rome. Trained as a canon lawyer, he spent more than forty years in papal service. On December 24, 1294, Benedict was elected pope of the Roman Catholic Church. He succeeded Celestine V, an eighty-year-old hermit who proved ill-suited for papal responsibilities and resigned after six months. Boniface's critics argued that he forced Celestine's resignation. Because of his fear of church schism, Boniface held Celestine in a castle against his will. Celestine died a year later in papal custody.

Papal Career

Upon assuming office, Boniface waged war on the Spiritual Franciscans, a religious order that supported absolute poverty, as well as Celestine. In August, 1296, Boniface declared them heretical. In Rome, he struggled continuously with members of the Colonna family, who were vocal critics of his administration. When members of the Colonna family refused to submit after organizing a mugging of the papal train in 1297, Boniface excommunicated them. He hired another member of the family to raze Colonna properties and completely destroyed the town of Palestrina, sowing salt into the ground. His declaration of the first papal jubilee year in 1300 and the promise of a plenary indulgence brought unprecedented pilgrims to Rome. He was one of the first popes to place images of himself around Rome; a contemporary portrait of him declaring the papal jubilee year still stands in the Lateran Church in Rome.

Boniface VIII is best known for his political struggles with the era's major rulers. His relationship with the French king Philip IV the Fair proved the most notorious. Exacerbated by both men's strong personalities, tensions centered on clerical taxation. Entering into war, the French king turned toward the clergy for financial support. In previous centuries, the clergy supported the Crusades. However, this was a secular war, and the French clergy and monks lodged a complaint with Boniface. In 1296, Boniface issued his papal bull *Clericis laicos*, in which he forbade secular taxation of the clergy without papal permission. Although Boniface later capitulated and canonized Philip's grandfather Louis IX in 1297, the situation turned grim when Philip imprisoned and tried a French bishop for treason in 1301. This assertion of secular power fueled another papal bull; in response, the first session of the Estates-General met in 1302, issuing a strong condemnation against Boniface.

Boniface VIII. (Library of Congress)

The medieval church's most notorious statement on papal power subsequently was issued. In *Unam Sanctam* (1302), Boniface stated that every human creature was subject to the pope. If temporal power erred, it must be judged by spiritual powers; however, only God judged the Papacy. In 1303, Boniface excommunicated Philip IV the Fair.

The aggressive Philip responded with mudslinging, accusing Boniface of heresy, blasphemy, simony, and sodomy. On September 7, 1303, Philip's men stormed Boniface's palace at Anagni, seized Boniface for a few days, and demanded his resignation. The local population intervened, yet thereafter Boniface remained in ill health. He died one month later in Rome.

Clericis laicos: Heavy Burdens (1296)

In 1296, Boniface issued his papal bull Clericis laicos, *in which he forbade secular taxation of the clergy without papal permission.*

Antiquity teaches us that laymen are in a high degree hostile to the clergy, a fact which also the experiences of the present times declare and make manifest; inasmuch as, not content within their own bounds, they strive after what is forbidden, and loose the reins in pursuit of what is unlawful. Nor have they the prudence to consider that all jurisdiction is denied them over the clergy—over both the persons and the goods of ecclesiastics. On the prelates of the churches and on ecclesiastical persons, monastic and secular, they impose heavy burdens, tax them and declare levies upon them. . . . And, with grief do we mention it, some prelates of the churches . . . do acquiesce, not so much rashly, as improvidently, in the abuses of such persons. We therefore, wishing to put a stop to such iniquitous acts, by the counsel of our brothers, of the apostolic authority, have decreed:

. . . persons, of whatever pre-eminence, condition or standing who shall impose, exact or receive such payments, or shall any where arrest, seize or presume to take possession of the belongings of churches or eccelsiastical persons which are deposited in the sacred buildings, or shall order them to be arrested, seized or taken possession of, or shall receive them when taken possession of . . . shall incur, by the act itself, the sentence of excommunication. Corporations, moreover, which shall be guilty in these matters, we place under the eccelesiastical interdict. . . . Notwithstanding any privileges whatever—under whatever tenor, form, or manner or conception of words—that have been granted to emperors, kings, and other persons mentioned above; as to which privileges we will that, against what we have here laid down, they in no wise avail any person or persons. Let no man at all, then, infringe this page of our constitution, prohibition or decree, or, with rash daring, act counter to it; but if any one shall presume to attempt this, he shall know that he is about to incur the indignation of Almighty God. . . .

Source: From *Select Historical Documents of the Middle Ages*, translated by Ernest F. Henderson (London: G. Bell and Sons, 1921).

Impact

Benedict XI succeeded Boniface but remained pope only for eight months before his death. Benedict was succeeded by Clement V, a Frenchman. Philip used his persuasion with the new pope to argue that Boniface should be tried posthumously. Although Clement initiated several delays and finally negotiated dropping the charges, the inquest—the Avignon trial (1310-1311)—and rumors that circulated throughout Europe contributed to the loss of prestige for the late medieval church.

Although Boniface VIII argued vigorously for papal supremacy, the medieval papacy lost ground against rising European nationalism and state government. The posthumous trial of Boniface indicates this loss of papal power and prestige. Writers—such as Dante in his *La divina commedia* (c. 1320, 3 vols; *The Divine Comedy*, 1802) and Giovanni Boccaccio in his *Decameron: O, Prencipe Galetto* (1349-1351; *The Decameron*, 1620)—used literature to critique Boniface and the late medieval Papacy.

Further Reading

Boase, T. S. R. *Boniface VIII*. London: Constable, 1933. The first significant biography of Boniface.

Menache, Sophia. *Clement V*. Cambridge, England: Cambridge University Press, 2003. Chapter 5 highlights Boniface's trial.

Paravicini-Bagliani, Agostino. *The Pope's Body*. Chicago: University of Chicago Press, 2000. Examines Boniface's use of imagery in his reign and in death.

Wood, Charles T., ed. *Philip the Fair and Boniface VIII: State vs. Papacy*. New York: Krieger, 1976. Addresses major issues in the church-state debate of the times.

—*Shelley Wolbrink*

See also: Alexander VI; Clement VII; Leo X; Urban VI.

Stede Bonnet

Barbadian pirate

Born: 1688; Barbados, British West Indies
Died: December 10, 1718; White Point, South Carolina
Also known as: Gentleman Pirate; Captain Thomas
Major offenses: Robbery and murder
Active: 1717-1718
Locale: The Caribbean and the Atlantic Coast
Sentence: Death by hanging

Early Life

Stede Bonnet (steed BON-eht), the son of Edward and Sarah Bonnet, was born on Barbados in 1688, prior to his christening being registered on July 29, 1688. His grandfather, Thomas Bonnet, had immigrated to Barbados, establishing a plantation. When Bonnet was approximately six years old, his father died. Guardians guided the estate of Bonnet and his two younger sisters while they matured.

In 1709, Bonnet married Mary Allamby. They resided on his sugarcane plantation near Bridgetown, the island's capital, and had three sons and one daughter. Bonnet became a major in the island's militia. He enjoyed a privileged, leisurely life. At taverns, Bonnet listened to privateers who docked at Bridgetown's harbor. He admired them, yearning to experience sea adventures like they described.

Criminal Career

In spring, 1717, Bonnet bought a ship, the *Revenge*, and decided to become a pirate. He secured his crew in taverns, requiring them to sign an agreement that he devised. Bonnet told people he planned to pursue trading when he left Barbados that summer. Once his pirating career commenced, his crew plundered and occasionally burned vessels along the Atlantic Coast. In September, 1717, a Spanish ship fired at the *Revenge*, wounding Bonnet. While Bonnet arranged for repairs in the Bahamas, he encountered Edward Teach (also known as Blackbeard). Considering Bonnet inept, Teach seized the *Revenge* several months later, forcing Bonnet aboard his vessel. In June, 1718, when Teach received a royal pardon, Bonnet regained the *Revenge*. Bonnet also secured a pardon and approval for privateering against Spanish vessels near the Virgin Islands.

Rescuing some of Teach's abandoned crew, Bonnet decided to resume piracy again, calling himself Captain Thomas and his ship the *Royal James*. On July 29, 1718, Bonnet captured the *Fortune* in Delaware Bay. Two days later, he seized the *Francis*. In August, Bonnet ordered his crew to sail up the Cape Fear River to careen his ship, remove barnacles, and fix leaks.

Enraged by piracy, South Carolina governor Robert Johnson approved Colonel William Rhett's request to pursue Bonnet. Rhett and his forces sighted Bonnet's ship by September 26, 1718. River sandbars trapped Bonnet's and Rhett's vessels while they fought, creating vulnerable targets. After the tide freed Rhett's ships, Bonnet surrendered.

Legal Action and Outcome

Rhett delivered Bonnet to authorities in Charleston on October 3. Officials confined Bonnet in the provost marshal's home, but he escaped on October 24. While Bonnet was a fugitive, his crew's trial began on October 28. A grand jury indicted them for two counts of piracy involving the *Francis* and *Fortune*. The trial concluded on November 5, with most of Bonnet's men receiving death sentences.

Rhett caught Bonnet on nearby Sullivan's Island, returning him to Charleston by November 6. Officials hanged twenty-two crew members two days later. Bonnet's trial began on November 10. Bonnet denied accusations that he seized the *Francis*, claiming he had been sleeping. Nonetheless, the court found him guilty. The next day, Bonnet pleaded guilty to piracy involving the *Fortune*. On November 12, Judge Nicholas Trott sentenced him to death for piracy and eighteen colonial casualties occurring during his initial capture.

Many locals, including Rhett, unsuccessfully attempted to secure clemency for Bonnet, who also wrote letters to the governor pleading for compassion. Officials hanged a stunned, silent Bonnet on December 10 and buried him in the marsh four days after his death.

Impact

Stede Bonnet posed a hazard to commercial and economic stability for colonial and international trade. Officials worried about disruptions and the loss of income from stolen and ruined goods. Although most friends expressed sadness that Bonnet deserted his family for selfish indulgences, many Barbadians ostracized Bonnet's wife and children. Writers often romanticized Bonnet's piracy, suggesting that he was the first pirate to make victims walk the plank. Several modern historical markers remind people of Bonnet's crimes.

Further Reading

Butler, Lindley S. *Pirates, Privateers, and Rebel Raiders of the Carolina Coast*. Chapel Hill: University of North Carolina Press, 2000. Chapter devoted to Bonnet provides one of the most accurate depictions of him based on primary records.

Pendered, Norman. *Stede Bonnet: Gentleman Pirate*. Manteo, N.C.: Times Printing, 1977. Includes details of Bonnet's family history and life in Barbados, which are unavailable in other accounts.

Seitz, Don C. *Under the Black Flag: Exploits of the Most Notorious Pirates*. Mineola, N.Y.: Dover, 2002. Section chronicling Bonnet compares his crimes to those of pirates active in the southern colonies and how their actions affected Bonnet.

—*Elizabeth D. Schafer*

See also: Samuel Bellamy; Anne Bonny; Sir Henry Morgan; John Rackham; Mary Read; Bartholomew Roberts; Edward Teach; Dominique You.

William H. Bonney

Frontier-era American outlaw

Born: November 23, 1859; New York, New York

Died: July 14, 1881; Fort Sumner, New Mexico Territory

Also known as: Billy the Kid; Billy Antrim; Kid Antrim; Billy Bonney; Henry McCarty (birth name)

Major offenses: Murder and cattle theft

Active: 1874-1881

Locale: New Mexico Territory

Sentence: Death; escaped prison while awaiting execution and was shot to death three months later

Early Life

William H. Bonney (BAW-nee) was born Henry McCarty in 1859 to Irish immigrants in New York City's slums. Not much is known about his early childhood. Sources suggest that young Henry lived with his widowed mother, Catherine, and his younger brother, Joe, in Indianapolis, Indiana, during the Civil War. In 1870 the family, along with Catherine's future husband, William Antrim, relocated to Wichita, Kansas, where Catherine operated a laundry. Diagnosed with tuberculosis in 1871, Catherine again moved her family, eventually landing in Santa Fe, New Mexico, where she married Antrim on March 1, 1873. The Antrims settled in Silver City, a mining community in the southwestern part of the territory. Henry, now known as Henry Antrim, attended school and reportedly was an ordinary teenager. When his mother died in September, 1874, however, the future outlaw's life changed direction.

William H. Bonney. (Library of Congress)

A MAN MORE SINNED AGAINST

"I don't blame you for writing of me as you have. You had to believe other stories, but then I don't know if any one would believe anything good of me anyway," Billy the Kid told a Las Vegas (New Mexico) *Gazette* reporter in 1880. The rumors, exaggerations, and lies about him had already spread. He knew the score. Still, the newspaper gave him a friendly description in 1881:

> He is about five feet eight or nine inches tall, slightly built and lithe, weighing about 140; a frank, open countenance, looking like a school boy, with the traditional silky fuzz on his upper lip; clear blue eyes, with a roguish snap about them; light hair and complexion. He is, in all, quite a handsome looking fellow, the only imperfection being two prominent front teeth slightly protruding like squirrel's teeth, and he has agreeable and winning ways.

In fact, far from the fiery-tempered sociopath that some accounts made him, Billy the Kid was widely liked, even by his foes in the Lincoln County War. He was said to be easygoing, cool under stress, and regularly cheerful. The historian- politician Miguel Antonio Otero, Jr. (1859-1944) wrote in his biography *The Real Billy the Kid* (Houston: Arte Público Press, 1998), "I have been told that Billy had an ungovernable temper; however, I never saw evidences of it. He was always in a pleasant humor when I saw him—laughing, sprightly, and good natured." As a young man, Otero was on the train that took Billy the Kid to jail. They talked at length. Otero admitted:

> I liked the Kid very much . . . and long before we reached Santa Fe, nothing would have pleased me more than to witness his escape. He had his share of good qualities and was very pleasant. He had a reputation for being considerate of the old, the young, and the poor; he was loyal to his friends and above all, loved his mother devotedly. He was unfortunate in starting life, and became a victim of circumstances. In looking back to my first meeting with Billy the Kid, my impressions were most favorable and I can honestly say that he was a man more sinned against than sinning.

CRIMINAL CAREER

Now lacking parental guidance, Henry began associating with rough characters. Just a year after Catherine's death, he found himself facing theft charges after stealing a bundle of clothing from a Chinese laundry. Not wanting to stand trial, Henry escaped through the local jail's chimney and made his way into Arizona.

Now nicknamed "The Kid" because of his youth and diminutive size, Henry worked as a teamster and cowboy around Camp Grant. During his two years in Arizona, Henry honed his skills as a gunman and horseman. While historians often describe the gunfighter as a cheerful and well-liked young man, nobody disagreed that he had a short and violent temper. That temper exploded on August 17, 1877, when seventeen-year-old Henry shot and killed Frank "Windy" Cahill, a much older and stronger man who had made a habit of verbally and physically abusing the teenager.

Now wanted for murder in Arizona, Henry escaped to New Mexico under the alias William "Billy" Bonney. Billy ended up in Lincoln County, New Mexico, where he worked as a cowboy for Englishman John Tunstall. In 1878, the county was dominated by the mercantile monopoly of Lawrence Murphy and James Dolan. Challenging the Murphy-Dolan alliance were Tunstall and a Scotsman named Alexander McSween, who sought to outbid their rivals for government contracts. Billy soon became involved in the Lincoln County War (1878-1879), in which Tunstall was killed by assassins from the Murphy-Dolan faction. During the war Billy rode with the "Regulators," a group of Tunstall employees who sought to avenge the death of their employer. For the following year, the two sides engaged in deadly retaliatory warfare. Billy's skills with a gun and his reckless bravado served the Tunstall-McSween faction well during the conflict. On March 9, 1878, the Regulators captured and killed Frank Baker and William Morton, both suspects in Tunstall's murder.

On April 1, 1878, Billy and several Regulators ambushed and killed Sheriff William Brady, an ally of the Murphy-Dolan faction. Just three days later, the Regulators battled Buckshot Roberts, a bounty hunter hired by the opposition, at Blazer's Saw Mill, about forty miles outside Lincoln. After a fierce battle, Dick Brewer, the leader of the Regulators, and Roberts lay dead or dying. The Lincoln County War climaxed in a five-day battle (July 15-19, 1878) in which McSween and several Regulators were also killed. On the final day of the battle, Billy led a gallant escape from a burning building under heavy gunfire.

LEGAL ACTION AND OUTCOME

In the years after the Lincoln County War, Billy teetered back and forth between ranching and rustling cattle. While the territorial governor pardoned most of the participants in the conflict, Billy was indicted for killing Sheriff Brady. He was arrested by the new sheriff, Pat Garrett, in December, 1880. After a questionable trial, the Kid was convicted of murder and sentenced to death. Just as he had several times before, Billy cheated his sentence before it could be carried out. On April 28, 1881, he killed two guards and escaped. The Kid's days were still numbered, as lawmen relentlessly hunted him. Finally, on July 14, 1881, Garrett tracked Billy to Fort Sumner, where he surprised the twenty-one-year-old outlaw under the cover of darkness. "¿Quién es? ¿Quién es? (Who is it?)" Billy asked as he heard someone enter the room where he slept. Without answering, Garrett fired two shots, killing Billy the Kid instantly.

Impact

Within months of William H. Bonney's death, books and serialized stories began creating the Billy the Kid legend. During the twentieth century, Hollywood movies solidified his status as an American icon. Some described him as a swaggering, homicidal maniac. Others portrayed him as an American Robin Hood who became an outlaw to protect the innocent and the helpless. Somewhere in between these extremes is the historic Billy the Kid. He came of age in a rough frontier world where violence was commonplace. He killed when he thought necessary but not nearly as often as stories suggest. Legend credits Billy the Kid with twenty-one killings. History, however, can confirm only four killings by the Kid's own hand and five or six in which he participated as a member of the Regulators.

Further Reading

Burns, Walter Noble. *The Saga of Billy the Kid.* New York: Grosset and Dunlap, 1926. A vivid and romanticized biography that helped create the image of Billy the Kid as an American Robin Hood.

O'Neal, Bill. *Encyclopedia of Western Gunfighters.* Norman: University of Oklahoma Press, 1979. This valuable collection of 587 gunfighter biographies provides a biography of Billy the Kid along with short descriptions of his criminal exploits and gunfights.

Tuska, Jon. *Billy the Kid: His Life and Legend.* Reprint. Albuquerque: University of New Mexico Press, 1997. A thoroughly researched book that examines fallacies and inaccuracies in previous books, novels, and movies.

Utley, Robert. *Billy the Kid: A Short and Violent Life.* Lincoln: University of Nebraska Press, 1989. An authoritative and objective account of Billy the Kid, written by an eminent Western historian.

—*Mark R. Ellis*

See also: Apache Kid; Tom Bell; Curly Bill Brocius; Butch Cassidy; Bob Dalton; Emmett Dalton; Bill Doolin; John Wesley Hardin; Doc Holliday; Jesse James; Tom Ketchum; Harry Longabaugh; Bill Longley; Joaquín Murieta; Johnny Ringo; Robin Hood; Belle Starr; Henry Starr; Hank Vaughan; Cole Younger.

Jules Bonnot

French car thief and murderer

Born: October 14, 1876; Pont-de-Roide, France
Died: April 28, 1912; Paris, France
Cause of notoriety: Bonnot was the most experienced member of the anarchist Bonnot gang, which committed violent crimes in France and Belgium.
Active: 1911-1912
Locale: Paris, France, and Belgium

Early Life

When Jules Bonnot (jool bon-oh) was five, his mother died, and he was put in the custody of his grandmother and father. During his teen years he committed various crimes, including assaulting a police officer, and was imprisoned twice. At age twenty-one, he was conscripted into the French army, where he served as an auto mechanic for three years and became an expert rifleman.

In 1901 he married Sophie-Louise Burdet and traveled to get work as a mechanic in Switzerland and in France. He then worked in factories and eventually joined the syndicalist movement, which advocated workers' ruling the workplace. At the time there was widespread unemployment. In 1907 Bonnot's wife left him, and by 1911 Bonnot could not find any work at all.

Anarchist Career

After joining an anarchist illegalist group in 1911, Bonnot contributed his knowledge of automobiles and his experience as a thief, while the anarchists provided an ideological justification for their continued crimes. The illegalists believed in crime as a lifestyle and that illegal acts required no moral justification. The notion of theft as a liberating act of class warfare was promoted in *L'Anarchie*, a weekly magazine published in Paris amid that city's great social and class conflict.

The gang members made national headlines when they robbed the Society General bank in December, 1911. They used a stolen automobile to flee the crime scene, and the incident was the first documented case of thieves using a getaway car. Although the group's founder was Raymond Callemin and its leader was Octave Garnier, the newspapers dubbed them the "Bonnot gang" after Bonnot, brandishing an automatic weapon, made a dramatic appearance at the office of the *Petit Parisien* newspaper. Other gang members included the writer Kibaltchiche, who later became Victor Serge, advocate of Russian Communism. Eventually, there were twenty members, mostly French and unemployed.

The gang committed an escalating series of crimes, including the murder and robbery of a wealthy man and his maid on January 2, 1912. French police started investigating anarchist organizations and made one arrest, while the gang moved into Belgium, shooting a policeman there, and continuing their robberies. They targeted expensive vehicles, enhancing their image as revolutionaries stealing from the rich.

In late March they shot three cashiers and an automobile driver during another high-profile bank robbery, flaunting their use of high-powered vehicles to escape the ill-equipped police. The government responded by increasing funding for law enforcement and by posting a reward for information. During the following weeks, some of the gang members were arrested, but Bonnot managed to avoid capture. He had become the most wanted criminal in France. He killed another policeman after almost being captured on April 24. Four days later, Bonnot was finally cornered in a house near Paris by a group of hundreds, including soldiers, firemen, and private citizens as well as police. Dynamite was used to destroy his cover, and after more gunfire, Bonnot was severely wounded. He died after being moved by the police, who wanted to discourage mob hysteria.

Impact

During his criminal career, Jules Bonnot was considered public enemy number one. His "motor bandits" gang was the most notorious French anarchist and illegalist group. In Europe, they were the first to use a getaway car in a bank robbery, and they used new technology such as repeating rifles. Their daring exploits made headline news. However, their legacy of violence also became the justification for a massive expansion of law enforcement powers and a fierce crackdown on all anarchist organizations. As a result, in August, 1913, French anarchist Communists distanced themselves from illegalist behavior and formed the Anarchist Communist Federation (FCA), which declared individualist anarchism and illegalism as capitalistic.

However, to the French proletariat, Bonnot and his gang remained folk heroes, comparable to Robin Hood and his Merrie Men. Souvenirs with portraits of gang members were sold. In popular culture, they became legendary, "tragic bandits" who inspired books, poetry, a movie, and musical recordings.

In 1969, the film *Bonnot's Gang* (*La Bande à Bonnot*) was released. Directed by Philippe Fourastié, the movie featured Bruno Cremer as Bonnot. Pino Cacucci's 2006 crime thriller, *Without a Glimmer of Remorse: The Remarkable Story of Sir Arthur Conan Doyle's Chauffeur*, is a fictional narrative about Bonnot.

In 2004, Milanese songwriter Giangilberto Monti released *La Belle Époque della Banda Bonnot*, a CD based on songs by Boris Vian and Monti's radio play about Bonnot. The play won Swiss National Radio's Prix Suisse in 2004. French pop star Joe Dassin recorded songs about the Bonnot gang on numerous albums released from 1986 to 2006.

Further Reading

Mell, Ezra Brett. *The Truth About the Bonnot Gang*. London: Coptic Press, 1968. A concise but detailed account of Jules Bonnot and anarchism, the Bonnot gang cult, and the economic and political implications of the gang's activities. Illustrated.

Parry, Richard. *The Bonnot Gang: The Story of the French Illegalists*. London: Rebel Press, 1987. The most complete and comprehensive study of the Bonnot gang—their lives, crimes, philosophy, and legacy. Index and bibliography.

Serge, Victor. *Memoirs of a Revolutionary*. Translated by Peter Sedgwick. Iowa City: University of Iowa Press, 2002. A close supporter of the Bonnot gang, the early anarchist Serge provides an intimate portrait of the group. Originally an outspoken advocate of illegalism, in these memoirs he criticizes the nihilistic direction of illegalism. Index and bibliography.

Skirda, Alexandre. *Facing the Enemy: A History of Anarchist Organization from Proudhon to May, 1968*. Oakland, Calif.: AK Press, 2002. Based on decades of scholarly research, this acclaimed work includes an analysis of the criminal and individualistic activities of the Bonnot gang. Illustrated; includes bibliography.

Varias, Alexander. *Paris and the Anarchists: Aesthetes and Subversives During the Fin-de-siècle.* New York: St. Martin's Press, 1996. This comprehensive analysis of anarchism in Paris in the late nineteenth century describes the class divisions, anarchist concerns, and terrorism that influenced the illegalists and the Bonnot gang. Illustrated, including maps.

—Alice Myers

See also: Cartouche; Jacques Mesrine.

Anne Bonny

Irish pirate

Born: c. 1697; Kinsale, County Cork, Ireland
Died: After 1720; place unknown
Also known as: Anne Cormac (birth name); Bonn
Major offenses: Piracy, assault, and theft on the high seas
Active: Early 1700's-1720
Locale: Around Cuba, Hispaniola, Jamaica, and throughout the Caribbean
Sentence: Death by hanging; temporarily suspended because of her pregnancy; no record exists of her actual execution

Early Life

Born in Kinsale, County Cork, Ireland, Anne Cormac, later known as Anne Bonny (BAH-nee), was the daughter of a wealthy lawyer and the family's maid. Although few historical facts are known, some sort of scandal resulted, and Anne, her father, and her mother sailed to the United States and settled in South Carolina. Anne met and married James Bonny, an occasional pirate, and they moved to New Providence (now Nassau) in the Bahamas. Anne subsequently left for sea with another pirate, John "Calico Jack" Rackham, becoming his mistress. She maintained a disguise as a man and called herself Bonn because male pirates considered it bad luck to sail with a woman.

Pirating Career

Bonny was reported to have had a violent temper, and there are many tales of her courage and daring, as well as her proficiency with sword and pistols, which gained her much notoriety. During this time, she discovered another woman, Mary Read, who was disguised as a man and sailed with the crew. She became friends with Read, and both built reputations as daring and dangerous pirates. The pirates were pursued at the time by the governor of the Bahamas, Captain Woodes Rogers, who was commissioned by the British government to rid the Caribbean of the pirate stronghold in New Providence. In late October of 1720, Captain Jonathan Barnet of the British Navy captured Rackham's ship and took the crew captive, including Bonny. They were taken to Jamaica, under Governor Nicholas Lawes, to stand trial and pleaded not guilty.

Legal Action and Outcome

Bonney and Read, along with Rackham's entire crew, were found guilty and sentenced to hang. All were hanged except for the two women, who "pled their bellies" because they were pregnant—it was illegal to execute a pregnant woman at the time. While Read apparently died in prison, Bonny simply disappeared, and no more was heard of her. She was rumored to have received a reprieve, and there is no record of her execution.

Impact

Among a number of female pirates who masqueraded as men, Anne Bonny and Mary Read were perhaps the best known. Bonny might have been an early feminist, rebelling against the oppressive role of women at the time, or simply a wild soul seeking adventure. She was known as courageous, bloodthirsty, and daring and became a pirate legend.

Further Reading

Canfield, R. "Something's Mizzen: Anne Bonny, Mary Read, Polly, and Female Counter Roles on the Imperialist Stage." *South Atlantic Review* 66, no. 2 (2001): 45-63. Explores the roles of Bonny and other women who dressed and fought as men and as pirates in the context of imperialist ambitions in the Caribbean.

Cordingly, David. *Under the Black Flag: The Romance and the Reality of Life Among the Pirates.* New York: Random House, 1995. Contains notes on historical sources, trial transcripts, and records. Discusses the case of Bonny and describes the life and times both of women who went to sea on merchant ships or with the navy and of the few who became pirates.

Defoe, Daniel. *A General History of the Robberies and Murders of the Most Notorious Pyrates*. Edited by Manuel Schonhorn. Mineola, N.Y.: Dover, 1999. This is a reprint of the classic work from 1725 written about pirates, including Bonny, and based on both historical records and unsubstantiated information.

—*Martha Oehmke Loustaunau*

See also: ʿAruj; Samuel Bellamy; Maurycy Beniowski; Charlotte de Berry; Stede Bonnet; William Dampier; William Kidd; Jean Laffite; Sir Henry Morgan; Grace O'Malley; John Quelch; John Rackham; Mary Read; Bartholomew Roberts; Edward Teach; Rachel Wall; Dominique You.

John Wilkes Booth

American assassin of President Abraham Lincoln

Born: May 10, 1838; near Bel Air, Maryland
Died: April 26, 1865; near Bowling Green, Virginia
Cause of notoriety: Booth assassinated President Abraham Lincoln soon after the end of the Civil War.
Active: 1865
Locale: Washington, D.C.

Early Life

John Wilkes Booth (jahn wihlks bewth) was one of ten children of the noted tragic actor Junius Brutus Booth. The younger Booth made his first theatrical appearance at seventeen and soon had established a solid reputation as an interpreter of many leading roles in the plays of William Shakespeare, particularly that of Romeo in *Romeo and Juliet* (c. 1595). Muscular, dark-haired, and incredibly handsome, Booth was perfect for the part.

Although he seldom prepared well for his roles, his innate ability and resplendent style carried him through his performances. Having mastered most of the major male roles in Shakespeare's plays, Booth toured the nation performing them. His good looks and outstanding talent made him irresistible to women.

Criminal Career

When the Civil War erupted in 1861, most of Booth's family supported the Union. Booth, on the other hand, was violently pro-Confederate. He deplored Abraham Lincoln and, by 1864, had devised a scheme to kidnap the president and hold him hostage, to be ransomed only on the release of Confederate prisoners of war.

When this plot failed to materialize, Booth devised another scheme. As the Union victory in the Civil War appeared inevitable, he met with several conspirators at Mary Surratt's boardinghouse in Washington, D.C., and with them outlined his plan to assassinate the president,

John Wilkes Booth. (Library of Congress)

Booth's Four Chances

John Wilkes Booth succeeded in assassinating President Lincoln after passing up three earlier opportunities, all which came to him because of his own soaring celebrity. He began acting in 1855. Five years later he was a star, his acting career flourishing. He was making $20,000 a year, and although based in Richmond, Virginia, he was in demand everywhere.

Booth was appearing as Duke Pescara in *The Apostate* when president-elect Lincoln attended a performance in New York while on his way to Washington, D.C. Booth, whose sympathies lay with the South, had not yet developed his deep loathing for Lincoln, so the president was only another audience member to him then. That changed once the Civil War started. Booth's hatred was swift and implacable. By the time that the president again saw him perform—on November 9, 1863—Booth could not disguise his feelings. This time the play was *The Marble Heart*, and the performance took place at Ford's Theater in Washington, D.C. Booth portrayed Raphael. A member of the president's party, Mary Clay, later recounted the evening:

> In the theater President and Mrs. Lincoln, Miss Sallie Clay and I, Mr. Nicolay and Mr. Hay, occupied the same box which the year after saw Mr. Lincoln slain by Booth. I do not recall the play, but Wilkes Booth played the part of the villain. The box was right on the stage, with a railing around it. Mr. Lincoln sat next to the rail, I next to Mrs. Lincoln, Miss Sallie Clay and the other gentlemen farther around. Twice Booth in uttering disagreeable threats in the play came very near and put his finger close to Mr. Lincoln's face; when he came a third time I was impressed by it, and said, "Mr. Lincoln, he looks as if he meant that for you." "Well," he said, "he does look pretty sharp at me, doesn't he?" At the same theater, the next April, Wilkes Booth shot our dear President.

Mary Clay misspoke the date by a year, and by then Booth had again come perilously close to Lincoln. He attended the second inaugural ball on March 4, 1865, with his fiancée, Lucy Hale. Afterward he said to a friend, "What an excellent chance I had to kill the President, if I had wished, on inauguration day!" Forty-one days later, he succeeded.

the vice president, and Lincoln's cabinet members. Booth, assuming the responsibility for killing Lincoln himself, wanted these assassinations to occur almost simultaneously.

On Good Friday, 1865, Booth learned from the manager of Ford's Theater, where he was well known and had often acted, that the president was expected to attend the evening performance of Tom Taylor's *Our American Cousin* (pr. 1865). The Lincolns were ambivalent about attending the play, but the president craved relaxation after an exhausting week. Mrs. Lincoln invited General and Mrs. Ulysses S. Grant to join them, but the Grants were about to leave town, so they declined their invitation.

Booth was determined to kill Lincoln that night. Early in the evening, he fortified himself with brandy at a bar near Ford's Theater. After the play began, he entered the theater and burst into the president's box, where he shot Lincoln, firing a single bullet from his derringer into the president's brain. An accomplice attacked Secretary of State William H. Seward at about the same time and almost killed him. Plans to assassinate Vice President Andrew Johnson went awry.

In the confusion following his shooting of Lincoln, Booth jumped onto the stage, but he became entangled in some drapery, causing him to land at an awkward angle and break his leg. Despite this injury, Booth limped from the theater, where David E. Herold joined him. The two rode to Maryland, stopping along the way to have Dr. Samuel Mudd set Booth's broken leg.

The fugitives hid out in Maryland for several days before making their way to Richard Garrett's farm near Bowling Green, Virginia. Meanwhile, Secretary of War Edwin M. Stanton launched a massive hunt to track down the fugitives. It was eleven days after the shooting and ten days after President Lincoln's death on April 15, 1865, that government agents tracked Booth to the farm where he was hiding.

With the farm surrounded, Herold, who had retreated into Garrett's tobacco barn with Booth, surrendered. Attempting to flush Booth from the barn, his pursuers set fire to the building. A shot rang out. It remains unclear whether Booth shot himself or Sergeant Boston Corbett fired the shot. At any rate, Booth, now dead, clearly could not be tried for Lincoln's assassination.

Legal Action and Outcome

Although John Wilkes Booth's death placed him beyond the scope of the law, various conspirators were arrested and, in May, 1865, those most obviously involved were brought to trial. Many were given long prison sentences, and, on July 6, after a speedy trial that was a mockery of justice, four were sentenced to be hanged. The sentence was carried out the following day before swarms of spectators gathered at Washington's Old Arsenal to witness the executions.

Impact

One impact of Lincoln's assassination, the first to befall an American president, was that presidential security was very much increased to prevent a recurrence of such a devastating event. A more historically important impact, however, was that Lincoln's death turned him into a martyr and greatly enhanced the nation's appreciation of him both as a man and as president. Scorned by many during his first term of office and reviled by many after his election to a second term, Lincoln assumed a hallowed position in American history. In most polls that measure the popularity of the American presidents, Lincoln's name leads the list.

Further Reading

Clark, Champ. *The Assassination: Death of the President.* Alexandria, Va.: Time/Life, 1987. An accessible account of Lincoln's assassination written for general audiences.

Clarke, Asia Booth. *John Wilkes Booth: A Sister's Memoir.* Edited and with an introduction by Terry Alford. Jackson: University of Mississippi Press, 1996. Booth's sister provides details about her brother's early life and upbringing. Somewhat biased but nevertheless valuable, as is the penetrating introduction.

Goodrich, Thomas. *The Darkest Dawn: Lincoln, Booth, and the Great American Tragedy.* Bloomington: Indiana University Press, 2005. Part 2 focuses on the actual assassination and serves as an excellent presentation.

Hanchett, William. *The Lincoln Murder Conspiracy.* Urbana: University of Illinois Press, 1986. Hanchett reviews the varied threads of the conspiracy aimed at eliminating Lincoln, his vice president, and members of his cabinet.

Higham, Charles. *Murdering Mr. Lincoln: A New Detection of the Nineteenth Century's Most Famous Case.* Beverly Hills, Calif.: New Millennium Press, 2004. Detailed information about plans to assassinate Lincoln with special emphasis in chapter 8 on the actual assassination.

—*R. Baird Shuman*

See also: Leon Czolgosz; Charles Julius Guiteau; Lee Harvey Oswald; Lewis Powell; Mary Surratt.

Lizzie Borden

Accused American murderer

Born: July 19, 1860; Fall River, Massachusetts
Died: June 1, 1927; Fall River, Massachusetts
Also known as: Lizzie Andrew Borden (full name); Lizbeth of Maplecroft; Lizbeth Andrews Borden
Cause of notoriety: Borden was tried and acquitted for the murders of her father and stepmother.
Active: 1892
Locale: Fall River, Massachusetts

Early Life

Lizzie Andrew Borden (LIH-zee AN-droo BOHR-dehn) was born to Andrew J. Borden and his wife, Sarah Morse, on July 19, 1860, in Fall River, Massachusetts. Her father had hoped for a boy, accounting for Lizzie's unusual middle name. She had an older sister, Emma, with whom she remained close throughout much of her life. Sarah Borden died when Lizzie was a small child of about two or three years old. A few years afterward, Mr. Borden married Abby Durfee Gray, a woman in her late thirties.

Lizzie called her stepmother "Mother" for many years and then alternately called her Mrs. Borden. She remained distant from both of her parents after her father

Lizzie Borden. (The Granger Collection, New York)

If Not Lizzie, Who?

More than a century following Lizzie Borden's murder acquittal, crime writers, Fall River residents, conspiracy buffs, and distinguished jurists continued to publish arguments for or against Borden's guilt. Some insist that she killed her father and stepmother to get control of the family wealth; others feel she did it while deranged in an epileptic fit. Those that think her to be innocent, if only partly, sometimes fix on other suspects.

- One theory has Lizzie's sister Emma as the murderer, with Lizzie's connivance. Again, the motive is envy over the portion of their father's estate dedicated to their stepmother in his will. Emma pretends to be out for the day and sneaks back for the murders. Lizzie allows herself to be arrested, and the sisters support each other in the cover-up.
- A second theory indicts Bridget, the Irish maid. Angered at having to wash windows on a blistering hot day, she quarrels with Mrs. Borden and later kills her. Later still, she kills Mr. Borden to prevent his reporting her earlier argument with his wife. A variation on this theory again has Lizzie as a co-conspirator who covers up the crime.
- An even stranger theory involves an illegitimate son of Mr. Borden, William. Mentally incapacitated and bitter at his father's treatment of him—and perhaps egged on by his half sisters—he does the killing. His sisters, their Uncle John Morse, the attending physician, and their lawyer all work together to protect William.
- From there, the speculations grow even more bizarre: Uncle Morse, the physician, and even a Chinese Sunday school student of Borden are all considered.
- The mystery endures into the twenty-first century. What most analysts of the case do agree upon, however, is that Borden's defense attorneys were far more skillful than the state's prosecutor. They made sure that two pieces of crucial evidence—Borden's conflicting testimony during the inquest and a report of her attempt to buy prussic acid (a poison) before the murders—were excluded from the trial. A friendly jury did not harm her chances either.

purchased property for Abby, despite his buying properties of equal value for Lizzie and Emma. This purchase, to which the rift is attributed, had seemingly indicated to both Lizzie and Emma that their father went to an extreme and expensive length to please his wife.

Lizzie had red hair and prominent pale eyes and liked to have her picture taken. In spite of the difficulties of her relationship with her father and stepmother in later years, Lizzie and her father were said to be very close.

Lizzie's father had begun his professional career as an undertaker in Fall River. He became a bank president and an astute businessman. At the time of his death, Mr. Borden was worth an estimated $250,000—a huge sum in 1892. Despite his acquired wealth, the family continued to live in the "unfashionable" part of Fall River. The children were reared in a home that was small, without running water or electricity and using food that was past its prime as a result of a lack of refrigeration. Such conditions are reported to have been against Lizzie's liking.

Like many women of her day, Lizzie had no formal career of which to speak. However, she busied herself with many social and religious-based organizations. She was an active member and secretary-treasurer for the Central Congregational Church, a member of the Ladies' Fruit and Flower Mission, a member of the Women's Christian Temperance Union, a board member of the Good Samaritan Charity Hospital, and she taught a Sunday school class for Chinese children.

The Murders

The Borden parents were both murdered at their home, killed by blows to the head with an ax. Lizzie was charged with the murders, which took place on August 4, 1892. At the time of the crime, her sister, Emma, was away visiting friends, and the family home was occupied by Lizzie, her parents, housekeeper Bridget Sullivan, and her biological mother's brother, John Morse, who was visiting from out of town.

Lizzie was suspected of having committed the murders for several reasons, including her conflicting answers at the inquest, her supposed lack of despair at her parents' deaths, her acknowledgment of the strain between her and her parents, and her attempted purchase of prussic acid. Others, such as members of the Fall River community, did not believe that a young woman from her background could have committed such a crime. Her sister and the church championed her innocence, while others testified against her.

Legal Action and Outcome

An inquest, preliminary hearing, and trial were held. Lizzie never took the stand in her own defense. However, she was acquitted of all charges, and her acquittal was initially cheered by the townspeople. This reception was short-lived, however, and Lizzie was to face great isolation from her community. She purchased a new home, added an "s" to her middle name, and became known as

Lizbeth of Maplecroft. She spent her years traveling to New York and Boston and befriending animals and people of the theater.

Lizzie died on June 1, 1927. She was followed in death, nine days later, by Emma. She and her sister were buried alongside their parents, stepmother, and baby sister, who had died shortly after birth. Much of Lizzie's money was left to the care of animals.

Impact

Much, but not all, of what has been written about Lizzie Borden states that she indeed was guilty of ax murders that resulted from ten blows to her father and twenty to her stepmother—numbers that vary in the verse that children have subsequently sung about the case:

> Lizzie Borden took an ax
> And gave her mother forty whacks.
> When she saw what she had done
> She gave her father forty-one.

The controversy and mystery surrounding Lizzie and the Fall River murders continued to fascinate people into the twenty-first century, as evidenced by the continual writing of books, a Web site, and a museum, all of which introduce new generations to the case.

Further Reading

Axlrod-Contrada, Joan. *The Lizzie Borden "Ax Murder" Trial: A Headline Court Case.* Berkeley Heights, N.J.: Enslow, 2000. Provides photographs of the main participants, transcript excerpts, and the known facts surrounding the murders. Also included are characterizations of the time period of the murders, along with a chronology of events.

Avery, Donald R. "The Case of Lizzie Borden." In *The Press on Trial: Crimes and Trials as Media Events*, edited by Lloyd Chiasson, Jr. Westport, Conn.: Greenwood Press. 1997. The chapter provides the reader with a detailed look at the specifics of the Borden case, as well as the role such media outlets (primarily newspapers and reporters) played both in the case and in shaping the public's view of the crime.

Masterton, Willie L. *Lizzie Didn't Do It!* Boston: Brandon, 2000. The author provides newspaper headlines, photographs, character sketches, and the coroner's statement in his discussion of the Borden case. Uses modern-day forensic analyses, as well as the identification of the likely assailant, to determine that Lizzie Borden was innocent of the crimes.

—*Nancy A. Horton*

See also: Marie Hilley.

Cesare Borgia

Italian duke and son of Pope Alexander VI

Born: 1475 or 1476; Rome, Papal States (now in Italy)
Died: March 12, 1507; Viana, Navarre (now in Spain)
Also known as: Archbishop of Valencia; Duke of Romagna; Duke of Valentinois
Cause of notoriety: Borgia strengthened the power of the papacy through cunning military strategy and murder plots. He was also accused of having incestuous relations with his sister, Lucrezia Borgia, allegations that were unproven.
Active: 1492-1507
Locale: Rome, Papal States (now in Italy)

Early Life

Cesare Borgia (CHEH-zash-reh BOHR-zhyah) was the illegitimate son of Pope Alexander VI (Rodrigo Borgia) and his mistress Vannozza dei Catanei. He was educated first at the Sapienza in Perugia and later at the University of Pisa. In 1492, at age seventeen, Cesare's ecclesiastic career was launched when he was appointed protonotary (the official keeper of canonization records and signatory to papal bull) of the Roman Catholic Church and bishop of Pampeluna. In the same year, his father ascended the papal throne and appointed him archbishop of Valencia. A year later, the pope gave Cesare the cardinalate.

In 1492, Cesare's sister Lucrezia had married Giovanni Sforza, and in 1497 this marriage was annulled, reportedly because of nonconsummation. Sforza, appalled at the fact that his manhood had been questioned, accused the Borgias of engaging in incestuous relations, allegations that were never proven. In that same year, Cesare's brother Giovanni, duke of Gandia, was murdered, and rumors began that Cesare had killed him out of jealousy. In 1498, Cesare renounced his ecclesiastical dignities and began his political career.

POLITICAL CAREER

Even before Cesare had renounced his religious career, Alexander VI began negotiations for Cesare's marriage to Carlotta of Aragon, the daughter of Federico, king of Naples. In 1498, Lucrezia married Alfonso, duke of Bisceglie, the illegitimate son of the former king of Naples, in order to persuade Carlotta's father to accept the marriage to Cesare. However, Federico refused, exclaiming that he would not have his daughter wed "a priest, the bastard son of a priest." In 1499, Cesare instead married Charlotte d'Albret, sister of the king of Navarre, and was appointed duke of Valentinois by Louis XII of France. Being of no further use to the Borgias, in 1500 the duke of Bisceglie was murdered, and Cesare was blamed for his death.

Having forged an alliance with Louis XII, Cesare was involved in the capture of Milan by the French. Alexander VI saw this as an opportunity to retake the fiefs of the Holy See in the Romagna region, which had repudiated papal authority, refused to pay their tributes, and on occasion even bore arms against the Church. Cesare carried out the mission with great success, capturing Imola, Forli, and Cesena between 1499 and 1500, and Rimini, Pesaro, Faenza, Urbino, Camerino, Piombino, and Elba between 1500 and 1502.

In 1501, Alexander VI appointed Cesare duke of Romagna. Though his administration of Romagna was praised by contemporaries as a model for good government and equitable treatment to all, Cesare was also capable of great cruelty. When, in 1501, he took Faenza after the surrender of its lord, the eighteen-year-old Astorre Manfredi, Cesare promised that he would not harm the young man. However, he broke his word when, after taking Astorre to Rome as his prisoner, he had him murdered. In 1502, Astorre's body was found in the Tiber River with a rock tied around his neck. Later that year, Cesare had two of his captains, Vitellozzo Vitelli and Oliverotto da Fermo, strangled for participating in a conspiracy against him.

Cesare was also known for his love affairs. After the fall of Forli, he took prisoner its ruler, Countess Caterina Sforza Riario, and is said to have had a love affair with her. Unlike his male prisoners, Caterina was eventually freed. While in Imola, ten of Cesare's soldiers abducted Dorotea Caracciolo, wife of Gianbattista Caracciolo, a Venetian army captain. An envoy was sent to Cesare demanding Dorotea's release, and soon rumors began that she had been a willing participant in her abduction and was having an affair with Cesare. Correspondence sent by Dorotea's husband and the Venetian ambassador to the Holy See finally persuaded Cesare to release the woman, who immediately took shelter at a convent for fear of retaliation from her husband.

By 1502, the king of France, Louis XII, had turned his back on Cesare, considerably diminishing Cesare's power. The death of Alexander VI in 1503 was also a major factor in Cesare's demise. Pius III was elected as Alexander's successor, appointing Cesare the Gonfaloniere of the Church, a prestigious communal post. However, the favor of the new pope did not prevent Cesare's loss of the territories that he conquered, with the exception of Cesena, Forli, Faenza, and Imola.

Pius III died suddenly, and Giuliano della Rovere, an enemy of the Borgias, assumed the throne as Pope Julius II in 1503, a move that cost Cesare dearly. He was forced to resign his strongholds in the Romagna and flee from Rome

CRUELTY AND CLEMENCY

Although one of Cesare Borgia's contemporaries, Andrea Boccaccio, described him as possessing a "marked genius and a charming personality . . . merry and fond of society," this good humor did not go to Borgia's head. Niccolò Macchiavelli, in his famous treatise on leadership The Prince *(1513)—which many scholars consider to be modeled after Cesare Borgia—notes that Borgia set a good example for princes: He would not allow compassion to undermine his power:*

Coming now to the other qualities mentioned above, I say that every prince ought to desire to be considered clement and not cruel. Nevertheless he ought to take care not to misuse this clemency. Cesare Borgia was considered cruel; notwithstanding, his cruelty reconciled the Romagna, unified it, and restored it to peace and loyalty. And if this be rightly considered, he will be seen to have been much more merciful than the Florentine people, who, to avoid a reputation for cruelty, permitted Pistoia to be destroyed. Therefore a prince, so long as he keeps his subjects united and loyal, ought not to mind the reproach of cruelty; because with a few examples he will be more merciful than those who, through too much mercy, allow disorders to arise, from which follow murders or robberies; for these are wont to injure the whole people, whilst those executions which originate with a prince offend the individual only.

Source: Niccolò Machiavelli, *The Prince*, translated by W. K. Marriott (New York: E. P. Dutton, 1908).

for fear that his life was in danger. Louis XII deprived him of his French dominions; only the king of Navarre offered him refuge. Cesare was killed on March 12, 1507, while fighting for the king against rebel troops.

Impact

Cesare Borgia possessed great political skill and was an able military strategist. By forging proper alliances and removing any obstacles along the way, even through murder, he was able to recover for the papacy the territories that had once avowed their fealty. In doing so, Cesare strengthened the power of the papacy and filled its coffers. His military prowess earned him the admiration of Florentine philosopher Niccolò Machiavelli, who, inspired by Cesare's actions, wrote *Il principe* (wr. 1513, pb. 1532; *The Prince*, 1640), a guide on how to conquer and then retain power over a Renaissance state.

Baldassare Castiglione, a diplomat and Renaissance author, also wrote about Cesare in his *Il libro del cortegiano* (1528; *The Book of the Courtier*, 1561). However, unlike Machiavelli, who praised Cesare's political prowess, Castiglione instead spoke of Cesare's gallantry and good looks. Machiavelli and Castiglione's works paint a picture of Cesare as a man with a complex personality: handsome and gallant but also hungry for power and capable of committing the most vicious acts.

Further Reading

Bradford, Sarah. *Phoenix: Cesare Borgia, His Life and Times*. London: Phoenix Press, 2001. Examines Cesare's life, including the accusations of treachery, incest, and murder levied against him.

Mallett, Michael Edward. *The Borgias; The Rise and Fall of a Renaissance Dynasty*. New York: Barnes and Noble, 1969. The authority on the history of the Borgia family. Includes extensive discussion of Cesare's political career.

Sabatini, Rafael. *The Life of Cesare Borgia of France*. Rockville, Md.: Wildside Press, 2003. A sympathetic account of Cesare's life. Argues that accusations of murder, incest, and other such acts exist only because it was Cesare's enemies who wrote the histories. Devotes a great deal of effort to dissipate those accusations as merely unfounded rumors.

—*Lilian H. Zirpolo*

See also: Alexander VI; Lucrezia Borgia.

Lucrezia Borgia

Italian noblewoman

Born: April 18, 1480; Subiaco, Papal States (now in Italy)

Died: June 24, 1519; Ferrara, Papal States (now in Italy)

Also known as: Lucretia Borgia; Duchess of Ferrara

Cause of notoriety: Borgia was accused of having incestuous relations, participation in assassination plots, and illicit affairs.

Active: 1492-1519

Locale: Papal States (now in Italy)

Early Life

Lucrezia Borgia (lew-CREE-shah BOHR-zhyah) was the daughter of Pope Alexander VI and his mistress Vannozza dei Catanei, with whom he fathered four children. Lucrezia lived with her mother until the age of three, when her father, then Cardinal Rodrigo Borgia, took her to Rome to live with his cousin, Adriana de Mila, the widow of Ludovico Orsini, from one of the oldest and most prestigious Roman families. Adriana brought members of the nobility into her home with whom Lucrezia developed close ties. Lucrezia became particularly fond of Giulia Farnese, the wife of Orsino Orsini, whom she considered an elder sister.

Lucrezia's early life was changed dramatically when, in 1492, her father was elected to the papal throne as Pope Alexander VI. She was only twelve at the time, and she, Adriana, and Giulia moved into a newly built palace that connected with St. Peter's Basilica through a private doorway. Her father could visit any time he pleased, and soon Giulia became his mistress. This marked the beginning of a life for Lucrezia surrounded by scandal. Surprisingly, her relationship with Giulia did not change.

Career

In 1492, at the age of twelve, Lucrezia was betrothed to Giovanni Sforza of Pesaro. The marriage, meant to strengthen papal relations with Milan, then ruled by the Sforza, was annulled in 1497 supposedly because of nonconsummation. Sforza, who felt his manhood ques-

Lucrezia: A Mixed Reputation

Lucrezia Borgia's evil reputation probably stems from the manipulations of men in her life, as suggested by Alexander VI's Master of Ceremonies, Johann Burchard, in a contemporary account. Borchard's assertions about incest, however, are now believed untrustworthy:

[Pope Alexander VI's] daughter had just turned seventeen and was at the height of her beauty. We now know that he was, in fact, her lover. Here, however, the tale darkens. Romans had scarcely absorbed the news that the father lusted for his daughter when they learned even more. Lucrezia was said to be unavailable to her father because she was already deeply involved in another incestuous relationship, or relationships—a triangular entanglement with both her handsome brothers. The difficulty, it was whispered, was that although she enjoyed coupling with both of them, each, jealous of the other, wanted his sister for himself.

Niccolò Cagnolo, on the other hand, found her to have a good disposition and a zest for life:

She is of middle height and graceful of form; her face is rather long, as is her nose; her hair is golden, her eyes gray, her mouth rather large, the teeth brilliantly white, her bosom smooth and white and admirably proportioned. Her whole being exudes good humor and gaiety.

Sources: Johannes Burchard, *Johannis Burchardi Argentinensis capelle pontificie sacrorum rituum magistri diarium, sive Rerum urbanarum commentarii (1483-1506)*, edited L. Thuasne (Paris: E. Leroux, 1883-1885). Niccolò Cagnolo quoted in Ivan Cloulas, *The Borgias*, translated by Gilda Roberts (New York: F. Watts, 1989).

tioned, accused the Borgias of engaging in incest. He claimed that Alexander VI wanted Lucrezia to divorce so that he could have her for himself. Soon, rumors spread that she was also having incestuous relations with her brothers Cesare and Giovanni. The Neapolitan poet Jacopo Sannazzaro in fact called Lucrezia the "daughter, bride, and daughter-in-law of the pope." The fact that Lucrezia's brother Cesare involved her in acts of violence did not help her reputation. In one incident, Cesare shot at unarmed criminals with a crossbow from a balcony in the Vatican while Lucrezia stood by his side and watched.

After the divorce, Lucrezia fled to the convent of San Sisto, Rome. Rumors began that she had been impregnated by Pedro Calderón, one of the pope's messengers. While her pregnancy was never confirmed, a baby did suddenly appear among the Borgias, and Calderón's body was eventually found floating in the Tiber River, the murder undoubtedly committed to ensure his silence. The child's paternity has been given variously to Calderón, Cesare Borgia, Giovanni Borgia, and the pope.

In 1498, Lucrezia was married to Alfonso, duke of Bisceglie, the illegitimate son of Alfonso II, former king of Naples. This was a political maneuver to bring Cesare closer to his goal of marrying Carlotta, daughter of Federico, the current Neapolitan king. Federico, however, refused Cesare's offer, and Cesare instead married Charlotte, sister of the king of Navarre. No longer of any use to the Borgias, Alfonso was brutally attacked on the steps of St. Peter's Basilica in 1500. A month later, he was strangled in his own bed.

In 1502, Lucrezia married Alfonso d'Este, and in 1505, the couple became the duke and duchess of Ferrara. At first, the d'Este family was against the union because of Lucrezia's dreadful reputation. However, it was in the family's best interest to accept the offer, since Cesare was engaging in war against the city-states of the Romagna and had made refugees of the princes who governed the region. The marriage would protect the Estes from a similar fate.

As duchess, Lucrezia presided over court with great skill and eventually won the respect of her husband's family and the people of Ferrara. She surrounded herself with writers and artists of renown, including the poet Pietro Bembo, with whom she exchanged correspondence. The contents of these letters have tempted historians to conclude that Lucrezia and the poet engaged in a torrid affair. Others believe that these letters were written in accordance with the Neoplatonic conventions of the day, which entail the use of an impassioned tone and do not necessarily imply a physical relationship. Moreover, Lucrezia had forged a solid relationship with Alfonso and his family, and her own seven children. At the age of thirty-nine, after almost two decades at Ferrara, Lucrezia died of complications in childbirth.

Impact

Part of the impact of Lucrezia Borgia's actions has to do with the fact that she was part of a society in which women were expected to remain in the domestic realm and not involve themselves in political affairs. However, the fact that she was the illegitimate daughter of a pope and the sister of Cesare Borgia, a key figure in papal politics, made Lucrezia's involvement in her family's affairs inevitable. All three of her marriages were arranged to further these men's aims, as were the annulment of her wedding to Giovanni Sforza and the murder of her second husband, the duke of Bisceglie. These intrigues led the nineteenth century French writer Victor Hugo to write an unsympathetic account of Lucrezia's life, *Lucrèce Borgia* (pr., pb. 1833; *Lucretia Borgia*, 1842), which became the basis for Gaetano Donizetti's 1834 opera on the same subject. Modern historians question whether the accusations of incest, conspiracy, and murder are in fact accurate. Most view Lucrezia as a victim of her father's and brother's political aspirations and recognize that in Ferrara, she acted with great kindness toward the populace and members of her court.

Further Reading

Bellonci, Maria. *Lucrezia Borgia*. London: Phoenix Press, 2003. A biographical account of Lucrezia's life vis-à-vis the political intrigues and maneuvers surrounding her at the papal court.

Bradford, Sarah. *Lucrezia Borgia: Life, Love, and Death in Renaissance Italy*. London: Viking, 2004. Portrays Lucrezia Borgia in a positive light, discrediting the view that she may have had some involvement in her husband's murder.

Gregorovius, Ferdinand. *Lucretia Borgia, According to Original Documents and Correspondence of Her Day*. Translated by Leslie Garner. New York: B. Blom, 1968. Examines archival documentation and letters in order to reconstruct the life and deeds of Lucrezia and her family.

Shankland, Hugh, ed. *The Prettiest Love Letters in the World: Letters Between Lucrezia Borgia and Pietro Bembo, 1503-1519*. Boston: D. R. Godine, 1987. Provides translations for the nine extant letters between Lucrezia and Bembo, now housed in the Biblioteca Ambrosiana in Milan.

—*Lilian H. Zirpolo*

See also: Alexander VI; Cesare Borgia.

Martin Bormann

Secretary and chief assistant to Adolf Hitler

Born: June 17, 1900; Wegeleben, near Halberstadt, Germany

Died: May 2, 1945; Berlin, Germany

Also known as: Martin Ludwig Bormann (full name)

Cause of notoriety: As a "model secretary" to Adolf Hitler, Bormann steadily gained influence within the Nazi apparatus, and by the end of World War II he was second only to Hitler in terms of real political power.

Active: 1933-1945

Locale: Germany

Early Life

Martin Bormann (BOHR-man), named after German theologian Martin Luther, was born near the town of Halberstadt in 1900. Educated in private schools, Bormann was a poor student. In 1918, he entered the German army, but he saw no active service during World War I. After the war, Bormann became a farm manager in Mecklenburg, where he joined a local anti-Semitic organization. In 1923, he was involved in the murder of a member of the organization and was tried for manslaughter rather than murder; he served one year in prison. In 1926, he moved to Weimar, becoming active in radical politics and officially joining Adolf Hitler's Nazi Party in February, 1927.

In 1929, he married Gerda Buch, the daughter of a fervent Nazi. Hitler and Rudolf Hess were witnesses. Gerda was the archetypal Aryan woman, five feet, eleven inches tall, while Bormann was dark, stocky, and only about five feet, seven inches in height. The marriage produced nine children. Gerda proved to be a submissive wife, in spite of Bormann's numerous infidelities. Bormann largely cut himself off from his own family, although his younger brother, Albert, served in Hitler's secretariat.

Nazi Career

In 1928, Bormann was summoned to Munich, the center of the Nazi movement, and was given a position in the Sturmabteilung (SA, or stormtroopers) Insurance Office. The classic bureaucratic insider, Bormann made himself indispensable. The insurance program was turned into a relief fund, and by 1930 Bormann was its administrator.

Martin Bormann. (AP/Wide World Photos)

The Nazi Party never gave publicity to financial matters, and Bormann, lacking any public charisma, remained a figure behind the scenes. The Great Depression gave the Nazis their opportunity to escalate their power, and in the September, 1930, elections, they became the second largest party in the Reichstag, or parliament. In late 1932, Hitler reorganized the party structure, placing the newly created Political Central Committee under Hess. On January 30, 1933, Hitler was appointed German chancellor, and in July Bormann became Hess's chief of staff.

Hitler's management style was to create rivalries intentionally among the leading Nazis, including Hermann Göring, Joseph Goebbels, Heinrich Himmler, Hess, and others. Hess, an incompetent idealist, would have been destroyed without Bormann, the bureaucrat. After Hess became deputy leader in late 1933, it was Bormann who dealt with Hitler on party matters rather than the distracted Hess, and it was through Bormann that Hitler issued his orders to party functionaries. However, Bormann was not just a conduit; he used his position to injure rivals and to promote loyal subordinates. He also had access to the so-called Adolf Hitler Endowment Fund, making payments as directed and liberally reallocating funds for gifts to Nazi officials. Bormann even purchased many of Hitler's gifts for his mistress, Eva Braun, and was largely responsible for the expansion of Hitler's mountain retreat at Berchtesgaden. Personally, Bormann was less avaricious than many in the Nazi Party, although over time, he acquired several residences and other properties.

Bormann's attendance upon Hitler was almost constant, both before and during World War II. He approached the apex of power in May, 1941, after deputy führer Hess secretly flew to Scotland in a confused attempt to make peace with Great Britain. It is unlikely that Bormann knew of Hess's plans, but he was the beneficiary, becoming head of the Party Chancellery after Hess's exit from the party. In April, 1943, Bormann became the official secretary to the führer, and from then on hardly anyone saw Hitler without first going through Bormann. His influence even extended into the Germany military, or Wehrmacht; by 1943, he was attempting to apply Nazi ideological criteria in military appointments. After the failed assassination attempt on Hitler in July, 1944, the Gestapo reported directly to Bormann regarding its investigations, and he was instrumental in forcing German field marshal Erwin Rommel to commit suicide.

Although Bormann was a baptized Christian, he was among the most vehement of the anti-Christians among the Nazi leadership, and he used his position in enforcing anti-Christian policies among other party members. He was also involved in propagating the anti-Semitic Nuremberg Laws in 1935, as well as other discriminatory actions against the Jews. His role in the "final solution" regarding the Jews was that of the bureaucrat whose signature, along with others, facilitated the horrors of the Holocaust. He was not in attendance at the Wannsee Conference of January, 1942 (in which various Nazi deputies discussed plans for the extermination of Jews), but it is likely that knew of its decisions beforehand. Bormann was also active in decisions affecting the Slavs of Eastern Europe, whether it was in establishing nonfraternization policies, introducing German military law, or encouraging Slavs to have abortions in order to reduce the birth rate of that "inferior" race.

By late 1944, German defeat became inevitable, and the declining state of Hitler's health raised the question of the führer's successor. Bormann probably did not aspire to the position, preferring to operate behind the scenes. His own preference would have been for a nonpolitical figure, perhaps a military officer such as Admiral Karl Dönitz, to take the lead. Bormann was with Hitler when the führer moved into the Berlin bunker in February, 1945. Although urged by Bormann and others to flee to the south and continue the resistance, Hitler refused, committing suicide on April 30. Bormann attempted to escape the city but failed; he apparently ingested a capsule of poison early in the morning of May 2 and died.

Impact

Martin Bormann's body disappeared in the chaos resulting from the Soviet capture of Berlin. He was condemned to death in absentia at the Nuremberg Trials in 1946, and for years Bormann sightings were reported worldwide, from Australia to Argentina. In 1972, Bormann's skeleton was discovered in Berlin and he was formally pronounced dead by a West German court in April, 1973. Bormann, like Joseph Stalin, is an example of a ruthless individual who achieved and maintained power through skills of private bureaucratic manipulation rather than through an electoral, democratic process or by use of charismatic rhetoric, like that of Hitler.

Further Reading

Bormann, Martin. *The Bormann Letters*. New York: AMS Press, 1981. A collection of Bormann's letters, many of which are revealing of the man and his power.

Evans, Richard J. *The Third Reich in Power*. New York: Penguin, 2005. The second volume in a major assessment of Hitler's Third Reich, which places Bormann in the context of the Nazi state.

Kilzer, Louis. *Hitler's Traitor*. Novato, Calif.: Presidio, 2000. The author, a Pulitzer Prize winner, theorizes that Bormann was a Soviet spy.

Lange, Jochen von. *The Secretary*. New York: Random House, 1979. A readable biography by a German journalist involved in the identification of Bormann's body.

—*Eugene Larson*

See also: Karl Dönitz; Joseph Goebbels; Rudolf Hess; Heinrich Himmler; Adolf Hitler.

Christopher John Boyce

American spy and bank robber

Born: February 16, 1953; Santa Monica, California
Also known as: The Falcon; Jim Namcheck; Tony Lester
Major offenses: Espionage, escape from federal custody, and bank robbery
Active: 1970-1981
Locale: Mexico City, Mexico; California; Idaho; Montana; and Washington State
Sentence: Forty years' imprisonment for espionage; three years' imprisonment for prison escape; twenty-five years' imprisonment for bank robbery

Early Life

Christopher John Boyce (BOYZ) was one of nine children born to Charles and Noreen Boyce. He grew up in an upper-middle-class area of Southern California. Boyce was an altar boy at the Roman Catholic church that he attended with his family in Palos Verde, California. During these early years, he developed an interest in peregrine falcons and a love of the outdoors (he was later nicknamed the Falcon).

Boyce dropped out of college. His father, a former Federal Bureau of Investigation (FBI) agent who was working in private security, helped him get a job at TRW, a defense-related American corporation. Boyce eventually was given a desk job that gave him access to the "vault," where, among other stored items, was information on satellite systems.

Criminal Career

Boyce soon teamed up with his boyhood friend Daulton Lee. Lee had become involved in drugs—he used and sold marijuana and cocaine (leading to his nickname, the Snowman). Boyce and Lee developed a plan to become involved in espionage and international intrigue by selling information on American satellite systems to agents of the Soviet Union. Their plan included making contact with Soviet intelligence agents through the Soviet embassy in Mexico.

Boyce decided that being a spy would be an adventure and would enable him to act on his growing antigovernment ideals. It appeared that Lee was more motivated by the seventy-seven thousand dollars reportedly paid to the pair by the Soviets. Boyce later said that he had received

Christopher John Boyce. (AP/Wide World Photos)

only about twenty thousand dollars of the money that the Soviets paid his partner, and he denied that money was his motive.

Legal Action and Outcome

In December, 1976, Lee was erroneously arrested in front of the Soviet embassy in Mexico City for the murder of a police officer. He was interrogated after a top-secret microfilm was found in his possession, and he confessed to being a Soviet spy. He also implicated Boyce, who was soon arrested. Boyce and Lee had separate jury trials for espionage. Their trials were held in front of the same judge in the federal district court in Los Angeles, California. Boyce testified on his own behalf, denying that he had any contact with the Soviets or their embassy in Mexico City. The jury apparently found Boyce unconvincing and came back with a guilty verdict after deliberating only a few hours. He was convicted of espionage on June 20, 1977, and sentenced to forty years in federal custody. Lee was also convicted in his jury trial. Both Lee and Boyce were sent to the U.S. penitentiary in Lompoc, California, to serve their sentences.

Boyce escaped from the penitentiary on January 21, 1980. He reportedly made a papier-mâché head to trick guards into thinking he was asleep in his cell. He hid for several hours in a small drainage hole inside the fence of the penitentiary. He then used a homemade ladder and pieces of tin to get through the fence.

After his escape, Boyce reportedly roamed the countryside for several days before finding a friend whom he knew from prison, who already had been released. His friend suggested that Boyce go up to Bonners Ferry, Idaho, and find a woman named Gloria White. According to the friend, White would help him.

Boyce located White in the Bonners Ferry area. White let Boyce stay at her cabin, and when Boyce expressed an interest in robbing banks, she taught him how to disguise himself using stage makeup. She also showed him that wearing baggy clothing and putting cotton in his mouth would make him look heavier and change his appearance.

During his nineteen months as a fugitive, Boyce robbed banks in Idaho, Washington State, and Montana. He became somewhat of a colorful local character when he purchased a mule and would often bring it with him when he came into Bonners Ferry. He also took flying lessons in Washington. It was reported that Boyce intended to fly to the Soviet Union via Alaska, where he believed he would receive a hero's welcome. Boyce eventually was arrested by U.S. Marshals in Port Angeles, Washington, on August 21, 1981.

In late 1981, he pleaded guilty to the escape charge and received in additional three-year sentence. Then, in March, 1982, Boyce was tried and convicted of bank robberies in Idaho, Washington, and Montana. He was sentenced to twenty-five years' imprisonment, to be served at the end of his previous sentences for espionage and escape. White was also convicted for her role as a co-conspirator in the robberies. Boyce was released on parole in California on March 14, 2003. His parole term was scheduled to expire on August 15, 2046.

Impact

The satellite secrets sold by Christopher John Boyce and Andrew Daulton Lee to the Soviets greatly compromised U.S. intelligence-gathering capabilities and slowed the progress of U.S. and Soviet disarmament talks. In October, 1979, the FBI relinquished authority to investigate escapes to the U.S. Marshals Service. Boyce's escape in January, 1980, became the first high-profile fugitive case investigated by the marshals. The event helped establish the marshals' reputation as fugitive investigators.

Boyce and Lee's adventures became the basis for Robert Lindsey's best-selling 1979 book, *The Falcon and the Snowman*, which was adapted to film in 1985 and starred Timothy Hutton and Sean Pean in the lead roles. Lindsey's book was followed by another in 1983, *The Flight of the Falcon*.

Further Reading

Lindsey, Robert. *The Falcon and the Snowman: A True Story of Friendship and Espionage*. New York: Simon & Schuster, 1979. A chronicle of the lives of Boyce and Lee up to and through the time of their trials and convictions for espionage.

_______. *The Flight of the Falcon*. New York: Simon & Schuster, 1983. An account of Boyce's escape from the penitentiary at Lompoc, his activities while a fugitive, and the massive manhunt leading to his arrest.

Serrano, Richard. "The Falcon and the Fallout." *The Los Angeles Times*, March 2, 2003. An account of Boyce's life at the time of his prison release.

—Gerald P. Fisher

See also: Aldrich Ames; Robert Philip Hanssen; Daulton Lee.

Belle Boyd

American spy for the Confederate States of America

Born: May 4, 1844; Martinsburg, Virginia (now in West Virginia)

Died: June 11, 1900; Kilbourn (now Wisconsin Dells), Wisconsin

Also known as: Maria Isabella Boyd (full name); Isabelle Boyd

Cause of notoriety: Boyd supplied Confederate officers with information on Union troop movements during the American Civil War and helped turn the tide of the Battle of Front Royal in the rebels' favor.

Active: 1861-1864

Locale: United States, mainly Shenandoah Valley

Early Life

Maria Isabella (Belle) Boyd was the first of eight children born to farmer and shopkeeper Benjamin Reed Boyd and his wife, Mary Rebecca Glenn. She was a spirited child skilled in riding horses. The Boyd family was relatively prosperous and owned several household slaves, including Belle's personal attendant, Eliza Hopewell Corsey.

Belle Boyd attended school in Martinsburg until age twelve. In 1856, her parents enrolled her in the Mount Washington Female Seminary near Baltimore, Maryland, where she studied French, literature, and music. Boyd graduated in 1860 as sectional tensions worsened between the Northern and Southern states. Keenly aware of the conflict, Boyd allied herself with the Southern cause of states' rights. On April 17, 1861, Vir-

Belle Boyd. (Library of Congress)

Belle on the Battlefield

Belle Boyd's own account of her daring exploits on the Civil War battlefield:

On the evening of the 23rd May [1862] I was sitting at the window of our room [at Front Royal], reading to my grandmother and cousin, when one of the servants rushed in, and shouted, or rather shrieked—"Oh, Miss Belle, I t'inks de revels am a-comin', for de Yankees are a-makin' orful fuss in de street." I immediately sprang from my seat and went to the door, and I then found that the servant's report was true. The streets were thronged with Yankee soldiers, hurrying about in every direction in the greatest confusion. . . .

I was in possession of much important information, which if I could only contrive to convey to General Jackson, I knew our victory would be secure. . . .

I put on a white sun-bonnet, and started at a run down the street, which was thronged with Federal officers and men. I soon cleared the town and gained the open fields, which I traversed with unabated speed, hoping to escape observation until such time as I could make good my way to the Confederate line, which was still rapidly advancing.

I had on a dark blue dress, with a little fancy white apron over it; and this contrast of colours, being visible at a great distance, made me far more conspicuous than was just then agreeable. The skirmishing between the outposts was sharp. . . . [A]lthough I was not hit, the rifle-balls flew thick and fast about me, and more than one struck the ground so near my feet as to throw the dust in my eyes. Nor was this all: the Federals in the hospital seeing in what direction the shots of their pickets were aimed, followed the example and also opened fire upon me. . . .

As I neared our line I waved my bonnet to our soldiers, to intimate that they should press forward, upon which one regiment, the 1st Maryland "rebel" Infantry, and Hay's Louisiana Brigade, gave me a loud cheer, and, without waiting for further orders, dashed upon the town at a rapid pace. . . .

They did not then know who I was, and they were naturally surprised to see a woman on the battle-field, and on a spot, too, where the fire was so hot. Their shouts of approbation and triumph rang in my ears for many a day afterwards, and I still hear them not unfrequently in my dreams. . . .

[T]o my unspeakable, indescribable joy, I caught sight of the main body fast approaching; and soon an old friend and connection of mine, Major Harry Douglas, rode up, and, recognising me, cried out, while he seized my hand—"Good God, Belle, you here! what is it?" "Oh, Harry," I gasped out, "give me time to recover my breath." For some seconds I could say no more; but, as soon as I had sufficiently recovered myself, I produced the "little note," and told him all, urging him to hurry on the cavalry, with orders to them to seize the bridges before the retreating Federals should have time to destroy them.

Source: Belle Boyd, *Belle Boyd in Camp and Prison* (London: Saunders, Otley, 1865).

ginia seceded from the Union, and Boyd's father joined the Confederate army.

Espionage Career

Strategically poised at the entrance to the Shenandoah Valley, Martinsburg was frequently occupied by Northern troops during the war. On July 4, 1861, Union soldiers came to the Boyd home and attempted to force the family to display an American flag. As her mother argued with one of the soldiers, Boyd shot and killed him. Though she was not punished for the incident, Union commanders placed troops around the family home. Boyd would flirt with these sentries in order to extract information on troop locations and plans. She would then dispatch an ally, such as her slave Eliza, with the information to Confederate officers. In October, 1861, Boyd was commissioned a courier in the Confederate Intelligence Service. In this capacity, Boyd transmitted information and stole medicine and other supplies for the Confederate army.

On May 23, 1862, Boyd accomplished her most celebrated act of espionage as Union troops advanced on Front Royal, Virginia, where Boyd was staying with family members. She ran through gunfire and artillery to the camp of Confederate general Stonewall Jackson. The information that she provided secured a Confederate victory at Front Royal and kept Union forces from capturing the rest of the Shenandoah Valley.

Boyd's deeds were well publicized in the press, and she was imprisoned in 1862 and 1863 for the threat that she posed to Union military efforts. After attempting to sail for England to act as a Confederate ambassador in 1864, Boyd was ordered to leave the United States. She moved to London and married a former Union soldier,

Samuel Wylde Hardinge, in 1865. That same year, Boyd had a daughter, Grace, and published her memoirs, *Belle Boyd in Camp and Prison*. After her husband's death, Boyd became a stage actor. She returned to the United States in 1866 and worked as an actor until 1869, when she married another Union veteran, named John Swainston Hammond. The couple had four children, one of whom died in infancy, before divorcing in 1884. The following year, Boyd married the actor Nathaniel Rue High and returned to the stage, performing dramatic adaptations of her wartime exploits. She was in Wisconsin to give one of these performances when she died of a heart attack.

Impact

Heralded in her lifetime as a Confederate heroine, Belle Boyd continued to fascinate historians into the twenty-first century as a woman who used her femininity to participate in the masculine realms of warfare and espionage. The United Daughters of the Confederacy preserved Boyd's memory in the late nineteenth and early twentieth centuries. Even if there is no uniform agreement regarding the importance of her espionage to Confederate war aims, Boyd challenged the nineteenth century assumption that women were uninterested in politics.

Further Reading

Kennedy-Nolle, Sharon. Introduction to *Belle Boyd in Camp and Prison*. Baton Rouge: Louisiana State University Press, 1998. This introduction to a revised edition of Boyd's memoirs emphasizes Boyd's use of conventional understandings of womanhood to accomplish quite unconventional ends.

Leonard, Elizabeth D. *All the Daring of the Soldier: Women of the Civil War Armies*. New York: W. W. Norton, 1999. Leonard places Boyd in the company of other women, Northern and Southern, who participated in the Civil War as soldiers or spies and explores their varied reasons for doing so.

Sigaud, Louis A. *Belle Boyd: Confederate Spy*. Richmond, Va.: Dietz Press, 1944. In one of the first scholarly biographies of Belle Boyd, Sigaud confirms the historical accuracy of much of Boyd's autobiography.

—*Francesca Gamber*

See also: Pauline Cushman.

Eva Braun

Mistress, and later wife, of Adolf Hitler

Born: February 6, 1912; Munich, Germany
Died: April 30, 1945; Berlin, Germany
Also known as: Eva Anna Paula Braun (full name)
Cause of notoriety: Unknown to most contemporary Germans and rarely appearing in public, Braun was Adolf Hitler's mistress. She committed suicide with him to avoid being captured alive by the Russians at the end of World War II.
Active: 1932-1945
Locale: Germany, mainly Munich, Berchtesgaden, and Berlin

Early Life

Eva Braun (AY-vah brown) was born into a lower-middle-class Catholic family. Her father, Friedrich Braun, was a teacher at an industrial college, and her mother, Franziska, was a dressmaker. Eva had an older sister named Ilse and a younger sister named Gretel. At convent school, she studied bookkeeping, French, typing, music, and drawing. However, her real interests were in sports, drama, and fashion.

At seventeen, she became an assistant to Heinrich Hoffmann, who was Adolf Hitler's personal photographer and an early member of the National Socialist Party (the Nazi Party). In 1929, she was introduced to "Herr Wolf," which was Hitler's nom de guerre. Uninterested in politics, she did not at first realize who Hitler was and only knew that she was attracted to him. In 1932, she became his mistress.

Domestic Career

Braun had become intimately involved with one of the most infamous, pathological, and evil figures in history. Totally devoted to Hitler, she was by all accounts completely excluded from his politics, including details of the Holocaust and military developments. She rarely appeared in public, and her relationship with Hitler was unknown to most Germans and even to most of Hitler's inner circle.

Much of Hitler's support and popularity came from women, so he needed to give the impression of being unattached and totally devoted to Germany. Eva often felt

Adolf Hitler and Eva Braun, circa 1940. (Hulton Archive/Getty Images)

neglected and isolated. She attempted suicide by shotgun in November, 1932. In May, 1935, she attempted suicide with an overdose of sleeping pills. After this second suicide attempt, Hitler bought her a villa in Munich and a car with a chauffeur. In 1936, Hitler brought Braun to live at Berghof, his mountain retreat in the Alps. While the world was embroiled in World War II, Braun led a sheltered life of leisure. Her favorite activities were reading romance novels, exercising, nude sunbathing, and watching films. She was also interested in photography and filmmaking.

By January, 1945, the Allies were regularly bombing Berlin, and the Soviets had begun their final offensive. Hitler had gone to his underground bunker in the Reich Chancellery gardens in Berlin. He told Eva not to come to Berlin, but on March 7, 1945, she traveled by special train to join him. On April 28, 1945, Hitler and Braun were married. On April 30, they committed suicide to avoid being captured alive.

Impact

Eva Braun was the Third Reich's mystery woman, a carefully guarded secret until after the war. She left diaries and home movies that have generated controversy and are of major significance for historians. Two diaries provide details about her personal life with Hitler. The National Archives at Washington, D.C., holds an authentic diary of twenty-two pages covering February 6 to May 28, 1935, both in German and in English translation.

A second, disputed diary covers the last few months of 1937 to July 23, 1944. According to Austrian filmmaker Luis Trenker, in the winter of 1944-1945 at the Kitzbuhel ski resort, Braun entrusted him with a sealed package, not to be opened until after her death. In December, 1945, Trenker took the package to a notary public for the opening. It contained an unsigned manuscript, apparently Braun's diary. A London publisher confirmed its authenticity, and it was first published in London in 1949 and then again in 1979 and 2000. However, in October, 1948, the Munich courts had declared the diary a forgery.

Braun's home movies of life at Berghof were filmed during the late 1930's and early 1940's. They are unique, candid views of the private life of Braun, Hitler, and Nazi leaders. They show Hitler relaxing and joking with friends and children. As World War II ended, the Allies discovered these films, which fascinated many people, some of whom Hitler and his policies had terrorized for more than a decade. The films were eventually published on videocassette in the 1980's and 1990's. In 2004, a complete DVD set was released.

Often considered Germany's most infamous woman, Hitler's secret mistress and later wife remained conspicuous in popular and social culture into the twenty-first century. She has been portrayed in modern media such as videos, television, and DVDs. Leonard Nimoy's *In Search Of* television series produced an episode titled "Eva Braun" in 1976. *The Bunker* was a 1980 film about the last weeks of Hitler's life. In 1991, *Hitler's Mistress, Eva Braun* was released on video. In 2003, *Adolf & Eva*, a DVD based on home videos and interviews, was released.

Further Reading

Braun, Eva. *The Diary of Eva Braun*. 1949. Reprint. Bristol, England: Spectrum International, 2000. The diary covers late 1937 to July 23, 1944, and this edition contains letters from Hitler to Braun. Also includes a commentary by Alan Bartlett. Illustrated.

Gun, Nerin E. *Eva Braun: Hitler's Mistress*. New York, Meredith Press, 1968. A lengthy biography based on interviews with Braun's closest acquaintances, including her mother and sisters. The author concludes that Braun and Hitler had an ordinary intimate relationship, rather than a perverted one. Illustrated, with index.

Knopp, Guido. *Hitler's Women*. New York: Routledge, 2003. This book about six of Hitler's women friends devotes the first chapter to Hitler's relationship with Braun. Illustrated. Includes bibliography and index.

Sigmund, Anna Maria. *Women of the Third Reich*. Richmond Hill, Ont.: 2000. Includes a chapter titled "Eva Braun: The Secret Love." Illustrated. Bibliography.

Thomas, W. Hugh. *The Murder of Adolph Hitler: The Truth About the Bodies in the Berlin Bunker*. New York: St. Martin's Press, 1996. Using forensic evidence from the archives of the former Soviet Union, the author, a British surgeon, concludes that Hitler was murdered by his own guards, while Braun was allowed to escape. Illustrated. Contains bibliography and index

—*Alice Myers*

See also: Magda Goebbels; Jiang Qing; Imelda Marcos; Eva Perón; Winifred Wagner.

Arthur Bremer

American assassin

Born: August 21, 1950; Milwaukee, Wisconsin

Also known as: Arthur Herman Bremer (full name)

Major offense: Attempted murder of presidential candidate George Wallace, governor of Alabama

Active: May 15, 1972

Locale: Laurel, Maryland

Sentence: Sixty-three years in prison, later reduced to fifty-three years

Early Life

As a child, Arthur Bremer (BREH-mur) had little communication with his parents. Bremer's father was a Milwaukee truck driver who went to work, paid the bills, argued with his wife, and occasionally drank alcohol to relieve his frustrations. In short, Bremer grew up in an uncommunicative and conflict-ridden household. Bremer became emotionally withdrawn, filled with anxiety, and compliant in his behavior. At the age of eight or nine, he began fantasizing about committing suicide by lying down on railroad tracks near his home. During this same time period, Bremer began to find some peace by attending church and thought about becoming a priest. However, his family then moved away, and he never returned to church. After he failed the fifth grade, he thought of commiting suicide but never attempted such a thing. He graduated from high school in 1968, an average student. Although his high school years were fairly uneventful, during his senior year his parents did notice that Bremer changed his behavior dramatically. His passive compliance began to disappear, and he turned into a very aggressive and outspoken person, often irritated by his parents.

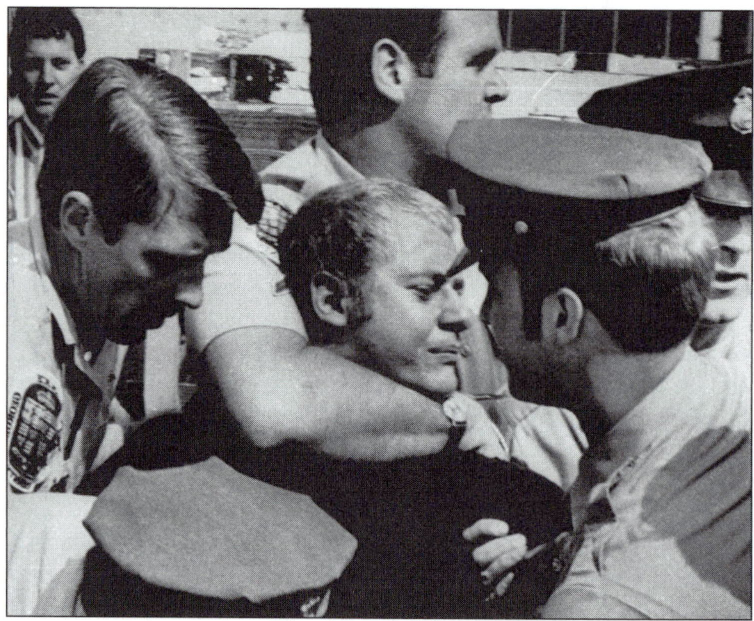

Arthur Bremer. (AP/Wide World Photos)

After high school, Bremer worked as a busboy at the Milwaukee Athletic Club and at an upscale restaurant. He also worked as a janitor at an elementary school for $2.70 per hour. Few coworkers remembered Bremer because he merely performed his menial tasks and rarely spoke to others. Bremer enrolled at the Milwaukee Technical College, where he took courses in psychology, photography, art, and writing in the fall, 1970, semester. He registered for spring courses but then dropped out and also moved out of his parents' house after a heated argument with his father. During this same time period, Bremer was demoted from busboy to kitchen worker because of his idiosyncratic habits such as mumbling to himself and whistling. After his demotion, Bremer filed a grievance with the Milwaukee Community Relations Commission.

While working at the elementary school, the twenty-one-year-old Bremer asked a fifteen-year-old student, Joan Pembrick, for a date. Pembrick would be the first and only love in his life. The two dated for roughly two months, but Pembrick quickly became frustrated with Bremer's immature behavior and offensive language.

Criminal Career

After Pembrick's mother informed Bremer that her daughter wanted to end their relationship, Bremer became obsessed with suicidal and homicidal fantasies. He felt that his life was meaningless, and he became even more alienated from society. Wishing for fame and notoriety, Bremer developed a plan to assassinate President Richard M. Nixon while he was visiting Canada on March 1, 1972, but Bremer was unable to get close enough to the president in order to carry out the assassination.

Bremer then decided to murder Alabama governor and presidential candidate George Wallace, believing that he could get close enough to shoot Wallace, who did not have as many security guards as President Nixon. On May 15, 1972, Bremer shot Wallace in Laurel, Maryland, after the presidential candidate delivered a speech before a crowd of roughly one thousand supporters. With a .38-caliber revolver, Bremer shot five times at Wallace, who survived the assassination attempt. However, one of the four bullets that hit Wallace lodged in the governor's spine, leaving him paralyzed for life.

Legal Action and Outcome

A Maryland jury found Bremer guilty of attempted murder after a five-day trial in which evidence was presented from eight psychiatrists and two psychologists who had examined Bremer. The psychologists and psychiatrists divided on the issue of Bremer's sanity. Ultimately, the jury concluded, based upon Bremer's diary, that he knew what he was doing when he attempted to kill Wallace and also understood the consequences of his actions. In the end, Bremer's motive was that of a sociopath who wanted to commit a perverse act to harm society and gain publicity for himself. In short, he committed a premeditated act of violence simply because he felt like it.

Bremer was imprisoned at the Maryland Correctional Institute and scheduled to be eligible for parole in 2015. Psychological records, however, suggested that Bremer would be a danger to society if released.

Impact

The assassination attempt on Wallace caused conspiracy theorists to speculate that Arthur Bremer had ties to the Republican Party and to Nixon's reelection campaign. Nixon reportedly met with Federal Bureau of Investigation agent Mark Felt to discuss such concerns about the assassination attempt. Wallace was convinced that

Nixon had ordered the assassination attempt and vowed revenge against Nixon by announcing that he would run for president in 1972 as a third-party candidate. Wallace, however, had to drop out of the race because of health problems related to the shooting.

Interestingly, Bremer's relationship with the fifteen-year-old Pembrick would later serve as inspiration for the Robert DeNiro character in the 1976 film *Taxi Driver*. DeNiro's character, a potential assassin named Travis Bickle, awkwardly tries to establish a relationship with an attractive young woman. Ironically, the Bickle character in *Taxi Driver* served as motivation for John Hinckley, Jr., to attempt the assassination of President Ronald Reagan in 1981.

Further Reading

Bremer, Arthur H. *An Assassin's Diary*. New York: Harper's Magazine Press, 1973. Bremer's diary, in which he states that he was not opposed to George Wallace's politics but that his primary motive was to achieve fame and notoriety. He also states that, prior to his assassination attempt on Wallace, he had also stalked President Richard Nixon.

Clarke, James W. "Arthur Herman Bremer." Chapter 6 in *American Assassins: The Darker Side of Politics*. Rev. ed. Princeton, N.J.: Princeton University Press, 1990. Clarke develops a typology for analyzing sixteen political assassins in American history.

Healy, Thomas S. *The Two Deaths of George Wallace: The Question of Forgiveness*. Montgomery, Ala.: Black Belt Press, 1996. Explores the mind of Arthur Bremer by tracing his movements prior to the assassination attempt on George Wallace.

—*Scott P. Johnson*

See also: Samuel Joseph Byck; Lynette Fromme; John Hinckley, Jr.; Richard Nixon; George C. Wallace; Giuseppe Zangara.

John R. Brinkley

American medical fraudster

Born: July 8, 1885; Jackson County, North Carolina

Died: May 26, 1942; San Antonio, Texas

Also known as: John Romulus Brinkley (full name); John Richard Brinkley; Goat Gland Doctor

Cause of notoriety: Brinkley claimed in his controversial "goat gland operation" to restore male virility. He was sued for malpractice and for libel and was indicted for mail fraud by the U.S. Postal Service.

Active: 1918-1942

Locale: Milford, Kansas; Villa Acuña, Mexico; and Del Rio, Texas

Early Life

John R. Brinkley (BRIHN-klee) was the son of John Brinkley, an unlettered country doctor, and Candice Burnett. Orphaned at age ten, the young Brinkley was raised by an aunt. He received his early education in Tuckaseigee, North Carolina, but never earned a diploma. In his mid-teens, he led a nomadic life and worked as a telegrapher. From 1907 through 1915 he received dubious credentials from schools of little repute, such as the Eclectic Medical University of Kansas City and the Bennett Medical College of Chicago.

Medical Career

In spite of his questionable degrees, Brinkley was licensed to practice medicine in Arkansas and later established his practice in Milford, Kansas. He began performing his notorious "goat gland operation" in 1918, which involved implantation of Toggenberg goat glands in human men and which Brinkley claimed could restore male fertility as well as virility. Soon the $750 rejuvenation operation was in high demand, and Brinkley became wealthy.

In 1923 he created Kansas's first radio station and only the fourth commercial station in the United States. KFKB (which stood for Kansas's First, Kansas's Best) became a powerful radio station which broadcast and promoted ads for Brinkley's secret remedies. Brinkley also organized a network of pharmacies in his radio coverage area, known as the National Dr. Brinkley Pharmaceutical Association, and prescribed medicine by number which one could get only at the local affiliated pharmacy, which sent a portion of the profits to Brinkley.

In 1928 Dr. Morris Fishbein, secretary of the American Medical Association, lambasted Brinkley for diagnosing illnesses over the radio as well as promoting medicines on the air. As a result, the State Medical Board of

Kansas revoked Brinkley's medical license in 1930. That year, the Federal Radio Commission would not renew his broadcasting license. Still widely popular, Brinkley next ran for governor, but none of his three campaigns—in 1930, 1932, and 1934—met with success.

In 1931 he received authority from Mexican officials to assemble the world's most powerful transmitter at Villa Acuña, Mexico. Under the call sign of XER, Brinkley used his new "border blaster" transmitter to reach listeners as far north as Canada. In 1933 he moved his entire medical staff and facilities across the border to the Roswell Hotel in Del Rio. The Mexican government issued a license for Brinkley to begin broadcasting from his 500-kilowatt transmitter under the new call letters XERA. The new AM station, with its powerful antennas, could broadcast throughout the United States and Canada, and even as far as the Soviet Union. Brinkley's fabulously lucrative business supported his flashy lifestyle. Estimates are that he earned twelve million dollars between 1933 and 1938. In 1938 he moved his medical activities to Little Rock, Arkansas.

About the time Brinkley moved back to Arkansas, he lost a libel suit against Fishbein, fought numerous malpractice suits, battled the Internal Revenue Service over back taxes, and was indicted for mail fraud by the U.S. Postal Service. Soon, Brinkley's station was out of business, and in January, 1941, he filed for bankruptcy. When World War II began in Europe, Brinkley further provoked the U.S. government by allowing Nazi sympathizers to broadcast their propaganda. In 1941, XERA was expropriated by the Mexican government, and three days later Brinkley suffered a massive heart attack. On May 26, 1942, he died in San Antonio of heart failure. He was buried in Memphis, Tennessee.

Impact

John R. Brinkley's role in exposing America's vulnerability to medical quackery cannot be understated, but he had an equally important impact on legislation to regulate radio broadcasting. Because of Brinkley's actions, in April of 1941 the Mexican government struck a deal with the United States to restrict cross-border links between U.S. radio studios and Mexican transmitters through the Communications Act of 1934, commonly known as the Brinkley Act, which led to the shutdown of XERA and placed limitations on the abuse of broadcasting.

Further Reading

Juhnke, Eric S. *Quacks and Crusaders: The Fabulous Careers of John Brinkley, Norman Baker, and Harry Hoxsey*. Lawrence: University Press of Kansas, 2002. A major contribution to the understanding of medical quackery of yesteryear and today, this book examines the careers of Brinkley, Baker, and Hoxsey.

Lee, R. Alton. *The Bizarre Careers of John R. Brinkley*. Lexington: University Press of Kentucky, 2002. Perhaps the most complete account of Brinkley's life, delivered in academic yet humorous detail.

Young, James Harvey. *The Medical Messiahs: A Social History of Health Quackery in Twentieth-Century America*. 1966. Reprint. Princeton, N.J.: Princeton University Press, 1992. Summarizes the development of patent medicines in America from the 1906 Pure Food and Drugs Act through the mid-1960's.

—*Wayne J. Pitts*

See also: Frank W. Abagnale, Jr.; Larry C. Ford; Linda Burfield Hazzard; Michael Swango.

Curly Bill Brocius

American West gunslinger and outlaw

Born: c. 1840; possibly in or near Crawfordsville, Indiana

Died: Probably March 24, 1882; probably near Iron Springs (now Mescal Springs), Arizona

Also known as: William Brocius Graham (birth name); William Brocius (full name); William Bresnaham; Curly Bill

Cause of notoriety: Brocius, as a member of the cattle-rustling and stagecoach-robbing Cowboys gang, associated with some of the best-known outlaws in the American West and was believed to be responsible for at least eight (and possibly thirty-two) murders.

Active: 1878-1882

Locale: Arizona, New Mexico, Texas, and Mexico

Early Life

Evidence suggests that William "Curly Bill" Brocius (BRO-shyuhs) began life in the 1840's as William Graham, a struggling farmer in pre-Civil War Indiana. Graham was married with three children. Tired of being poor, Graham accepted five hundred dollars to perform military duty in place of a drafted wealthy man. When the Civil War ended in 1865, Graham did not return home but wandered the South. Returning to Indiana in 1869, Graham found his wife had remarried and had had another child. Angry, Graham left Indiana.

Brocius has been described as somewhat heavyset, with dark skin, dark eyes, and thick, curly black hair. A portion of his left ear was missing, shot off by a Texas Ranger. In a separate incident, Brocius was shot in the left side of the neck, the bullet exiting his right cheek. No documented photographs of Brocius exist, though one photograph shows a man fitting his description with a bullet-wound scar to the right cheek. All life descriptions of Brocius share one common trait: Curly Bill was unburdened by a conscience.

Criminal Career

Records of Brocius's criminal career first appear in the late 1870's, when he rode with cattle rustlers led by John Kinney, a central figure in the Lincoln County War. In 1878, Brocius, then using the alias William Bresnaham, helped rob an army wagon suspected of harboring cash. One soldier died in the attack, and after a shoot-out with Texas Rangers, Brocius was captured. He was charged with attempted robbery but not murder, and he was con-

Bill Gets a Bullet

On May 26, 1881, the Arizona Weekly Star *reported a typical brawl involving Curly Bill and the Cowboys:*

The notorious Curly Bill, the man who murdered Marshal White at Tombstone last fall and who has been concerned in several other desperate and lawless affrays in South Eastern Arizona, has at last been brought to grief and there is likely to be a vacancy in the ranks of out border desperados. The affair occurred at Galeyville Thursday. A party of 8 or 9 cowboys, Curly Bill and his partner Jim Wallace among the number, were enjoying themselves in their usual manner, when deputy Sheriff Breakenridge of Tombstone, who was at Galeyville on business, happened along.

Wallace made some insulting remark to the deputy at the same time flourishing his revolver in an aggressive manner. Breakenridge did not pay much attention to this "break" of Wallace but quietly turned around and left the party. Shortly after this, Curly Bill, who it would seem had a friendly feeling for Breakenridge, insisted that Wallace should go and find him and apologize for the insult given. . . . By this time Curly Bill who had drank just enough to make him quarrelsome, was in one of his most dangerous moods and evidently desirous of increasing his record as a man killer. He commenced to abuse Wallace, who, by the way, had some pretensions himself as a desperado and bad man generally and finally said, "You d-d Lincoln county s-of a b—, I'll kill you anyhow." Wallace immediately went outside the door of the saloon, Curly Bill following close behind him. Just as the latter stepped outside, Wallace, who had meanwhile drawn his revolver, fired, the ball entering penetrating the left side of Curly Bill's neck and passing through, came out the right cheek, not breaking the jawbone. A scene of the wildest excitement ensued in the town. . . .

The wounded and apparently dying desperado was taken into an adjoining building, and a doctor summoned to dress his wounds. After examining the course of the bullet, the doctor pronounced the wound dangerous but not necessarily fatal, the chances for and against recovery being about equal. Wallace and Curly Bill have been Partners and fast friends for the past 4 or 6 months and so far is known, there was no cause for the quarrel, it being simply a drunken brawl.

victed and sentenced to five years in prison. He escaped and arrived in Arizona in 1878 with a cattle herd bound for the San Carlos Apache Indian Reservation.

Upon his arrival in Tombstone, Brocius began his association with the outlaw gang that called itself the Cowboys, led by Newman "Old Man" Clanton. The Cowboys were a loose confederation whose principal occupation was stealing cattle and robbing stagecoaches, though members were free to pursue individual acts of criminal enterprise. The gang was protected by local law enforcement, notably Tombstone sheriff John Behan. Behan used Brocius as his "tax collector," and Curly Bill gained a reputation for shooting "taxpayers" who did not pay Behan's extortionary demands.

In 1881, during a drunken rampage in Tombstone, Brocius was asked to disarm by Marshal Fred White. While Brocius was surrendering his revolvers, one discharged and mortally wounded the marshal. Deputy Sheriff Wyatt Earp, arriving soon after, clubbed Brocius and arrested him. White gave a dying statement to witnesses that the shooting was accidental. Brocius was acquitted subsequently of a murder charge, with Earp testifying on his behalf regarding the accidental nature of White's death. Despite this, Brocius never forgave Earp for humiliating him with a pistol-whipping in front of Tombstone residents and his Cowboy associates.

Following Old Man Clanton's death in 1881, Curly Bill Brocius became the primary leader of the Cowboys. At that time the gang had more than four hundred members in Arizona, New Mexico, and old Mexico and had become the largest rustling operation in American history. In some instances, gang members rustled thousands of head of cattle at a time, and they did so with a total disregard for the international border with Mexico. This angered Mexican officials and President James Garfield, who ordered the gang be stopped at all costs.

In July, 1881, Brocius and Johnny Ringo rode to New Mexico for a revenge killing of two store owners who had killed two Cowboys during an attempted robbery. During this time, the men also led an attack on a cattle herd, killing six men. Brocius was out of Tombstone during the infamous gunfight at the O.K.Corral. Angered by the deaths of his comrades by the Earps and John "Doc" Holliday, Brocius masterminded the attack on Virgil Earp and the killing of Morgan Earp. These attacks began the legendary vendetta involving the Earps and the Cowboys.

The death of Curly Bill Brocius is linked to the legendary Earp vendetta ride. In March, 1882, after receiving information that Brocius and other Cowboys were near Iron Springs, Arizona, Wyatt Earp, Holliday, and three other men rode to the area. The Earp posse was ambushed by the Cowboys; during the battle and at point-blank range, Curly Bill and Wyatt Earp faced each other, both discharging double shotgun blasts. Pellets from Brocius's gun tore through Earp's clothing. Earp's double blast took Brocius in the stomach, nearly tearing him in half.

Impact

Despite the presidential order against the Cowboys, as well as his reputation as a killer and countless known criminal acts, Curly Bill Brocius's influence was such that he was never formally wanted for any crime in Arizona. The character of Brocius recurred in several well-known Hollywood films, including *Hour of the Gun* (1967), *Tombstone* (1993), and *Wyatt Earp* (1994).

Further Reading

Breakenridge, William M. *Helldorado: Bringing the Law to the Mesquite*. New York: Houghton Mifflin, 1928. Memoirs of Sheriff Breakenridge and the only firsthand account of the Earp vendetta ride that does not come from an Earp family member.

Gatto, Steve. *Curly Bill: Tombstone's Most Famous Outlaw*. Lansing, Mich.: Protar House, 2003. A good biography of the life and times of Brocius.

Marks, Paula M. *And Die in the West: The Story of the O.K. Corral Gunfight*. Norman: University of Oklahoma Press, 1996. An in-depth look at the events leading up to and following the famous gunfight, including the Earp vendetta ride.

Turner, Alford E., ed. *The Earps Talk*. College Station, Pa.: Creative, 1980. A book of documented interviews with Wyatt Earp, Jesse James, and Virgil Earp.

Walters, Lorenzo D. *Tombstone's Yesterday: True Chronicles of Early Arizona*. Glorieta, N.M.: Rio Grande Press, 1928. Documented stories from Tombstone locals about the lawless days of the late nineteenth century.

—*Randall L. Milstein*

See also: Wyatt Earp; Doc Holliday; Johnny Ringo.

William Brodie

Scottish carpenter, businessman, and burglar

Born: September 28, 1741; Edinburgh, Scotland
Died: October 1, 1788; Edinburgh, Scotland
Also known as: Deacon Brodie; John Dixon
Major offenses: Theft attended with housebreaking
Active: August, 1786-March 8, 1788
Locale: Edinburgh, Scotland
Sentence: Death by hanging

Early Life

The firstborn son of a prosperous Edinburgh cabinetmaker and descendant of a landed family from northern Scotland, William Brodie (BROH-dee) studied classics at the high school of Edinburgh before following his father's trade, although he romantically desired a career at sea. In 1781, when the older Brodie suffered a paralysis, William succeeded him as deacon of the Wrights (president of Edinburgh's guild of carpenters; not an ecclesiastical title) and member of the town council, whose monopoly on public building contracts advanced young Brodie's profession. Inspired by Macheath, the dashing highwayman of John Gay's popular *The Beggar's Opera* (pr., pb. 1728), Brodie kept two separate mistresses and dressed like a dandy in satin breeches and silk stockings. He was a gambler with his own cockfighting flock, and he frequented an irreverent mock-Masonic club that nicknamed him Sir Lluyd (pronounced "lewd").

Criminal Career

In August, 1786, using a counterfeit key, Brodie and three accomplices stole £800 from a bank in the Royal Exchange, then whimsically returned £250 to the town council chambers. That autumn, they robbed two goldsmiths and a jeweler. In 1787, they stole more than three hundred pounds of tea from a grocer and deposited packages of tea along the road back to Edinburgh. As winter approached, they robbed a shoemaker's shop and a silk shop and stole Edinburgh University's silver mace. Exasperated, the Home Department at Whitehall offered King George's full pardon to any gang member who betrayed his fellows.

In March, Brodie and his fellow thieves broke into the Excise Office but found only petty cash. Two days later, John Brown, a gang member already evading deportation for crimes in England, seized the pardon by confessing to the sheriff-clerk. Brodie fled to London, and the sheriff-clerk offered two hundred pounds as reward for his capture.

Next, calling himself John Dixon, Brodie sailed to Holland. He entrusted letters to Edinburgh friends to the care of a Scottish tobacconist, who delivered them to the sheriff-clerk instead. Brodie planned to escape to the United States, but in Amsterdam he befriended a man who forged Scottish bank notes; there, a London public office clerk arrested him.

Legal Action and Outcome

At Brodie's trial for the bungled attempt on the Excise Office, his advocate (attorney) objected to Brown's testimony as an inadmissible report of a convicted felon. However, the presiding justice overruled the objection, declaring that the king's pardon, which removed all past convictions, made Brown's word legitimate. The jury voted conviction, and the justice sentenced Brodie to hang.

Awaiting execution on the gibbet (gallows) that he had helped design, Brodie acted cheerful, secretly hoping to thwart the noose with a steel collar and prompt removal of his body from the gallows. Though the plan evidently failed, those who later opened Brodie's unmarked grave found it empty.

Impact

William Brodie became legendary in Edinburgh, where, in the twenty-first century, his statue continues to stand on the High Street across from a large pub sign which depicts him as both the elegant town councilman and a masked thief. Robert Louis Stevenson adapted Brodie's double life into his somber science-fiction thriller *The Strange Case of Dr. Jekyll and Mr. Hyde* (1886). In *The Prime of Miss Jean Brodie* (1961), Muriel Spark named her defiant, flamboyant protagonist after Brodie's sister.

Further Reading

Edwards, Owen Dudley. "Stevenson, Jekyll, Hyde, and All the Deacon Brodies." *Folio* 1 (2000): 9-12. Asserts that it was not the historical Brodie but Stevenson's tempestuous collaboration with William Ernest Henley on a melodrama that inspired his subsequent novella.

Gibson, John S. *Deacon Brodie: Father to Jekyll and Hyde*. Edinburgh, Scotland: Paul Harris, 1977. Lively account of Brodie's life and its transformation into popular legend.

McNally, Raymond T., and Radu R. Florescu. *In Search of Dr. Jekyll and Mr. Hyde*. Los Angeles: Renaissance Books, 2000. Brief Brodie biography and comprehensive annotated bibliography of theatrical and cinematic adaptations of the Jekyll and Hyde story.

—*Gayle Gaskill*

See also: Charles Peace; Rob Roy; Jack Sheppard; Dick Turpin; Jonathan Wild.

Marcus Junius Brutus

Roman politician

Born: c. 85 B.C.E.; Rome (now in Italy)

Died: October 23, 42 B.C.E.; near Philippi, Macedonia (now in Greece)

Also known as: Marcus Junius Brutus Caepio (full name); Quintus Caepio Brutus

Cause of notoriety: As the leader of the plot to assassinate Roman dictator Julius Caesar, Brutus attempted to restore the Roman Republic but instead brought forth the Roman Empire.

Active: March 15, 44 B.C.E.

Locale: Rome

Early Life

Marcus Junius Brutus (BREW-tuhs) came from noble stock. His reputed paternal ancestor, Lucius Junius Brutus, helped overthrow the last king of Rome, Lucius Tarquinius Superbus, in 510 B.C.E. and then became one of the first two consuls of the Roman Republic. His mother, Servilia Caepionis, was descended from Gaius Servilius Ahala, who had murdered the would-be tyrant Spurius Maelius in 439.

Brutus grew up in a time when the Roman Republic was already in serious decline, afflicted by political violence and civil war. Gnaeus Pompeius Magnus (better known as Pompey the Great) treacherously killed Brutus's father in 77 during the revolt of Marcus Aemilius Lepidus. Quintus Servilius Caepio subsequently adopted Brutus, who then took the name Quintus Caepio Brutus. Marcus Porcius Cato (also known as Cato the Younger), Brutus's uncle and one of the fiercest adherents of the conservative faction in Roman politics, played a major role in Brutus's education. Brutus's rhetorical skill and deep commitment to philosophy were well known.

Military Career

Brutus served under Cato in Cyprus in 58 and was a *monetalis* (in charge of the mint) probably in 55. Some of his coins featured portraits of his famous ancestors Lucius Brutus and Ahala. In 54, Brutus married Claudia, daughter of Appius Claudius Pulcher. He served as quaestor in Cilicia under his father-in-law the following year.

In spite of having close connections to Julius Caesar (Caesar had an affair with Servilia and some believed him to be Brutus's father) and ample reason to hate Pompey the Great, his father's murderer, Brutus chose to side with Pompey in the civil war between Caesar's forces and those of Pompey; it began in 49. Caesar pardoned Brutus after Pompey's defeat at Pharsalus in 48.

Brutus did well under Caesar's new regime. He be-

Marcus Junius Brutus. (Library of Congress)

came a pontifex (a member of a Roman guild of priests) and, in 46, governed Cisalpine Gaul as a proconsul. The following year, Brutus divorced Claudia and married his cousin Porcia, Cato's daughter. Brutus became urban praetor in 44 and was promised the consulship for 41. However, Brutus became disenchanted with Caesar's increasingly autocratic rule. His friend Gaius Cassius Longinus brought Brutus into a large conspiracy against Caesar, and he came to play a leading role. On March 15, 44, the conspirators stabbed Caesar to death at a meeting of the senate. Chaos ensued as Republicans and those loyal to Caesar jockeyed for power.

By summer, the assassins had been forced to leave Italy. Brutus went to Athens and soon began to raise troops and money. Cassius did the same in Asia. Meanwhile, in Italy, Marcus Antonius (better known as Marc Antony) and Marcus Aemilius Lepidus (son of the Lepidus mentioned above), two of Caesar's chief lieutenants, formed a shaky alliance, called the Second Triumvirate, with Caesar's grand nephew and heir, Gaius Octavius (who later became the emperor Augustus). Together they tried and condemned the assassins in absentia, brutally suppressed local resistance through proscriptions, and prepared to avenge the death of Caesar.

In the fall of 42, the combined forces of Brutus and Cassius met with the army of the Second Triumvirate, led by Antony and Octavian (as Augustus was then called), at Philippi. In the first battle, Brutus defeated Octavian, but Cassius, following his own defeat at the hands of Antony, committed suicide. In a second battle several days later, Brutus was defeated, and he, too, committed suicide.

A Changing Reputation

Of all differences in literary viewpoint, the one between the Italian poet Dante Alighieri (1265-1321) and the English playwright William Shakespeare (1564-1616) over Brutus's reputation is among the most profound. In Inferno *(part 1 of his epic* The Divine Comedy, *translated by John Ciardi, 1954), Dante places Brutus in the center of Hell, one of the three most damned of all humans. There, frozen in a lake, is three-headed Satan:*

In every mouth he worked a broken sinner
between his rake-like teeth. Thus he kept three
in eternal pain at his eternal dinner.
For the one in front the biting seemed to play
no part at all compared to the ripping: at times
the whole skin of his back was flayed away.
"That soul that suffers most," explained my Guide,
"is Judas Iscariot, he who kicks his legs
on the fiery chin and has his head inside.
Of the other two, who have their heads thrust forward,
the one who dangles down from the black face
is Brutus: note how he writhes without a word."

Shakespeare ends his tragedy Julius Caesar *(pr. c. 1599-1600) with two short speeches by Brutus's principal enemies, Mark Antony and Octavius, as they stand over his body:*

Antony: This was the noblest Roman of them all.
All the conspirators save only he
Did that they did in envy of great Caesar;
He only in a general honest thought
And common good to all, made one of them.
His life was gentle, and the elements
So mixed in him that Nature might stand up
And say to all the world "This was a man!"

Octavius: According to his virtue let us use him,
With all respect and rites of burial.
Within my tent his bones tonight shall lie,
Most like a soldier, ordered honourably.

The judgment of Brutus's older contemporary, the orator Cicero, is more balanced: Brutus, he wrote, demonstrated that he had the courage of a man and the brains of a child.

Impact

Marcus Junius Brutus became a controversial figure in history. In antiquity, many admired his principled stand against tyranny, but others condemned the assassination of Caesar as the betrayal of a friend. Dante Alighieri's *La divina commedia* (c. 1320; *The Divine Comedy*, 1802) placed Brutus in the lowest circle of hell, while William Shakespeare, in his *Julius Caesar* (pr. c. 1599-1600), has Antony call Brutus "the noblest Roman of them all." Opponents of monarchy, autocracy, and federalism, as well as assassins such as Lorenzo de' Medici and John Wilkes Booth, have looked to Brutus for inspiration. Scholars, however, are more apt to note his usurious lending practices and lapses of political and military judgment.

Further Reading

Clark, Martin L. *The Noblest Roman: Marcus Brutus and His Reputation*. London: Thames and Hudson, 1981. A brief biography of Brutus with chapters on his historical reception and literary impact.

Morstein-Marx, Robert. *Mass Oratory and Political Power in the Late Roman Republic*. Cambridge, England: Cambridge University Press, 2004. Chapter 4, "The Voice of the People," includes a discussion of Brutus's attempts to sway popular opinion in Rome following the assassination.

Sedley, David. "The Ethics of Brutus and Cassius." *Journal of Roman Studies* 87 (1997): 41-53. Explores the role of Platonic philosophy in Brutus's decision to assassinate Caesar.

—*David B. Hollander*

See also: John Wilkes Booth; Cassius Chaerea.

Louis Buchalter

American gangster and killer

Born: February 6, 1897; New York, New York
Died: March 4, 1944; Sing Sing Prison, Ossining, New York
Also known as: Lepke Buchalter; Judge Louis; Louis Buckhouse (birth name)
Major offense: Murder in the first degree and numerous gang-related crimes
Active: 1916-1939
Locale: New York, New York
Sentence: Death by electrocution

Early Life

Louis Buchalter (BOOK-uhl-ter) was born in 1897 on New York City's lower East Side, home at that time to many Russian Jewish immigrants. His father ran a hardware store, and his siblings achieved success in life by honest means. Louis, known as Lepke, although quiet by nature, was drawn to street crime and rapidly made a name in the extortion rackets of New York's garment district.

Criminal Career

By the era of the Great Depression in the 1930's, Buchalter's vicious tactics had allowed him to rise to boss of New York's labor and industrial rackets. He had also become prominent in both the national gang syndicates and in the newly powerful Jewish-Italian gangs of New York City, where he was associated with Lucky Luciano. Buchalter was involved in prostitution, hijacking, narcotics, and extortion—and soon a new form of criminal behavior: murder for hire. He headed the Brooklyn-based Murder, Inc., one of the most vicious organized gangs of murderers in urban history. Under contracts from other gangsters, the hit men of Murder, Inc. killed hundreds of citizens and rival criminals, the most famous being gangster Dutch Schultz in 1935. Buchalter is alleged to have committed scores of the murders himself.

Legal Action and Outcome

Buchalter's first conviction was on a charge of theft in May, 1916. He was in and out of prison throughout the following two decades. Pursued by the police and the Federal Bureau of Investigation throughout the 1930's, Buchalter went into hiding in 1936. In 1939, he gave himself up and was sentenced to a fourteen-year term in Leavenworth Federal Penitentiary on a narcotics charge. In 1940, a Murder, Inc. hit man, Abe "Kid Twist" Reles, informed on Buchalter for four murders. Brought from Leavenworth for trial, Buchalter was quickly convicted of murder in the first degree and sentenced to death. After losing appeals all the way to the U.S. Supreme Court, Buchalter was executed in Sing Sing Prison's electric chair on March 4, 1944.

Impact

The unassuming Louis Buchalter was a particularly vicious criminal, seizing control of New York City's lucrative labor and extortion rackets. His notoriety chiefly arises from two factors. First, Murder, Inc., which he headed, was an original entity in organized crime: a syndicate that carried out contract killings nationwide in an efficient and businesslike manner, using the most vicious methods, such as shotgun blasts, bludgeoning by lead pipes, assaults with ice picks, and stranglings. Second, Buchalter is commonly described as the only crime boss ever to be executed in the United States. His execution in 1944 brought about the quick end of Murder, Inc. and the Jewish gangs of New York City. While Buchalter was perhaps not outdone in brutality, he is the only syndicate chief to have paid the ultimate penalty.

Further Reading

Cohen, Rich. *Tough Jews: Fathers, Sons, and Gangster Dreams in Jewish America*. New York: Simon and Schuster, 1998. Cohen presents a sociological and anecdotal account of the Jewish gangsters of pre-World War II New York and their lingering presence in the psyche of modern Jewish America.

Feder, Sid, and Burton Turkus. *Murder, Inc.: The Story of the Syndicate*. Cambridge, Mass.: Da Capo Press, 2003. Cowritten by the Brooklyn County assistant district attorney who prosecuted members of Murder, Inc., and helped send seven of them to the electric chair. An inside story of the rise and fall of the syndicate murderers.

Fox, Stephen. *Blood and Power: Organized Crime in Twentieth-Century America*. New York: William Morrow, 1993. Portrays organized crime in modern America and the interplay among corrupt politicians, Hollywood celebrities, and rival ethnic groups.

Kavieff, Paul. *The Life and Times of Lepke Buchalter: America's Most Ruthless Labor Racketeer*. Fort Lee, N.J.: Barricade Books, 2006. The first full-length biography of Buchalter also focuses on the New York City underworld.

—Howard Bromberg

See also: Joe Adonis; Albert Anastasia; Vincent Coll; Joe Colombo; Carlo Gambino; Sam Giancana; John Gotti; Sammy Gravano; Henry Hill; Richard Kuklinski; Meyer Lansky; Lucky Luciano; Salvatore Maranzano; Carlos Marcello; Dutch Schultz.

Ted Bundy

American serial killer

Born: November 24, 1946; Burlington, Vermont

Died: January 24, 1989; Florida State Prison, Starke, Florida

Also known as: Theodore Cowell (birth name); Theodore Nelson; Theodore Robert Bundy (full name)

Major offenses: Murder, kidnapping, and attempted kidnapping

Active: 1974-1979

Locale: King County, Washington; Salt Lake City, Utah; Colorado; and Tallahassee, Florida

Sentence: Two death sentences and three ninety-year sentences

Early Life

Theodore (Ted) Robert Bundy (BUHN-dee) was born Theodore Cowell to Eleanor Louise Cowell in a home for unwed mothers in 1946 in Vermont. He was raised for the first few years of life with his grandparents and his mother in Philadelphia, Pennsylvania, believing that his mother was his sister and his grandparents were his parents. Some believe that this early life influenced Bundy in later years and shaped his life course.

Ted and his mother moved to Tacoma, Washington, in 1950, and shortly thereafter Louise married and changed her son's name to Theodore Robert Bundy.

Ted Bundy. (AP/Wide World Photos)

Bundy stayed in Washington throughout his schooling and was a proficient student, graduating from high school and continuing on to college in Washington.

Bundy appeared in his early adulthood to have a bright future despite some problems in college, including a failed relationship with a girlfriend, Stephanie Brooks. He was an honor student and active in the political scene in Washington, particularly with the Republican Party, and worked at the Seattle Crisis Clinic. He was a man with many accomplishments and a seemingly ideal citizen.

Criminal Career

Many believe Bundy's first murder occurred in 1974, when a young woman was taken from her basement apartment in Seattle; only bloodstains were left behind. A wave of abductions of young women around the King County area in Washington followed. Skeletal remains of the missing women were found later in the foothills of the Cascade Mountains. Bundy often rendered his victims unconscious and took them to remote locations, where he strangled them. All his victims were young females, most in their college years.

After Bundy moved to Utah in 1974, disappearances of young women also began there. In 1978, Bundy entered the Chi Omega sorority house in Florida and beat five girls, killing two by strangulation and biting one of the deceased on her left buttock; the teeth imprints eventually helped to convict Bundy. A month after the sorority attacks, Bundy abducted, assaulted, and killed a twelve-year-old girl, Kimberly Leach.

Legal Action and Outcome

Bundy was first arrested in Utah in 1975 for suspicion of burglary. He was then identified in a lineup for an attempted kidnapping that had occurred in 1974 and sentenced to one to fifteen years in prison on the charge. In 1977, he was extradited to Colorado to stand trial for a 1975 murder. In June, 1977, Bundy escaped from jail and was recaptured six days later. He escaped a second time in December, 1977, and fled to Tallahassee, Florida. He was arrested there in February, 1978, as he drove a stolen car.

After his arrest in Florida, Bundy was indicted on two counts of murder and three of attempted murder. He went on trial in June, 1979, and was found guilty. Then, in 1980, Bundy was found guilty of the Leach murder and received a death sentence for that crime.

Ultimately, Bundy was given two death sentences and three ninety-year sentences. He spent the next ten years on death row, using legal tactics to delay his execution. In January, 1989, the state of Florida executed Bundy for the death of Leach.

Evil Wears a Smile

Ted Bundy was by all accounts affable, handsome, and extremely intelligent—fortunate in having come from a good family where he enjoyed a happy childhood. His disturbed personality and evil deeds were only magnified by those facts. In sentencing Bundy to death, Judge Edward Cowart expressed the incomprehensibility of a wasted life—and demonstrated how easy it was to be taken in by Bundy's charm:

It is ordered that you be put to death by a current of electricity, that current be passed through your body until you are dead. Take care of yourself, young man. I say that to you sincerely; take care of yourself. It's a tragedy for this court to see such a total waste of humanity as I've experienced in this courtroom. You're a bright young man. You'd have made a good lawyer, and I'd have loved to have you practice in front of me, but you went the wrong way, partner. Take care of yourself. I don't have any animosity to you. I want you to know that. Take care of yourself.

Impact

Although not the first serial murderer in American history, Ted Bundy was one of the most intriguing because of his charm and ability to manipulate his victims and the legal system. Bundy enjoyed taunting the police and baiting the media, reveling in the attention. Scholars are still unsure of the exact number of Bundy's victims because of the fact that Bundy never fully confessed, although he had been connected to the deaths of at least thirty women. Even up until the last minute, Bundy tried to manipulate and con his way out of execution by offering to confess to his crimes; ultimately his ploy did not work.

Further Reading

Michaud, Stephen, and Hugh Aynesworth. *Ted Bundy: Conversations with a Killer*. New York: Signet, 1989. The authors were able to interview Bundy preceding his execution in 1989; this is a transcription of those interviews.

Nelson, Polly. *Defending the Devil: My Story as Ted Bundy's Last Lawyer*. New York: Wm. Morrow, 1994. Nelson provides insight into the litigation surrounding Bundy's crimes.

Rule, Ann. *The Stranger Beside Me*. 4th ed. New York: W. W. Norton, 2000. Written by a woman who had been friends with Bundy, the book describes Bundy's life and criminal career. The fourth edition adds information about the impact Bundy had on society.

—*Jenephyr James*

See also: Joe Ball; David Berkowitz; Paul Bernardo; Kenneth Bianchi; Angelo Buono, Jr.; Andrei Chikatilo; Jeffrey Dahmer; Albert DeSalvo; John Wayne Gacy; Ed Gein; Karla Homolka; Leonard Lake; Henri Désiré Landru; Charles Ng; Dennis Rader; Richard Speck; Aileen Carol Wuornos.

Angelo Buono, Jr.

American serial killer

Born: October 5, 1934; Rochester, New York
Died: September 21, 2002; Calipatria State Prison, Calipatria, California
Also known as: Hillside Strangler
Major offense: Murder
Active: October 17, 1977-February 16, 1978
Locale: Los Angeles, California
Sentence: Life in prison without the possibility of parole in nine separate sentences

Early Life

Angelo Buono (BOH-noh) was born in Rochester, New York. After his parents' divorce, Buono, then five years of age, moved with his mother and sister to Glendale, California. In his youth, Buono developed a lifetime preoccupation with sexual violence against women and idolized the high-profile sex offender Caryl Chessman. Buono received poor grades in school and dropped out at the age of sixteen. As a juvenile, he was arrested several times for larceny and auto theft, sent to a reformatory school, escaped from the institution, and was later recaptured in December, 1951. In his early twenties, Buono became a husband and father. During his lifetime, he married four times and had eight children. Buono physically and sexually abused several of his wives and one of his female children. He was again arrested for larceny and auto theft in his thirties. In his forties, Buono, then separated from his latest wife, began an automobile upholstering business out of his home.

Criminal Career

In 1976, Buono's cousin, Kenneth Bianchi, moved to Los Angeles. In order to supplement their incomes, Buono and Bianchi became pimps to several prostitutes. It was the anger resulting from the escape of two of the prostitutes employed by the cousins that led them to start killing women in the fall of 1977. The team would pose as police officers in order to lure victims back to Buono's residence. The victims were raped and tortured, and their nude bodies were then dumped on hillsides in the Los Angeles area. Their ten victims were young women ranging in age from twelve to twenty-eight, with such occupations as a prostitute, a student, and an aspiring actress and model. Police attention intensified after the bodies of two schoolgirls, the third and fourth victims, were discovered.

Legal Action and Outcome

In 1978, Bianchi moved to Bellingham, Washington, and the next year, he was arrested for the murders of two local women. Bianchi claimed that he had dissociative identity disorder and implicated Buono in the Los Angeles murders. After admitting to fabricating his defense, Bianchi accepted a plea bargain that spared him the death penalty if he would testify against his cousin. Buono was arrested in October of 1979 for the murders of the young women in the Los Angeles area. In the early stages of the trial, the judge rejected a motion by the district attorney to dismiss the case against Buono based on lack of evidence. Thus two deputy attorneys general were appointed to prosecute the case.

Buono's defense team argued that Bianchi was the sole perpetrator of the murders; however, eyewitness testimony and circumstantial evidence directly implicated Buono in the murders. He was convicted of nine of the ten first-degree murder charges in October of 1983. The jury opted against a sentence of capital punishment, and Buono was sentenced to life imprisonment without the possibility of parole. He died in prison on September 21, 2002, at the age of sixty-seven, of a heart condition.

Impact

With intense media reporting, the Hillside Strangler murders produced widespread panic in the Los Angeles area, especially among young women. The trial of Angelo Buono, Jr., moreover, was one of the longest in

American history, beginning on November 16, 1981, and ending on November 18, 1983. Bianchi alone testified for approximately six months. Additionally, the judge and jury visited the different sites where the bodies were found, which is unusual in criminal trials.

Further Reading

Boren, Roger W. "The Hillside Strangler Trial." *Loyola Law Review* 33, no. 2 (January, 2000): 705-725. California Court of Appeals justice Roger W. Boren details his experience as the prosecutor in the Buono trial.

O'Brien, Darcy. *Two of a Kind: The Hillside Stranglers*. New York: New American Library, 1985. Award-winning author O'Brien uses police reports, court transcripts, and interviews with witnesses to provide a detailed account of the murders and Buono's trial.

Schwartz, Ted. *The Hillside Strangler*. Sanger, Calif.: Quill Driver Books, 2001. Focusing mostly on Bianchi, *New York Times* best-selling author Schwartz provides a comprehensive narrative, based on interviews with Bianchi, his psychiatrists, and police officers assigned to the case, of the murders and police efforts to apprehend the Hillside Stranglers.

—*Margaret E. Leigey*

See also: Joe Ball; David Berkowitz; Paul Bernardo; Kenneth Bianchi; Ted Bundy; Andrew Cunanan; Jeffrey Dahmer; Albert DeSalvo; Albert Fish; John Wayne Gacy; Ed Gein; Karla Homolka; Leonard Lake; Charles Ng; Dennis Rader; Richard Speck; Aileen Carol Wuornos.

Guy Burgess

British spy

Born: April 16, 1911; Devonport, Devon, England
Died: August 30, 1963; Moscow, Soviet Union (now Russia)
Also known as: Guy Francis de Moncy Burgess (full name)
Cause of notoriety: Burgess was a double agent for the Soviet Union, and his espionage damaged relations between U.S. and British intelligence agencies.
Active: c. 1934-1951
Locale: Cambridge and London, England; Washington, D.C.; and Moscow, Soviet Union

Early Life

Guy Burgess (gi FRAN-sihs BUHR-jihs) was the son of Royal Navy commander Malcolm Kingsford de Moncy and Evelyn Mary (née Gilman) Burgess. He attended Eton College and the Royal Naval College at Dartmouth, but his poor eyesight precluded a navy career. Instead, in 1930, he enrolled at Trinity Hall College, Cambridge, where he developed the behaviors and made the personal contacts that would shape the rest of his life.

Burgess quickly established a reputation at Cambridge as a brilliant student, a flamboyant homosexual, and an incipient alcoholic. He was introduced by fellow student Anthony Blunt to the prestigious Cambridge debating society known as the Apostles, a group that also included Kim Philby and Donald Duart Maclean, men who would later become spies with Burgess. Burgess also joined the Communist Party. Many members of his generation believed that communism offered the best hope of combating the rise of fascism in Europe, but in Burgess's own case, the rebellious nature of the act may have been equally appealing.

Espionage Career

Burgess's academic career failed to develop, but in 1936, he joined the British Broadcasting Corporation (BBC) as a producer. In this position, he met many of the leading political figures of his day, including British prime minister Winston Churchill. Sometime during the early 1930's, Burgess was also recruited as a secret agent of the Soviet Union, becoming a member of a ring of spies that later came to be labeled variously as the Cambridge Five, the Cambridge Apostles, and the Cambridge Ring. (Whether Burgess became a spy in Cambridge or on a trip he took to Moscow in 1934 is unclear.) Publicly, Burgess renounced his membership in the Communist Party and took increasingly pro-German positions.

In another public move, Burgess joined the British Secret Intelligence Service (SIS) in late 1938. In his new employment, he was able to win an intelligence position for Philby, who had also become a Soviet agent. When Burgess's own job was eliminated in 1940, he returned to the BBC. Subsequently, he held several positions with the British Foreign Office in which he routinely passed secret documents to his Soviet controllers. His final posting in the early 1950's took him to the British embassy in Washington, D.C. There, Burgess lived with Philby, who was unable to curb his colleague's increasingly outrageous behavior; Burgess was sent home in 1951.

During this time, British intelligence officials were growing increasingly concerned over security leaks from the foreign office. Their suspicions were focused not on Burgess, however, but on another officer and former Apostle: Maclean. It was later revealed that Maclean had also been recruited as a Soviet agent during the 1930's. In the official British reconstruction of events, Philby became aware of the investigation and ordered Burgess to help Maclean escape. The two disappeared on May 25, 1951, but Burgess unexpectedly accompanied Maclean all the way to the Soviet capital of Moscow, where the two reappeared publicly in 1956. Burgess spent the rest of his life in the Soviet Union, where he died at a relatively early age of a heart attack apparently brought on by alcoholism.

Impact

Although Guy Burgess helped damage relations between British and American intelligence agencies, the extent of his impact on world affairs is unclear. The secrets he passed to the Soviets were presumably important, but his most significant gift to his country's enemies was probably his recruitment of Philby into British intelligence. The issue is clouded by suspicions that British intelligence officials may have been aware of the Cambridge Ring earlier than was officially admitted. If this scenario was the case, the trio could have been used by British official to channel disinformation—that is, false and misleading documents—to the Soviets.

Burgess's impact on the British public is clearer. The treason of Burgess and his fellow agents (Blunt would be publicly unmasked only in 1979) was a blow to the morale of ordinary British citizens, and the resulting climate of dismay is reflected in spy novels written by John le Carré, Len Deighton, Graham Greene, and John Banville. Burgess himself is the subject of an acclaimed 1983 television film titled *An Englishman Abroad*, the screenplay of which was written by playwright Alan Bennett.

Further Reading

Boyle, Andrew. *The Fourth Man: The Definitive Account of Kim Philby, Guy Burgess, and Donald Maclean and the Man Who Recruited Them to Spy for Russia*. New York: Dial Press, 1979. The book that publicly revealed the identity of the fourth member of the Cambridge Ring, Anthony Blunt. Includes a bibliography.

Hamrick, S. J. *Deceiving the Deceivers: Kim Philby, Donald Maclean, and Guy Burgess*. New Haven, Conn.: Yale University Press, 2004. Revisionist account suggesting that British intelligence knew about the spying activities of Philby, Maclean, and Burgess earlier than previously revealed. Includes detailed notes.

Modin, Yuri. *My Five Cambridge Friends: Burgess, Maclean, Philby, Blunt, and Cairncross*. New York: Farrar, Straus, & Giroux, 1994. Memoir by the KGB agent who handled the Cambridge Ring, managed Burgess and Maclean's defection, and befriended Burgess in Moscow.

Piadyshev, Boris. "'Burgess. Guy Burgess.' (In the Service of a Foreign Power)." *International Affairs: A Russian Journal of World Politics, Diplomacy, and International Relations* 51 (2005): 179-190. Informal memoir by a retired Soviet diplomat.

—Grove Koger

See also: Anthony Blunt; John Cairncross; Donald Duart Maclean; Kim Philby.

William Burke
Irish murderer

Born: 1792; Orrery, Ireland
Died: January 28, 1829; Edinburgh, Scotland
Major offense: Murder
Active: 1828
Locale: West Port, Edinburgh, Scotland
Sentence: Death by hanging

Early Life

Much of what is known about William Burke (buhrk) comes from a broadside (a news sheet) published after his execution. While most of its substance is likely to be mere rumor and some pure invention, it alleges that Burke came from a good family and worked as a servant for a year after leaving home at eighteen, at which point he then served in the Donegal Militia. He married and had seven children; all but one died. He moved to Scotland to work as a "navvy" on the New Union Canal, and he began a relationship with Nell (Helen) McDougal, whom he met in Maddiston; the two scraped together a living buying and selling secondhand clothing. In 1827, they often stayed at a lodging house in Tanners Close, West Port, which was run by Maggie Laird—she had inherited the lodge from her dead husband. Laird was living with an Ulsterman named William Hare.

Criminal Career

When one of Laird's tenants, Mr. Donald, died on November 27, 1827, owing four pounds' rent, Hare allegedly conspired with Burke to steal the body from its coffin and sell it to the school of anatomy in Surgeons Square, run by Robert Knox. The two men were paid seven pounds, ten shillings, and they allegedly embarked upon a career as "resurrection men" (body snatchers). Assisted by Laird and McDougal, the men reportedly lured poor people (often prostitutes) to the lodging house, got them drunk, smothered them, and then sold their bodies. The broadside reported the number of their victims as sixteen. The one murder with which Burke was actually charged was that of an Irishwoman, Mary Docherty; Burke and Hare had been denounced by two fellow lodgers, James and Ann Gray, who had discovered Docherty's body.

Legal Action and Outcome

Following their arrest, Hare and Laird were recruited to give evidence for the crown against Burke and McDougal. Burke was convicted, although the verdict on McDougal was "not proven." Burke was hanged at Liberton Wynd, to the great delight of an enraged crowd. His body was then passed on to the University Medical School for dissection; his skeleton still remains there as an exhibit. Burke's confession exonerated Knox. McDougal allegedly fled West Port with a lynch mob at her heels and went to Australia, while Hare is said to have ended up as a blind beggar. Burke subsequently lent his name to the dubious profession of "burking"—a vocation that probably existed largely in the imaginations of writers and rumormongers. Knox eventually redeemed his reputation by becoming a pioneering physical anthropologist of the racist type that was typical of his era.

Impact

William Burke became the principal scapegoat of a contemporary moral panic regarding the treatment of the dead. At the time, a growing crisis of anxiety existed in Britain, which was manifest in exaggerated fears of premature burial and a dramatic increase in the ceremonial ritual of nineteenth century funerals. The advancement of medical science was dependent on knowledge of anatomy and physiology that could be gained only by empirical inquiry, but the demand for specimens generated considerable popular resentment, which was easily deflected from physicians to the "resurrection men" who did the dirty work of grave robbing. The characters of Burke and Hare became legendary through lurid literary works based on their case, including Robert Louis Stevenson's *The Body Snatcher* (1881) and James Bridie's play *The Anatomist* (pr. 1930). Actor Boris Karloff, who had earlier played Frankenstein's monster, was cast as Burke in the 1945 film version of Stevenson's story. The 1948 film *The Crime of Burke and Hare* was censored and redubbed as *The Greed of William Hart*, but *The Flesh and the Fiends* (1959) and *Burke and Hare* (1972) avoided censorship, as did *The Doctor and the Devils* (1985), based on a script by Dylan Thomas.

Further Reading

Bailey, Brian. *Burke and Hare: The Year of the Ghouls.* Edinburgh, Scotland: Mainstream, 2002. A modern sensationalist account aimed at the Edinburgh tourist trade.

Douglas, Hugh. *Burke and Hare: The True Story.* London: Robert Hale, 1973. A typical item of modern "true crime" reportage; includes a reasonable summary of the historical evidence.

Edwards, Owen Dudley. *Burke and Hare*. Edinburgh, Scotland: Polygon, 1981. A more balanced account than that of Bailey, but nonetheless focused on the more sensational aspects of the case.

Roughhead, William, ed. *Burke and Hare*. Edinburgh, Scotland: William Hodge, 1921. Includes early attempts to uncover reliable historical data and isolate them from broadside-based rumor; a work to which all subsequent accounts are heavily indebted.

—Brian Stableford

See also: Jack the Ripper.

Aaron Burr

American politician, third vice president of the United States (1801-1805)

Born: February 6, 1756; Newark, New Jersey

Died: September 14, 1836; Port Richmond, Staten Island, New York

Cause of notoriety: Burr was indicted but not tried for the 1804 murder of political enemy Alexander Hamilton during a duel; he was also charged but not convicted of treason in his plan to detach Western states and territories from the American union.

Active: 1804-1807

Locale: New York

Early Life

The son and grandson of Protestant divines who were presidents of the College of New Jersey (now Princeton University), Aaron Burr (EHR-ehn buhr) abandoned the study of theology in 1774 for the law. In 1775, he joined the Continental Army, where he distinguished himself for bravery. Promoted to major and appointed to the staff of General George Washington by Congress, he lasted only ten days; Washington always distrusted Burr, and as president, he refused to appoint Burr to any office.

Political Career

Burr served in the New York Assembly, 1784-1785, before becoming state attorney general. In 1791, he defeated Philip Schuyler, Alexander Hamilton's father-in-law, in an election for U.S. senator, earning Hamilton's unremitting enmity. Burr was the Republican candidate for vice president in 1796 and 1800.

Burr transformed the Tammany Society from a social club into an organization that dominated New York City's politics. He won control of the state legislature in 1800, guaranteeing the Republicans New York's electoral votes (then still cast by the legislature) and victory in the presidential contest. Every Republican elector voted for both Burr and Thomas Jefferson; under existing constitutional provisions, the tie went to the House of Representatives for decision. Although everyone knew Jefferson was the presidential candidate, Federalists ignored Hamilton's vigorous denunciation of Burr as unfit for the office and supported him, deadlocking the House for thirty-six ballots before permitting Jefferson's victory.

Jefferson suspected Burr had secretly collaborated with Federalists and froze him out of his administration. Knowing he would not be renominated, Burr unsuccessfully ran against the Republican candidate for governor

Aaron Burr.

The Burr-Hamilton Duel

The political rivalry between Aaron Burr and Alexander Hamilton ended with a bang, but there is reason to believe that death was never the real intention of either man. It is not clear how friendly the two ever were to each other, yet they worked together amicably, at least at first. Beginning in 1783, they shared a law practice in New York and often had dinner together. When, twenty years later, bitter and angry with each other, Burr challenged Hamilton to a duel, it may have been a bluff. Historians speculate that he may have expected Hamilton simply to apologize.

Hamilton did not back down, however, and on July 11, 1804, the two traveled from New York, where dueling was illegal, to Weehawken, New Jersey. The night before the duel, Hamilton wrote in a letter, "I have resolved, if our interview is conducted in the usual manner, and it pleases God to give me the opportunity, to reserve and throw away my first fire, and I have thoughts even of reserving my second fire." He proved true to this intention. When the two had taken up their Wogdon dueling pistols and assumed the agreed twenty-foot distance from each other, Hamilton fired first and missed. Although some feel that Hamilton intended to miss, others think the pistol may have misfired: It had a hair trigger, and dueling pistols were not very accurate even at short distances.

Burr then fired, but not at a "kill zone" such as the mid-chest or head. He shot Hamilton in the abdomen just above the right hip, and historians wonder if Burr's intention was only to wound Hamilton. A rib deflected the bullet upward into Hamilton's chest cavity, mauling his spine and liver. He died thirty-six hours later.

Burr later learned of Hamilton's letter and dismissed its statement out of hand. He never apologized to Hamilton's family for the killing, and he savored the adulation, mainly from Southerners, for defending his honor. However, he once admitted, "Had I read Sterne more and Voltaire less, I should have known the world was wide enough for Hamilton and me."

of New York in 1804 while still vice president. Once again, Hamilton attacked Burr's character. This time Burr asked him to retract or apologize; when Hamilton equivocated, Burr challenged him to a duel in which he killed Hamilton on July 11, 1804.

The Conspiracy

Almost universal condemnation of Burr throughout the North ended any possible political future, and Burr turned his attention westward. Exactly what he intended is unclear. Historians disagree, as did Burr's contemporaries; he told various people different things, keeping his actual intentions to himself. On August 6, less than one month after the duel, the British minister to the United States informed his government that Vice President Burr had offered to detach the territory west of the Appalachians from the Union; on March 29, 1805, the minister added that Burr desired $500,000 and dispatch of a British naval squadron to the mouth of the Mississippi. Burr received no British cash, but a similar appeal to the Spanish minister brought him $10,000. When Burr sought Andrew Jackson's approval in May, he did not mention disunion but talked of attacking Spanish territory. Some followers believed Burr intended to seize control of the West and use its military power to conquer Mexico.

Burr expected cooperation from General James Wilkinson, commander of American armed forces in the West, including using his troops to carry out Burr's goals. However, when Burr informed Wilkinson in July, 1806, that he was coming down the Mississippi with a band of armed men, Wilkinson panicked and sent Jefferson a translation of Burr's coded message, carefully edited to minimize his own participation in the plot. Jefferson ordered federal officers to apprehend Burr and transfer him to Richmond, where he would be tried for treason.

Legal Action and Outcome

Jefferson proclaimed Burr's guilt, but the spectacular and lengthy 1807 trial did not go as he expected. The United States chief justice John Marshall presided over the Richmond criminal trials as part of his circuit court duties and used the occasion to frustrate the president he disliked. Reversing a ruling he had made in February, 1807, in *Ex parte Bollman* that to be guilty of conspiracy to commit treason, it was not necessary to be physically present when an act took place. Marshall now insisted on a literal interpretation of the Constitution: The prosecution had to produce two witnesses to Burr's engaging in an overt act of treason. The prosecution could not do this, and Marshall's ruling effectively directed the jury to acquit.

Despite his acquittal, Burr had few prospects in the United States. In 1808, he traveled to Europe, ignoring the Napoleonic Wars as he tried and failed to interest Britain or France in his latest plan. The precise nature of the plan is unclear—even in letters to his daughter, the one person in whom he confided, Burr identified his project only as "X." Returning to the United States in 1812, he resumed his law practice. In 1833, at age seventy-seven,

Burr married Elizabeth Jumel, a wealthy, fifty-year-old widow. Within a year, she sued for divorce, accusing him of infidelity and of wasting her fortune.

Impact

The death of Hamilton from Aaron Burr's pistol shocked Americans and discredited dueling throughout the North more effectively than prohibitory legislation. Marshall's ruling in Burr's trial precluded use of treason accusations as political weapons in the United States. By insisting on a rigid interpretation of the Constitution, Marshall eliminated forever the British doctrine of constructive treason, in which anyone aware of a plot against the government is as guilty as someone who acts.

Burr's ambiguous intentions have been a boon to historical conspiracy buffs, who still debate whether he planned treason. When late nineteenth century archival research revealed Burr's negotiations with the British and Spanish ministers, his defenders argued that he had merely told them what they wanted to hear. Since only Burr and his daughter knew his actual intentions, no theory can be conclusively proved or disproved.

Further Reading

Fleming, Thomas. *Duel: Alexander Hamilton, Aaron Burr, and the Future of America*. New York: Basic Books, 1999. Places the duel in the political and personal context of the long-standing enmity of the two.

Lomask, Milton. *Aaron Burr*. 2 vols. New York: Farrar, Straus and Giroux, 1979, 1982. The standard, detailed narrative of Burr's life.

Melton, Buckner F. *Aaron Burr: Conspiracy to Treason*. New York: John Wiley & Sons, 2002. Suggests Burr planned treason in 1804-1806.

Vidal, Gore. *Burr*. New York: Random House, 1973. Vidal writes an imagined memoir of Burr based on historical facts.

Wheelan, Joseph. *Jefferson's Vendetta: The Pursuit of Aaron Burr and the Judiciary*. New York: Carroll & Graf, 2005. Portrays Jefferson as a vindictive persecutor of Burr.

—Milton Berman

See also: Simon Cameron.

Richard Girnt Butler

Official spokesperson for the Aryan Nations

Born: February 23, 1918; Bennett, Colorado
Died: September 8, 2004; Hayden, Idaho
Also known as: Richard Gernt Butler
Cause of notoriety: Butler was the voice of anti-Semitism for the neo-Nazi movement in North America.
Active: 1960's-2004
Locale: Idaho

Early Life

Born in Bennett, Colorado, in 1918, Richard Girnt Butler (BUHT-luhr) moved during the Great Depression to Los Angeles, where he studied aeronautical engineering. During World War II, he served in the United States Army and was stationed in India. While the European community sought to eliminate Nazi aggression during the war, Butler became an admirer of Adolf Hitler and set out to learn more about the German leader's resolve to purge society of those races he claimed to be inferior. Butler returned to the United States believing that his own government many times acted contrary to the best interests of its Caucasian citizens.

It was at Lockheed in Southern California where Butler met William Potter Gale, a fellow veteran and leader of a local paramilitary group called the California Rangers. Gale introduced Butler to Christian Identity—a religious belief that claims God's chosen people are not Jewish but in fact are of European descent.

During the 1960's, Butler associated himself with the Christian Defense League, an anti-Semite organization. Its founder, Wesley Swift, mentored Butler and later appointed him to the position of director. Following Swift's death in 1971, Butler attempted to legitimize the Christian Identity faith by blending the Christian Defense League into a newly formed religious sect, the Church of Jesus Christ Christian. Soon thereafter, Butler moved this new ministry to a compound near Hayden Lake, Idaho, in an attempt to establish a homeland of racial purity—an Aryan nation.

Militant Career

Butler's philosophy of racial solidarity flowed from a patchwork of diverse ideas. Combining religious bigotry with white nationalism, Butler transformed an otherwise heartless paramilitary organization into a passionate congregation focused upon preaching a message of racial purity in hopes of making the Pacific Northwest a homeland for the Caucasian race. While Butler's interpretation of Christian doctrine differed only slightly from the mainstream, his exaggerations of parables and prophecies were highly shocking to some. For example, Butler compared Hitler with Jesus Christ, suggesting that they were two of the greatest individuals who had ever lived.

Butler was well known for his friendship with Robert Matthews and his support of the Order, a white separatist organization. During 1983 and 1984, the Order committed bombings, conducted armed robberies, and assassinated a Jewish radio personality from Denver. That same year, Matthews was killed during a confrontation with federal agents.

Although neatly hidden from the public eye, Butler's compound became host to white power advocates from all walks of life. In addition to hosting the annual World Congress of Aryan Nations, Butler promoted youth training camps and survivalist schools for the paramilitarily inclined. All of this, Butler claimed, would ready his people for the coming race war. It would be his associations with militant groups, however, that would ultimately contribute to the demise of the Aryan Nations in the Pacific Northwest. In 1998, armed members of Butler's security fired shots from inside the compound at a minority family repairing their car out on the roadway. Represented by the Southern Poverty Law Center, the minority family prevailed in a civil trial in which a Kootenai County jury found that Butler had been negligent in the training and supervision of the security detail. This action caused the Aryan Nations to claim bankruptcy and ultimately led to the loss of Butler's compound in Hayden Lake.

IMPACT

The white supremacy movement might have remained fragmented were it not for the networking machine of Richard Butler's organization. For years his message to the Caucasian race came by way of newsletters, radio programs, demonstrations, pickets, and parades. Butler will best be remembered, however, for his ability to unite disparate racist factions under the umbrella of Christian Identity.

FURTHER READING

Abanes, Richard. *American Militias*. Downers Grove, Ill.: Intervarsity Press, 1996. A fact-filled contemporary account of the militia phenomenon in the United States in the late twentieth century.

Ezekiel, Raphael S. *The Racist Mind*. New York: Penguin Books, 1995. Ezekiel interviews four different types of people belonging to the hate movement in the United States.

Landau, Elaine. *The White Power Movement: America's Racist Hate Groups*. Brookfield, Conn.: Millbrook Press, 1993. Offers a historical account of the white power movement and broadly examines the philosophical roots of racial hatred.

—Douglas A. Orr

SEE ALSO: Willis A. Carto; David Duke; Matthew F. Hale; Robert Jay Mathews; Tom Metzger; William Joseph Simmons; Gerald L. K. Smith; J. B. Stoner; Randy Weaver.

Joey Buttafuoco

American statutory rapist

Born: March 11, 1956; New York, New York
Also known as: Bad Boy
Major offense: Statutory rape
Active: May 17, 1992
Locale: Massapequa, Long Island, New York
Sentence: Four months in jail

Early Life

Joey Buttafuoco (buh-tah-FEW-koh) worked in his father's car repair shop in Baldwin on Long Island for much of his life. His father was a convicted child molester who served time in prison in New York. Buttafuoco married his wife Mary Jo in 1977. They had a son, born in 1980, and a daughter, born in 1983.

Criminal Career

Buttafuoco met sixteen-year-old Amy Fisher in May, 1991, when she took her car to his repair shop. The two soon began a sexual relationship. In May, 1992, Fisher, then seventeen, had a friend drive her to Buttafuoco's home, where she rang the doorbell. When Mary Jo Buttafuoco answered the door, Fisher shot her in the head. The shooting shocked the quiet suburban area of Massapequa and created a media frenzy around all three members of the love triangle. Of particular surprise was Mary Jo's devotion to Joey. Not only did she remain married to him, but she also publicly supported his version of the events that led to the shooting.

Legal Action and Outcome

Fisher, who said Joey told her to shoot Mary Jo, was the only person to be charged in the immediate aftermath of the crime; the county prosecutor announced the statutory rape case against Joey closed in October, 1992. In February, 1993, Joey Guagenti, who had driven Fisher to the Buttafuocos' house, was sentenced to six months in jail for obtaining the gun used in the shooting. At that time the county prosecutor announced that he was reopening the statutory rape case against Buttafuoco.

After more than a year of maintaining his innocence and arguing that he and Fisher (who had come to be known as the Long Island Lolita) shared nothing more than a few slices of pizza, Joey pleaded guilty to one count of third-degree, or statutory, rape in October, 1993. The prosecution had spent the previous year gathering evidence, including eyewitness accounts and hotel receipts with Joey's signature. Fisher served seven years for first-degree assault and was released in 1999, in part because of support for her parole by Mary Jo.

In 1995 Joey was arrested for soliciting a prostitute on Hollywood Boulevard who was actually an undercover police officer. The following year he moved to Los Angeles with Mary Jo to pursue an acting career. While repairing cars and hosting a local public access television show, he also made cameo appearances in several movies. In 2003, Joey divorced Mary Jo, who remained partially paralyzed from the shooting.

In March, 2004, Joey was sentenced to one year in jail and ordered to surrender his mechanic's license after pleading guilty to felony insurance fraud. In March, 2005, he married a Croatian woman, Evanka Franjko, in Las Vegas. In August, 2005, he pleaded not guilty to charges of possessing ammunition, a violation of his pro-

Joey Buttafuoco leaves the Nassau County Courthouse with his wife Mary Jo. (Jeff Christensen/Reuters/Landov)

bation. After losing his license to repair cars, Buttafuoco was employed by an ice cream concession company. In February, 2006, Joey and Fisher reunited for the coin toss at the Lingerie Bowl III (models playing football in bikinis), a pay-per-view event aired during Super Bowl halftime.

Impact

The Joey Buttafuoco-Amy Fisher story inspired three made-for-television movies, one released in 1992 and two in 1993. Mary Jo appeared on the television talk show *Oprah* in June, 2005, with her daughter, Jessica, who reported that while she still spoke with her father, her brother had changed his name and terminated contact with him. Amy Fisher began making public appearances on talk shows at around the same time, feeding the public's appetite for news of her life after the affair. In interviews she took full responsibility for shooting Mary Jo Buttafuoco and recanting earlier claims that Joey Buttafuoco had conspired with her.

Further Reading

Dominguez, P. *Amy Fisher: Anatomy of a Scandal—The Myth, the Media, and the Truth Behind the Long Island Lolita Story*. Lincoln, Neb.: Writers Club Press, 2001. Provides an in-depth biography of Amy Fisher, exploring her childhood and teenage years and following her through her release from prison.

Fisher, Amy, with Sheila Weller. *Amy Fisher: My Story*. Reprint. New York: Pocket Books, 1993. In Fisher's first written account, the focus is on her experiences growing up and the details of her relationship with Buttafuoco.

Fisher, Amy, and Robbie Woliver. *If I Knew Then*. New York: IUniverse, 2004. Fisher describes her relationship with Buttafuoco and her experiences of being sexually assaulted while incarcerated.

—*Gennifer Furst*

See also: Roscoe Arbuckle.

Mary Butters

Irish witch

Born: Late 1700's; Ireland
Died: Early 1800's; Ireland
Also known as: Carnmoney witch
Major offenses: Accused of witchcraft and three murders
Active: August 1807 (prior to August 21, 1807)
Locale: Carrickfergus (Carrigfergus), Ireland
Sentence: Discharged by proclamation

Early Life

Very little is known of Mary Butters (BUH-turz) except for the events immediately surrounding her trial. A ballad written about her was later copied in an abridged form, but her name was copied as Mary "Butlers," probably adding to the difficulties of finding Mary Butters in history.

Criminal Career

Butters was known to the locals as a "wise woman." Alexander Montgomery, a local tailor also known as Sawney, owned a cow that was producing milk, but Sawney's wife could not make butter from that cow's milk. According to local superstitions, such cows were probably bewitched. Sawney asked Butters to "heal" his cow, and Butters arrived one evening in August at about 10:00 p.m. She first spoke some magic words. As part of the procedure she made Sawney and Carnaghan, a young man from town, go out to the barn and stand in front of the cow, wearing their waistcoats inside out. In the house, the chimney, all windows, and any cracks or openings were sealed by Butters, by Sawney's wife and son, and by a woman from town, Margaret Lee.

Butters then boiled some of the milk from the cow with some crooked nails and pins, and the house filled with smoke. The two men waited until morning, then found everyone inside the house lying on the floor. All but Butters had died. The men picked up Butters, threw her outside, and kicked her until she woke up. She claimed that a black man with a club killed the others and beat her unconscious. Many believed he was sent by the witch or warlock that Butters was trying to drive out or away from the cow.

Legal Action and Outcome

Butters was jailed until the spring of 1808, when the assizes (court sessions) were held. The trial was held in the town of Carrickfergus at the Carnmoney Meeting-House. Although all the jurors believed that the three vic-

The Ballad of Mary Butters

The Mary Butters affair inspired this ballad, which appeared in a 1908 issue of the Ulster Journal of Archaeology:

In Carrick town a wife did dwell
Who does pretend to conjure witches.
Auld Barbara Goats, or Lucky Bell,
Ye'll no lang to come through her clutches,

A waeful trick this wife did play
On simple Sawney, our poor tailor.
She's mittimiss'd the other day
To lie in limbo with the jailor.

This simple Sawney had a cow,
Was aye as sleekit as an otter;
It happened for a month or two
Aye when they churn'd they got nae butter,

Rown-tree tied in the cow's tail,
And vervain glean'd about the ditches;
These freets and charms did not prevail,
They could not banish the auld witches.

The neighbour wives a' gathered in
In number near about a dozen;
Elspie Dough, and Mary Linn,
An' Kate M'Cart, the tailor's cousin.

Aye they churn'd and aye they swat,
Their aprons loos'd, and coost their mutches
But yet nae butter they could get,
They blessed the cow but curst the witches.

Had Sawney summoned all his wits
And sent awa for Huie Mertin,
He could have gall'd the witches' guts,
An' cur't the kye to Nannie Barton.

But he may shew the farmer's wab,
An' lang wade through Carnmoney gutters;
Alas! it was a sore mis-jab
When he employ'd auld Mary Butters.

The sorcerest open'd the scene
With magic words of her invention,
To make the foolish people keen
Who did not know her base intention,

She drew a circle round the churn,
And washed the staff in south-run water,
And swore the witches she would burn,
But she would have the tailor's butter.

When sable Night her curtain spread
Then she got on a flaming fire;
The tailor stood at the cow's head
With his turn'd waistcoats in the byre.

The chimney covered with a scraw
An' every crevice where it smoak'd,
But long before the cock did craw
The people in the house were choak'd.

The muckle pot hung on all night,
As Mary Butters had been brewing
In hopes to fetch some witch or wight,
Whas entrails by her art were stewing.

In this her magic a' did fail;
Nae witch nor wizard was detected.
Now Mary Butters lies in jail
For the base part that she has acted.

The tailor lost his son and wife,
For Mary Butters did them smother;
But as he hates a single life
In four weeks' time he got another.

He is a crouse auld canty chiel,
An' cares nae what the witches mutter
He'll never mair employ the Deil,
Nor his auld agent Mary Butters.

At day the tailor left his post
Though he had seen no apparition,
Nae wizard grim, nae witch, nor ghost,
Though still he had a stray suspicion

That some auld wizard wrinkled wife
Had cast her cantrips o'er poor brawney
Cause she and he did live in strife,
An' whar's the man can blame poor Sawney.

Wae sucks for our young lasses now,
For who can read their mystic matters,
Or tell if their sweethearts be true,
The folks a' run to Mary Butters.

To tell what thief a horse did steal,
In this she was a mere pretender,
An' has nae art to raise the Deil
Like that auld wife, the Witch of Endor.

If Mary Butters be a witch
Why but the people all should know it,
An' if she can the muses touch
I'm sure she'll soon descry the poet.

Her ain familiar aff she'll sen'
Or paughlet wi' a tu' commission
To pour her vengeance on the man
That tantalizes her condition.

tims had died because of suffocation from the fumes of the "brew" Butters created, they also said that she had done so to help a sick or bewitched cow. Butters was discharged by proclamation. Some later sources claim that Butters had also killed the cow, but there is no textual evidence to support this.

IMPACT

Sawney remarried four weeks after the trial ended and left his job (and possibly the town), in part out of fear of his wife returning from the dead. Mary Butters's tale seems to be one of many examples of how such superstitions and beliefs pervaded this region. The ballad written by a local individual about the event ridicules Butters, Sawney, and the entire affair. The exact date of its composition is uncertain, but if it was written before the trial, as seems to be the case, it may have contributed to the outcome and dismissal of Butters instead of a guilty verdict and execution. Because there are no mentions of her in historical texts following the trial, the specific impact of her case outside her region and period are uncertain. However, similar attributes and beliefs continued to appear in trial transcripts and other accounts more than one hundred years later.

FURTHER READING

O'Brien, Lora. *Irish Witchcraft from an Irish Witch.* Franklin Lakes, N.J.: The Career Press, 2005. Provides history of witches, witchcraft, folklore, superstitions, and belief systems in Ireland. Also includes a short account of what is known about Mary Butters and a complete version of the ballad written about her.

Rhŷs, John. *Celtic Folklore: Welsh and Manx.* Two vols. 1901. Reprint. Oxford, England: Clarendon Press, 1971. A good introduction and analysis of Celtic folklore from early pre-Celtic history to the nineteenth century, including beliefs and practices of witchcraft.

Seymour, John D. *Irish Witchcraft and Demonology.* 1913. Reprint. London: Portman Books, 1989. Provides a summary of the history of witchcraft in Ireland, from the Middle Ages to 1911, as well as a brief passage on Mary Butters in particular. Also includes the entire text of the ballad.

Ulster Journal of Archaeology (1908). Contains the first known print edition of the ballad of Mary Butters.

—*Michael T. Martin*

SEE ALSO: Tamsin Blight; Margaret Jones; Lady Alice Kyteler; Florence Newton; Dolly Pentreath; Elizabeth Sawyer; Mother Shipton; Joan Wytte.

SAMUEL JOSEPH BYCK

Alleged American hijacker and murderer

BORN: January 30, 1930; Philadelphia, Pennsylvania
DIED: February 22, 1974; Baltimore, Maryland
ALSO KNOWN AS: Sam Byck
CAUSE OF NOTORIETY: Byck attempted to hijack an airplane with the intention of crashing it into the White House and assassinating President Richard M. Nixon.
ACTIVE: November, 1968; February 22, 1974
LOCALE: Baltimore-Washington International Airport

EARLY LIFE

Samuel Joseph Byck (bihk) was born in Philadelphia, the oldest of three brothers in a Jewish family. Byck viewed his father as a failure because of his financial difficulties, but he also saw his father as a kind person. After failing to complete high school and working odd jobs, he entered the army at age twenty-four. He left the army after two years with an honorable discharge.

In 1957, Byck married a woman within a month of his father's death, an act that his Jewish family felt was in bad taste. He tried to be a good husband and father to his four children but could not hold employment; this fact placed stress on his marriage. He failed in every job and business venture. His two brothers were financially successful, and he was jealous of them. Byck disowned his brothers, pretending that they had died by holding a Jewish ceremony to mourn their deaths.

CRIMINAL CAREER

In November, 1968, Byck was arrested for receiving stolen goods, but his case was thrown out of court in May, 1969. In 1969, Byck became angry at the federal government for rejecting his application for a twenty-thousand-dollar loan from the Small Business Administration to promote his business idea of selling at shopping centers the automobile tires from school buses. Byck was admitted to a psychiatric hospital for anxiety after his loan application was rejected; there, he was diagnosed as a manic-depressive (suffering from bipolar disorder).

Byck viewed his mental health problems as a product of his bad marriage and financial troubles, but he also viewed his personal problems as symptomatic of the political corruption of the Richard Nixon administration. He began to identify with the poor and minorities in society who were disadvantaged by the political system, and he perceived successful persons, such as his brothers, as "sell-outs."

Byck had been questioned by the Secret Service because he had suggested in conversations that someone should kill Nixon. The Secret Service, however, did not view him as a threat. He attended the inauguration of Nixon in 1973 and spoke with police officers and security personnel. On Christmas Day, 1973, Byck dressed up as Santa Claus and demonstrated outside the White House.

Byck and his wife eventually divorced, and he was allowed to see his children for only one hour per week. This was unbearable for him so he began to plot the assassination of Nixon because he wanted his life to mean something. Byck became inspired by a man named Jimmy Essex, who killed six people by shooting from the top of a hotel in New Orleans. Byck devised a plan he called Operation Pandora's Box: He would hijack an airplane and crash it into the White House. Byck made tape recordings about his life frustrations and mailed the recordings to famous people such as composer Leonard Bernstein and physician Jonas Salk.

On February 22, 1974, Byck attempted to hijack Delta Flight 523 at the Baltimore-Washington International Airport. Byck shot and killed a police officer and then shot and killed one of the pilots before he was shot through a window of the plane by a police officer. As he lay wounded, Byck shot himself in the temple to end his own life.

Impact

The Federal Aviation Administration published a document in 1987 on Samuel Byck's attempted hijacking to remind people about the potential dangers involved in civil aviation. In 2004, Byck gained notoriety when Sean Penn portrayed him in the film *The Assassination of Richard Nixon*. Byck also is portrayed in the Stephen Sondheim and John Weidman musical *Assassins*, which opened on Broadway in 2004. Finally, Byck gained some attention in the early twenty-first century when the 9/11 Commission mentioned his attempt to fly an airplane into the White House.

Further Reading

Clarke, James W. "Samuel Byck." In *American Assassins: The Darker Side of Politics*. Princeton, N.J.: Princeton University Press, 1982. In a book in which Clarke develops a typology for analyzing sixteen political assassins throughout American history, chapter 4 is devoted to Byck.

Sondheim, Stephen, and John Weidman. *Assassins*. 1991. Reprint. Bronxville, N.Y.: PS Classics, 2004. The script, lyrics, and musical score for a Broadway play based upon assassins and would-be assassins of presidents of the United States.

—*Scott P. Johnson*

See also: John Wilkes Booth; Arthur Bremer; Leon Czolgosz; Lynette Fromme; Charles Julius Guiteau; Richard Lawrence; Lee Harvey Oswald; Giuseppe Zangara.

JOHN CAIRNCROSS

British spy for the Soviet Union

BORN: July 25, 1913; Lesmahagow, near Glasgow, Scotland
DIED: October 8, 1995; England
CAUSE OF NOTORIETY: Cairncross's espionage undermined British attempts to deceive the Soviets during World War II and aided Soviet efforts against Nazi Germany.
ACTIVE: c. 1939-1951
LOCALE: Bletchley Park, Milton Keynes, England

EARLY LIFE

John Cairncross (KARN-kraws) was born in 1913 in Scotland, one of eight children. Following initial studies at Glasgow University, he completed a degree in both French and German at the Université Paris Sorbonne and acquired a degree in modern languages from Trinity College, Cambridge University. While at Trinity, Cairncross met four other young men—Donald Duart Macean, Anthony Blunt, Kim Philby, and Guy Burgess—who, together with Cairncross, would later become spies and came to be called variously the Cambridge Five, the Cambridge Ring, or the Cambridge Apostles. Cairncross was seduced into the group largely by Burgess. After graduating from Trinity, Cairncross began work at the British Foreign Office in 1936 after having achieved the highest score ever on both the foreign office and the home office exams. He secretly joined the Communist Party in 1937.

ESPIONAGE CAREER

While it is impossible to gauge precisely when Cairncross began passing information to the Soviets, most historians point to 1939 as the beginning of his career, when he first passed information to Burgess about British politicians and their attitudes toward Nazi Germany. In 1940, Cairncross became the secretary to Lord Maurice Hankey, the minister responsible for the various intelligence services in Britain. Upon Hankey's leaving office, Cairncross was assigned to the Government Code and Cipher School at Bletchley Park, Milton Keynes, England, where he decrypted communications intelligence. Cairncross states in his 1997 autobiography that at one point he attempted to stop passing information to the KGB (the Soviet intelligence agency) because he believed that the British government would not deliberately withhold such information from its allies. However, when he discovered that broken German codes continued to be kept from the Soviets, he returned to espionage. Cairncross passed along information concerning British knowledge of Soviet ciphers, the German Luftwaffe bases in the Soviet Union, German Tiger tanks, and the order of battle for the 1943 spring German offensive in the Soviet Union. Cairncross later wrote that the information he supplied helped the Russians win the Battle of Kursk in July-August of 1943. Cairncross later was awarded the Order of the Red Banner by the Soviets for his espionage work.

At the end of World War II, Cairncross went to work for the British treasury. He was fired from the treasury when papers were found in his handwriting inside Burgess's residence, although no charges were filed against him. He then went to work for the United Nations Food and Agricultural Organization in Rome and retired to southern France.

After the MI5 (a division of the British intelligence agency) questioned Blunt in 1964, Blunt named Cairncross as a Soviet spy, and Cairncross, in exchange for full immunity, made a full confession to his espionage activity during the war.

IMPACT

John Cairncross and the Cambridge Five were an example of the way in which the disenchanted youth of Britain became susceptible to Soviet influence during an era when many intellectuals held Marxist theory in high regard and expressed disgust with Western governments' appeasement of the Germans. The inability of MI5 to move quickly better enabled the activities of the Cambridge Five and highlighted the ineptitude of British counterintelligence to discover Soviet spies who had entered its ranks during and after World War II. The lack of prosecutions for the majority of the Cambridge Five, including Cairncross, was mainly a result of the British government's embarrassment at counterintelligence failures and its desire to maintain secrecy. The public did not learn the identity of Cairncross until two KGB defectors identified him in 1990.

FURTHER READING

Cairncross, John. *The Enigma Spy*. London: Century, 1997. In his autobiography, Cairncross portrays his acts as patriotic, alleges that only the Soviets could have defeated Nazi Germany, and denies giving the Soviets any atomic secrets.

Gannon, James. *Stealing Secrets, Telling Lies*. Washington, D.C.: Brassey's, 2001. An account of the secrets stolen by Cairncross and his role in aiding the Soviet Union.

Volkman, Ernest. *Espionage*. New York: J. Wiley and Sons, 1995. Documents Cairncross's activities and his involvement with the Cambridge Five.

—Michael W. Cheek and Dennis W. Cheek

See also: Anthony Blunt; Guy Burgess; Donald Duart Maclean; Kim Philby.

Caligula

Third Roman emperor (r. 37-41 c.e.)

Born: August 31, 12 c.e.; probably Antium, Latium (now in Anzio, Italy)
Died: January 24, 41 c.e.; Rome (now Italy)
Also known as: Gaius Caesar Germanicus (birth name)
Cause of notoriety: As ruler of Rome, Caligula engaged in bizarre and dictatorial behavior.
Active: March 16, 37-January 24, 41 c.e.
Locale: Rome, Italy

Early Life

Caligula (kuh-LIHG-yew-lah) was born Gaius Caesar Germanicus and was the third of six children born to Augustus's granddaughter, Agrippina the Younger, and his grandnephew, Germanicus, also the grandson of Augustus's wife Livia. He accompanied his parents on military campaigns and was given the nickname Caligula from the little boots (*caliga*) that he wore. His parents were involved in, and were the victims of, the dynastic struggles

Caligula, shown seated. (Library of Congress)

Suetonius on Caligula

The Roman biographer Suetonius was born less than three decades following Caligula's assassination. In his biography of Caligula, he described the Roman emperor's legendary cruelty:

The following are special instances of [Caligula's] innate brutality. When cattle to feed the wild beasts which he had provided for a gladiatorial show were rather costly, he selected criminals to be devoured. . . . Many men of honourable rank were first disfigured with the marks of branding-irons and then condemned to the mines, to work at building roads, or to be thrown to the wild beasts; or else he shut them up in cages on all fours, like animals, or had them sawn asunder. Not all these punishments were for serious offences, but merely for criticising one of his shows, or for never having sworn by his Genius. He forced parents to attend the executions of their sons, sending a litter for one man who pleaded ill health, and inviting another to dinner immediately after witnessing the death, and trying to rouse him to gaiety and jesting by a great show of affability. . . .

He was very tall and extremely pale, with an unshapely body, but very thin neck and legs. His eyes and temples were hollow, his forehead broad and grim, his hair thin and entirely gone on the top of his head, though his body was hairy. Because of this to look upon him from a higher place as he passed by, or for any reason whatever to mention a goat, was treated as a capital offence. While his face was naturally forbidding and ugly, he purposely made it even more savage, practising all kinds of terrible and fearsome expressions before a mirror.

He was sound neither of body nor mind. As a boy he was troubled with the falling sickness, and while in his youth he had some endurance, yet at times because of sudden faintness he was hardly able to walk, to stand up, to collect his thoughts, or to hold up his head. He himself realised his mental infirmity, and thought at times of going into retirement and clearing his brain. It is thought that his wife Caesonia gave him a drug intended for a love potion, which however had the effect of driving him mad. He was especially tormented with sleeplessness; for he never rested more than three hours at night, and even for that length of time he did not sleep quietly, but was terrified by strange apparitions. . . .

Source: C. Suetonius Tranquillus, *The Lives of the Twelve Caesars*, translated by J. C. Rolfe (New York: Macmillan, 1914).

that wracked Augustus's family for years. Germanicus was poisoned, and Agrippina was arrested and finally executed by Tiberius. Caligula's two older brothers were also executed on suspicion of treason. Caligula himself must have lived in a constant state of terror. He lived with his great grandmother Livia, then with his grandmother Antonia. In 31 C.E., he joined Tiberius in the emperor's retreat on the isle of Capri. When Tiberius died, Caligula was named his coheir along with Tiberius's grandson Tiberius Gemellus, who was executed a few months later.

The Roman public greeted Caligula's accession with joy. He was the descendant of Augustus for whom everyone had been waiting. In the early months of his reign, Caligula spent money lavishly on public works projects, entertainment, and donations to the people of Rome. He recalled exiles and repaid those who had been hurt by the imperial tax system. However, beneath Caligula's flamboyant exterior lurked the signs of a psychopath. Ancient sources report that even as a youth he displayed a fondness for watching executions, had trouble sleeping, and showed various other symptoms of a disturbed personality.

Political Career

Caligula had not been given any training for government, as Tiberius had been under Augustus. He found that he could do anything he wanted. Even a stable personality would have trouble coping with that much power, and Caligula was, in the judgment of all the admittedly hostile ancient sources, far from stable. A few months into his reign, he suffered from some unspecified illness that seemed to have affected his personality. Thereafter, his depravity knew no limits. He married one of his sisters, forced himself on the wives of prominent Romans, and compelled men to watch the executions of their family members. He even appointed his favorite racehorse to the Senate and invited people to dine at the new "senator's" house.

Caligula posed a serious danger to Rome because of his erratic decisions in military affairs. The army faced real threats on the frontiers, especially in Germany, but Caligula treated the soldiers as his pawns. The most famous incident that is cited as evidence of his madness was when he had his troops collect seashells to bring back to Rome as part of a triumph, a triumph in which he dressed up Gauls as conquered Germans.

The fatal flaw in the principate as Augustus had structured it was that there was no check on the ruler's power and no way to remove him, short of assassination. Augustus and Tiberius, both competent rulers, had lived into their seventies. Faced with the prospect of a deranged emperor who might live for years and resentful of his treatment of them, a handful of his Praetorian Guards, with the connivance of a few senators, managed to isolate Caligula in a passageway and murder him on January 24, 41 C.E. He was not yet thirty years old.

Impact

Caligula did not rule long enough to have significant impact on Roman imperial policy, but he left his mark in other ways. Augustus and Tiberius had tried to disguise the fact that the principate was a monarchy. Caligula began the process of turning it into an Oriental despotism. He considered himself a god and demanded that people recognize his divinity. Later emperors, such as Domitian, would return to that position. Caligula also was the first Roman politician to express open antipathy toward Jews. His attempts to place his statue in the temple in Jerusalem heightened tensions between the Jews and Romans so much that war would have broken out in 41 if Caligula had not been assassinated. Finally, Caligula was the first emperor to show his successors the extent of self-indulgence and depravity that an unchecked ruler could explore.

Further Reading

Barrett, Anthony A. *Caligula: The Corruption of Power*. New York: Simon & Schuster, 1989. A comprehensive biography of Caligula. Barrett challenges the common notion that Caligula was insane but argues that he did lack any sense of moral responsibility and was utterly unprepared to govern Rome.

Ferril, A. *Caligula: Emperor of Rome*. London: Thames & Hudson, 1991. Provides superficial treatment, taking hostile ancient sources as truth, which argues that Caligula was as mad as generally believed.

Malloch, S. J. V. "Gaius's Bridge at Baiae and Alexander-*Imitatio*." *Classical Quarterly* 51 (2001): 206-217. Discusses how Caligula's building of a bridge over the bay of Naples and other aspects of his behavior at that time demonstrate his desire to imitate Alexander the Great and establish himself as a powerful ruler.

Noy, David. "'A Sight Unfit to See': Jewish Reactions to the Roman Imperial Cult." *Classics Ireland* 8 (2001): 68-83. Analyzes the way in which Caligula's hostility toward Judaism was a departure from the toleration displayed by his predecessors and successors.

Wardle, D. "Caligula and His Wives." *Latomus* 57 (1998): 109-126. Ancient accounts of Caligula's marriages were biased by those who wanted to make his behavior appear bizarre. While he diverged from Roman practices, Caligula had reasons for each of his marriages.

Woods, D. "Caligula's Seashells." *Greece and Rome* 47 (2000): 80-97. One piece of evidence for Caligula's insanity is his order to his troops to gather seashells from the English Channel and bring them back to Rome to display to the Senate. Woods notes, however, that "seashells" was a slang term for a type of British boat. The term was misinterpreted by Caligula's later detractors in order to disgrace him.

—Albert A. Bell, Jr.

See also: Cassius Chaerea; Domitian; Herod Antipas; Pontius Pilate.

William Calley

U.S. Army lieutenant

Born: June 8, 1943; Miami, Florida
Also known as: William Laws Calley, Jr. (full name)
Major offenses: War crimes, specifically the murders of Vietnamese civilians in the My Lai massacre
Active: March 16, 1968
Locale: South Vietnam
Sentence: Life in prison; reduced to parole after three and one-half years served

Early Life

William Calley (CAY-lee) grew up in an upper-middle class home in Miami Shores, Florida. He graduated from high school in Miami and attended Palm Beach Junior College in Lake Worth, Florida. After leaving community college, Calley worked as a conductor for the Florida East Coast Railroad.

Calley's military career began in 1966, when he enlisted in the United States Army, as the Vietnam War was escalating. Upon his completion of basic training, Calley was transferred to Fort Lewis, Washington, where he began training as a clerk-typist. Calley was accepted to Officer Candidacy School in 1967, receiving only six months of junior officer training before his battalion was deployed to Vietnam.

Calley commanded little respect in the military and was remembered as being ordinary but power hungry and lacking intelligence. His superiors made fun of him openly, and his subordinates had no regard for him.

Criminal Career

On March 16, 1968, Lieutenant Calley, under the command of Captain Ernest Medina, led his men of the First Platoon, Charlie Company, First Battalion Americal Division into the hamlet of Song My, near the village of My Lai in South Vietnam. Calley ordered his men to shoot and kill everyone in the hamlet, which was made up primarily of elderly men, women, and children. Calley and his troops rounded up the civilians and shot them to death in the streets and in ditches. The women who survived were gang-raped by U.S. soldiers before they were murdered. The exact number of massacre victims is unknown but was estimated to be around five hundred.

During the summer of 1969, the U.S. Army launched an investigation into Operation My Lai, after ex-GI Ronald Ridenhour reported the illegal massacre of innocent civilians to U.S. authorities. Colonel William Wilson headed the investigation, interviewing any soldier who had involvement in, or knowledge about, My Lai. In June, 1969, Wilson met with Warrant Officer Hugh Thompson, who had threatened to turn his guns against U.S. soldiers if they shot another innocent My Lai civilian. Thompson offered much-needed information and identified Calley from a photograph as the leader of the massacre. He told Colonel Wilson that approximately seventy-five to one hundred bodies of those murdered by Calley and his troops had been placed in an open ditch. After ten weeks, Colonel Wilson submitted his report to Lieutenant General William Peers. The Peers report is still used to prosecute officers in cases of murder and rape.

Legal Action and Outcome

Calley was charged with six specifications of premeditated murder for the deaths of 109 Vietnamese citizens on September 5, 1969. His trial began November 17, 1969, and lasted until March 29, 1971, the longest court-martial in U.S. history. Throughout the trial, Calley

Lt. William Calley, Jr., during his court-martial at Fort Benning, Georgia. (AP/Wide World Photos)

asked to be exonerated of his crimes, maintaining that he was following orders and protecting his troops.

The practice of military courts is to exonerate an officer who has committed a crime while carrying out orders if there exists a question about the trial's legality or the officer's mental capabilities. Calley underwent psychological evaluations that determined he was of average intelligence and fully aware of his actions. Because the court deemed the order to kill children and unarmed civilians incapable of resistance unquestionably illegal, and Calley's evaluations proved him to be mentally sound, he was not eligible for exoneration.

On March 31, 1971, Calley was found guilty for the deaths of at least twenty-two civilians and the attempted murder of one baby. Upon his sentencing, Calley read a statement in which he justified his actions by saying he had to protect his troops from danger. He neglected to mention that the victims were all unarmed and that there were no U.S. casualties. He was sentenced to life in prison.

On April 1, 1971, President Richard M. Nixon ordered that Calley be released from prison and placed under house arrest pending his appeal. Nixon stated that Calley and the trial were being exploited by the media and antiwar activists to undermine the United States' actions in Vietnam. On August 20, 1971, the commanding general of Fort Benning reduced Calley's sentence to twenty years. In 1973, Secretary of the Army Howard Calloway reduced Calley's sentence to ten years. By September 9, 1974, Calley was paroled, having served just three and one-half years of his sentence under house arrest.

THE CHAIN OF COMMAND

According to many commentators, two tragedies resulted from the My Lai operation: the deaths of hundreds of civilians and a cover-up by the military. Just as officers must obey the lawful orders of their superiors, so are those superiors responsible for the behavior of their juniors. That responsibility follows the chain of command upward to the person who holds final responsibility—the U.S. president as commander in chief. However, superior officers are not held accountable for the actions of their subordinates when the junior officer is not sane or knowingly violates the law. Although fourteen officers were initially charged for the massacre, only two other officers besides Lieutenant William Calley were tried at courts-martial. Critics claim that Calley was a scapegoat to protect high-ranking officers. In the chain of command in Vietnam, they were:

- **General William C. Westmoreland**, commander of Military Assistance Command, Vietnam. He later became chief of staff, the highest-ranking post in the U.S. Army. He retired in 1972 and died in 2005.
- **Lieutenant General Robert E. Cushman, Jr.**, commander of the III Marine Amphibious Force. After leaving Vietnam in 1969, he became deputy director of the Central Intelligence Agency (CIA) and then commandant of the Marine Corps from 1972 to 1975, the service's top post. He died in 1985.
- **Major General Samuel W. Koster**, commander of the American Division (U.S. Army). Koster became commander of the U.S. Military Academy at West Point, a prestigious post. Charges alleging dereliction of duty and failure to obey lawful orders during the aftermath of My Lai were eventually dropped; however, he received a letter of censure and was demoted to brigadier general.
- **Colonel Oran K. Henderson,** commander Eleventh Infantry Brigade. Because he performed a perfunctory investigation of the massacre, he was indicted for dereliction in the performance of his duties, failure to obey lawful regulations, false swearing, and making a false official statement. He was acquitted of all charges in a 1971 court martial. He left the army and became director of the Pennsylvania Emergency Management Agency. He died in 1998.
- **Lieutenant Colonel Frank Barker**, Jr., commander of Task Force Barker. He died a few weeks after the massacre in a helicopter crash.
- **Captain Ernest Medina**, C Company. He was acquitted in a 1971 court martial and went to work at the Enstrom Helicopter Manufacturing Company, owned by his lawyer, F. Lee Bailey.

IMPACT

The United States had already been divided over its involvement in Vietnam. By 1970, the antiwar movement was gaining momentum, while President Nixon was under pressure to defend his foreign policies. Nixon feared that the United States would lose negotiating power with North Vietnam should the North Vietnamese learn that the United States was divided over the outcome of the war. Although many urged Nixon to open a government investigation into the massacre and examine all involved, Nixon felt it was politically expedient to let the military control the proceedings.

The psychological impact of the massacre and William Calley's conviction on American citizens was intense. Reactions to the outcome of Calley's trial were as diverse across the United States as were feelings about the war. Those who opposed the U.S. involvement in

Vietnam saw it as another global atrocity perpetrated by the United States. Those who supported the war viewed the trial as another abuse by the media to further domestic and international hatred toward the American position in Vietnam. Almost everyone, however, saw Calley as a scapegoat who took the entire blame for the massacre, which should have been distributed among Captain Medina and other officers.

Further Reading

Belknap, Michal R. *The Vietnam War on Trial: The My Lai Massacre and the Court Martial of Lieutenant William Calley*. Lawrence: University Press of Kansas, 2002. Belknap's balanced portrayal of Calley as both a criminal and a victim. The book offers a modern perspective on why the Vietnam War was so controversial.

Bilton, Michael, and Kevin Sim. *Four Hours in My Lai*. New York: Penguin Books, 1993. A gut-wrenching account of the atrocities that occurred in My Lai, depicted through eyewitness testimony, survivors' accounts, and military investigations.

Olson, James S., and Randy Roberts. *My Lai: A Brief History with Documents*. New York: Bedford/St. Martin's Press, 1998. A thorough look into the military's investigation of the My Lai massacre.

—*Sara Vidar*

See also: Reginald Dyer; Baruch Goldstein; Richard Nixon; William Clarke Quantrill.

Roberto Calvi

Chairman of Italy's Banco Ambrosiano

Born: April 13, 1920; Milan, Italy
Died: June 12, 1982; London, England
Also known as: God's banker; Gian Roberto Calvini
Cause of notoriety: Calvi created phantom holding companies outside of Italy that were used for illegal export and laundering of Italian currency; his actions triggered the largest European bank collapse to that date since World War II.
Active: 1975-1982
Locale: Milan and Rome, Italy
Sentence: Four years' imprisonment; murdered after his release pending appeal

Early Life

Roberto Calvi (roh-BEHR-toh KAHL-vee) was born the son of an official at Banco Ambrosiano. After graduating from high school, Calvi enlisted in the Fascist Italian Army and served in an Italian cavalry unit on the Russian front. Having survived World War II, in 1943 he joined Banco Ambrosiano, against his family's wishes that he study commerce or law.

Financial Career

In his more than twenty-eight years at Ambrosiano, Calvi ascended to the post of chairman and transformed the small Milanese lender into a bank with foreign departments and international ties. Michele Sindona, a Sicilian with Mafia connections, introduced Calvi to the director of the Vatican Bank, Chicago native Bishop Paul C. Marcincus, who then began entrusting Vatican Bank business to Calvi. Under bank auspices, Calvi established a secret operation for converting weakening Italian lira from the Vatican and possibly the Mafia and the Masons into other currencies, the U.S. dollar in particular. Calvi laundered the money, hidden among ordinary deposits, via banks around the world.

Legal Action and Outcome

In 1979, an investigation of Italian businessman Licio Gelli revealed him to be the headmaster of the secret Masonic lodge Propaganda Due, or P2. While Masonic lodges are not barred under Italian law, P2 was considered a secret organization and was thus illegal. A search of Gelli's home revealed a partial but nevertheless long list of P2 members, including officials in the Vatican, the Italian Catholic Church, politicians, members of the government, Mafia figures, and officers in the army and its intelligence branches.

Calvi's name was on the list, and he was soon investigated. He was fingerprinted and his passport taken away; then in 1981 he was formally charged, arrested, tried, and sentenced to four years in prison. Calvi was released pending an appeal, and he retained his position at the bank. In 1982 Banco Ambrosiano collapsed upon the discovery of massive debts. Large amounts of the money had been moved via the Vatican Bank, which was Ambrosiano's main shareholder. Calvi fled to England, possibly lured by the set-up promise of a partial bailout by the Church organization Opus Dei. To flee, Calvi used a false passport and a private plane hired by a "fixer" with Mafia connections.

Murder in London

Within days, Calvi's body was found hanging from London's Blackfriars Bridge. His suit had been stuffed with rocks, but his pockets held more than fourteen thousand dollars in cash in various currencies. London police declared the death to be a suicide, despite evidence to the contrary. A 1992 exhumation and autopsy revealed that Calvi had been suffocated before hanging, and the case was reopened. In 2005, Licio Gelli was indicted in Calvi's murder; Gelli's statement to the court implicated several others. On October 5, 2005, a trial in Rome commenced of five people charged with Calvi's murder. These were businessman Flavio Carboni, his former girlfriend Manuela Kleinzig, Mafia member Pippo Calò, Roman gangster Ernesto Diotallevi, and Calvi's bodyguard and driver Silvano Vittor.

Impact

Roberto Calvi structured a virtually impenetrable web of money-laundering banks and oversaw payments to P-2 members, bribes of political figures and, reputedly, the dispensing of funds for the Vatican to the Solidarity trade union movement in Poland. The scandal following Banco Ambrosiano's collapse led to the Bank of Italy receiving new powers, allowing it to become a vigorous watchdog as well as the central bank. The many sources on Calvi's life and death include a full-length Italian feature film, *I banchieri di dio* (2001; *God's Bankers*) and an Arts & Entertainment Network biography first broadcast in October, 2005.

Further Reading

Cornwell, Rupert. *God's Banker: The Life and Death of Roberto Calvi*. London: Unwin, 1984. Arguably the most detailed account of the scandal.

Gurwin, Larry. *The Calvi Affair: Death of a Banker*. London: Macmillan, 1983. Detailed, clearly written, with photographs.

Jones, Tobias. *The Dark Heart of Italy*. New York: North Point Press, 2004. The Calvi affair is presented within a chapter on the difference between Catholicism of individuals and Vatican manipulations.

Raw, Charles. *The Moneychangers: How the Vatican Bank Enabled Roberto Calvi to Steal $250 Million for the Heads of the P2 Masonic Lodge*. London: Harvill, 1992. More than 485 pages, relentlessly prosecutorial in tone; individual chapters, however, provide compelling information, documents, and photographs.

Williams, Paul L. *The Vatican Exposed: Money, Murder, and the Mafia*. Amherst, N.Y.: Prometheus Books, 2003. Historical account of how the Vatican Bank came to be and how Calvi became its banker.

—*Robert B. Youngblood*

See also: Martin Frankel; Nick Leeson.

Simon Cameron

American secretary of war (1861-1862)

Born: March 8, 1799; Maytown, Pennsylvania
Died: June 26, 1889; Donegal Springs, near Maytown, Pennsylvania
Cause of notoriety: Cameron, as war secretary under President Abraham Lincoln during the Civil War, bungled war efforts and was accused of administering the war department with blatant favoritism.
Active: 1860-1862
Locale: Washington, D.C.

Early Life

As a young man, Simon Cameron (CAM-ruhn) apprenticed in the newspaper industry and soon invested in several local newspapers. Recognizing that political connections would help him make money, Cameron used his business enterprises to lead him into politics. As his financial interests diversified into mining and transportation, Cameron rose in prominence in the Democratic Party, presiding over the Pennsylvania delegation at the 1832 Democratic National Convention and serving in 1837 on Pennsylvania's Constitutional Convention. These political connections led to his association with James Buchanan, a powerful Pennsylvania senator, who arranged Cameron's major appointment as Indian commissioner to the Winnebago tribe. However, rumors soon circulated that Cameron was skimming money from the Winnebagos' annuity payments, and he resigned. Thereafter, rumors of corruption followed Cameron wherever he went.

Political Career

In 1845, Buchanan became secretary of state, and Cameron ran in the special election to fill Buchanan's Senate seat. Believing that the Whig Party's economic platform was more agreeable to his burgeoning economic interests, Cameron appealed to the Pennsylvania Whigs for support. Cameron won the election but angered Democrats in the process. Unable to straddle the differences between the Democratic Party he represented and the Whig Party to which he owed his office, Cameron declined to run for reelection in 1848 and returned to Pennsylvania. Alienated from his Democratic supporters, Cameron determined to create a new base of political support. By 1855, Cameron's influence rivaled that of Buchanan, and he ran for the Senate on the American (Know-Nothing) Party ticket; he lost the election.

The following year, Cameron again switched parties, this time to the new Republican Party. This move eventually led to a successful Senate campaign. As a Republican senator from a prominent state, Cameron wielded some influence on the selection and support for the Republican presidential candidate in 1860. At the Republican Convention in Chicago, Cameron could not collect enough support for a presidential nomination for himself, but he did exert enough influence to earn a major appointment from any candidate whom he decided to back. When the supporters of Lincoln promised a cabinet position for his support, Cameron backed Lincoln.

Once Lincoln became president, Cameron hoped to become secretary of the treasury in order to help his personal business interests. Instead, in December, 1860, Lincoln named Cameron as the secretary of war. However, rumors of Cameron's shady business dealings and constant shifting between political parties worried Lincoln (one congressman told Lincoln that Cameron was so greedy, he would steal a red-hot stove), and Lincoln temporarily withdrew the nomination. The president needed the support of Pennsylvania in the looming secession crisis, so in March, 1861, he offered Cameron the position once again.

Cameron proved unable to meet the challenge of his position. First, he lacked the experience necessary to make military decisions. As the standoff at Fort Sumter, in the harbor at Charleston, South Carolina, intensified, Cameron provided little leadership and made few proactive decisions. Once the Civil War began, Cameron provided little advice to the president on how to conduct the war. Second, Cameron lacked the ability to control the bureaucracy at the War Department. As volunteers flooded into military service, Cameron failed to organize the department to accommodate them. Moreover, the new army constantly lacked weapons, supplies, uniforms, or anything else to shape it into an effective force. Third, Cameron deviated from the Lincoln administration's established policy on slavery. In the annual report issued every year from the War Department, Cameron stated that it was his belief that not only should the government seize slaves from their owners, but also the slaves should be armed as soldiers. Cameron did not clear the report with Lincoln beforehand, and Lincoln ordered Cameron to withdraw the statement.

Finally, Cameron came under scrutiny for the rampant corruption at the War Department. Employing the "spoils system" of the day, Cameron placed friends and business associates in key positions for procuring equipment for the army, opening him to charges of corruption when those associates paid too much for defective rifles, sick horses, and shoddy equipment. Cameron blatantly exploited his knowledge of government business and military strategies to invest in companies soon to receive supply and transportation contracts. For instance, he invested heavily in the Central Pennsylvania Railroad, knowing that the company was to receive large sums of money from the government to haul army supplies, thus making a huge profit for himself in the process. Ever the businessman, Cameron saw no conflict of interest in acting on this insider information.

Congress soon began an investigation of the War Department, and Lincoln, wishing to minimize the damage, decided to remove Cameron before the investigation could issue its report. Lincoln named Cameron as the new ambassador to Russia, and Cameron left the country just as the congressional investigation results, highly critical of Cameron's leadership, became public. Unhappy as ambassador, Cameron left Russia almost as soon as he arrived. He tried to run for his Senate seat in 1862 after returning to Pennsylvania, but he lost the election. Refusing to return to Russia, Cameron remained in Pennsylvania and resumed his position as political insider. Cameron ran a powerful Pennsylvania political machine, and no one could be elected without his behind-the-scenes support. He retired from politics in 1877 and died in his hometown in 1889.

Impact

Simon Cameron's weaknesses as war secretary during the early years of the Civil War were in part responsible for early Union defeats that threatened the young nation's survival. Cameron's successor as secretary of war, Edwin Stanton, proved a brilliant choice. Stanton soon got the War Department under control and properly received the credit for leading the department through the Civil War. The corruption of Cameron foreshadowed the rampant corruption that plagued presidents throughout the rest of the nineteenth century. Cameron is credited with the saying that "the definition of an honest politician is someone who, when he is bought, stays bought."

Further Reading

Bradley, Erwin S. *Simon Cameron, Lincoln's Secretary of War: A Political Biography.* Philadelphia: University of Pennsylvania Press, 1966. The only dedicated biography of Cameron, the book claims that charges of corruption were overstated and Cameron did the best he could in an impossible situation.

Crippen, Lee F. *Simon Cameron: Antebellum Years.* New York: DaCapo Press, 1972. A study of Cameron's development as a businessman and politician, good background for understanding Cameron's dubious reputation.

Goodwin, Doris K. *Team of Rivals: The Political Genius of Abraham Lincoln.* New York: Simon & Schuster, 2005. An extensive study of Lincoln's cabinet, with a good discussion of the delicate political decision to remove Cameron from office.

—*Steven J. Ramold*

See also: Bobby Baker; Aaron Burr; Charles W. Colson; John D. Ehrlichman; Albert B. Fall; H. R. Haldeman; E. Howard Hunt; G. Gordon Liddy; Thomas Joseph Pendergast; Leander Perez; William Marcy Tweed.

Billy Cannon

American football hero and counterfeiter

Born: August 2, 1937; Philadelphia, Mississippi
Also known as: William Abb Cannon (full name)
Major offense: Counterfeiting
Active: December 1, 1989-November 19, 1990
Locale: Baton Rouge, Louisiana
Sentence: Five years in a federal penitentiary and a ten-thousand-dollar fine; served two and a half years in Texarkana federal prison and time in a Baton Rouge halfway house

Early Life

Billy Cannon (CAN-nuhn) was born in Philadelphia, Mississippi, and grew up in a working-class area of Baton Rouge, Louisiana, known as Istrouma. He enjoyed an outstanding football career in high school and at Louisiana State University (LSU). He was awarded the 1959 Heisman Trophy as the outstanding national collegiate football player and was instrumental in the team's gaining the national championship that year. He then went on to have a successful eleven-year career in professional football with the Houston Oilers and Oakland Raiders.

As a youth, Cannon was known to participate in various acts of general delinquency and violence. However, because he was such an outstanding athletic talent, several adults defended him, and victims rarely pressed charges. He once received a ninety-day suspended sentence and probation when one beating victim decided to press charges. Once his professional athletic career developed, Cannon associated with high-profile celebrities and was known to frequent horse races.

Criminal Career

Cannon demonstrated determination to develop a successful life after football. He attended the University of Tennessee and Loyola University of Chicago dental schools during the off seasons of his football schedule. His successful Baton Rouge orthodontic practice reportedly earned as much as $300,000 per year.

Canon's financial problems began to surface in the early 1980's, when he was involved in numerous lawsuits tied to poor investments and reported gambling. At the time he faced these problems, Cannon associated with John Stiglets, a t-shirt printer and convicted counterfeiter. Cannon funded operations for the printing of approximately six million dollars' worth of one-hundred-dollar bills.

A man who was caught passing the bad bills named Cannon as the ringleader of the counterfeiting operation. More than fifty federal agents worked on the case, and Cannon's phones were wiretapped. Cannon ultimately took the investigators to his property, where he had been secretly hiding the bills in water coolers.

Legal Action and Outcome

Because Cannon pleaded guilty to counterfeiting and cooperated with the investigators and prosecutors, there is little public information about his counterfeiting operation. Although he was sentenced to five years in prison, he was released from the federal prison in Texarkana after quietly serving two and a half years and continuing his term at the Salvation Army halfway house in Baton Rouge.

Cannon's license to practice dentistry was restored after his release from prison, but he faced serious financial problems and filed for bankruptcy in 1995 after failing to restore his dental practice. Bankrupt, his private orthodontic practice closed, and his Heisman Trophy reportedly sold to a Baton Rouge restaurateur, Cannon accepted a job as the head of the Angola State (Louisiana) Penitentiary Dental Clinic, where he led a relatively quiet life working and raising racehorses.

Billy Cannon. (AP/Wide World Photos)

Impact

Billy Cannon is primarily remembered for his football accomplishments, as well as for being one of twenty players who played with the American Football League for its full ten-year existence. In spite of his significant achievements that mean so much to football fans throughout the state of Louisiana, no significant book has ever been written on his life. The main character of a 1981 novel written by Frank Deford and titled *Everybody's All-American*, LSU football star Gavin Grey, shares many similarities with Cannon, but the author claims his book is not a biographical depiction of Cannon. While Cannon continued to enjoy fame for his football heroics, he angrily declined to make any public comment on his criminal career.

Further Reading

Deford, Frank. *Everybody's All-American*. New York: Viking Press, 1981. Although *Sports Illustrated* writer Deford has denied that his novel, set in the late 1950's, is a portrayal of Cannon, the parallels between his life and that of protagonist Gavin Grey are patent, even if the crimes are different.

Goodman, Michael J. "An Utter Disaster: Former Football Star Billy Cannon." *The Sporting News*, May 29, 1995. A detailed interview with Cannon around the time of his bankruptcy, likely his most candid thoughts on his criminal actions.

Martin, Maggie. "Football Exploits Still Defining Moments for Billy Cannon." *Shreveport Times*, August 21, 2005, p. C1. Discusses Cannon's football exploits in an attempt to resurrent Cannon's reputation.

Peter, Josh. "Still Running." *Times-Picayune*, December 31, 2003, p. C1. This newspaper article mentions Cannon's willingness to talk about his football days and resistance to talk about his criminal actions.

—*John C. Kilburn, Jr.*

See also: O. J. Simpson.

Al Capone

American gangster

Born: January 17, 1899; Brooklyn, New York
Died: January 25, 1947; Palm Island, Florida
Also known as: Alphonse Gabriel Capone (full name); Scarface
Major offenses: Income tax evasion, contempt of court, and carrying concealed deadly weapons
Active: 1920's-1930's
Locale: Chicago, Philadelphia, and New York
Sentence: One year for carrying concealed deadly weapons and released nine months later for good behavior; eleven years in federal prison for income tax evasion, plus a fine of $50,000, $7,692 in court costs, and payment of $215,000 plus interest due on back taxes; concurrent six-months' imprisonment for contempt of court

Early Life

Alphonse "Al" Capone (kah-POHN) was born January 17, 1899, in Brooklyn, New York, to Italian emigrants Gabriele and Teresina Raiola Capone. Alphonse soon joined two neighborhood gangs—the Forty Thieves Juniors and the Brooklyn Rippers. He quit school at age fourteen after fighting with a teacher. For a few years, he worked at odd jobs around Brooklyn and then joined the notorious Five Points Gang headed by Frankie Yale in Manhattan. He became bartender and bouncer in Yale's bar, the Harvard Inn. At Harvard Inn, Capone insulted the sister of Frank Gallucio, a thug who then slashed Capone's right cheek with a switchblade knife, leaving him scarred for life and earning him the nickname Scarface.

In 1918, Capone met an Irish girl, Mary (Mae) Coughlin, at a dance. On December 4, 1918, she gave birth to their son, Albert "Sonny" Francis Capone, and they were married on December 30, 1918, in Brooklyn. In 1919, they moved to Long Island in order to be close to Yale's business on "Rum Row." In New York, Capone was linked to two murders but was never tried. However, after Capone had a fight with a rival gang member, Yale sent him to Chicago to get a break from the New York scene. The Capone family moved to 7244 South Prairie Avenue in Chicago, where Capone launched his career as one of the most notorious gangsters in American history.

Criminal Career

In Chicago, Capone worked for underworld boss Johnny Torrio, who quickly recognized Capone's talents for gang leadership. By 1922, Capone was Torrio's second in command and was soon made a full partner in Torrio's prostitution rackets, saloons, and gambling houses in Chicago. In 1925, after Torrio barely survived an assassination attempt, he turned the business over to Capone and left Chicago. Between 1925 and 1930, Capone expanded Chicago's vice industries into a multimillion-dollar business. He controlled distilleries and breweries, nightclubs, speakeasies, gambling houses, racetracks, and brothels; combined, these enterprises earned him $100 million a year.

By 1928, Capone's crime gang numbered more than one thousand experienced gunmen, and Capone could truthfully say he "owned" Chicago. At least half of the city's police force was on Capone's payroll. He bribed aldermen, state's attorneys, legislators, governors, Congress members, and mayors, including Chicago's own mayor, William "Big Bill" Thompson.

In 1928, Capone's Chicago headquarters included the Four Deuces on South Wabash and the Metropole and Lexington Hotels on South Michigan Avenue. He maintained suburban headquarters in Cicero and reputed

Al Capone. (Library of Congress)

Scarface and Free Enterprise

Al Capone once proudly said,

I make my money by supplying a public demand. If I break the law, my customers, who number hundreds of the best people in Chicago, are as guilty as I am. The only difference is that I sell and they buy. Everybody calls me a racketeer. I call myself a businessman.

In 1930, British journalist Claud Cockburn interviewed Capone. Cockburn asked what Capone would have done if he had not become a gangster and related Capone's reply:

"[S]elling newspapers barefoot on the street in Brooklyn." He stood up as he spoke, cooling his finger-tips in the rose bowl in front of him. He sat down again, brooding and sighing. Despite the ham-and-corn, what he said was quite probably true and I said so, sympathetically. A little bit too sympathetically, as immediately emerged, for as I spoke I saw him looking at me suspiciously, not to say censoriously. My remarks about the harsh way the world treats barefoot boys in Brooklyn were interrupted by an urgent angry waggle of his podgy hand. "Listen," he said, "don't get the idea I'm one of these goddam radicals. Don't get the idea I'm knocking the American system. The American system. . . ." As though an invisible chairman had called upon him for a few words, he broke into an oration upon the theme. He praised freedom, enterprise, and the pioneers. He spoke of "our heritage." He referred with contemptuous disgust to Socialism and Anarchism. "My rackets," he repeated several times, "are run on strictly American lines and they're going to stay that way."

His vision of the American system began to excite him profoundly and now he was on his feet again, leaning across the desk like the chairman of a board meeting, his fingers plunged in the rose bowls.

"This American system of ours," he shouted, "call it Americanism, call it Capitalism, call it what you like, gives to each and every one of us a great opportunity if we only seize it with both hands and make the most of it." He held out his hand towards me, the fingers dripping a little, and stared at me sternly for a few seconds before reseating himself.

Source: Claud Cockburn, *In Time of Trouble: An Autobiography* (London: Rupert Hart-Davis, 1956).

hideouts in Indiana, Tennessee, and Arkansas. In 1928, Capone bought an estate in Palm Island, Florida, to which he retreated when his men carried out planned gangland killings. He was there on February 14, 1929, when his henchmen, led by John "Machine Gun" McGurn, ambushed Bugs Moran's gang on Chicago's North Side. In what became known as the St. Valentine's Day Massacre, Capone's gunmen slaughtered six Moran gang members and a friend in the S-M-C Cartage Company garage. Moran escaped the carnage because he was late to the meeting and never entered the building. Though Capone's connection was obvious, no person was ever prosecuted for the crime. The massacre did, however, end Moran's control of the North Side; his gang vanished, leaving Chicago open to Capone's takeover. Moreover, the incident brought Capone's criminal activities under scrutiny at the Federal Bureau of Investigation (FBI) and eventually led to his conviction for income tax evasion in 1931.

Legal Action and Outcome

When Capone resisted a federal grand jury subpoena to appear in court on March 12, 1929, on the grounds that he was too ill to attend, the FBI obtained evidence to the contrary, and Capone was ordered to appear on March 20. He completed his testimony on March 27 and was arrested for contempt of court; he was released on a five-thousand-dollar bond. On May 17, 1929, Capone was arrested in Philadelphia for carrying a concealed deadly weapon and sentenced to one year in prison. He was released nine months later for good behavior, on March 17, 1930.

Meanwhile, the U.S. Treasury Department had filed charges of tax evasion against Capone. On June 16, 1931, Capone pleaded guilty to tax evasion, bragging to the press that he had a deal to serve two and a half years in prison. The federal judge rejected the deal, and Capone changed his plea to not guilty. Tried and convicted on October 18, 1931, Capone was sentenced November 24, 1931, to eleven years in prison, fined $50,000 and court costs, and ordered to pay $215,000 plus interest due on back taxes; the six-month contempt of court sentence ran concurrently. He was released November 16, 1939, having paid all fines and taxes and having served seven and a half years in the federal penitentiary at Atlanta and Alcatraz.

Capone was unable to return either to Chicago or to gangland politics. A victim of syphilitic paresis, his mentality had deteriorated in prison to that of a twelve-year-old person. He retired to Palm Island, Florida, and lived in seclusion until his death from stroke and pneumonia on January 25, 1947.

Impact

During Prohibition and the Great Depression era, the historical and social conditions for immigrants were such that many turned to organized crime as a source of jobs and income. Al Capone's career as a powerful crime boss during this period remains a popular subject of literature and film. He became a mythic figure as public enemy number one and was romanticized in magazines, books, films, and television.

Further Reading

Bergreen, Laurence. *Capone: The Man and the Era.* New York: Simon & Schuster, 1994. Describes the rise of Capone to crime syndicate leadership during the 1920's and 1930's.

Kobler, John. *Capone: The Life and World of Al Capone.* New York: Da Capo Press, 1992. A biography of Capone as a famous crime boss and unrecognized philanthropist.

Ruth, David E. *Inventing the Public Enemy: The Gangster in American Culture, 1918-1934.* Chicago: University of Chicago Press, 1996. Provides a commentary on the cultural impact of organized crime.

—*Marguerite R. Plummer*

See also: Bugs Moran; Dion O'Banion; Hymie Weiss.

Willis A. Carto

Far-right politician and founder of the Liberty Lobby

Born: July 17, 1926; Fort Wayne, Indiana
Also known as: Frank Tompkins; Samuel P. Foner; John Henry; J. W. Young; E. L. Anderson; Willis Allison Carto (full name)
Cause of notoriety: Carto was a primary perpetuator of organized anti-Semitism in the United States during the last half of the twentieth century.
Active: 1955-2001
Locale: United States

Early Life

Of French Protestant descent, Willis A. Carto (CAR-toh) was born in Fort Wayne, Indiana, and raised in Mansfield, Ohio. After high school, he joined the U.S. Army and fought in World War II. Carto returned to Ohio after his service and attended Denison University and the University of Cincinnati Law School. He graduated from neither institution and began working for the Household Finance Company of San Francisco as an account collector. At this time, he began his involvement in right-wing politics.

Political Career

Carto became affiliated with the far right in the early 1950's, when he joined the racist Congress of Freedom as its director. He also established the group Liberty and Property and *Right*, a journal that promoted anti-Semitic and racist thought. Francis Yockey, a Nazi sympathizer, greatly influenced Carto's ideology. Yockey wrote a virtually incomprehensible racist and anti-Semitic treatise titled *Imperium* that Carto hailed as foundational to the far right movement. Carto later had it reprinted.

In 1957, Carto established the Liberty Lobby. Headquartered in Washington, D.C., this organization's primary mission was to marshal public hostility toward Jews. One of its chief weapons was *The Spotlight*, a weekly periodical that began publication in 1975. The newspaper attempted to appeal to a wide array of readers by disguising its ideology with appeals to patriotism and populism. At the height of its success in 1981, *The Spotlight*'s weekly circulation reached 300,000 copies.

In 1968, Carto joined George Wallace's presidential campaign as a leader of Youth for Wallace. After the campaign, Carto and William Pierce, an activist for the American Nazi Party, transformed Youth for Wallace into the National Youth Alliance. Disagreement between Carto and Pierce prompted a split in 1970. Pierce ultimately asserted control and renamed the organization the National Alliance. It later became one of the most infamous neo-Nazi groups in the United States.

Carto founded the Institute for Historical Review (IHR) in 1979. Promoting itself as a center for scholarship, the IHR sponsored conferences and generated "revisionist" publications that denied the existence of the Holocaust. These publications included the *Journal of Historical Review*. In 1984, Carto helped form the Populist Party, which fielded three presidential candidates before disbanding: Bob Richards (in 1984), a former Olympic athlete; David Duke (in 1988), a former imperial wizard of the Ku Klux Klan; and Bo Gritz (in 1992), a former Green Beret.

Shortly thereafter, Carto's fortunes began to fade. In 1993, the IHR Board of Directors accused him of gross financial mismanagement and dismissed him from its staff. A lengthy, acrimonious court battle ensued. In 1996, a Superior Court judge decreed that Carto owed the IHR approximately six million dollars. Carto and the Liberty Lobby promptly filed for bankruptcy, managing to prolong the case for three additional years.

Despite Carto's precarious financial situation, in 1998 he managed to acquire a controlling interest in Resistance Records, a distribution center for hate-themed music. He quickly lost control of the company to rival William Pierce. In 2001, a federal bankruptcy court refused to grant Chapter 11 protection to the Liberty Lobby. The organization was forced to cease operations, although as late as 2006 a volunteer staff was making *The Spotlight* available online.

Impact

For nearly five decades, Willis A. Carto was prominent in far right-wing politics. His vast media network furthered his ability to disseminate racism, conspiracy theories, and Holocaust denial propaganda. However, his reputation within the movement was tarnished by his quarrelsome nature and apparent interest in financial gain. At the time of this writing, his influence on the movement has waned significantly.

Further Reading

Berlet, Chip, and Matthew M. Lyons. *Right-Wing Populism in America: Too Close for Comfort*. New York: Guilford Press, 2000. Discusses the Liberty Lobby's relationship to the John Birch Society and the mixture of nativism, conspiracism, and populism that both groups espoused.

George, John, and Laird Wilcox. *Nazis, Communists, Klansmen, and Others on the Fringe*. Buffalo, N.Y.: Prometheus Books, 1992. Devotes a chapter to Carto's rise to power in far right politics.

Mintz, Frank P. *The Liberty Lobby and the American Right: Race, Conspiracy, and Culture*. Westport, Conn.: Greenwood Press, 1985. This essential text examines the ground from which the Liberty Lobby sprang and traces its evolution through the height of its influence.

—*Beth A. Messner*

See also: Richard Girnt Butler; Frank Collin; David Duke; Matthew F. Hale; David Irving; Jean-Marie Le Pen; Robert Jay Mathews; Tom Metzger; William Luther Pierce III; George Lincoln Rockwell; Savitri Devi; William Joseph Simmons; Gerald L. K. Smith; J. B. Stoner; George C. Wallace; Randy Weaver.

Cartouche

French highwayman

Born: 1693; Paris, France
Died: November 28, 1721; Paris, France
Also known as: Louis-Dominique Garthauszien; Louis-Dominique Cartouche; Louis-Dominique Bourguignon (birth name); Lamarre; Petit
Major offense: Theft
Active: 1711-1721
Locale: Paris, France
Sentence: Execution by strangulation

Early Life

The semilegendary figure Louis-Dominique Cartouche (kar-tewsh) was born to a German mercenary soldier who found himself in Paris and decided to stay and learn a trade. He became a cooper, married Catherine Lamarre, and had two daughters, followed by Cartouche in 1693, and two more sons. The father's family name, Garthauszien, became Cartouche. The boy's family life was shared with his cousins, one of whom, Jacques, had spent ample time in prison. Cartouche was free to investigate all kinds of places with his friends but soon was obliged by his father to learn coopering. Incapable of making and repairing the barrels, he accompanied his uncle to Rouen on business. Returning, he tried the trade again, but he wanted to be free.

At age eighteen, Cartouche spotted a laundress who liked presents. Penniless, Cartouche decided to pilfer from his poor father. He then began to try his criminal skill in other places and found success. His career as a thief was launched.

Criminal Career

Cartouche had two lives. In one, he was an extraordinarily adept thief who began practicing on girls who were selling fruit. He soon worked his way into bigger jobs. He stole money from a servant, who unexpectedly returned to his room, leaving Cartouche hiding on top of a huge armoire for two days. In his other life, he was an eighteenth century Robin Hood, stealing from the rich and giving to the poor. He held up a bank with a toy pistol, stole a large sum, and gave it all to the poor.

Cartouche's reputation was such that thieves from all over Paris came to him to learn from and to work for him, forming a group of about 140 men. Cartouche called for elections of a leader, and he was chosen unanimously. His rules resembled a religious order: Anyone caught disobeying would be severely punished. One young man who acted foolishly was killed, and the word spread quickly.

Legal Action and Outcome

Secret orders came from the regent himself, Philippe II, Duke of Orléans, to find Cartouche, but the thief—a master at disguise and protected by the many people who had benefited from or admired him for his good deeds—eluded capture. Caught once and imprisoned, he escaped. He managed to get to a house through a tunnel, but the dog barked and woke up the household, making escape impossible. He was taken to Châtelet Prison and later transferred to the Conciergérie, where the notorious and the nobility awaited trial and sentencing. Following a brief trial, Cartouche was sentenced to have his legs, thighs, and kidneys crushed alive on a scaffold on Execution Square and then, with the face looking up to heaven, to be placed on a wheel and strangled. The execution was carried out on November 28, 1721.

Impact

Cartouche is remembered as the French equivalent of Robin Hood, the chief of Parisian thieves and, to the lower bourgeoisie and the poor, a great eighteenth century hero. He stole, but not just for himself. The reputation and legend of Cartouche are larger than the figure on which that legend is based. He was celebrated in ballads, artworks, and romances, including the swashbuckling film *Cartouche* (1962), directed by Philippe de Broca and starring Jean-Paul Belmondo and Claudia Cardinale.

Further Reading

Defoe, Daniel. *The Life and Actions of Lewis Dominique Cartouch: Who Was Broke Alive upon the Wheel at Paris, Nov. 28, 1721*. London: Printed for J. Roberts, in Warwick-Lane, 1722. Defoe's *Histoire de la vie et du procès de Louis Dominique Cartouche*, offering a wonderful contemporary insight, is available in some larger university libraries.

Fleuret, Fernand. "Cartouche, Mandrin et la littérature de Colportage." In *De Ronsard à Baudelaire*. Paris: Mercure de France, 1935. The books of a traveling peddler include a story about Cartouche in chapter 7. Fernand denies the early life story of some biographers such as Lüsenbrink. The rest is a lively repertoire of Cartouche's escapades and a description of his courage facing death. In French.

Henry, Gilles. *Cartouche, Le bandit de la Régence: Le brigand*. Paris: Tallandier, 2001. A biographical novel with detailed descriptions that give a real sense of the man and thief. The early life is entirely different from Lüsenbrink's work. In French.

Lüsenbrink, Hans-Jürgen. *Histoires curieuses et véritables de Cartouche et de Mandrin*. Paris: Montalba, 1984. An erroneous tale of Carthouche's early life and details of popular eighteenth century bandits are an introduction to *Histoire de la vie et du procès de Louis-Dominique Cartouche* (Story of the life and trial of Louis-Dominique Cartouche). In French.

—*Patricia J. Siegel*

See also: William Brodie; Claude Duval; Charles Peace; Rob Roy; Jack Sheppard; Dick Turpin; Jonathan Wild.

Sante Jeronimo Caserio

Italian anarchist and terrorist

Born: September 8, 1873; Motta Visconti, near Milan, Italy
Died: August 16, 1894; Lyon, France
Major offense: Murder
Active: June 24, 1894
Locale: Lyon, France
Sentence: Death by decapitation

Early Life

Sante Jeronimo Caserio (SAHN-tay yay-RO-nih-moh cah-SAY-rih-yoh) was born the second youngest of eight children to a poor family in the Milan province. His father, Giovanni, who was a peasant and boatman on River Ticino, finished out his life in a psychiatric institution for mental disorders that were linked with scabies. The young Caserio was a rather reserved boy but had a marked altruistic inclination. He wanted to enter a seminary and is reported to have been very pious. He started work at the age of ten as an apprentice in the local bakery, and at fourteen, he found work in Milan. There, he became acquainted with anarchist propaganda, inspired by the ideas of the Russian revolutionary Mikhail Bakunin, who predicated violent methods of action ("propaganda by fact") based on individual assassinations. During this period, the authoritarian methods of the Italian head of state Francesco Crispi exacerbated class conflicts in Italy and created a situation of great tension, which would eventually culminate with the assassination in 1900 of King Umberto I.

After his imprisonment for distributing socialist propaganda on May Day, 1892, Caserio fled to Switzerland, took part in numerous anarchist meetings, and emigrated to France. In the spring of 1894, he worked in a bakery in Sète, in southern France, and was member of an anarchist club known as the Oaktree Hearts.

Criminal Career

It is not clear whether Caserio decided alone to assassinate Marie-François Sadi Carnot, the president of the French Republic (1837-1894), or if he was designated by a group of comrades, as was stated later during his trial. Historians do know that after taking leave from his work in 1894, Caserio bought a knife and took the train to Vienne, where he decided to continue his journey to Lyon by road in order to avoid police detection.

On the evening of June 24, President Carnot was expected at the Grand Théâtre in Lyon for a gala given in his honor. When Caserio, a slim and rather unimpressive young man, stepped forward toward the president's carriage with a newspaper in his hand, the guards did not take any notice. Caserio suddenly produced his knife and—yelling "Long live the revolution! Long live anarchy!"—he stabbed the president with incredible force. The blade penetrated eleven centimeters into the liver, and the president died three hours after the assault.

Legal Action and Outcome

Caserio was immediately arrested, and his trial began on August 2, 1894. He refused assistance from an Italian lawyer who wanted to plead, based on Caserio's father's medical record, irresponsibility on grounds of disturbed mental heredity. Caserio made no attempt to deny his responsibility and claimed his action was retaliation against President Carnot's refusal to grant mercy to anarchist Auguste Vaillant, who had been executed a few months earlier. When his death sentence was pronounced, Caserio exclaimed, "Long live the social revolution!" He was beheaded in the early morning of August 16 and is reported to have whispered again, "Long live anarchy!" seconds before the blade of the guillotine descended on his neck.

Impact

The assassination of the French president by Sante Jeronimo Caserio caused an outbreak of violence against Italian immigrants in France in a context of acute rivalry and tension over colonial matters between the two countries. The day following the murder, the widow of the president received an anonymous letter containing a photograph of Ravachol (François-Claudius Königstein), who had been executed in 1892, with the words "He is well avenged." However, despite more anarchist threats, Caserio's act was the last of a long list of political assassinations in France.

Further Reading

Gallas, John, and Clifford Harper. *The Ballad of Santo Caserio*. London: Agraphia Press, 2003. A poem about Caserio's life with illustrations and a biographical note.

Maîtron, Jean. *Le Mouvement anarchiste en France*.

Paris: Gallimard, 1991. A thorough account of anarchist movement history in France from the mid-nineteenth century to World War I. In French.

Miller, Paul B. *From Revolutionaries to Citizens: Antimilitarism in France, 1870-1914.* Durham, N.C.: Duke University Press, 2002. Provides good contextual history of France and Europe during the era in which Caserio lived and anarchists flourished.

—*Frank La Brasca*

See also: Leon Czolgosz; Nicola Sacco; Bartolomeo Vanzetti.

Butch Cassidy

American bank robber and horse rustler

Born: April 13, 1866; Beaver, Utah

Died: Possibly November 7, 1908; possibly San Vicente, Bolivia

Also known as: Robert LeRoy Parker (birth name); George Parker; George Cassidy; Lowe Maxwell; James Ryan; Robin Hood of the West

Cause of notoriety: Cassidy and his Wild Bunch Gang were responsible for countless robberies and thefts, becoming folk legends in the process.

Active: 1894-1896

Locale: American West and Southwest, Argentina, and Bolivia

Early Life

Robert LeRoy Parker, who would later come to be known as Butch Cassidy (CAS-ih-dee), was born in Beaver, Utah, on April 13, 1866. Known as Roy as a child, Cassidy was the oldest of thirteen children born to Mormon pioneers from England. During his childhood, the Parkers spent much of their time in Circleville, Utah, as homesteaders. As a teenager, Roy worked on ranches throughout western Utah. It was while working on such ranches that he came under the tutelage of an unscrupulous rancher named Mike Cassidy; Roy would later adopt Cassidy's last name. Originally taking the name George Cassidy, Roy would later be labeled with the nickname "Butch" as a result of his work with local Utah butcher Charlie Crouse. It has been largely speculated that Roy assumed a new identity to avoid bringing shame to his family name.

Roy's first run-in with the law came at a young age, when he let himself into a closed shop in order to steal a pair of pants (legend has it that he left an "IOU" note, promising to return and pay the merchant). Cassidy began his more consistent criminal activity as a cattle rustler. He disliked the manner in which larger ranchers would drive small-time ranchers out of business and began his criminal career rustling from the larger ranches. As his actions were initially designed to hurt the substantial landowners and help the small ones, he was labeled the Robin Hood of the West. Cassidy was convicted for horse theft on July 4, 1894. He received a two-year sentence in the prison at Laramie, Wyoming, and was released on January 6, 1896.

Butch Cassidy.

Butch Cassidy Rides Again . . . and Again

Nothing could elevate a nineteenth century desperado's reputation and turn him into a folk hero more readily than a spectacular or mysterious death. Butch Cassidy had both. In fact, he seems to have died frequently and on three continents.

Historians Daniel Buck and Anne Meadows looked into the many reports of Cassidy's death. In their 2006 Internet article "Butch and Sundance: Still Dead?" they report that the rumors had become laughable even before the two outlaws left for South America. A turn-of-the-century article in the *Vernal Express* (Utah), for instance, jokes,

> Butch Cassidy is receiving as much unsolicited notoriety as a New York Tammany leader. He has been reported killed a dozen times in the last five years, and yet every time a notorious train or bank robbery occurs, Butch comes to life and is credited with being the leader of the gang. He certainly must have more lives than a whole family of cats.

According to Buck and Meadows, Cassidy was first reported dead in 1898, when he was 32, and last in 1978, when he was 112. In between, under various aliases, he was reported to have died on numerous dates and in numerous places, including in Chile in 1904, 1906, 1908, 1909, 1911, 1912, 1913, and 1935; Bolivia in 1908 and 1909; Utah in 1913 and 1955; on an island off Mexico's coast in 1932; Arizona and Georgia in 1936; and Washington, California, and Oregon in 1937. There were also rumors of his dying in Denver, Colorado, in the late 1930's; a small Nevada mining town in the early 1940's; and in Ireland at an unknown date. The Sundance Kid, while not dying quite so often, had a similar series of fates.

Buck and Meadows explain, "Their 1908 deaths in Bolivia did not become common—albeit controversial—knowledge until decades later." Thus, in addition to innocent misidentifications, rumors and hoaxes had free rein.

Cassidy robbed his first bank in June, 1889, when he and three partners held up the San Miguel Valley Bank in Telluride, Colorado. While fleeing with their twenty-thousand-dollar bounty, Cassidy and his gang were among the first to make use of the Outlaw Trail, a long, dangerous route running through Mexico, Utah, Wyoming, and Montana. The trail linked together a series of hideouts, including the infamous Robbers' Roost in Utah and Wyoming's Hole-in-the-Wall.

After his time in prison between 1894 and 1896, Cassidy returned to the rustler's life along the Arizona-Utah border. At this time, he began to assemble what would become his most renowned gang, the Wild Bunch—a group of seasoned cowboys, robbers, and rustlers. Membership often changed and rarely exceeded ten people, but the gang's more prominent members included Flat Nose George Curry, Harvey "Kid Curry" Logan, Bill Carver, Elzy Lay, and Harry "Sundance Kid" Longabaugh.

On August 13, 1896, the Wild Bunch made off with seven thousand dollars from a bank in Montpelier, Idaho. Cassidy and his gang then robbed the Pleasant Valley Coal Company payroll of eight thousand dollars. Known for intricate planning, the gang would set up check points with new horses to replace their tired horses after a heist. Thus, law enforcement officers would be chasing fresh horses on their own tired horses.

Following the Coal Company holdup, the gang began bringing in larger sums of money in robberies throughout South Dakota, New Mexico, Nevada, and Wyoming, including an estimated seventy thousand dollars from a train robbery near Folsom, New Mexico. However, by this time, the Wild Bunch had an array of law enforcement officers on their trail wherever they traveled. Operatives of the Pinkerton National Detective Agency were specifically tracking Cassidy, known to be the leader of the gang.

In 1900, the gang is said to have asked Utah governor Heber Wells for amnesty in exchange for mending their criminal ways. When this idea failed, the band disbanded under the heat of law enforcement pursuit, and the members went in separate directions. After the gang disbanded in 1902, Cassidy traveled to England and then met up with Longabaugh (the Sundance Kid) and his girlfriend, Etta Place, in Fort Worth, Texas. The three then traveled to Argentina.

After farming for a time, Cassidy and Sundance went back to robbing payrolls and trains in Argentina and Bolivia until they were supposedly killed by soldiers in San Vicente, Bolivia, on November 7, 1908. However, the exact circumstances of their deaths remain unknown. In one account, two polite American bandits robbed a coal-mine payroll in early November, 1908, and hid in San Vicente, where they celebrated their success. Three days later, they were surrounded by Bolivian soldiers and killed in a gunfight. The bandits were buried in unmarked graves and assumed to be Cassidy and Sundance. Another legend has it that Cassidy put Sundance out of his misery after he was seriously wounded and then turned the gun on himself. Yet another legend has it that it was not Cassidy and Sundance whom soldiers killed but two other bandits. This legend concludes with Cassidy traveling to Europe, later returning to the United States as William Phillips and marrying a woman named Gertrude Livesay. The Phillips family is said to have lived a law-abiding life in Arizona and then in Washington. William Phillips, after nearing bankruptcy and returning to Utah and Wyoming to look for some buried caches from the Wild Bunch days, was diagnosed with cancer and died on July 20, 1937.

Impact

Butch Cassidy's legend has had more influence on American perceptions of the Old West than perhaps any other. Known as the Robin Hood of the West, Cassidy, for right or wrong, became known as a gentleman criminal. His image was that of the working-class hero standing up for the little guy against larger ranchers. As a holdup man and bank robber, Cassidy was known to be polite and as gentle as possible. This mode of operation, along with what has been viewed as his general good nature, has made Cassidy the Old West's quinessential "good guy" criminal. His legend was solidified in film in 1969 with the release of *Butch Cassidy and the Sundance Kid*, starring Paul Newman as Cassidy and Robert Redford as Sundance.

Further Reading

Kelly, Charles. *The Outlaw Tail: A History of Butch Cassidy and His Wild Bunch.* Omaha: University of Nebraska Press, 1996. Kelly weaves together the lives of Cassidy and his contemporaries. The historical analysis includes depictions of both the famous Hole-in-the-Wall and Robber's Roost hideouts.

Meadows, Annie. *Digging up Butch and Sundance.* Lincoln, Neb.: Bison Books, 2003. After finding out that Butch and Sundance had lived for several years in their beloved Patagonia, the author and her husband set out to trace the final days of the pair. The couple unearthed documents, followed leads, and analyzed DNA evidence in an attempt to trace the demise of the two outlaws. Eventually, they traced their deaths to San Vicente, Bolivia, in 1908. This, for many, has become the accepted location in which Cassidy and Sundance Kid were finally shot and killed.

Patterson, Richardson. *Butch Cassidy: A Biography.* Omaha: University of Nebraska Press, 1998. Devoted to the life and times of Cassidy.

—*Ted Shields*

See also: Salvatore Giuliano; Harry Longabaugh; Robin Hood.

Paul Castellano

American Mafia boss

Born: June 20, 1915; Brooklyn, New York
Died: December 16, 1985; New York, New York
Also known as: Constantino Paul Castellano (full name); Big Paul; PC; Big Pauly
Cause of notoriety: As head of the Gambino Family, Castellano oversaw labor racketeering and the corruption of businesses and public officials.
Active: 1934-1985
Locale: New York

Early Life

Paul Castellano (kahs-tehl-LAN-oh) was born in Brooklyn in 1915 to Sicilian immigrants. His father was a butcher who sold Italian lottery tickets in their neighborhood. Paul dropped out of school by the eighth grade and began selling lottery tickets and helping his father in the butcher shop. In 1934 the nineteen-year-old Castellano spent three months in jail in Connecticut for armed robbery. In 1937 he married Nina Manno, who was the sister-in-law of Carlo Gambino, a rising Mafia member in the crime "family" of Albert Anastasia. Gambino was married to Castellano's sister Katharine. As Gambino rose within the New York Mafia, Castellano would assume greater and greater criminal responsibilities. In October, 1957, Anastasia was murdered in a barber's chair in New York, and Gambino became boss of what became known as the Gambino Family.

Criminal Career

Gambino appeared to be a slight and unassuming man at first sight. He had a fearsome reputation, however, as an underworld figure. During the time of his brother-in-law's leadership, Castellano's fortunes grew. His principal assets were his diplomatic ability in the underworld and his success in corrupting legitimate businesses. Castellano's main interest was the meat business. He and his sons controlled meat distribution concerns and had influence with labor unions. Castellano would force supermarket chains to carry certain brands, and he would "encourage" butcher shops and other outlets to stock his brand and not others. Gambino, as he was dying in 1976, anointed Castellano as his successor.

Castellano became head of the Gambino Family in 1976. The group was already divided between street criminals, such as John Gotti, and businessmen, such as Castellano. As Castellano gained both prominence and wealth, he abandoned the Brooklyn and Queens neighborhoods in which he had spent his younger days for a fashionable mansion on Staten Island. He also forbade the members of his Family from becoming involved in the narcotics trade. Over the next several years, tensions between the two factions became more pronounced as Castellano became more isolated. Castellano's organization was heavily involved in labor racketeering and the corruption of businesses and public officials. The group's street crew, headed by Aniello Dellacroce (and later John Gotti), carried on traditional criminal activities such as hijacking, loan-sharking, and bookmaking.

Paul Castellano after his hearing in May, 1959. (AP/Wide World Photos)

Legal Action and Outcome

In 1983 the Federal Bureau of Investigation (FBI) planted an electronic listening device in Castellano's home. The bug revealed many of the inner workings of the Gambino Family as well as sordid details of Castellano's personal life. Over the next two years, the FBI gathered evidence against Castellano and several other members of the Gambino Family. Finally, a joint federal task force arrested Castellano and several other members of organized crime's ruling body, "The Commission." On February 25, 1985, FBI agents arrested many, if not all, of the major organized crime figures in New York, including Castellano.

Castellano never went to trial for his many alleged crimes. On December 16, 1985, while arriving for dinner at a favorite restaurant, he and his bodyguard were ambushed and killed by unidentified men. Many blamed the murder on Gotti, the leader of the street crew for the Gambinos and representative of the new guard of Mafia leaders.

Impact

The impact of Castellano's death was greater than that of his life. Paul Castellano represented the last link to the older, more traditional Mafia. His death signaled an end to that tradition and ushered in the era of Gotti, the dapper don. Gotti was a high-profile street thug whose many trials and acquittals were widely covered by the New York media. However, the criminal organization that Gotti inherited was a shell of its former self. The impact of FBI investigations and federal prosecutions destroyed much of the effectiveness of the older criminal organization, and new criminal groups became more powerful over the prevailing years.

Further Reading

Cummings, John, and Ernest Volkman. *Gombata: The Improbable Rise and Fall of John Gotti and His Gang*. New York: Avon Books, 1990. Chronicles the career of John Gotti, who assumed control of the Gambino Family after Castellano's death. Shows the deep differences in style and personality between Castellano and Gotti.

Maas, Peter. *The Valachi Papers*. New York: Putnam's, 1968. Firsthand account of a small-time Mafia member gives some interesting views of the early period of

Mafia organization from the 1930's to the 1950's.

O'Brien, Joseph, and Andris Kurins. *Boss of Bosses: The FBI and Paul Castellano*. New York: Dell, 1991. This book by two FBI agents is a blow-by-blow account of the FBI's attack on the Gambino Family. Examines both technical and ethical aspects of the case.

—*Charles C. Howard*

See also: Joe Adonis; Albert Anastasia; Louis Buchalter; Vincent Coll; Joe Colombo; Carmine Galante; Carlo Gambino; Sam Giancana; Vincent Gigante; Salvatore Giuliano; John Gotti; Sammy Gravano; Henry Hill; Richard Kuklinski; Meyer Lansky; Salvatore Maranzano; Carlos Marcello; Joseph Profaci; Arnold Rothstein; Dutch Schultz.

Fidel Castro

Cuban revolutionary and premier (1959-)

Born: August 13, 1926 or 1927; Birán, Cuba

Also known as: Fidel Castro Ruz (full name); El Barbudo (the Bearded One); Maximum Leader

Cause of notoriety: Castro was both revered and reviled as a Communist revolutionary, the dictator of Cuba, and an enemy of the United States.

Active: 1959-present

Locale: Cuba

Early Life

Fidel Castro (fee-DEHL CAST-roh), who would lead the Cuban Revolution of 1959 to victory and establish the first socialist state in the Western Hemisphere, was born in the eastern Cuban province of Oriente to a Spanish landowner, Ángel Castro, and his second wife, Lina Ruz. Fidel benefited from his father's wealth, attending Jesuit primary school and college, along with his brother Raúl, before enrolling at the University of Havana to study law in 1945. His student days, by his own admission, were filled with political militancy rather than study, yet Castro managed to receive a law degree in 1950, the same year he married for the first time.

Political Career

On the brink of what appeared to be a brilliant career in law and politics and having announced an intention to run for congress in 1952, Castro's plans were dashed when General Fulgencio Batista y Zaldívar launched a coup that year, suspending all political parties.

Castro soon gathered a band of followers around him, including his brother, to overthrow Batista by force of arms. On July 26, 1953, several dozen of Castro's men tried to storm the Moncada army barracks in his home province of Oriente, hoping to spark a national revolt. Instead, the rebels were either killed or captured, and Castro went on trial for sedition. His bold move against the dictatorship and the political program outlined during the concluding speech at his trial, "History Will Absolve Me," had gained him huge popular support, and Batista granted amnesty to Castro and his remaining partisans in 1956. They quickly escaped to Mexico, where Castro plotted an armed invasion of Cuba with the aid of Argentine revolutionary Ernesto "Che" Guevara.

Fidel Castro. (Library of Congress)

It's Dangerous at the Top

"If surviving assassinations were an Olympic event," Fidel Castro told an interviewer, "I would win the gold medal." Indeed, one writer claims that 637 conspiracies to assassinate the Cuban leader were uncovered during his first forty years in office.

Although the Central Intelligence Agency (CIA) had pondered earlier efforts, the U.S. intelligence community, under intense pressure from the administration of President John F. Kennedy, began an intensive campaign to get rid of Castro following the disastrous Bay of Pigs invasion in April, 1961. Called Operation Mongoose, it included ideas that later came to be considered as legendarily perverse or inane: hiring Mafia hit men or getting Castro to handle an exploding cigar or seashell, a poisoned wet suit, or hair-removal powder. The hair powder, a CIA agent later explained, was meant to make Castro's whiskers fall out so that Cubans would laugh him out of power.

In 1967, the *CIA Inspector General's Report on Plots to Assassinate Fidel Castro* distinguished five separate phases to the planning:

a. **Prior to August 1960:** All of the identifiable schemes prior to about August 1960, with one possible exception, were aimed only at discrediting Castro personally by influencing his behavior or by altering his appearance.

b. **August 1960 to April 1961:** The plots that were hatched in late 1960 and early 1961 were aggressively pursued and were viewed by at least some of the participants as being merely one aspect of the over-all active effort to overthrow the regime that culminated in the Bay of Pigs.

c. **April 1961 to late 1961:** A major scheme [using Mafia assassins] that was begun in August 1960 was called off after the Bay of Pigs and remained dormant for several months, as did most other Agency operational activity related to Cuba.

d. **Late 1961 to Late 1962:** That particular scheme was reactivated in early 1962 and was again pushed vigorously in the era of Project MONGOOSE and in the climate of intense administration pressure on CIA to do something about Castro and his Cuba.

e. **Late 1962 until well into 1963:** After the Cuban Missile Crisis of October 1962 and the collapse of Project MONGOOSE, the aggressive scheme that was begun in August 1960 and revived in April 1962 was finally terminated in early 1963. Two other plots were originated in 1963, but both were impracticable and nothing ever came of them.

Source: Fabián Escalante Font, *CIA Targets Fidel: Secret 1967 CIA Inspector General's Report on Plots to Assassinate Fidel Castro* (Melbourne, Australia: Ocean Press, 1996).

Setting shore in Oriente, Castro, with only a few dozen poorly trained men, mounted a guerrilla campaign against the Cuban army. From the mountains Castro called for land redistribution and the restoration of democracy, winning him the support of both the peasantry and the Cuban middle class. His organization, called Movimiento 26 de Julio (July 26 Movement or M-26), swelled to several thousand fighters while Batista's forces lost control of the countryside. On January 1, 1959, the dictator fled Havana, and Castro proclaimed the triumph of the Cuban Revolution.

Relations with the Soviets and Americans

The execution of some of Batista's collaborators, the declaration of a land-reform program limiting the size of private holdings, and increased trade with the Soviet Union earned Castro the wrath of the Eisenhower administration in the United States, which broke diplomatic relations with Cuba, installed a trade embargo, and begat plans to oust his regime. The scheme to overthrow Castro using Cuban exiles trained by the United States came to rueful fruition under President John F. Kennedy. The failed Bay of Pigs invasion in April, 1961, boosted Castro's fortunes at home and made him a hero in much of Latin America. Proclaiming himself a Marxist-Leninist and hoping to forestall yet another invasion, Castro accepted the offer of Soviet premier Nikita S. Khrushchev to install nuclear missiles in Cuba in 1962. The United States naval blockade that followed the discovery of the missiles and their subsequent withdrawal proved a humiliating setback for Castro, who was now beholden on Soviet economic aid to keep his revolution afloat. This episode came to be known as the Cuban Missile Crisis and was the closest the world came to nuclear war in the twentieth century.

During the next two decades, Castro realigned the Cuban government and economy along Soviet lines. Cuba was officially designated a one-party regime in 1965, with Castro serving as both first secretary of the Cuban Communist Party and head of state. Property in land and industry, with few exceptions, came under government control. Castro supported dozens of guerrilla movements throughout Latin America, only to see them all founder; the one in Bolivia cost the life of confidant Guevara in 1967.

The year 1970 was the low point of the Cuban Revolution. The attempt to harvest ten million tons of sugar turned into a colossal bungle, with Castro accepting personal responsibility. This disaster, along with the U.S. embargo, led to food shortages and strict rationing of almost all commercial goods. However, Castro still enjoyed the full support of the Soviet Union, and with Russian aid to Cuba estimated at one million dollars a day during the 1970's, his regime remained firmly entrenched. The late 1970's saw Castro dispatching Cuban troops to Angola and Ethiopia to bolster pro-Soviet regimes.

Castro was stunned in 1980 when hundreds of thousands of Cubans took up his offer to leave the island by way of Mariel harbor. The 1980's also witnessed a worsening of ties between Cuba and the Soviets as Mikhail Gorbachev enacted liberalizing reforms that were anathema to Castro. After the collapse of the Soviet Union in 1991 and the loss of Russian subsidies, Castro had no choice but to open the Cuban economy to market forces.

Impact

Fidel Castro had an immense influence on global politics, something rare for a Latin American. His political, economic, and military decisions have had deep repercussions in North America, South America, and Africa. On the domestic scene, he divided a nation, driving more than one million Cubans into exile in the United States. One of the last staunch defenders of Marxism-Leninism, he vowed "Socialism or Death!" In July, 2006, it appeared that the latter might be imminent when Castro entered the hospital for a mysterious gastrointestinal ailment and shortly thereafter handed the reins of government to his brother Raúl.

Further Reading

Coltman, Leycester. *The Real Fidel Castro*. New Haven, Conn.: Yale University Press, 2003. The author once served as Britain's ambassador to Cuba, giving him close access to Castro. His viewpoint is remarkable, because unlike many American biographers, Leycester has no ax to grind against Castro, nor does he overlook his subject's many policy failures.

Quirk, Robert E. *Fidel Castro*. New York: W. W. Norton, 1993. Exhaustively researched, the volume nevertheless classifies as an ad hominem attack on Castro filled with personal gossip rather than objective analysis.

Skierka, Volker. *Fidel Castro: A Biography*. Translated by Patrick Camiller. Cambridge, England.: Polity Press, 2004. Offering a thematic rather than chronological approach, Skierka examines the roots of Castro's most important decisions, from applying guerrilla warfare in the mountains to opening up Cuban socialism to market forces.

Szulc, Tad. *Fidel: A Critical Portrait*. New York: Morrow, 1986. Castro cooperated with, although withheld official approval of, this biographer. Szulc focuses mainly on his subject's life before the 1959 revolution. His grasp of Cuban history is slight, and the reader should apply caution to the more fanciful allegations, including that Castro received funding from the Central Intelligence Agency (CIA) during the fight against Batista.

—Julio Pino

See also: Fulgencio Batista y Zaldívar; Che Guevara; Nikita S. Khrushchev.

CATILINE

Roman politician

BORN: c. 108 B.C.E.; place unknown
DIED: Early January 62 B.C.E.; near Pistoria, Etruria (now Pistoia, Italy)
ALSO KNOWN AS: Lucius Sergius Catilina (full name)
MAJOR OFFENSE: Treason by conspiracy against the Roman state
ACTIVE: 63-62 B.C.E.
LOCALE: Rome, Italy
SENTENCE: Death

EARLY LIFE

The early life of Catiline (CA-tuh-lin) is obscure. He came from an impoverished patrician family with declining political distinction. Little else is known of his parents or his childhood. He served in the Social War of 91-88 B.C.E., a revolt of Rome's Italian subjects and allies. Catiline next supported the bloodthirsty dictator Lucius Cornelius Sulla. Early in the 70's, Catiline served abroad, probably in Cilicia.

POLITICAL CAREER

Catiline held the praetorship (an elected office with judicial duties) in 68 B.C.E. and then was governor of Africa (Tunisia) for two years; he was tried for peculation (embezzlement) but was acquitted. He next ran for consul, the highest office in the Roman Republic, in 63, competing with Marcus Tullius Cicero. Catiline was defeated by Cicero and Gaius Antonius Hybrida in the consular election of 63.

Catiline allegedly organized conspiracies and assassination attempts in 65 and 64, which failed to materialize. In 63, he organized a conspiracy against the state, building his support among the poor, the landless, indebted aristocrats, and impoverished Sullan veterans. Catiline's platform offered debt cancellation, which was opposed by the wealthy. His plan in 63 was to assassinate the following year's consuls, massacre the Senate, and set fire to the city of Rome.

On October 18, Cicero was given letters warning of

Cicero denounces Catiline in this nineteenth century painting.

Catiline's plot and read them in the Senate. The Senate passed the so-called Ultimate Decree on October 21, which empowered it to suspend civil law. Cicero denounced Catiline and his conspiracy in the Senate on November 8 in a address that came to be called the First Catilinarian Oration, and Catiline stormed out. Catiline left the city that evening to raise an army with his second in command, Gaius Manlius, while his followers continued to conspire in the city of Rome. On November 9, the Senate declared Catiline and Manlius public enemies. Cicero then addressed the people of Rome in his Second Catilinarian Oration.

On December 2, Cicero proved Cataline's conspiracy when the envoys of the Allobroges, a German tribe, turned over incriminating letters. Cicero had suborned the Allobroges, recruited earlier by the Catilinarians. Cicero read the letters in the Senate on December 3 and again spoke before the people in his Third Catilinarian Oration. The conspirators were taken into custody.

Legal Action and Outcome

On December 5, the Senate debated the judgment of the conspirators, and Cicero gave another oration, his Fourth Catilinarian Oration. Julius Caesar spoke in favor of clemency, while Cato the Younger favored execution; the senators voted for execution. The conspirators were strangled in prison that day. In January of 62, Antonius defeated Catiline and his army in a battle near Pistoria; Catiline and his followers died bravely.

Impact

Catiline is presented by Cicero and Sallust as an archetypal rebel, bandit, or criminal—bold and daring, committing every kind of transgression, and encouraging his followers likewise. However, he is also depicted as deranged or troubled by guilt. Cicero alleged that Catiline seduced the Vestal virgin Fabia and that he killed his own son in order to marry a new wife, Aurelia Orestilla, who did not want stepchildren. Catiline reportedly bound his followers by human sacrifice, swearing an oath over the blood and flesh of his victims.

Catiline's supporters reflected Roman social tensions: A great influx of wealth from successful warfare had caused extravagance and greater social inequality. Cicero's and Sallust's depictions of Catiline's supporters suggest that Catiline practiced "class warfare" against the wealthy; however, the Catilinarians were not modern social revolutionaries, as they intended to enrich themselves.

The suppression of the conspiracy also set a precedent for the suspension of civil law (that is, imposition of martial law) in order to prosecute treason or terrorism. Cicero aggrandized his reputation through his suppression of Catiline.

Further Reading

Cicero. *Orations: In Catilinam I-IV, Pro Murena, Pro Sulla, Pro Flacco.* Translated by C. MacDonald. Cambridge, Mass.: Loeb Classical Library, 1977. A primary contemporary source, this translation shows Cicero as highly rhetorical, putting himself in the best possible light and Catiline in the worst.

Everitt, Anthony. *Cicero: The Life and Times of Rome's Greatest Politician.* New York: Random House, 2001. A chapter discusses Catiline and Cicero's role in the discovery and suppression of the conspiracy.

Sallust. *The Jugurthine War: The Conspiracy of Catiline.* Translated by S. A. Handford. New York: Penguin Books, 1963. A good primary source of information about the events.

—*Sara Elise Phang*

See also: Marcus Junius Brutus; Fulvia; Flavius Josephus; Lucius Cornelius Sulla.

NICOLAE CEAUŞESCU

Communist leader of Romania (1965-1989)

BORN: January 26, 1918; Scorniceşti, Romania
DIED: December 25, 1989; Târgovişte, Romania
ALSO KNOWN AS: Nicolae Andruta Ceauşescu (full name); Genius of the Carpathians
MAJOR OFFENSE: Genocide and illegal gathering of wealth
ACTIVE: 1965-1989
LOCALE: Romania
SENTENCE: Death

EARLY LIFE

A son of a peasant, Nicolae Andruta Ceauşescu (nih-kohl-ay ahn-DROO-tah chow-SHEHS-koo) at a young age became active in the Romanian communist movement. He was imprisoned several times for his Communist Party activities. In prison, he met the future first secretary of the Romanian Communist Party, Gheorghe Gheorghiu-Dej. After escaping in 1944, Ceauşescu held a variety of posts within the Communist Party and then, after the communist takeover in 1948, within government ranks. After the death of Gheorghiu-Dej in March, 1965, Ceauşescu was chosen first secretary of the central committee of the Communist Party. In December, 1967, he assumed the office of president of the state council and effectively became the ruler of Romania.

Nicolae Ceauşescu with his wife, Elena. (AP/Wide World Photos)

POLITICAL CAREER

Initially, Ceauşescu was a popular leader, charting an independent course in international affairs and challenging the Soviet Union on several fronts. Nationally, Ceauşescu maintained a communist, centralized administration and allowed for little dissent or opposition. His secret police maintained rigid controls over free speech, dissent, and the media. Obsessed with power, he created a personality cult, giving himself the titles of Conducător (Leader) and Geniul din Carpa i (Genius of the Carpathians). His administration was very insular; his wife, Elena, and other members of his family held many of the most important positions in the government.

In 1966, in an effort to increase the population and labor force, Ceauşescu outlawed abortion and contraception, instituted higher taxes for childless couples, discouraged divorce, and prohibited sex education. The birthrate almost doubled, and infant mortality increased greatly, as did unwanted pregnancies. The result was an enormous increase in handicapped, orphaned, and abandoned children, who were placed in dismal state-run institutions.

In 1972, Ceauşescu instituted a program of urban and rural "systematization," with the goal of increasing the amount of land available for farming while also increasing the number of people available for new industries. The program of resettlement, demolition, and construction resulted in more than eleven million people being resettled and the destruction of numerous historic buildings and churches. Moreover, Ceauşescu's impractical economic policies and mismanagement resulted in an extreme downturn in the economy. As a result of his opposition to the Soviet Union, Ceauşescu was able to borrow heavily from the West in order to finance economic development programs and briefly keep the economy afloat. Politically, Ceauşescu continued to concentrate his power by overhauling the military and security forces and blending the party and state power structures.

By the late 1970's and early 1980's, relations between his regime and the West soured, largely because of the deteriorating human rights situation and Ceauşescu's attempts to blame the West for the country's economic problems. The result was a nation with a dysfunctional economy and enormous foreign debt. In 1982, Ceauşescu introduced a draconian austerity program in attempt to repay the foreign debt. Most of the country's production was exported, resulting in extreme shortages of food, medicine, fuel, and other necessities. As a result, thousands of Romanians died, and millions more lived under near-starvation conditions. Meanwhile, Ceauşescu and his family continued to live lavishly.

By 1989, Ceauşescu's goal of eliminating foreign debt was achieved, but the social cost to the people of Romania was enormous. Protests of Ceauşescu's human rights abuses and economic and social policies became more frequent. On December 16, demonstrations broke out in Timisoara in western Romania. The next day, protesters marched on the Communist Party headquarters in the city, and Ceauşescu ordered his security forces to fire on the crowd. As many as four thousand people died during the days following the initial confrontation. Demonstrations spread to Bucharest, and on December 22, the Romanian Army defected to the protesters, thus ending the Ceauşescu regime. Ceauşescu and his wife were captured, and on Christmas Day, after a short military trial in which they were convicted of genocide and illegal gathering of wealth, they were both executed by a firing squad.

Impact

After the fall of Nicolae Ceauşescu, Romania became known as the "land of the orphans." After Ceauşescu was removed from power, more than 100,000 handicapped and orphaned children were found living in miserable conditions in orphanages and on the streets. The legacy of Ceauşescu remained in subsequent years, as Romania had the highest children's rate of human immunodeficiency virus (HIV) and acquired immunodeficiency syndrome (AIDS) in Europe. Romania began the transition from communism in 1989 with a largely obsolete industrial base and an unmotivated, unhealthy, and unproductive population. For years following Ceauşescu's rule, the people of Romania suffered greatly. The situation improved somewhat in the twenty-first century, but Romania remained a nation with extensive poverty and rampant corruption.

Further Reading

Behr, Edward. *Kiss the Hand You Cannot Bite: The Rise and Fall of the Ceauşescus*. New York: Villard, 1991. An analysis of the rise and fall of Ceauşescu's dictatorship in Romania, with an emphasis on both the historical roots of Ceauşescu's rise to power and the psychological makeup of this sociopath.

Deletant, Dennis. *Ceauşescu and the Securitate: Coercion and Dissent in Romania, 1965-1989*. Armonk, N.Y.: M. E. Sharpe, 1996. An authoritative account of the Ceauşescu years, providing a history of the oppressors and the oppressed. It is the first major work to use the archives of the Romanian secret police.

Gallager, Tom. *Romania After Ceauşescu*. Edinburgh, Scotland: Edinburgh University Press, 1995. A firsthand account of Romania after the fall of Ceauşescu in 1989. The author argues that former communists have exploited nationalism and ethnic tensions to retain power and prevent a transition to an open political system.

Kilch, Kent. *Children of Ceauşescu*. New York: Umbrage Editions, 2002. A portrait of children with AIDS in present-day Romania.

—*Jerome L. Neapolitan*

See also: Enver and Nexhmije Hoxha; Wojciech Jaruzelski; Tito.

BEATRICE CENCI

Italian noblewoman

BORN: February 6, 1577; Rome (now in Italy)
DIED: September 11, 1599; Rome
MAJOR OFFENSE: Murder
ACTIVE: September 9, 1598
LOCALE: L'Aquila, Naples (now in Italy)
SENTENCE: Death by decapitation

EARLY LIFE

Beatrice Cenci (beh-ah-TREE-cheh CHEHN-chee) was born into an old, respected, and powerful Roman family. Her paternal grandfather, Cristoforo Cenci, dramatically increased the Cenci fortune through financial transactions such as embezzling the papal treasury. Her father, Francesco Cenci, was a criminally violent and depraved nobleman. Her mother, Ersilia Santacroce, died on April 18, 1584, when Beatrice was only seven. Beatrice and her sister Antonina were educated at the Monastery of Monte Citorio. They were brought home by Francesco when he married Lucrezia Petroni in 1593. Within two years, Antonina married and died in childbirth; Rocco, one of Beatrice's nefarious brothers, was killed in a duel; and Francesco took Beatrice and Lucrezia to a castle at La Petrella del Salto in the Abruzzi mountains. By April, 1595, La Petrella had become the women's prison.

CRIMINAL CAREER

Subjected to cruel and allegedly unnatural treatment by Francesco, Beatrice and Lucrezia contemplated escape, but they were literally trapped. Beatrice had written to relatives begging to be released from her father's control through either of two means available to a young woman—to become a wife or a nun—but no help came. Beatrice and Lucrezia, with the help of other family members and retainers, devised a plot to do away with Francesco.

In 1598, Olimpio Calvetti, the warden of the castle and likely Beatrice's lover, along with Marzio Catalano, murdered Francesco by driving a spike into his head, then threw the corpse over a balcony. The Cenci family claimed it was an accident, pointing to a hole in the balcony through which Francesco allegedly fell, but priests and villagers cleaning the blood-encrusted corpse disputed the tenuous evidence.

LEGAL ACTION AND OUTCOME

Calvetti attempted to escape to the hills but was ambushed and beheaded. Catalano, interrogated while incarcerated in the Tordinona Prison, died in custody. For the Cencis, there was no clemency, despite the ethical ambiguity of their situation: Beatrice, Lucrezia, and Beatrice's brother Giacomo were sentenced to death. Romans sympathized immensely with Beatrice, with thousands weeping during the procession and execution. Beatrice and Lucrezia were publicly beheaded; Giacomo was tortured, then drawn and quartered and his skull crushed; and the youngest Cenci brother, Bernardo, made to observe the executions of the others, was sentenced to life imprisonment, although he was released soon thereafter. Clement VIII, who purportedly benefited greatly from the Cenci executions, confiscated Cenci property. Legend claims that public sympathy for Beatrice ran so high that young girls were said to have placed garlands on her newly severed head.

IMPACT

The lasting impact of Beatrice Cenci has proven to be the legend that grew after her death—that of a young girl, beautiful in her innocent purity, embodying the figures of victim and villain, martyr and murderer. Some histori-

Guido Reni's portrait of Cenci, now believed to be of a different woman.

ans assert that Beatrice was not an innocent victim but a woman in her twenties entrusted by Francesco with household management, temporarily imprisoned because she was carrying Calvetti's child.

Perhaps because of the ethical ambiguity of her situation and its pathetic universality, Cenci also became the subject of legend in literature and art. She has been examined, cross-examined, adored, and reviled in literature, including in works such as Percy Bysshe Shelley's *The Cenci* (pb. 1819), Alfred Nobel's tragedy *Nemesis* (1896), Alberto Moravia's *Beatrice Cenci* (pr. 1955), and Antonin Artaud's *Les Cenci* (pr. 1935). A haunting portrait attributed to Baroque painter Guido Reni was long thought to be that of Cenci and gained fame by allegedly sparking Shelley's interest in the woman; however, modern-day art authorities believe that the image most likely is not that of Cenci. Other themes explored in works about Cenci range from religious hypocrisy and aristocratic corruption to the examination of self and soul and the functioning of the human psyche under duress.

Further Reading

Burkhardt, Jacob. *The Civilization of the Renaissance in Italy*. Reprint. New York: Random House, 1982. Considered by many to be the masterwork on Beatrice's milieu.

Jack, Belinda. *Beatrice's Spell: The Enduring Legend of Beatrice Cenci*. New York: Other Press, 2005. Explores the effect of Beatrice on authors.

Ricci, Corrado. *Beatrice Cenci*. 2 vols. Translated by Morris Bishop and Henry Longan Stuart. New York: Boni and Liveright, 1925. Foundation for many twentieth century interpretations of Cenci's story, Ricci's account draws on Antonio Bertolotti's *Francesco Cenci e la sua famiglia* (1879), the first modern account to rely on primary sources.

—*Donna Berliner*

See also: Lucrezia Borgia.

Cassie L. Chadwick

Canadian swindler

Born: October 10, 1857; Eastwood, Ontario, Canada
Died: October 10, 1907; Ohio Penitentiary Hospital, Columbus, Ohio
Also known as: Elizabeth Bigley (birth name); Mrs. E. G. Thomas; Lydia Scott; Madam Lydia Devere; Mrs. Hoover
Major offenses: Forgery, conspiracy against the government, and conspiracy to wreck the Citizens' National Bank of Oberlin, Ohio
Active: 1879-1905
Locale: Ohio
Sentence: Nine and a half years in prison for forgery, paroled after four years; fourteen years in prison and seventy-thousand-dollar fine for conspiracy charges

Early Life

Cassie Chadwick (KAH-see CHAHD-wihk) was born as Elizabeth Bigley in southern Ontario, Canada, to Daniel Bigley, a railroad section hand, and his wife, Alice, a homemaker. She displayed early wayward traits when she adopted the name of Mrs. E. G. Thomas and spent extravagantly in the nearby town of Woodstock, backing the bills she ran up by showing merchants a forged letter, allegedly from a London attorney, that said that she was a widow who had inherited eighteen hundred dollars. She was arrested in 1879 but was found not guilty by reason of insanity, presumably to avoid sentencing a young girl to prison; her courtroom antics, including making faces at the jurors, probably also influenced this decision. She moved to Toronto briefly and then relocated to Cleveland, Ohio, living with her married sister.

Criminal Career

Chadwick set up shop in Toledo as a fortune-teller (first as Lydia Scott and then as Madam Lydia Devere). She was married to Wallace Springsteen for just eleven days and in 1889 was convicted for forging the name of Richard Brown, a prominent Youngstown, Ohio, citizen, in order to pay for her purchases. She was sentenced to nine and a half years in the Ohio Penitentiary. She was paroled after four years and opened a brothel in Toledo in 1893. She then met and married Dr. Leroy S. Chadwick and in short order saw him off to Paris, sending him his monthly annuity to keep him abroad.

Using her standing as Chadwick's wife to gain social legitimacy, Chadwick launched a grand plan of fraud. She enlisted the aid of a prominent Ohio lawyer to accompany her to New York City. She left the lawyer in a carriage in front of the Fifth Avenue mansion of steel magnate Andrew Carnegie, the richest bachelor in the United States. She remained inside the house (apparently meeting with a housekeeper) for about twenty minutes. Back in the carriage, she told the lawyer that she was Carnegie's illegitimate daughter and let him glimpse a trust deed for $2 million, allegedly from Carnegie. When Carnegie died, she declared, she stood to inherit about $400 million.

The lawyer arranged for her to deposit the trust deed in the Wade Park Bank in Cleveland. Had the bank president opened the sealed envelope, he readily would have discovered that the deed was a crude forgery. Using the deposit and the promise of more to come, Chadwick borrowed what has been variously estimated at between $2 million and $20 million from banks throughout the nation, commonly offering bank officials exorbitant interest and personal bonuses. A primary target was the Citizens' National Bank in the college town of Oberlin, Ohio, which she ultimately plunged into bankruptcy. She also accumulated more than $100,000 of the personal funds of its president, Charles Beckwith.

Legal Action and Outcome

The Chadwick ruse came to a halt when a Brookline, Massachusetts, bank demanded payment of its loan. When Chadwick stalled, it filed criminal charges. Other banks soon joined in the quest for their money. Arrested in 1905, Chadwick underwent a two-week trial in Cleveland, during which her lawyer portrayed her as a helpless female being oppressed by wealthy male capitalists. The prosecutor countered by noting that she had deprived widows and orphans—the bank's depositors—"of their hopes of peace and prosperity in their old age." The jury convicted Chadwick on seven counts of conspiracy, and the judge imposed a fourteen-year prison sentence. Chadwick died in the prison hospital two years after she was incarcerated. The cause of death was a heart attack and what the prison physician described as an overindulgence in rich food.

Both Beckwith and a bank cashier, A. T. Spear, later would be charged with violation of federal banking laws for cashing Chadwick's checks when she did not have funds on deposit to cover them. Beckwith died before he could be tried; Spear received a seven-year sentence. Carnegie, who had never had any relationship to Chadwick, later would make good the bank's losses, besides endowing a library at Oberlin College.

Impact

The case involving Cassie Chadwick made clear to early twentieth century Americans that swindling was not exclusively a male crime. It also put bankers on notice that they had to tighten up the scrutiny of those seeking loans, rather than succumb to the charms and unsupported claims of applicants.

Further Reading

Butts, Ed. *She Dared: True Stories of Heroines, Scoundrels, and Renegades*. Toronto, Ont.: Tunda Books, 2005. One of the chapters summarizes the life and con career of Chadwick.

"*Chadwick v. United States*." *Federal Reporter* 141 (November 17, 1905): 225-247. A discussion of the criminal charges against Chadwick plus the court's review and rejection of her arguments for a reversal of the verdict.

Crosbie, John S. *The Incredible Mrs. Chadwick: The Most Notorious Woman of Her Age*. New York: McGraw-Hill Ryerson, 1975. The author is subjective with some of the facts of the Chadwick saga, using, he says, the kind of inventiveness of which Chadwick herself would be proud.

DeGrave, Kathleen. *Swindler, Spy, Rebel: The Confidence Woman in the Nineteenth-Century*. Columbia: University of Missouri Press, 1995. Chadwick is portrayed in the context of female swindlers of her time. Her ladylike appearance and genteel behavior are said to have fooled men who were accustomed to gallant behavior toward seemingly respectable women.

Wells, Joseph T. *Frankensteins of Fraud: The Twentieth Century's Top Ten White-Collar Criminals*. Austin, Texas: Obsidian, 2000. The first chapter provides a sprightly discussion of Chadwick's background, personality, and exploits.

—*Gilbert Geis*

See also: John R. Brinkley; Megan Louise Ireland; Henri Lemoine; Victor Lustig; Charles Ponzi; Alexandre Stavisky.

Cassius Chaerea

Roman assassin

Born: Date unknown; place unknown
Died: 41 c.e.; place unknown
Major offenses: Treason, conspiracy, and regicide
Active: January 24, 41 c.e.
Locale: Rome
Sentence: Execution

Early Life

Very little is known of the early life of Cassius Chaerea (cas-SEE-uhs ki-REE-a) except for some passing references to his high-mindedness and bravery. As a soldier, he served in Germany and helped to quell a mutiny by disaffected legionnaires. The Roman historian Tacitus describes him as a high-spirited youth and handy with a sword. In this action, he single-handedly cleared a passage through an armed and hostile throng of rioters.

Criminal Career

Later in his career, Emperor Gaius Caesar Caligula appointed Chaerea tribune in the Praetorian Guard, a cohort of elite soldiers who had the honor of guarding the emperor. However, his relationship with the emperor was hardly friendly. Caligula was renowned for his capricious and sometimes monstrous antics. It was perhaps because of Chaerea's high-pitched voice that Caligula would taunt him—referring to him as "wench" (soft and effeminate). When Chaerea was on guard duty, the emperor would give him watchwords like "love" or "venus." Furthermore, on those occasions when Chaerea was called upon to thank the emperor, Caligula would offer his hand to be kissed and then withdraw it only to make an indecent gesture. No doubt these actions were offensive to the tribune, who was known for his nobility and his love of the virtues of the old Roman Republic. Certainly Chaerea must have been disgusted by the licentious behavior of the emperor and whatever role he himself was forced to play in satisfying the ruler's desires. In all, these insults provided a powerful motive for his decisive action against Caligula.

Other Roman noblemen wanted Caligula eliminated because of his hostility against the senate and aristocracy. They plotted against him and decided that he would be dispatched during the Palatine games—festivities produced in honor of Rome's first emperor, Augustus. On the fourth day of these proceedings, the emperor was attacked in transit from the theater to his palace, which took him through a tunnel. He had paused to compliment some Grecian boys of noble birth who had composed a song in his honor. In the narrow confines of this tunnel, the assailants fell upon Caligula. Chaerea is said to have struck the first blow to the emperor's neck, shouting "Take this"; these words, interestingly, were part of ritual pronouncements for blood sacrifices. It is rumored that this wound was not intended to be mortal. Caligula enjoyed watching a slow death, and it was thought appropriate by his assailants that he too should suffer one. After he fell, others present joined in the mayhem, stabbing the prostrate body savagely even though it was clear that he was dead. It is rumored that some even tasted his flesh. Thirty sword wounds later, the conspirators were run off by the emperor's loyal but tardy German bodyguards. The guards managed to slaughter some of the conspirators and a few innocent senators but not before Caligula's wife and baby daughter were also murdered.

Legal Action and Outcome

What had begun as Cassius Chaerea's plan to assassinate one of Rome's worst tyrants ended in an attempt to execute the remainder of the enture Julio-Claudian line by not only Chaerea but severed sympathetic senators as well—as the assassinations of Caligula's wife and daughter attest. The attempt failed, however, with the succession of Claudius , who decreed that the memory of the unfortunate event be expunged, and he extended clemency to many. However, Chaerea was not granted clemency and was either executed or forced to commit suicide as an example to those who would dare conspire against the emperor.

Impact

After the murder of Caligula at the hands of Cassius Chaerea, some noblemen hoped for a return to the Roman Republic with a significant role being apportioned to the aristocracy. These hopes were soon dashed by Claudius, who was backed by authority of the Praetorian Guard.

Further Reading

Barrett, Anthony A. *Caligula: The Corruption of Power*. New Haven, Conn.: Yale University Press, 1989. A stimulating account of the assassination, which relies heavily on the histories of the ancient historian Flavius Josephus.

Levick, Barbara, *Claudius*. New Haven, Conn.: Yale University Press, 1990. Levick discusses the hypothesis that Claudius may have been involved in the assassination plot.

Suetonius. *Lives of the Caesars*. Translated by Catherine Edwards. New York: Oxford University Press, 2000. Suetonius, a prominent Roman historian, provides a lively account of the achievements and foibles of the Roman emperors as the height of imperial power. The assassination is described in the chapter on Caligula.

Winterling, Aloys. *Caligula, eine Biographie*. Munich, Germany: C. H. Beck, 2003. Winterling argues that Chaerea acted as an agent of the freedman, Callistus. In German.

—*Edward W. Maine*

See also: Caligula; Flavius Josephus; Lucius Cornelius Sulla.

Houston Stewart Chamberlain

Anglo-German race theorist

Born: September 9, 1855; Southsea, England
Died: January 9, 1927; Bayreuth, Germany
Also known as: Houston Stuart Chamberlain
Cause of notoriety: An eloquent anti-Semite and devout believer in German superiority, Chamberlain was a friend and confidant to Kaiser Wilhelm II and Adolf Hitler.
Active: Late nineteenth century-1927
Locale: Germany

Early Life

Born in Southsea, England, Houston Stewart Chamberlain (CHAYM-buhr-lihn) was an infant when his mother died. His father, a career military officer, sent the boy to France to live with relatives. He suffered from what was believed to be lung problems, so after a brief time in an English military school, Houston was sent on a tour of European health spas. He was supervised by a Prussian tutor, Otto Kuntze.

Kuntze was a fervid believer in German superiority, and his constant propagandizing, in addition to the rampant anti-Semitic sentiment so prevalent in Europe at that time, helped produce in Chamberlain a philosophy that the Nazis would later admire. Later, Houston declared that he had no desire to return to the land of his birth and announced that he intended to remain in Europe to read, write, and publish his views.

Intellectual Career

Living in Cannes, France, and then Florence, Italy, Chamberlain displayed a growing antipathy to England, the land of his birth, and rarely returned there. He studied at the University of Geneva and then worked on a dissertation in natural sciences in Dresden, Germany, where he became infatuated with the German language, history, and culture. Often ill, he had ample time for reading, thinking, and, especially, writing.

Houston Stewart Chamberlain.

Chamberlain's Views on Civilization

In 1899, Houston Stewart Chamberlain made his belief in racial superiority clear in The Foundations of the Nineteenth Century:

Scarcely anyone will have the hardihood to deny that the inhabitants of Northern Europe have become the makers of the world's history. At no time indeed have they stood alone, either in the past or in the present; on the contrary, from the very beginning their individuality has developed in conflict with other individualities, first of all in conflict with that human chaos composed of the ruins of fallen Rome, then with all the races of the world in turn; others, too, have exercised influence—indeed great influence—upon the destinies of mankind, but then always merely as opponents of the men from the north. What was fought out sword in hand was of but little account; the real struggle . . . was one of ideas; this struggle still goes on to-day. If, however, the Teutons were not the only peoples who moulded the world's history, they unquestionably deserve the first place: all those who from the sixth century onwards appear as genuine shapers of the destinies of mankind, whether as builders of States or as discoverers of new thoughts and of original art, belong to the Teutonic race. The impulse given by the Arabs is short-lived; the Mongolians destroy, but do not create anything; the great Italians of the *rinascimento* were all born either in the north saturated with Lombardic, Gothic and Frankish blood, or in the extreme Germano-Hellenic south; in Spain it was the Western Goths who formed the element of life; the Jews are working out their "Renaissance" of to-day by following in every sphere as closely as possible the example of the Teutonic peoples. From the moment the Teuton awakes, a new world begins to open out, a world which of course we shall not be able to call purely Teutonic—one in which, in the nineteenth century especially, there have appeared new elements, or at least elements which formerly had a lesser share in the process of development, as, for example, the Jews and the formerly pure Teutonic Slavs, who by mixture of blood have now become "un-Teutonised"—a world which will yet perhaps assimilate great racial complexes and so lay itself open to new influences from all the different types, but at any rate a new world and a new civilisation.

Source: Houston Stewart Chamberlain, *The Foundations of the Nineteenth Century*, translated by John Lees (London: John Lane, 1911).

His most famous work was *Die Grundlagen des neunzehnten Jahrhunderts* (1899; *The Foundations of the Nineteenth Century*, 1910), which he wrote in German. This work asserted the supremacy of Western civilization and attributed this dominant position to the influence and power of the Germanic people. Chamberlain was leery of any group or organization that he believed had universalist intentions, such as the Roman Catholic Church, international economic systems, and, primarily, Jews.

Chamberlain believed the Germanic (or Aryan) people were heirs to an incredible historical legacy. He saw his adopted and beloved culture as directly descended from classical Greece and Rome. He asserted that when the German tribes toppled the Western Roman Empire in 476 C.E., the empire had been fatally weakened by encroaching Jewish influence. Jews were disparaged because of their perceived lack of assimilation, supposed adherence to internationalist theological and economic beliefs, and non-Indo-European origin. He also believed that Jesus was only Jewish by religion, not race, a position of dubious defensibility even then.

In addition to being influenced by Kuntze, Chamberlain was also heavily influenced by the writings of Count Joseph Arthur de Gobineau and the music of Richard Wagner. Gobineau had also asserted the superiority of Aryan Germans but feared the debasement of Aryans through loathsome but inevitable miscegenation, especially with Jews. In Wagner, Chamberlain found the musical expression of all things German; he would eventually marry the composer's daughter.

Chamberlain denounced England's entrance into World War I as part of the anti-German Triple Entente. He was granted German citizenship and was honored with the Iron Cross for his propaganda efforts against the Allied cause. In the fall of 1923, he met Adolf Hitler and was apparently quite impressed, declaring the younger man to be Germany's eventual savior. Hitler was impressed as well and visited Chamberlain shortly before Chamberlain's death in 1927.

Impact

Houston Stewart Chamberlain was well educated and seemingly very intelligent. He was also a skilled writer, philosopher, and adept disseminator of propaganda. However, many of his views have been repudiated and are considered by many to be repugnant and abhorrent. He was an apologist for anti-Semites, race baiters, and bigots in general and perhaps helped pave the way for the rise of fascist ideology. His impact was substantial but, sadly, not benevolent.

Further Reading

Herman, Arthur. *The Idea of Decline in Western History*. New York: Free Press, 1997. Herman, while critical of Chamberlain personally and Chamberlain's ultranationalist views, provides basic factual information.

Lindsey, Hal. *The Road to Holocaust*. New York: Bantam Books, 1989. This work contains only a brief mention of Chamberlain but does acknowledge his importance, while placing him in the proto-Nazi context.

Rubenstein, Richard. *Approaches to Auschwitz: The Holocaust and Its Legacy*. Atlanta: John Knox Press, 1987. This work discusses the Nazi manipulation of Chamberlain's views.

—Thomas W. Buchanan

See also: Julius Evola; Elisabeth Förster-Nietzsche; Savitri Devi; Winifred Wagner.

Whittaker Chambers

American spy and informer

Born: April 1, 1901; Philadelphia, Pennsylvania

Died: July 9, 1961; Westminster, Maryland

Also known as: Jay Vivian Chambers (full name); David Whittaker Chambers (alias); David Breen (alias); Lloyd Cantwell (alias); Karl or Carl (alias); Bob (alias); Harold Phillips (alias); Arthur Dwyer (alias); Charles Adams (alias); Charles Whittaker (alias); George Crosley (alias); John Kelly (literary pseudonym)

Cause of notoriety: Chambers, a onetime Communist spy, became notorious less for his own espionage than for making accusations of espionage against Alger Hiss.

Active: 1932-1950

Locale: Baltimore, Washington, D.C., New York City, and Westminster, Maryland

Early Life

Despite the best efforts of his mother, the upbringing of Whittaker Chambers (WIHT-uh-kur CHAYM-burz) in Lynbrook on New York's Long Island was anything but respectable or conventional. His mother was an unsuccessful actress, and his father was an artist who at one point abandoned the family to live with a male lover. Chambers's grandmother frightened the family by brandishing scissors and knives and claiming that people were trying to kill her, and his only brother committed suicide.

In high school Chambers kept to himself but was teased and called derisive names like Girlie and Stinky. He had bad teeth because his mother would not pay for dentist visits, and he got in trouble at his graduation ceremonies by predicting that one of his classmates would end up as a prostitute. He began to feel like an outcast and briefly ran off to Baltimore and New Orleans before enrolling at Columbia University in 1920.

At Columbia he got in trouble for a political satire about Jesus that he published in *The Morningside*, the student literary annual. He left the university as a result and in 1923 traveled to Europe, where he was attracted by Communist political protests.

On his return he began reading political literature, including a pamphlet by Vladimir Ilich Lenin, and he joined the Communist Party in 1925, working for its newspaper, *The Daily Worker*. He supplemented his income with translation work, making the first English translation of the famous animal story *Bambi* (1928). After a split in the Communist Party in 1929, Chambers was forced to leave but returned to its good graces in 1931 through a series of short stories he submitted to the Communist literary journal, *The New Masses*.

Political Career

Chambers became editor of *The New Masses* and then, in 1932, was recruited for special underground work, which consisted of espionage for the Soviet Union. For the following six years Chambers worked as a courier, transmitting government documents to agents of the GRU, the Soviet military intelligence department.

In 1938, in the wake of purges in the Soviet Union and among its agents abroad, Chambers escaped from the Communist underground and went into hiding for a year until he was able to surface with a job writing for the book section of *Time* magazine. Now a committed anti-Communist, Chambers wrote extensively about the dangers of Communism and the Soviet Union, alienating some of his fellow journalists, who thought him biased and extreme.

Concerned about the Nazi-Soviet pact of August, 1939, Chambers reported to the U.S. State Department on some of his past espionage activities, but no action was taken then or in the early 1940's after he was interviewed by the Federal Bureau of Investigation.

After World War II, however, the House Committee on Un-American Activities (HUAC) became interested in Soviet espionage and subpoenaed Chambers, who accused several individuals of having been secret members of the Communist Party. One of these individuals was Alger Hiss.

Whittaker Chambers. (AP/Wide World Photos)

The Alger Hiss Case

After a distinguished career at the State Department, Hiss had just become president of the Carnegie Endowment for International Peace. He denied being a Communist and sued Chambers for slander. Chambers then added to his allegations, saying Hiss had been not only a Communist but a spy. Led by Congressman Richard Nixon, HUAC continued hearings on these matters; a grand jury began investigating them as well, leading to two charges of perjury against Hiss.

To support his accusations, Chambers produced various documents, including the so-called Pumpkin Papers, microfilm of stolen government documents that he had hidden in a pumpkin on his farm in Maryland. The documents included materials typed on what appeared to be Hiss's typewriter and notes made in his handwriting, and seemed to indicate that a Communist spy ring had been active in Washington. After a mistrial, a second trial found Hiss guilty of perjury in January, 1950.

Impact

The Hiss-Chambers case divided the United States. Many on the left saw the conviction of Hiss as a frame-up intended as part of an attack on liberals and Democrats. Conservatives saw it as an important blow against Soviet espionage. Whittaker Chambers himself saw his actions as part of the worldwide struggle against Communism on behalf of Christianity, to which he had become converted.

Whether or not Hiss was guilty—and by the end of the twentieth century most commentators were convinced that he was—the effect of Chambers's charges against him was to provide support for Senator Joseph McCarthy's attacks on supposed Communists in the 1950's, which cost many innocent liberals their jobs. Chambers himself was involved in one such incident which ruined the career of the diplomat Edmund Clubb.

Chambers had reservations about McCarthy's attacks, but he expressed them only privately, and he himself, in such writings as *Witness* (1952), tended to lump liberals together with Communists, thus contributing to the McCarthyist mind-set.

President Ronald Reagan posthumously awarded a Medal of Freedom to Chambers in 1984 and praised him for aiding the struggle against Communism. Perhaps in some distant way Chambers contributed to the fall of the Soviet Union. In the short term, his charges against Hiss fanned the flames of Cold War hysteria.

Further Reading

Chambers, Whittaker. *Witness*. New York: Random House, 1952. Chambers's autobiography, describing the lure of Communism, his life as a spy, and his upbringing.

Roazen, Paul. "The Strange Case of Alger Hiss and Whittaker Chambers." *Queen's Quarterly* (December, 1999): 518-533. Discusses the split among intellectuals over the Hiss-Chambers case.

Swan, Patrick, ed. *Alger Hiss, Whittaker Chambers, and the Schism in the American Soul*. Wilmington, Del.:

ISI Books, 2003. Collection of articles written between 1950 and 2001 by various writers analyzing the Hiss-Chambers case.

Tanenhaus, Sam. *Whittaker Chambers: A Biography*. New York: Random House, 1997. Full-scale biography, tracing Chambers's life from childhood through his Communist and post-Communist periods, with emphasis on the Hiss hearings and trials.

Weinstein, Allen. *Perjury: The Hiss-Chambers Case*. 2d ed. New York: Random House, 1997. Provides biographical information on Hiss and Chambers and massive detail on the Hiss hearings and trials.

—*Sheldon Goldfarb*

See also: Alger Hiss; Joseph McCarthy; Richard Nixon.

Mark David Chapman

American murderer

Born: May 10, 1955; Fort Worth, Texas

Major offense: Second-degree murder in the death of John Lennon

Active: December 8, 1980

Locale: Central Park West, New York City, New York

Sentence: Twenty years to life imprisonment

Early Life

The formative years of Mark David Chapman (CHAP-muhn) in Decatur, Georgia, were troubled by an oversolicitous mother and an emotionally detached, abusive father. Early in life he imagined he was the ruler or hero of a city of "little people" whom he either had to save or had to destroy because of their waywardness. He became addicted to drugs and obsessed with the pop music group the Beatles but at sixteen rejected his past and turned to evangelical Christianity. His disillusionment with the Beatles increased both with the claim by musician John Lennon that the Beatles were more popular than Jesus and with the 1971 release of Lennon's *Imagine* album, which called forth an idealist vision of a world beyond religious sectarianism, capitalist consumerism, and international war. Chapman psychologically identified with Holden Caulfield, the antisocial protagonist of J. D. Salinger's *The Catcher in the Rye* (1951), who ran away to New York to sort out his life.

Before Chapman made his own way to New York City, he worked for the Young Men's Christian Association (YMCA) in Georgia, Russia, and Beirut, Lebanon. He then attended Dekalb Community College in Clarkson, Georgia, and fell in love with Jessica Blankenship. He followed her to the conservative Christian Covenant College in Tennessee but left as a result of a mental breakdown.

Criminal Career

In the 1970's, Chapman worked as an armed security guard but became dissatisfied with life and flew to Hawaii, where he twice attempted suicide. In 1979, he traveled to Asia and married Gloria Abe, a Japanese American travel agent who had arranged his trip and who reminded him of Yoko Ono, Lennon's wife. The couple returned to Hawaii, where he again became obsessed with Caulfield and began debating with his "little people" whether to kill Lennon.

On October 30, 1980, he flew to New York to kill Lennon, convinced that Lennon was a phony for rejecting Christianity and a hypocrite for singing about an ideal world without borders and war and people without greed or money. Unable to buy bullets in New York, Chapman left to buy them in Georgia and returned on November 10. However, Abe convinced him to return home, where his demons were temporarily quelled.

Chapman returned to New York City on December 6; two days later he staked out Lennon in front of Lennon's residence, the Dakota. That afternoon, he had Lennon autograph *Double Fantasy*, the recently released album by Lennon and Ono, before the couple departed for their recording studio. When they returned at 10:50 p.m., Chapman, with *The Catcher in the Rye* in his pocket, shot Lennon with four hollow-point cartridges. Lennon died shortly thereafter.

Legal Action and Outcome

Chapman was charged with second-degree murder. The threat of public lynching was so great that he was transferred from Bellevue Hospital, where he had been taken for a psychiatric examination, to Rikers Island jail. After dozens of tests, six psychiatrists were prepared to testify that Chapman was psychotic; three were prepared to testify that his delusions fell short of the legal definition of psychosis. Chapman rejected the advice of his lawyer and the defense psychiatrists and pleaded guilty, saying that was what God wanted. On June 22, 1981, his plea that he intentionally caused the death of Lennon was accepted, and he was sentenced to twenty years to life in Attica State Prison. Despite being a model prisoner, he was denied parole in 2000, 2002, and 2004.

Impact

For many Americans, the assassination of Lennon signaled the end of an era. Mark David Chapman murdered a highly visible icon for peace activism and the counterculture that dominated the United States and Europe from the mid-1960's through the mid-1970's. The Chapman case brought to light the relatively new phenomenon of abnormal psychology associated with crimes against celebrities and highlighted the ongoing problematic way that psychopathic individuals are treated in the American justice system. Lennon is still mourned by friends and fans, and Chapman has refused any treatment for his illness while in prison.

Further Reading

Bresler, Fenton. *Who Killed John Lennon?* New York: St. Martin's Press, 1989. A speculative account claiming that Chapman was programmed by the Central Intelligence Agency (CIA) through drugs and hypnosis to assassinate Lennon for political reasons.

Hamilton, Sue. *The Killing of a Rock Star: John Lennon (Days of Tragedy).* Edited by John Hamilton. Minneapolis: Abdo & Daughters, 1989. Brief children's version of Lennon's biography and Chapman's role in killing him.

Jones, Jack. *Let Me Take You Down: Inside the Mind of Mark David Chapman, the Man Who Shot John Lennon.* New York: Villard Books, 1992. Based on personal interviews, the book gives a thorough account of Chapman and the mental conditions that led him to murder Lennon.

—*Jules Simon*

See also: John Hinckley, Jr.; Yolanda Saldívar.

Charles II

King of Spain (1665-1700)

Born: November 6, 1661; Madrid, Spain
Died: November 1, 1700; Madrid, Spain
Also known as: Carlos II; Charles the Mad; the Bewitched (el hechizado);
Cause of notoriety: A physically deformed and mentally incompetent king, Charles II was the last of the Habsburg Dynasty to rule Spain.
Active: 1665-1700
Locale: Spain

Early Life

Little about the childhood of Charles (chahrlz) II was normal. When his father, Philip IV, died in 1665, Charles ascended to the Spanish throne when he was only four years old. Even more remarkable, however, was the boy's physical and mental condition. He was descended from Isabella of Portugal and Joan the Mad, both of whom suffered from mental illness, and intermarriage among the Spanish and Austrian Habsburgs created profound genetic problems for the boy. Of his eight great-grandparents, seven were direct descendants of Joan the Mad, and the boy's father was his mother's uncle. The child's head was overlarge, his Habsburg lower jaw protruded so far that he could never chew his food properly, his tongue was so large that he had difficulty speaking, and he suffered from rickets, epilepsy, and perhaps acromegaly. Philip IV, an infamous philanderer, may have infected his wife, Mariana of Austria, with syphilis, which she then could have passed to Charles. The boy was also mentally impaired, which made the rudiments of education difficult. Given all his physical and mental deficiencies, he seemed unlikely to survive childhood.

Royal Career

Even without his disabilities, the four-year-old Charles would have been unable to rule when his father died, and Philip designated Queen Mariana to govern as regent until Charles was fourteen. Until six or seven years of age, Charles could barely stand by himself and could not walk unassisted, leaving observers to remark that the crown was firmer on his head than the ground under his feet. Although Charles had intermittent, brief periods of limited lucidity, the empire was ruled by his mother and her Jesuit confessor, Everard Nithard; his illegitimate half brother, Juan José of Austria; the royal *validos* (favorites), the duke of Medinaceli and the Duke of Oropesa; and most important, the various councils representing the autonomous Spanish realms. The king's rare public roles included presiding over the Inquisition's great 1680 *auto-da-fé* (act of faith) in Madrid.

Even when he came of age and the regency ended, his condition prevented Charles from governing, and he could not command respect from his subjects. This reduced his only significant role to that of begetting an heir. In 1679, he married Marie Louise, the niece of France's Louis XIV. The marriage proved sterile, and the fun-loving queen lapsed into depression and morbid obesity before dying in 1689. Within three months, he wed Maria Anna of Neuberg. Some suspected that he was the victim of a curse: Only witchcraft could impede God's anointed from procreating the much desired heir. He thus became known as Charles the Bewitched (*el Hechizado*). Charles submitted to exorcism but was still unable to father a child.

By 1696, the ruling houses of Europe knew that Charles's own death would touch off a dynastic struggle. The Austrian Habsburg archduke Karl and the Bourbon Philip of Anjou, Louis XIV's grandson, emerged as the chief candidates to succeed the Bewitched. Spanish political leaders were chiefly concerned that the empire not be dismembered. Charles died on November 1, 1700.

Charles II.

Impact

Charles's will named Philip of Anjou as his heir. Castilians willingly accepted the change in dynasty, but it touched off a major European conflict, the War of the Spanish Succession (1701-1713). Catalonia supported the Habsburg candidate, largely to assert its autonomy from Madrid. Philip V withstood the Habsburgs and their allies and then suppressed the attempted Catalan secession.

Further Reading

Kamen, Henry. *Spain in the Later Seventeenth Century, 1665-1700.* New York: Longman, 1980. The foremost English-language history of Charles II's reign, it devotes little attention to the king and focuses instead on the beginnings of Spain's recovery following its disastrous mid-century decline.

Langdon-Davies, John. *Carlos: The King Who Would Not Die*. Englewood Cliffs, N.J.: Prentice-Hall, 1963. One of several works about Spain by a prolific writer of popular history, this is the most detailed account in English of Charles's life, although it devotes little attention to the historical context in which he ruled. An edition published in London is *Charles, the Bewitched.*

Lynch, John. *The Hispanic World in Crisis and Change, 1598-1700.* Oxford, England: Blackwell, 1992. Chapters 9-10 provide an excellent overview of Charles II's reign and its consequences for the empire and Europe.

—*Kendall W. Brown*

See also: Joan the Mad.

Charles VI

King of France (r. 1380-1422)

Born: December 3, 1368; Paris, France
Died: October 21, 1422; Paris, France
Also known as: Charles le Bien-Aimé; Charles the Mad
Cause of notoriety: Charles VI' s insanity compromised France's position during the Hundred Years' War.
Active: 1388-1422
Locale: Paris, France

Early Life

Charles (shahrl-luh) VI was born in Paris on December 3, 1368. He was the son of Charles V and Jeanne de Bourbon. In 1380, he became king at the age of eleven. His coronation took place on November 4 in Reims Cathedral, the traditional site for crowning French kings. Until 1388, he ruled under the guidance of his uncles, with Philip II, the duke of Burgundy, playing the most important role. It proved a difficult period for France as the uncles spent extravagantly and depleted the treasury. Their insistence upon new tax levies caused uprisings among the people throughout France and Flanders. In 1385, Charles VI married Isabeau de Bavière.

Royal Career

In 1388, Charles VI assumed the full authority of his throne. He dismissed his uncles and chose his brother Louis of Valois, duke of Orléans, as his counselor. He summoned his father's ministers, the Marmousets, back to the court. These ministers, who were not members of the nobility, but of humble origin, had received their name of Marmousets, meaning "little fellows," from the court nobility who resented them. Under the leadership of Olivier de Clesson, they implemented conservative and reasonable practice to govern the country.

In August, 1392, Charles VI suffered his first attack of insanity. In April of that same year, he had been afflicted with a mysterious illness, which had caused his hair and nails to fall out and subjected him to bouts of fever and bizarre behavior. His first episode of insanity occurred while he was riding with some of his soldiers in search of Pierre de Craon, who had attempted to murder de Clesson. Charles VI suddenly attacked and killed four of his soldiers before he could be subdued. Although he had occasional periods of lucidity, he had lost his ability to govern effectively. When he was not totally incapacitated by his delusions, he tended to follow the advice of whoever was with him at the moment. Charles died in Paris on October 21, 1422. He was buried in Saint Denis Basilica near Paris.

Impact

Charles VI's illness and incapacity to rule placed France in a precarious position. France was fighting England in the Hundred Years' War (1337-1453), and the country was in a state of anarchy. Two noble factions, the Burgundians and the Armagnacs, fought for control of the kingdom. Queen Isabeau, who served as regent during her husband's periods of insanity, repeatedly changed her allegiance. At times, she allied herself with the Burgundian faction and at other times with the Armagnacs. She entered into secret negotiations to place Henry V of England on the throne of France. France suffered a dev-

Charles VI.

astating defeat at Agincourt in 1415. Then on May 21, 1420, under the influence of Isabeau and the duke of Burgundy, Charles VI signed the Treaty of Troyes, which recognized Henry V as the successor to the French throne.

With the subsequent deaths of both Charles VI and Henry V, the French throne remained in contention. The English laid claim to the throne by the Treaty of Troyes and the French by Salic laws of inheritance for Charles VI's son Charles. The throne remained in question until the divinely inspired Joan of Arc appeared at Chinon and escorted Charles to Reims, where he was crowned Charles VII, king of France.

FURTHER READING

Bachman, Clifford R. *The Worlds of Medieval Europe*. New York: Oxford University Press, 2003. Thorough presentation of the period's economic, social, and political currents. Chapter 17 deals with the events of the fourteenth century. Includes a chart of the Valois dynasty.

Findling, John E., and Frank W. Thackery, eds. *Events That Changed the World Through the Sixteenth Century*. Westport, Conn.: Greenwood Press, 2001. Chapter 3 presents a detailed account of the Hundred Years' War and explains the problems involved in succession to the French throne in the absence of a male heir.

Henneman, John Bell. *Olivier de Clesson and Political Society in France Under Charles V and Charles VI*. Philadelphia: University of Pennsylvania Press, 1996. Detailed account of the machinations of the uncles of Charles VI and their motivation, and the roles played by Olivier de Clesson and the Marmousets.

—*Shawncey Webb*

SEE ALSO: Charles II; Joan the Mad; Peter the Cruel; Richard III.

HENRI CHARRIÈRE

French convict and author

BORN: November 16, 1906; Ardèche, France
DIED: July 29, 1973; Madrid, Spain
ALSO KNOWN AS: Papillon; Papi
MAJOR OFFENSES: Murder, repeated escapes from prison
ACTIVE: 1932-1945
LOCALE: Paris, France, and French Guiana
SENTENCE: Hard labor for life for murder; repeated sentences of solitary confinement for prison escapes

EARLY LIFE

Henri Charrière (ahn-ree shah-ree-eh) was born in Ardèche, France, on November 16, 1906. His father was the headmaster of a village school. His mother died when he was very young.

CRIMINAL CAREER

After completing his obligatory military service, Charrière went to Paris and became involved with the city's underworld, gaining his livelihood as a safecracker and petty thief. While in the navy, he had a very large butterfly tatooed on his chest, which earned him the name of Papillon (French for "butterfly"). Charrière was framed for the murder of the pimp Roland le Petit.

LEGAL ACTION AND OUTCOME

Although he adamantly insisted on his innocence, Charrière was found guilty. On October 26, 1932, he was sentenced to hard labor for life. He was briefly imprisoned at Caen, then transferred to the French penal colony Devil's Island in French Guiana. At the colony, all prisoners were identified by a number, determined by the time of their arrival there. Charrière became prisoner number 51367. Over the following thirteen years, Charrière attempted escape repeatedly and actually succeeded numerous times.

His first escape occurred in 1933, while he was being treated at a prison hospital and successfully escaped with two companions. They managed to sail as far as Colombia before they were caught and re-imprisoned. Charrière broke out again and traveled to Guajira, where he stayed for six months. Charrière found peace and security among the Wayuus natives who lived there. Intent upon proving his innocence, he left the safety of the island but was recaptured. He was incarcerated at Santa Marta and then at Barranquilla. In 1934 he was extradited to French Guiana. He made numerous attempts to escape, for which he was sentenced to two years in solitary confinement.

In 1936 he was sent to the island of Royale, where he followed an unsuccessful escape by killing the informer who had thwarted his attempt, resulting in an eight-year term of solitary confinement. Such a sentence was tantamount to a sentence of death. Charrière, however, was released from solitary confinement after nineteen months after he tried to save a little girl from drowning in shark-infested waters. While this courageous act earned him his release from solitary confinement, his transfer was officially attributed to medical reasons. He tried to escape from the hospital but was nearly killed in the rough waters.

He next requested a transfer to Devil's Island. Although escape from the island was considered impossible, Charrière succeeded. He threw himself off a cliff and, using a bag of coconuts as a raft, drifted to freedom. Shortly thereafter, he was captured again in Venezuela and imprisoned in El Dorado. He was released on October 18, 1945. He stayed in Venezuela, became a citizen, married, and bought a nightclub in Caracas. An earthquake hit Caracas in 1967, and Charrière was financially ruined. He then wrote his autobiography *Papillon* (1969; English translation, 1970), which became a best-seller. Charrière died of throat cancer in 1973, still a fugitive from French justice.

Impact

Through his autobiography *Papillon*, Henri Charrière brought his extraordinary life to the attention of the world and became a folk hero who exemplified indomitable courage and determination to live as a free man. The 1973 film *Papillon*, based on his book, further affirmed his fame as a symbol of the human will to survive, to fight injustice, and to be free. Composer Aldemaro Romero wrote "Ballad to Papillon" in Charrière's honor.

Further Reading

Ceaser, Mike. "Where Desert Meets City: Linked to the Harsh la Guajara Peninsula, These Natives Face the Intersection of Tradition and Modernity." *America* (English edition) 56 (November/December, 2004). Treats the culture of the Wayuus tribe, with which Papillon lived for six months.

Charrière, Henri. *Banco: The Further Adventures of Papillon*. New York: Morrow, 1973. Translated by Patrick O'Brian. Continues the autobiography of Papillon in Venezuela; the French edition contains more material.

_______. *Papillon*. Translated by June P. Wilson and Walter B. Michaels. 1970. Reprint. New York: HarperCollins, 2001. Charrière's story of his imprisonment, repeated attempts to escape, and eventual escape from Devil's Island.

Redfield, Peter. *Space in the Tropics: From Convicts to Rockets in French Guiana*. Berkeley: University of California Press, 2000. Treats conditions in the penal colony, hardships resulting from the climate and topography, attitudes toward prisons and punishment.

—*Shawncey Webb*

See also: Jacques Mesrine; Willie Sutton.

Cheng I Sao

Chinese pirate leader

Born: 1775; Canton, China
Died: 1844; Canton, China
Also known as: Ching Shih; Hsi Kai
Cause of notoriety: Cheng I Sao commanded a large fleet of pirate vessels that operated along the south China coast.
Active: 1802-1810
Locale: South China Sea

Early Life

The early life and circumstances of Cheng I Sao (chehng shyoh) are the subjects of several contradictory legends. One version has her as a prostitute, another as the daughter of a rival pirate family. The most widely accepted story presents her as one of twenty village maidens captured in a raid and brought before the pirate commander Cheng I. Her beauty so impressed him that he ordered her untied, whereupon she lunged at him, ready to scratch out his eyes. This show of courage convinced him that the young woman, then known as Hsi Kai, would be a good pirate's wife.

In 1801 she married Cheng I, who already led a sizable pirate fleet. Under sponsorship of the Tay-son dynasty in Vietnam, Cheng I had turned a few dozen junks into a unified privateer fleet. By 1802, when a new Vietnamese regime threw them out, he and Cheng I Sao had

The Widow Ching

The audacity and scale of Cheng I Sao's career are well known: some four hundred ships, seventy thousand followers, and a long run of profitable piracy. However, much about her remains vague. It takes a poet, sometimes, to imagine key details that history neglects. In "The Widow Ching—Pirate," Jorge Luis Borges does just that. To him the Widow Ching "was a sapling-thin woman of sleepy eyes and caries-riddled smile. Her oiled black hair shone brighter than the sun." Moreover, her negotiated retirement from "freelance piracy" in 1810 is like a fable in Borges's retelling:

> And yet each evening, lazy flocks of weightless dragons rose high into the sky above the ships of the imperial fleet and hovered delicately above the water, above the enemy deck. These cometlike kites were airy constructions of rice paper and reed, and each silvery or red body bore the identical characters. The widow anxiously studied that regular flight of meteors, and in it read the confused and slowly told fable of a dragon that had always watched over a vixen, in spite of the vixen's long ingratitude and constant crimes. The moon grew thin in the sky, and still the figures of rice paper and reed wrote the same story each evening, with almost imperceptible variations. The widow was troubled, and she brooded. When the moon grew fat in the sky and the red-tinged water, the story seemed to be reaching its end. No one could predict whether infinite pardon or infinite punishment was to be let fall upon the vixen, yet the inevitable end, whichever it might be, was surely approaching. The widow understood. She threw her two swords into the river, knelt in the bottom of a boat, and ordered that she be taken to the flagship of the emperor's fleet.
>
> It was evening; the sky was filled with dragons—this time, yellow ones. The widow murmured a single sentence, "The vixen seeks the dragon's wing," as she stepped aboard the ship.

The chroniclers report that the vixen obtained her pardon, and that she dedicated her slow old age to opium smuggling. She was no longer "the Widow"; she assumed a name that might be translated as "The Luster of True Instruction."

Source: Jorge Luis Borges, *A Universal History of Iniquity*, translated by Andrew Hurley (New York: Penguin, 2001).

set up operations along the Chinese coast with seven separate fleets, identified by colors, under their command. Cheng I Sao had demanded half her husband's wealth in lieu of silks as a wedding gift, and her talent for organization had already paid off.

Pirate Career

Cheng I was killed in 1807. Cheng I Sao then dressed in the chieftain's robes with embroidered dragons, secured his swords in her sash and donned his war helmet, and went before his captains to present her case for succeeding him. Citing the many prizes taken by her own fleet, the White, and her part in her husband's successes, she apparently met no significant opposition. As commander, her first act was to appoint her adopted son, Chang Pao, as admiral of the Red Fleet.

For the following few years, Cheng I Sao led a pirate confederacy unmatched in its size or strength. It is estimated to have included some seven hundred ships and up to seventy thousand individuals. No vessel operating in the South China Sea or adjacent waters was safe from them.

Her pirates operated under strict rules and discipline. Only sailors of the imperial navy were automatically executed when captured. Other captives were held for ransom or put to work on the fleet's ships. Cheng I Sao referred to booty as "trans-shipped goods" and set up a warehouse for their safekeeping, keeping written records of all goods held. She also established a string of banking offices along the shore, to sell safe passages and collect other fees. Within a few months her pirates so dominated the coast and waters of Kwangtung that the government sought help from British and Portuguese ships in order to defeat them. When this failed, in 1810 the governor offered amnesty.

Cheng I Sao negotiated a settlement that allowed her pirates to retain their wealth and even win some social advancement. Her adopted son, Chang Pao, now her husband, was appointed lieutenant colonel of a regiment in Fukien. She lived there with him for twelve years and upon his death returned to Canton, where she reportedly ran a gambling house but otherwise led a quiet life until her death in 1844.

Impact

Despite its brutalities, a career with Cheng I Sao's pirate enterprise offered poor villagers and peasants a route to a better life. Later histories and popular lore have kept her life story from falling into obscurity. Strangely enough, Western writers have seemed more fascinated with her attainments than Chinese historians, who tend to attribute most of her deeds to her male partner Chang Pao.

Further Reading

Klausmann, Ulrike, Marion Meinzerin, and Gabriel Kuhn. *Women Pirates and the Politics of the Jolly Roger*. Montreal: Black Rose Books, 1997. Historical overview of women pirates in the China Sea to the late twentieth century.

Murray, Dian H. "Cheng I Sao in Fact and Fiction." Chapter 12 in *Bold in Her Breeches: Women Pirates Across the Ages*, edited by Jo Stanley. London: Pandora, 1995. Long article that attempts to separate the core facts from the gloss of romantic legend. Points out Cheng I Sao's relative neglect by Chinese sources.

Weatherly, Myra. *Women Pirates: Eight Stories of Adventure*. Greensboro, N.C.: Morgan Reynolds, 1998. Explains the economic context and Cheng I Sao's mode of operation. Helpful map.

Wren, Laura Lee. *Pirates and Privateers of the High Seas*. Berkeley Heights, N.J.: Enslow, 2003. Retells major engagements of the pirate fleet, including a little-known mutiny within its ranks.

—*Emily Alward*

See also: Samuel Bellamy; Charlotte de Berry; Stede Bonnet; Anne Bonny; William Dampier; William Kidd; Sir Henry Morgan; Grace O'Malley; John Quelch; John Rackham; Mary Read; Bartholomew Roberts; Edward Teach.

Andrei Chikatilo

Ukrainian serial killer

Born: October, 16, 1936; Yablochnoye, Ukraine, Soviet Union (now in Ukraine)
Died: February 14, 1994; Novocherkassk, Ukraine, Soviet Union (now in Ukraine)
Also known as: Forest Strip Killer; Rostov Ripper; Andrei Romanovich Chikatilo (full name)
Major offense: Fifty-three murders
Active: 1978-1990
Locale: Soviet Union
Sentence: Fifty-two death sentences; executed by gunshot

Early Life

Andrei Chikatilo (ahn-DRAY cheh-kah-THAY-loh) was born in Yablochnoye, Ukraine. Chikatilo suffered a traumatic upbringing as Soviet premier Joseph Stalin's agricultural collective plan caused mass starvation in his village. When Chikatilo's older brother, Stefan, disappeared, he was thought to have been cannibalized by villagers—an act that was not uncommon. Chikatilo lived with his mother, who beat and publicly ridiculed him. During World War II Chikatilo witnessed the violence and brutality of the Germans, and fantasized about luring invading troops into the woods and murdering them.

Chikatilo was a good student, but he failed his university entry examinations. After his service in the Soviet army, he completed correspondence courses and began teaching in Novoshakhtinsk in 1971. Unable to command respect and accused of indecent behavior, he frequently changed schools. He ultimately became a factory buyer and salesman; his position offered him access to victims across the country. After an arranged marriage to his wife, Feyina, in 1963, he had two children, Lyudmila and Yuri.

Criminal Career

Chikatilo's criminal career began in Shakhty in 1978; he attempted to rape a nine-year-old. When she would not cooperate, he stabbed her, beginning a lifelong connection for him between violence and sexual excitement. Chikatilo murdered again in 1982, killing seven people. His victims were prostitutes, young runaways, and vagrants he would lure into the forest. He would attempt consensual intercourse but achieved orgasm only by stabbing his victims. Over the summer of 1983, he killed four women and children. He then relocated to Novocherkassk and murdered two women in 1985. In 1987 he killed three young boys in Revda, Zaporozhye, and Leningrad. By 1988, Chikatilo had left Rostov, after killing nine people. He murdered two women and seven boys in 1990. His crimes were becoming more brutal, involving mutilation and cannibalism.

Legal Action and Outcome

In 1984 Chikatilo, who was observed acting suspiciously at a bus station, was arrested. A knife, rope, and lubricant were found in his briefcase. Chikatilo's blood did not match semen samples found on the victims. Later it was discovered that Chikatilo was a "non-secretor," meaning his blood type can be determined only through blood samples, not semen. Without physical evidence of murder, authorities detained him on minor charges; he served three months of a one-year sentence.

By late 1985, police officer Issa Kostoyev was handling the serial murder investigations. Kostoyev brought in a psychiatrist to profile the killer, the first time that method was employed in the Soviet Union. On November 6, 1990, Chikatilo killed his final victim, Sveta Korostik. When he emerged from the woods with blood on his face, he was questioned and released. On November 20, the police observed Chikatilo and arrested him. Between November 30 and December 5, 1990, Chikatilo broke under pressure and confessed to fifty-six murders. He was charged with fifty-three murders, as three victims were not found. The police previously had recorded only thirty-six killings.

Chikatilo stood trial on April 14, 1992, caged in the courtroom because of his disruptiveness. In October of 1992, he was found guilty of fifty-two murders and received a death sentence for each. He was executed by a gunshot to the back of his head on February 14, 1994.

Impact

At the time Andrei Chikatilo was at large, Soviet policy barred the media from reporting a killing spree; serial killers were seen as a Western phenomenon. As a result, the public did not know of any such danger. After Chikatilo's conviction, the government was forced to publicize the serial killings and debunk the rumors that had surrounded the victims' disappearances. Chikatilo's crimes forced authorities to set aside propaganda and acknowledge that violence does not occur only in "hedonistic capitalist nations."

Chikatilo's notorious murders served as fodder for true crime novels as well as films, including *Citizen X* (1995) and *Evilenko* (2004). Similarities between Chikatilo and Hannibal Lector, the antagonist of Thomas Harris's novel *The Silence of the Lambs* (1988), are discernible.

Further Reading

Krivich, Michail. *Comrade Chikatilo*. Fort Lee, N.J.: Barricade Books, 1993. A shockingly candid look into the life of Chikatilo.

Lourie, Richard. *Hunting the Devil*. New York: HarperCollins, 1993. An in-depth examination of Chikatilo's crimes and the detective who caught him.

Vronsky, Peter. *Serial Killers: The Method and Madness of Monsters*. Goleta, Calif.: Berkley Trade, 2004. A comprehensive account of serial killers, their histories, and their motives.

—*Sara Vidar*

See also: Kenneth Bianchi; Ted Bundy; Angelo Buono, Jr.; Jeffrey Dahmer; Albert DeSalvo; Albert Fish; John Wayne Gacy; Ed Gein; Leonard Lake; Charles Ng; Dennis Rader; Charles Sobraj; Joseph Stalin.

Christian VII

King of Denmark and Norway (1766-1808)

Born: January 29, 1749; Copenhagen, Denmark

Died: March 13, 1808; Rendsburg, Schleswig (now in Germany)

Cause of notoriety: When Christian II became incapacitated to rule his country as a result of mental illness, he left the task to his ministers, his doctor, and his son, Frederick VI.

Active: 1766-1808

Locale: Europe, mainly Denmark, Norway, and Germany

Early Life

Christian (KRIHS-chehn) VII was the son of Frederick V of Denmark and his first wife, Louisa, the daughter of George II of Great Britain. From a very early age, Christian showed clear signs of suffering from severe mental problems, now believed to have been schizophrenia. Christian's condition was worsened by the brutal beatings and abuses that he received from his royal chamberlain, Detlev Reventlow.

Royal Career

Christian was crowned king at the age of seventeen upon his father's death on January 14, 1766. That same year, he married Caroline Mathilde, the daughter of Frederick, prince of Wales. The marriage produced two children, Prince Frederick VI and Princess Louise Augusta, duchess of Augustenborg. After showing no love or respect for his wife and even publicly humiliating her, Christian had the marriage annulled in 1772 under pressure from

King Christian VII.

his paternal grandmother, Sophie Magdalene of Brandenburg-Kulmbach. Caroline Mathilde retained her title as queen of Denmark but was exiled to Celle, Germany, where she lived until the end of her life.

During his life, Christian was influenced by several powerful individuals. The most prominent was Johann Friedrich Struensee (1737-1772), who in 1768 became physician to the mentally ill king. Struensee gained Christian's trust and rose steadily in power. He had a passionate love affair with Queen Caroline Mathilde, who was pathetically lonely. In 1771, Christian appointed Struensee as privy cabinet minister, who, as a result, enjoyed practically unlimited powers. He carried out several Enlightenment reforms; the most important was the freedom of the press. However, the general ill will against Struensee (called "the dictator" by many), which had been smoldering throughout the autumn of 1771, found expression in a secret conspiracy against him. In 1772, Struensee was overthrown and condemned to death for *lèse majesté* (an offense against a sovereign).

Christian was only nominally the king from 1772 onward. Danish statesman Andreas Peter Bernstorff became chief minister in 1773, a position that he held until 1797, with a brief interlude between 1780 and 1784. As minister, he successfully kept Denmark at peace: He sought friendship with Sweden and kept Denmark neutral in the French Revolutionary Wars. From 1784 to 1808, Christian's son and successor, Frederick VI, acted as regent. The period of collaboration between Frederick VI and Bernstorff is considered one of the most prosperous times for Denmark: It undertook a liberal program of social, economic, and educational reform, including the abolition of serfdom.

The king ultimately sank further into mental illness and became unresponsive to external stimuli. His symptoms included deliriums, paranoia, hallucinations, and even intentional self-mutilation. Christian VII died at age fifty-nine on March 13, 1808, in Rendsburg, a town at the Kiel Canal in the northeastern part of Schleswig, Germany. The death was likely caused by a brain aneurism. His body was buried at the Cathedral of Roskilde in Roskilde, Denmark.

Impact

In spite of Christian II's deficiencies as a king, it is clear that, for a short time at least, general opinion was relatively favorable to him: Outside his narrow court circle, few believed that Christian VII was really mad, feeling only that his will had been weakened by the influence of others. During his rule, many important reforms were passed, but Christian cared little whether the Danish people approved of them.

Further Reading

Brown, John. *Memoirs of the Courts of Sweden and Denmark: During the Reign of Christian VII of Denmark and Gustavus III and IV of Sweden.* New York: Grolier Society, 1818. A collection of the original memoirs of the most influential figures of the reigns of Christian VII, which offer the reader an opportunity to explore the political and social intricacies of eighteenth century Denmark.

Nors, P. *The Court of Christian VII of Denmark.* London: Hurst & Blackett, 1928. One of the best English-language accounts covering Christian VII's life and rule. Its chapters cover such topics as Queen Caroline Mathilde, Frederick V, Johann Friedrich Struensee, the Danish revolution of 1660, and much more.

—*Concepción Sáenz-Cambra*

See also: Charles II; Charles VI; Joan the Mad; Ludwig II.

JOHN REGINALD HALLIDAY CHRISTIE

English serial killer

BORN: April 8, 1899; Halifax, Yorkshire, England
DIED: July 15, 1953; London, England
MAJOR OFFENSE: Murders of seven women
ACTIVE: 1948-1952
LOCALE: 10 Rillington Place, Notting Hill, London
SENTENCE: Death by hanging

EARLY LIFE

John Reginald Halliday Christie (KRIHS-tee) was born at Black Boy House in Boothtown, Halifax, near Sheffield, the son of a carpet designer. He won a scholarship to Halifax Secondary School, sang in the local church choir, and was a Boy Scout. He served in World War I, initially with the Fifty-second Nottinghamshire and Derby Regiment and subsequently with the West Yorkshire section of the Duke of Wellington's Regiment. Christie was injured by mustard gas—a seemingly traumatic experience that rendered him speechless for three years, although doctors could find nothing physically amiss. When the war was over, he returned to live in Halifax; after marrying Ethel Waddington, a typist, he recovered his power of speech.

CRIMINAL CAREER

Christie served several prison sentences for theft—and one for assault—in the 1920's and early 1930's, when he and Ethel became separated. After his release on remission from the last of these sentences, Ethel joined him in London, where they took the ground-floor flat at 10 Rillington Place, an end-of-terrace house in Notting Hill. He obtained work as a clerk but suffered from either continual ill health or chronic hypochondria. He recovered sufficiently to serve as a reserve policeman during World War II, receiving two commendations.

In 1948, Timothy Evans, a van driver, and his pregnant wife, Beryl, moved into one of two first-floor flats above Christie's. According to Evans, when Beryl became pregnant for a second time in 1949 she did not want the baby, and Christie volunteered to abort it; Christie then told Evans that the abortion had gone wrong and told him to leave London, saying that he would put the surviving baby daughter up for adoption.

Evans initially did as he was told but then went to the police; when the bodies of his wife and daughter were found strangled in the washhouse at 10 Rillington Place, Evans was arrested. He made a confession that he subsequently retracted. Christie was the chief prosecution witness at Evans's trial for the murder of his daughter; the charge of murdering his wife was not tried. Evans was convicted and hanged in July, 1949. When Christie left 10 Rillington Place in 1953, however, six more bodies were discovered on the premises. Ruth Furst, a nurse, had been missing since 1943; Muriel Eady, a former work colleague of Christie, had been missing since 1944; the others—Ethel Christie and three prostitutes—had apparently been killed in rapid succession in 1952-1953.

LEGAL ACTION AND OUTCOME

Christie was arrested on the riverbank in Putney on March 31, 1953, after an intense manhunt during which his photograph was given extensive exposure in the newspapers. He confessed to murdering his wife and was also charged with the other five murders. He then confessed that he had also murdered Beryl Evans. He pleaded not guilty by reason of insanity but was convicted of murder and hanged at Pentonville a month later.

IMPACT

John Reginald Halliday Christie's confession to Beryl Evans's murder resulted in a special enquiry by the Home Office into Timothy Evans's conviction. Although Christie had not confessed to murdering the child, and Evans had not been tried for the murder of his wife, it seemed likely that Christie must have been guilty of that crime as well and that Evans had been wrongly executed. This probable error became a key factor in the political pressure that resulted in the abolition of the death penalty in England. Evans received a posthumous pardon in 1966.

Christie became a key example of a sexually motivated serial killer, offering abundant scope to journalists and other amateur psychoanalysts. Ludovic Kennedy's successful dramatization of the case was released in 1971 as the film *10 Rillington Place*, starring Richard Attenborough as Christie. The name of Rillington Place was changed to Ruston Close before the houses were torn down and rebuilt as Bartle Road.

FURTHER READING

Chance, John Newton. *The Crimes at Rillington Place*. London: Hodder & Stoughton, 1961. One of the popularizations hastily written to cash in on the publicity surrounding Kennedy's book, by a prolific writer of popular crime thrillers.

Eddowes, John. *The Two Killers of Rillington Place*. London: Little, Brown, 1994. The most significant development of the unorthodox thesis that Evans was, in fact, as guilty as Christie and that the two worked in collusion.

Furneaux, Rupert. *The Two Stranglers of Rillington Place*. London: Panther, 1961. The most immediate contradiction of Kennedy's polemical assertion that the hanging of Evans was a terrible miscarriage of justice.

Jesse, F. Tennyson, ed. *The Trials of Timothy John Evans and John Reginald Halliday Christie*. London: William Hodge, 1957. An anthology reflective of the intense debate generated by the case, with special relevance to Evans's conviction and its relevance to the political argument for the abolition of capital punishment.

Kennedy, Ludovic. *Ten Rillington Place*. London: Victor Gollancz, 1961. A best-selling dramatization by a leading journalist, supportive of the view that Evans was mistakenly convicted and hanged; primarily interesting for its painstakingly researched but highly speculative analysis of Christie's psychopathological history.

—*Brian Stableford*

See also: William Burke; Albert DeSalvo; Ed Gein; Jack the Ripper; Henri Désiré Landru.

Benjamin Church

American colonist and spy

Born: August 24, 1734; Newport, Rhode Island
Died: January, 1778; at sea
Also known as: Benjamin Church, Jr. (full name)
Major offense: Criminal correspondence with the enemy British
Active: 1774-1775
Locale: Massachusetts
Sentence: Life in prison, later commuted to voluntary exile

Early Life

Benjamin Church was the son of Benjamin Church, Sr., a merchant of Boston, and was the grandson of another Benjamin Church, who was a colonel in the colonial forces during King Philip's (Metacom's) War in 1675. The young Church attended Boston Latin School and graduated from Harvard College in 1754. He studied medicine under Dr. Joseph Pynchon and continued his studies in London. While there, he married Hannah Hill. Upon his return to Boston, he soon built a fine reputation as a physician and surgeon.

Treasonous Career

In addition to his medical practice, Church was a published poet, philosopher, orator, and newspaper editor. He was a member of both the Provincial Congress of Massachusetts and of the Sons of Liberty, together with John and Samuel Adams, Joseph Warren, Paul Revere, John Hancock, and others. Church was rather extravagant in his personal life, having built an elegant country house in Raynham near Boston in 1768 and also maintaining a mistress. Apparently this lifestyle was supported with periodic payments by the British for his spying activities. On the other hand, Church was the first physician on the scene following the Boston Massacre and was also a participant in the Boston Tea Party.

Apparently, it was upon Church's information that the British marched to seize colonial supplies at Concord, which resulted in the Battle of Lexington and Concord (1775). Later Church was named the first surgeon general of the Continental Army. During a trip to occupied Philadelphia, supposedly to obtain needed medicines for the army, Church met with British general Thomas Gage. A communication in cipher from Church to Gage—forwarded by Church's mistress to Major Kane of the British army in Boston—was intercepted, was deciphered, and led to Church's arrest and court-martial. It was later deduced that Church had begun spying for and communicating with the British perhaps as early as 1774.

Curiously, Church also had connections with two other notorious individuals. When Benedict Arnold offered in 1775 to capture Ticonderoga, it was Church who endorsed the plan and secured for Arnold a commission as colonel to carry it out. Also, Charles Lee was one of those serving on the examining board for Church's court-martial.

Legal Action and Outcome

At his 1775 court-martial, Church was sentenced to life imprisonment "and debarred from the use of pen, ink, and paper." He was subsequently confined to jail at Norwich, Connecticut. While there, he became seriously ill and as a consequence was allowed on May 13, 1776, to return on parole to Massachusetts. His subsequent petition for voluntary exile to the West Indies was approved, but the vessel on which he departed in 1778 was lost at sea and never heard from again.

Impact

Benjamin Church goes down in history along with those, such as Benedict Arnold and Charles Lee, who will be remembered by Americans as traitors to the revolutionary cause. Had Church's treachery not been discovered early, he might have had a substantial impact on the outcome of the War for Independence, because of his outstanding reputation and involvement with leading American politicians. As a result of the disclosure of his treachery and his subsequent early demise, however, he had little contemporary impact and has virtually disappeared from popular history.

Further Reading

French, Allen. *General Gage's Informers*. 1932. Reprint. Westport, Conn.: Greenwood Press, 1968. The primary study that shaped twentieth century assessments of Church, based on Paul Revere's reminiscences of Church's treasonous activities, Church's performance as director of the Continental Army hospital, and the patriots' response to the captured letter. French concludes, after having discovered several letters from Church to Gage, that Church was truly a traitor.

Kiracofe, David. "Dr. Benjamin Church and the Dilemma of Treason in Revolutionary Massachusetts." *New England Quarterly* 70, no. 3 (1997): 443-462. Analyzes Church's behavior in light of the lack of treason laws in his day, his background (he was from a prominent Massachusetts family), his status as a Whig, and the pained reactions of his colleagues. Concludes nevertheless that he was guilty of treason.

Norwood, William Frederick. "The Enigma of Dr. Benjamin Church: A High-Level Scandal in the American Colonial Army Medical Service." *Medical Arts and Sciences* 10, no. 2 (1956): 71-93. A substantial analysis of why Church undertook his treasonous activities.

Walker, Jeffrey B. *Devil Undone: The Life and Poetry of Benjamin Church, 1734-1778*. New York: Arno Press, 1982. Looks beyond the treason to assess Church's entire career and varied talents.

—Jack H. Westbrook

See also: Benedict Arnold; Charles Lee.

Clement VII

Roman Catholic pope (1523-1534)

Born: May 26, 1478; Florence (now in Italy)
Died: September 25, 1534; Rome, Papal States (now in Italy)
Also known as: Giulio de' Medici (birth name)
Cause of notoriety: Clement's pontificate was rife with failures, including the inability to halt the spread of the Protestant Reformation and the fall of Rome. He also struggled with King Henry VIII of England over Henry's desire to divorce his wife, which ultimately led to the king's break with the Catholic Church.
Active: 1521-1534
Locale: Rome, Papal States

Early Life

Giulio de' Medici, the future Pope Clement (KLEH-mehnt) VII, was born in the kingdom of Florence (now in Italy) and was the illegitimate son of Giuliano de' Medici and his mistress, Fioretta. Shortly after Giulio's birth, his father was assassintated. Giulio was raised as a prince by his uncle, Lorenzo de' Medici (also called Lorenzo the Magnificent), who was the ruler of the Florentine Republic.

Papal Career

In 1513, Giulio began his career in the Church when his birth status was legitimized by his cousin, Pope Leo X, and he was appointed as the archbishop of Florence and a cardinal. By 1517, Giulio had made himself a vital part of Leo X's administration and was named vice chancellor. This role made him responsible for a number of policies, including those that brought measures against ecclesiastical reformer Martin Luther. By 1519, Giulio was governing all of Florence.

Clement VII. (Library of Congress)

With the death of Leo X in 1521, Giulio played a significant part in the selection of the next pope; his name was mentioned as a candidate for that role. Ten years later, with the death of Pope Adrian VI, Giulio de' Medici was elected to the Papacy and took the papal name Clement VII.

Clement VII came to the Papacy during troubled times. Kingdoms were at war, and the impact of the Protestant Reformation was beginning to be felt in northern Europe and Scandinavia. Charles V of Spain hoped for the Church's support in the war with Francis I of France, so he supported Clement in his bid for the Papacy. However, fearful that he might end up under the complete domination of Charles (Spain already ruled all of southern Italy), Clement VII signed agreements with the French. In early 1525, Charles's troops met the French army, and after battling, the Spanish emerged victorious, taking Francis I as prisoner. Upon hearing this news, Clement decided to align himself with Charles; all of Italy then fell under Spanish protection.

After a series of subversive plots, Clement realigned the Papacy with Venice and Milan against the Spanish. In September, 1526, Spanish forces plundered the Vatican, leading to the imprisonment and ransom of Clement VII. When Clement's own troops found that he had paid the ransom but had not paid them, they turned on him. The result was the brutal eight-day sack of Rome in May, 1527.

The pope's final crisis came at the same time as the siege of Rome. An emissary from Henry VIII, king of England, came to Rome asking to allow Henry to divorce his wife, Queen Catherine of Aragon, Charles V's aunt, and marry Anne Boleyn. Clement vacillated on this decision, giving a number of decrees on the subject. He understood that if he allowed the divorce, he would incur the wrath of Charles. A decision not to allow Henry VIII to divorce was finally given in March, 1534. Henry was excommunicated. Significant religious upheaval occurred as Henry left the Church and started the Church of England. In September, 1534, Pope Clement VII passed away in Rome.

Impact

Pope Clement VII was not known as a man of action; decision making was not one of his strengths. He was politically astute and seemed to fare well as a second in command yet did not function well as a leader. Aside from the death and other violence associated with the sack of Rome, the plundering of the Vatican, and other wars fought, Clement is also credited with the lack of response to the Protestant Reformation in Germany and the country's subsequent departure from the Church, as well as the loss of the Great Britain as a result of his decision on Henry's divorce.

A man of continual intrigue, Clement VII did not seem to have a worldview beyond Florence. However, he was also known as a Renaissance pope. He was a patron of the arts and supported artists such as Benvenuto Cellini, Raphael, and Michelangelo. He commissioned Michelangelo's *Last Judgment* (1537-1541) for the Sistine Chapel shortly before his death.

Further Reading

Gouwens, Kenneth, and Sheryl E. Reiss, ed. *The Pontificate of Clement VII: History, Politics, Culture*. Burlington, Vt.: Ashgate, 2005. This collection of essays draws on what the publisher terms "long-neglected sources" to reassess one of the most controversial popes.

Kelly, J. N. D., ed. *The Oxford Dictionary of Popes*. Rev. ed. New York: Oxford University Press, 2005. This text has a chronological discussion of each of the Catholic Church's popes. Dates and times of service are indicated and some biographical data is given.

Tobin, Greg. *Selecting the Pope: Uncovering the Mysteries of Papal Selection*. New York: Barnes and Noble, 2003. The author discusses the process for selection of a pope, documenting how the process has changed through time and some of the irregularities that have occurred.

—*Robert Stewart*

See also: Leo X.

Jacques Clément

French Dominican friar

Born: c. 1567; Serbonnes, France
Died: August 1, 1589; Saint-Cloud, near Paris, France
Cause of notoriety: A fervent supporter of the French League during the sixteenth century civil war in France and a religious fanatic, Clément assassinated King Henry III.
Active: August 1, 1589
Locale: Gondi mansion, Saint-Cloud, France

Early Life

In 1589, Jacques Clément (zhahk kleh-mah), a Dominican friar in the Parisian Order of Preachers, was an unknown young monk in his twenties. He was a partisan of the French League—the Roman Catholic noble faction opposing the Huguenots (Protestants) and the Crown—during the French Wars of Religion (c. 1550-1598). Engrossed by fanaticism, Clément purportedly proclaimed his will to vanquish heresy by exterminating the Huguenots and reported having a vision in which an angel urged him to slay the "tyrant." He was supported (if not manipulated) in his efforts by the French League, which likely promised that he would become a hero or a saint if he succeeded.

Criminal Career

Clément became instrumental to the league's cause in 1589, a year when the political scale began tipping in favor of the king. The ambivalent Catherine de Médicis, the queen of France as the wife of King Henry II, died, and the Guise brothers—Henry I, duke of Guise, and Louis II, cardinal of Guise—the leaders of the League, were killed. Henry III (1551-1589) then formed an alliance with his remote cousin Henry Bourbon, king of Navarre, the prospective heir to the throne and a notorious Huguenot. In May, 1589, the armed forces of the two Henrys started marching upon Paris. On July 31, they prepared to lay siege on the rebel city.

Henry III was then headquartered in Saint-Cloud, in the house of Gondi. On August 1, Clément obtained letters for the king—probably counterfeit—and presented himself at Saint-Cloud pretending to bring news from imprisoned royalists. When Clément was ushered in, Henry III was sitting on his close-stool, and Clément requested a word in private. After the king's attendants withdrew, Clément assaulted the vulnerable monarch: Drawing a knife from under his cloak, the friar stabbed Henry III in the lower belly. After calling for help, Henry III pulled the poisoned dagger out, which also pulled out his bowels. A guard rushed in and immediately executed Clément. Before the king died the next morning, he recognized Henri of Navarre as his heir in public and in his presence.

Impact

The assassination of Henry III exposed a fanaticism heretofore unseen in early modern France. Jacques Clément's fanatic sacrifice made him a divine zealot and a martyr in the eyes of the league and its allies, including Pope Sixtus V, who briefly considered canonizing Clément. Although Clément was extolled by Catholic radicals, his murderous act brought a Protestant ruler to the throne. King Henry III, nevertheless, exhorted his heir to convert to Catholicism with a view to regaining national unity.

Clément's regicide reveals how diminished the sacredness of the "Lord-Anointed" king had become by the sixteenth century. Clément's crime put an end to the Valois dynasty; Henri of Bourbon, king of Navarre (as Henry III of Navarre), became Henry IV and thus began the Bourbon Dynasty. The new king, however, had to fight armed rebellion and propaganda for ten more years and had to abjure his Protestant faith before he finally earned national legitimacy. Henry IV himself was assassinated by a fanaticized monk—François Ravaillac—in 1610.

Further Reading

Garrisson, Janine. "Paris and the Assassination of Henri III." In *A History of Sixteenth Century France, 1483-*

1598, translated by R. Rex. New York: St. Martin's Press, 1995. Aptly focuses on the frenzied seditious state of the French League after the execution of the duke of Guise, the dissolution of the Estates-General, and King Henry III's alliance with Huguenot Henry of Navarre.

Knecht, Robert J. "The Assassination of Henry III (1 August 1589)." In *The Rise and Fall of Renaissance France*. London: Fontana Press, 1996. One of the most detailed accounts of the regicide in the English language. Clear and concise background information on extremist Leaguer propaganda and the French Salic Law.

_______. *The Valois: Kings of France, 1328-1589*. London: Hambledon, 2005. Recounts the regicide, mentioning modern historical research on its causes and consequences.

Potter, David, ed. and trans. "The Assassination of Henry III." In *The French Wars of Religion: Selected Documents*. London: Macmillan, 1997. A generally accurate but partial translation of the testimony of the main eyewitness.

—*Corinne Noirot-Maguire*

SEE ALSO: Guy Fawkes; John Felton; Giuseppe Fieschi; John Parricida; Jack Ketch.

DOROTHY CLUTTERBUCK

British high priestess

BORN: January 19, 1880; Bengal, India

DIED: January 12, 1951; Highcliffe, England

ALSO KNOWN AS: Dorothy St. Quintin Fordham (married name); Old Dorothy

CAUSE OF NOTORIETY: Clutterbuck was a high priestess who is believed to have initiated the father of modern Wicca and paganism, Gerald Brosseau Gardner, into the New Forest Coven and provided him with a ritual and verbal history of witchcraft that connected it firmly to pre-Christian times. Some doubt her existence, claiming that Gardner invented her to serve his own purposes.

ACTIVE: 1930's-1951

LOCALE: Highcliffe, England

EARLY LIFE

Dorothy Clutterbuck (KLUHT-tuhr-buhk) was born to Thomas St. Quintin Clutterbuck, a captain serving with the Fourteenth Sikhs Regiment, and Ellen Anne Morgan in Bengal, India, and was baptized in Paul Church, Umbala, on February 21, 1880. Clutterbuck's father eventually attained the rank of lieutenant colonel, which at the time would have afforded Clutterbuck an upper-middle-class upbringing.

Clutterbuck eventually returned to Britain under unknown circumstances in 1933 to reside at Mill House, Lymington Road, Highcliffe, where, according to lists kept by the register of electors at the Christchurch Town Hall, she married Rupert Fordham sometime in 1937 or 1938. Very little else is known about Clutterbuck's early life, a fact that Gerald Gardner attributed to her desire to remain anonymous until after her death.

WITCHCRAFT CAREER

Although most of Clutterbuck's life is a mystery that cannot be substantiated, Gardner claimed that Old Dorothy Clutterbuck was the high priestess who initiated him into the New Forest Coven in September, 1939. During this initiation, Gardner first heard the term "Wicca," which has since come to refer to modern witchcraft. According to Gardner, at that time Clutterbuck was leading an authentic coven of witches in traditional pagan ritual and worship, the last remains of a tradition that could trace its lineage and rituals directly to pre-Christian times. Gardner claimed these rituals and practices to be authentically traditional although fragmented. He also maintained that between the fifteenth and nineteenth centuries in Europe much magical knowledge and witchcraft lore were lost as a result of widespread executions of women presumed to be witches. During these times of persecution, Gardner claimed that several witches maintained and preserved this magical lore, passing it down from generation to generation. After Clutterbuck's death at the age of seventy in 1951, Gardner identified her as the heir to and caretaker of one of these ancient lines of magical knowledge; however, since Clutterbuck had died, it was impossible to verify his claims. Ironically, the year that Clutterbuck died was when the repeal of antiwitchcraft legislation in Britain occurred, which, had Clutterbuck been alive, might have allowed her the freedom to confirm or deny without fear of criminal prosecution Gardner's many claims regarding her role in shaping the path of modern-day witchcraft.

Impact

For many years, skeptics and opponents of paganism maintained that Clutterbuck was a convenient manifestation of Gardner's active imagination and a useful tool to lend credibility to his claims that Wicca and paganism have legitimate, traceable roots and histories. If Gardner's claims are true, his initiation provided him with invaluable access to and knowledge of one of the world's oldest and most secretive religions. Doreen Valiente's research in the early 1980's into the life and death of Dorothy Clutterbuck established birth, death, marriage, and residential records for Clutterbuck, placing her in very close proximity to Gardner during his initiation and matching his description of an older, upper-class woman living in a large house in Highcliffe. This verification coincided with an improved perception of Wicca as a genuine religion with its own traditions and beliefs. Additional research has revealed little else about Clutterbuck or any further verification of Gardner's claims.

Gardner on Witchcraft

Gerald Gardner, a British civil servant and anthropologist, claimed to have met Dorothy Clutterbuck and to have been initiated into the rites of modern witchcraft, or Wicca (from the Old English word for "knowledge"). In his book Witchcraft Today, *he described English witches as follows:*

I have been told by witches in England: "Write and tell people we are not perverts. We are decent people, we only want to be left alone, but there are certain secrets that you mustn't give away." So after some argument as to exactly what I must not reveal, I am permitted to tell much that has never before been made public concerning their beliefs, their rituals and their reasons for what they do; also to emphasise that neither their present beliefs, rituals nor practices are harmful. . . .

What are they then? They are the people who call themselves the Wida, the "wise people," who practise the age-old rites and who have, along with much superstition and herbal knowledge, preserved an occult teaching and working processes which they themselves think to be magic or witchcraft. They are the type of people who were burned alive for possessing this knowledge, often giving their lives to turn suspicion away from others. . . .

What can [their] Power be? The easy answer is Mind over Matter. If you believe a thing firmly enough, you will imagine things. While I can believe that Mind has much to do with it, this answer does not satisfy me. Superstition is believing without evidence; science is testing a thing and only believing it when you obtain adequate proof. For this reason science is continually and quite rightly changing its views; they may often confuse cause with effect, as when an early Egyptian scientist noticed that at the coming of the Dog Star the Nile rose, and, to the great benefit of agriculture, was able to predict the annual flooding. That later on it was discerned that the Dog Star did not actually cause the floods, but simply rose at the time of the floods, made no difference to this.

I think that thousands of years ago some medicine men found that by directing the Massed Power of Mind they got good results in hunting. Whether this power affected the animal or the hunter did not matter, it produced results, and they called this Power, Magic. . . .

Source: Gerald Gardner, *Witchcraft Today* (London: Rider, 1954).

Further Reading

Farrar, Janet, and Stewart Farrar. *A Witches' Bible: The Complete Witches' Handbook*. Custer, Wash.: Phoenix, 1984. Describes in detail various aspects of Clutterbuck's influence on modern-day Wiccan rituals. Appendix A provides robust historical documentation of Clutterbuck's life and death, as well as her association with known occultists and spiritualists.

Heselton, Philip. *Wiccan Roots: Gerald Gardner and the Modern Witchcraft Revival*. London: Capall Bann, 2000. Heselton provides a well-researched history of the people and circumstances behind Gardner's initiation into a coven of witches in 1939, including sources and explanations that differ from those provided by Ronald Hutton.

Hutton, Ronald. *The Triumph of the Moon*. New York: Oxford University Press, 2001. Hutton provides significant evidence supporting the existence of Clutterbuck as Gardner described her, including many indications that she was likely involved in or at the very least aware of alternative spiritual traditions suchas Theosophy, Rosicrucianism, and offshoots of Freemasonry, all of which have found their way into modern-day pagan rituals.

Valiente, Doreen. *Witchcraft for Tomorrow*. New York: St. Martin's Press, 1978. Valiente's book was the first to cite historical records that confirmed some of the information that Gardner had provided about Clutterbuck and placed Clutterbuck in Highcliffe in the 1930's and 1940's.

—*Sally A. Lasko*

See also: Tamsin Blight; Mary Butters; Dolly Pentreath; Elizabeth Sawyer; Mother Shipton; Joan Wytte.

Roy Cohn

American attorney

Born: February 20, 1927; New York, New York
Died: August 2, 1986; Greenwich, Connecticut
Also known as: Roy Marcus Cohn (full name)
Cause of notoriety: A Senate lawyer who earned prominence during the Joseph McCarthy era, Cohn was widely unpopular but wielded tremendous political power.
Active: 1930's-1954
Locale: United States; mostly New York

Early Life

Roy Cohn (kohn) grew up an only child in the Bronx. His father, a New York State judge, was a power broker for one of New York's old-style political bosses. At the age of nine, Cohn told President Franklin Roosevelt that he agreed with Roosevelt's attempt to "pack" the U.S. Supreme Court. Cohn graduated from Columbia University Law School at the age of twenty and began working for the U.S. attorney in Manhattan.

Legal and Political Career

While working in the U.S. attorney's office, Cohn helped to prosecute a number of high-profile anticommunist cases. He received publicity for his zealous prosecution of William Remington, a former Commerce Department employee. Cohn obtained a conviction of perjury against Remington relating to Remington's membership in the Communist Party. Cohn also prosecuted eleven Communist Party leaders for sedition under the Smith Act. One of the prosecutors in the Alger Hiss case, Cohn received widespread fame in the conviction of Julius and Ethel Rosenberg for espionage in 1951. His cross-examination of Ethel's brother produced testimony considered to be responsible for the Rosenbergs' execution. The damaging testimony was later determined to be perjured, and Cohn was accused of being aware of its falsity from the beginning. Cohn, however, was proud of his role in the Rosenberg case and in his autobiography claimed that his influence on Judge Irving Kaufman, the trial judge, caused the judge to impose the death penalty on the Rosenbergs.

McCarthy's Anticommunist Crusade

Cohn's role in the Rosenberg case caught the attention of Federal Bureau of Investigation (FBI) director J. Edgar Hoover, who recommended the twenty-four-year-old Cohn to Senator Joseph McCarthy. Shortly after beginning work for McCarthy, Cohn was selected as chief counsel for the Senate Subcommittee on Investigations chaired by the senator. Cohn was chosen over young attorney Robert F. Kennedy for the position.

Cohn quickly gained power in the subcommittee nearly equal to that of McCarthy. He became famous for his aggressive questioning of suspected communists. He performed as if he were a prosecutor, rather than chief counsel. He called suspected communists before the subcommittee and grilled them about their sexual tendencies. He subpoenaed gay individuals in the arts and threatened to publicize their homosexual tendencies unless they named suspected communists. (The other members of the subcommittee probably did not know that Cohn, himself, was gay.)

In October, 1953, the subcommittee began investigating communist infiltration into the military. With Cohn's help, McCarthy attempted to discredit Robert Stevens, the secretary of the Army. President Dwight Eisenhower, in a move designed to discredit the work of McCarthy and his subcommittee, arranged to have the subcommittee hearing televised so that the entire United States could witness the bullying tactics of the subcommittee.

The U.S. Army then passed information to well-known columnist Drew Pearson that Cohn had abused congressional privilege by trying to prevent his friend David Schine from being drafted, and when that failed Cohn had tried to pressure the Army to grant Schine special privileges. Pearson published the allegations on December 15, 1953. As a result of the televised hearings, the tactics of Cohn and McCarthy were exposed. Senators, embarrassed by their performances in the televised hearings, voted on December 2, 1954, to censure McCarthy by a vote of sixty-seven to twenty-two. Cohn was forced to resign.

Roy Cohn, right, confers with Joseph McCarthy at a committee hearing. (AP/Wide World Photos)

After Cohn quit the subcommittee, he became a high-powered attorney in New York City. His clients included Donald Trump, Mafia figures Tony Salerno and John Gotti, and the Archdiocese of New York.

Cohn was a grandnephew of Joshua Lionel Cowen, founder of Lionel Model Train Company. In 1959, when Joshua and his son Lawrence became involved in a family dispute over control of the company, Cohn and a group of investors bought the majority of their stock and took control of the company. Under Cohn's leadership, sales declined, and the company suffered significant financial losses. Cohn was forced to resign from the business in 1963. In the 1970's and 1980's, he was indicted three different times by the federal government for perjury and other professional misconduct. In New York he was accused of financial improprieties involving city contracts and private investments. He was never convicted. For more than twenty years he was the subject of inquiries by the Internal Revenue Service (IRS). By the time of his death in 1986, the IRS had seized all of his assets.

Shortly before his death, Cohn was disbarred by the state of New York on grounds of unethical and unprofessional conduct. The disbarment proceeding found that Cohn had mismanaged client funds, had provided false information in his application to practice law in Washington, D.C., and had forced a dying man to sign a codicil to his will naming Cohn as the executor of his estate. At the time of Cohn's death from complications of acquired immunodeficiency syndrome (AIDS), he was broke and living on an expense account from his former law firm. It was estimated that at the time of his death, he owed the IRS more than seven million dollars.

IMPACT

Roy Cohn will forever be remembered for his high-profile role in the Red Scare of the 1930's, 1940's, and 1950's. Perhaps the most prominent image captured in footage of the McCarthy hearings is that of Army attorney Joseph Welch testifying before McCarthy, with Cohn at his side. McCarthy complained vehemently of Welch's baiting Cohn in order to hide his own attempt to paint one of the Army attorneys on Welch's staff as a Communist. Welch responded with an apology to Cohn, "I meant to do you no personal injury," followed by one of the most famous lines in all American rhetoric, directed to McCarthy: "Have you left no sense of decency?" With that, McCarthy and cohorts such as Cohn were branded as what they were, and the tide of political intolerance began to turn.

Further Reading

Cohn, Roy M., with Sidney Zion. *The Autobiography of Roy Cohn*. New York: Lyle Stuart, 1988. Cohn presents in casual and matter-of-fact manner his back-door dealings, illegal and secret ex parte meetings to rig cases, as if there was nothing wrong with conducting business in this fashion.

Gillespie, Nick. "TV and Tailgunner Joe." *Reason* 35, no. 10 (March 1, 2004): 64. Gillespie discusses how Joseph McCarthy destroyed people's careers and lives with the help of Roy Cohn.

Marqusee, Mike. "Critical Essay." *The Nation* 279, no. 20 (December 13, 2004): 30. The author discusses the claim made by a witness that prosecutor Roy Cohn had induced him to lie in court proceedings.

Morgan, Ted. *McCarthyism in Twentieth Century America*. New York: Random House, 1999. A discussion of the tactics of the Senate subcommittee and the subcommittee's witch hunts.

—*Cliff Roberson*

See also: John Gotti; Alger Hiss; J. Edgar Hoover; Joseph McCarthy; Ethel Rosenberg; Julius Rosenberg.

Schuyler Colfax

U.S. vice president (1869-1873)

Born: March 23, 1823; New York, New York
Died: January 13, 1885; Mankato, Minnesota
Cause of notoriety: Colfax allegedly accepted a bribe in the form of stock in Crédit Mobilier, a large railroad construction company. Although he was investigated by Congress, he was never impeached.
Active: 1865-1867
Locale: Washington, D.C.

Early Life

The father of Schuyler Colfax (SKI-ler KOHL-fax) died four months prior to his son's birth. Young Schuyler grew up poor and at the age of ten began working in a retail store to help support his mother and grandmother. In 1836, his mother remarried, and the family moved to Indiana, where Schuyler initially worked in his stepfather's store. Colfax became the deputy auditor of St. Joseph County, Indiana, in 1841. He later became a legislative correspondent for an Indiana newspaper and in 1845 bought a partial interest in a South Bend newspaper that was the major Whig supporter in northern Indiana. He married a childhood friend, Evelyn Clark, in 1844.

Political Career

In 1850, Colfax ran for Congress as a Whig candidate but was narrowly defeated. As a Republican, he was elected to the House of Representatives in 1854 on an antislavery ticket and served as congressman until becoming vice president of the United States in 1869 under President Ulysses S. Grant. Cofax served his last six years in Congress as Speaker of the House.

Colfax had long been a beloved man in Congress. He taught Sunday school, often spoke at temperance meetings, and was considered a Christian statesman. In fact, his abstinence from drinking hard liquor was one reason he was nominated for vice president: It was felt that he would balance the hard-drinking Grant. Colfax's image changed when a September 4, 1872, article in the powerful *New York Sun* accused him and other noted politicians of accepting stock in the Crédit Mobilier in exchange for their influence in Congress.

Crédit Mobilier was the construction company that

Schuyler Colfax. (Library of Congress)

built the transcontinental railroad on behalf of the Union Pacific Railroad. The objective of the bribes was to ensure that there would be no interference from Congress to delay federal money being funneled into railroad construction. To make the matter of taking bribes even worse, it was determined that one of the purposes of Crédit Mobilier, besides building the railroad, was to defraud the government by overcharging for construction of the tracks. Insiders at the Union Pacific Railroad had created the construction company to enable them to pay themselves millions of dollars to build the railroad. Thus, Crédit Mobilier was a scandal of gargantuan proportions even before it was connected to the acceptance of bribes by politicians.

Crédit Mobilier was formed by Thomas Durant of the Union Pacific Railroad to construct the transcontinental railroad, primarily because the separate corporation would allow Durant to line his own pockets without oversight from either the railroad company or Congress. President Abraham Lincoln had been an avid supporter of the transcontinental project and provided unwavering support. When he was assassinated in April, 1865—before any tracks had yet been laid—Durant and his successor, Oakes Ames, worried that Congress would vote to cut its losses and abandon the government contracts. Their solution was to obtain support from congressional leaders by selling them stock in the company at bargain prices.

The investigation disclosed that Colfax had received twenty shares of stock in Crédit Mobilier and dividends from that investment totaling twelve hundred dollars. Colfax asserted that he had never owned any stock that he had not purchased. Similarly, he claimed never to have received the supposed twelve hundred dollars in dividends.

Beware a Beautiful Smiler

Schuyler Colfax retired from politics at the relatively young age of forty-seven, but he later enjoyed a lucrative career on the lecture circuit giving talks about President Abraham Lincoln. He declined later invitations to run for public office, abhorring the thought of serving the "many headed public," and never lived down his scandalous reputation, as this rhyme from a contemporary newspaper attests:

A beautiful smiler came in our midst,
Too lively and fair to remain;
They stretched him on racks till the soul of Colfax
Flapped up into Heaven again,
May the fate of poor Schuyler warn men of a smiler,
Who dividends gets on the brain!

Source: Mark O. Hatfield, with the Senate Historical Office, *Vice Presidents of the United States, 1789-1993* (Washington, D.C.: Government Printing Office, 1997).

Legal Action and Outcome

Colfax was the subject of a congressional investigation by the House Judiciary Committee. The investigation determined that Colfax had indeed deposited that amount into his bank account just two days after the supposed dividend payment. After two weeks, Colfax explained that the deposit had been a campaign contribution from a friend who had since died. Even his strongest supporters doubted this story. The money, even if it had been contributed, would have been perceived as a bribe to get Colfax to buy government supplies from the donor.

Colfax was never impeached because his alleged crime took place before he became vice president, and he was nearing the end of his term in office at the time of the investigation. Because of the stigma attached to the accusation, Colfax was not renominated for the 1872 election. Following his retirement from politics, he lectured throughout the United States on the topic of morality in government and on his relationship with former president Lincoln. Some of Colfax's fellow congressmen accused of bribe-taking were formally censured, but no criminal or civil charges were ever filed against any of the individuals involved in the Crédit Mobilier scandal.

Impact

Even though he was not found guilty, Schuyler Colfax saw his political career destroyed by the scandal. Partially because of the Crédit Mobilier incident and the failure of the transcontinental railroads to make their bond payments, the Panic of 1873 ensued. The result was a disastrous collapse on Wall Street followed by a depression that lasted several years. Although Colfax had played a minor role, media coverage of this economic collapse led many investors to blame him for it.

Further Reading

Ambrose, Stephen E. *Nothing Like It in the World: The Men Who Built the Transcontinental Railroad, 1863-1869*. New York: Simon & Schuster, 2000. Although this volume does not devote much attention to Colfax, it is an excellent overview of the history of the transcontinental railroad and the Crédit Mobilier of America.

Moore, Ambrose Yoemans. *The Life of Schuyler Colfax*. Philadephia: T. B. Peterson & Brothers, 1868. This is a laudatory biography, published while Colfax was running for vice president. Probably a sponsored biography to help the campaign, it is nonetheless a good source of information on Colfax's early life.

Smith, Willard H. *Schuyler Colfax: The Changing Fortunes of a Political Idol*. Indianapolis: Indiana Historical Bureau, 1952. A well-researched biography that emphasizes the way the public viewed Colfax before and after the scandal. The chapter on the Crédit Mobilier is probably the best source on Colfax's involvement in the scandal.

—Dale L. Flesher

See also: Oakes Ames; Jim Fisk.

Vincent Coll

American gangster

Born: July 20, 1908; Rosses, County Donegal, Ireland
Died: February 8, 1932; New York, New York
Also known as: Mad Dog Coll; Mad Mick
Cause of notoriety: "Mad Dog Coll" was a Mafioso bootlegger, loan shark, enforcer, kidnapper, and hit man whose attempt to establish his own empire ultimately failed with his death at the age of twenty-three.
Active: 1920-1932
Locale: Greater New York City area

Early Life

The infamous gangster Vincent Coll (kohl) was born in the Rosses of County Donegal, Ireland, on July 20, 1908. At the age of one, Vincent emigrated with his family to the United States and settled in the Bronx, New York. Vincent experienced much heartache and personal tragedy from an early age. Before he turned twelve, his father deserted the family, and soon thereafter five of Vincent's siblings, along with this mother, died from a combination of disease and poverty. His only remaining friend was his older brother, Peter, who became Vincent's partner in crime throughout the late 1920's and early 1930's.

Vincent and his brother embarked on a rash of minor criminal acts throughout the Hell's Kitchen section of New York. As a consequence, Vincent was consigned to a Catholic boys' reformatory. After serving his time there, he and Peter decided to enlist to become Mafia enforcers and rumrunners for the infamous Jewish gangster Dutch Schultz, a decision that sparked the formidable yet short career of Coll.

Criminal Career

Vincent and Peter excelled at their job of inflicting pain and suffering—and in some cases death—on any threat to Schultz and his enterprise. In 1931, after a few years of apprenticeship, Coll asked Schultz for a percentage of the illegal alcohol profits, but Schultz turned down the request. His denial enraged Coll, causing him to break away from his mentor to form his own criminal operation. He recruited Peter and some other low-ranking Schultz enforcers to assist him in establishing his criminal gang, which would attempt to operate in both the Bronx and Harlem.

In order to establish himself as a mobster, Coll and his crew chose to send a strong message to Schultz and other mobsters: that they were now legitimate and deserved respect in the crime underworld. With this aim, Coll assassinated two of Schultz's top-ranking lieutenants. In retaliation, Schultz had Coll's brother, Peter, shot the following day. Peter's death sent Vincent into an insatiable rage and ignited a war between Coll and Schultz. More than twenty men from both gangs were killed during this gang war.

However, it was Coll's murder plot in Spanish Harlem that made him one of the most notorious gangsters of all time and gave him his nickname of Mad Dog. During a failed assassination attempt on two of Schultz's officers, Coll opened fire on a crowd of innocent citizens that included five children. When the gunfire ceased, adults and children lay severely injured, including a five-year-old boy who ultimately died from the gunshot wounds. Coll was later acquitted of the boy's murder and continued his illicit operations.

Lacking sophistication in business, Coll had to find a way to finance his war against Schultz. He turned to kidnapping famous celebrities with mob connections as well as rival mobsters and their crews; he also offered murder for hire. Coll was recruited and paid by famous mob boss Salvatore Maranzano to kill rival boss Lucky Luciano and his crew. Ironically, Luciano discovered the plot and had Maranzano killed. In the end, Coll was paid twenty-five thousand dollars without having to lift a finger.

On February 8, 1932, at the age of twenty-three, Coll was gunned down in broad daylight while standing in a telephone booth. He was demanding a ransom from reputed mobster Owney Madden at the time. Coll's body was literally torn in half by bullets fired by Schultz's hitmen.

Impact

Vincent Coll was one of the most violent mobsters of the Prohibition era and the quintessential Irish immigrant mobster who survived tragedy and poverty only to find an ultimately destructive way of survival. His brutal crimes and misdeeds gave him the reputation as one of the most prolific hit men and racketeers in the history of organized crime. His early death made him a symbol of the violent and wasteful lifestyle of mid-twentieth century crime families. Two films, both titled *Mad Dog Coll*, have fictionalized Coll's life. One released in 1961 starred John Davis Chandler as Coll, and one released in 1993 starred Christopher Bradley in the title role.

Further Reading

Delap, Breandán. *Mad Dog Coll: An Irish Gangster*. Dublin: Mercier Press, 1999. An unbiased account of Coll's life, from his tragic upbringing to his trademark violent behavior, which ultimately landed him on the Federal Bureau of Investigation's most wanted list.

Reppetto, Thomas. *American Mafia*. New York: Holt, 2004. A chronicle of the Mafia's rise to power in the United States from 1890 to 1951. Includes an excellent bibliography.

Sifakis, Carl. *The Mafia Encyclopedia*. 2d ed. New York: Facts on File, 1999. Comprehensive overview of organized crime personalities, power clashes, hangouts, hideaways, and rackets.

—*Paul M. Klenowski*

See also: Joe Adonis; Albert Anastasia; Paul Castellano; Joe Colombo; Carmine Galante; Carlo Gambino; Sam Giancana; Vincent Gigante; Salvatore Giuliano; John Gotti; Sammy Gravano; Henry Hill; Richard Kuklinski; Meyer Lansky; Lucky Luciano; Salvatore Maranzano; Carlos Marcello; Joe Masseria; Joseph Profaci; Arnold Rothstein; Dutch Schultz.

Frank Collin

Founder of the National Socialist Party of America

Born: November 3, 1944; Chicago, Illinois
Also known as: Frank Joseph Collin (full name); Frank Joseph
Cause of notoriety: Collin proposed a march by neo-Nazis in a Jewish suburb of Chicago and saw the Supreme Court uphold his group's right to march.
Active: 1960's-1980
Locale: Illinois

Early Life

Frank Collin (CAWL-ihn) was born in Chicago. His father, Max Cohn, was a furniture store owner and a German-born Jew who spent time in Germany's Dachau concentration camp. Max Collin became a naturalized American citizen in 1946, changing his name from Cohn to Collin.

Frank Collin attended Southern Illinois University from 1962 to 1964, where he claimed a fellow student introduced him to the National Socialist Party. Collin left Southern Illinois University in June, 1964, and enrolled at Hiram Scott College in Scotts Bluff, Nebraska. In 1967 he returned to Southern Illinois University. Between 1967 and 1969 he became increasingly involved with National Socialism. Eventually he dropped out of college to devote all his time to the Nazi Party.

Political Career

Collin joined George Lincoln Rockwell's American Nazi Party in the 1960's. Later he became the Midwest coordinator for its successor, the National Socialist White Peoples Party (NSWPP). In 1970 Collin was expelled from the NSWPP after it was revealed that his father was Jewish. Collin then formed the National Socialist Party of America (NSPA) and set up headquarters in Chicago. Its membership was less than one hundred and consisted primarily of young men and adolescents. Its activities generally consisted of marches and rallies, which attracted attention and frequently ended in clashes between party members and opponents.

In 1975, Collin ran for alderman in Chicago and received 16 percent of the vote. In October, 1976, he received national publicity when he announced plans to hold a rally in Skokie, Illinois, a predominately Jewish suburb of Chicago. The Skokie Park District Board of Commissioners responded by passing an ordinance requiring prospective marchers to obtain a permit at least thirty days in advance of the parade date and to post an insurance bond equal to $350,000. In June, 1977, Collin requested a permit for the National Socialist Party of America to march in front of Skokie Village Hall. In response, the Village Board passed three ordinances. The first required a $350,000 indemnity bond to be posted in advance of any march. The second prohibited the distribution of printed material that promoted hatred of groups of people. The third prohibited demonstrations by individuals wearing military-style uniforms. The Village of Skokie then denied the NSPA the right to march in military-style uniforms.

Frank Collin. (© Chip Berlet/Courtesy, PRA)

Collin challenged these actions in court with the assistance of the American Civil Liberties Union. In January, 1978, the Illinois Supreme Court upheld the First Amendment right of the Nazis to march and declared that the swastika was symbolic of political speech. The Federal District Court of the Northern District of Illinois, the U.S. Court of Appeals for the Seventh Circuit, and the U.S. Supreme Court refused to prohibit the march. On May 25, 1978, the Village of Skokie issued a permit allowing the NSPA to demonstrate in front of the Village Hall. Collin, however, cancelled the march. In its place, he and about twenty-five followers held a rally in Marquette Park in Chicago on July 9, 1978. While Collin and the NSPA never marched in Skokie, he received national publicity for his movement. In addition, a made-for-television film titled *Skokie* was aired in 1981.

In 1980 Collin was convicted of sexually molesting adolescent boys at his party headquarters. For these crimes he served three years at Pontiac State Prison. Following his release from prison, Collin changed his name to Frank Joseph and established himself as an author, editor, and neo-pagan. He wrote several books, including *The Destruction of Atlantis* (1987). He also wrote articles for *Fate* magazine and served as editor of *The Ancient American*.

Impact

Frank Collin's neo-Nazi organization had almost no support from or appeal to Americans. However, he is remembered because of his attempt to march in Skokie and the First Amendment issues his effort raised.

Further Reading

George, John, and Laird Wilcox. *American Extremists*. Amherst, N.Y.: Prometheus Books, 1996. Examines a number of American extremist groups, including the National Socialist Party of America and other neo-Nazi groups.

Strum, Philippa. *When the Nazis Came to Skokie: Freedom for Speech We Hate*. Lawrence: University of Kansas Press, 1999. A detailed analysis of the First Amendment issues related to the proposed march through Skokie.

—*William V. Moore*

See also: Richard Girnt Butler; Willis A. Carto; David Duke; Matthew F. Hale; Jean-Marie Le Pen; Robert Jay Mathews; Tom Metzger; William Luther Pierce III; George Lincoln Rockwell; William Joseph Simmons; Gerald L. K. Smith; J. B. Stoner; Randy Weaver.

JOE COLOMBO

American Mafia boss

BORN: June 16, 1923; Brooklyn, New York
DIED: May 22 or May 23, 1978; Newburgh, New York
ALSO KNOWN AS: Joseph Anthony Colombo, Sr. (full name)
CAUSE OF NOTORIETY: A hit man for the Profaci crime family, Colombo later became boss of the family and renamed it after himself. He ran gambling operations, extortion and loan-sharking rackets, and other criminal enterprises. He also organized a civil rights league supposedly created to protect the rights of Italian Americans.
ACTIVE: 1945-1971
LOCALE: New York, New York

EARLY LIFE

Joe Colombo (koh-LUHM-boh) was born in Brooklyn, New York, in 1923. His parents were Anthony "Nino" and Catherine Colombo. Nino was a Brazilian immigrant born to Italian parents. He became a small-time extortionist and all-around minor hood. In 1938 or 1939, the elder Colombo was found murdered in his car, alongside his presumed mistress Christina Oliveri, the wife of a Profaci soldier. The two had been strangled with a cord.

While little is known of Joe's early life, he attended New Utrecht High School and served in the U.S. Coast Guard from 1942 to 1945. He was discharged after being diagnosed with a nervous disorder. After his military service, Colombo worked as an associate for the Profaci crime family. He ran dice games, worked as an enforcer on the docks, and eventually took over the Mafia-operated gambling enterprises in Brooklyn and Long Island.

CRIMINAL CAREER

Joe, along with the Gallo brothers ("Crazy Joe" and Larry) and two others, formed a five-man hit squad for Profaci. In the early 1960's, Joseph Bonanno of the Bonnano crime family contacted Joe Magliocco (who later became boss of the Profaci family and an ally of Bonanno) to carry out the assassination of several key Mafia figures, including Carlo Gambino and Stefano Magaddino of Buffalo, New York. Magliocco, in turn, gave the contract to his top enforcer, Joe Colombo.

Colombo, however, presumably out of an instinct for self-preservation, decided to go to each target of Bonanno's victim list and warn him of the plan. Bonanno was subsequently kidnapped by his cousin Magaddino, and Colombo took control of the Profaci family as a reward for thwarting the mass murder, renaming the family after himself.

Colombo's leadership was marked by internal strife. He called unwanted attention to the Mafia by picketing offices of the Federal Bureau of Investigation (FBI) for its 1970 arrest of his son, Joe Jr. He alienated the Gallo brothers because of his greed, skimming heavily from the soldiers' operations. Colombo further displeased his fellow mobsters by forming the Italian American Civil Rights League, an organization supposedly dedicated to celebrating Italian heritage and, ironically, to combat the gangster stereotype of Italian Americans.

Colombo's penchant for creating public spectacles culminated at a "Unity Day" rally on June 28, 1971. As the crowd formed for the rally, an African American man with press credentials shot Colombo in the head three times. The shooter, named Jerome Johnson, was then immediately killed by an unidentified man who managed to escape. Observers believe that Joe Gallo set up the murder because of Gallo's known alliance with African American criminals and "Crazy Joe's" hatred of Colombo. Colombo did not die that day, but he remained in a vegetative state until his death in 1978.

IMPACT

Joe Colombo's 1960's-style social activism and public persona anticipated the flashiness and popular appeal of John Gotti in the 1980's but in his own time stirred consternation among law enforcement agencies and his fellow mobsters alike. Nevertheless, Colombo appealed to many honest Italian Americans, fifty thousand of whom attended the first Unity Day rally and proclaimed Colombo "man of the year." Similarly, Colombo's son Christopher achieved a celebrity status, starring in a 2005 HBO "reality"-style special that profiled the Mafia scion as he served a modified house-arrest while facing charges for racketeering, loan-sharking, and extortion. Such mob figures who attempt to develop a positive (or at least public) image may speak to the romanticism that, for some, still clings to certain aspects of mob life.

FURTHER READING

Capeci, Jerry. *Jerry Capeci's Gang Land*. New York: Alpha Books, 2003. A compilation of journalist and

Mafia expert Capeci's columns in the *New York Daily News* covering organized crime activity in New York City from 1989 through 1995.

Raab, Selwyn. *Five Families: The Rise, Decline, and Resurgence of America's Most Powerful Mafia Empires*. New York: St. Martin's Press, 2005. Recounts the history of the New York crime families; spotlights major figures and events of organized crime in New York.

Talese, Gay. *Honor Thy Father*. New York: World, 1971. Biographical sketch of Joe Bonanno's reign, from the Castallammerese War until the infamous Banana Wars.

—*David R. Champion*

See also: Joe Adonis; Albert Anastasia; Paul Castellano; Vincent Coll; Carmine Galante; Carlo Gambino; Sam Giancana; Vincent Gigante; John Gotti; Sammy Gravano; Henry Hill; Richard Kuklinski; Meyer Lansky; Salvatore Maranzano; Carlos Marcello; Joe Masseria; Joseph Profaci; Arnold Rothstein; Dutch Schultz.

Charles W. Colson

Special counsel to the president in the Nixon administration

Born: October 16, 1931; Boston, Massachusetts
Also known as: Charles Wendell Colson (full name); Chuck Colson
Major offense: Obstruction of justice
Active: 1970-1973
Locale: Washington, D.C.
Sentence: One to three years' imprisonment; served seven months

Early Life

Charles Wendell Colson (KOHL-suhn) was born in Massachusetts, the son of an attorney. He attended Browne and Nichols, a private preparatory school, and then entered Brown University in 1949 on a full Navy ROTC scholarship. Commissioned in the Marine Corps, he served as a platoon commander on exercises in the Caribbean. After his graduation from Brown, Colson re-

Charles W. Colson. (AP/Wide World Photos)

Nixon on Colson

In his memoirs, Richard Nixon recalled the 1974 election and Colson's role in it:

John Mitchell was going to be my campaign manager, but he would have his hands full organizing and running the Committee to Re-elect the President. Increasingly I turned to Chuck Colson to act as my political point-man. Colson had joined the administration in late 1969 in the role of White House liaison with special interest groups. He worked on policy matters with energy and devotion. He spent hours with labor groups, veterans' organizations, ethnic minorities, and religious groups. He was positive, persuasive, smart, and aggressively partisan. His instinct for the political jugular and his ability to get things done made him a lightning rod for my own frustrations at the timidity of most Republicans in responding to attacks from the Democrats and the media. When I complained to Colson I felt confident that something would be done, and I was rarely disappointed.

Source: Richard Nixon, *RN: The Memoirs of Richard Nixon* (New York: Grosset and Dunlap, 1978).

signed from the Corps and switched his commission to the Reserves. Interested in law, he took a job in Washington, D.C., which allowed him to attend classes at night at George Washington University School of Law. With his law degree in hand, Colson and another attorney, a close friend, opened a firm with offices in Boston and Washington. The practice soon became successful.

Colson had been politically active in the Republican Party as early as 1948. He learned a great deal about the rough-and-tumble electoral politics from his experience in several Boston political campaigns. After managing Leverett Saltonstall's successful senatorial campaign in 1960, he tried to deflect Barry Goldwater's presidential nomination in 1964 in favor of Richard Nixon. Although the effort was unsuccessful, he and Nixon formed an enduring political bond. Colson was again active in Nixon's presidential campaign in 1968, and he was appointed special counsel to the president when Nixon took office the following year.

Criminal Career

Colson quickly became known as President Nixon's "hatchet man" because of his performance of political "dirty tricks" and his willingness to operate at the edge, or sometimes slightly beyond the boundaries, of law. A favorite trick was to release or leak disparaging stories about political opponents while knowing them to be false. Because President Nixon trusted him, Colson was often able to operate independently of the normal chain of command in the White House, which led through H. R. Haldeman, the president's chief of staff, and John Ehrlichman, the chief domestic policy adviser.

During the course of the investigations of the Watergate scandal, information regarding an earlier crime emerged. The White House had sent operatives to discover what they could about military analyst Daniel Ellsberg. Ellsberg had given the Pentagon Papers—a classified government study of the origins of the war in Vietnam—to *The New York Times*. The White House investigators broke into the office of Ellsberg's psychiatrist in order to find material with which Ellsberg could be discredited. Although Colson was not the progenitor of this operation, he learned of it almost immediately and did everything he could to prevent knowledge of it from becoming public.

Then, on June 17, 1972, the Watergate break-in took place. Five burglars, later shown to be affiliated with and to have been paid by the Committee to Re-elect the President (CRP), broke into the offices of the Democratic National Committee in the Watergate Hotel. Several of them were former White House operatives. Their purpose was to obtain political intelligence by bugging the Democrats' telephones. They were caught and arrested by the District of Columbia police.

Colson had decided to resign his White House office after President Nixon's first term. He had been dissatisfied with the tenor of his life for some time. He resigned his office in March, 1973, and resumed his legal practice. During the summer of 1973, Colson underwent a profound religious conversion, becoming, to use his own words, "born again." Although initially much derided in the press, his deep commitment to Christianity gives impetus to his life and activities after his conversion. When the Watergate investigation focused on Colson, he decided to tell everything he knew without the benefit of a plea bargain or guaranteed minimum sentence.

Legal Action and Outcome

Colson pleaded no contest to one count of obstruction of justice for his role in the Ellsberg burglary; all other charges were dropped. Judge Gerhard Gesell sentenced Colson to a term of imprisonment of one to three years. Colson was confined at Fort Holabird, Maryland, and at a federal work camp near Maxwell Air Force Base in Alabama. During his imprisonment, he worked actively to promote Christianity and to help other prisoners. After seven months, Judge Gesell reduced his sentence to time served, perhaps because Judge John Sirica, before whom some of the other Watergate defendants had pleaded guilty, freed them. Colson was released on January 31, 1975.

Impact

The manifold illegal activities associated with the Watergate scandal—many not involving Charles Colson at all—had the long-term effect of reducing public confidence in the government and in the presidency in particular. For a long time, Colson's name was associated with many of the vilest acts of the Nixon administration. However, his commitment to prison ministries, which continued long after his release from prison, slowly demonstrated the sincerity of his conversion.

Further Reading

Ambrose, Stephen. *Nixon*. 3 volumes. New York: Simon & Schuster, 1987-1991. An illuminating and balanced discussion of Nixon, his personality, career, and presidency. The Watergate material can be found in volume III, *Ruin and Recovery*.

Colson, Charles W. *Born Again*. Old Tappan, N.J.: Chosen Books, 1976. Colson discusses his career, Watergate activities, conversion to Christianity, and the effect of his religious consciousness on his behavior.

Safire, William. *Before the Fall: An Inside View of the Pre-Watergate White House*. Garden City, N.Y.: Doubleday, 1975. A fascinating, laudatory view of the accomplishments of the Nixon administration before Watergate destroyed it.

White, Theodore H. *Breach of Faith: The Fall of Richard Nixon*. New York: Atheneum, 1975. Excellent history of the Watergate affair; Colson's role discussed at length.

—Robert Jacobs

See also: John D. Ehrlichman; H. R. Haldeman; E. Howard Hunt; G. Gordon Liddy; James W. McCord, Jr.; John Mitchell; Richard Nixon.

Commodus

Roman emperor (180-192 c.e.)

Born: August 31, 161 c.e.; Lanuvium, Latium (now Lanuvio, Italy)
Died: December 31, 192 c.e.; Rome (now in Italy)
Also known as: Marcus Aurelius Commodus Antoninus (full name); Lucius Aelius Aurelius Commodus (birth name); Hercules Romanus
Cause of notoriety: Politically inept and self-indulgent, Commodus ushered in a period of decline for the Roman Empire during his reign.
Active: 180-192 c.e.
Locale: Italy, mainly Rome

Early Life

Lucius Aelius Aurelius Commodus (KAWM-uh-dus), son of Marcus Aurelius and Annia Faustina, was born on August 31, 161 c.e., at Lanuvium (near Rome). Most of his youth was spent with his father campaigning along the Danube. Although no Roman emperor had been in a position to select his own son as successor since the time of the Flavians (69-96 c.e.), it would appear that Marcus Aurelius, convinced that the security of the empire was at stake, was determined to prepare Commodus for that role. Despite concerns about the youth's health and his predilection for nonroyal activities such as whistling, singing, dancing, and pottery-making, Commodus was accorded all of the titles and powers of an heir apparent. In 177 c.e., faced with uprisings in Gaul, Mauretania, and the Nile Delta, Commodus was proclaimed a co-Augustus. When Marcus Aurelius died on March 17, 180 c.e., at Vindobona (modern Vienna), Commodus became princeps.

Political Career

Although Marcus Aurelius attempted to educate his son in the proper methods of government and generalship, these efforts were largely wasted. Some of the ancient authorities are of the opinion that Commodus was not an evil man, but there is general agreement that he was a weak, malleable vessel who was easily influenced by a cortege of sycophants. Convinced by his associates that an emperor's place was in Rome, not in the wilds of Germany, he broke off his father's war with the Marcommani and Quadi in favor of a policy of conciliation and accommodation. That decision was to have far-reaching repercussions. Legions throughout the empire quickly lost confidence in the new emperor. There were mutinies

Machiavelli on Commodus

The author of the famous Renaissance treatise on leadership, The Prince, *Niccolò Machiavelli, had this to say about Commodus:*

But let us come to Commodus, to whom it should have been very easy to hold the empire, for, being the son of Marcus, he had inherited it, and he had only to follow in the footsteps of his father to please his people and soldiers; but, being by nature cruel and brutal, he gave himself up to amusing the soldiers and corrupting them, so that he might indulge his rapacity upon the people; on the other hand, not maintaining his dignity, often descending to the theatre to compete with gladiators, and doing other vile things, little worthy of the imperial majesty, he fell into contempt with the soldiers, and being hated by one party and despised by the other, he was conspired against and was killed.

Source: Niccolò Machiavelli, *The Prince*, translated by W. K. Marriott (New York: E. P. Dutton, 1908).

in Britain, Gaul, Spain, and even Dacia (now southeastern Europe). Some of the disaffected soldiers turned to banditry and took to pillaging the countryside. Plague, famine, and widespread corruption in the government were other factors that weakened both the economy and the morale of the people.

A stronger emperor might have been able to effect solutions, but Commodus evinced little interest in the drudgeries of government business, preferring to leave such matters in the hands of disreputable minions while immersing himself in a life of debauchery and leisurely activities. Through royal favors and entertainment spectacles, he sought to win the support of the masses and the army, but his self-indulgent approach did not endear him to everyone. In 182 C.E., some members of the Senate, aided by the emperor's sister Lucilla, who was jealous of her lost influence at court, conspired to assassinate Commodus. The plot failed, and Lucilla and others of distinction were put to death. Thereafter, no one was above suspicion, especially those of senatorial rank. In the purge that followed, many faithful servants of the empire and some members of Commodus's inner circle perished.

In the meantime, Commodus had abandoned himself to a life of sensual delights—feasting, drinking, and cavorting, according to ancient sources, with a harem of several hundred women and an equal number of boys. Chief among the emperor's concubines was a Christian named Marcia, whose influence may have provided some measure of protection for the oft-persecuted Church. The lurid descriptions of Commodus's sexual appetite have almost certainly been exaggerated, but there can be little doubt that he stood alone among the emperors of Rome in his passion for the circus, gladiatorial combat, and wild beast shows. One source asserts that on 735 occasions, Commodus donned the accouterments of the gladiator and hunter and descended into the arena, where he bested his opponents and dispatched lions, leopards, hippopotami, camels, and rhinoceroses with unerring accuracy. So comfortable was Commodus in this role that he adopted the name of Hercules Romanus.

In the end, Commodus's megalomaniacal behavior and cruelty proved more than even his obsequious companions could stomach. An assassination plot hatched by the praetorian prefect Quintus Aemilius Laetus and other members of the emperor's court was carried to completion on December 31, 192 C.E., when a young wrestler strangled Commodus while he slumbered in a drunken stupor in his bath.

Impact

It is, perhaps, ironic that Marcus Aurelius, the last of the so-called good emperors, would eschew that principle that had brought the empire to its peak—the selection of a successor on the basis of merit—in favor of bestowing the emperorship on his youthful, unproven son Commodus. While it would be incorrect to blame Commodus for all of Rome's problems, there can be no doubt that his reign ushered in a period of decline from which the empire would never really recover. Often compared with the infamous Nero, Commodus was a miserable failure as an emperor. In the words of one historian, Commodus "is one of the few Roman emperors of whom nothing good can be said."

Further Reading

Boatwright, Mary T., Daniel J. Gargola, and Richard J. A. Talbert. *The Romans from Village to Empire*. New York: Oxford University Press, 2004. General history of Rome from the earliest period to Constantine the Great. A short overview of Commodus's reign suggests that the abandonment of the Germanic wars might have been the culmination of a process begun by his father.

Glay, Marcel Le, Jean-Louis Voisin, and Yann Le Bohec. *A History of Rome*. 3d ed. London: Blackwell,

2005. A history of Rome from the earliest period through the collapse of the empire in the fifth century. Written primarily for students, each section, including that telling of Commodus's reign, is accompanied by an annotated list of important points.

Hekster, Olivier. *Commodus: An Emperor at the Crossroads*. Amsterdam: Gieben, 2002. First biography of Commodus in almost a half century. A somewhat sympathetic study that suggests that Commodus's reign was a "crossroads" that signaled the approach of difficult times.

—Larry W. Usilton

See also: Caligula; Domitian; Nero.

Anthony Comstock

American reformer

Born: March 7, 1844; New Canaan, Connecticut
Died: September 21, 1915; Summit, New Jersey
Also known as: Fair Flower of Puritanism
Cause of notoriety: Comstock was the author and enforcer of the 1873 federal Comstock Law, which banned for more than sixty years the advertisement, publication, or sale of contraception or information about abortion. His name came to be associated with moralistic censorship.
Active: 1868-1915
Locale: New York, New York

Early Life

Born in rural western Connecticut of a prosperous farmer and a devout Congregationalist mother who died when he was ten, Anthony Comstock (CAHM-stawk) retained his early fundamentalist upbringing for his entire life. After his older brother died at the Battle of Gettysburg during the Civil War, Comstock enlisted in the Seventeenth Regiment of the Connecticut Infantry. Posted away from battle in Florida for most of his one and a half years' service in the Union Army, he joined the Christian Commission and distributed temperance and religious tracts to his fellow soldiers; established prayer meetings for his regiment, which he attended up to nine times a week; and not only refused to drink whiskey but also poured his ration onto the ground. By his own admission, he was an unpopular man.

Reformist Career

After briefly trying his luck in Connecticut and Tennessee without success, Comstock settled in New York City, which was then the American center for the commercialized sex industry. Prostitutes roamed the streets and advertised in newspapers. Local printers sold pornographic books, photographs, and other materials. Concert saloons staged salacious shows, and immoral acts were committed at fancy balls. Comstock, working first as a porter and then as a salesman in a dry-goods notion house, was horrified. He determined to destroy the industry that produced this way of life.

He began his lifelong battle in 1868 by purchasing a sexually explicit book from a popular bookseller, taking it straight to the captain of the local police precinct, and accompanying the captain to the bookseller's arrest and the seizing of his stock. In 1871, Comstock married Maggie Hamilton, a woman ten years his senior. A daughter was born to them but died about six months later, and his wife did not become pregnant again. This circumstance might have amplified his anger toward women who casually terminated pregnancies or who used birth control devices to prevent them.

Anthony Comstock. (Library of Congress)

THE CENSOR'S NEMESIS

A ferocious antismut crusader, Anthony Comstock was widely feared because he was effective. He boasted in a 1914 report that he sent 3,697 people to court on charges, of whom 2,740 were convicted and jailed or fined. Later sources claim that he directly caused the destruction of 160 tons of literature and artwork. Despite his legal and political influence, some among his victims were not daunted.

In 1910, the feminist writer Emma Goldman published an article, "The White Slave Traffic," exposing widespread prostitution in America. Comstock had the U.S. Post Office stop the article's distribution. When Goldman's associate asked Comstock about it, he initially denied responsibility but then backed down and allowed the distribution.

In her lecture "Victims of Morality" (1913), Goldman wrote,

> Not so very long ago I attended a meeting addressed by Anthony Comstock, who has for forty years been the guardian of American morals. A more incoherent, ignorant ramble I have never heard from any platform. The question that presented itself to me, listening to the commonplace, bigoted talk of the man, was, how could anyone so limited and unintelligent wield the power of censor and dictator over a supposedly democratic nation?

Birth control activist Margaret Sanger was another of Comstock's targets. Comstock objected to literature about contraception and believed it conducive to lust and licentiousness. He had Sanger and her husband arrested for distributing her 1914 pamphlet *Family Limitation*. The charges against Sanger were dismissed, but her husband was convicted of selling a single copy. Comstock himself attended the trial, where he fell ill with the pneumonia that led to his death soon afterward.

As sometimes happens to the fiery and righteous, Comstock could be tricked into harming his own cause. Any denunciation from him made the object of it immediately intriguing to the public. A case in point was an incident engineered by Harry Reichenbach, later famous for producing motion-picture publicity stunts. While working at an art gallery, he egged Comstock into demanding the removal of a painting of a naked girl bathing in a lake. The picture, *September Morn*, was instantly popular, selling thousands of lithograph copies.

In 1872, Comstock requested and received from Morris Ketchum Jesup, a founder of the Young Men's Christian Association (YMCA), thirty thousand dollars to purchase the equipment and stock of a pornography printer. He arranged for the printing plates to be taken to a laboratory in Brooklyn and supervised their destruction by acid. This act so impressed Jesup that he introduced Comstock to other wealthy YMCA supporters. Together, they founded the New York Society for the Suppression of Vice (NYSSV). Although the first of its kind in the country, the NYSSV was soon joined by similar organizations in many major U.S. cities.

Comstock was hired as the NYSSV's full-time agent. In 1880, he wrote the first of two books, *Frauds Exposed*, and successfully lobbied Congress to pass the federal Act of the Suppression of Trade in, and Circumstances of, Obscene Literature of Articles and Immoral Use, which came to known more simply as the Anti-Obscenity Act or the Comstock Law. This act authorized NYSSV and similar organizations to assist the police department in its enforcement of the law. Two years later, Congress strengthened Comstock's power by naming him special agent of the U.S. Post Office. Over time, the NYSSV made some seven hundred arrests, was responsible for the imprisonment of more than three hundred people, and levied fines totaling more than sixty-two thousand dollars for "obscene offenses" as defined in the act, including imparting of information about and sale of contraceptives. Comstock and his agents received a fee for each arrest.

Although the Comstock Law allowed up to a five-thousand-dollar fine and ten years in prison, judges and juries were more reluctant than Comstock and his agents to impose the maximum sentences or often any punishment at all. Comstock came to regard the justice system with a jaundiced eye. Judges were cautious about enabling what they saw as the possibility of unchecked federal power, and jurors and prosecutors were concerned about the right to privacy. Even presidents pardoned people who had been sentenced to jail on birth control charges.

Comstock's belligerence and courtroom histrionics—chronicled in editorials, cartoons, and poems—might have been partly responsible for these judicial leniencies. His fervor made him unpopular personally, but some found appealing his efforts to solidify Victorian morals into law. In 1915, Secretary of the Navy Josephus Daniels, a fundamentalist Christian, banned the sale of chemical prophylactics on navy ships and started a campaign through talks and pamphlets to teach men abstinence through self-control. By then, Comstock had been dead for several months.

Impact

Anthony Comstock has been variously termed "the fair flower of Puritanism," "the most famous prude and busybody in American history," "a fanatical figure," "a charismatic purist," and finally, a hypocrite, the latter because he did not pursue aristocratic physicians and druggists even though he had successfully fought an amendment to his law that would have exempted doctors from giving birth control information or devices to their patients. However, one biographer noted that Comstock was not an isolated fanatic, and, while his fervor was unique, his ideas represented prevailing attitudes about sexual matters. He viewed abortion as permissible only when a woman's life was in danger, and, while admitting that birth control was desirable when pregnancy might endanger a woman's life, he preferred "natural methods" (which he never defined in writing because that would have been an obscenity) and emphasized abstinence (which he considered character-building). One of his objections to "man-made" contraception was his belief that it encouraged lewdness and lust and allowed the practice of licentiousness without consequences.

The Comstock Law spawned "little Comstocks" in twenty-four states. Largely because of Comstock's efforts, information about birth control, as well as the sale of devices, became unavailable to many people, especially poor women. Margaret Sanger, who opened the first birth control clinic in the United States, was arrested as a result of Comstock's efforts and left the country several times. However, after Comstock's death, there was considerably less enthusiasm for enforcing the law. It was not until 1961 that the U.S. Supreme Court ruled Connecticut's law against the use of contraceptives unconstitutional, and until 1972 that Massachusetts law, which made contraception illegal for unmarried couples, was also ruled as unlawful. The term "comstockery," originally coined by playwright George Bernard Shaw, was used to refer to the strict censorship of materials deemed obscene.

Further Reading

Bates, Anna Louise. *Weeder in the Garden of the Lord: Anthony Comstock's Life and Career*. Lanham, Md.: University Press of America, 1995. A standard biography that details Comstock's life and explores his impact on American morality.

McBridge-Stetson, Dorothy. *Women's Rights in the USA: Policy Debates and Gender Roles*. New York: Routledge, 2004. Puts birth control debates into the context of U.S. history, including the role of Comstock and the women's movement.

Tone, Andrea. *Devices and Desires: A History of Contraceptives in America*. New York: Hill & Wang, 2001. The early section of the book examines how the passage of the Comstock Act criminalized contraception and set important precedents for future family planning efforts.

—*Erika E. Pilver*

See also: Madame Restell.

Janet Cooke

American journalist and fraud

Born: July 23, 1954; Toledo, Ohio
Also known as: Janet Leslie Cooke (full name)
Cause of notoriety: Cooke's feature story, "Jimmy's World," appeared in *The Washington Post* and subsequently won a Pulitzer Prize, which the writer returned after admitting that she had fabricated the work.
Active: September 29, 1980
Locale: Washington, D.C.

Early Life

Janet Cooke (kook) was born into a middle-class family in Toledo, Ohio. Her father, who worked for Toledo Edison, gave Janet a typewriter when she was five years old. While in elementary school, she wrote poetry. She attended Vassar College for one year and received a bachelor of arts degree from the University of Toledo. She then worked as a reporter for the *Toledo Blade* for two years.

Journalism Career

In July of 1979, Cooke sent a letter of inquiry to Ben Bradlee, executive editor of *The Washington Post*, stating that she felt herself qualified to work for a major newspaper. She included copies of six stories she had written for the *Toledo Blade* and a resume that stated she had graduated Phi Beta Kappa from Vassar in 1976. This fact, later proven false, caught Bradlee's attention. Cooke was invited to interview with the *Post* staff, all of whom were very impressed by both Cooke's resume and her performance in the interview. Thus, after a cursory verification of her credentials, the *Post* hired her on January 3, 1980.

Cooke was assigned to the "District Weekly" section and worked under Vivian Aplin-Brownlee. Her first byline appeared just two weeks after she was hired. On February 21, her first major story appeared. It covered a police patrol along 14th Street, the center of Washington D.C.'s drug traffic. Cooke was ambitious and had set her sights on a position working for the Metro section of the paper and on a Pulitzer Prize. On September 29, 1980, her story "Jimmy's World," about an eight-year-old heroin addict, appeared in the *Post*. Public reaction was intense. A citywide search was made for Jimmy; everyone wanted to help him, but he could not be found, and Cook said she was unable to remember where he lived. Doubts about Jimmy's existence and the story's veracity arose among *Post* staff members and in the public sector.

The newspaper not only maintained that the story was authentic but also nominated it for a Pulitzer Prize. Cooke was awarded the Pulitzer on April 13, 1981, but she had little time to enjoy her success. The editors of the *Toledo Blade* noticed inconsistencies in Cooke's biography accompanying the announcement of her award. Further inquiry revealed that her credentials were falsified. The *Post* confronted Cooke, who admitted that both her credentials and the story were fraudulent. On April 15, the *Post* publicly admitted that Cooke had made up the story. The Pulitzer was returned, and Cooke resigned from the paper. Her journalism career was at an end.

In 1982, she appeared on television's *Phil Donahue* show; she blamed the high-pressure work environment at the *Post* for her bad judgment in fabricating the story. She subsequently worked as a salesclerk, married, divorced, and moved to Kalamazoo, Michigan, where she worked again in sales. In 1996, Mike Sager interviewed her for *Gentlemen's Quarterly* magazine. Columbia TriStar Pictures purchased the film rights to her story.

Impact

Janet Cooke's reportorial misconduct had a far-ranging impact on the field of journalism. For the general public, the credibility of the press was now suspect. Cooke had lied about her credentials and presented fiction as factual

Janet Cooke learns she has won the Pulitzer Prize. (AP/Wide World Photos)

reporting. At the *Post*, a new policy improved internal communication and placed greater responsibility for story accuracy on editors. Within the profession, the Cooke case resulted in a reevaluation of the rights of reporters to work independently and maintain confidentiality for their sources. The Cooke case also reemphasized the responsibility of editors to ensure truth in reporting.

Further Reading

Cooke, Janet. "Jimmy's Story." *The Washington Post*, September 29, 1980. Cooke's emotionally charged but fabricated story that won the Pulitzer Prize and ruined her journalism career.

Iggers, Jeremy. *Good News, Bad News: Journalism Ethics and the Public Interest*. Boulder, Colo.: Westview Press, 1998. Fully examines the Janet Cooke case, its importance for journalism, and ethics in journalism.

Nemeth, Neil. *News Ombudsmen in North America: Assessing an Experiment in Social Responsibility*. Westport, Conn.: Praeger, 2003. Looks at role of ombudsman in monitoring and checking veracity of news reported. Examines the Janet Cooke case in the light of who was responsible for the story.

Seitz, Don Carlos. *Joseph Pulitzer: His Life and Letters*. Whitefish, Mont.: Kessinger, 2004. Examines Pulitzer's career, his beliefs about journalism and journalists' responsibilities, his efforts to raise the standards of journalism, and his establishment of the Pulitzer Prize.

—*Shawncey Webb*

See also: Billy Cannon; Susanna Mildred Hill; Megan Louise Ireland; Clifford Irving; Victor Lustig; Joseph Weil.

D. B. Cooper

American skyjacker

Born: Mid-1920's; place unknown

Died: Possibly November 24, 1971; Southwest Washington

Also known as: Dan Cooper

Cause of notoriety: Cooper carried a bomb on board a passenger airliner; upon his threat to detonate it he was given money, with which he escaped midair, never to be caught.

Active: November 24, 1971

Locale: Oregon and Washington State

Early Life

Because D. B. Cooper (KEW-puhr) was never caught or positively identified, information on his early life or why he committed his crime is not available.

Criminal Career

On November 24, 1971, a man identifying himself as Dan Cooper entered the Portland International Airport in Oregon. Witnesses would later describe him as slender, about forty-five years of age, of medium height, and dressed in a dark suit with a pearl tiepin. He purchased a ticket for Northwest-Orient Airlines flight 305 to Seattle, scheduled to leave at 4:35 p.m. Shortly after takeoff, Cooper summoned flight attendant Florence Schaffner and handed her a note that said he had a bomb in his briefcase. Cooper's demands for $200,000 in cash and four parachutes equipped with manual ripcords were forwarded to authorities by the pilot, Captain William Scott.

When the plane landed at Seattle-Tacoma International Airport, Cooper released the passengers in exchange for the parachutes and money, which amounted to twenty-one pounds of twenty-dollar bills. Cooper kept the crew as hostages. He then ordered Scott to fly the plane to Mexico City but not to exceed 10,000 feet in altitude or 150 knots airspeed. The plane could not reach Mexico City, so Cooper agreed to Scott's request to refuel in Reno, Nevada. Shadowed by three U.S. Air Force aircraft, Scott turned the plane toward Reno. At 8:24 p.m., over the wilderness of Washington and Oregon, Cooper let down the plane's aft stairway and parachuted into the night. The tailing Air Force pilots did not observe Cooper's parachute escape. When the plane landed in Reno, Cooper, two of the parachutes, and the money were gone.

In the following days, the Federal Bureau of Investigation (FBI) conducted an extensive ground search for Cooper. In the process, the skyjacker's name became irrevocably changed. Questioning suspects with similar names, the FBI interviewed someone named D. B. Cooper. He had no connection to the crime, but in the subsequent news reporting "Dan" Cooper became known as

"D. B." Cooper. Despite an intense eighteen-day manhunt and months of follow-up searches, authorities failed to locate either the skyjacker or the money. Although Cooper left fingerprints behind, the FBI could not find a match.

In subsequent years, the FBI investigated many leads, but all proved fruitless. In 1979, fifty-eight hundred dollars of the ransom money was unearthed near the Columbia River, suggesting that Cooper made it to the ground intact. Whether he lived has remained under speculation. Cooper parachuted wearing the clothes that he wore onto the aircraft, so investigators doubted he survived the frigid descent or the wilderness conditions when he landed. Moreover, no more ransom money has resurfaced, suggesting that Cooper did not live to spend the money. Some researchers, however, believe that he survived, suggesting that Cooper carried additional clothing with him in his briefcase. Supporting this theory, Cooper left behind his tie and its distinctive pearl tiepin, implying that he changed his attire before escaping.

Four months after Cooper's crime, a nearly identical skyjacking occurred in California. An FBI investigation led to Richard McCoy, a former Green Beret. In McCoy's home, police found money from the California skyjacking. McCoy received a forty-five-year prison sentence, but he escaped and later died in a shoot-out with police in 1974. The similarity of the skyjackings convinced many investigators that McCoy was D. B. Cooper.

Deathbed Confession

"I'm Dan Cooper," said Duane Weber to his wife as he lay dying in a Florida hospital in 1995. Jo had been married to the antiques dealer for seventeen years, yet she had no idea what he was talking about. Duane had always been secretive about his past. "Oh, let it die with me," he told her, apparently annoyed at her puzzlement.

A year later, Jo learned from a library book that "Dan Cooper" was the name used by an airline hijacker in 1971; he was better known as D. B. Cooper. The book also gave the hijacker's description: mid-forties, six feet tall, 170 pounds, black hair, and a chain-smoking bourbon drinker. In 1971, Jo remembered, Weber had been black-haired, an inch taller than six feet, 185 pounds, and a chain-smoking bourbon drinker. Moreover, the match between the composite sketch of the hijacker made by the Federal Bureau of Investigation (FBI) and a photo of her husband was striking. What she really found strange, however, was a pencil notation in the book. It appeared to be in her husband's handwriting, and it named the Washington town where the placard from the rear ramp of the Northwest-Orient Airlines jet had landed.

Then Jo recalled certain items and incidents from Duane's life that seemed to relate to the Cooper hijacking: a white bag the couple owned that matched the description of the canvas bag in which the $200,000 ransom was stowed; a mysterious Northwest ticket stub for a Seattle-Portland flight that her husband disclaimed as unimportant but later disappeared; and another of Duane's deathbed comments, this one referring to a bucket in which he had buried $173,000. Above all, Jo particularly recalled a 1979 vacation to Washington State. They stopped by the Columbia River not far from Portland, and her husband continued to the river edge by himself. Was he searching for something? In the same area, a boy found nearly $5,800 of the ransom money four months later.

All that was uncovered that might relate the case to Duane was considered circumstantial evidence, and the FBI remained skeptical. The FBI did compare Duane's fingerprints with the sixty-six unidentified fingerprints taken from the hijacked plane. There was no match; however, the FBI was unclear that any of the prints came from "Dan Cooper" in the first place. While the former lead agent in the case was intrigued, the FBI dropped the Weber investigation in 1998 for lack of solid evidence; nonetheless, Duane remained among the most likely of several candidate Coopers.

Source: Cooper quoted in *U.S. News and World Report*, July 24, 2000.

Impact

D. B. Cooper's audacious act set off a wave of copycat crimes, most of which failed miserably. Cooper's exploits did demonstrate, however, the woeful state of U.S. airport security, which increased dramatically afterward. Perpetuating Cooper's fame, a device that became known as the Cooper vane was subsequently added to all Boeing 727-model craft to prevent the rear door from opening while in flight.

Further Reading

Calame, Russell, and Bernie Rhodes. *D. B. Cooper: The Real McCoy*. Salt Lake City: University of Utah Press, 1991. Trying to put the Cooper case to rest, Calame, an FBI agent, claims that convicted skyjacker Richard McCoy was D. B. Cooper.

Himmelsbach, Ralph P., and Thomas K. Worcester. *Norjak: The Investigation of D. B. Cooper*. West

Linn, Oreg.: Norjak Project, 1986. Written by the FBI agent in charge of the Cooper investigation, this book discredits many of the Cooper theories.

Tosaw, Richard T. *D. B. Cooper: Dead or Alive?* Ceres, Calif.: Torsaw, 1984. Written by another FBI investigator, the book postulates that Cooper drowned in the Columbia River, which explains the found money and the fact that his body and parachutes were never recovered.

—*Steven J. Ramold*

See also: Samuel Joseph Byck; Theodore Kaczynski; Ilich Ramírez Sánchez.

Charlotte Corday

French assassin

Born: July 27, 1768; farm of Ronceray, Normandy, France
Died: July 17, 1793; Paris, France
Also known as: Marie-Anne Charlotte de Corday d'Armont (birth name); Angel of Anger; Angel of Justice; Angel of Assassination
Major offense: Murder of French revolutionist Jean-Paul Marat
Active: July 13, 1793
Locale: Paris, France
Sentence: Execution by guillotine

Early Life

Charlotte Corday (SHARH-laht kohr-DAY) was born into minor Norman nobility, the second of four children of Jacques François de Corday and Charlotte-Marie Gaultier des Authieux. Corday's father was a descendant of the dramatist Pierre Corneille: He was the great-grandson of Marie Corneille, the sister of Corneille. The day after Corday's birth, she was baptized in the nearby Church of Saint-Saturnin de Lignerits.

The family lived in several places in Normandy when Corday was a child. At age eight, she moved in with her uncle, Charles Adrien de Corday, a parish priest and later, an abbot. In 1782, she entered the girls' boarding school of l'Abbaye aux Dames in Caen. There, she became interested in politics. She was naturally conservative and religious but believed that the power of the king should be limited. When revolutionary pressures closed l'Abbaye aux Dames in 1791, Corday moved in with a cousin at 148 rue St.-Jean in Caen.

Criminal Career

Before the French Revolution (1789-1799), Jean-Paul Marat was a physician, scientist, philosopher, and friend of Benjamin Franklin. In September, 1789, he began

Charlotte Corday, assassin of Jean-Paul Marat, in a famous painting from 1860.

publishing an underground revolutionary journal called *L'Ami du Peuple* (friend of the people); he soon was also known as the Friend of the People. A hateful, spiteful man, his writings were full of vitriol toward anyone connected with the monarchy. The oppressed lower classes, the sansculottes, loved him.

The Girondins were moderate republicans who supported a constitutional monarchy. Their implacable enemies were the Montagnards—the radical left faction consisting mainly of the Cordeliers, led by Marat and Georges Danton—and the Jacobins, led by Robespierre. Marat especially detested the Girondins, seeing them as royalist appeasers and counterrevolutionaries, all deserving the guillotine.

By 1792, Corday was an avowed Girondin. When the sansculottes and Montagnards succeeded in overthrowing the Girondins on June 2, 1793, she decided to act. She blamed all that had gone wrong during the revolution on Marat's exhortations to violence. On July 9, she took the mail coach from Caen to Paris and got a room at the Hôtel de Providence, where she wrote her manifesto *Adresse aux Français amis des lois et de la paix* (address to the French people, friends of law and peace), explaining what she was about to do and why. On July 13, after buying a knife at a kiosk in the Palais-Royal, Corday gained admission to Marat's home at 30 rue des Cordeliers by a ruse, promising to betray Girondins from Caen. Since Caen was known as a hotbed of Girondist sentiment, Marat was eager for this information. He suffered from seborrheic dermatitis, a painful skin condition that drove him to spend most of his time in the bathtub. She found him there and stabbed him once in the heart. Marat's death cries brought help. She was instantly arrested without resistance.

Legal Action and Outcome

On the morning of July 17, Corday was brought to the Palais de Justice for trial. Referring to July 13 as the Day of the Preparation of Peace, she calmly admitted the murder, insisting that she had acted alone, that she had killed one man to save one hundred thousand, that she had been a republican before the revolution, and that she never lacked the will or energy to do what was morally correct and honorable. She went to the guillotine that evening, believing that she had righted a great wrong and that history would judge her favorably.

Impact

How one regards Charlotte Corday is a function of one's own political views. Sympathizers with Marat see her as a reactionary villain; those who consider Marat a monster admire her as a courageous tyrannicide. Monarchists in general and the British in particular glorified her immediately after her death. They compared her with the biblical Judith of Bethulia, who used her beauty to gain audience with the invading Assyrian general Holofernes, then got him drunk and killed him, becoming a heroine to the oppressed Hebrews. Corday herself was inspired by the story of Judith.

Corday's admirers called her the Angel of Anger, the Angel of Justice, the Angel of Assassination, and other names. German revoltionary Adam Lux deemed her more gallant than Brutus, the murderer of Julius Caesar. Lux died on the guillotine in November, 1793, for writing a pamphlet praising Corday. Throughout the nineteenth century, the English-speaking world saw her as essentially heroic. Thomas Carlyle wrote in his monumental *The French Revolution* (1837) that Marat was "squalid" but that Corday apparently did not foresee that killing him would make him a martyr, in turn having the undesired effect of emboldening his allies and making the Reign of Terror even worse.

Further Reading

Debriffe, Martial, ed. *Charlotte Corday*. Paris: France-Empire, 2005. One of a stream of French tributes to Corday that includes works by such notables as Alphonse de Lamartine, Jules Michelet, and André Chénier.

Gelbart, Nina Rattner. "The Blonding of Charlotte Corday." *Eighteenth-Century Studies*. 38, no. 1 (Fall, 2004): 201-221. Interesting speculation on why Corday's admirers persist in describing her as blond, even though her hair was brown.

_______. "Death in the Bathtub: Charlotte Corday and Jean-Paul Marat." In *The Human Tradition in Modern France*, edited by K. Steven Vincent and Alison Klairmont-Lingo. Wilmington, Del.: SR Books, 2000. Pages 17-32 provide a study of contemporary attitudes toward Corday, especially in view of her gender.

Gottschalk, Louis R. *Jean Paul Marat: A Study in Radicalism.* Chicago: University of Chicago Press, 1967. An authoritative analysis of Corday's victim, which provides a deeper understanding of why she chose Marat as a target.

Montfort, Catherine R. "For the Defense: Charlotte Corday's Letters from Prison." *Studies on Voltaire and the Eighteeneth Century* 329 (1995): 235-247. A sympathetic view of Corday's last hours.

Scherr, Marie. *Charlotte Corday and Certain Men of the Revolutionary Torment*. New York: AMS Press, 1970. Classic study of the Girondist faction and its enemies, with focus on Corday, Marat, Danton, and Robespierre.

Shearing, Joseph. *The Angel of the Assassination: Marie-Charlotte de Corday d'Armont, Jean-Paul Marat, Jean-Adam Lux: A Study of Three Disciples of Jean-Jacques Rousseau*. New York: H. Smith and R. Haas, 1935. Written by Marjorie Bowen under the pseudonym Joseph Shearing, this book remains a standard about Corday.

—*Eric v.d. Luft*

See also: Marie-Antoinette; Jean-Paul Marat; Robespierre.

Frank Costello

Italian American Mafia kingpin

Born: January 26, 1891; Lauropoli, Calabria, Italy
Died: February 18, 1973; New York, New York
Also known as: Francesco Castiglia (birth name); Prime Minister of the Mob
Major offenses: Contempt of Congress and tax evasion
Active: 1920's-1973
Locale: United States, mainly New York, New York
Sentence: Eighteen months' imprisonment for contempt of Congress, of which he served fourteen months; five years' imprisonment for tax evasion, of which he served forty-two months

Early Life

Frank Costello (caws-TEHL-oh) was born Francesco Castiglia in Italy, and at the age of four years, he sailed to the United States, carried by his mother in a large cooking pot. He despised his father's acceptance of poverty in their East Harlem ghetto, so he left school in the fifth grade and turned to various street crimes: purse-snatching, petty theft, and rifling vending machines. One day, in the balcony of a film theater, he met Lucky Luciano; both boys were kicked out of the theater for throwing trash at the audience below.

Criminal Career

In 1914, Costello, a Roman Catholic, met and married a Jewish girl, Loretta Geigerman. A year later, he was sentenced to one year in prison for carrying a concealed weapon. Thereafter, he resolved to work with persuasion rather than with weapons and used his skill at meeting the right people to work in his favor. His circle of close acquaintances included Owney Madden, a beer baron who became a celebrity gangster, and Arnold Rothstein, a businessman who reputedly fixed the 1919 World Series. Costello also worked with other known mobsters, including Meyer Lansky, Bugsy Siegel, Vito Genovese, Vincent Alo, Joseph Doto (better known as Joe Adonis), and William Vincent Dwyer, who was later elected mayor of New York.

During Prohibition, Costello, working in partnership with Lansky under Luciano's leadership, made a fortune in bootlegging with such daring tactics as using seaplanes to keep hijackers away from his boats filled with alcohol. However, he was soon arrested and charged with organizing a multimillion-dollar liquor ring and bribing the coastguard to let liquor into the country. The jury in this case was hung, and Costello went free on January 20, 1927.

After Prohibition, Costello focused on slot machines. When Mayor Fiorello La Guardia attempted to prosecute Costello's operation, Costello moved it to New Orleans, where it found tacit protection from Senator Huey Long, the former governor of Louisiana. Costello poured his profits into joint ventures with friends in order to build swanky nightclubs and casinos in New York and Florida, as well as regional vice centers around the country. Later, along with Luciano and Lansky, Costello invested heavily in Siegel's dream to build the casino capital of the world in Las Vegas, Nevada, where gambling was legal.

Costello inherited valuable connections with Democratic politicians in New York from Rothstein, who was killed in 1928. Because Costello's Mafia niche was his skill with political influence, his friends counted on him to protect their illegal activities by bribing police, politicians, and judges. He accompanied Jimmy Hines, Manhattan's Democratic party boss, to the Democratic National Convention, where he helped Franklin D. Roosevelt win the presidential nomination in 1932.

Costello wielded enormous political influence during the 1930's and 1940's. Legend has it that, during this period, no judge reached the bench in New York without Costello's approval. In 1940, Costello used his political influence to arrange a payoff to police in exchange for silencing a witness who had turned into an informer. Abe "Kid Twist" Reles began telling authorities what he knew about forty-nine mob killings. However, while in police custody, Reles mysteriously fell to his death from a hotel window.

In 1934, after mob leader Luciano was jailed and left Genovese in charge as his underboss, Genovese fled to avoid prosecution for the murder of mobster Ferdinand Boccia. Captured by Army officers in Italy, Genovese was returned to the United States after World War II. However, before trial, the key witness against him was poisoned in his prison cell, and Genovese was released on June 11, 1946. Costello had served as "caretaker" while Genovese was away, but Genovese began to resume power upon his return, a move contested by Costello. The power struggle between the men had repercussions more than a decade later, when Genovese's bodyguard, Vincent Gigante, shot Costello at point-blank range on May 2, 1957. The bullet grazed Costello's skull but did not kill him. True to the Mafia code, Costello refused to identify his assailant in court.

Legal Action And Outcome

During the 1950's, Costello was in and out of courtrooms and jails. He was subpoenaed to appear before the Kefauver Committee investigations into organized crime in March, 1951. However, his reluctance to answer questions before the Senate committee led both to his conviction of contempt of the Senate and to a sentence of eighteen months in prison; he served fourteen months. In April, 1954, Costello was convicted of evading federal tax on $51,095 income. He served forty-two months of a five-year sentence.

Costello faced more trouble in 1957 after police—investigating the attempt on Costello's life by Gigante—found a note in Costello's coat pocket that proved the mob was behind the buildup of Las Vegas. Costello was sent to prison for fifteen days for contempt of court for refusing to answer questions about the murder attempt.

Lengthy legal maneuvers to deport Costello came to a surprising end in February, 1961, when the United States Supreme Court overturned his deportation order. The high council of the American Mafia then allowed Costello to take most of his money into retirement with his wife on Long Island.

Impact

With his dapper dress, dignified bearing, and diplomatic aplomb, Frank Costello brought to organized crime more than a veneer of civility. To a degree, he was able to suppress violence and prevent Las Vegas and New York from becoming violent cities, as Chicago had become. Known as the Prime Minister of the Mob, he was a peacemaker who reconciled opposing factions, adjudicated disputes, and brought about significant results.

Costello was, foremost, a bridge between the underworld and the political powers of his era. Despite his penchant for crime, he was a practical man who took a long-range view of what needed to be accomplished. He saw that both bootlegging and gambling supplied public demands, which were soon to be declared legal and operated as government monopolies.

At a time when the Mafia was abandoning its old ways and reorganizing itself according to principles of business management, Costello perfected the art of political corruption. A man with old-fashioned moral values, he understood the benefits and detractions of bribery. He shunned drug dealing and ordered his associates not to engage in it. Because he hated fascism, he supported Roosevelt and other politicians who waged war against Adolf Hitler and Benito Mussolini. Likewise, because he hated bigotry, he supported politicians who respected diversity and who put equality on the national agenda.

Further Reading

Katz, Leonard. *Uncle Frank: The Biography of Frank Costello*. New York: Drake, 1973. A sympathetic portrait drawn principally from published accounts and interviews with people who knew Costello. Photographs and index are included.

Raab, Selwyn. *Five Families*. New York: St. Martin's Press, 2005. Definitive history of the rise and fall of New York's most powerful mobs, written by a *New York Times* reporter.

Reppetto, Thomas. *American Mafia*. New York: Holt, 2004. A chronicle of the Mafia's rise to power in the United States from 1890 to 1951. Includes an excellent bibliography.

—*John L. McLean*

See also: Joe Adonis; Vito Genovese; Meyer Lansky; Huey Long; Lucky Luciano; Arnold Rothstein; Bugsy Siegel.

Charles E. Coughlin

Canadian Roman Catholic priest, radio broadcaster, and Nazi sympathizer

Born: October 25, 1891; Hamilton, Ontario, Canada
Died: October 27, 1979; Birmingham, Michigan
Also known as: Charles Edward Coughlin (full name); Father Coughlin; Radio Priest
Cause of notoriety: Coughlin was a Catholic priest who used radio to communicate his pro-Nazi, anti-Semitic message to his followers during the Great Depression.
Active: 1930's
Locale: United States

Early Life

Charles Edward Coughlin was the only child of Thomas and Melia Coughlin. His mother encouraged her son to enter the priesthood. Following his mother's wishes, Coughlin entered St. Basil's Seminary after his graduation from St. Michael's College in Toronto. After being ordained on June 29, 1916, he became a professor at Assumption College in Windsor, Ontario. In 1923, Coughlin, dissatisfied with the vows of poverty required by the Basilian Order, left Assumption College and accepted a position as an assistant pastor at St. Leo's Cathedral in Detroit, Michigan. After assisting in several parishes in the Detroit area, Michael Gallagher, the Catholic bishop of Detroit, offered Coughlin a position as head pastor of a small church in Royal Oak, Michigan, a working-class suburb of Detroit. At the time, the Shrine of the Little Flower congregation consisted of twenty-five families. Coughlin, a skilled orator, began to generate support and money for his church by broadcasting his sermons over a local radio station. His first broadcast was on October 3, 1926. Initially, his talks targeted children; however, as his reputation and popularity grew, Coughlin began to express his views on politics.

Father Coughlin's Credos

During an radio broadcast on November 11, 1934, Father Coughlin listed his tenets for social justice:

1. I believe in liberty of conscience and liberty of education, not permitting the state to dictate either my worship to my God or my chosen avocation in life.
2. I believe that every citizen willing to work and capable of working shall receive a just, living, annual wage which will enable him both to maintain and educate his family according to the standards of American decency.
3. I believe in nationalizing those public resources which by their very nature are too important to be held in the control of private individuals.
4. I believe in private ownership of all other property.
5. I believe in upholding the right to private property but in controlling it for the public good.
6. I believe in the abolition of the privately owned Federal Reserve Banking system and in the establishment of a Government owned Central Bank.
7. I believe in rescuing from the hands of private owners the right to coin and regulate the value of money, which right must be restored to Congress, where it belongs.
8. I believe that one of the chief duties of this government owned Central Bank is to maintain the cost of living on an even keel, and arrange for the repayment of dollar debts with equal value dollars.
9. I believe in the cost of production plus a fair profit for the farmer.
10. I believe not only in the right of the laboring man to organize in unions but also in the duty of the Government, which that laboring man supports, to protect these organizations against the vested interests of wealth and of intellect.
11. I believe in the recall of all non-productive bonds and therefore in the alleviation of taxation.
12. I believe in the abolition of tax-exempt bonds.
13. I believe in broadening the base of taxation according to the principles of ownership and the capacity to pay.
14. I believe in the simplification of government and the further lifting of crushing taxation from the slender revenues of the laboring class.
15. I believe that, in the event of a war for the defense of our nation and its liberties, there shall be a conscription of wealth as well as a conscription of men.
16. I believe in preferring the sanctity of human rights to the sanctity of property rights; for the chief concern of government shall be for the poor because, as it is witnessed, the rich have ample means of their own to care for themselves.

Broadcasting Career

By 1930, the Columbia Broadcasting System (CBS) network was playing Father Coughlin's radio program throughout the United States. As a result of this exposure, Father Coughlin's popularity and reputation grew, and within a year he was receiving an estimated eighty thousand letters a week from supporters. At first, Coughlin's political attachés focused on communism and the Soviet Union. He characterized communism as antifamily since the Soviet Union had made divorce easy and asserted that these ideas were spreading to the United States. Many of Coughlin's assertions were contradictory. While he warned about the dangers of the concentration of wealth in the hands of the few, he also warned of the dangers of socialism and communism. When he began to attack President Herbert Hoover too harshly, CBS refused to renew his contract. Coughlin then organized his own radio network, which eventually grew to more than thirty stations nationwide.

In 1932, Coughlin was a staunch supporter of Franklin Delano Roosevelt for president and supported Roosevelt's New Deal; however, within a few years, Coughlin became disillusioned with the slow process of reform. He began to attack Roosevelt and began to refer to him as a liar and as "double-crossing Roosevelt."

In November, 1934, Coughlin established the National Union for Social Justice. The purpose of the organization was to affirm the sanctity of private property. It advocated monetary reform and the replacement of the gold standard with the silver standard.

In 1936, Father Coughlin helped form a third party, the Union Party, which nominated North Dakota congressman William Lemke for president. Coughlin said he would retire if Lemke did not receive 9,000,000 votes. When Lemke received only 900,000 votes, Coughlin briefly retired; however, he resumed his broadcasts in 1937.

When Father Coughlin returned to radio, his tone was more radical. He began to express sympathy for the fascist policies of German leader Adolf Hitler and Italian leader Benito Mussolini and claimed that Roosevelt's New Deal was a communist conspiracy. Coughlin became increasingly anti-Semitic and claimed that Jewish manipulation of the economy was responsible for the Great Depression.

As Europe moved toward war, Coughlin advocated isolationism and claimed that Jewish financiers were behind efforts to involve the United States in the war. In 1938, his magazine *Social Justice*, printed *The Protocols of the Elders of Zion*, a forged document that claimed to be the minutes of Jewish leaders plotting to take over the world.

Following U.S. entry into World War II, a federal grand jury indictment was directed at Coughlin and his operations, and he was stripped of his second-class mailing privileges by the United States government. In addition, the bishop in Detroit ordered Coughlin to stop his radio broadcasts and to return to his duties as a parish priest. Father Coughlin remained as the pastor of the Shrine of the Little Flower until his retirement in 1966. He died in 1979.

Impact

Father Charles E. Coughlin (KAHG-lihn) was the forerunner of modern televangelists. He was the first religious leader to use the electronic media to communicate with supporters. Although Coughlin's original message was religious, he moved into the political world during the Great Depression. At its peak, his radio program reached more than thirty million listeners a week. Through his broadcasts, Father Coughlin became the most visible member of the radical right in America during the 1930's. He is considered one of the major political demagogues of the twentieth century even though he never served in an elected position.

Further Reading

Brinkley, Alan. *Voices of Protest: Huey Long, Father Coughlin, and the Great Depression*. New York: Alfred A. Knopf, 1983. An excellent volume that analyzes two major demagogues of the 1930's, Huey Long and Charles Coughlin, within the context of Depression-era politics in America.

Carpenter, Ronald H. *Father Charles E. Coughlin: Surrogate Spokesman for the Disaffected*. Westport, Conn.: Greenwood Press, 1998. This book is part of the Great American Orators series. It includes copies of some of Coughlin's speeches, and it analyzes Coughlin's rhetoric and his appeal to disaffected Americans during the Depression.

Warren, Donald. *Radio Priest: Charles Coughlin, the Father of Hate Radio*. New York: Free Press, 1996. A biography of Coughlin that shows the link between Coughlin's radio talk show and contemporary conservative radio talk shows.

—William V. Moore

See also: Mildred Gillars; William Joyce; Tokyo Rose.

Bettino Craxi

Italian Socialist Party chairman (1976-1993); prime minister of Italy (1983-1987)

Born: February 24, 1934; Milan, Italy
Died: January 19, 2000; Hammamet, Tunisia
Also known as: Benedetto Craxi (full name); Ghino di Tacco
Major offenses: Bribery and corruption
Active: 1979-1993
Locale: Milan and Rome, Italy
Sentence: Tried in absentia and convicted to five years' imprisonment; fled to Tunisia to avoid jail time

Early Life

The son of a socialist lawyer, Bettino Craxi (beht-TEE-noh KRAHK-see) received an antifascist upbringing. From childhood, he took an active part in Socialist Party campaigns. Not given to scholarly pursuits, Craxi managed to pass the admission test to university; he left its law school not long afterward. A student trip to Prague converted Craxi into a fervent anticommunist, and he immediately rededicated himself to Socialist Party work, thereby gaining party office. In that capacity, he helped eliminate the communist, left-leaning wing of his party and later allied it with the capitalist forces of northern Italy.

Political and Criminal Career

Craxi was appointed the head of the Socialist Party in 1976, a position in which he served until 1993. A decade earlier, Craxi effected a historical coup. The collapse of the government and the resulting political paralysis enabled the first Socialist president of Italy, Alessandro (Sandro) Pertini, to charge Craxi with forming a coalition government, which Craxi succeeded in doing. His vigor, quasidictatorial leadership of the party, maltreatment of his enemies, badgering public speeches, and grandstanding appearances on television, however, created a backlash among the public and his fellow politicians.

The 1985 hijacking of the *Achille Lauro* cruise ship proved to be the most significant international event of Craxi's premiership. Three Arab men representing the Palestine Liberation Front (PLF) took control of the ship, held all passengers hostage, and murdered a Jewish American man, Leon Klinghoffer, who was confined to a wheelchair. Craxi maintained that Italian jurisdiction prevented him from handing over the terrorists to the United States, who wanted the men because of Klinghoffer's murder. In part because Craxi had been supporting fellow socialist leaders in the Arab-Muslim world, he arranged to fly the perpetrators to Africa in order to stand trial there. American president Ronald Reagan's response was to order U.S. fighter jets to force the Italian plane to the ground at the U.S. military base in Sicily. Incensed by this infraction of Italian sovereignty, Craxi had Italian troops surround the base. Reagan initially backed down, a move that raised Craxi's standing in the Muslim world and in some Western countries. However, shortly thereafter, Western fear of terrorism, renewed pro-American sentiment, and early signs of Craxi's corruption initiated Craxi's downfall.

In the 1990's, judges in Milan began to investigate political party financing in an initiative called *Mani pulite* (Italian for "clean hands"). Craxi quickly became a target of the investigation in part because of his residence in an

Bettino Craxi. (AP/Wide World Photos)

expensive Rome hotel and his ownership of a villa in Tunisia. The investigation also alleged that Craxi used personal acquaintance rather than merit to appoint political colleagues and granted political favors to people, especially within the media. Any support that Craxi had maintained to that point withered, and he was publicly accused of corruption and bribery.

Legal Action and Outcome

Brought up on corruption charges in 1992, Craxi delivered a notorious speech in parliament, his last, admitting that he had indeed accepted illegal contributions but maintained that every other member of the Chamber of Deputies had also done so. In effect, he did not proclaim himself innocent but pointed out that all politicians were guilty of corruption. Craxi challenged any fellow legislator who had not accepted bribes to stand up. Nobody did.

Craxi was tried for bribery and corruption in 1993 and sentenced in absentia to a prison term of five years. He escaped imprisonment by fleeing to his villa in Tunisia in 1994, where, under the protection of socialist dictator Ben Ali, he remained until his death from complications of diabetes in January, 2000.

Impact

Bettino Craxi was the longest governing post-World War II Italian prime minister. He became the most visible symbol of a widespread system of political corruption, which came to be known as *tagentopoli* (Italian for "bribeville"). Although he accomplished many of his goals during his tenure—including attaining Group 7 (G7) membership for Italy and renegotiating Benito Mussolini's 1929 concordat with the Vatican, thereby removing Roman Catholicism as the official state religion—Craxi earned the distrust and enmity of Italians both for damaging relations with the United States during the *Achille Lauro* incident and for his blatant corruption.

Further Reading

Bufacchi, Vittorio, and Simon Burgess. *Italy Since 1989: Events and Interpretations*. New York: St. Martin's Press, 1998. Chapter 4 illuminates the culture of big-business bribery in northern Italy, particularly within Italy's business center, Milan.

Di Scala, Spencer M. *Renewing Italian Socialism: Nenni to Craxi*. New York: Oxford University Press, 1988. Contains many references to Craxi, including an authoritative description of the reformation of his party and his personal influence on its electoral gains, enabling his rise to power.

Ginsborg, Paul. *A History of Contemporary Italy*. London: Macmillan, 1990. Provides good context for the years of Craxi's rule. Includes an excellent bibliography.

_______. *Italy and Its Discontents: Family, Civil Society, State, 1980-2001*. New York: Palgrave Macmillan, 2003. Another good contextual study of the years surrounding Craxi's rise to and fall from political prominence.

—Robert B. Youngblood

See also: Benito Mussolini.

Aleister Crowley

British occultist

Born: October 12, 1875; Leamington, Warwickshire, England

Died: December 1, 1947; Hastings, England

Also known as: Edward Alexander Crowley (full name); Great Beast; 666; Wickedest Man in the World

Cause of notoriety: Crowley, a controversial author and a founder of mystic and magic occult philosophies, was also known for his hedonism and sexual adventurism.

Active: 1890-1947

Locale: England

Early Life

Edward Alexander Crowley (KROW-lee) was born in 1875 to Edward and Emily Crowley and was raised in a strict environment influenced by staunch Victorian and religious principles. His father, Edward, was a successful brewer who later became a staunch preacher before passing away when Crowley was eleven years old. Crowley was a rebellious and oppositional child who resisted the strict religious practices of his parents by developing a deep skepticism of religious faith. He reportedly tortured a cat and was sexually active with older women while still a teenager. His antisocial behavior was severe enough that his nickname, the Great Beast (a biblical reference to the anti-Christ), was supposedly given to him by his own dismayed mother. This moniker was later used by Crowley himself.

Occultist Career

While at Cambridge University, Crowley deepened his philosophy of skepticism and distrust of conventional morality and created his own occult belief system based on a combination of Western secret occult societies and some of the Eastern mystic traditions. During this time, he pursued wide-ranging sexual activities with both men and women, although he tried to keep his homosexuality a secret. He also began his prolific writing career and authored a number of homoerotic and sexually charged poems, often under pseudonyms. These works gained notoriety and referenced necrophilia, bestiality, and other deviant acts. He developed an interest in mountain climbing and continued to build a lifestyle and belief system that comprised free will, hedonism, and scientific skepticism tinged with mystical elements.

At the age of twenty-three, Crowley joined a magic-mystic oriented society called the Hermetic Order of the Golden Dawn. This organization represented a mix of numerology, astrology, and other beliefs and rites associated with magic. Crowley later left the society because of bitter disputes with its leadership over various issues, including an alleged copyright dispute over a particular ritual that Crowley supposedly appropriated from its originator.

Crowley continued his search for spiritual or mystical meanings and traveled the globe. He married his wife Rose in 1893, and she joined him in his travels. During this time, he wrote much of his influential work, including *Book of the Law*, which was published posthumously in 1973. He claimed to have transcribed this work, with the assistance of Rose, from the Egyptian god Horus (also called Aiwass). It was this book that contained the phrase "Do what thou wilt shall be the whole of the law," which became the foundation of a mystic-spiritual roadmap later known as Thelema. "Do what thou wilt" became closely associated with the notorious hedonism of Crowley, although some defenders believe that it has a higher meaning that refers to the self-actualized will of enlightened people.

According to Crowley, his *Book of the Law* (which he maintained he only channeled from beyond and did not truly author) ushered in a new magical age based upon the law of Thelema. Crowley formed the Astrum Argentium (the Silver Star) to propagate his philosophy.

Do What Thou Wilt

In The Book of the Law *(written in 1904 but published posthumously in 1976), which Aleister Crowley claimed to have transcribed from the Egyptian god Horus, he outlined the foundation of a mystic-spiritual new age based on "Thelema":*

39. The word of the Law is Thelema.
40. Who calls us Thelemites will do no wrong, if he look but close into the word. For there are therein Three Grades, the Hermit, and the Lover, and the man of Earth. Do what thou wilt shall be the whole of the Law.
41. The word of Sin is Restriction. O man! refuse not thy wife, if she will! O lover, if thou wilt, depart! There is no bond that can unite the divided but love: all else is a curse. Accursed! Accursed be it to the aeons! Hell.
42. Let it be that state of manyhood bound and loathing. So with thy all; thou hast no right but to do thy will.
43. Do that, and no other shall say nay.
44. For pure will, unassuaged of purpose, delivered from the lust of result, is every way perfect.
45. The Perfect and the Perfect are one Perfect and not two; nay, are none! . . .
48. My prophet is a fool with his one, one, one; are not they the Ox, and none by the Book? . . .
72. I am the Lord of the Double Wand of Power; the wand of the Force of Coph Nia—but my left hand is empty, for I have crushed an Universe; & nought remains.
73. Paste the sheets from right to left and from top to bottom: then behold!
74. There is a splendour in my name hidden and glorious, as the sun of midnight is ever the son.
75. The ending of the words is the Word Abrahadabra.

The comment: Do what thou wilt shall be the whole of the Law. The study of this Book is forbidden. It is wise to destroy this copy after the first reading. Whosoever disregards this does so at his own risk and peril. These are most dire. Those who discuss the contents of this Book are to be shunned by all, as centres of pestilence. All questions of the Law are to be decided only by appeal to my writings, each for himself. There is no law beyond Do what thou wilt. Love is the law, love under will. The priest of the princes, Ankh-f-n-khonsu.

In 1910, Crowley joined and later took on a leadership role with the Ordo Templi Orientis—another secret, ritual-based society that might have influenced the future Scientology founder L. Ron Hubbard.

Aside from promulgation of his ideas and beliefs about human existence, magic (which he spelled "magick" to differentiate it from stage magic), and free will, Crowley invited, and possibly enjoyed, notoriety for other behaviors. He set up the Abbey of Thelema, in Cefalu, Sicily, members of which were rumored to engage in drug abuse, sexual rituals, and animal sacrifices. The rumors surrounding the Abbey led to his expulsion from Italy. During World War I, he penned pro-German propaganda, which he later claimed was really part of a patriotic effort on his part to discredit the Germans. His interpersonal style was often described as arrogant, self-aggrandizing, and abusive, which undoubtedly added to his unsavory reputation among many people.

Despite his notoriety and prolific writings, Crowley died in poverty in 1947. Many of his works were self-published and quickly banned. His addiction to heroin and an unsuccessful lawsuit in 1934 also served to drain his funds. It has been reported that his last words were "I am perplexed," although this is not substantiated by a mistress who was with him at the time of his death.

Impact

Aleister Crowley was certainly influential within the mystic-magick subcultures, and many of his written works became available only after his death. Aside from his mystical philosophical base of influence stemming from his activities and writings associated with the Astrum Argentium and the Ordo Templi Orientis, one can find references to Crowley in the popular culture. His face appears among the multitude on the Beatles' *Sergeant Pepper's Lonely Hearts Club Band* album cover. Hard metal musician Ozzy Osbourne wrote a song about him, and Jimmy Page, the guitarist for the British band Led Zeppelin, is reported to have been interested by Crowley's work and bought a rural house once owned by the occultist.

In general, Crowley's massive output of writings (often poetic, symbolic, or obscure while peppered with verbose sexual references), combined with his overall unconventional behavior, generated to some an image of Crowley as a pioneer. Crowley's supporters consider him a feminist (despite his systematic womanizing) and an advocate of human freedom of will, while others admire him as a nonconforming free spirit with deep mystical insights. Detractors of Crowley call him a self-publicizing charlatan, a misogynist, and a manipulative abuser of his followers. Regardless of one's opinion of Crowley, it is clear that his controversial artistic and philosophical tenor influenced current ideas about the occult and secret societies.

Further Reading

Crowley, Aleister, John Symonds, and Kenneth Grant. *The Confessions of Aleister Crowley: An Autobiography*. New York: Penguin, 1989. An account of Crowley's ideas of Scientific Illuminism as well as a description of his life and controversial actions, told by Crowley himself.

Regardie, Israel. *The Eye in the Triangle: An Interpretation of Aleister Crowley*. Phoenix, Ariz.: Falcon Press, 1982. A biography of Crowley that emphasizes his appreciation of mystery novels and explores how the novels influenced his writing.

Sutin, Lawrence. *Do What Thou Wilt*. New York: St. Martin's Press, 2000. This book recounts the life history of Crowley, discussing the many aspects of Crowley and his work, including his studies of yoga and Eastern mystic disciplines.

—David R. Champion

See also: Dorothy Clutterbuck; L. Ron Hubbard; Anton Szandor LaVey.

Andrew Cunanan

American serial killer

Born: August 31, 1969; Rancho Bernardo, California

Died: July 23, 1997; Miami, Florida

Also known as: Andrew Phillip Cunanan (full name); Andrew De Silva; Lieutenant Commander Cummings

Cause of notoriety: Cunanan engaged in a killing spree that left five people dead, including well-known fashion designer Gianni Versace. He committed suicide before he could be arrested.

Active: April 25-July 23, 1997

Locale: San Diego, California; Minneapolis and Rush City, Minnesota; Chicago, Illinois; Pennsville, New Jersey; and Miami, Florida

Early Life

Growing up in San Diego, California, Andrew Phillip Cunanan (coo-NAN-an) attended the upper-class Bishop's School, graduating in 1987. A cross-country runner and good student, he obscured his middle-class background from his classmates, most of whom were from upper-class families. In the school yearbook, students named Andrew "the most likely to be remembered." A year after Cunanan finished high school, his father, Modesto, who had been in the United States Navy and was a stockbroker, returned to his native Philippines, presumably to escape investigation about questionable business dealings. Cunanan followed Modesto to the Philippines but soon returned, dismayed by the squalid conditions in which his father lived. Modesto also had a violent streak, which might have had an impact on Cunanan's decision.

Cunanan then distanced himself from his family, using assumed names and passing himself off as a Hollywood film official or prosperous antique merchant. He frequented gay bars and had numerous gay contacts. He was also not above bartering sexual favors for money.

Cunanan was physically attractive and glib, projecting a self-assurance that masked his intrinsic phoniness. He was extravagant, usually picking up the check when he was out with people for meals or drinks. People considered him a rich, if somewhat improvident, acquaintance. He financed his generosity by taking money from the older men whom he allowed to seduce him. He also sold illicit drugs to raise money in order to maintain his deceit.

Criminal Career

As the acquired immunodeficiency syndrom (AIDS) epidemic erupted, Cunanan feared that he was HIV-positive, although a postmortem test revealed otherwise. Some people theorized that it was Cunanan's fear of the disease that sparked his murderous spree of five people and his eventual suicide.

Cunanan left San Diego on April 25, 1997, going first to Minneapolis, where, on April 29, he bludgeoned twenty-eight-year-old Jeffrey Trail to death. Trail was a friend of David Madson, who had recently moved to Minnesota. On May 3, Madson's body was found on the shore of East Rush Lake, north of Minneapolis. He was shot three times. The following day, the body of real estate developer Lee Miglin was found in Chicago; Miglin's throat was cut, his Lexus was missing, Madson's car was found near the Miglin house. The Lexus was discovered on May 9 near the office of William Reese, a cemetery caretaker, who was then found shot to death in his office. Reese's Chevrolet pickup truck was missing.

More than two months passed before Cunanan's next murder, which was that of fashion designer Gianni Versace at the gates of his Miami mansion on July 15. Reese's Chevrolet truck, bearing stolen license plates, was found in a nearby garage. On July 23, Cunanan, who had hidden on an unoccupied houseboat after the Versace murder, was found dead in an upper bedroom of the boat; he had shot himself in the mouth and had died instantly.

Impact

Andrew Cunanan's crimes made national headlines, especially after the murder of Versace, both as authorities tried to locate Cunanan and as news broke of Cunanan's subsequent suicide. Cunanan left behind many clues to his identity and his whereabouts at crime scenes, including a pawn ticket with his thumbprint on it. Investigators later learned that the pawnbroker had turned it over to the police, who then failed to pursue the lead. Following the events surrounding the killing spree, law enforcement authorities became more vigilant in checking details that might connect crimes under investigation to other crimes.

Further Reading

Clarkson, Wensley. *Death at Every Stop*. New York: St. Martin's Press, 1997. Accurate account of Cunanan's murderous rampage that began in California and ended in Florida.

Crowley, Harry. "Homocidal Homosexual." *The Advocate*, September 2, 1998, 27-31. Focuses on the media coverage of Versace's murder and the search for his killer.

Indiana, Gary. *Three Month Fever: The Andrew Cunanan Story*. New York: HarperCollins, 1999. A thorough analysis of Cunanan's killing spree.

Orth, Maureen. *Vulgar Favors: Andrew Cunanan, Gianni Versace, and the Largest Failed Manhunt in U.S. History*. New York: Delacorte, 1999. Orth packs considerable detail into this book's lengthy discussion and gives an excellent summary of the gruesome events surrounding Cunanan's crime spree.

Thomas, Evan. "End of the Road." *Newsweek* 130, no. 5 (August 4, 1997): 22-28. Comprehensive account of Cunanan's murderous spree before his suicide.

—R. Baird Shuman

See also: Joe Ball; David Berkowitz; Kenneth Bianchi; Ted Bundy; Angelo Buono, Jr.; Albert DeSalvo; Albert Fish; John Wayne Gacy; Ed Gein; Karla Homolka; Leonard Lake; Charles Ng; Dennis Rader; Richard Speck; Charles Starkweather; Aileen Carol Wuornos.

Pauline Cushman

American actor and Civil War spy

Born: June 10, 1833; New Orleans, Louisiana
Died: December 2, 1893; San Francisco, California
Also known as: Harriet Wood (birth name); Pauline C. Fryer
Cause of notoriety: During the American Civil War, Cushman was captured by Confederate soldiers and sentenced to death for being a Union spy, but she was freed by the Union army before her punishment could be carried out.
Active: 1861-1863
Locale: Southern United States

Early Life

Born as Harriet Wood into a mixed Creole heritage with Spanish, French, and African roots, Pauline Cushman (KUHSH-man) lived in New Orleans until she was ten, when her father opened a trading post in the frontier city of Grand Rapids, Michigan. There, on the edge of wilderness, Harriet learned to ride and to read trail signs, and gained other outdoor skills that served her well in her later adventures.

At age eighteen, Harriet went to New York City, seeking a theatrical career. Hired by Thomas Placide, manager of the New Orleans Varieties, to perform in his music hall, she took the stage name Pauline Cushman. Her bright, flashy style of singing and acting quickly won a following. In 1853, she married Charles Dickson, a fellow musician-actor. When the Civil War broke out in 1861, Dickson enlisted in the Union army. He died a year later in one of the army camps. Devastated, Cushman joined a touring company, performing *The Seven Sisters* in the border states between the North and South.

Espionage Career

Cushman had always been a Union patriot, although her brother was in the Confederate army. She apparently reported some information about opposition spies while performing in St. Louis. Her first known assignment, however, originated in Louisville, a city nominally under Union control but full of Southern sympathizers. Two Confederate officers offered her three hundred dollars to give a toast onstage to Jefferson Davis, president of the Confederacy. Cushman played for time and reported the offer to the local provost marshal. To her surprise, he asked her to do it and then gave her an oath of allegiance. In his mind, the public toast could establish Cushman as a Confederate loyalist, enabling her to travel in the South and gather information.

The plan worked. Cushman started following Confederate forces, claiming to be looking for her brother. She would usually be admitted to the camp and invited to ride through the area. Although she asked no questions about defenses or military power, this approach gave her the opportunity to observe Confederate soldiers and take mental notes. Visiting the hospitals, she asked about medical supplies and the number of casualties. By riding between camps and crossing rebel lines frequently, she also gained detailed information about country roads and terrain in Tennessee, northern Georgia, and other sparsely mapped areas where Union forays were planned.

Pauline Cushman. (Library of Congress)

Her background in riding and outdoor activities suited her for such explorations, and her beauty and charm won the confidence of Confederate officers, who often offered her help and news.

Her most ambitious assignment began in May, 1863, when General William Rosecrans charged her to discover the location and strength of the Army of Tennessee. Prepared with a specially made gray uniform, she managed to cross into Confederate territory. However, security measures there had become tighter. Captured by scouts, she made several nearly successful escape attempts. The discovery of sketches hidden in her boots increased her jeopardy. When she was brought before Confederate General Braxton Bragg, he put her under guard at a farmhouse and instituted a trial. She was sentenced to be hanged as a spy.

However, fate intervened. Rosencrans's advance reached Shelbyville before her sentence could be carried out. The Confederate army evacuated, leaving Cushman behind to be rescued by the Union forces. Now too recognizable to spy actively again, Cushman continued to provide Northern forces with information on the Southern terrain until the war's end.

Postwar, Cushman toured the country with a lively lecture on her spying adventures. She moved to California in 1872 and married twice again. When her stage career faded, she supported herself as a seamstress until her death of a morphine overdose at age sixty.

Impact

Although no action by Pauline Cushman clearly determined a battle's outcome, the mass of data she supplied certainly aided the campaigns of Union generals. Her quiet fingering of Confederate spies in St. Louis and Louisville also helped the success of the Union war effort.

Further Reading

Caravantes, Peggy. *Petticoat Spies: Six Women Spies of the Civil War.* Greensboro, N.C.: Morgan Reynolds, 2002. A summary account of Cushman's life and career.

Eggleston, Larry. *Women in the Civil War.* Jefferson, N.C.: McFarland & Company, 2003. Detailed coverage of Cushman's work as a scout and spy, emphasizing its match with her loyalties and skills.

Markle, Donald E. *Spies and Spymasters of the Civil War.* New York: Hippocrene Books, 2004. Discusses Cushman's career as part of the larger espionage effort in the war.

—*Emily Alward*

See also: Belle Boyd.

George A. Custer

American cavalry commander

Born: December 5, 1839; New Rumley, Ohio
Died: June 25, 1876; Little Bighorn River, Montana Territory (now Montana)
Also known as: George Armstrong Custer (full name); Autie; Fanny; Son of Morning Star; Yellow Hair
Cause of notoriety: Custer led the U.S. cavalry forces that engaged in the indiscriminate killing of noncombatants during wars against the Plains Indians.
Active: 1867-1876
Locale: Great Plains, United States

Early Life

George Armstrong Custer (KUHS-tuhr) was born into a large rural family in Ohio. Although an indifferent student, he qualified to teach grammar school by age sixteen. The next year, he entered the United States Military Academy at West Point, New York. Custer graduated last in the class of 1861 and entered the cavalry. Two years later, during the Civil War, he was the nation's youngest general (by brevet).

Military Career

Like many other officers in the drastically reduced postwar Regular Army, Custer used political connections to receive the highest rank and position that he could. Although his brevet of major general ended with the disbanding of the Third Division of Michigan Volunteers, he secured the rank of lieutenant colonel in the Seventh Cavalry, which was headquartered at Fort Riley, Kansas. The cavalry faced the American Indian tribes of the Southern Cheyenne, Arapahos, Oglala, Brule Sioux, Kiowas, Comanches, and Plains Apaches. Custer was initially unsuccessful as an officer on the plains, earning a year's suspension in October, 1867, as punishment for a host of shortcomings. He returned to active duty in time for the Southern Plains War of 1868-1869. In late November, 1868, Custer led the Seventh Cavalry in pursuit of a band of Cheyenne, which, under the leadership of Black Kettle, was pursuing General Philip Sheridan in an attempt to make peace.

The attack on Black Kettle's camp on the Washita River in what is now western Oklahoma on November 27, 1868, set the pattern for Custer's method of fighting the Plains Indians. For Custer, the problem with Indian fighting lay not in assembling superior numbers of soldiers or in massing firepower, but in surprise. Without surprise, Indian villages would quickly disperse, making decisive battle impossible. From Custer's perspective, Indian villages needed to be attacked at dawn and from multiple directions to achieve decisive results. During these attacks, the line between warrior and noncombatant blurred, and soldiers would often kill women and children.

Equally important, the Washita campaign entrenched dissension within the officers corps of the Seventh Cavalry. Custer left the battlefield before learning the whereabouts of a subordinate officer and his patrol. Some junior officers of the cavalry felt that Custer had abandoned his men in hostile country. Moreover, Custer lacked the maturity to heal the rift during the long interludes between campaigns—during his decade on the frontier, Custer fought far fewer battles with Indians than he had against Confederates during the Civil War.

George A. Custer. (Library of Congress)

Demise

Many tribes of the northern plains, particularly the Sioux, bitterly resented Custer's expedition into the sacred Black Hills in 1874, which was in violation of the Treaty of Fort Laramie of 1868. The treaty barred white Americans from the Great Sioux Reservation. Indian resentment had united many elements from several tribes and filled them with the desire for a fight.

During the 1876 campaign of the Great Sioux War, Custer's famous luck ran out. That June, the army began a campaign to crush the Sioux and Cheyenne, who resisted the government's attempts to confine them to reservations. Most of these northern Plains Indians coalesced around Sitting Bull of the Hunkpapa Sioux, whose village swelled to around seven thousand people that month. The Seventh Cavalry had been looking for the village throughout the month, finally discovering its location neat the Little Bighorn River on the morning of June 25. Custer, as usual, feared dispersal of the Indians more than their numbers. He was considering running for president and wanted a large victory to aid his election efforts. Concerned that his presence was known, Custer personally led five companies of the Seventh Cavalry in a midday headlong attack into the massive village. All the officers and men with Custer, 261 in all, died in the ensuing battle.

Sitting Bull's Little Bighorn

After defeating a cavalry attack by Major Marcus Reno's force, Sitting Bull led his warriors against Custer's battalion:

We then turned to attack the other division which was coming down from the end of the camp. Just as we met them a great thunder storm came on and the lightning killed some men and horses. I then called out that the Great Spirit was fighting for us and we attacked the second division. About forty of the soldiers had been dismounted and were trampled to death in a short time. After the thunder storm the soldiers fired very little and we knocked most of them from their horses with our coup sticks and they were killed immediately.

The Americans fired very wild and did not do us much harm. There were only twenty-five Sioux killed in the battle. After we had nearly disposed of the second division there were five soldiers [from Major Reno's force] living and I told my men to let them go. We did not kill the Interpreter.

I did not recognize Custer in the fight but only thought I did but could not tell for certain. There is no truth in the story that Custer was the last man to die and that he killed himself. I saw two soldiers shoot themselves. The Sioux were following them and in a few moments would have killed them but they killed themselves by putting their pistols to their heads and firing.

I believe that General Custer was killed in the first attack. We found what all of us thought was his body and it was in the middle of the camp. He had his hair cut short. There were seven hundred and nine Americans killed. We counted them by putting a stick upon each body and then taking up the sticks and counting them. We found seven hundred and seven carbines and two might have been lost in the river.

Source: "Sitting Bull's Own Narrative of the Custer Fight," *The Canadian Historical Review* 16, no. 2 (June, 1935).

Impact

The loss of the Seventh Cavalry caused great shock throughout the United States and led to massive public support for aggressive pursuit and ultimate destruction of independent bands of American Indians on the high plains. At Little Bighorn, George A. Custer died, but a legendary Custer was born. The mythic Custer—loving husband, dashing leader, Indian expert—came from Custer's memoirs, and later, from his wife; until her death in 1933, Elizabeth Custer maintained the heroic image of her late husband. Following the 1960's, a decade in which the history and rights of minorities began to be recognized and better understood, Custer became more controversial. Opinions of his legacy run from considering him a talented battle leader who was respected by his enemies to seeing him as a symbol of American arrogance, racism, and genocide.

Further Reading

Barnett, Louis. *Touched by Fire: The Life, Death, and Mythic Afterlife of George Armstrong Custer*. New York: Henry Holt, 1996. A revisionist history that argues Custer spent the years after the Civil War trying to reclaim the excitement of that era. While he accepted the racist attitudes of American culture toward Native Americans, he likewise loathed the lower-class men he commanded in the postwar army.

Sklenar, Larry. *To Hell with Honor: Custer and the Little Bighorn*. Norman: University of Oklahoma Press, 2000. Sympathetic portrayal of Custer as an army leader. Sklenar argues that poor support by subordinate officers rather than poor decisions by Custer at Little Bighorn doomed Custer, although given the size of the Indian encampment and talent of the native leaders, victory for Custer might have been impossible anyway.

Utley, Robert M. *Cavalier in Buckskin: George Armstrong Custer and the Western Military Frontier*. Norman: University of Oklahoma Press, 1988. Standard military biography of Custer. Utley depicts him to be a competent battle leader during the Civil War but argues that Custer's immaturity created dissension within the officer corps of the Seventh Cavalry.

Welch, James. *Killing Custer: The Battle of the Little Bighorn and the Fate of the Plains Indians*. New York: W. W. Norton, 1994. The career of Custer and his demise at Little Bighorn provide the framework for a study from an American Indian perspective of relations between the United States and the tribes of the West in the second half of the nineteenth century.

—*Barry M. Stentiford*

SEE ALSO: William Calley; Reginald Dyer; James Wilkinson.

MOLL CUTPURSE

British thief and pawnbroker

BORN: c. 1584; London, England
DIED: July 26, 1659; London, England
ALSO KNOWN AS: Mal Cutpurse; Mary Frith (birth name); Merry Moll; Mary Thrift; Mrs. Mary Markham
MAJOR OFFENSES: Purse snatching, public immorality, prostitution, and bawdry
ACTIVE: 1600-1644
LOCALE: London
SENTENCE: Jailed in Bridewell Prison, 1611; committed to Bethlehem insane asylum in 1644

EARLY LIFE

Biographical records for Mary Frith, later known as Moll Cutpurse (KUHT-puhrs), are nonexistent, and contemporary accounts are largely fabrications. Extant court records indicate that Cutpurse was low-born and semiliterate and turned early to thievery as a career. She was indicted in 1602, along with two female accomplices, for purse snatching, a charge for which she was arrested several additional times.

CRIMINAL CAREER

By 1608, Frith had earned a reputation as "Moll Cutpurse." She dressed in unconventional male attire, which gave her greater freedom to pursue her trade in the infamous Southwark area of London, where brothels, theaters, and alehouses offered ample criminal opportunities. On September 8, 1609, she was arrested for burglary.

LEGAL ACTION AND OUTCOME

Cutpurse acquired infamy for her scandalous onstage appearance at the Fortune Theater on April 11, 1611, at which she sang and played her lute. She was accused of transgressing against laws for women's attire and behavior and regulations against unlicensed musical entertainment and faulted as an underworld criminal mocking the style of London gentlemen. Indicted on charges of public immorality, Curpurse was committed to Bridewell Prison. On Christmas Day, 1611, the unrepentant Cutpurse was again arrested in St. Paul's churchyard on charges of prostitution and bawdry (pimping) and remanded to Bridewell. Her drunken public penance in February, 1612, however, proved yet another opportunity for entertainment, not remorse. Nevertheless, the incarcerations in Bridewell were severe enough to deter her from further activities as an actor and musician in the theater or in taverns.

By 1614, Cutpurse pursued a more lucrative career as a pawnbroker and intermediary between authorities and London's criminal world. A marriage of convenience on March 23, 1614, to Lewknor Markham, a member of the gentry of Nottingham, provided some respectability for her business as a licensed broker. A court record of the case of the robbery of Henry Killigrew in February, 1621, attests to Mary Markham's (Cutpurse's married name) participation in the recovery of the stolen money.

The Bridewell Court Books for 1644 note that Mary Frith was released from imprisonment for insanity in Bethlehem Hospital; the wily transgressor was probably feigning madness, since her roaring ways were still subject for pamphlets and poems in 1645 and 1647. She created her will on June 6, 1659, and died on July 26, 1659. She left a significant amount of money to relatives and paid for her own burial within, not outside, St. Bridget's Church on Fleet Street in London.

IMPACT

Moll Cutpurse's extravagant reputation endures more in literature than in life. Her transvestism inflamed contemporary anxiety about the increasing number of females who dressed and behaved as men, a controversy that climaxed in the pamphlets *Hic Mulier: Or, The Man-Woman* and *Haec Vir: Or, The Womanish-Man* (1620), which attacked and defended cross-dressed women. She was the subject of a questionable anonymous biography published in 1662 titled *The Life and Death of Mrs. Mary Frith. Commonly Called Mal Cutpurse*. Cutpurse's exploits as actor and singer were popularized in Thomas Middleton and Thomas Dekker's comedy *The Roaring Girl: Or, Moll Cutpurse* (pr. c. 1610, pb. 1611) and in Nathan Field's play *Amends for Ladies* (pr. 1611, pb. 1618). More recently, the fictional virago has been analyzed in literary debates as both a rebellious champion of women's sexual and personal autonomy and, more conservatively, as a one-woman army defending conventional gender hierarchies and institutions.

Further Reading

Baston, Jane. "Rehabilitating Moll's Subversion in *The Roaring Girl*." *Studies in English Literature, 1500-1900* 37, no. 2 (Spring, 1997): 317-335. Opposing the scholarly view that Cutpurse represented a radical criticism of patriarchal society, Baston argues that the play depicts no subversion of gender or class institutions.

Rose, Mary Beth. "Women in Men's Clothing: Apparel and Social Stability in *The Roaring Girl*." *English Literary Renaissance* 14, no. 3 (Autumn, 1984): 367-391. Rose views the play as simultaneously lauding Moll's defiance of Jacobean society and dismissing her as an aberrant, nonthreatening outsider.

Ungerer, Gustav. "Mary Frith, Alias Moll Cutpurse, in Life and Literature." *Shakespeare Studies* 28 (2000): 42-84. An analysis of the historical figure, with a chronological survey of available documentary biographical records.

—*Marion S. McAvey*

See also: Charles Peace; Jack Sheppard; Dick Turpin; Jonathan Wild.

Cypselus of Corinth

Ancient Greek ruler (c. 657-627 b.c.e)

Born: Early seventh century b.c.e.; Corinth, Greece
Died: 627 b.c.e.; place unknown
Also known as: Kypselos of Korinthos
Cause of notoriety: Cypselus was known for his political tyranny while ruling Corinth and became a symbol of brutality that accompanies total power.
Active: c. 657-627 b.c.e.
Locale: Corinth, Greece

Early Life

The early life of Cypselus (SIHP-suh-luhs) is mired in legends and cannot be reconstructed in detail. He was born in Corinth at a time when Greek cities were ruled by aristocratic clans. The Corinthians were governed by the Bacchiadae, a clan that claimed descent from an early king, Bacchis. Legends say that Cypselus's mother Labda saved him from these rulers by hiding him in a cedar chest (a *kypselē*) and that he spent his youth in exile. These stories—akin to the story of Moses in the bulrushes—are likely not true. He grew up in Corinth, even though his father Aetion was not from the ruling aristocracy, and rose to prominence through his rabble-rousing. He overthrew the Bacchiadae and took power c. 657 b.c.e., probably with a good deal of support.

Political Career

Cypselus's control over Corinth represents perhaps the earliest Greek tyrannical dynasty. Later accounts say that Cypselus held power over Corinth without personal bodyguards and that he redefined the tribal system of Corinth in order to allow native-born Corinthians a say in public affairs. Such measures suggest that a sizable portion of the population was on his side. However, this popular empowerment did not lead to decent governance; he used his power to strip the prosperous of their wealth, driving many into exile if not execution, and motivating Greek historian Herodotus's story that he stripped the women of Corinth naked in order to please his own wife.

Upon Cypselus's death, his son Periander took power, solidifying the new dynasty, the Cypselids (descendants of Cypselus). Periander became famous for even greater cruelty. Herodotus, writing two hundred years later, said that Periander asked the tyrant Thrasybulus of Samos how to maintain control of a city; Thrasybulus walked through a cornfield, lopping off the tops of the tallest plants. (The philosopher Aristotle reversed the story and said that Thrasybulus asked Periander.) Thus the metaphor of the "tall poppies" was born of a sense that Periander and his father had been brutal despots, maintaining their power by ruthlessly destroying anyone of stature.

Upon Periander's death, the tyranny passed to a nephew, the younger Cypselus, also called Psammetichus, who was then killed. Cypselus the elder therefore established a classic two-generation tyranny: The founder claims power with some popular support; the son reverts to unmitigated brutality; and the next, incompetent successor loses it all.

IMPACT

Evaluations of Cypselus must be ambiguous; to many Greeks he was far from notorious. On one hand, he brought order to Corinth, presided over its rise as an economic power, spread its influence through colonies, and ended civil strife. Periander was called one of the "seven sages" of ancient Greece, a group that included the philosopher Thales and the lawgiver Solon. However, Cypselus and Periander maintained rule by subjecting the people of Corinth to unseemly repression. Herodotus cites Cypselus as a harsh tyrant who left his city prosperous but whose son extended his father's brutality without limits. The impact of Cypselus on Corinth lasted for generations, but his true relevance in history is in the very idea of tyranny—for this he is justly condemned.

Cypselus became a symbol of brutality that accompanies total power even when attended by popular consent and claims to divine sanction. He held office by force, the essence of tyranny. The Greeks, and the tradition of liberty and self-government that has followed, properly reject the notion that a strongman's club is a legitimate way to avoid anarchy. Thanks to the example of Cypselus and his son, no dictator can claim that his purges are good because they maintain order.

FURTHER READING

Andrewes, A. *The Greek Tyrants*. New York: Prometheus, 1956. An account of early Greece with a dedicated focus on tyrants.

Herodotus. *Histories*. Translated by A. de Selincourt. New York: Penguin, 2003. The classic ancient account of archaic Greece; see especially book 5, section 92.

Murray, O. *Early Greece*. 2d ed. Cambridge, Mass.: Harvard University Press, 1993. A comprehensive but reader-friendly account of preclassical Greece.

Salmon, J. B. *Wealthy Corinth: A History of the City to 338 B.C.* New York: Oxford University Press, 1984. A close look at Corinth, including a discussion of its economic rise during the time of Cypselus.

—John Lewis

SEE ALSO: Alcibiades of Athens; Phalaris; Polycrates of Samos.

LEON CZOLGOSZ

American assassin

BORN: 1873; Detroit, Michigan
DIED: October 29, 1901; Auburn Prison, Auburn, New York
ALSO KNOWN AS: Leon Frank Czolgosz (full name); Fred C. Nieman
MAJOR OFFENSE: Murder of President William McKinley
ACTIVE: September 6, 1901
LOCALE: Buffalo, New York
SENTENCE: Convicted of first-degree murder; executed by electrocution

EARLY LIFE

Leon Frank Czolgosz (CHEWL-gawsh) was born into brutal poverty with parents who were Polish immigrants. His mother died when Czolgosz was twelve while she was giving birth to a child. At the age of fourteen, Czolgosz began working in the steel and glass factories of Cleveland and Pittsburgh. Because he was earning only four dollars a day, Czolgosz joined a union and went on strike, but this resulted in his being fired. Czolgosz and his family usually had little money left for housing and medical care. As a young man, he had only one girlfriend, who broke up with him; after this relationship, he was too shy to talk to women. Czolgosz was always fairly quiet and withdrawn. He was also known to sleep a great deal, and he refused to eat food prepared by his stepmother because he feared that she might poison him.

Czolgosz was influenced by the Haymarket Square bombing in 1886—a labor rally in Chicago during which a bomb exploded, killing eleven persons. Anarchists were arrested for the crime, although there was little evidence against them. Czolgosz was angry that five anarchists were executed for the bombing and saw this as an

Nieman, No Man

Leon Czolgosz rightly used the alias "Fred Nieman"; the surname means "no man" in German, and it referred to his rejection by the far-left radicals and anarchists among whom he sought acceptance. Suspicious of Czolgosz, Abraham Isaak, the editor of the radical periodical Free Society, *issued a warning in his paper regarding the possibility that Czolgosz might be a spy in their midst:*

Attention!
The attention of the comrades is called to another spy. He is well dressed, of medium height, rather narrow shouldered, blond, and about 25 years of age. Up to the present he has made his appearance in Chicago and Cleveland. In the former place he remained a short time, while in Cleveland he disappeared when the comrades had confirmed themselves of his identity and were on the point interested in the cause, asking for names, or soliciting aid for acts of contemplated violence. If this individual makes his appearance elsewhere, the comrades are warned in advance and can act accordingly.

injustice against the labor movement. He also rejected religion, believing that God had abandoned the working class.

Criminal Career

In the 1896 presidential election between Republican William McKinley and Democrat William Jennings Bryan, McKinley represented the wealthy industrialists, and Bryan represented the working poor. Czolgosz believed that money from the wealthy industrialists swayed the election to McKinley. In 1897, the Lattimer Mines Massacre in Pennsylvania occurred during which police killed Slavic miners who were peacefully demonstrating. The police officers were later acquitted, which contributed to Czolgosz's nervous breakdown in the fall of 1897. Czolgosz absorbed the radical literature of his day and was obsessed with the need for radical social change. He was a follower of Emma Goldman, an anarchist and feminist who was a great speaker. Czolgosz heard her speak on a number of occasions and also had brief conversations with her. Anarchists thought that Czolgosz might be a government spy and sent out a warning to others to watch out for him. He often used the alias Fred C. Nieman.

In 1900, King Humbert I of Italy was assassinated by an anarchist named Gaetano Bresci. Bresci held that he had killed the king for the sake of the common person. Czolgosz found in Breschi his hero, a man who had the courage to sacrifice himself for a cause. Inspired by Breschi, Czolgosz sought to assassinate President McKinley because he was wealthy and indifferent to the working class. Czolgosz heard McKinley speak in Buffalo at the Pan-American Exposition about the prosperity of the United States, while so many of the working poor suffered. On September 6, 1901, Czolgosz went to the exposition with a pistol concealed in a handkerchief bandaged around his right hand. McKinley was standing in a receiving line greeting people when Czolgosz shot McKinley twice at point-blank range. McKinley died eight days later.

Leon Czolgosz imprisoned. (Library of Congress)

Legal Action and Outcome

When Czolgosz was arrested, police found a folded newspaper clipping about Bresci in Czolgosz's pocket. Czolgosz pleaded guilty and did not express any regret. He was sentenced to death and executed by electrocution on October 29, 1901.

Impact

After the assassination, the government sought to eliminate anarchists who were blamed for McKinley's death. While some anarchists condemned Leon Czolgosz, others, such as Goldman, praised him as a brave martyr. Oddly enough, the McKinley assassination provided the United States with a more progressive leader in Theodore Roosevelt, who was more sympathetic to the working class. Roosevelt pushed for the creation of the departments of labor and commerce and also weakened the power of large corporations.

Further Reading

Clarke, James W. *American Assassins: The Darker Side of Politics*. Princeton, N.J.: Princeton University Press, 1982. Clarke develops a typology for analyzing political assassins throughout American history.

Johns, A. Wesley. *The Man Who Shot McKinley*. South Brunswick, N.J.: A. S. Barnes, 1970. Johns provides a new perspective on the assassin of President McKinley.

MacDonald, Carlos F. "The Trial, Execution, Autopsy, and Mental Status of Leon F. Czolgosz, Alias Fred Nieman, the Assassin of President McKinley." *American Journal of Insanity* 58 (January, 1902): 369-386. Provides a contemporary psychological analysis of Czolgosz.

—Scott P. Johnson

See also: John Wilkes Booth; Emma Goldman; Charles Julius Guiteau; Lee Harvey Oswald.

Jeffrey Dahmer

American serial killer

Born: May 21, 1960; Milwaukee, Wisconsin
Died: November 28, 1994; Columbia Correctional Institution, Portage, Wisconsin
Also known as: Jeffrey Lionel Dahmer (full name)
Major offenses: Murder, cannibalism, and sexual assault
Active: June 18, 1978; November, 1987-July, 1991
Locale: Bath, Ohio; Milwaukee, Wisconsin
Sentence: Fifteen consecutive life sentences; ten years on sixteen counts of murder

Early Life

Jeffrey Lionel Dahmer (DAH-muhr) had a troubled childhood. He had difficulty making friends and was a loner who was fascinated with death, bodies, flesh, and taxidermy. He had a collection of roadkill and insects preserved in chemicals. Dahmer was also fond of impaling the heads of animals on stakes and mounting the bodies on trees behind his house. By high school, Dahmer had alienated his peers and was shy around female students. He consistently sought attention with his odd behavior and by faking seizures. Dahmer was probably also influenced by the divorce of his parents, Lionel and Joyce. His parents fought over the custody of his younger brother David but not over his custody (mainly because Dahmer was already eighteen and custody was not an issue). Both his father and his mother tried to pressure Dahmer to side with them, pitting Dahmer against each one. His mother eventually received custody of David and moved to Wisconsin, and Lionel moved out of the house shortly thereafter; both effectively abandoned Dahmer.

Criminal Career

On June 18, 1978, Dahmer met eighteen-year-old hitchhiker Stephen Hicks and brought him back to the empty home that Dahmer now occupied. The two engaged in sexual intercourse and afterward, when Hicks tried to leave, Dahmer struck him in the head with a barbell. Dahmer used a sledgehammer to smash Hicks's body, and then he buried the remains in the woods behind the house.

Although Dahmer committed his first murder in 1978, he did not kill again until 1987. Between 1978 and 1987, Dahmer joined the army, from which he was discharged in 1981 because of his alcohol problem. In 1982, Dahmer moved in with his grandmother near Milwaukee and began going to gay bars and bringing men home with him. Dahmer killed again in 1987, when he picked up Steven Toumi in a gay bar. Dahmer took Toumi to a hotel, where the two men got drunk and lost consciousness. According to Dahmer, when he awoke, Toumi was dead, and Dahmer proceeded to take the body to his grandmother's house, where he engaged in necrophilia, dismembered the body, and threw the body parts in the trash. Dahmer continued his pattern of meeting men at gay bars; taking them back to his grandmother's house, where he drugged them; having sex with them (either alive, dead, or both); and then dismembering the body.

Dahmer moved from his grandmother's house to his own apartment in November, 1988. The next day, he brought a thirteen-year-old boy to his apartment, where he tried to drug the boy with sleeping pills. However, the boy escaped, and Dahmer was arrested the next day for sexual assault, to which he pleaded guilty and was given a sentence of five years' probation. However, despite this encounter with the law, Dahmer continued killing men.

In March, 1989, Dahmer picked up a twenty-four-year-old African American male, whom he took to his grandmother's house. There, the two engaged in intercourse, and then Dahmer drugged the man and strangled him. Dahmer disposed of the body but kept the head, boiling it until only the skull remained. As he murdered and dismembered several more men, Dahmer continued this act of keeping a souvenir of his victims. Dahmer eventually transitioned from engaging in necrophilia and collecting skulls and body parts to engaging in cannibalism.

On July 22, 1991, Dahmer picked up another man, Tracy Edwards, whom he took back to his apartment. Edwards managed to escape and was able to notify police. The officers responded to Dahmer's apartment. They smelled a rancid odor and found pictures of dismembered bodies and skulls and a full human skeleton. Dahmer was finally arrested, and his murderous career ended.

Legal Action and Outcome

After his arrest in 1991, Dahmer pleaded guilty by reason of insanity to the murder charges. The jury found Dahmer sane on all sixteen counts of murder. Wisconsin did not allow the death penalty, so the judge sentenced Dahmer to fifteen consecutive life sentences plus ten years on all counts. Dahmer was sent to the Columbia Correctional Institution to serve his time. However, on November 28, 1994, Dahmer was beaten to death by another inmate.

Jeffrey Dahmer at his preliminary hearing. (AP/Wide World Photos)

Impact

Jeffrey Dahmer's crimes were shocking, not only in number but also in what he did with the bodies. Dahmer had confessed to the murders and admitted to necrophilia and cannibalism, but the question of why he committed these crimes remained, fascinating psychologists and criminal investigators. The crimes also had an impact on the justice system itself. Investigators learned of an incident in May, 1991, during which one of Dahmer's eventual victims escaped from Dahmer, only to be returned to him by the responding officers, who deemed the event "a lover's quarrel." The fourteen-year-old boy soon became Dahmer's twelfth and youngest victim. Law officers were forced to consider the ways in which they handle such seemingly innocent events. Moreover, Dahmer committed several of his crimes while on probation for his 1988 arrest, calling into question the efficacy of probation and the criminal justice system in general.

Further Reading

Dahmer, Lionel. *Father's Story*. New York: William Morrow, 1994. Written by Dahmer's father, who discusses his son's life from the unique perspective of someone who was close to and loved Dahmer, despite his crimes.

Davis, D. *The Milwaukee Murders: Nightmare in Apartment 213, the True Story*. New York: St. Martin's Press, 1991. Discusses in depth the life and crimes of Dahmer, although it was published before Dahmer was killed in prison.

Jaeger, R. W., and M. W. Balousek. *Massacre in Milwaukee: The Macabre Case of Jeffrey Dahmer*. Oregon, Wisc.: Waubesa Press, 1991. Discusses the life and crimes of Dahmer, as well as the aftermath of the murders and the consequences of the crimes for the police and the public.

Masters, B. *The Shrine of Jeffrey Dahmer*. London: Hodder and Stoughton, 1993. Discusses the life of Dahmer and his crimes.

—*Jenephyr James*

See also: Joe Ball; David Berkowitz; Paul Bernardo; Kenneth Bianchi; Ted Bundy; Angelo Buono, Jr.; Andrei Chikatilo; Albert DeSalvo; Albert Fish; John Wayne Gacy; Ed Gein; Leonard Lake; Charles Ng; Dennis Rader; Gilles de Rais; Richard Speck; Aileen Carol Wuornos.

Bob Dalton

American Old West outlaw

Born: May 13, 1869; near Belton, Cass County, Missouri

Died: October 5, 1892; Coffeyville, Kansas

Also known as: Robert Rennick Dalton (full name)

Cause of notoriety: Dalton, along with other members of the Dalton Gang, terrorized the American Old West with bank robberies, train robberies, and cattle theft.

Active: c. 1887-1892

Locale: California, Kansas, New Mexico Territory (now mostly New Mexico), and Indian Territory (now Oklahoma)

Early Life

Robert (Bob) Rennick Dalton (DAHL-tuhn) was one of fifteen children born to Lewis and Adeline (Younger) Dalton. The Dalton family was constantly on the move, living at one time or another in Missouri, Kansas, Indian Territory (now Oklahoma), and California. The older Dalton children were all law-abiding, respectable citizens. Frank Dalton, for example, was killed in the line of duty while serving as a deputy U.S. marshal under Judge Isaac C. Parker (known as the Hanging Judge because of his preferred sentences). However, four Dalton boys—Bob, Bill, Grattan, and Emmett—eventually became outlaws. It is unclear why the younger Daltons robbed trains and banks while the older siblings minded the law—perhaps the fact that Lewis Dalton had abandoned the family while the younger boys were still in their formative years had an impact. The Dalton brothers also proudly claimed kinship to the infamous James-Younger Gang (with Jesse James and Cole Younger being its most famous members), which might have also played a role in pushing the Dalton boys into criminal activities.

Outlaw Career

After the death of brother Frank, Grattan replaced his fallen brother as a deputy marshal, and he soon appointed brothers Bob and Emmett as his assistants. Bob also served the Osage Nation as chief of Indian police. During the late 1880's, Indian Territory was a raucous and dangerous place where bootlegging, horse theft, and murder reached epidemic levels. Within this world, the Dalton brothers wore badges but also began engaging in crime. Their life of crime began with horse and cattle theft in Indian Territory. However, it soon progressed to murder when Bob shot and killed Charles Montgomery, a man who courted Bob's sweetheart while he was out of town.

By 1890, the Dalton brothers' quasi-law enforcement careers had ended, and they turned to the more profitable career of full-time horse thieving. With warrants for their arrest in Indian Territory and Kansas, the brothers fled the region. Grattan joined several brothers in California, while Bob and Emmett moved to New Mexico, where they found themselves wanted by the law after robbing men playing a faro game. Emmett retreated to Indian Territory, while Bob joined his brothers in California. Once again, trouble followed Bob. When a train was robbed at Alila, California, by masked gunmen, law officers targeted Bob, Grattan, and Bill Dalton. Although authorities arrested Bill and Grattan, Bob managed to elude capture and returned to Indian Territory. There, he resumed his criminal career by heading a gang of outlaws, which included Emmett Dalton, Bill Doolin, George "Bitter Creek" Newcomb, and Bill Powers, among others. Grattan then rejoined his brothers after escaping from California authorities in September, 1891. For the next year, the Dalton Gang robbed at least four trains within and surrounding Indian Territory and were blamed for dozens of other robberies.

The Dalton Gang made a fatal mistake on October 5, 1892. Five gang members—Bob, Grattan, and Emmett Dalton, along with compatriots Dick Broadwell and Powers—attempted to do what their heroes in the James-Younger Gang had never done: simultaneously rob two banks. The gang chose Coffeyville, Kansas, for the robberies. The robberies, however, were poorly conceived. The Dalton brothers had lived near Coffeyville ten years earlier, and their brother Frank was buried in the town cemetery. As they rode into town, citizens immediately recognized the Daltons, who, by 1892, were well-known criminals. Confident of their abilities, however, Bob and Emmett entered the First National Bank, while Powers, Broadwell, and brother Grattan robbed the Condon Bank across the street. Word quickly spread throughout town that the Dalton Gang was robbing the town banks. Citizens armed themselves, some borrowing guns from local businesses, and began surrounding the banks from concealed positions. Although Bob and Emmett exited the First National Bank with more than twenty-one thousand dollars, they were forced to retreat back into the bank when armed citizens opened fire. They then retreated through a back door, where they were met by the other three robbers.

Trapped in an alley and under heavy gunfire, the Dalton Gang fought tenaciously to escape. Wielding a Winchester rifle, Bob killed three citizens and wounded another, while Grattan reportedly killed Marshal Charles Connelly. One by one, however, the Dalton Gang succumbed to the relentless shoot-out. John Kloher, a Coffeyville liveryman, killed Bob with a bullet to the chest, probably making Bob the first of the gang to die. When Grattan tried to avenge his brother, Kloher fatally wounded him too. Coffeyville marksmen knocked Broadwell and Powers from their horses as they attempted to escape. Emmett, the only member of the gang still mounted, perhaps could have escaped, but he returned to the alley and attempted to rescue his dying brother Bob. Armed citizens then fired on Emmett, riddling the twenty-year-old bandit with more than twenty bullets. When the shooting stopped, four Dalton Gang members and four Coffeyville citizens lay dead or dying. Surviving members were soon dead or in prison. Doolin and Bill Dalton, who did not participate in the raid, were later killed by lawmen. Emmett, the sole survivor of Coffeyville, pleaded guilty to second-degree murder and served nearly fifteen years in the Kansas State Penitentiary.

Impact

The Coffeyville Raid, as it came to be known in history, is perhaps the most famous of the frontier-era bank robberies. During the raid, the Dalton Gang met its end by the quick actions of the citizens of Coffeyville. Historians often point to the failed bank robberies as the point at which the outlaw-driven frontier era began to fade away. Citizens, fed up with criminal activity, sent a message to would-be robbers by killing members of the Dalton Gang.

Further Reading

Barndollar, Lue Diver. *What Really Happened on October 5, 1892: An Attempt at an Accurate Account of the Dalton Gang and Coffeyville*. Coffeyville, Kans.: Coffeyville Historical Society, 1992. An illustrated history of the Daltons' failed bank robberies.

O'Neal, Bill. *Encyclopedia of Western Gunfighters*. Norman: University of Oklahoma Press, 1979. This valuable collection of 587 gunfighter biographies provides a biography of Bob Dalton, as well as short descriptions of his criminal activity and gunfights. Biographies of Emmett, Grattan, and Bill Dalton are also included.

Smith, Robert Barr. *Daltons! The Raid on Coffeyville*. Norman: University of Oklahoma Press, 1996. A detailed examination of the deadly Coffeyville Raid.

—*Mark R. Ellis*

See also: Emmett Dalton; Bill Doolin; Jesse James; Cole Younger.

Emmett Dalton

American outlaw

Born: May 3, 1871; Kansas City, Missouri
Died: July 13, 1937; Hollywood, California
Also known as: Em
Major offenses: Murder and robbery
Active: 1890-October 5, 1892
Locale: Northeast Oklahoma and southeast Kansas
Sentence: Life in prison; pardoned after fourteen years

Early Life

Emmett Dalton (EHM-eht DAHL-tuhn) was the eleventh of fifteen children born to James Lewis and Adeline Dalton. Named after an Irish criminal who was hanged on the gallows in England, Emmett was a first cousin of the notorious Cole Younger and his brothers. Dalton received little formal education. He and his older brother Bob developed a close relationship, and Bob protected his younger brother during times of trouble.

For a few months in 1889, Dalton served as a lawman alongside his brothers Bob, Bill, and Grattan in Fort Smith, Arkansas. Later that year, the four brothers served with Indian police on the Osage Indian Reservation. Bored by the lack of action and tired of the meager pay, the brothers turned to cattle rustling but soon discovered ventures that brought more money.

Criminal Career

In 1890, Emmett and Bob Dalton drifted into New Mexico. After feeling that they were cheated in a faro card game, they held up the players and took back their money—and more. "Wanted" posters were issued for their arrest. Bob headed to California, while Emmett returned home to his family in Kingfisher, Oklahoma, to spend time with his childhood sweetheart, Julia Johnson.

In the spring of 1891, Emmett joined with his brothers Bob and Grat to form a formidable outlaw gang that included Bill Doolin, George Newcomb, Charley Bryant, Dick Broadwell, and Bill Powers. On May 9, 1891, the gang robbed the Texas Express train near Whorton, Oklahoma, taking about fourteen thousand dollars. A few weeks later, they took nineteen thousand dollars in currency and silver from a train near Lelietta, Oklahoma. Emmett and Bob then left the gang, with hopes of going straight.

After a few months, Grat talked his brothers into rejoining the gang. Their next heist occurred near Red Rock, Oklahoma, where they took eleven thousand dollars from a Santa Fe train. On July 14, 1892, they stopped a train near Adair, Oklahoma, and got away with close to seventeen thousand dollars. On October 5, 1892, Emmett, Bob, and Grat Dalton, along with Bill Powers and Dick Broadwell, attempted to rob two banks at the same time in Coffeyville, Kansas. After they took twenty-four thousand dollars from the banks, an ensuing gun battle led to the death of four Coffeyville citizens and all of the outlaws except Emmett Dalton. He received twenty-three gunshot wounds but survived.

Legal Action and Outcome

For his participation in the Coffeyville robberies, Emmett was charged with first-degree murder. A preliminary hearing was held on January 16, 1893. The evidence against Dalton was sufficient for him to be held for trial without bail. His trial took place at the Montgomery County Courthouse in Independence, Missouri, in March, 1893. Dalton's lawyer, Joseph Fritch, convinced Dalton to plead guilty to second-degree murder so that he would receive a lighter sentence. The judge unexpectedly sentenced Dalton to life imprisonment in the Kansas State Penitentiary in Lansing, Kansas. Because of his good behavior, Dalton was granted an unconditional pardon on November 2, 1907, after serving fourteen and one-half years.

Impact

Emmett Dalton is a classic example of a reformed outlaw. He was involved in the first simultaneous double bank robbery in outlaw history. While he was in prison, his model behavior led to his early release. He married Julia Johnson and became an exemplary citizen, living first in Tulsa, Oklahoma, and then in Hollywood, California. He became a real estate agent, author, and actor. With the collaboration of Jack Jungmeyer, Dalton wrote the story of the Dalton gang, *When the Daltons Rode* (1931). The book was made into a film in 1940. Stories of the Dalton gang have been portrayed in magazines, movies, and television shows.

Further Reading

Barndollar, Lue Diver. *What Really Happened on October 5, 1892: An Attempt at an Accurate Account of the Dalton Gang and Coffeyville*. Coffeyville, Kans.: Coffeyville Historical Society, 1992. Discusses the outlaw days of Emmett, Bob, and Grat Dalton, with a detailed account of the Coffeyville escapade.

Dalton, Emmett. *Beyond the Law*. 1918. Reprint. Gretna, La.: Pelican, 2002. Dalton recounts his life and memories of the Dalton gang.

_______. *When the Daltons Rode*. Garden City, N.Y.: Doubleday, Doran, 1931. Dalton's memoir. Illustrated.

Pryor, Alton. *Outlaws and Gunslingers: Tales of the West's Most Notorious Outlaws*. Roseville, Calif.: Stagecoach, 2001. Reviews the lives of twenty-seven famous gunfighters of the Old West, including the Dalton brothers.

—*Alvin K. Benson*

See also: Bob Dalton; Bill Doolin; Jesse James; Cole Younger.

William Dampier

English pirate, naturalist, and explorer

Born: August, 1651; East Coker, Somerset, England
Died: March, 1715; London, England
Cause of notoriety: Dampier engaged in piracy in the Caribbean Sea and the Pacific Ocean; he circumnavigated the globe and carried out scientific observations during his voyages.
Active: c. 1679-1708
Locale: Caribbean coast, Panama, South America, Southeast Asia, and Australia

Early Life

After the death of his tenant-farmer parents, the guardians of William Dampier (DAM-peer) apprenticed the teenage boy to a shipmaster. Dampier mastered his trade and enjoyed life at sea, especially a long voyage to the East Indies in 1671-1672. He volunteered for the Royal Navy in 1673 during the Third Anglo-Dutch War. In 1674 Dampier accepted a position on a Jamaica sugar plantation but quarreled with the manager and left the following year for the Bay of Campeche, Mexico, to engage in the logwood trade (a valuable source of dyestuff). After a 1676 hurricane destroyed his stock, Dampier joined a group of buccaneers who raided nearby Spanish towns. Dampier acquired sufficient funds from his logwood business and piracy to return to England in 1678 and marry. The following year he acquired a small estate in Dorsetshire.

Piracy Career

Dampier left England in the spring of 1679 for a short trading voyage to Jamaica that stretched to twelve years, during which he took part in several pirate cruises and circumnavigated the globe. Despite difficult conditions, Dampier preserved careful notes on what he saw. In 1680 he joined a buccaneer fleet of some dozen vessels and nearly five hundred men that captured and looted the city of Portobello on the north coast of the Isthmus of Panama. Attempting to imitate Henry Morgan's highly lucrative 1670 seizure of Panama City, Dampier and his companions crossed the isthmus to the Pacific side but found the city too well defended. After unprofitable raids along the coast of South America, the buccaneers painfully struggled back, taking twenty-three days to walk 110 miles to the Atlantic. Dampier then joined a group that raided Spanish possessions along the Caribbean coast.

In 1683 Dampier enlisted in a fleet that sailed around Cape Horn to attack the Pacific coast of South America, provisioning at the Galápagos Islands, where the unique natural life fascinated him. Unsuccessful in raiding coastal cities, and failing to capture the extremely valuable Manila galleon, Dampier's captain decided in 1686 to try his luck in the Philippines, depending on Dampier's navigational skills to guide the ship across the Pacific. In 1688 Dampier left his pirate companions and spent eighteen months traveling in Southeast Asia before returning to England in 1691 aboard an East India Company ship, the third Englishman to circumnavigate the world, and the first in more than a century.

During the following six years Dampier transformed the notes and journals he had painstakingly protected during his voyages into a book that won him fame. His narrative of buccaneering adventures and detailed sketches of exotic places and customs made *A New Voyage Round the World* popular in 1697. His accurate, precise descriptions of weather, scenery, people, plants, and animal life won Dampier the respect of scientific and literary England.

William Dampier. (Library of Congress)

Dampier always referred to his companions as privateers—piracy being a crime punishable by hanging. However, it does not appear that any commander Dampier joined had government authorization to raid Spanish possessions in America, which legal privateering required, nor were they concerned with whether Britain was at war with Spain when looting Spanish ships and towns.

His literary fame won Dampier command of ships for his next two voyages. The Royal Navy sent him on an exploratory voyage (1699-1701) to the seas around Australia, but he did little exploring and lost his ship. Returning home, Dampier was court-martialed, convicted of mistreating his officers and men, and fined his entire three year's pay. In 1703 Dampier commanded a privateering expedition to the Pacific. Although he now had authentic letters of marque (authorization papers), he captured so few prizes that he lost money for his investors. He did, however, complete a second circumnavigation. His service as pilot in a 1708 privateering fleet that captured a Manila galleon earned him considerable prize money while providing a third circumnavigation of the globe.

Dampier in the New World

William Dampier's travelogue A New Voyage Round the World *(1697) is often matter-of-fact, even prosaic, but at times the wonder of discovery comes through clearly:*

In this Sea we made the best of our way toward the Line, till in the Lat. of 24 S. where we fell in with the main Land of the *South America.* All this course of the Land, both of *Chili* and *Peru* is vastly high. . . . The Land . . . is of a most prodigious Heighth. It lies generally in Ridges parallel to the Shore, and 3 or 4 Ridges one with another, each surpassing other in heighth; and those that are farthest within Land, are much higher than others. They always appear blue when seen at Sea; sometimes they are obscured with Clouds, but not so often as the high Lands in other parts of the World, for here are seldom or never any Rains on these Hills, any more than in the Sea near it; neither are they subject to Fogs. These are the highest Mountains that ever I saw. . . .

The *Gallapagos* Islands are a great number of uninhabited Islands, lying under, and on both sides of the Equator. The Eastermost of them are about 110 Leagues from the Main. . . . They are some of them 7 or 8 Leagues long, and 3 or 4 broad. . . . Some of the Westermost of these Islands, are nine or ten Leagues long, and six or seven broad; the Mould deep and black. These produce Trees of great and tall Bodies, especially Mammee-trees, which grow here in great Groves. In these large Islands there are some pretty big Rivers; and in many of the other lesser Islands, there are Brooks of good Water. The *Spaniards* when they first discover'd these Islands, found Multitudes of Guanoes, and Land-turtle or Tortoise, and named them the *Gallapagos* Islands. I do believe there is no place in the World that is so plentifully stored with these animals. The Guanoes here are fat and large as any that I ever saw; they are so tame, that a Man may knock down twenty in an Hour's Time with a Club.

Source: William Dampier, *A New Voyage Round the World* (London: James Knapton, 1697).

Impact

William Dampier's enduring reputation came from his literary and scientific achievements, not from bloody exploits as a pirate, though he undoubtedly witnessed more gore than he recorded. Other seventeenth century buccaneer authors, A. O. Exquemelin and Basil Ringrose, attracted readers with lurid accounts of violence and looting, but Dampier downplayed criminal aspects of his life as a pirate.

Major English literary figures eagerly borrowed Dampier's descriptions of pirate life and exotic places and people. Daniel Defoe used Dampier's books in his *A General History of the Robberies and Murders of the Most Notorious Pyrates* (1724-1728). Defoe's portrayal of Robinson Crusoe's island closely matched Dampier's depiction of the Islas las Aves in *A New Voyage Round the World by a Course Never Sailed* (1724). Jonathan Swift openly praised Dampier in *Gulliver's Travels* (1726). Samuel Taylor Coleridge admired Dampier and drew on his work for *The Rime of the Ancient Mariner* (1798).

Dampier's scientific reputation grew over succeeding centuries. His precise descriptions of natural phenomena were adopted by eighteenth century dictionaries and encyclopedias. Captain James Cook consulted Dampier's books during his explorations of the Pacific. Cook and Admiral Horatio Nelson praised the information on winds, tides, and currents contained in Dampier's 1699 "Discourse on Winds"; the Royal Navy continued to cite Dampier's observations well into the twentieth century. Charles Darwin used Dampier's detailed information in formulating his theory of evolution.

Dampier's extreme admirers implausibly claim he was uninterested in monetary gain and sailed with pirates only for scientific purposes. More realistic defenders assert that the value of his scientific and literary contributions far outweighs whatever illegal acts he committed during his pirate career.

Further Reading

Cordingly, David. *Under the Black Flag: The Romance and Reality of Life Among the Pirates*. New York: Harcourt Brace, 1995. Provides detailed context for Dampier's accounts of pirate life.

Preston, Diana, and Michael Preston. *A Pirate of Exquisite Mind: Explorer, Naturalist, and Buccaneer—The Life of William Dampier*. New York: Walker, 2004. A carefully researched, highly laudatory biography of Dampier.

Shipman, Joseph P. *William Dampier: Seaman-Scientist*. Lawrence: University of Kansas Libraries, 1962. Brief, judicious evaluation of Dampier's scientific contributions.

Williams, Glyndr. *The Great South Sea: English Voyages and Encounters, 1570-1750*. New Haven, Conn.: Yale University Press, 1997. Records criticisms as well as praise of Dampier's exploratory voyages in the South Pacific.

—*Milton Berman*

See also: Charlotte de Berry; Stede Bonnet; Anne Bonny; William Kidd; Sir Henry Morgan; Grace O'Malley; John Quelch; John Rackham; Mary Read; Bartholomew Roberts; Edward Teach.

François Darlan

French admiral and Vichy politician

Born: August 7, 1881; Nérac, France

Died: December 24, 1942; Algiers, Algeria

Also known as: Jean-Louis-Xavier-François Darlan (full name)

Cause of notoriety: Commander of the French armed forces during World War II, Darlan was a traitor in the eyes of his fellow French because of his collaborationist stance.

Active: 1940-1942

Locale: France and North Africa

François Darlan.

Early Life

Jean-François Darlan (zhah frahn-swah dahr-lah) was born August 7, 1881, in Nérac, France. He graduated from the naval academy in 1902 and became an officer in the French navy that year. Darlan remained in the navy until 1929, reaching the rank of rear admiral, at which point he was called upon to rebuild the navy. He became chief of staff in 1936 and was admiral of the fleet by 1937. He was given command of the entire French navy in 1939.

Naval and Political Career

During World War II, after the Germans began their occupation of Paris in 1940, Darlan fully supported the Vichy prime minister, Marshal Philippe Pétain, and Darlan's loyalty was rewarded by his being allowed to retain control over the French navy.

Darlan ordered a large portion of the fleet to French North Africa. On July 3, 1940, the British decided to de-

Charles de Gaulle's Appeal of June 18

With the rise of the Nazi-installed Vichy government, led by Philippe Pétain, François Darlan, Joseph Darnand, and others, the commander of the French Free Forces, General Charles de Gaulle, issued his "Appeal of June 18," a famous radio speech aired by the British Broadcasing Corporation on that date in 1940. De Gaulle's words prompted the French Resistance, the struggle against against Nazi occupation that would last through World War II:

The leaders who, for many years, were at the head of French armies, have formed a government. This government, alleging our armies to be undone, agreed with the enemy to stop fighting. Of course, we were subdued by the mechanical, ground and air forces of the enemy. Infinitely more than their number, it was the tanks, the airplanes, the tactics of the Germans which made us retreat. It was the tanks, the airplanes, the tactics of the Germans that surprised our leaders to the point to bring them there where they are today.

But has the last word been said? Must hope disappear? Is defeat final? No!

Believe me, I speak to you with full knowledge of the facts and tell you that nothing is lost for France. The same means that overcame us can bring us to a day of victory. For France is not alone! She is not alone! She is not alone! She has a vast Empire behind her. She can align with the British Empire that holds the sea and continues the fight. She can, like England, use without limit the immense industry of United States.

This war is not limited to the unfortunate territory of our country. This war is not finished by the battle of France. This war is a world-wide war. All the faults, all the delays, all the suffering, do not prevent there to be, in the world, all the necessary means to one day crush our enemies. Vanquished today by mechanical force, we will be able to overcome in the future by a superior mechanical force.

The destiny of the world is here. I, General de Gaulle, currently in London, invite the officers and the French soldiers who are located in British territory or who would come there, with their weapons or without their weapons, I invite the engineers and the special workers of armament industries who are located in British territory or who would come there, to put themselves in contact with me.

Whatever happens, the flame of the French resistance must not be extinguished and will not be extinguished. Tomorrow, as today, I will speak on Radio London.

Source: Charles de Gaulle, *The Speeches of General de Gaulle* (New York: Oxford University Press, 1944).

stroy the fleet at Mers El Kébir rather than risk its falling into German hands. This decision resulted in more than thirteen hundred French naval dead and intensified Darlan's hatred of the English. Despite his Anglophobia, Darlan continued to deny the Germans control of the remaining ships.

In 1941, however, Darlan replaced Pierre Laval as Pétain's deputy, and he was also made minister of foreign affairs, defense, and the interior. This left Darlan, in effect, the head of government. He quickly adjusted to his new power. He promoted ties with Germany and strove to create an alliance between the Vichy government and the Nazi Party. The Nazis, however, did not see Darlan as loyal as they had Laval; they viewed Darlan as more of an opportunist. The Germans forced him to relinquish his posts and return power to the more obviously pro-Nazi Laval.

On November 7, 1942, Darlan traveled to Algiers, Algeria, to visit his son, who had been hospitalized with polio. The following day, there was an attack on the Vichy government, carried out by four hundred poorly armed members of the French Resistance. The resistance managed to occupy and gain control of major strategic points in Algiers, including the general government and staff offices, officers' barracks, and telephone lines. They also rounded up and arrested most of the Vichy government officials and personnel, including Darlan. This paved the way for an Allied forces occupation.

General Mark W. Clark of the Allied command negotiated an agreement with Darlan in which the latter would convince the French collaborators to stop all hostilities, and Darlan would remain the head of the French administration. To Darlan's shock, only some of the French troops followed his commands, while others continued to fight alongside the Germans. Darlan was removed from the Vichy government for his collaboration with the Allies, and southern France was invaded by Germany in Operation Attila.

Thinking that the French would follow Darlan more willingly than they would someone from the Allied forces, American general Dwight D. Eisenhower agreed with Darlan's nomination of himself to the post of high commissioner of France for North and West Africa. Darlan's appointment was met with criticism from the commander of the free French forces, Charles de Gaulle,

English prime minister Winston Churchill, and other Allied officials.

While in Algiers, a twenty-year-old French monarchist and member of the resistance, Ferdinand Bonnier de La Chapelle, entered Darlan's headquarters on December 24, 1942, and shot him twice. Darlan died a few hours later. De La Chapelle was arrested and executed by firing squad on December 24, 1942.

Impact

As hatred and mistrust of the Vichy government grew in France and in other countries, so did support for the French Resistance. François Darlan and other members of the Vichy government had a profound effect on French daily life and on the psyche of the nation. While many French citizens joined the resistance, standing up against the Nazis and supporting their country, many others sided with the Vichy government, dividing France into confused and, at times, contradictory factions. With the Allied forces' ultimate victory in World War II, those who supported the Vichy regime claimed that they had been forced to do so by the Germans, and many who joined the resistance when a German defeat was inevitable claimed to have been against the Nazis and Vichy throughout the war. On the whole, France and its citizens were left in a state of confusion and shame.

Further Reading

Alexander, Martin S. *The Republic in Danger: General Maurice Gamelin and the Politics of French Defense, 1931-1940*. New York: Cambridge University Press, 2002. Written for those who already possess an understanding of French politics during the Vichy era, this book offers an excellent account of France's involvement in World War II and the internal conflict occurring simultaneously within France.

Burrin, Philippe. *France Under the Germans: Collaboration and Compromise*. New York: New Press, 1998. Explores the reasoning and rationale behind the compromises France made with the Nazis and their ramifications for France's citizens.

Jackson, Julian. *France: The Dark Years, 1940-1944*. New York: Oxford University Press, 2003. Takes the controversial stance that the Vichy government was not an oppressive force thrust upon France by the Germans but rather a powerful faction of French fascists and anti-Semites.

Melton, George E. *Darlan*. Westport, Conn.: Praeger, 1998. A thorough biography of Darlan, covering his childhood, career development, involvement in World War II, and assassination, of which Melton offers a complete picture.

Paxton, Robert O. *Vichy France*. New York: Columbia University Press, 2001. A thoroughly researched and well-documented account of the Vichy government and its decision-making processes.

—*Sara Vidar*

See also: Joseph Darnand; Jacques Doriot; Adolf Hitler; Pierre Laval; Philippe Pétain.

Joseph Darnand

Vichy head of the secret police

Born: March 19, 1897; Coligny, Ain, Rhône-Alpes France

Died: October 10, 1945; Châtillon, Seine, France

Also known as: Aimé-Joseph Darnand (full name)

Major offense: Collaboration with the enemy

Active: July, 1941-June 25, 1945

Locale: France

Sentence: Death by firing squad

Early Life

Joseph Darnand (dahr-nahn) was born in Coligny; his father was a railroad employee. Darnand was eighteen years old and working as a cabinetmaker when World War I began and he volunteered for duty. During the course of the war he received seven citations for bravery, including a medal awarded personally by General Philippe Pétain. Darnand developed an intense loyalty to Pétain.

After the war, he worked again as a cabinetmaker, then founded a transportation company in Nice. During this time, he became a member of several right-wing political organizations, some of which were paramilitary. In 1925, he joined Action Française; then in 1928 he became a member of les Croix-de-Feux. In 1936, he became a member of the neo-fascist Parti Populaire Français, founded by Jacques Doriot.

Darnand once again volunteered for military service at the beginning of World War II. He was mobilized in

1939 and fought along the Maginot line. He was captured and was a prisoner of war in the camp at Pithiviers but managed to escape and rejoin Pétain's forces. After the armistice, Darnand returned to Nice. There he was very active in the Légion Française des Combattants (French Legion of Veterans), which was approved by the Vichy government. He was in charge of a recruiting office for the Legion des Volontaires Françaises Contre le Bolchevisme (LVF).

Criminal Career

Soon Darnand found the organization's policies too moderate and in July, 1941, established the Service d' Ordre Legionnaire, whose purpose was to combat the opponents of Pétain's National Revolution by fighting against the French Resistance and by aiding in the finding and arresting of Jews. On January 1, 1943, the organization was officially recognized and renamed the Milice Française, which was, in reality, the secret police of the Vichy government. In October, 1943, Darnand swore an oath of loyalty to Adolf Hitler and became a member of the Waffen Schutzstaffel (SS). Two months later, he was named head of the Milice. In this position, he worked with the German forces to strengthen the effort against the French Resistance (Maquis). The Milice, under his direction, carried out summary executions at random and assassinations of politicians opposed to Vichy and Hitler. Darnand also established a special force to combat the black market. He continued to play a major role in the Vichy regime and was named secretary of the interior in December of 1943. In September, 1944, he followed Pétain to Germany. There, at Sigmaringen, he joined Pétain's government in exile.

Legal Action and Outcome

Darnand was captured by the English on June 25, 1945, in northern Italy, where he had been sent in pursuit of French partisans. French authorities, who returned him to France. He was brought to trial before the Haut Cour de Justice, where he was judged and condemned to death by firing squad on October 3, 1945. The sentence was carried out at Fort Châtillon on October 10, 1945.

Impact

Joseph Darnand made a major contribution to the Vichy government's fight against the French Resistance. His establishment of the Milice, an all-French police force, strengthened the Vichy regime's ability to find and interrogate those working in the resistance. Darnand provides insight into one aspect of the mentality of collaboration. He had heroically served France in World War I and had defended the Maginot line against the German invasion, yet during the late 1930's and early 1940's, he had become convinced of the value of fascism as a political ideology and of its appropriateness as a form of government for France. Coupled with his devotion to Pétain, this belief inspired him to work with the Germans.

Further Reading

Gildea, Robert. *Marianne in Chains: In Search of the German Occupation, 1940-45*. London: Pan, 2003. Looks at interaction between the army of occupation and local officials and how ordinary French citizens responded to the occupation. Archival and personal interview sources.

Jackson, Julian. *France: The Dark Years, 1940-44*. New York: Oxford University Press, 2003. Comprehensive and detailed, this work discusses collaborators, resistance workers, the social and political atmosphere of the period, and the Vichy regime. Distinguishes between myths and realities of the war years.

Ousby, Ian. *Occupation: The Ordeal of France, 1940-1944*. London: Pimlico, 1999. Extensive treatment of the Vichy regime, especially its policy of persecuting Jews, communists, and dissenters.

—*Shawncey Webb*

See also: François Darlan; Jacques Doriot; Adolf Hitler; Pierre Laval; Philippe Pétain.

Richard Walther Darré

German minister of food and agriculture (1933-1942)

Born: July 14, 1895; Buenos Aires, Argentina
Died: September 5, 1953; Munich, West Germany (now Germany)
Major offenses: War crimes, namely furnishing propaganda used by the Nazis to persecute Jews
Active: July, 1933-March, 1942
Locale: Germany
Sentence: Seven years in prison; commuted for health reasons

Early Life

Richard Walther Darré (RIK-hard VAHL-tur DAHR-ray) was born in Buenos Aires to immigrant German farmers. He was educated in Germany and briefly in England before he returned to Germany, where he served with distinction in the German army during World War I. At the cessation of hostilities, he took up the study of agronomics. While working as an executive in agricultural firms and as an labor organizer for various farming groups, he began writing treatises, applying his radical ideas about plant growth to the evolution of human populations and races.

Political Career

In 1928 Darré published *Das Bauerntum als Lebensquell der nordischen Rasse* (the peasantry as life source of the Nordic race), a book celebrating the concept of "blood and soil." Darré's thesis was that the German peasant deserved to be celebrated as the preserver of German character and integrity and that the highest form of European culture resided in his native land. This work and others brought Darré to the notice of high-ranking members of the National Socialist (Nazi) Party, particularly Heinrich Himmler. In 1930, Darré joined the Nazi Party and began a meteoric rise toward national leadership in the Nazi political machine. By 1932, he was known to Adolf Hitler, who appreciated Darré's arguments about the need to preserve racial purity among the Germans and the importance of the peasantry in Germany's history and future.

Darré's writings on the superiority of the German race and his glorification of farming life contributed to the cult of Aryanism and to programs designed to eliminate Jews and subjugate Slavic peoples. Within the Nazi Party, Darré was given assignments to promote agricultural policies that favored the small farmers; he also assumed a leadership role in what would become the Schutzstaffel (SS), the political police in Hitler's Third Reich. When the Nazis came to power in 1933, Darré was made minister of food and agriculture; he was also made head of the Race and Settlement Office in the SS, approving marriages for SS officers and leading efforts to settle SS men in farming communities. By 1938, however, he had fallen out with SS leadership and was relegated to duties in agriculture. When German agricultural production began failing during the early years of World War II, Hitler lost confidence in Darré and relieved him of his duties as minister in 1942.

Legal Action and Outcome

In November, 1947, Darré was indicted for war crimes and tried at Nuremberg with twenty other Reichministers in 1948. On April 13, 1949, he was sentenced to seven years' imprisonment. He was released the following year for health reasons, however, and retired to Munich, where he died in 1953.

Impact

Richard Walther Darré's writings on the Aryan race provided tools used by the Nazis to persecute Jews and to subjugate Slavic peoples. His work as agriculture minister was less effective, however, and his policies may have helped shorten the war by denying Germany necessary foodstuffs to support both the military and the general populace. The relatively light sentence he received at the Nuremberg trials suggests that, by the end of hostilities, he was no longer considered one of Hitler's inner circle and therefore not as culpable for the Nazis' policies of terror and extermination as others in the regime.

Further Reading

Bramwell, Anna. *Blood and Soil: Richard Walther Darré and Hitler's Green Party*. Abottsbrook, England: Kensal Press, 1985. Controversial biography linking Darré's efforts at promoting ecological causes to late twentieth century ecological movements.

Corini, Gustavo. "Richard Walther Darré: The Blood and Soil Ideologue." In *The Nazi Elite*, edited by Ronald Smelser and Rainer Zimmerman. New York: New York University Press, 1993. Excellent summary of Darré's career, highlighting both his work as the leader of agricultural programming and his contributions to Nazi ideology.

Nicholls, David. *Adolf Hitler: A Biographical Companion*. Santa Barbara, Calif.: ABC-CLIO, 2000. Describes Darré's rise to prominence in the Nazi Party and his racist ideology glorifying the German peasants.

Stephens, Piers. "Blood, Not Soil: Anna Bramwell and the Myth of 'Hitler's Green Party.'" *Organization & Environment* 14, no. 2 (2001): 173-187. Reviews Darré's career in an attempt to de-link his ideology from that of postwar ecological movements.

—Laurence W. Mazzeno

See also: Dietrich Eckart; Elisabeth Förster-Nietzsche; Adolf Hitler; Albert Speer.

Richard Allen Davis

American murderer

Born: June 2, 1954; San Francisco, California
Major offenses: Murder, robbery, burglary, kidnapping, lewd act involving a child, and assault with a deadly weapon
Active: October 1, 1993
Locale: Petaluma, California
Sentence: Death

Early Life

Richard Allen Davis (DAY-vihs) was born in San Francisco. His father, Robert, who worked as a truck driver and longshoreman, was an alcoholic who was absent much of the time. His mother, Evelyn, who stayed home with the children, was abusive and emotionally neglectful. Richard's early childhood was unstable, as the family relocated frequently. His parents divorced when he was eleven. Richard began getting in trouble with law enforcement authorities at an early age. His first encounter, at age twelve, resulted in his arrest for burglary. Later that same year, after being arrested for forgery, he was placed in a juvenile detention center, where he remained until his father obtained custody of him. Davis attended school through the tenth grade, when he dropped out and joined the Army. He was enlisted in 1971-1972 but was then discharged after developing a morphine addiction.

Criminal Career

Through the years, Davis continued his criminal career, with seventeen arrests for various crimes, including robbery, burglary, theft, three separate kidnapping charges, sexual assault, public drunkenness, possession of marijuana, and numerous parole and probation violations. By the time Davis was thirty-nine, he had spent more than fourteen years in prison and had a rap sheet eleven pages long. He was last paroled on June 27, 1993, after serving eight years of a sixteen-year sentence for kidnapping. Three months after his release, he kidnapped and murdered Polly Klaas, a twelve-year-old girl.

In the autumn of 1993, Polly Hannah Klaas was having a slumber party at her home with two friends. While her mother and sister slept in the next room, Davis entered the home, gagged and tied up Polly's friends, and abducted Polly at knifepoint. Later that night, police received a phone call regarding a suspicious man seen near a car in a ditch. Law enforcement officers assisted Davis in pulling his car out of the embankment, allowing him to continue on his way. It is believed that Polly was still alive at that time. The officers at the scene were unaware of the abduction because the appropriate alert had not been dispatched to patrol cars, for fear that the press would hear the information over the scanner.

Legal Action and Outcome

Polly's disappearance prompted a communitywide search that lasted sixty-five days. At the end of this time, Davis was arrested after forensic evidence—a palm print found in Polly's bedroom—matched his print in the computer network. Four days later, Davis confessed to strangling the child. He led the police to the body, which was located in a shallow grave in a wooded area of Cloverdale, California. On December 7, 1993, Davis was charged with the kidnapping and murder of Polly Klaas. At trial, Davis conceded to all charges except the sexual assault allegation. On June 18, 1996, the jury found him guilty on all counts, and on September 26, 1996, he was sentenced to death. As of 2006, he was awaiting execution on death row in San Quentin State Prison.

Impact

Richard Allen Davis's arrest for the kidnapping and murder of Polly Klaas was a catalyst for passage of the "three strikes law" in California, which mandated harsher penalties and longer prison terms for violent repeat offenders. Marc Klaas, Polly's father and an activist for crime prevention programs, lobbied for this law and helped obtain the signatures needed for its passage. Klaas's advocacy was also instrumental in passing the Amber Alert notification system at state and national levels. Klaas formed the KlaasKids Foundation, an organization devoted to protecting children from violent crimes through education and community events. BeyondMissing, another organization founded by Klaas, works to find missing children. The Polly Klaas Foundation, of which Polly's mother was a director, was also established to promote children's safety.

Further Reading

Bortnick, Barry. *Polly Klaas: The Murder of America's Child.* New York: Pinnacle Books, 1995. A true-crime book on the Klaas kidnapping and murder.

Filler, D. M. "Making the Case for Megan's Law: A Study in Legislative Rhetoric." *Indiana Law Journal* 76 (Spring, 2001): 315. A review of arguments by legislators regarding the need for sex-offender legislation, including a discussion of Polly Klaas's murder.

Jenkins, Philip. *Moral Panic: Changing Concepts of the Child Molester in Modern America.* New Haven, Conn.: Yale University Press, 1998. Explores the evolution of legislation related to sex crimes against children and how the murder of Polly Klass was a catalyst for predator legislation.

Klaas, Marc. "Sex Offender Registries Protect Our Children." *Corrections Today* 65, no. 1 (February, 2003): 23-24. An article by Polly's father, advocating the monitoring of sex offenders.

Vitiello, M. "'Three Strikes' and the Romero Case: The Supreme Court Restores Democracy." 30 *Loyola of Los Angeles Law Review* 30, no. 1643 (June, 1997). A review of California's "three strikes" legislation, which passed as a result of Polly Klaas's murder.

—Lisa A. Williams-Taylor

See also: Ira Einhorn; Albert Fish; Gilbert Gauthe.

Tino De Angelis

American corporate commodities tycoon

Born: 1915; Bronx, New York
Also known as: Anthony De Angelis (full name)
Major offenses: Conspiracy and transporting forged warehouse receipts across state lines
Active: 1957-November, 1963
Locale: Bayonne, New Jersey
Sentence: Twenty years' imprisonment; paroled in less than seven years

Early Life

Anthony "Tino" De Angelis (dee AN-jehl-ihs) was born the son of Italian immigrants. While still a teenager, he worked as a butcher in a meat market. In 1938, he started his own slaughterhouse and earned more than $100,000 the first year. At some point, De Angelis began perpetrating a fraud against the National School Lunch Act program by selling spoiled meat. He later began selling substandard vegetable oil products to Europe while its infrastructure was struggling with the aftermath of World War II.

Criminal Career

Sometime in the late 1950's or early 1960's, De Angelis, through his company, the Allied Crude Vegetable Oil Refining Corporation, began the scam that was to make him infamous: his purported control of the world's supply of soybean oil. However, most of the salad oil he controlled did not exist. To store the salad oil, De Angelis acquired a tank farm in Bayonne, New Jersey, just across the Hudson River from New York City. He filled the forty-two-foot-tall storage tanks almost completely with water and topped them off with vegetable oil. Since oil floats on water, the ingredient at the top of each tank was indeed oil; however, water formed the majority of the tank's contents. Even the small amount of oil on top was pumped from tank to tank via interconnecting pipes. De Angelis then obtained loans using as collateral the valuable salad oil that was supposedly in the tanks. When inspectors and auditors checked the contents of the tanks, all they could see was oil. A subsidiary of American Express, American Express Field Warehousing Company, guaranteed that the oil was really in the tanks.

Lending money on the basis of warehouse receipts is a common banking practice. Banks assume that the receipts prove the existence of the inventory. De Angelis used warehouse receipts to borrow from brokerage companies, and the brokers, in turn, used the same receipts as collateral on loans from banks. Thus, there were many loans but no collateral to support them. In addition to fooling warehouse workers, De Angelis also forged his own warehouse receipts, resulting in the appearance that he owned more salad oil than existed in the entire country.

Legal Action and Outcome

De Angelis was convicted of conspiracy and transporting forged warehouse receipts across state lines. He was sentenced to twenty years in prison, but he was paroled in only seven years, serving from August, 1965, to June, 1972. However, he apparently did not learn any lessons from incarceration; upon release, he was twice more convicted of similar crimes.

Tino De Angelis. (Courtesy, *The Jersey Journal*)

Impact

The "salad oil swindle" received less publicity than similar scams because it was uncovered during the week that President John F. Kennedy was assassinated, in November, 1963. As a result, the media and American population had more compelling news with which to be concerned than a commodities con in New Jersey. However, at that time, it was one of the biggest frauds in history. The result of Tino De Angelis's scheme for investors amounted to losses of at least $150 million. One brokerage firm, Ira Haupt & Co., was quickly liquidated because of its losses to De Angelis, and another firm, Williston and Beane, was taken over by Merrill Lynch. The American Express Field Warehousing Company also went out of business, but the parent company made good the losses. At least twenty banks that had loaned money to De Angelis also lost money. New procedures for auditing warehoused inventories were subsequently created, thus affecting accountants and auditors. The crime's impact on brokerage firms ultimately led to the passage of the 1971 Securities Investor Protection Act, which provided insurance against losses at securities dealers.

Further Reading

Eichenwald, Kurt. "Economy and Business: After a Boom, There Will Be Scandal." *The New York Times*, December 16, 2002, p. C3. A retrospective article on how scandals most often occur in boom times.

Miller, Norman C. *The Great Salad Oil Swindle*. New York: Coward-McCann, 1965. This is the complete story of De Angelis written by a *Wall Street Journal* staff writer who won a Pulitzer Prize for his coverage of the case. Includes an extensive index.

Phalon, Richard. *Forbes Greatest Investing Stories*. New York: John Wiley & Sons, 2001. This volume includes stories with lessons for investors, including a chapter titled "Swindle of the Century: Anthony De Angelis."

—*Dale L. Flesher*

See also: John R. Brinkley; Megan Louise Ireland; Henri Lemoine; Victor Lustig; Charles Ponzi; Alexandre Stavisky.

Léon Degrelle

Leader of the Rexist movement

Born: June 15, 1906; Bouillon, Belgium
Died: March 31, 1994; Málaga, Spain
Also known as: José León Ramírez Reina; Léon Joseph Marie Degrelle (full name)
Cause of notoriety: A leader of the extreme right in his native Wallonia region, Degrelle collaborated with the Nazis, fought in the Waffen Schutzstaffel (SS) on the Eastern Front, and escaped to Spain to become a strident Holocaust denier and an apologist for Fascist- and Nazi-inspired movements.
Active: 1930-1945
Locale: Belgium, Eastern Europe, Spain

Early Life

The family of Léon Degrelle (duh-GREHL) originated in France, and, as fervent Catholics, emigrated in protest over the anticlerical policies of the Third Republic. They set up a brewery business in the town of Bouillon, in the French-speaking Wallonia provinces of southern Belgium. There enjoying fewer restrictions on the Church, Léon Degrelle was given a rigorous Catholic education. He was publishing a weekly newspaper by the age of twenty and had studied law for two years at the University of Louvain. He worked for a while as a foreign correspondent and in 1930 entered the political arena, founding and directing the Rexist movement, which originally operated within the framework of the Catholic Party.

The name "Rexist" derived from the Latin *Christus Rex* (Christ the king), and the movement became increasingly extreme in its platform, espousing fascistic totalitarianism, anti-Semitism, and Walloon separatism—so much so that the Rexists split from the Catholic Party in 1935 to advance their own candidates for public office. The Rexist Party, under Degrelle's leadership, captured thirty-four parliamentary seats in the 1936 election but held only four seats by 1939, at least in part because of the unpopularity of the aggressive policies of Nazi Germany and Fascist Italy, with which the Rexists were identified.

Nazi Career

On May 10, 1940, after Germany's blitzkrieg on Belgium, Degrelle was arrested as a subversive and sent to a prisoners' camp in France. He was freed when France surrendered to Germany on June 21, 1940. Returning to Belgium, he collaborated with the German occupiers in the hope of governing Wallonia under Nazi rule. His Rexist Party split, some members forming a resistance movement, and Degrelle was excommunicated by the Vatican on August 19, 1943. He was not granted power, which remained in the hands of the German military governor.

Frustrated, Degrelle recruited a Walloon unit to serve in the Nazi forces on the eastern front in what was termed a "crusade against Bolshevism." This "Legion Wallonie" would be engaged from 1941 to 1945 and ended as a unit in the elite Waffen Schutzstaffel (SS). Degrelle, denied an officer's commission, joined as a private but worked through the ranks to become a general and would command the legion from February 13, 1944, until it disbanded on May 5, 1945. Wounded seven times in action, Degrelle was awarded the Knight's Cross by Nazi dictator Adolf Hitler.

Legal Action and Outcome

Degrelle was tried in absentia in liberated Belgium and sentenced to death on December 29, 1944. He fled to Norway, where he boarded an airplane and flew to neutral Spain, crash landing on May 8, 1945. Severely injured, he was protected by Spanish dictator Francisco Franco and lived for a while incognito under the pseudonym of José León Ramírez Reina. He became a building contractor and was granted Spanish citizenship. Several attempts to extradite him failed, and the death sentence lapsed in 1974. He remained controversial as an unabashed supporter of neofascist causes and for his lectures, books, and articles (including an "Open Letter" to Pope John Paul II) that tried to cast doubt on the veracity of the Holocaust.

Impact

The Rexist movement, already marginalized before World War II, had little effect on political affairs in Belgium from 1940 to 1945. Léon Degrelle consequently became, aside from his military exploits and propaganda value to the Nazis, a less than consequential figure. During the postwar years, he served as a lightning rod for various groups fostering anti-Semitism and Holocaust denial.

Further Reading

Blom, J. C. H., and E. Lamberts. *History of the Low Countries*. Translated by James C. Kennedy. Oxford, England: Berghahn Books, 1999. Degrelle's fanatical commitment to fascism is blamed for alienating the middle class and causing Rexism's decline.

Brodsky, Alexandra Fanny. *A Fragile Identity: Survival in Nazi-Occupied Belgium*. New York: Radcliffe Press, 1998. Though Rexism is mentioned only peripherally, this account provides an invaluable background for placing the movement in its historical context.

Kieft, David Owen. *Belgium's Return to Neutrality: An Essay in the Frustrations of Small-Power Diplomacy*. Oxford, England: Clarendon Press, 1972. Takes a view opposed to that of Blom and Lamberts by asserting that Degrelle's abilities were Rexism's greatest assets.

—*Raymond Pierre Hylton*

See also: Willis A. Carto; Francisco Franco; Adolf Hitler; David Irving; Savitri Devi.

Eugene de Kock

South African commander of secret police

Born: January 29, 1948; South Africa
Also known as: Prime Evil
Major offenses: Six murders, one manslaughter, and three counts of conspiracy to murder
Active: 1983-1991
Locale: South Africa
Sentence: Two life sentences plus 212 years

Early Life

Eugene de Kock (kohk) grew up in a conservative Afrikaner family, descendants of the Dutch who settled South Africa beginning in the seventeenth century. His early life was shaped by the policy of apartheid, the strict separation of whites and blacks set forth by the conservative Afrikaans government with the blessing of the Dutch Reformed Church. His father, a heavy drinker, was physically abusive to his wife and ridiculed the young de Kock for stuttering.

Criminal Career

De Kock initially led the South African Army's counterinsurgency unit, called Koevoet, in Namibia. In 1983, he was appointed director of Vlakplaas, a unit of the secret police devoted to fighting political opponents of the apartheid regime. Originally formed in 1981, the unit's headquarters was on a "death farm" where security forces tortured and killed antiapartheid suspects. The Vlakplaas unit was known as the "death squad." Promoted to colonel, de Kock received promotions for the efficiency of his work. His own men were the first to call him "Prime Evil" for his actions. The Vlakplaas unit operated until the African National Congress came into power in 1994.

Legal Action and Outcome

In 1996, de Kock was put on trial. He confessed to more than one hundred acts of torture and murder. In 1998, he was convicted of six murders, one manslaughter, and three counts of conspiracy to murder. He was sentenced to two life terms plus 212 years for other crimes.

To deal with the trauma of decades of apartheid, Bishop Desmond Tutu and President Nelson Mandela set up a Truth and Reconciliation Commission (TRC), which granted amnesties in return for the truth about some crimes. De Kock applied for amnesty for more than one hundred crimes, including the six murders for which he was convicted. To the surprise of many, some of the widows and families of men he had killed supported his amnesty application. They reportedly felt that he had told the truth about the death squad, while many members of the former regime had refused to cooperate with the commission. One widow explained that knowing who had killed her husband had given her enough peace to move forward with her life. De Kock was granted amnesties in 2000 for some crimes not related to his two life sentences, including the bombing of the offices of an antiapartheid church group.

De Kock maintained in his appearances before the TRC that he was following political orders when he committed the atrocities. He also later testified for the prosecution in the trial of former South African president Pieter Wilhelm Botha. He expressed remorse for his crimes and a desire to atone for them. Imprisoned in C-Max, the maximum-security section of Pretoria's central prison, de Kock was expected to spend the rest of his life in jail.

Impact

Although guilty of many horrific crimes, Eugene de Kock had a remarkable effect on South Africans' thinking about how governments or other social entities affect the actions of individuals. His trial raised questions about the law and how it focuses only on the actions of the individual but fails to address crimes of the system or structure in which those actions take place. De Kock's life has given philosophers, sociologists, religious scholars, and others the opportunity to examine questions about the nature of evil and the importance and meaning of forgiveness.

Further Reading

Daley, Suzanne. "A Sentence for 'Prime Evil.'" *The New York Times*, 145, November 3, 1996; "Killer Tells of Rewards for Defending Apartheid." *The New York Times*, 147, June 4, 1998; and "South Africa Confronts Brutalities of One Man." *The New York Times*, July 19, 1999. Three of many articles by Daley covering the trial of Eugene de Kock and its aftermath.

De Kock, Eugene. *A Long Night's Damage: Working for the Apartheid State*. Saxonwold, South Africa: Contra Press, 1998. De Kock's own account of his career and crimes.

Gobodo-Madikizela, Pumla. *A Human Being Died That Night*. Boston: Houghton Mifflin, 2002. Written by an African psychologist who consulted with the TRC and based on interviews with de Kock, this book examines the nature of evil and the meaning of forgiveness.

—*Rebecca Lovell Scott*

See also: Winnie Mandela; Hendrik Frensch Verwoerd.

John DeLorean

American automobile engineer

Born: January 6, 1925; Detroit, Michigan

Died: March 19, 2005; Summit, New Jersey

Also known as: John Zachary Delorean (full name); John De Lorean

Cause of notoriety: After securing numerous investments to build his DeLorean Motor Company, John DeLorean struggled with the automobile plant's monetary losses and became involved in narcotics trafficking in order to earn money to keep his company afloat.

Active: 1975-1984

Locale: Detroit, Michigan; Belfast, Northern Ireland; New York, New York; and Los Angeles, California

Early Life

John DeLorean (deh-LOR-ee-uhn) was born John Delorean and grew up in an Eastern European migrant community on the east side of Detroit. He was the first of four sons born to Zachary and Kathryn Pribak Delorean. While Zachary made a respectable income working in the automotive industry, he was known to drink excessively and act violently. John's parents divorced when he was in high school, but he continued to live with his mother until he first married, at the age of twenty-nine.

DeLorean was a talented student and attended Cass Technical High School and then the Lawrence Institute of Technology. His studies were interrupted by his Army service in 1943, but he eventually returned to complete his degree. He went on for graduate degrees in engineering from the Chrysler Institute and business at the University of Michigan.

Business Career

DeLorean experienced a rapid rise in the General Motors corporate structure, but he was also suspected to hold investments in outside ventures that made profits through dealing with General Motors—a clear conflict of inter-

John DeLorean. (AP/Wide World Photos)

est. These accusations, as well as personal friction with others at General Motors, led management to ask him to resign. Publicly, DeLorean stated that he quit; he then began a media campaign criticizing General Motors for its failures in the automotive industry.

DeLorean's carefully managed public image, including his marriage to his third wife, supermodel Christina Ferrare, added even more luster to his storybook life. For many years, he was the subject of numerous tales applauding him for his courage to speak out about the problems with the Detroit auto manufacturers.

In the mid-1970's, he formed the DeLorean Motor Company (DMC) with a factory in Northern Ireland built largely through British government investments. Other investors included high-profile celebrities such as Johnny Carson and Sammy Davis, Jr. DeLorean's company produced only one type of car: The DMC-12 gull-wing stainless steel sports car was unique, and buyers aggressively pursued ordering the cars before they were available. However, the reality of design flaws, production delays, and inflated sales projections led to significant monetary losses. In order to gain more financial support, DeLorean falsified numerous claims about the vehicle.

DeLorean's Two Car Coups

John DeLorean's legend among car enthusiasts derives primarily from two of his novel creations: the Pontiac GTO and his namesake, the DeLorean sports car.

The GTO's name was an allusion to Ferrari's Grand Turismo Omologato, the most chic of 1960's sports cars. DeLorean's car was not chic, but it was powerful—a "muscle car." DeLorean's design team put a 389-cubic-inch-displacement, 325-horsepower V-8 engine into the medium frame of a Tempest so that the GTO had loads of power for a budget price.

It could accelerate from zero to sixty miles per hour in 7.5 seconds. It could do a quarter mile in 14.8 seconds. Young men loved it; they nicknamed it the Goat. Pontiac hoped to sell 5,000 in its first year, 1964, but at year's end, 32,450 had been sold. Later models had even bigger engines.

However, it was the DeLorean itself that made its inventor the cynosure of public attention. As a sports car, it had many problems—it was sluggish and the driver's compartment was cramped—yet that hardly mattered. It had two qualities that endeared it to the American public. First, it was the product of a maverick company, a daring go-it-alone venture. Second, it looked unlike anything else on the highways. The wedge-shaped body was the work of Ital Design, the same firm that designed the Lotus Esprit. Its "gull-wing" doors flipped out and up like those of a race car. The power plant was a six-cylinder sports engine developed by Peugeot, Renault, and Volvo (the PRV6) with 2.8 liters displacement. It was a sleek 166 inches long, 73.1 inches wide, and 44.9 inches high.

Unfortunately, its price, twenty-five thousand dollars, put it beyond the reach of many buyers when it debuted in 1981. By 1982, DeLorean had to end its production, having made about 9,200 of the cars.

Their rarity helped keep DeLoreans exotic. They were a marvel to see flash by on the highways. They looked, in fact, like a glimpse of the world of tomorrow. In the science-fiction comedy film *Back to the Future* (1985), Michael J. Fox exclaims to Christopher Lloyd, "Are you telling me you built a time machine . . . out of a DeLorean?" Lloyd replies, "The way I figured it, if you're gonna build a time machine into a car, why not do it with some style?" The joke worked so well because the combination seemed in keeping with the DeLorean bravado—almost.

Legal Action and Outcome

After a desperate attempt to earn money to keep operations afloat, DeLorean was arrested in a federal sting operation at a hotel near the Los Angeles airport. He was charged for his role in offering to fund the sale of one hundred kilograms of cocaine with a potential street value of fifty million dollars. In August of 1984, DeLorean was acquitted of these criminal charges based on the arguments that he was entrapped in the sale and that once he found out about the illegality, he feared for the safety of his family.

Impact

While John DeLorean's criminal actions associated with drug dealing were somewhat significant, his actions related to the failed DeLorean Motor Company venture had a far greater impact on the lives of several thousand people. More than twenty-five hundred workers lost their jobs in Northern Ireland. Those employed by the vehicle plant and those additional workers employed by the suppliers were left without jobs. Numerous investors lost an estimated total of $250 million.

Further Reading

Fallon, Ivan, and James Strodes. *Dream Maker: The Rise and Fall of John Z. De Lorean.* New York: G. P.

Putnam's Sons, 1983. Offers a biography of DeLorean's youth and rapid rise in the corporate structure at General Motors. Also details his building of the complex multinational operation that would become the failed corporations related to his automotive ventures. Because his criminal trial was still pending at publication time, few details related to his cocaine trafficking case are shared.

Haddad, William. *Hard Driving: My Years with John DeLorean*. New York: Random House, 1985. Haddad, a fifteen-year business associate and top executive with DeLorean Motor Company, details the complexity of his admiration for and disaffection with the talented but untrustworthy DeLorean.

Levin, Hillel. *Grand Delusions: The Cosmic Career of John De Lorean*. New York: Viking Press, 1983. This journalistic account details the rationale for the numerous complex corporations and unconventional business tactics used by DeLorean in his attempt to build an automotive empire.

—*John C. Kilburn, Jr.*

SEE ALSO: Ivan Boesky; Martin Frankel; Michael Milken.

ALBERT DESALVO

Rapist and suspected serial murderer

BORN: September 3, 1931; Chelsea, Massachusetts
DIED: November 25, 1973; Walpole State Prison, Massachusetts
ALSO KNOWN AS: Boston Strangler; Green Man; Measuring Man
MAJOR OFFENSE: Rape
ACTIVE: June 14, 1962-January 4, 1964
LOCALE: Boston, Massachusetts
SENTENCE: Life in prison

EARLY LIFE

Albert DeSalvo (duh-SAL-voh) was born in Boston in 1931, where he grew up in an abusive home. His father, Frank DeSalvo, had a history of legal infractions and incarcerations and also physically abused his wife and children. DeSalvo's father was absent for much of his son's childhood, divorce finally split the family in 1944. Albert compiled a number of juvenile arrests, primarily for property crimes.

DeSalvo joined the Army in 1948 and was first stationed in Germany. While in Germany, he met and married a German woman, Irmgard Beck. He brought her back to the United States with him when he was transferred to Fort Dix, New Jersey, in 1954. At this point, DeSalvo's life appeared stable, with a military career, a wife, and a child who was born in 1955. Later, however, he was charged with molesting a nine-year-old girl in New Jersey. Because the family of the child declined to press charges against DeSalvo, he received an honorable discharge from the Army in 1956 and returned to Boston.

CRIMINAL CAREER

Once back in Boston, DeSalvo's involvement in property crime reemerged, and he was arrested several times for breaking and entering over the following years. After a 1960 arrest for suspicion of burglary, police learned of DeSalvo's involvement in repeated predatory sexual behavior. At the time of this arrest, authorities had been searching for a suspect whom they had named the Measuring Man. This suspect had been posing as a talent scout, approaching women's homes and gaining entrance with the hoax. Once inside, this man would take the women's measurements while intimately touching them. DeSalvo confessed to being the Measuring Man and was convicted of breaking and entering and assault and battery, ultimately serving eleven months in prison.

After being released from prison, DeSalvo's sexual offenses turned from perversion and assault to rape. He began breaking into homes across four states over the next few years, tying up his female victims, and raping them. The perpetrator of this series of rapes became known as the Green Man, because of the green pants typically worn during the attacks. Overlapping this period was a series of murders that would become known as the Boston Strangler murders. From 1962 to 1964, thirteen women were raped and murdered; most were strangled, and the killer sometimes left the bodies in different poses.

LEGAL ACTION AND OUTCOME

In 1965, nine months after the last of the Boston Strangler murders, DeSalvo was arrested in the Green Man case after a woman identified his picture to police. While awaiting trial, DeSalvo bragged to another inmate that he was the Boston Strangler and then later described the killings to the inmate's attorney, F. Lee Bailey. DeSalvo described the women who were murdered, as well as crime scenes, to Bailey, who gave the information to the police.

The prosecutor's office decided to prosecute DeSalvo for only the Green Man crimes, and he was sentenced to life in prison after being convicted of the rapes. He was stabbed and killed in his prison cell on November 25, 1973. His killer was never identified.

Impact

The Boston Strangler case was one of the most notorious crime sprees of the 1960's, and it led to a number of books and movies. It brought attention to the deliberate and calculated methods used by some serial rapists and caused a controversy over the credibility and value of confessions in the criminal process. The case also launched the career of attorney F. Lee Bailey, who gained additional fame defending Patty Hearst, Sam Sheppard, and O. J. Simpson.

Although Albert DeSalvo reportedly confessed to the murders, controversy still surrounds the identity of the Boston Strangler. Indeed, a new group of books have been released that challenge the assertion that Albert DeSalvo was the Boston Strangler.

Further Reading

Junger, Sebastien. *A Death in Belmont*. New York: W. W. Norton, 2006. Junger examines the 1963 slaying of Bessie Goldberg, of whose murder housecleaner Roy Smith was convicted; Goldberg has long been thought to have been a victim of the Boston Strangler.

Kelly, Susan. *The Boston Stranglers: The Public Conviction of Albert DeSalvo and the True Story of Eleven Shocking Murders*. New York: Pinnacle Books, 2002. Follows the life of Albert DeSalvo and contends that he was not the Boston Strangler.

Rae, William. *Confessions of the Boston Strangler*. New York: Pyramid Books, 1967. Focuses on the Boston Strangler case and examines the confessions of Albert DeSalvo.

Sherman, Casey. *A Rose for Mary: The Hunt for the Real Boston Strangler*. Urbana, Ill.: Northeastern University Press, 2003. Like Kelly, Sherman, the nephew of the strangler's last victim, argues in this meticulously researched volume against DeSalvo as the murderer of all eleven women and examines why experts think there was more than one murderer.

—Brion Sever

See also: Joe Ball; David Berkowitz; Kenneth Bianchi; Ted Bundy; Angelo Buono, Jr.; Andrei Chikatilo; John Reginald Halliday Christie; Andrew Cunanan; Jeffrey Dahmer; Albert Fish; John Wayne Gacy; Ed Gein; Karla Homolka; Leonard Lake; Charles Ng; Dennis Rader; Richard Speck; Aileen Carol Wuornos.

Phoolan Devi

Indian bandit and Parliament member (1996-1998, 1999-2001)

Born: August 10, 1963; Gorha Ka Purwa, Uttar Pradesh, India
Died: July 25, 2001; New Delhi, India
Also known as: Bandit Queen
Major offenses: Robbery, kidnapping, and alleged murder
Active: February 14, 1981-February, 1983
Locale: Uttar Pradesh and Madhya Pradesh, northern India
Sentence: Eleven years in prison

Early Life

Phoolan Devi (FEW-lan DEH-vee) was born into poverty in Uttar Pradesh to a farmer in the lower caste of Mallahs. She faced great strife at an early age due to familial struggles over land rights. She was married at the age of eleven to a man twenty years her senior, who beat her and forced her into manual labor. She was repeatedly beaten and raped before the age of eighteen.

Devi was kidnapped by a local gang and forced to accompany them on bandit raids throughout Uttar Pradesh. She was taken as a mistress by the gang's leader, Vikram Mallah, whose death she allegedly avenged, making her a wanted woman.

Criminal Career

Upon the death of Mallah, Devi changed gangs, aligning herself with those who were briefly in power in the shifting world of Indian bandits, known as dacoits. She sought refuge among those gangs that could offer her protection from her increasing number of enemies. Finding loyalty among bandits a difficult task, Devi started her own gang, with Man Singh, in the treacherous terrain of the Chambal Ravines.

Devi claimed not to have been present at the infamous Behmai Massacre on February 14, 1981, at which she allegedly murdered the two brothers who killed Vikram Mallah, Sri Ram Singh and Lala Ram Singh. In addition to the vengeful slaughter of the Ram brothers, Devi and her gang were named in the murder of twenty-two upper-caste Thakur (landowners) who had humiliated and reportedly raped Devi.

Legal Action and Outcome

Devi was charged with fifty-five criminal counts of theft, kidnapping, and murder upon her arranged surrender in February, 1983. She claimed she would surrender to authorities only if the Indian congress guaranteed that neither she nor her fellow gang members would be hanged for their crimes. Her surrender to police was a public spectacle; her violent actions had given her legendary status as a warring champion among the lower castes. Before ten thousand people, Devi laid down her rifle and bayonet. She served eleven years in prison before she was paroled in 1994 by the lower-caste minister of the Congress Party.

Labeled a modern-day Robin Hood, Devi was a heroine among the poor and the lower-caste women, which helped her earn a seat in the Samajwadi Party of Parliament in 1996, with an agenda focused on justice for the lowest castes. Her life was threatened on many occasions by upper-caste protesters. The widows of the massacred Thakur men called for a retrial and a death sentence. On July 25, 2001, Devi was shot three times in the head by three masked gunmen in front of her New Delhi home, while on a break from Parliament. She died at the age of thirty-seven.

Impact

Around the time of her release from prison, a film about Phoolan Devi's life titled *The Bandit Queen* (1994) was released to supportive viewers who accepted the film's violent details of her earlier rape and the string of murders as truthful. Devi predicted that a dramatization of her life, such as seen in the film, and her implication in the Behmai Massacre would make her a target for revenge. Her 1996 autobiography, *I, Phoolan Devi: The Autobiography of India's Bandit Queen*, predictably gives a less criminal interpretation of her life, with her actions reflecting earlier traumas in her life revolving around the lingering caste structure and sexual abuse.

Further Reading

Alexander, Gemma, ed. *Heroic and Outrageous Women*. Edison, N.J.: Castle Books, 2002. A compendium of notorious women in history, with a section of Devi's personal statements.

Burns, John F. "India's 'Avenging Angel': Candidate of Low Castes." *The New York Times*, May 6, 1996, p. A3. An analysis of Devi's early political career and her candidacy for Parliament.

Devi, Phoolan. *I, Phoolan Devi: The Autobiography of India's Bandit Queen*. London: Little, Brown, 1996. This ghostwritten autobiography of Devi provides a more intimate look at her early life, giving probable cause for disputed criminal events in her teenage years.

Devi, Phoolan, with Marie-Thérèse Cuny and Paul Rambali. *The Bandit Queen of India: An Indian Woman's Amazing Journey from Peasant to International Legend*. Guilford, Conn.: Lyons Press, 2003. Contains details of Devi's early life and political career.

—Emilie B. Sizemore

See also: Robin Hood.

Legs Diamond

American mobster and racketeer

Born: 1897; Philadelphia, Pennsylvania
Died: December 18, 1931; Albany, New York
Also known as: Jack Moran (birth name); Gentleman Jack; Clay Pigeon; John Thomas Diamond; Jack Diamond; John Thomas Noland
Cause of notoriety: Diamond, an important figure in Mafia-related bootlegging operations during Prohibition, was referred to as the "clay pigeon of the underworld" because he had been shot and wounded on several occasions.
Active: 1920-1931
Locale: New York, New York

Early Life

Raised in Philadelphia by Irish immigrant parents, Jack Moran—who would become infamous under his alias Jack "Legs" Diamond (DI-muhnd)—and his younger brother Eddie received a limited public school education. After Jack's mother, Sara, died in 1913, his father, John, a menial laborer, moved the two boys to Brooklyn. However, Jack and his brother soon became involved with a group of hoodlums known as the Boiler Gang. Jack served in the U.S. Army during World War I, but he later went absent without leave (AWOL). He was charged with desertion and spent a year in the military prison at Leavenworth, Kansas. He married Alice Kenny in 1920 and held a series of odd jobs for a short time.

Criminal Career

Diamond may have received his nickname "Legs" for three reasons. First, Diamond was a good dancer in Philadelphia as a youth. Second, during his early days as a petty thief, he always managed to evade the law. Finally, fellow gangsters dubbed Diamond a liar and a cheat. He earned the reputation among his cohorts as a double-dealer who never maintained a sense of loyalty to the mob family.

Diamond became a member of Hudson Dusters, a small gang in New York City that robbed packages from delivery trucks. He eventually became a bodyguard for Jacob "Little Augie" Orgen, a major racketeer. When Diamond helped in the killing of Augie's main rival, Nathan "Kid Dropper" Kaplan, the mob kingpin rewarded him with some of his bootlegging enterprises. Louis "Lepke" Buchalter and Jacob Gurrah Shapiro soon began to attempt a takeover of Orgen's garment district operations.

In 1927, Orgen was killed on the lower East Side in a drive-by shooting. Diamond was severely wounded in the attack, but he survived despite a heavy loss of blood. With money no longer an object, he began to participate in a decadent night life, often partying with his mistress, Marion "Kiki" Roberts, and spending many of his evenings in the Hotsy Totsy Club on Broadway. Two years later, on June 13, 1929, he and one of his henchmen, Charles Entratta, killed William "Red" Cassidy after a scuffle in the club. Entratta and Diamond then went into hiding, but for lack of evidence they were never prosecuted. Although twenty-five people had witnessed the crime, none came forward to testify.

Diamond soon began working for Buchalter, a move that put him in conflict with bootlegging mobster Dutch Schultz, who wanted to move his base of operations into Manhattan. Schultz placed a contract hit out on Diamond. In October, 1929, three men stormed into the hotel room where Diamond and his mistress were staying, shooting him five times; he survived.

Legs Diamond. (AP/Wide World Photos)

Diamond decided to travel to Europe and stay there until his safety could be guaranteed, but upon his arrival the authorities in each port city refused to let him off his ship. Diamond returned home; two years later, he was shot again after emerging from a hotel. In December, 1931, his good luck finally ran out; he was in Albany, New York, when two hit men entered the room where he was sleeping and fired three bullets into his head. The men who killed him were never caught.

Impact

Legs Diamond was a celebrity during his lifetime. Newspaper accounts relished in his underworld exploits during Prohibition, and he achieved legendary status for surviving so many attempts on his life. The criminal career of Diamond reflected the rise of organized crime during the 1920's and 1930's. Gambling, prostitution, and loan sharking were prominent vices in the late nineteenth century, spurred by alliances between local political machines and gangsters. However, with the passages of the Eighteenth Amendment and the Volstead Act, the outlawing of alcohol caused an increase in liquor trafficking on a national scale. Italian and Irish mobsters began to vie for control of the lucrative bootlegging business during Diamond's era. Diamond proved to be the enforcer between these warring factions until he became a liability for the powerful crime syndicates.

Further Reading

Levine, Gary. *Jack "Legs" Diamond: Anatomy of a Gangster*. Rev. ed. New York: Purple Mountain Press, 1995. Levine interviewed known associates of Diamond and policemen who dealt with him in order to produce this biography.

Nash, Jay Robert. *Bloodletters and Badmen: A Narrative Encyclopedia of American Criminals, from the Pilgrims to the Present*. New York: J. B. Lippincott, 1973. Arranged in alphabetical order by last name, a series of entries on memorable gangsters, criminals, and murderers. The author traces their backgrounds, crimes, and prison sentences.

Reppetto, Thomas A. *American Mafia: A History of Its Rise to Power*. New York: H. Holt, 2004. Overview of the rise of organized crime in the United States; the author asserts that the Mafia retained its power in part because of the fragmentation found in law enforcement agencies.

Sifakis, Carl. *The Mafia Encyclopedia*. 2d ed. New York: Facts On File, 1999. Comprehensive overview of organized crime personalities, power clashes, hangouts, hideaways, and rackets.

—Gayla Koerting

See also: Louis Buchalter; Arnold Rothstein; Dutch Schultz.

Porfirio Díaz

President of Mexico (1876-1880, 1884-1911)

Born: September 15, 1830; Oaxaca, Mexico
Died: July 2, 1915; Paris, France
Also known as: José de la Cruz Porfirio Díaz (full name); Porfirio Díaz Mori
Cause of notoriety: Díaz wielded dictatorial power during the early years of the Mexican republic, often continuing his regime through rigged elections and violent suppression of opponents and critics.
Active: 1876-1911
Locale: Mexico

Early Life

José de la Cruz Porfirio Díaz (pohr-FEER-yoh day la krewz DEE-ahs) was born in 1830 to Petrona Mori, of Mixtec Indian ancestry, and José Faustino Díaz, who died when Porfirio was three years old. He began his formal education in a Roman Catholic seminary, then continued at the Institute of Arts and Sciences. When the United States invaded Mexico in 1846, Díaz decided on a military career and began to organize his fellow students. By 1856, he had become a captain in the National Guard. Díaz's first battle came during the War of Reform (1857-1861), and he fought in thirty-seven battles during the next decade. The War of Reform was fought over the Constitution of 1857 and the Laws of Reform, which attempted to shift political power from the rich landowners and the Catholic Church to the common people. The reform movement was led by Benito Juárez, who later became Mexico's president. For his performance on behalf of the Liberals during this war, Díaz was promoted in 1859 to lieutenant colonel and again in 1860 to chief of the mountain brigade in Oacaxa. In 1861, he attained the rank of general.

The War of the French Intervention was the second war of Díaz's career. In 1863, on the pretense of reclaiming Mexican debts (but with the cooperation of a group of wealthy monarchist Mexicans), the French Army of Napoleon III invaded Mexico. The French were initially defeated on May 5, 1863 (a date celebrated as Cinco de Mayo among Mexicans), but they eventually took control of the country, making Archduke Ferdinand Maximilian Joseph Habsburg the emperor of Mexico (r. 1864-1867). Díaz suffered some defeats but became famous for his successes, especially the final battle at Puebla on April 2, 1867, when Maximilian's forces were finally defeated.

Political Career

Díaz's political career began when he ran unsuccessfully for president against the immensely popular Juárez in 1867. Díaz ran against Juárez again in 1871, but Congress declared Juárez the winner after no candidate had won a majority. However, Juárez died in office in 1872, leaving as president his successor, Sebastian Lerdo de Tejáda. When Lerdo was reelected in 1876, Díaz rebelled. Declaring Lerdo's reelection unconstitutional under the Constitution of 1857, Díaz led a coup against Lerdo in 1876 and made himself president. Díaz was succeeded in 1880 by a handpicked successor, thereby running Mexico in fact if not in name; in 1884, he was again elected president. Díaz's reelections after his first term in office violated the very principles of the 1857 Constitution, which Díaz had invoked in order to overthrow Lerdo in 1876. His reelections in the years that followed continued to violate the spirit of that constitution.

From the beginning, the aim of Díaz's administration was to make Mexico into a modern country like those of Europe, with an emphasis on economic growth and industrialization. To some extent, this effort was a success. Foreign investments flowed into Mexico, mining became important, railroads were built, and much of the country became connected by telegraph and, later, by telephone. In Mexico City, a canal, general hospital, legislative palace, and national theater were all built.

Still, the modernization of Mexico brought little benefit to the vast majority of the population. The gap between the rich and the poor widened. Mexicans worked in the mines and in industry for low wages. Often, workers were paid in scrip or vouchers that could be cashed only at the "company store." The lives of workers' families were difficult, and the modernization brought by the Díaz regime offered them little hope for the future.

Small farmers also suffered during this period. During Spanish colonial times, much agricultural land be-

Justice, According to Porfirio Díaz

British commentators Channing Arnold and Frederick J. Tabor Frost, contemporaries of Porfirio Díaz, described Mexico at the height of his power:

Law and order is represented by a blend of a rough-and-ready justice, a sort of legalized lynch-law, with an official law administration venal to a high degree. . . .

Even to the casual observer the difficulty of governing Mexico must seem inexpressibly great. President Díaz has succeeded not so much because he does not know what mercy means or because a rifle bullet is his only answer for those who question his authority, but because he is endowed with superhuman tact. The iron heel, like that of Achilles, has its vulnerable spot if pressed too hard upon a people's throat, and so he has little dodges by which he appears to his subjects to exercise a judicious clemency. If some redoubtable criminal is captured, some monarch of murderers, Díaz knows well that among his thousands of crime-loving fellow countrymen the brute will have a large following. His execution will mean the declaration of a vendetta against the police. So he is put on his trial, condemned to death, and within twenty-four hours the president commutes his sentence to one of twenty years' incarceration in the penitentiary. After about a week there, he is taken out one evening, as usual, into the prison yard for exercise under a small guard of soldiers. One of these sidles up to him and suggests that as the night is dark he might make a bolt for it. The convict believes it a genuine offer, sprints off, and is dropped at thirty yards like a rabbit by the five or six soldiers who have been waiting under the shadow of the farther wall. The next morning the official newspaper states, "Last night the notorious criminal So-and-So, to whom His Excellency the President recently extended clemency, made an attempt to escape while being exercised in the prison yard, and was shot dead by the sentries." Thus everybody is pleased, except possibly the convict, and the president, without the least odium to himself, has rid the country of another blackguard.

Source: Channing Arnold and Frederick J. Tabor Frost, "The Rule of Porfirio Díaz, 1909," in *Canada, South America, Central America, Mexico, and the West Indies*, edited by Eva March Tappan, volume 11 in *The World's Story: A History of the World in Story, Song, and Art* (Boston: Houghton Mifflin, 1914).

Porfirio Díaz. (Library of Congress)

longed to haciendas, or huge estates owned by rich families in which workers lived in almost feudal conditions. Because Díaz relied for political support in part on the support of hacienda owners, his administration saw the growth of these enormous estates, often by the seizure of land from small farmers and Indians. Conditions in Díaz's Mexico often led to uprisings, but these were repressed with force; their leaders were shot. Newspaper editors who opposed Díaz, as well as workers who went on strike, were jailed and often killed.

As the years passed, Díaz's reelections drew increasing opposition, until, in the early twentieth century, the Mexican Liberal Party published a list of twenty-eight points, which eventually led to the Mexican Revolution. A Liberal leader, Francisco Madero, proposed reforms to Díaz in 1910. Díaz rejected them, and Madero became a candidate for president, running against Díaz for the Anti-Reelection Party in 1910. Díaz engineered a fraudulent election to retain power and ordered that Madero be jailed. As a result of these actions, rebels such as Pancho Villa, Pascual Orozco, and Emiliano Zapata began the Mexican Revolution. In 1911, Díaz was driven from office and sailed to Paris, where he died four years later.

Impact

The administration of Porfirio Díaz brought modernity to Mexico at a terrible price. Poverty worsened, and government by personal fiat left few democratic traditions on which reforms could be built. Many of the problems Díaz caused—including a landless peasantry and polarized wealth—persisted into the twenty-first century, nearly one hundred years after Díaz was driven from office.

Further Reading

Garner, Paul. *Porfirio Díaz*. New York: Longman, 2001. Garner's book has been described as the "current standard" biography. Includes bibliography and indexes.

Meyer, Michael C., and William H. Beezley, eds. *The Oxford History of Mexico*. New York: Oxford University Press, 2000. Within this collection, three essays together cover the period of Díaz's life and provide good historical context: Josefina Vasquez's "War and Peace with the United States" (pp. 339-370), Paul Vanderwood's "Betterment for Whom? The Reform Period, 1855-1875" (pp. 371-397), and Robert M. Buffington and William E. French's "The Culture of Modernity" (pp. 397-432).

Perry, Laurens Ballard. *Juárez and Díaz: Machine Politics in Mexico*. De Kalb: Northern Illinois University Press, 1978. A hefty study at nearly five hundred pages, focusing on the primary political issues faced by Mexico since the early twentieth century—in large part the legacy of Díaz. Includes bibliography and index.

Shorris, Earl. *The Life and Times of Mexico*. New York: W. W. Norton, 2004. Not a chronological narrative, this history covers bits and pieces on Díaz's career throughout a rather creative text. A fascinating book to read, factual regardless of its unorthodox approach. Particularly useful is the chapter titled "The Defeat of August Comte" (pp. 189-214).

—*Timothy C. Frazer*

See also: Pancho Villa; Emiliano Zapata.

John Dillinger

American bank robber

Born: June 22, 1903; Indianapolis, Indiana
Died: July 22, 1934; Chicago, Illinois
Also known as: John Herbert Dillinger, Jr. (full name)
Cause of notoriety: During the Great Depression, many Americans made heroes of outlaws who took what they wanted at gunpoint. Dillinger was perhaps the most famous of these outlaws, earning celebrity and admiration both for his criminal audacity and for his affable, polite manner.
Active: September, 1924-June, 1934
Locale: Midwestern United States
Sentence: Ten to twenty years' imprisonment for assault and two to fourteen years for conspiracy to commit a felony in 1924; served nine years

Early Life

Raised in Mooresville, Indiana, John Dillinger (DIHL-ihn-juhr) was born to a farmer who also ran a small grocery. His mother died when he was three, and John was raised by his older sister. A natural athlete and an excellent baseball player, Dillinger nonetheless had no particular life direction, and he quit school in the seventh grade. In 1923, after joyriding in a stolen car, Dillinger was forced to enlist in the navy to avoid punishment. He soon deserted the military and got a dishonorable discharge. He married sixteen-year-old Beryl Hovious in 1924, the same year in which he and an ex-convict tried to rob a grocer by hitting him over the head with an iron bolt. Dillinger pleaded guilty in order to get a reduced sentence; his partner received only a few months in jail. Sentenced to ten to twenty years' imprisonment for assault and two to fourteen years for conspiracy to commit a felony, Dillinger went to a reformatory, and his wife divorced him. He was transferred to the Michigan City Penitentiary in Indiana, where he met bank robbers Harry Pierpont and Homer Van Meter, both of whom agreed to form a gang with him upon release. Dillinger was paroled in May, 1933.

Criminal Career

In September, 1933, Dillinger robbed his first bank. He also threw guns over the wall of Michigan City to break his friends out of jail but was arrested in Dayton, Ohio, before the reunion. Dillinger was held in a Lima, Ohio, jail, but his gang freed him by killing the town sheriff. The subsequent robbery spree attracted great publicity. The gang walked into the Auburn, Indiana, police station, took police hostage, and stole guns and bulletproof vests. In Peru, Indiana, the gang struck again. Newspapers widely reported it, and the gang was admired for its audacity. There was scant sympathy for banks or for law enforcement among the public during the Great Depression; many Americans rooted for criminals.

Indiana police captain Matt Leach blamed Dillinger for bank robberies throughout his region, inflating Dillinger's notoriety. Dillinger disliked Leach and taunted him through the mail. Although not the gang's leader (a position held by Pierpont), Dillinger became its star. He looked like actor Humphrey Bogart, and he was affable and polite. The public viewed him as a small-town boy gone bad as a result of a too-harsh jail sentence.

The gang robbed banks about twice a month, hiding out in Chicago or St. Paul. Each bank was cased, and getaways were meticulously planned. In January, 1934, the gang robbed a bank in East Chicago, during which Dillinger killed an officer. Someone triggered an alarm, and the robbers walked out with hostages. Officer William O'Malley fired shots into Dillinger's bulletproof vest, but Dillinger killed him with a machine gun.

Several gang members were recognized and arrested in Tucson, Arizona, in January, 1934. Dillinger was sent to jail in Crown Point, Indiana; gang members Pierpont and Charles Makley were sent to Lima, Ohio, for trial. Dillinger escaped in March using a smuggled wooden gun and driving away in the chief deputy's car. Driving over state lines violated a federal law, so Dillinger became a target of the Federal Bureau of Investigation (FBI). Pierpont and Makley got death sentences for killing the sheriff. Dillinger was then declared public enemy number one. He visited his family in Mooresville, and a photograph of him smugly holding the wooden pistol from his escape was widely distributed.

In April, 1934, the gang—now including infamous robber George "Baby Face" Nelson—hid out at Little Bohemia Lodge in Wisconsin, but they were recognized and surrounded by FBI agents. The FBI opened fire in the dark and killed three innocent men exiting the lodge. The gang escaped out back windows.

In an attempt to avoid recognition, Dillinger and Van Meter had plastic surgery in May, 1934. Their last robbery was in South Bend, Indiana, in June, 1934. A wild shoot-out occurred with police, and civilians were hit; Van Meter was wounded but used his machine gun to kill an officer. Dillinger hid in Chicago with brothel owner Anna Sage.

Legal Action and Outcome

Sage offered to betray Dillinger in exchange for not being deported back to Romania, to which the authorities agreed. On July 22, 1934, Sage told the FBI that Dillinger was going to take her and a friend to the Biograph Theater to see a gangster film that evening. Dillinger entered the theater at 8:30 P.M., and dozens of agents took their positions outside. As Dillinger exited at 10:35 P.M., agents approached him from behind and either executed him on the spot or shot him as he ran up an alley. Whatever the truth, he died after being shot through the back of his head and in his torso. He was thirty-one years old. Van Meter was killed in St. Paul a month after Dillinger's death, and Pierpont and Makley were executed. Sage was deported to Romania.

Impact

The death of John Dillinger edged J. Edgar Hoover closer to becoming a national icon. Within two years, G-men (FBI agents) replaced bank robbers as national heroes. Dillinger's photograph became the official target on FBI's firing ranges and remained so into the twenty-first century. It was reported that Hoover hung Dillinger's death mask in his office as a favorite memento.

Dillinger continued to fascinate writers and filmmakers as a smiling "rogue hero," who seemingly was more bad boy than criminal. Bryan Burrough, in his book *Public Enemies: America's Greatest Crime Wave and the Birth of the FBI, 1933-1934* (2004), relates a visit to Dillinger's grave, where he imagined touching his face. Many films have been made about Dillinger, although most were critical failures. *Dillinger* (1945) starred Lawrence Tierney; *Dillinger* (1973) starred Warren Oates and an excellent supporting cast, but its screenplay had little to do with historical reality. *Public Enemy Number One*, a documentary produced for the television series *The American Experience*, was aired by the Public Broadcasting Service in 2001.

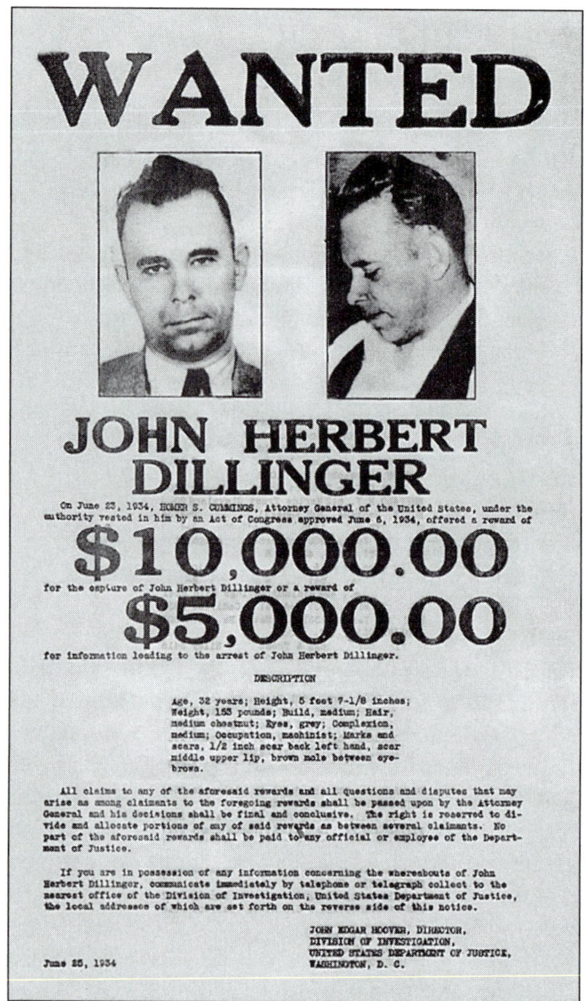

John Dillinger's "wanted" poster. (NARA)

Further Reading

Burrough, Bryan. *Public Enemies: America's Greatest Crime Wave and the Birth of the FBI, 1933-1934.* New York: Penguin Books, 2004. Recounts Dillinger's robberies in exciting detail and in chronological sequence along with discussion of other criminals of the era. The reader comes to understand how short and packed with violence the public enemy era was.

Girardin, G. Russell, with William J. Helmer. *Dillinger: The Untold Story.* Bloomington: University of Indiana Press, 1994. Girardin interviewed Dillinger's attorney and various criminal cohorts in the 1930's, giving an intimate portrayal of Dillinger. The manuscript was unpublished until 1994.

Matera, Dary. *John Dillinger: The Life and Death of America's First Celebrity Criminal.* New York: Carroll & Graf, 2004. Details Dillinger's youth and personal traits but is somewhat speculative about Dillinger's thoughts and motives.

—*Jim Pauff*

See also: Ma Barker; Pretty Boy Floyd; Baby Face Nelson; Henry Starr; Willie Sutton.

Françoise Dior

French neo-Nazi activist

Born: April 7, 1932; Paris, France
Died: 1993; France
Also known as: Marie Françoise Suzanne Dior (full name)
Major offenses: Posting swastikas on the walls of the British embassy and arson of Jewish synagogues
Active: 1962-1993
Locale: Britain and France
Sentence: Four months' imprisonment for painting swastikas; eighteen months for arson

Early Life

Françoise Dior (frahn-swahz dyohr) was born to Madeleine Leblanc, who had her daughter out of wedlock with a Hungarian nobleman named Valentin de Balla. Leblanc's subsequent marriage to Raymond Dior, the brother of the renowned French fashion designer Christian Dior, made Françoise officially part of the aristocratic and royalist Dior family. Her world was dominated by the occupying German Army, whose soldiers and their uniforms impressed her.

Dior learned about Adolf Hitler's idea that the Aryan race was superior to all others, and it appealed to her because she herself was among the elite. Later in life, Dior remembered fondly the compliment that a German Schutzstaffel (SS) soldier paid her when he commented on what a lovely Aryan girl she was.

Following family tradition, Dior married the royalist Comte Robert-Henri de Caumont La Force, a French nobleman. Following French custom, the couple wed in Paris in a civil ceremony and the following day in a traditional Roman Catholic Mass. Two years later, their daughter, Anne-Marie Christiane, was born. Settling into the everyday life of being a wife and mother was difficult for Dior; the eventual revelation of her liaison with a former Cuban ambassador caused her divorce from La Force.

Political and Criminal Career

In 1962, Dior arrived in London, having put her daughter in the custody of her parents. A rally in Trafalgar Square, led by Colin Jordan, had made newspaper headlines, and Dior wanted to meet Jordan, who, along with John Tyndall and Martin Webster, had just founded the National Socialist Movement (NSM). Immersing herself in the activities of the NSM, Dior made Jordan take notice of her, and he began escorting her around town until he went to prison for offenses against the public order. With Jordan incarcerated, Tyndall decide to pursue Dior romantically, and shortly thereafter the two were engaged. However, Tyndall was also imprisoned for what were called offenses against the public order. Jordan was released before Tyndall, and in haste Dior married Jordan in early October, 1963. News of their wedding attracted widespread media attention; the public was shocked that Christian Dior's niece was associating with the NSM. Patriotic Londoners pelted the couple with rotten eggs as they left the wedding ceremony. To formalize their devotion to neo-Nazism, they cut their fingers and let their blood fall on the pages of Hitler's *Mein Kampf* (1925-1927; *My Struggle*, 1933). The marriage ended in divorce two years later.

Legal Action and Outcome

Dior was among thirty-four people convicted for burning Jewish synagogues, but she was not caught until several years later. In 1965, she was appointed French representative of the World Union of National Socialists, and in March, 1966, she returned to Paris absolutely broke. Her mother agreed to support her provided that the court be in charge of her finances: She wanted to prevent Dior from ruining her future through donations to suspect causes.

In October, 1966, in a French case in which she was tried according to French law and in her absence, Dior was found guilty of a crime committed before she married Jordan: posting swastikas on the walls of the British embassy. She served four months in a jail in Nice, France. Upon release, she and her secretary, Terence Cooper, went to England, where they stayed with the Cooper family. There, in 1968, Dior was arrested and sent to prison for eighteen months for the arson of several London synagogues. She and Cooper settled in Normandy after her release. After ten years, they separated. During this time, she allegedly committed incest with her own daughter; in 1978, Dior learned that her daughter had committed suicide.

Dior spent the last years of her life concocting schemes to acquire money—from her mother, by investing in a Parisian nightclub, by mortgaging her property, and by marriage to Comte Hubert de Mirleau in a loveless union which he likely considered an investment in the Dior family wealth. Having abused her body through years of drinking, smoking, and promiscuity, Dior died of lung cancer at the relatively young age of sixty.

IMPACT

Françoise Dior stands as an example of the two decadent influences in mid-twentieth century Europe: the persistence of racist neo-Nazism and the self-indulgence and sense of entitlement of a dying aristocracy. Dior's outrageous behavior and dismaying use of her inheritance simultaneously encapsulate these social trends and mark a wasted life.

FURTHER READING

Goodrick-Clarke, Nicholas. *Hitler's Priestess: Savitri Devi, the Hindu-Aryan Myth, and Neo-Nazism.* New York: New York University Press, 1998. A recounting of Dior's acquaintance with Savitri Devi, one of the earliest promoters of neo-Nazism.

Walker, Martin. *The National Front.* Glasgow, Scotland: Fontana/Collins, 1977. A brief, two-page discussion reviews Dior's marriage and her conviction in 1968.

—*Patricia J. Siegel*

SEE ALSO: Frank Collin; Savitri Devi.

THOMAS DIXON, JR.

American author and Baptist preacher

BORN: January 11, 1864; Shelby, North Carolina
DIED: April 3, 1946; Raleigh, North Carolina
CAUSE OF NOTORIETY: Dixon's 1905 novel *The Clansman* was adapted in 1915 to become director D. W. Griffith's *The Birth of a Nation*, a silent-film blockbuster with racist overtones.
ACTIVE: 1880's-1930's
LOCALE: North Carolina and New York, New York

EARLY LIFE

Thomas Dixon (DIHK-suhn), Jr., was born as the Civil War drew to a close, the third of five children, to a Baptist minister and farmer who had married the daughter of a wealthy South Carolina planter. The family fell on hard times at the war's end, and as Dixon's father struggled to make ends meet, opening a hardware store and then turning to farming again, he found solace by actively participating in the Ku Klux Klan (KKK), a white supremacist vigilante organization of hooded men who saw themselves as guardians of Southern honor and opposed those who worked for African American advancements during Reconstruction. Dixon's favorite uncle, Colonel Lee Roy McAfee, was also a leading member of the Klan. These early experiences with the KKK presumably influenced Dixon's later literary career.

Dixon, a bright student, had earned his master's degree at Wake Forest College before he reached the age of twenty. He then went to Johns Hopkins University to do graduate work in history and politics. There, he befriended fellow student Woodrow Wilson, who would later become the president of the United States. Dixon left graduate school to try various careers—first, he toured as a thespian in a Shakespearean troupe; next, he returned to North Carolina, where he took a seat in the state legislature and was awarded a law degree from Greensboro Law School in 1886. He left politics as he

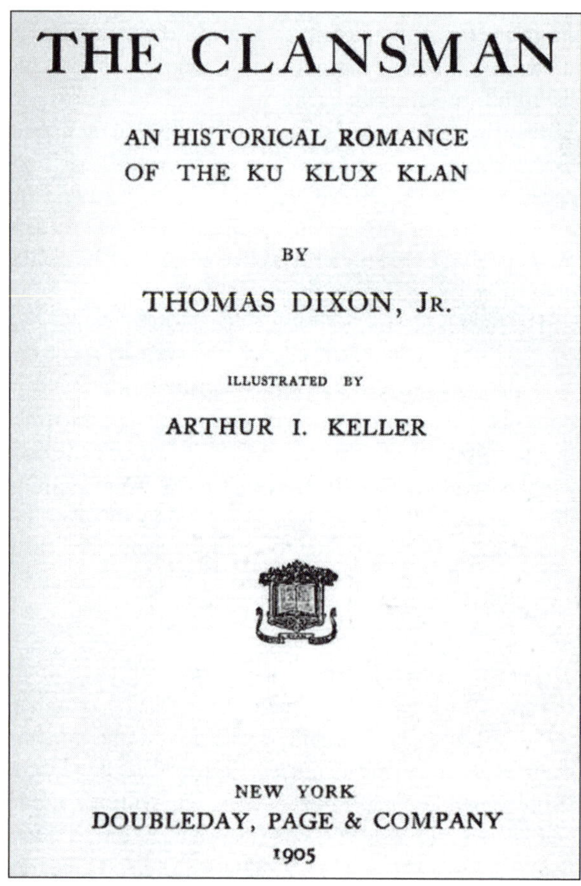
THE CLANSMAN

AN HISTORICAL ROMANCE OF THE KU KLUX KLAN

BY

THOMAS DIXON, JR.

ILLUSTRATED BY

ARTHUR I. KELLER

NEW YORK
DOUBLEDAY, PAGE & COMPANY
1905

Cover page of Dixon's The Clansman.

left the stage and, following in his father's footsteps, was ordained a Baptist minister in October, 1886.

Dixon was a charismatic public speaker who took strong positions on current political and social concerns. A series of pastoral appointments led to his six years' service at the Twenty-third Street Church in New York, where his congregation included such influential Americans as John D. Rockefeller. He then left the Baptists and started his own nondenominational People's Church in New York City in 1895.

Writing and Speaking Career

By 1899, Dixon had tired of the ministry, so he resigned his position at the People's Church and began a popular four-year speaking tour of the country on the topic of Christianity's relevance for modern society, which reached up to five million Americans. Incensed by the image of the South conveyed in the popular novel written by Harriet Beecher Stowe, *Uncle Tom's Cabin* (1852), Dixon wrote a trilogy of novels intended to show Reconstruction from his perspective: white culture being imperiled by the bestial nature and impulses of African Americans and the way in which the KKK arose to confront that challenge. These books—*The Leopard's Spots: A Romance of the White Man's Burden* (1902), *The Clansman: An Historical Romance of the Ku Klux Klan* (1905), and *The Traitor: A Story of the Fall of the Invisible Empire* (1907)—were all best sellers, and their popularity afforded Dixon increasing status in the literary field.

With this success, Dixon decided to devote himself to correcting what he called "social evils" through literature. He wrote seventeen more novels, though none of them garnered the acclaim of his first trilogy. A second trilogy—*The One Woman: A Story of Modern Utopia* (1903), *Comrades: A Story of Social Adventure in California* (1909), and *The Root of Evil* (1911)—attacked socialism. In later books, Dixon warned against other "causes": the emancipation of women in *The Foolish Virgin: A Romance of Today* (1915), pacifism in *The Fall of a Nation: A Sequel to "The Birth of a Nation"* (1916), and miscegenation in *The Flaming Sword* (1939). In the latter work, Dixon criticized the calls for social justice by African American leaders W. E. B. Du Bois and James Weldon Johnson.

From the Preface to *The Clansman*

In his preface to The Clansman, *Thomas Dixon's racism, bigotry, and belief in white supremacy are unmistakable:*

To the Reader

"The Clansman" is the second book of a series of historical novels planned on the Race Conflict. "The Leopard's Spots" was the statement in historical outline of the conditions from the enfranchisement of the Negro to his disfranchisement.

"The Clansman" develops the true story of the "Ku Klux Klan Conspiracy," which overturned the Reconstruction régime.

The organisation was governed by the Grand Wizard Commander-in-Chief, who lived at Memphis, Tennessee. The Grand Dragon commanded a State, the Grand Titan a Congressional District, the Grand Giant a County, and the Grand Cyclops a Township Den. The twelve volumes of Government reports on the famous Klan refer chiefly to events which occurred after 1870, the date of its dissolution.

The chaos of blind passion that followed Lincoln's assassination is inconceivable to-day. The Revolution it produced in our Government, and the bold attempt of Thaddeus Stevens to Africanise ten great states of the American Union, read now like tales from "The Arabian Nights."

I have sought to preserve in this romance both the letter and the spirit of this remarkable period. The men who enact the drama of fierce revenge into which I have woven a double love-story are historical figures. I have merely changed their names without taking a liberty with any essential historic fact.

In the darkest hour of the life of the South, when her wounded people lay helpless amid rags and ashes under the beak and talon of the Vulture, suddenly from the mists of the mountains appeared a white cloud the size of a man's hand. It grew until its mantle of mystery enfolded the stricken earth and sky. An "Invisible Empire" had risen from the field of Death and challenged the Visible to mortal combat.

How the young South, led by the reincarnated souls of the Clansmen of Old Scotland, went forth under this cover and against overwhelming odds, daring exile, imprisonment, and a felon's death, and saved the life of a people, forms one of the most dramatic chapters in the history of the Aryan race.

Thomas Dixon, Jr.
Dixondale, Va., December 14, 1904.

Source: Thomas Dixon and Arthur I. Keller, preface to *The Clansman: An Historical Romance of the Ku Klux Klan* (New York: Doubleday, Page, 1905).

Impact

The racist attitude of Thomas Dixon, Jr., toward African Americans had the greatest impact when D. W. Griffith transformed *The Clansman* into the epic silent film *The Birth of a Nation* (1915). This film was highly influential: It received great critical acclaim and suggested the new possibilities for epic storytelling through cinema. President Woodrow Wilson happily commended the film following a publicized private viewing at the White House, and millions of average Americans flocked to see it on the big screen; it generated huge commercial success. Embedded in the film is the same racist story conveyed in the novel: The members of the KKK are portrayed as chivalrous defenders of white womanhood against the ever-looming onslaught of lustful African American men, who are unable to control their animal urges.

The years following the film saw an upturn in the number of race riots and lynching reports throughout the country. Moreover, during the 1920's, the KKK would be reborn on a significant national level as a racist vigilante force dedicated to promoting and protecting the interests of white Protestant Americans. Dixon recognized the suggestive power of the new film medium and produced five Hollywood motion pictures himself based on some of his works from the period between 1915 and 1919, but none was critically or financially successful.

Further Reading

Dixon, Thomas, Jr. *The Clansman: An Historical Romance of the Ku Klux Klan*. 1905. Reprint. Lexington: University Press of Kentucky, 1970. This reprint makes Dixon's original work accessible to the modern reader.

Eby, Carl. "Slouching Toward Beastliness: Richard Wright's Anatomy of Thomas Dixon." *African American Review* 35 (Fall, 2001): 439-458. Eby summarizes how Dixon propagated the myth of black men as beasts and then evaluates how author Richard Wright parodied this notion in his groundbreaking novel *Native Son*, first published in 1940.

Gilman, Susan. *Blood Talk: American Race Melodrama and the Culture of the Occult*. Chicago: University of Chicago Press, 2003. This scholarly work traces the development and popularity of a literary subgenre, the "race melodrama," from the period of Reconstruction through World War I. The author discusses strong connections between this emergent format and an interest in secret ritual and the occult. Dixon's Klan trilogy receives much attention in the first half of the book as it epitomizes the integration of the two themes.

Lang, Robert, ed. *The Birth of a Nation*. New Brunswick, N.J.: Rutgers University Press, 1994. This script of the classic film includes supplementary contextualizing writings, including Dixon's personal response to *The Boston Globe* criticism of the film's explicit racial hatred.

—*Scot M. Guenter*

See also: David Duke; Julius Evola; Nathan Bedford Forrest; Elisabeth Förster-Nietzsche; Arthur de Gobineau; George Lincoln Rockwell; William Joseph Simmons; Gerald L. K. Smith; Benjamin Tillman.

William Dodd

British clergyman and author

Born: May 29, 1729; Bourne, Lincolnshire, England
Died: June 27, 1777; Tyburn, London, England
Also known as: Macaroni Parson
Major offense: Forgery
Active: February, 1777
Locale: London, England
Sentence: Death by public hanging

Early Life

William Dodd (dawd) was born the eldest of six children to the Reverend William Dodd and Elizabeth Dixon. He entered Clare College, Cambridge, to study mathematics in 1746, graduating in 1749 with a good degree. Having written poetry at university, his ambitions were literary, and he settled in London, where he spent the remainder of his life. He wrote poetry, a play, and a student philosophy textbook. In 1751, he secretly married sixteen-year-old Mary Perkins and leased an expensive house in the fashionable part of London. This move anticipated a life of overextending himself financially in order to keep up the appearance of success and to enjoy society life, parties, beautiful women, flamboyant clothes, and horse races. Eventually this led to his nickname, the Macaroni Parson.

Criminal Career

Despite the success of several poems in 1749 and the 1752 publication of *The Beauties of Shakespeare*, Dodd came to realize that literature was not going to sustain his ambitions. He returned to Cambridge to be ordained into the Church of England. For the next ten years, he combined writing and preaching, becoming noted for his fashionable sermons. He gained several lectureships, became prebend (a clergyman earning a stipend) at Brecon Cathedral, was appointed chaplain to King George II, and served as editor of the *Christian Magazine* from 1760 to 1767.

In 1765, Dodd became tutor to the son of the earl of Chesterfield and subsequently opened a small private school. In 1766, he gained his LLD (doctor of laws) to enhance his standing, marking the high point of his career. However, from this point on, he ran deeper into debt. Bids to obtain lucrative church livings failed, as did other ventures. Dodd was fired as editor and lost his royal chaplaincy, and his tutoring and school career came to an end. Preaching styles changed, and he lost his popularity. Although he was involved in many charities and became grand chaplain to the Freemasons in 1775, this position failed to bring the patronage that he desired. Dodd left England briefly to join his former pupil, now the new earl of Chesterfield. On his return, the earl paid some of his debts and provided him a small income.

In a desperate bid to fend off creditors, Dodd forged a bond in the name of the earl for four thousand pounds, claiming that the earl wanted the money secretly. He presented the bond to a broker, Lewis Robertson, but it lacked any signatures. Robertson, trusting the integrity of Dodd, finally found a banker, Messrs. Fletcher and Peach, to forward the money. Dodd filled in one of the signatures, and Robertson filled in another. However, the forgery quickly became known when the bond was shown to the earl, who immediately disowned it.

Legal Action and Outcome

Dodd was arrested and taken before Sir Thomas Halifax, the lord mayor of London. Dodd still had most of the money and offered to find the rest immediately. He claimed he would have paid the money back in six months and asked for the case to be settled privately, but neither of the attorneys acting for the earl or Halifax was willing. Fraud was a capital offense at this time, so the case was brought to the Old Bailey, the highest criminal court in London, on February 22, 1777.

The jury found Dodd guilty but recommended clemency, and the court delayed sentencing on technical grounds. This enabled a number of campaigns to be run on behalf of Dodd in the newspapers and by Oxford and Cambridge universities; the largest petition gained more than twenty thousand signatures. Dodd asked the well-known writer Dr. Samuel Johnson to intervene; Johnson did, writing speeches and sermons for Dodd to deliver. Johnson's efforts were unsuccessful, however. The lord chief justice, Lord William Murray Mansfield, considered this a high-profile case and felt that any leniency he showed would set a bad precedent. Dodd was thereupon sentenced on May 14, 1777, to the full punishment of death by public hanging, which was carried out at Tyburn on June 27, 1777.

Impact

Ironically, William Dodd had preached against the death penalty only a few years before his own death, at a time when the death penalty was given for many crimes against property. Widespread revulsion against such a harsh punishment soon generated campaigns to reduce the list of capital offenses; they were successful, and fraud and forgery ceased to be hanging offenses. It was almost another century, however, before public hanging ceased, and another century before the death penalty was abolished in the United Kingdom altogether.

Further Reading

Boswell, James. *Life of Johnson*. Vol. 3. Edited by George Birkbeck Hill. Kila, Mont.: Kessinger, 2004. Relates Dr. Johnson's efforts on behalf of Dodd in this commentary on the original Boswell text of 1791.

Howson, Gerald. *The Macaroni Parson: Life of the Unfortunate Doctor Dodd*. London: Hutchinson, 1973. A definitive biography of Dodd, giving a list of all the available sources.

Langbein, John H. *The Origins of Adversary Criminal Trial*. Oxford, England: Oxford University Press, 2003. Explains the technical delays in sentencing in Dodd's trial.

—*David Barratt*

See also: Arthur Orton.

Samuel K. Doe

President of Liberia (1980-1990)

Born: May 6, 1950; Tuzon, Grand Gedeh, Liberia
Died: September 9, 1990; Monrovia, Liberia
Also known as: Samuel Kanyon Doe (full name); Chairman Doe
Cause of notoriety: A brutal military dictator of Liberia whose regime stifled freedom of the press, Doe banned political activity, used the army to terrorize the population, and perpetrated human rights abuses and numerous political murders.
Active: 1980-1990
Locale: Liberia

Early Life

Samuel Kanyon Doe (doh) was born May 6, 1951, in Tuzon, Grand Gedeh, Liberia, to poor, uneducated parents who were members of the rural Krahn tribe. Doe had only a primary school education when he decided to become a career soldier. He received training from the American Green Berets and rose to the rank of master sergeant in the Liberian Army. On April 12, 1980, a group of noncommissioned officers led by Doe staged a successful, though bloody, military coup, killing President William R. Tolbert in his bed and executing thirteen of his aides.

Political Career

After taking power, Doe pledged a return to civilian rule and true democracy. In reality, he surrounded himself mostly with members of the Krahn ethnic group and formed an authoritarian regime called the People's Redemption Council. Doe forced the Soviet Union out of Liberia and forged a strong relationship with the United States, allowing the United States to have exclusive rights of use of Liberia's ports and land. Over the next four years, the Doe regime became increasingly dictatorial and oppressive of ethnic groups other than the Krahn tribe.

In 1985, a ban on political parties ended, and elections were held. Doe's National Democratic Party of Liberia (NDPL) was declared the winner. It was widely accepted

Samuel K. Doe (right) in Washington, D.C., with Ronald Reagan. (AP/Wide World Photos)

that the elections were rife with fraud, and it was highly unlikely that the NDPL had actually won. On January 6, 1986, Doe was sworn in as Liberia's twentieth president and the first of the Second Republic.

The international community did not react to the election fraud, and the United States was pleased that Doe remained in power because of his favorable policies toward the United States. In the years following the election increased human rights abuses, corruption, and ethnic conflicts occurred. However, the decline of communism and the Cold War, coupled with increased fiscal austerity in the United States, resulted in aid to Liberia being greatly reduced. Thus, the already faltering economy of Liberia stalled even further, resulting in a dramatic decline in the standard of living for the people of Liberia during the Doe regime.

The faltering economy, favoritism toward the Krahn tribe, and human rights abuses resulted in substantial anger and resentment toward Doe among Liberians. A revolt against Doe by the National Patriotic Front of Liberia (NPFL) was led by Charles Taylor, a former Doe ally. It began with an invasion from Côte d'Ivoire on December 24, 1989. The NPFL was quickly joined by thousands of people from different tribes. On September 9, 1990, Doe was captured and killed in Monrovia by faction leader Prince Yormie Johnson.

Impact

Following the death of Chairman Doe, chaos overtook Liberia, and civil war among rival factions continued until 2003. It is estimated that in the twelve-year civil war, nearly 200,000 Liberians died and hundreds of thousands of refugees fled the country. This catastrophic civil war cannot be totally blamed on Doe, but clearly his policy of fomenting ethnic strife was a contributing factor. Doe also left a country mired in extreme poverty and enormous foreign debt. In November, 2005, Ellen Johnson-Sirleaf was elected president of Liberia, becoming the first female president of an African nation.

Further Reading

Ellis, Stephen. *The Mask of Anarchy: The Destruction of Liberia and the Religious Dimensions of an African Civil War.* New York: New York University Press, 1999. Examines the economic, political, and cultural roots of the Liberian civil war, with a special emphasis on the role of religion.

Hyman, Lester. *United States Policy Toward Liberia, 1822 to 2003: Unintended Consequences?* Cherry Hill, N.J.: Africana Homestead Legacy, 2003. This book argues that the United States has made numerous poor decisions concerning Liberia and that these decisions had unintended negative consequences.

Pham, John-Peter. *Liberia: Portrait of a Failed State.* Chicago: Reed Press, 2004. A complete history of Liberia, including the Doe regime and its aftermath.

—Jerome L. Neapolitan

See also: Sani Abacha; Idi Amin; Omar al-Bashir; Jean-Bédel Bokassa; Mengistu Haile Mariam; Mobutu Sese Seko; Robert Mugabe; Muhammad Siad Barre; Charles Taylor.

Domitian

Roman emperor (r. 81-96 c.e.)

Born: October 24, 51 c.e.; Rome (now in Italy)
Died: September 18, 96 c.e.; Rome
Also known as: Titus Flavius Domitianus (full name); Caeser Domitianus Augustus
Cause of notoriety: As a paranoid tyrannical ruler of Rome, Domitian used torture, executions, espionage, and suppression of basic rights to maintain control of his subjects.
Active: 81-96 c.e.
Locale: Rome (now in Italy)

Early Life

Domitian (doh-MIHSH-yuhn) was the youngest son of Roman emperor Vespasian (r. 69-79 c.e.) and his first wife, Domitilla. Contrary to a literary tradition associating his family with poverty, they enjoyed a high degree of status in Roman society prior to Nero's fall in 69. Domitian was known as a poet and the author of a treatise on baldness in these early years. When his father was proclaimed emperor on July 1, 69, Domitian was seventeen years old and was persecuted by Vitellius, the third emperor after the death of Gaius Claudius Nero. Domitian escaped only with great difficulty from the burning religious center of Rome, the Capitolium, on December 19, 69. His father's troops occupied the city the following day.

Ten years later, in 79 c.e., Vespasian was succeeded by Domitian's elder brother Titus. Two months after the inauguration of Titus, the famous eruption of Mount Vesuvius near Naples occurred, which destroyed Pompeii and Herculaneum. Titus died two years later, on September 13, 81, and was succeeded by Domitian, who was proclaimed emperor by the praetorians (elite troops in Rome). The following day, this proclamation was accepted by the senate. There is no evidence that Domitian had murdered his brother or that he had intrigued to become emperor.

Political Career

During the first years of his reign, Domitian was a prudent and competent administrator, particularly of justice and of the ruling of the provinces of the entire Roman Empire, which stretched from the Atlantic Ocean to modern-day Iraq and from northern Africa to Germany. Domitian sought to purify moral and religious norms by punishing priests who had neglected their religious duties. Similarly, he executed vestals (priestesses of the goddess Vesta, the ancient Roman goddess of the hearth), applying brutal kinds of execution as had been common long before his reign.

During his reign, Domitian undertook several wars in the northern parts of the empire, such as Germania, Pannonia, Dacia (now Germany, Hungary, and Romania). At the end of the 80's and the beginning of the 90's of the first century C.E., Domitian gradually turned into a despotic ruler. His administration of justice, which initially had been praiseworthy, soon came to be used as an instrument of the emperor's cruelty.

As a result of Domitian's tyranny, his reign gained unenviable notoriety. Paranoid fear, easily wounded pride, and vanity led Domitian to take delight in the misfortune and suffering of his victims, mostly loyal and excellent senators or military commanders. One of these commanders, Gnaeus Julius Agricola, the commander and governor of the province of Britannia, became known because of a book written by his son-in-law, Tacitus, the well-known Roman historian of the time. In his short work on the life of Agricola, Tacitus described the career and death of his father-in-law and offered, persuasively, an insight into life under a despotic regime: Intellectuals were regarded as a potential danger for the ruler and were therefore expelled, actions of protest were suppressed by military force, spies were present everywhere, arrest could occur with no legal control, and torture and execution were the order of the day.

Suetonius on Domitian

In The Lives of the Twelve Caesars, *the Roman historian Suetonius, who lived in the second half of the first century C.E., during Domitian's lifetime, rehearses Domitian's career as emperor:*

In the earlier part of his reign . . . he often gave strong proofs not merely of integrity, but even of liberality. . . . But he did not continue this course of mercy or integrity, although he turned to cruelty somewhat more speedily than to avarice.

After his victory in the civil war he became even more cruel, and to discover any conspirators who were in hiding, tortured many of the opposite party by a new form of inquisition, inserting fire in their privates; and he cut off the hands of some of them. . . .

His savage cruelty was not only excessive, but also cunning and sudden. . . . To abuse men's patience the more insolently, he never pronounced an unusually dreadful sentence without a preliminary declaration of clemency, so that there came to be no more certain indication of a cruel death than the leniency of his preamble. . . . In this way he became an object of terror and hatred to all, but he was overthrown at last by a conspiracy of his friends and favourite freedmen, to which his wife was also privy. . . slain on the fourteenth day before the Kalends of October in the forty-fifth year of his age and the fifteenth of his reign. . . .

He was tall of stature, with a modest expression and a high colour. His eyes were large, but his sight was somewhat dim. He was handsome and graceful too, especially when a young man, and indeed in his whole body with the exception of his feet, the toes of which were somewhat cramped. In later life he had the further disfigurement of baldness, a protruding belly, and spindling legs, though the latter had become thin from a long illness. He was so conscious that the modesty of his expression was in his favour, that he once made this boast in the senate: "So far, at any rate, you have approved my heart and my countenance." He was so sensitive about his baldness, that he regarded it as a personal insult if anyone else was twitted with that defect in jest or in earnest; though in a book "On the Care of the Hair," which he published and dedicated to a friend, he wrote the following by way of consolation to the man and himself:

> Do you not see that I am too tall and comely to look on? And yet the same fate awaits my hair, and I bear with resignation the ageing of my locks in youth. Be assured that nothing is more pleasing than beauty, but nothing shorter-lived.

Source: C. Suetonius Tranquillus, *The Lives of the Twelve Caesars*, translated by J. C. Rolfe (New York: Macmillan, 1914).

Domitian was married to Domitia Longina in 70 C.E. They had a son, who died at the age of two or three. Domitian had many concubines, and his erotic extravagances were notorious. There were also rumors of an incestuous affair with Flavia Julia, the daughter of his deceased brother Titus. Julia's husband Sabinus was accused of conspiracy and executed by Domitian. Julia died in 89 C.E., at the age of twenty-eight, perhaps as a result of an abortion demanded by her imperial lover.

During the last three years of his reign, from 93 C.E. to September, 96 C.E., Domitian's regime of terror became especially intolerable. In the end, the emperor's paranoia turned against his family. Thus, the husband of Domitian's sister Domitilla, Flavius Clemens, was executed in 95 C.E.; Domitilla herself was sent to Pandateria, a small island in the Gulf of Naples. Her bodyguard Stephanus and Domitian's own wife persuaded officers of the praetorian guard to assist them in a conspiracy. On September 18, 96 C.E., Stephanus, with the help of some officers, killed the emperor during his dinner in the palace. The Roman senate gave orders to abolish all inscriptions throughout the empire featuring Domitian's name. This official act was called *Damnatio Memoriae*—the damnation of the memory of the Emperor Titus Flavius Domitianus.

Impact

Ancient historians—such as Tacitus, Dio Cassius, and Suetonius (the latter wrote a biography of Domitian)—depict the emperor as a brutal, despotic paranoiac. Modern scholars use these accounts but take their biases into account in attempting to draw a more objective and fairer portrait of Domitian, the third and last emperor of the Flavian Dynasty. He made a number of economic and military improvements—including increasing the number of military fortifications in North Africa, building roads, and returning the debased coinage to its Augustan level of silver—but at the expense of heavy taxation and social upheaval.

The remains of Domitian's reign are visible even in the twenty-first century. He is famous for his architectural program: He gave orders to restore temples and official buildings all across the empire. In Rome, two huge palaces on the Palatine hill were built, the Domus Augustana and the Domus Flavia; their ruins are now important remains of imperial Rome. Domitian also established new games for the Roman people. Furthermore, his commissioned stadium remains well known: Rome's famous Piazza Navona.

Further Reading

Rolfe, John C., ed. *Suetonius*. 2 vols. Reprint. London: Heinemann, 1959-1960. An English translation of the Latin biographies by the Roman author Suetonius.

Rutledge, Steven H. *Imperial Inquisitions: Prosecutors and Informants from Tiberius to Domitian*. London: Routledge, 2001. Concentrates on Domitian's despotic and tyrannic features.

Southern, Pat. *Domitian. Tragic Tyrant*. New York: Routledge, 1997. Offers a balanced view of Domitian, based on historical sources.

—*Gerhard Petersmann*

See also: Caligula; Elagabalus; Galerius; Nero.

KARL DÖNITZ

German Nazi admiral

BORN: September 16, 1891; Grünau, near Berlin, Germany
DIED: December 24, 1984; Aumühle-Bilenkamp, near Hamburg, West Germany (now Germany)
MAJOR OFFENSES: War crimes, including planning, initiating, and waging wars of aggression
ACTIVE: 1914-1946
LOCALE: Germany and the North Atlantic Ocean
SENTENCE: Ten years' imprisonment

EARLY LIFE

Karl Dönitz (kahrl DYEW-nihts) was born in 1891 in the Berlin suburb of Grünau. He graduated from the Imperial Naval Academy in 1913 and was serving as second lieutenant when World War I broke out in 1914. In 1916, he was given command of a submarine. In the infancy of submarine warfare, commanders operated independently, with very limited ability to communicate with one another, so Dönitz was free to develop his own strategies. He concluded that only a coordinated attack by multiple submarines could succeed against a convoy and was testing this theory in the Mediterranean when another of the submarines missed the rendezvous. Dönitz was captured and became a British prisoner.

Released in 1919, Dönitz rejoined a German navy sadly curtailed by the Treaty of Versailles. For fifteen years, he served in various peacetime capacities on surface vessels. Those years were not wasted. In his own words:

> The very impotence [of the Weimar Navy] was an added incentive to try ever more zealously to counterbalance our weakness . . . our object was to evolve and perfect by constant practice tactics which would give a weaker adversary some prospect of preventing the enemy of using his superior forces to their full extent.

When the Treaty of London (1935) allowed Germany to add submarines to its navy, Adolf Hitler asked Dönitz to assume command of this branch.

NAVAL CAREER

Unable to persuade Admiral Erich Raeder to devote the resources he believed necessary, Dönitz nonetheless succeeded in turning Germany's infant submarine fleet into an efficient fighting force by the time war broke out with Britain in 1939. In the ensuing naval war, Germany sought to cripple Britain by cutting off shipments of crucial supplies. Operating in "wolf packs," German submarines were able to attack heavily armed convoys, disabling warships and sinking freighters.

After the United States entered the war in 1941, Dönitz instituted Operation Drumbeat: coordinated attacks on American supply ships in the western Atlantic. Naval historians acknowledge that Germany nearly won the Battle of the Atlantic and credit the extreme strategic efficiency of the German U-boats. Dönitz replaced Raeder as commander in chief of the navy in 1943.

The case against Dönitz as a war criminal rests principally on two directives issued a year after the war commenced: the declaration of unrestricted submarine warfare and cessation of attempts to rescue crews of sunken ships. Both directives were violations of rules of naval

Karl Dönitz. (AP/Wide World Photos)

warfare, and both were subsequently followed by Britain and the United States. International standards had permitted combatants to stop and search neutral vessels but banned sinking unarmed vessels of any nationality. A submarine can determine a vessel's status only by surfacing, and the treaty did not anticipate the possibility of rapid air response. For the Germans, declaring unrestricted submarine warfare had become a necessary strategy in 1942.

The directive against rescuing crews arose from the *Laconia* incident. On September 12, 1942, a German U-boat torpedoed a liner carrying British troops and eighteen hundred Italian prisoners of war (POWs) off the coast of West Africa. The captain called for assistance. Four other Axis submarines responded and were proceeding for Senegal under a Red Cross flag with packed decks and lifeboats in tow when an American bomber attacked. The submarines submerged and escaped; many of the seamen and POWs drowned. The decision to abandon similar rescue attempts in the future was understandable.

On April 29, 1945, Hitler appointed Dönitz to succeed him as Germany's führer. For the next twenty days, Dönitz concentrated efforts on evacuating people from the projected Soviet sector, anticipating that the Russians, who had borne the brunt of German's war crimes, would retaliate in kind. Those twenty days as Nazi Germany's head of state probably helped secure his conviction and incarceration, not so much for his military actions as for his potential, as a man still much admired, to serve as a nucleus for revived German nationalism.

Legal Action and Outcome

Of all the Nazi officials convicted by the International Military Tribunal at Nuremberg, Dönitz was perhaps the least guilty. Direct involvement in the Holocaust or other crimes against humanity formed no part of the indictment against him. Whether he was as ignorant of them as he claimed at his defense is debatable but not entirely implausible.

In contrast to most aspects of World War II, the Battle of the Atlantic was a relatively clean military operation with clear strategic objectives. Both sides violated maritime laws framed before air power became a factor in naval battles, and attempts to establish which side acted first led to the conclusion that several British and American naval commanders could equally well have been convicted.

Dönitz argued in *Zehn Jahre und zwanzig Tage* (1990; *Ten Years and Twenty Days*, 1990) that that which constitutes an "aggressive war" is a political decision, and holding a military officer culpable for diligently serving his country in a war subsequently determined (by the victors) to have been inadequately justified creates an impossible dilemma: It appears to require a man to violate his oaths of allegiance and refuse orders based on personal assessment of an ambiguous situation.

Impact

Karl Dönitz's notoriety as a war criminal, which was never very great to begin with, faded over time. Being Hitler's successor made him a rallying point for revived Nazi sentiments in the years following World War II, but his fame ended long before his death. He is remembered mainly as a brilliant, innovative naval strategist, and his career is studied closely by military historians and students at naval academies throughout the world.

Further Reading

Dönitz, Karl. *Ten Years and Twenty Days*. Translated by R. H. Stevens. Annapolis, Md.: Naval Institute Press, 1990. A very readable account, in Dönitz's own words, of his naval career, brief tenure as führer, and trial.

Edwards, Bernard. *Dönitz and the Wolf-Packs: U-Boats at War*. London: Brockhampton Press, 1999. A popular, illustrated account of the Battle of the Atlantic, emphasizing individual sea battles.

Harris, Whitney R. *Tyranny on Trial: The Trial of the Major German War Criminals*. Dallas: Southern Methodist University Press, 1999. A good account of the Nuremberg Trials, with some information on Dönitz.

Padfield, Peter. *Dönitz, the Last Führer: Portrait of a Nazi War Leader*. New York: Harper and Row, 1984. Complete biography; concludes that the Nazi affiliation is significant.

—Martha A. Sherwood

See also: Adolf Hitler.

Black Donnellys

Irish Canadian victims of vigilante violence

James Donnelly

Born: March 7, 1816; Tipperary County, Ireland
Died: February 4, 1880; Biddulph Township, Ontario, Canada

Johannah Donnelly

Born: September 22, 1823; Tipperary, Ireland
Died: February 4, 1880; Biddulph Township, Ontario, Canada

James Donnelly, Jr.

Born: December 8, 1841; Ireland
Died: May 15, 1877; Biddulph Township, Ontario, Canada

William Donnelly

Born: 1845; London, Canada West
Died: March 7, 1897; Appin, Ontario, Canada

John Donnelly

Born: 1847/1848; Biddulph Township, Canada West
Died: February 4, 1880; Biddulph Township, Ontario, Canada

Patrick Donnelly

Born: April 15, 1849; Biddulph Township, Canada West
Died: May 18, 1914; Thorold, Ontario, Canada

Michael Donnelly

Born: September, 1850; Biddulph Township, Canada West
Died: December 9, 1879; Waterford, Ontario, Canada

Robert Donnelly

Born: November 9, 1853; Biddulph Township, Canada West
Died: June 14, 1911; Lucan, Ontario, Canada

Thomas Donnelly

Born: August 30, 1854; Biddulph Township, Canada West
Died: February 4, 1880; Biddulph Township, Ontario, Canada

Jenny Donnelly

Born: October, 1856; Biddulph Township, Canada West
Died: September 3, 1917; Glencoe, Ontario, Canada

Also known as: Donnelly family
Cause of notoriety: After engaging in violent acts in their township, several members of the Donnelly family were murdered by a local vigilante group.
Active: February 4, 1880
Locale: Biddulph Township, Middlesex County, Ontario, Canada

Early Lives

James Donnelly (DON-uh-lee) and his future wife, Johannah Magee, were born in the county of Tipperary, Ireland. They were likely both Roman Catholics in the village of Borrioskane. The early 1800's were tough times for Irish Catholics. They had been persecuted by the Protestants following the 1690 Irish Uprisings and were denied access to land, education, and economic opportunities. Catholics were vulnerable to food shortages and many starved to death. Their lives were also complicated politically by fighting between Protestants and Catholic vigilante groups. Many Catholic secret societies operated at night, when they torched structures, maimed animals, and attacked people. Tipperary was at the center of much of this violence, and Irish families who emigrated to the United States often transported these traditional social mores with them.

Farming Career

In 1840, James married Johannah in Ireland, and a few years later, he emigrated alone to Canada West. Johannah remained in Ireland, where she raised their eldest son, James, until they also immigrated. Travel across the Atlantic Ocean was a terrible experience for ship passengers, and many did not survive the voyage. The young family reunited in London, the former capital of Upper Canada, which was a thriving community located on the edge of the wilderness. Within a few years, the Donnelly family moved north to the township of Biddulph in Ontario. There, they cleared and farmed one hundred acres, although they did not have legal ownership of the land, a fact that resulted in lawsuits and violence.

Eventually James and Johannah had a total of seven sons and one daughter. All the children worked the land to eke out a meager subsistence. In the 1860's, a school operated on one corner of the property, although many of the Donnelly children did not have clothes to attend classes. Surrounding farms tended to be poor and run by Catholics, while the nearby town of Lucan was under the control of prosperous Protestant merchants.

Biddulph Township gained a reputation for lawless behavior, and several murders occurred, as well as arson and animal thefts or maimings. In most cases, the perpetrators were not brought to justice, and local offshoots of the Irish secret societies were blamed for the violence. Most local events were characterized by drunken fights, and in 1857, James, Sr., killed a neighbor at a barn raising, resulting in seven years in the Kingston Penitentiary. In the following decades several of the Donnelly sons also appeared in court because of local feuds, often over land or women. Eventually, most of the sons gained some prosperity as drivers and owners of a local stagecoach business, which also involved them in violent altercations with competing businesses.

Historical records suggest that the family was violent, as were most of their neighbors; the Donnellys were nonetheless respected for their hard work. However, the arrival of Father John Connelly, who took over St. Patrick's Catholic Church in early 1879, marked a change in the Donnellys' reputation. The priest fostered community perceptions of the Donnelly boys as troublemakers and socially isolated them from other Catholics. He established a Catholic vigilante society to battle crime, symbolized to him by the Donnelly family. Township tensions escalated and ultimately resulted in a group of thirty-five men, including local constable James Carroll, attacking the main Donnelly farmhouse in the early hours of February 4, 1880. The crowd brutally killed the two parents, their son Thomas, and Bridget, a visiting Irish niece, and then torched the house. In their bloodlust, the murderers did not notice a neighboring boy, Johnny O'Connor, escape. The violent mob then marched through the snow to Will Donnelly's house, where they shot and killed his brother John by mistake. They did not break into the house, where they would have discovered Will, his pregnant wife, Norah, and a neighbor.

Legal Action and Outcome

Everyone returned to their farms and went about their normal business on the day following the murders, although there were souvenir hunters who visited the scene of the crime. Most people knew who was involved. In the four days after the murders, thirteen arrests were made by the police. Among those arrested was Constable Carroll, who was the only man brought to trial; he was ultimately acquitted.

Impact

The deaths of the Donnelly family members and the resulting trial fascinated the Canadian public. After the murders, the family was pilloried in the press since it was otherwise difficult to understand such a horrendous act of violence. The final verdict also had political implications. The premier of Ontario, Sir Oliver Mowat (who also acted as the attorney general), needed to secure Irish Catholic votes for the upcoming election, and his office undermined much of the prosecution's efforts to convict the murderers.

Further Reading

Edwards, Peter. *Night Justice: The True Story of the Black Donnellys*. Toronto, Ont.: Key Porter Books, 2004. A persuasive explanation of the Donnelly deaths, which focuses on Biddulph local history and the social mores imported from Ireland.

Feltes, Norman N. *This Side of Heaven: Determining the Donnelly Murders, 1880*. Toronto, Ont.: University of Toronto Press, 1999. A Marxist framework that examines farming production and transportation networks and argues that economic history strongly determined the murders.

Reaney, James C., ed. *The Donnelly Documents: An Ontario Vendetta*. Toronto, Ont.: The Champlain Society, 2004. An edited collection of the historic documents that relate to the family and their lives in Canada.

—*Susan J. Wurtzburg*

See also: Irish Invincibles; Molly Maguires.

Bill Doolin

American bank robber and bandit

Born: 1858; near Clarksville, Johnson County, Arkansas
Died: August 24, 1896; Lawson, Oklahoma Territory
Also known as: King of the Oklahoma Bandits; William Doolin (full name)
Cause of notoriety: Doolin committed his early bank and train robberies in the company of the Dalton brothers; he later headed his own gang, the Wild Bunch.
Active: 1891-1896
Locale: Indian Territory, Oklahoma, and Texas

Early Life

Bill Doolin (DEW-lihn) was born to Michael "Mack" Doolin and Artemina Beller in Johnson County, Arkansas, in 1858. His father had had four children from his first marriage and two children with his second wife. The Doolins acquired a small farm in Big Piney Creek, thirty miles northeast of Clarksville, Arkansas, which Doolin helped run after his father's death.

Although illiterate, Doolin was a hard worker and was skilled with tools. He found employment with a ranch owner, Oscar D. Hasell, building corrals and other structures. Hassell also taught Doolin simple bookkeeping. Doolin worked for several ranchers and cattlemen until 1889, when the government vacated the Indian Territory of Oklahoma to make room for homesteaders. On March 14, 1893, Doolin married Edith Ellsworth, a preacher's daughter. The two had one son, whom they named Jay.

Criminal Career

Doolin's first brush with the law occurred on July 4, 1891, while he was working at the Bar X Bar Ranch. He and some friends had ridden into Coffeyville, Kansas, to celebrate Independence Day with a keg of beer. Kansas was a dry state, and authorities tried to confiscate the beer. A shoot-out ensued, wounding two police officers and forcing Doolin to flee the area.

Once on the run, Doolin met up with Bob and Emmett Dalton as well as other outlaws. His shooting skills, intelligence, and fairness made Doolin a natural leader among Western bandits. By September of 1891, he was riding with the Dalton gang and participated in train robberies in Leliaetta, Indian Territory; Red Rock, Oklahoma Territory; and Adair, Indian Territory. Doolin did not accompany the Daltons on their fatal attempt to rob two banks simultaneously in Coffeyville, Kansas, on October 5, 1892. On that day gang members, including two Daltons, were shot to death.

With the demise of the Dalton gang, Doolin recruited new men for his own gang, which became known as the Wild Bunch. The gang robbed a passenger train in Cimarron, Kansas, on June 11, 1893, but a posse of lawmen was ready for them and ambushed the gang as they were escaping. Doolin was shot in the left foot and limped for the rest of his life. Three months later, rumors of the Wild Bunch hiding in Ingalls, Oklahoma Territory, were circulating. On September 1, 1893, thirteen sheriffs entered the town and found the gang in a saloon. A shoot-out ensued, later dubbed the Battle of Ingalls, after which three marshals and two innocent bystanders were dead, and many were hurt. Members of the Wild Bunch escaped with minor wounds.

Over the next two years the gang continued its robbery spree. On April 3, 1895, the Wild Bunch ambushed and robbed a passenger train in Dover, Oklahoma Territory. Again, a posse was ready, and a shoot-out began

Bill Doolin.

which resulted in "Tulsa Jack" Blake's death. Now infamous, the gang disbanded after the Dover heist. Over the next few months, former members of the Wild Bunch were killed by bounty hunters or in shoot-outs. A realist, Doolin contacted his attorney to arrange a plea bargain in which he would surrender in exchange for a guaranteed short sentence. The authorities would not agree to the terms, and Doolin went into hiding in Eureka Springs, Arkansas.

Legal Action and Outcome

Deputy Marshall Tilghman, who had long been tracking Doolin, learned of the outlaw's location. There he surprised Doolin and brought him to Guthrie, Kansas, to stand trial for his crimes. While in prison awaiting trial, Doolin and "Dynamite Dick" Clifton, along with twelve other prisoners, escaped.

Missing his family and tired of running from the law, Doolin decided to return home, in order to take his wife and son to an undisclosed location. Deputy Marshall Heck Thomas heard of the plan. When Doolin was seen helping his wife, Edith, load a wagon, Deputy Thomas organized a stakeout. When Doolin later returned to his house he was met with gunfire. He died on August 24, 1896.

Impact

Although his crimes instilled fear in Western settlers, Bill Doolin enjoyed a reputation for being reasonable, sincere, and levelheaded. His intelligence and fairness gained him respect among fellow outlaws, members of the community, and—ironically—certain law officials.

When Oklahoma became a state in 1907, its government felt increased pressure to ensure the safety of its citizens. Several laws were passed spelling out police powers and instilling fear among local gangs. Amid rising instances of bank and train robberies, several states enacted rewards and bounties, ranging from one thousand to fifteen thousand dollars, for the capture of Doolin and other criminals, "dead or alive." Civilian vigilantes and sheriffs' posses legally pursued bandit gangs, armed with both muscle and authority. These raids and bounties resulted in the deaths of Doolin and other members of the Wild Bunch. They also served as warnings for other gangs and signified the end of the romantic Western shoot-outs.

Further Reading

Drago, Harry S. *Outlaws on Horseback*. Lincoln: University of Nebraska Press, 1998. Focuses on train and bank robbers and provides a riveting account of Bill Doolin's life as a bandit and his associations with other Wild West outlaws.

Lewis, Jon E. *The Mammoth Book of the West: The Making of the American West*. New York: Carroll & Graf, 2001. Lewis offers the reader a comprehensive account of life in the Wild West and mentions all of the key players who were involved. A good reference for Doolin and members of the Wild Bunch.

O'Neal, Bill. *Encyclopedia of Western Gunfighters*. Norman: University of Oklahoma Press, 1991. A factual look at the outlaws who roamed the Old West.

Reasoner, James. *Draw: The Greatest Gunfights of the American West*. New York: Berkley, 2003. Paints a historically accurate picture of the bandits and gunfighters. Reasoner does not romanticize bank robbers and bandits as some writings do but offers an objective look at the West.

Wellman, Paul I. *A Dynasty of Western Outlaws*. Norman: University of Oklahoma Press, 1998. Focusing on the late 1800's and early 1900's, Wellman's book provides a thorough examination of life in the Wild West and its outlaws. Also contains maps and family trees.

—*Sara Vidar*

See also: Apache Kid; Tom Bell; William H. Bonney; Curly Bill Brocius; Butch Cassidy; Bob Dalton; Emmett Dalton; John Wesley Hardin; Doc Holliday; Jesse James; Tom Ketchum; Harry Longabaugh; Bill Longley; Joaquín Murieta; Johnny Ringo; Belle Starr; Henry Starr; Hank Vaughan; Cole Younger.

Jacques Doriot

French Fascist

Born: September 26, 1898; Bresles, Oise, France
Died: February 22, 1945; near Mengen, Germany
Cause of notoriety: Doriot, a French Fascist who hated the Bolsheviks' influence in Europe, collaborated with the Germans occupying France in World War II.
Active: 1936-1945
Locale: France

Early Life

Jacques Doriot (zhahk doh-ree-oh) was born in Bresles, Oise, France, on September 26, 1898. His father was a blacksmith. Doriot moved to the Paris suburb of Saint-Denis and worked there as a metalworker and as a mechanic. By 1916 he was committed to advancing Socialist politics and became a member of the French Socialist party the Section Française de l'Internationale (SFIO). In 1917, he joined the French army and participated in World War I combat. He was taken prisoner and remained in a prison camp until the war ended in 1918. Upon his release, he returned to France and received the Croix de Guerre for his wartime service.

Political Career

In 1920, Doriot became a member of the Parti Communiste Français (PCF), in whose activities he played a very prominent role. In 1922, he became a member of the presidium of the executive committee of the Comintern. The following year, he accepted the position of secretary general of the French Federation of Young Communists. Also in 1923, he participated in a protest against the French occupation of Germany's Ruhr Valley. After writing a number of pamphlets espousing violence as a means of protest, he was sent to prison. While incarcerated, however, he was elected by the suburb of Saint-Denis to serve in the French chamber of deputies. His election resulted in his release from prison in 1924. In 1931, he was elected mayor of Saint-Denis. He held this office for several years and also continued to represent Saint-Denis in the chamber of deputies, where he was by now one of the major Communist leaders.

In 1934, Doriot was expelled from the Communist Party, as his ideology clearly differed from that of the party's mainstream. Doriot was in favor of an alliance with the Socialists and other leftist parties, while the main Communist leadership was shifting toward fascism under the leadership of Maurice Thorez and the Komintern. Doriot was also highly opposed to the parties' susceptibility to Soviet influence. In May of 1936, Thorez, with Leon Blum and Roger Salengro, led the Front Populaire, a coalition of leftist parties, to victory in the elections. This same year, Doriot, who vehemently opposed the Front Populaire, created a new party, Le Parti Populaire Français (PPF). The PPF's organization and structure closely resembled that of the Fascist Party, and its membership comprised both Communists and Fascists.

Personally, Doriot had been shifting ideologically from communism to fascism. As the Front Populaire shifted away from fascism and came to advocate coalition with the Socialists—which was Doriot's original position—he evolved ideologically in exactly the opposite direction. By 1936, having renounced his former communist beliefs and alliance, Doriot was a strong supporter of Adolf Hitler and fascism. He also established a newspaper, *La Liberté*, to disseminate the PPF's political views. Increasingly attracted to fascism, Doriot visited Spain and was a supporter of Francisco Franco during the Spanish Civil War. Doriot became friends with John Amery, a British Fascist, and traveled with him in Austria, Italy, and Germany.

After Germany's defeat of France in 1940, Doriot advocated collaboration and supported Philippe Pétain's Vichy government and the German occupation of northern France. Doriot lived for a while in Vichy France but was soon back in Paris, where he participated in anti-Bolshevik broadcasts on Radio Paris. In 1941, he and a fellow collaborator, Marcel Déat, founded the Légion des Volontaires Français (LVF). The organization, whose complete name was actually the Légion des Volontaires Français Contre le Bolchévisme, was a military division of the Wehrmacht. The French volunteers who joined the unit fought on the Russian front in the ranks of the German army and wore German uniforms. Doriot fought with the LVF and participated in the German invasion of Russia in June, 1941. When the LVF was no longer a viable fighting force after it suffered heavy losses, Doriot fought as a member of the German army and received the Iron Cross in December, 1943. When the Vichy government fell in 1944, Doriot fled to Germany with fellow collaborators Joseph Darnand and Déat. The three served the exiled Vichy government at Sigmaringen. Doriot was killed in an air raid on February 22, 1945, near Mengen, Germany.

Impact

Jacques Doriot played an extremely active and important role in French politics from 1920 to his death in 1945. From a working-class milieu, he was typical of many of the early Socialists who became affiliated with the Communist movement in France. Doriot, however, was atypical in his strong opposition to Russian influence and his sincere belief that the defeat of Bolshevism would unite Europe. He saw in fascism and in the German state the means to eradicate the Russian influence in France and in Europe as a whole. Doriot and his political activity before and during World War II elucidate an aspect of wartime collaboration based on ideological belief which is often not taken into account by those who study the French collaboration with the German invaders. Doriot's career is representative of the importance of political theory in French culture and of the confusion and instability that plagued French politics during the first half of the twentieth century.

Further Reading

Allardyce, G. "The Political Transition of Jacques Doriot." *Journal of Contemporary History* 1, no. 1 (1966): 56-74. Discusses in detail how and why Doriot left the Communist Party and became a Fascist.

Arnold, Edward J. *The Development of the Radical Right in France, from Boulanger to Le Pen*. Basingstroke, England: Macmillan, 2000. Traces Fascism in France from 1887 to 1998. Discusses Doriot's role in its development.

Morgan, Philip. *Fascism in Europe, 1919-1945*. London: Routledge, 2002. Good coverage of Fascism in Italy and Germany. Contains a useful bibliography.

Payne, Stanley G. *A History of Fascism, 1914-1945*. London: UCL, 1995. Defines Fascism and treats Doriot's efforts to establish the LVF. Presents the Fascist movement in a historical framework.

—*Shawncey Webb*

See also: François Darlan; Joseph Darnand; Francisco Franco; Adolf Hitler; Pierre Laval; Philippe Pétain.

Diane Downs

American murderer

Born: August 7, 1955; Phoenix, Arizona

Also known as: Elizabeth Diane Frederickson (birth name)

Major offenses: Murder, attempted murder, and assault

Active: May 19, 1983

Locale: Near Marcola, Oregon

Sentence: Life in prison for murder; fifty years for attempted murder and assault

Early Life

Diane Downs (di-AN downz), the daughter of Wes and Willadene Frederickson, resented her strict Baptist parents dictating how she and her four younger siblings lived. While a junior at Moon Valley High School, she met Steven Downs. After graduation, she briefly attended Pacific Coast Baptist Bible College while he served in the U.S. Navy. The two married in 1973. Downs gave birth to her first daughter, Christie, the following year, then her second daughter, Cheryl, in 1976.

Downs occasionally left, then reunited with, her husband, whom she considered too demanding. She gave birth to a coworker's son, Danny, in 1979. After her divorce in 1981, Downs pursued other affairs, often with married men. She secured postal employment in Chandler, Arizona, where she met Lew Lewiston, with whom she initiated a romantic relationship despite his disinterest in her children. In February, 1983, Downs was devastated when Lewiston informed her of his decision to remain married to his wife. Downs moved to Springfield, Oregon, where her father was postmaster. She asked Lewiston to relocate there as well.

Criminal Career

On the evening of May 19, 1983, Downs took her children to visit a friend at Marcola, near Springfield. Returning home on rural Old Mohawk Road, Downs parked the car and shot her children, then herself, with a pistol. After 10:30 p.m., she blared her horn outside the emergency entrance at McKenzie-Willamette Hospital, screaming that a stranger had attacked her family. While medical personnel focused on saving Downs's children, the hospital receptionist alerted police. Downs's youngest daughter died soon afterward. Physicians performed surgery on Downs's two surviving children.

Police arrived at the hospital and questioned Downs, who told them a disheveled white man had motioned for her to stop driving and demanded her keys. According to her, he had become agitated, shot her children, then her, and ran away. Officers searched the area for the man and the yellow car Downs said she had seen nearby.

Legal Action and Outcome

Police considered Downs a possible suspect because they observed her erratic behavior at the hospital and believed her wound was self-inflicted. For several months, detectives and Deputy District Attorney Frederick A. Hugi investigated the shooting. Their forensic examinations and interviews provided information that contradicted Downs's claims and suggested she had attempted to kill her children, in the hope of reconciling with Lewiston. Police arrested Downs on February 28, 1984, incarcerating her in the Lane County Jail at Eugene. A grand jury issued indictments for one murder count, two attempted murder counts, and two assault counts.

Downs's trial started on May 10, 1984, at the Lane County Courthouse. Her daughter stated that Downs had shot her and her siblings. Expressing her love for her children, Downs denounced the prosecution's statements. On June 16, jurors unanimously declared Downs guilty of murder, attempted first-degree murder, and first-degree assault. Two months later, Judge Gregory Foote sentenced Downs to life imprisonment extended by fifty years.

Incarcerated in the Oregon Women's Correctional Center at Salem, Downs escaped on July 11, 1987. She was at large for ten days before police apprehended her. A judge added five years to Downs's sentence, transferring her first to New Jersey's Correctional Institution for Women and then to the Valley Prison for Women in California.

Impact

Because of public fascination with Diane Downs's case, media worldwide focused on Downs during her trial and continued to cover her story after she was convicted. In 1984, a thirty-minute documentary featured her trial. Talk-show host Oprah Winfrey broadcast her interview with Downs in September, 1988. ABC television aired a four-hour movie depicting the murder in November, 1989. Appealing to her supportive fans, Downs published a book in the late 1980's. Hugi, the deputy district attorney, and his wife adopted Downs's children in 1986.

Further Reading

Downs, Elizabeth Diane. *Diane Downs: Best Kept Secrets*. Springfield, Oreg.: Danmark, 1989. Downs cites information she says authorities overlooked, describing herself as an innocent victim of faulty law enforcement practices.

Meyer, Cheryl L., and Michelle Oberman. *Mothers Who Kill Their Children: Understanding the Acts of Moms from Susan Smith to the "Prom Mom."* New York: New York University Press, 2001. Provides contextual analysis that examines such relevant topics as child abuse, domestic violence, and legal strategies.

Rule, Ann. *Small Sacrifices: A True Story of Passion and Murder*. New York: Signet, 2003. Thoroughly discusses Downs's life and how investigators proved her guilt. Includes excerpts from Downs's journals and letters.

—*Elizabeth D. Schafer*

See also: Magda Goebbels; Marie Hilley; Darlie Routier; Susan Smith; Andrea Yates.

Francis Drake

British seaman, privateer, and pirate

Born: c. 1540; Crowndale, near Tavistock, Devonshire, England
Died: January 28, 1596; at sea off Porto Bello, Panama
Also known as: Sir Francis Drake; El Draque (Spanish for dragon); The Dragon
Cause of notoriety: Although considered a patriot and hero by some, Drake conducted numerous raids on Spanish and Portuguese ships, settlements, and cities in search of loot and to weaken these countries politically and militarily.
Active: 1562-1596
Locale: Spain, Portugal, the Caribbean, the Canary Islands, Africa, South America, Florida, California, and the Philippines

Early Life

Francis Drake (drayk) was one of twelve sons of Edmund Drake, a curate and vicar in Devonshire, England. As a boy, Drake lived with his uncle, William Hawkins, a merchant and seaman. Drake and his cousin John Hawkins went on trading voyages; as they grew older they participated in plundering and slaving, learning seamanship and raiding tactics. A slaving raid to Africa and sale of the slaves in the Caribbean in 1562-1563 occurred during Drake's first trip to the Americas.

Pirating Career

Drake's first command may have been the *Judith*, one of seven ships that Hawkins took on a slave raid to Africa and on a subsequent trading expedition to the Caribbean in 1567-1568. The *Judith* expedition ended in disaster at San Juan de Ulúa near Veracruz, Mexico, when a Spanish fleet attacked the British, and Drake sailed away—an action that strained relations between Drake and Hawkins. Drake perpetrated several raids in Panama, which culminated in a spectacular success: capturing a mule train of gold and silver in April, 1573. Drake became a wealthy man, and his daring capture made the Spanish take notice of him.

From November, 1577, until September, 1580, Drake embarked on a voyage that resulted in the globe's second circumnavigation (after the Magellan expedition of 1519-1522). The public purpose was trade and exploration, but the real reason was to raid Spanish settlements on the Pacific coast of South and Central America. The voyage was marred by Drake's execution of Thomas Doughty, one of the commanders and a onetime friend, for mutiny. However, because of the tremendous treasure Drake brought back and because of the trouble he had caused the Spanish, he was knighted in England.

Drake's next major undertaking was his 1585-1586 raid on the West Indies and Saint Augustine, Florida, which helped precipitate the Anglo-Spanish War (1585-1604). Although not profitable for the "investors," the voyage damaged Spanish prestige and forced Spain to allocate greater resources defending its American possessions.

Drake increased his notoriety in the eyes of the Spanish with a daring raid on Cádiz, Spain, in April, 1587, disrupting preparations for the Armada of 1588. During this time, Drake was vice admiral and participated in the defense of England. His reputation suffered when he broke ranks with the British fleet to capture the Spanish ship *Rosario* as a prize. In 1589, Drake, in concert with Sir John Norris, commander of land forces, raided Spain and

Francis Drake. (Library of Congress)

Portugal. Drake's final military expedition in 1595-1596 reunited him with Hawkins in an attempt to repeat the raid of a decade earlier; however, this time the Spanish were well prepared for the British fleet.

Hawkins died in November, 1595, and was buried at sea off the coast of San Juan, Puerto Rico. On January 28, 1596, Drake died from dysentery and was buried at sea in a lead coffin off the coast of Porto Bello, Panama.

The Dragon's Circumnavigation

In the fall of 1580, after sailing thirty-six thousand sea miles around the world, Francis Drake returned to England a rich hero. It had been an adventure on an epic scale—buccaneering, trading, sea battles, storms, mutiny, near wreck, contact with exotic Americans, and discovery—and it all began with deception. When Drake led five ships from England in 1577, his men thought they were headed for the Nile River in Africa on a trading voyage. Instead, Drake sailed for the Straits of Magellan at the tip of South America. One captain mutinied. Drake, undaunted, executed him, discarded two damaged ships, and sailed on.

Down to three ships, the fleet had a long, stormy passage into the Pacific Ocean, losing its smallest ship and its crew. Once safely in the Pacific, Drake renamed his flagship the *Golden Hind* and rallied his crew. Before them lay largely unprotected Spanish colonies along the coast of Chile, Peru, and Central America. These they pillaged at will (seldom killing victims or losing crew members), and they captured several vessels, including a rich treasure ship, the *Cacafuego*. Drake had to stop twice for extended repairs, first on an island off Mexico and then somewhere near the most northern point of his voyage—between 42 and 49 degrees north, along Oregon or Washington. In one bay he stayed five weeks, enjoying friendly relations with the indigenous peoples. He named the country Nova Albion and left a metal plaque to commemorate his stay. It has never been found.

Drake's expedition then turned west, making landfall after sixty-eight days, probably on an Indonesian island. Drake cruised for several months among the islands, trading for spices, making other deals, and surviving a collision with a reef. Then he sailed for the tip of Africa and home, laden with cargo and booty. It is no wonder that the Spanish hated him and called him the Dragon.

Impact

Sir Francis Drake's exploits against the Spanish were supported by Elizabeth I (r. 1558-1603) and helped develop interest in colonizing the Americas because of the wealth and geographical knowledge he helped obtain. The Spanish regarded him as a tremendous threat and dubbed him "el Draque," or the dragon, because of his reddish hair and his ferocity and tenacity. He did, however, leave military engagements at crucial times, and, fearful of challenges to his authority, he had men executed. Nonetheless, his audacity, his patriotism, his anti-Catholicism, and his service to a popular, historically significant monarch assured him a legendary place in British history.

Further Reading

Bawlf, Samuel. *The Secret Voyage of Sir Francis Drake, 1577-1580*. New York: Penguin, 2004. This book presents a powerful argument that the purpose of this voyage was to find the Strait of Anian (the Northwest Passage) and that Drake sailed as far north as Vancouver Island.

Cummins, John G. *Francis Drake: Lives of a Hero*. New York: St. Martin's Press, 1997. A comprehensive biography that focuses on Drake's reputation and his exploits.

Kelesey, Harry. *Sir Francis Drake: The Queen's Pirate*. New Haven, Conn.: Yale University Press, 1998. A scholarly study that presents Drake as an adventurer whose primary focus was on obtaining riches.

—*Mark C. Herman*

See also: Samuel Bellamy; Charlotte de Berry; Stede Bonnet; Anne Bonny; William Dampier; William Kidd; Sir Henry Morgan; Grace O'Malley; John Quelch; John Rackham; Mary Read; Bartholomew Roberts; Edward Teach.

David Duke

American white supremacist

Born: July 1, 1950; Tulsa, Oklahoma
Cause of notoriety: Duke, a member and leader of numerous white supremacist groups in the United States and Europe—including the Knights of the Ku Klux Klan, the National Association for the Advancement of White People, and the European-American Unity and Rights Organization—concerned many when he ran for some major political offices.
Active: Beginning 1964
Locale: Louisiana

Early Life

David Duke (dewk) was born in 1950, the second child of Major David H. Duke and Maxine Crick Duke. His father was an engineer with Shell Oil Company. In 1954, the Duke family moved to the Netherlands when Major Duke was offered a position at the headquarters of Royal Dutch Shell. In 1955, the family moved to New Orleans, where they lived for the next fourteen years. During this period Duke's father's work required him to spend extensive time away from home. His mother began to drink heavily, and young Duke, a reclusive child, found himself alone much of the time. In 1964, Duke was introduced to the Citizens Councils, a segregationist group in New Orleans. He began to read various books written by segregationists, and by the time he entered John F. Kennedy High School in New Orleans, he had become active in right-wing politics. His activism culminated with Duke joining the Knights of the Ku Klux Klan in New Orleans in 1967 at the age of seventeen.

Political Career

Duke's public career began in 1969, when he was a student at Louisiana State University (LSU). He became a leader of the National Socialist Liberation Front, a group affiliated with the neo-Nazi National Socialist White People's Party. He began to give talks at Free Speech Alley on campus and quickly became known as the LSU Nazi. In spring, 1970, Duke picketed a speech by civil rights attorney William Kunstler at Tulane University, wearing a Nazi shirt and a swastika armband and carry-

David Duke, in Ku Klux Klan robes. (AP/Wide World Photos)

ing a placard that said "Kunstler Is a Communist-Jew" and "Gas the Chicago 7," the latter in reference to a liberal group who were arrested following riots at the 1968 Democratic National Convention in Chicago.

Following a rebuke from his father, Duke left the National Socialist Liberation Front. In January, 1972, he created a short-lived organization called the National Party in New Orleans, which was intended to be a political youth group for the Ku Klux Klan. That same year Duke became more active in the Knights of the Ku Klux Klan. He began to market the group as a more progressive type of Klan that accepted women as equals and admitted Roman Catholics. From 1976 to 1980, Duke served at the Grand Wizard of the Knights of the Ku Klux Klan. During this time he became a well-known Klan leader through his use of the national media. Duke left the Klan in 1980 and established the National Association for the Advancement of White People, a white supremacist group that he described as a white rights lobby organization.

In 1988, Duke became involved in electoral politics, running for president first as a Democrat and then as the candidate of the Populist Party, a racist and anti-Semitic party. His name was placed on the ballot in eleven states, and he received approximately forty-seven thousand votes. A year later he joined a field of seven candidates seeking a state house seat in Metairie, Louisiana, and was elected. In 1990, he ran for the U.S. Senate against Democratic incumbent J. Bennett Johnston. Although Johnston was reelected, Duke received 43.5 percent of the vote and 60 percent of the white vote. In 1991, Duke ran for Louisiana governor. Although he was defeated, he nevertheless received more than 700,000 votes. Finally, in 1992, Duke sought the Republican presidential nomination. Duke attempted to mainstream his extremist views; however, his campaign quickly collapsed.

After the 1992 race, Duke withdrew from the political process and concentrated on raising money. He reentered the political arena in 1996, when he competed in the U.S. Senate primary in Louisiana. Duke received 140,910 votes and finished fourth in a field of fifteen candidates. In 1998, Duke finished third in the race for the first congressional district seat in Louisiana.

Following his 1998 defeat, Duke once again became a white rights activist. In January, 2000, he formed a new group, the National Organization for European American Rights (NOFEAR), for the purpose of defending the rights and heritage of European Americans in the United States. In 2001 and 2002, Duke lived in Europe, where he toured and gave speeches. In 2003, he created the European-American Unity and Rights Organization (EURO).

Legal Action and Outcome

In 2002, Duke pleaded guilty to federal charges of mail fraud and tax evasion, for which he received a fifteen-month jail sentence. Duke was charged with a six-year scheme in which he mailed supporters and asked for donations so that he could keep his house; he claimed that he had lost his life savings, which investigators later proved as false. For the tax fraud charge, Duke had to pay a ten-thousand-dollar fine, cooperate fully with the Internal Revenue Service, and pay all money still owed from his 1998 taxes. Following his release from prison in 2004, Duke continued his racist activities in the United States and Europe.

Impact

David Duke was perhaps the best-known white supremacist in the United States from the early 1970's to the end of the twentieth century. Good-looking, shrewd, and articulate, Duke received an inordinate amount of media attention. He attempted to mainstream his message when he ran for political office, capitalizing on race and class resentment. In the 1990's, he began to use the Internet to spread his message in the United States. During the early years of the twenty-first century, Duke expanded his base to include Europe. By 2005, he had managed to create a European base by exploiting the same working-class fears of minorities in Europe that he had so successfully exploited within the United States.

Further Reading

Bridges, Tyler. *The Rise of David Duke*. Jackson: University Press of Mississippi, 1994. A detailed exposé and biography on Duke written by a reporter for *The New Orleans Times-Picayune*.

Kuzenski, John C., Charles S. Bullock III, and Ronald Keith Gaddie. *David Duke and the Politics of Race in the South*. Nashville, Tenn.: Vanderbilt University Press, 1995. An academic analysis of Duke's campaigns for public office and how race was a factor in them.

Powell, Lawrence. *Troubled Memory: Anne Levy, the Holocaust, and David Duke's Louisiana*. The story of a Holocaust survivor who worked to defeat Duke in the 1991 Louisiana gubernatorial campaign.

—*William V. Moore*

See also: Richard Girnt Butler; Willis A. Carto; Matthew F. Hale; Jean-Marie Le Pen; Robert Jay Mathews; Tom Metzger; George Lincoln Rockwell; William Joseph Simmons; John Tyndall.

John E. du Pont

American murderer

Born: c. 1939; France
Also known as: John Eleuthere du Pont (full name)
Major offense: Murder
Active: January 26, 1996
Locale: Foxcatcher Farms, Newton Square, Delaware County, Pennsylvania
Sentence: Thirteen to thirty years in prison or a mental institution

Early Life

John Eleuthere du Pont (dew-PAHNT) was born into one of the United States' wealthiest families. The great-great-grandson of Eleuthere I. du Pont de Nemours, the founder of the world's largest chemical company, he was born to William du Pont, Jr., and Jean Liseter Austin. For most of his life, he lived with his mother and apparently had a disturbed childhood. His early odd behavior evolved into that of a rather bizarre character: He displayed signs of paranoia and lived in constant fear for his life. In spite of these difficulties, in 1965 du Pont received a bachelor of science degree in zoology from the University of Miami. He became an accomplished ornithologist and published numerous articles about birds, even naming twenty-four new species.

Later in life, du Pont became interested in the sport of wrestling, financially supporting the wrestling program at Villanova University. In 1988, Villanova canceled the program, and du Pont turned his Pennsylvania estate (named Foxcatcher) into a training camp for wrestlers. In spite of his earlier marriage to Gale Wenk, his homosexuality became apparent at about this time.

Criminal Career

Throughout the 1980's, du Pont's behavior became increasingly bizarre and more troublesome to both his family and his employees. In 1988, a former employee, Andrew Metzger, filed a lawsuit against du Pont for sexual harassment and settled out of court for $555,000. In October, 1995, Dan Chaid, one of du Pont's wrestlers, contacted local police, claiming that du Pont had pointed a machine gun and had made threatening gestures at several people at his Foxcatcher estate while intoxicated. The police took no action. On January 26, 1996, at his Foxcatcher estate, du Pont approached thirty-six-year-old former Olympic wrestler David Schultz while Schultz was fixing his car radio. After a brief exchange of words and for no apparent reason, du Pont fired his gun three times and killed Schultz. Afterward he fled into his mansion and prepared himself for the arrival of police.

Legal Action and Outcome

The police tried to persuade du Pont to surrender but with no success. Du Pont used his cache of weapons and his skill as a marksman to keep officers at a distance. After a two-day standoff, the police were able to trick du Pont into emerging from his house by shutting off his heat. He was taken into custody without incident.

On January 28, 1996, du Pont was charged with the murder of Schultz. His trial lasted for slightly more than one year and received considerable media attention. Public opinion was that du Pont's great wealth and status would somehow buy him out of serving a long prison sentence. During the trial, it was determined that du Pont was mentally ill, but on February 26, 1997, the court found him guilty of third-degree murder; it also found him to be mentally ill. He was sentenced to between thirteen and thirty years in either prison or a mental institution, whichever best suited his mental state until completion of his sentence. The court recommended that he receive treatment for paranoid delusions. In addition, he was required to pay $742,107 as reimbursement of the court costs. Later, a wrongful death civil suit was filed by David Schultz's widow, Nancy. That suit was settled in 1999 for $35 million.

Impact

To many people, the conviction of John E. du Pont was a pleasant surprise. As District Attorney Patrick Meehan pointed out in his remarks about the verdict, du Pont was "the wealthiest murder defendant in the history of the United States" to be convicted of third-degree murder. The jury did not accept the defense argument that du Pont should be found innocent on grounds of insanity, despite testimony to his unpredictable behavior with the wrestlers on his estate, his paranoia, and his habit of carrying a sidearm. Nevertheless, du Pont was judged capable of understanding that his actions were wrong. His conviction was hailed as a tribute to justice and to the legal system—in glaring contrast to trials of other notable and wealthy figures, including O. J. Simpson—which many concluded had not served justice.

Schultz's wife Nancy, who witnessed her husband's murder, went on to care for their two children and to oversee the Dave Schultz Wrestling Club, which supports amateur wrestlers. Du Pont's name was removed from Villanova University's wrestling club soon after his conviction.

Further Reading

Ordine, Bill, and Ralph Vigoda. *Fatal Match*. New York: Avon Books, 1998. An account of the shooting and subsequent trial.

Palmer, Mark. "The Day Wrestling Died." In *The Life and Legacy of Dave Schultz*. http://revwrestling.com. A five-part article details the relationship between du Pont and wrestler Schultz (with emphasis on Schultz), providing the reader with good background information and insight into this tragic murder.

Smith, Carleton. *Blood Money: The Du Pont Heir and the Murder of an Olympic Athlete*. New York: St. Martin's Press, 1996. Traces du Pont's life from his ancestors to his capture and arrest; coverage predates the trial. Considers du Pont's motivations for shooting Schultz to be based in du Pont's disappointed aspirations for a sports career as well as his paranoid delusions.

—Paul P. Sipiera

See also: Jean Harris; O. J. Simpson.

Claude Duval

French highwayman

Born: 1643; Domfront, Normandy, France
Died: January 21, 1670; Tyburn, England
Also known as: Claude Duvall; Claude Du Vall; Claude Du Val; True Gentleman of the Road; Feather in the Cap of Highway Gentility
Major offense: Highway robbery
Active: 1666-1670
Locale: Roads leading to London, especially Holloway between Highgate and Islington
Sentence: Death by hanging

Early Life

Claude Duval (clawd dew-vahl) was born in 1643 in Normandy, France. He was probably the son of a miller. By the time he was fourteen, he was working as a stable boy in Rouen. There, an English nobleman, the duke of Richmond, hired Duval as groom for his horses. Richmond, with other English Royalists loyal to Charles II, had gone to France when the monarch had fled there in self-imposed exile. When Charles II returned to England after the fall of Oliver Cromwell, Duval accompanied the duke of Richmond as his footman.

Criminal Career

While in the service of the duke, Duval had become fluent in English and had learned the manners and etiquette of a gentleman. It is said that he found the inspiration for his career when he read the death-cell confessions of a convicted highwayman. By 1666, Duval was actively engaged in robbing travelers. He plied his trade on the roads leading to London, particularly Bath road and Portsmouth road. Duval gave a totally new image to his profession. While most highwaymen were unkempt, rough fellows capable of violence toward their victims, Duval was impeccably dressed in a long black coat, high leather boots which folded over at the top, a white ruff of lace at his throat, and a black mask. He was as dashing, elegant, and gallant as a gentleman. He soon made a name for himself in English society; it was very fashionable to be robbed by him.

Although Duval carried pistols, he never fired them or did harm to his victims. He was particularly attentive to his female victims and is said to be the first highwayman whose gallantry made women actually hope to be robbed by him. Women traveled to Hounslow Heath for that very purpose. He once played a flageolet duet and then danced a courante with a woman victim on that very heath. He then robbed her husband, saying that he had not paid for the music. In spite of his fashionableness and his popularity, Duval was eventually apprehended by the authorities. He was arrested at Mother Maberley's tavern, the Hole-in-the-Wall on Chandos Street in London. He was taken to Newgate prison.

Legal Action and Outcome

On January 17, 1670, Duval appeared before Judge Sir William Morton. He was convicted of six robberies. He was accused of other robberies, but there was insufficient evidence to convict him on the additional charges. He was sentenced to be hanged. Many people, including the ladies of the court and Charles II, opposed his death sentence, but Sir Morton refused to change it. On January 21, 1670, Duval was hanged at Tyburn. His body was taken to Tangier Tavern. His wake almost caused a riot as disconsolate women wept and attempted to touch his body. He was buried at Saint Giles.

Impact

Claude Duval changed the image of the highwayman during his lifetime. As much as, and perhaps more than, any other highwayman, he contributed to the image of the highwayman as a gentleman thief. As a dashing gallant for whom women swooned, Duval's greatest impact was in the areas of legend and fiction. The image he had created was romanticized in popular fiction during the 1880's and later. Made larger than life, he became the archetype for the fictional highwayman character. Throughout the 1800's, he appeared as a romanticized character in the ever-popular penny dreadfuls and dime novels. The character still appears in romance novels set in post-Restoration England.

Further Reading

Ash, Russell. *Discovering Highwaymen*. Princes Risborough, Buckinghamshire, England: Shire, 1999. Discusses backgrounds, methods, and localities in which highwaymen operated and favorite inns and taverns of highwaymen. Also considers factual information in regard to legends created about highwaymen.

Blackwood, Gary L. *Highwaymen (Bad Guys)*. Salt Lake City, Utah: Benchmark Books, 2001. Although written for young readers, this book contains useful information on the times in which highwaymen were active and on the extensive romanticizing of highwaymen.

Cox, Randolph. *The Dime Novel Companion: A Source Book*. Westport, Conn.: Greenwood Press, 2000. Information about the romanticizing of Claude Duval and the many fictions in which he appeared as a character. Contains chronologies of publications, lists of authors, and publishers of these novels.

—*Shawncey Webb*

See also: Charles Peace; Jack Sheppard; Dick Turpin.

François Duvalier

President of Haiti (1957-1971)

Born: April 14, 1907; Port-au-Prince, Haiti
Died: April 21, 1971; Port-au-Prince, Haiti
Also known as: Papa Doc
Cause of notoriety: As Haitian president, Duvalier waged an unremitting campaign of repression through terror, torture, detention, and murder.
Active: 1957-1971
Locale: Haiti

Early Life

François Duvalier (frahn-swah dew-vahl-yay) was born in one of the poorer districts of the Haitian capital, Port-au-Prince, despite the fact that his father, Duval Duvalier, had attained a higher level of education than most average Haitians; he had been trained as an elementary schoolteacher on his native island of Martinique. Immigrating to Haiti, Duval married Uritia Abraham. The family's finances were always precarious in part because Duval—as a foreigner—was prohibited from teaching during the 1915-1922 administration of President Philippe Sudré Dartiguenave, though Duval was ultimately reinstated and in 1930 was appointed a justice of the peace.

The young Duvalier attended and graduated from the Lycée Alexandre Pétion in Port-au-Prince and went to medical school, graduating in 1934. That same year, the occupation of Haiti by the U.S. Marine Corps, which had begun in 1915, came to an end. During the ensuing fifteen years, François identified himself with radical nationalist ideas, including those of the negritude movement, which was a widespread literary and ideological movement led by francophone black intellectuals, writers, and politicians. As a follower of the movement, Duvalier stressed his country's African heritage and placed himself in opposition both to the mulatto elite who dominated Haitian political and economic life and to American corporate interests. He was among the young intellectuals to found an active student nationalist group called Le Groupe des Griots, and, under the pseudonym "Abderrahman," he contributed articles for the newspaper *Action nationale* that were highly critical of his society's ruling institutions. Duvalier married Simone Ovide Faine on December 27, 1939; they would have three daughters, Marie-Dénise, Simone, and Nicole, and a son, Jean-Claude.

Duvalier's first significant appointment was with the

Inter-American Affairs Commission, where in 1943 he participated in a campaign to eradicate yaws, a contagious tropical disease, and to treat other diseases prevalent among the rural population. After becoming director of the Gressier Clinic, Duvalier expanded his work deep into the hinterland, organizing mobile clinics to service the more inaccessible regions. Developing a reputation as a healer, Duvalier discovered that he could cultivate support among the rural peasantry by identifying with the traditional vodun (commonly termed Voodoo) faith and the often clandestine village societies and networks. By 1948, he had become accepted as a full-fledged *houngan*, or vodun priest. It was then too that he became known as "Papa Doc," an affectionate term that he later leveraged for his political career. He studied public health for one year at the University of Michigan (1944-1945), returning to Haiti to assist in malaria eradication efforts.

POLITICAL CAREER

In 1946, Dumarsais Estimé, Duvalier's former schoolteacher, became president of Haiti and appointed Duvalier, his young protégé, as director for public health. In 1948, Duvalier advanced to the rank of undersecretary for labor and in 1949 to that of minister for health and labor. However, in 1950, Estimé was overthrown by a military coup and Paul Eugène Magloire ascended to power. From 1954 to 1956, Duvalier joined Clément Barbot in fomenting acts of rebellion against Magloire's regime, and in 1957 Duvalier ran for president. In a controversial contest marred by intimidation and voting irregularities, Duvalier's support both from the rural, vodun-dominated, predominantly black areas and from the army enabled him to defeat his mulatto opponent, Louis Dejoie, and he was inaugurated on October 22, 1957.

Shortly thereafter, Duvalier consolidated his power into nearly absolute control by suspending civil liberties; torturing, jailing, or driving into exile anyone opposed to his policies; and eventually creating the Tontons Macoutes, a rural militia that was personally loyal to him and was employed in brutalizing the population into compliance. Weathering a revolt in 1958 and a 1959 invasion organized by Cuban leader Fidel Castro, Duvalier was able to play on U.S. fears of further communist inroads into the Caribbean. He was therefore able to secure massive amounts of foreign aid from Washington, D.C., and support from the U.S. Marine Corps in training the Tontons Macoutes.

In 1963, Duvalier quelled an uprising led by his former chief associate Barbot and narrowly avoided war with the Dominican Republic. Moreover, although much of his foreign aid from the United States that year was cut off by the administration of

DUVALIERVILLE

Papa Doc Duvalier once said, "God and the people are the source of my power. I have twice been given the power. I have taken it, and damn it, I will keep it." Money helped, too, and to get it he decided in 1961 to build his own model city, Duvalierville, based on the pattern of Brazil's then-new capital, Brazilia.

First, Duvalier instituted a series of "taxes." He sent his paramilitary thugs, the Tontons Macoutes, to businesses, both Haitian and foreign-owned, in order to gather contributions of up to forty thousand dollars each. The Tontons Macoutes made the choice simple: Pay or get beaten. Duvalier managed to accumulate some six million dollars a year this way, even though American, British, French, Canadian, Italian, and German diplomats registered official complaints on behalf of their nationals. He practically gutted the national tobacco company and placed high taxes on vehicles. He also diverted funds sent from the U.S. government as part of an Agency for International Development (AID) program.

For the site of Duvalierville, Duvalier chose Cabaret, a city twenty miles from Port au Prince, because its population had overwhelmingly voted for him in 1957. He kept most of the project money for himself, and those contractors and financiers he favored with the rest did very little work. Houses were bulldozed, but only a few were rebuilt, none of them in the grandiose style that Duvalier had promised as a testament to himself and his governance.

When the administration of President John F. Kennedy learned how its foreign aid was being misused for Duvalierville, officials first discussed a possible "military solution." Kennedy, however, ordered that the State Department look for and provide support to someone to replace the dictator. In the meantime, AID money dried up, as did deliveries of equipment under the Military Assistance Program. Duvalier survived the setback, although Duvalierville did not.

In 1986, an angry mob looted what they could from Duvalierville after François's son, Jean-Claude Duvalier ("Baby Doc"), and his family fled to France. Thereupon the town reverted to its original name, Cabaret. All that remained of the renovations was a cluster of buildings overgrown by jungle and a local population just as poor as before Duvalier started his utopian project.

John F. Kennedy, Duvalier was so well established within Haiti that he had himself installed as lifetime president on June 22, 1964. Thereafter, he became increasingly less visible to the public, suffering from diabetes and heart ailments, and wielded his patriarchal tyranny from the confines of his presidential palace and through the Tontons Macoutes organization, which seemed to become more vicious and pervasive as years passed. In January, 1971, Duvalier designated his nineteen-year-old son, Jean-Claude (Baby Doc) Duvalier, as his successor. The senior Duvalier died of a heart attack on April 21, 1971.

Impact

As one of the twentieth century's consummate political operatives and survivors, François Duvalier proved to be unerringly adept at depicting himself both as a benevolent father figure intent on securing the best interests of his populace and as the anticommunist stalwart whose vigilance was essential for staving off the Red Menace in Latin America. In reality, Haiti remained the Caribbean country with the lowest levels of income and living standards and with mortality rates among the highest within the Western Hemisphere. The problems evident in 1957 were largely unchanged or had worsened by 1971, when the dictatorship of Jean-Claude Duvalier began.

Further Reading

Condit, Erin. *François and Jean-Claude Duvalier*. Philadelphia: Chelsea House, 1989. Amply illustrated volume that offers a succinct description of the manner in which the Duvaliers retained their grasp on power through religious-psychological manipulation and intimidation.

Heinl, Robert Debs, and Nancy Gordon Heinl. *Written in Blood: The Story of the Haitian People, 1492-1995*. Rev. ed. Lanham, Md.: University Press of America, 1996. The section on François Duvalier lays its primary stress on his purposeful identification with vodun beliefs and his exploitation of the U.S. government's "Cold War" anxieties.

Nicholls, David. *Haiti from Dessalines to Duvalier: Race, Colour, and National Independence in Haiti*. Rev. ed. New Brunswick, N.J.: Rutgers University Press, 1996. Contains a detailed explanation of the formative influences and overriding purposes behind the rise to power of François Duvalier.

—*Raymond Pierre Hylton*

See also: Fulgencio Batista y Zaldívar; Fidel Castro; Jean-Claude Duvalier; Rafael Trujillo.

Jean-Claude Duvalier

President of Haiti (1971-1986)

Born: July 3, 1951; Port-au-Prince, Haiti
Also known as: Baby Doc; Bébé Doc
Cause of notoriety: Duvalier continued the oppressive policies of his father's previous administration until uprisings against the regime's repression and blatant corruption led to his overthrow and exile.
Active: 1971-1986
Locale: Haiti

Early Life

Jean-Claude Duvalier (zhahn clohd dew-vahl-yay) was born the youngest and only son in a family of four children of Dr. François Duvalier and his wife Simone Ovide Faine. His older female siblings were named Marie-Dénise, Nicole, and Simone. At the time of his son's birth, Dr. Duvalier was a former minister for health and labor under President Dumarsais Estimé, whose government had been overturned in 1950. Dr. Duvalier, who was even then known as Papa Doc, conspired to subvert the regime of President Paul Eugène Magloire and in 1957 succeeded in winning a contested election to the Haitian presidency. In short order, Papa Doc established a heavy-handed dictatorship bolstered by cadres of locally based paramilitary units known as the Tontons Macoutes.

On April 26, 1963, while being dropped off at school in Port-au-Prince, Jean-Claude and his sister Simone narrowly escaped abduction during Clément Barbot's kidnap-revolution plot against Papa Doc. Barbot was one of the members of Papa Doc's security apparatus who had turned against him. Because Jean-Claude led a lavish and well-protected life, he gained the not wholly warranted reputation as a shallow playboy—a reputation that would cause opponents to underestimate his intelligence and genuine political skills. Jean-Claude was in his first year of law school at the University of Haiti when, in January, 1971, his ailing father publicly named him to be his successor as president-for-life.

Jean-Claude Duvalier. (AP/Wide World Photos)

POLITICAL CAREER

On April 22, 1971, the day after Papa Doc's death, Jean-Claude was elected to the presidency. At the age of nineteen, he was the world's youngest chief executive. Though the constitution mandated that Jean-Claude not take office until the age of twenty-one, the Haitian Assembly and a contrived plebiscite changed the constitution to enable his succession. Because Haitians recognized that Jean-Claude would perpetuate Papa Doc's power and mystique, the youthful president was nicknamed Baby Doc.

During the early years of Jean-Claude's presidency, a ruling council of twelve, selected long in advance by François Duvalier, performed most of the administrative tasks, but Jean-Claude steadily—and, in fact, at a more accelerated pace than expected—took the reins of government. Among those who rose to heights of major influence were Jean-Claude's mother (nicknamed Mama Doc), Interior Minister Luckner Cambronne, and, until August, 1971, his eldest sister and secretary, Marie-Dénise. Jean-Claude would gradually maneuver away from the old guard that remained from his father's regime in order to map a new course for his presidency: In September of 1972, Cambronne was fired, and in 1980, Mama Doc lost significant influence after Jean-Claude's marriage to Michèle Bennett, the daughter of mulatto businessman Ernest Bennett.

In a significant departure from the policies of his father's later years, Jean-Claude improved foreign relations with the United States, and, in return for modest liberalization, a substantial amount of American foreign aid poured into the country. He officially did away with the Tontons Macoutes (who nevertheless still flourished underground in the rural areas), replacing them with the more sophisticated Léopard Batallion. Because Jean-Claude encouraged a moderate degree of freedom of the press, the sanctioning of some political parties, incentives for foreign (mainly American) corporations to locate and invest in Haiti, the restoration of some civil liberties, and the astute positioning of Haiti as anticommunist card, he gained the image of a "liberalizing" leader and enjoyed further American support during the administration of Jimmy Carter.

However, upon the election of Ronald Reagan to the American presidency in 1980, Duvalier rolled back his reforms, regrouped the Tontons Macoutes, and reverted to an increasingly repressive domestic policy. Because of his growing orientation toward the despised middle-class mulatto elite which had long opposed his father, Jean-Claude steadily lost support with rural Haitians, the Tontons Macoutes, and adherents of the traditional vodun (Voodoo) faith. Jean-Claude's regime during the 1980's became noted for its conspicuous spending and rampant corruption. Some of the first lady's relatives reputedly became involved in cocaine trafficking.

Public unrest mounted through 1984 and into 1985, and after police opened fire in a schoolyard in Gonaives while chasing demonstrators and killed three schoolchildren, riots and insurrection spread throughout the rural regions. On February 7, 1986, the dictator and his family fled Haiti aboard a cargo plane and went into exile in France.

After fleeing Haiti, the Duvaliers engaged in lawsuits with the Haitian government over millions of dollars allegedly purloined from public funds. Jean-Claude and Michèle Duvalier divorced, and Mama Doc died in 1997. Following the overthrow of President Jean-Bertrand Aristide in early 2004, Jean-Claude announced his intention to return to Haiti. He attempted to get his name on the presidential ballot as the candidate of the Party for National Unity for the 2006 elections, but he failed.

Impact

Though Jean-Claude Duvalier demonstrated much of his father's political acumen and survived in power for nearly fifteen years, the conditions under which the average Haitian lived during his presidential tenure remained those of grinding poverty, illiteracy, fear, and frustration. Though American businesses provided some minimum-wage employment around the urban center of Port-au-Prince, the overall state of the Haitian economy worsened during Duvalier's years in power.

Further Reading

Condit, Erin. *François and Jean-Claude Duvalier*. New York: Chelsea House, 1989. This book attempts to moderate the assumption of Jean-Claude as being nothing more than a decadent blunderer and offers a somewhat more balanced picture of the younger dictator.

Ferguson, James. *Papa Doc, Baby Doc: Haiti and the Duvaliers*. New York: Basil Blackwell, 1987. Amply illustrated and easy to read, this volume pursues the classic theme of mild reform being the surest path to a despotic regime's downfall.

Heinl, Robert Debs, and Nancy Gordon Heinl. *Written in Blood: The Story of the Haitian People, 1492-1995*. Rev. ed. Lanham, Md.: University Press of America, 1996. The section on Jean-Claude depicts an individual trapped by his family's past alliances, ultimately leaving Haiti in conditions worse than ever before.

Nicholls, David. *Haiti from Dessalines to Duvalier: Race, Colour, and National Independence in Haiti*. Rev. ed. New Brunswick, N.J.: Rutgers University Press, 1996. Useful for its skillful analysis in setting the historical background of the Duvaliers' regimes.

—*Raymond Pierre Hylton*

See also: François Duvalier.

Reginald Dyer

British general in the colonial Indian Army

Born: October 9, 1864; Murree, Punjab, India (now in Pakistan)

Died: July 23, 1927; Long Ashton, England

Also known as: Reginald Edward Harry Dyer (full name); Rex Dyer; Butcher of Amritsar

Cause of notoriety: Dyer was the commander of British colonial troops who fired upon a crowd of nonviolent Indian political protesters in an enclosed quadrangle, killing more than 379 and wounding hundreds.

Active: April 13, 1919

Locale: Amritsar, Punjab, India (now in Pakistan)

Early Life

Born in India, Reginald Dyer (DI-uhr) was raised in Simla by second-generation colonial parents. He attended the local Bishop Cotton School and in 1885, he was commissioned into the Queen's (Royal West Surrey) Regiment. As an officer, he served in riot-control duties in Belfast and saw combat in the Third Burma War in 1886-1887. He also fought in several engagements in the Northwest Frontier around the beginning of the twentieth century. During World War I, he commanded the Eastern Persian cordon, a mountainous region of northwest Pakistan.

Military Career

Stern in manner and with a condescending opinion of the Indians in his jurisdiction, Dyer was the quintessential imperial British officer. In 1919, Indian nationalists protested the enactment of repressive legislation to curb sedition. Demonstrations and strikes were held throughout India. In the Punjab, where Dyer was a brigadier general in command of an infantry brigade, the arrest of two Indian politicians sparked a riot. Martial law was declared, and a ban on all public meetings was imposed. In Amritsar, an estimated twenty thousand people gathered in defiance of the ban at an enclosed lot called Jallianwala Bagh. Under Dyer's command, 150 colonial troops appeared at the entrance and ordered the crowd to disperse. However, with the military blocking the only entrance, the protesters could not leave. Dyer gave the order to fire point-blank into the unarmed crowd. For ten minutes, the troops fired their rifles until their ammunition was exhausted. Unofficial sources estimated that 1,000 were killed; the government declared 379 dead and 1,200 wounded. The exact figure was never known.

Dyer intended the massacre to teach "the natives" a lesson, perhaps in retaliation for the murder of Europeans and the beating of a woman missionary during earlier rioting. A few days later, Dyer issued an order that Indians using a street where the missionary had been assaulted would have to crawl down it. Local newspapers interpreted the order as a racial insult.

Impact

The massacre triggered mass riots in the Punjab, and the government placed much of the area under martial law. In October, 1919, an official inquiry committee investigated the massacre. Reginald Dyer obstinately refused to explain his actions and was severely censured for a mistaken notion of duty. In Britain, the bitter debate that followed the massacre almost caused the fall of the Liberal government. Majority opinion was probably against Dyer, but he became a hero among the British in India and in conservative circles at home. His defenders in the House of Lords and the Tory press took the line that a brave army officer was being condemned for doing his duty. A London newspaper, *The Morning Post*, set up a fund to save Dyer from poverty, and many people, especially Britons living in India, made contributions.

In March, 1920, the House of Commons relieved Dyer of his command and forced his retirement. The Amritsar Massacre, the worst atrocity perpetrated by the British in the twentieth century, did more than anything else to undermine Britain's moral legitimacy in India and provoked the rapid rise of the Indian nationalist movement.

Dyer returned to Britain, where he lived as a recluse until his death from a severe stroke in 1927. He was given a full although unofficial military funeral in London. In 1961, the Republic of India built a martyrs' monument at the site of the Amritsar Massacre.

Further Reading

Collett, Nigel. *The Butcher of Amritsar: General Reginald Dyer*. London: Hambledon & London, 2005. A detailed critical biography by a former lieutenant colonel of the British Army who commanded a Gurkha regiment.

Colvin, Ian Duncan. *The Life of General Dyer*. Edinburgh, Scotland: W. Blackwood & Sons, 1929. The book that established the Dyer legend was sponsored by Dyer's wife and written by a right-wing reporter for *The Morning Post*. Colvin's facts are biased, but the book represents the attitudes of many Britons during a time when the British Empire was in decline.

Fein, Helen. *Imperial Crime and Punishment: The Massacre at Jallianwala Bagh and British Judgment, 1919-1920*. Honolulu: University Press of Hawaii, 1977. A sociologist expounds on "the universe of obligation"—the tendency for members of a dominant class to disregard members of lower classes who commit crimes, as exemplified by Dyer at Amritsar.

—*Theodore M. Vestal*

See also: William Calley; George A. Custer.

Felix Dzerzhinsky

Founder of the Soviet secret police

Born: September 11, 1877; Kojdanów, Russian Empire (now Dzyarzhynsk, Belarus)

Died: July 20, 1926; Moscow, Soviet Union (now in Russia)

Also known as: Felix Edmundvich Dzerzhinsky (full name); Feliks Dzierżiński; Iron Felix; Shield of the Revolution; Bloody Felix; Knight of the Revolution; Felix the Goodheart

Cause of notoriety: Founder and head of the brutal Soviet secret police, Dzerzhinsky gathered agency after agency under his central control.

Active: 1917-1926

Locale: Soviet Union

Early Life

Felix Dzerzhinsky (FEE-lihks dyuhr-ZHEEN-skee) was born into a Polish noble family in the Russian Empire in 1877. He attended school in Vilnius, where he became associated with the Socialist movement. He became a founder of the Social Democratic Party of Lithuania and later helped found the Social Democratic Party of the kingdom of Poland and Lithuania along with Rosa Luxemburg. He was a Communist activist in the areas of Kowno and Warsaw from 1897 to 1899. In the early 1900's, he began to gravitate toward the Russian Social Democratic Party, and by 1906 he was named a member of the Central Committee of the party. He then began to split his activities between St. Petersburg and Warsaw.

Dzerzhinsky was imprisoned frequently between 1908 and 1917. He spent eleven years in and out of prison or exile. In February of 1917 he was released from prison as part of a general amnesty. He became a loyal supporter and ally of Vladimir Ilich Lenin upon Lenin's return to Russia in April, 1917. Dzerzhinsky was involved in the

Felix Dzerzhinsky.

planning of the October Revolution, and for his efforts was elected to the Bolshevik Central Committee in August of 1917. He was to remain a member of the Central Committee from 1917 to 1926.

Political Career

Following the October Revolution, Lenin appointed Dzerzhinsky to head the All-Russian Extraordinary Commission for to Combat Counterrevolution and Sabotage (Cheka, Vecheka, or the Soviet secret police). The Cheka was meant to be only a temporary creation until the revolution had stabilized society. It operated on the same organizational basis as the Okhrana, the czarist secret police, but incorporated the viciousness and cruelty of the Oprichnina, the secret police of Czar Ivan IV (Ivan the Terrible).

The Cheka operated as a state-within-the-state, using terror, fear, and torture as weapons against those who opposed the Bolshevik regime. Dzerzhinsky described the Cheka as an instrument for the settling of accounts with counterrevolutionaries. He described a Chekist as having a "warm heart, a cool head and clean hands." He was chosen by Lenin because he was willing to sacrifice "anyone" in defense of the revolution. To him, all forms of torture were permissible, from the impaling of priests to the skinning alive of Socialist opponents. No forms of torture were beyond the pale in the settling of accounts.

What few restraints there were on the Cheka dissolved after the assassination of Moisei Uritskii, the Petrograd Party chief, and the attempted assassination of Lenin by Fanya Kaplan. Dzerzhinsky, released from his remaining fetters, let loose the "Red Terror." Dzerzhinsky, who had began to see himself as the Robespierre of the Russian Revolution, would travel around Russia in an armored train, dispensing swift, inflexible "justice." He presided over the executions of thousands of people.

In addition, the application of class terror was taken to a new extreme, and executions based on class origin became the norm. Mass arrests of wealthy or successful farmers (kulaks) were instituted, and concentration camps (precursors to the Gulags) were developed to detain family members of possible anti-Bolshevik partisans. Sweeping arrests of Mensheviks and Social Revolutionaries were carried out under the premise that such elements were provoking the workers in Petrograd and Moscow. Zionists and Roman Catholics were also targeted. The appearance of legality was maintained as so-called kangaroo courts fabricated evidence. Dzerzhinsky instituted the process by which the condemned was forced to sign a confession just before he or she was executed.

Dzerzhinsky turned his attention to cleansing the military after the Kronstadt revolt of 1921. Thirty thousand soldiers and sailors were killed in crushing the military base revolt. The Cheka then began to penetrate every facet of daily life, in order to ensure the security of the state. By 1922, Lenin and Dzerzhinsky realized that the Cheka had gained a vile reputation for shedding as much innocent blood as guilty. In an attempt to assuage popular concerns, the Cheka in February of 1922 was renamed the State Political Directorate, or GPU. Nothing really changed except the name, which later became the Joint State Political Directorate (OGPU) and then the People's Commissariat for Internal Affairs (NKVD). Dzerzhinsky remained in charge of the secret police until his death in July of 1926.

Dzerzhinsky held many other political positions and accepted whatever task was given to him. In 1919, he was named commissar of internal affairs. During the Polish-Soviet War of 1920 he was appointed to the short-lived Polish Provisional Revolutionary Committee. He became people's commissar of transport in 1921, thus putting all forms of transportation under Cheka supervision. In 1924, he became chairman of the Supreme Council of the National Economy, which focused on the rapid development of heavy industry.

Following Lenin's death in 1924, Dzerzhinsky became a staunch supporter of Joseph Stalin, whom he had already started to move toward, ideologically. Dzerzhinsky was put in charge of the embalming of Lenin's body and its placement in the Kremlin tomb. He became a virulent opponent of Nikolay Bukharin and Lev Kamenev, who were open to further decentralization of the economy. Like Stalin, Dzerzhinsky was a devoted centralist. He died from a sudden heart attack at the Fourteenth Party Congress in July of 1926. He received a hero's burial at the Kremlin Wall. Stalin was later buried next to him.

IMPACT

As the person who implemented the Red Terror, Felix Dzerzhinsky was responsible for the deaths of thousands. He set the design of many future reincarnations of the Cheka, from the NKVD to the Committee for State Security (KGB) and its successor, the Federal Security Service of the Russian Federation (FSB). He created what became known in the Soviet Union and Russia as the Siloviki, or higher police. The Siloviki under Dzerzhinsky infiltrated all aspects of Soviet society in order to control and manipulate the population. As of 2006, the FSB still had agents in all nongovernmental civic organizations, a policy the Vladimir Putin administration sought to restrict and in some cases outlaw. In any case, Dzerzhinsky and his legacy endured. It is no wonder that one of the first statues torn down in the 1989 revolution in Russia was that of Dzerzhinsky.

FURTHER READING

Andrew, Christopher. *The Sword and Shield.* New York: Basic Books, 1999. Gives a history of the Soviet and Russian secret police, from the founding of the Cheka to the FSB.

Conquest, Robert. *The Great Terror.* New York: Oxford University Press, 1998. Conquest is the authority on the Terror, in which Dzerzhinsky played a dominant role.

Kromova, C. *Dzerzhinsky: A Biography.* Moscow: Progress, 1988. A classic Soviet biography of the founder of the Cheka, portraying him as the great protector of the revolution and a hero.

Pipes, Richard. *Russia Under the Bolshevik Regime.* New York: Knopf, 1994. Pipes is an authority on the rise of the Bolsheviks. This book traces how Dzerzhinsky gathered committee after committee under the general control of the Cheka.

—*David Stefancic*

SEE ALSO: Lavrenty Beria; Ivan the Terrible; Lazar Kaganovich; Fanya Kaplan; Nikita S. Khrushchev; Vladimir Ilich Lenin; Vyacheslav Mikhailovich Molotov; Symon Petlyura; Robespierre; Joseph Stalin; Vasili Vasilievich Ulrikh; Andrey Vyshinsky; Genrikh Yagoda; Nikolay Ivanovich Yezhov; Andrey Aleksandrovich Zhdanov.

Wyatt Earp

American lawman

Born: March 19, 1848; Monmouth, Illinois
Died: January 13, 1929; Los Angeles, California
Also known as: Wyatt Berry Stapp Earp (full name)
Cause of notoriety: An unrelenting lawman of the American West, Earp helped precipitate the shoot-out at the O.K. Corral and afterward conducted a remorseless vendetta against outlaws.
Active: 1881
Locale: Tombstone, Arizona; other frontier towns

Early Life

Wyatt Earp (WI-at urp), Western lawman and perhaps outlaw, was at the center of the most famous gunfight in the history of the American West: the shoot-out at the O.K. Corral. Earp was born in 1848 in Monmouth, Illinois. His father was a farmer and sometime constable and justice of the peace. Earp grew up on the American frontier, engaging in farming, buffalo hunting, stagecoach driving, and gambling. His first wife died early in their marriage. Of his many siblings, two brothers, Virgil and Morgan, would participate in the famous shoot-out. Wyatt's exceptionally close bond with his brothers would always figure prominently in his life and subsequent legend.

Law Enforcement Career

In 1869, Earp received his first appointment as an officer of the law, taking the place of his father as a constable of Lamar, Missouri. Over the following decade, Earp held various deputy and sheriff posts, earning a reputation for courageous and firm enforcement of the law. Although he was the most famous lawman of the American West, Earp was accused of his share of criminal actions. In 1871, he was indicted in Arkansas for horse stealing; he fled the jurisdiction.

As a marshal in wild Dodge City from 1875 to 1878, Earp formed his famous friendships with John Henry "Doc" Holliday and Bat Masterson. Helping to drive out the desperadoes and bandits of Dodge City, Earp became especially adept at disarming and arresting outlaws without allowing gunfire.

Showdown at the O.K. Corral

Earp was the central figure in the gun battle at the O.K. Corral, the most famous shoot-out of the American West. In 1879, Earp, accompanied by his brothers, arrived in Tombstone, Arizona, a wild boomtown of silver strikes and cattle rustlers. By 1880, Virgil Earp was the deputy U.S. marshal of Tombstone, assisted by Wyatt as deputy sheriff and Morgan as a special deputy. As such, the Earp brothers came into conflict with the "cowboys"—a current name for the cattle rustlers, thieves, and stagecoach robbers operating on both sides of the United States-Mexico border.

On October 26, 1881, the Earp brothers and Doc Holliday confronted the Clanton and McLaury brothers, notorious cowboy rustlers whom Wyatt suspected of a recent stagecoach robbery. (Wyatt Earp and Ike Clanton had been trading threats for days.) At about three in the afternoon, at the O.K. Corral, the two sides faced each other in a blaze of gunfire. In thirty seconds, the gunfight was over. Of the lawmen, Virgil and Morgan Earp were seriously injured; of the cowboys, Frank and Tom McLaury and Billy Clanton were killed. Ike Clanton escaped unscathed, although he would be gunned down in 1887 by Jonas Brighton.

Wyatt Earp.

Legal Action and Outcome

As there was some testimony that the Earps had fired first or had provoked the shooting, they and Holliday were charged with first-degree murder. After the judge and grand jury refused to indict the Earps, the cowboys decided to take revenge, ambushing and shooting Virgil and killing Morgan. Wyatt then set out over the next few months on his notorious "Earp vendetta ride," tracking down and killing at least three of the cowboys suspected in the attacks on his brothers. Although charged with several murders arising from his vendetta ride, Earp fled Arizona in 1882 and defeated extradition efforts.

Impact

In the most mythologized era of American history—that of the late nineteenth century Wild West—Wyatt Earp is perhaps the most mythic figure of the law. His fearless imposition of law and order on the lawless frontier is most celebrated in the showdown at the O.K. Corral. Although a relatively minor dispute, the drama of four closely related lawmen facing four cattle-rustling brothers has become the archetypal gun battle of the frontier.

Although Earp is a legendary lawman, a crosscurrent of opinion has always found sympathy for the Clantons and McLaurys, gunned down while lightly armed. However, Earp's legend has prevailed, in some part due to his longevity and the fact that he was never injured during his law career. Earp lived the last decades of his life in Los Angeles, sought out by the new film industry of Hollywood. Thus, it is not surprising that Earp's greatest impact has come in the cultural mythologizer of the Old West: the American movie Western. Of the countless film versions of Earp's life and of the events of Tombstone, most notable are *My Darling Clementine* in 1946 (Henry Fonda as Wyatt Earp); *The Life and Legend of Wyatt Earp*, television series (1955-1961); *Gunfight at the O.K. Corral* in 1957 (Burt Lancaster as Wyatt Earp); *Hour of the Gun* in 1967 (James Garner as Wyatt Earp); *Tombstone* in 1993 (Kurt Russell as Wyatt Earp); and *Wyatt Earp* in 1994 (Kevin Costner as Wyatt Earp).

How to Face Down a Desperado

This excerpt from Wyatt Earp's unpublished autobiography, written around 1926 with mining engineer John H. Flood, Jr., concerns his shoot-out with Clay Allison in Dodge City, Kansas:

Front Street in Dodge City was always the busiest thoroughfare in town, within reasonable allowances of course. Never anything like a rush occurred before the hour of ten A.M. It was ten o'clock before the housewives completed the household chores: it was ten o'clock before the cowmen of the trail herds got around from the night before: it was ten o'clock with the banks and it was ten o'clock with the stores: and it was ten o'clock before the city marshal got around although his hour was not supposed to start until one in the afternoon. And it is very likely that he would not have changed his schedule but this morning he had buckled on his guns and started out at nine o'clock: some one had reported that Clay Allison was in town. If he were in town, Earp wanted to give him every opportunity to complete his business and then get out.

[After Allison walked into Wyatt Earp on Front St.] Earp could feel the warmth of the conspirator's body as he leaned against him; the pulsations beat against his own and then there was a throb; something that felt like nerves, and the tenseness of muscles at the drawing of a gun. Earp was watching Allison and the movement of his forty-five; gradually, it was slipping forward from its holster while the marshal stood silently and looked on.

Now the assassin's thumb reached towards the hammer—quietly—then he felt a thrill, something that made his side turn cold, the side against that of the city marshal. Then he raised his eyes to another pair of eyes, and flinched, and dropped his gaze to the ground; he saw a movement at his side and he thought his end had come. Earp was two seconds ahead of him on the draw, and Allison knew that he had lost his play, and he edged out onto the walk. . . .

"I'm going around the corner for a moment," he said.

"Well you'd better go or I'll make you!" and Earp watched him closely as he backed down the street.

But he didn't return, and several moments later, when the marshal looked for him around the corner, he had disappeared.

Further Reading

Barra, Allen. *Inventing Wyatt Earp: His Life and Many Legends*. New York: Carroll and Graf, 1998. A biography that focuses on the mythology of Earp, especially as rendered in the Hollywood Western.

Lake, Stuart. *Wyatt Earp: Frontier Marshall*. 1931. Reprint. New York: Pocket Books, 1994. The first significant biography of Earp, based on several interviews with him in 1927. Lake's legendary portrayal of Earp is widely considered to contain exaggerations and embellishments.

Lubet, Steven. *Murder in Tombstone: The Forgotten Trial of Wyatt Earp*. New Haven, Conn.: Yale University Press, 2004. A meticulous analysis of the 1881 preliminary trial of the Earps and Holliday on first-degree murder charges. Lubet speculates that a lesser manslaughter charge might have secured convictions.

Terfertiller, Casey. *Wyatt Earp: The Life Behind the Legend*. New York: John Wiley and Sons, 1997. A modern biography that carefully retells Earp's life, including the often-neglected fifty-year period after the O.K. Corral shoot-out.

—Howard Bromberg

See also: Curly Bill Brocius; Doc Holliday; Johnny Ringo.

Bernard Ebbers

Co-founder of WorldCom, Incorporated

Born: August 27, 1941; Edmonton, Alberta, Canada
Also known as: Bernard John Ebbers (full name); Bernie Ebbers; Telecom Cowboy
Major offenses: Business accounting fraud and securities fraud
Active: Late 1990's-2002
Locale: Clinton, Mississippi
Sentence: Twenty-five years in federal prison

Early Life

Bernard Ebbers (EHB-uhrz) was born in Edmonton, Alberta, and was the second of five children. Because his father was a traveling salesman, the family moved quite frequently between Canada and the United States. After graduating from high school, Ebbers attempted college but failed out of both the University of Alberta and Calvin College. Finally, after moving back to Edmonton and working as a bouncer and a milkman, Ebbers decided to give college one more try. He tried out for a basketball scholarship at Mississippi College in Clinton, Mississippi, and ultimately made the team. He received his degree in physical education in 1966 and a year later married the young woman he had been dating throughout his senior year, Linda Piggott.

After a few years of teaching and coaching basketball in rural Mississippi, Ebbers decided to open his own business, a motel. As the popularity of his motel grew, he sought and received monies from his friends to allow him to open a chain of hotels. His hotels grew in popularity, and throughout the 1970's Ebbers generated a healthy profit from his first business venture.

In September, 1983, Ebbers partnered with several associates to form the Long Distance Discount Service (LDDS) corporation. As its founders realized, the telephone company, American Telephone & Telegraph (AT&T), was forced by the federal government to rent long-distance phone lines at discounted rates to small regional companies, which would then resell the lines' bandwidth capacity to small businesses. LDDS sought to capitalize on the financial opportunity presented by this situation. Ebbers, who within two years was named chief executive officer of LDDS, turned the company into a multimillion-dollar success. Over the following fifteen years, LDDS acquired other long-distance resellers and additional businesses, purchasing more than seventy-five companies in all. In 1989, LDDS issued a public stock offering, which gave Ebbers the ability to buy still more companies. In 1995, Ebbers changed the name of the LDDS corporation to WorldCom. WorldCom went on to purchase two major telecommunication giants, MFS Communications and MCI Communications. These multibillion-dollar acquisitions made Ebbers as well as investors and employees throughout WorldCom extremely wealthy, very quickly.

At the peak of his career in 1999, Ebbers's net worth was estimated to exceed 1.4 billion dollars. He was ranked as number 174 on the *Forbes* magazine list of the four hundred richest people in the world. His assets included Canada's largest cattle ranch, a minor-league hockey team, a lumber yard, a trucking company, a yacht company, and multiple lavish homes throughout Canada and the United States. The Telecom Cowboy, as he was referred to in the late 1990's, was a financial paragon. Then a fateful error in 1999 caused Ebbers and members of his executive staff to become known as some of the most sinister corporate criminals of modern times.

Criminal Career

In 1999, Ebbers announced that WorldCom would attempt to buy its largest competitor, Sprint Communications. This acquisition was halted by both U.S. and European antitrust regulators, who noted that such a purchase would turn WorldCom into a monopoly. To appease regulators, whose concerns included WorldCom's gaining

Bernard Ebbers. (AP/Wide World Photos)

too much of a stronghold in the fiber-optic Internet market, Ebbers opted to purchase only Sprint's traditional telephone services. This choice proved to be a major mistake, as copper telephone lines were a thing of the past. As a result, the price of WorldCom stock plummeted. Furthermore, the Internet market was slowly losing its economic viability, causing WorldCom stock to plunge further, from a record sixty-four dollars a share down to nine dollars.

During this downturn, Ebbers started to sell his millions of shares of WorldCom stock, some of which he had purchased with monies borrowed from banks and other financial institutions. The WorldCom board of directors offered Ebbers an unprecedented $400 million in loans so that he would not continue to forfeit his major position of power in the company—and also so that other investors would not panic and attempt to liquidate their stock. Ebbers accepted the loans. When the story was made known, those in the business and financial worlds were outraged by the actions of Ebbers and the attempted financial cover-up that took place under his watch as CEO of WorldCom. In 2002, Ebbers resigned from WorldCom and was given a generous pension.

That same year, an internal auditor alerted federal investigators to suspicious financial records she had uncovered at WorldCom. In summary, WorldCom executives, including Ebbers, had been misleading investors and regulators about their financial statements, mainly listing expenses as assets in order to protect the company throughout its financial turmoil in 2000-2002. By 2003, state and federal investigators had uncovered what was called the largest accounting fraud in U.S. history.

Legal Action and Outcome

Ebbers, along with his chief executive cabinet, faced both federal and state criminal charges for their parts in the WorldCom debacle. A federal judge found Ebbers guilty of nine felony counts, ranging from securities fraud to filing false financial statements. On July 13, 2005, Ebbers was sentenced to twenty-five years in prison, a sentence he appealed.

Impact

The name Bernard Ebbers became equated with the term "corporate criminal." Ebbers's fraudulent activities led to the largest accounting fraud ever recorded in U.S. history. The economic impact of WorldCom's fall not only caused twenty thousand employees to lose their jobs but also caused millions of investors to lose their life savings—a total of $180 billion. Ebbers was largely responsible for these losses, and he received the toughest sentence to date handed to the chief executive officer of a *Fortune* 500 company.

Further Reading

Brody, Keith, and Sancha Dunstan. *The Great Telecoms Swindle: How the Collapse of WorldCom Finally Exposed the Technology Myth.* Oxford, England: Capstone, 2003. This analysis of the telecom boom of the late 1990's and 2000 highlights the role that Ebbers and WorldCom played.

Jeter, Lynne. *Disconnected: Deceit and Betrayal at*

WorldCom. New York: Wiley, 2003. Provides an in-depth look at the greatest accounting fraud in American history and the man who was deemed responsible for it, Bernard Ebbers.

Malik, Om. *Broadbandits: Inside the $750 Billion Telecom Heist.* New York: Wiley, 2003. Offers a unique overview of the many players involved in the fraudulent activities surrounding the telecom industry, with special emphasis given to Ebbers and WorldCom.

—*Paul M. Klenowski*

See also: Jim Bakker; Ivan Boesky; Martin Frankel; Kenneth Lay; Michael Milken; Mou Qizhong; Jeffrey Skilling.

Dietrich Eckart

German journalist and playwright

Born: March 23, 1868; Neumarkt, Germany

Died: December 26, 1923; Berchtesgaden, Germany

Cause of notoriety: During the Nazi movement's formative years, Eckart promoted the nationalistic and racist ideology of the party. Through the nationalism that pervades his writings, he attempted to create an intellectual foundation for Nazi racism.

Active: 1918-1923

Locale: Germany

Early Life

The son of middle-class parents, Dietrich Eckart (DEE-trihk EHK-art) studied medicine at the University of Erlangen but left medical school in 1891 to pursue journalism and to write plays and poetry. In 1899 he moved to Berlin but had limited success with his writing career. His interests began to focus on social class and race as well as the notion of a higher intellectual and leadership class. This interest led him into the area of mysticism that emphasized race and identified the Aryan group as the most superior. For Eckhart, such an outlook evolved into intense anti-Semitism. He moved to Munich and in later years joined organizations that emphasized the concept of racial status in relation to the Jews, who were portrayed as inferior and also dangerous. Eckhart's plays and numerous other writings emphasized German nationalism, Aryan racial identity and superiority, and German mythology.

Political Career

Eckart became active in German politics following World War I. He edited an anti-Semitic periodical, *Auf gut Deutsch* (1918-1920; in plain German). He opposed the Versailles treaty signed by the newly created Weimar Republic in June, 1919, and supported the "stab in the back" theory (*Dolchstoss*) that blamed German Jews and socialists for Germany's having lost the recent war. Eckart joined the Thule Society, a conservative organization that emphasized German nationalism along with the study of the occult. Rudolf Höss and Arthur Rosenberg, later important Nazi Party leaders, also joined the Thule group at this time.

Eckart was one of the founders of the German Workers' Party (Deutsche Arbeiterpartei) in 1919, later renamed the National Socialist German Workers' Party (National Sozialistiche Deutsche Arbeiterpartei, or NSDAP). Adolf Hitler assumed leadership of the party in 1920. Between 1921 and 1923 Eckart edited the party newspaper *Volkischer Beobachter*, a racist and extremist publication. He wrote the nationalist song *Deutschland erwache* (Germany awake) as the party's patriotic anthem.

Eckart first met Hitler in 1919, and they collaborated in the early years of the Nazi movement. Eckart introduced Hitler to his contacts in Munich and thus to a wider segment of society among which to solicit financial support. Eckart's public hostility toward Jews, including Friedrich Ebert, president of the German republic, resulted in Eckart's indictment on charges of defaming of the president in early 1923. To escape arrest, he went into hiding in Berchtesgaden in southern Germany. His influence in the Nazi Party gradually declined, and the leadership removed him as *Volkischer Beobachter* editor in March, 1923. Eckart privately criticized Hitler for his delusions of grandeur, and the two men became estranged. In November, 1923, Eckart was in Munich but played no important role in Hitler's Beer Hall Putsch, which sought to take power in Bavaria. The plot collapsed, and authorities arrested Hitler, Eckart, and others. Eckart was released and died soon after. A plain tombstone, bearing only his name, marks his grave at Berchtesgaden.

IMPACT

Although not as well known as other Nazi leaders of later years, Dietrich Eckart actively promoted the nationalistic and racist ideology of this extremist and militant movement in its formative years. His writings and nationalist outlook attempted to provide a credible intellectual foundation for the party's racist beliefs. In addition to his newspaper work, he also used occultist philosophy, German mythology, and the Nazi theory of "positive Christianity" to portray Judaism as the primary enemy of civilization. Hitler's apparent appreciation of Eckart included reference to him as his "fatherly friend" and a tribute to Eckart in his book *Mein Kampf* (1925-1927; English translation, 1933). However, Eckart never held meaningful power in the party, and Hitler's primary focus on politics and power, rather than philosophical thinking, left Eckart behind as an interesting but fringe member of the Nazi movement. On his deathbed, Eckart allegedly made a statement taking credit for finding and promoting Hitler as Germany's political savior.

FURTHER READING

Anderson, Ken. *Hitler and the Occult*. Amherst, N.Y.: Prometheus Books, 1995. Places Eckart in the context of the Thule Society and its occult practices.

Kershaw, Ian. *Hitler, 1889-1936: Hubris*. New York: Norton, 1999. Traces Eckart's relations with Hitler in the early 1920's.

Levenda, Peter. *Unholy Alliance: A History of Nazi Involvement with the Occult*. 2d ed. New York: Continuum, 2002. Describes Eckart's occult beliefs and his relations with Hitler.

Stegmann-Gall, Richard. *The Holy Reich: Nazi Conceptions of Christianity, 1919-1945*. New York: Cambridge University Press, 2003. Discusses Eckart's role in the Nazi theory of "positive Christianity" used to support its racist views.

—*Taylor Stults*

SEE ALSO: Julius Evola; Savitri Devi.

JOHN D. EHRLICHMAN

White House domestic policy chief under President Richard M. Nixon

BORN: March 20, 1925; Tacoma, Washington
DIED: February 14, 1999; Atlanta, Georgia
ALSO KNOWN AS: John Daniel Ehrlichman (full name)
MAJOR OFFENSES: Conspiracy, perjury, and obstruction of justice
ACTIVE: 1970-1973
LOCALE: Washington, D.C.
SENTENCE: Four to eight years' imprisonment; served eighteen months

EARLY LIFE

John D. Ehrlichman (EHR-lihk-man) was born in Tacoma, Washington, in 1925. During World War II, he joined the Air Force at the age of eighteen. While in the service, he became a lead navigator for Eighth Air Force bombing missions over Europe. After twenty-six combat missions, Ehrlichman was awarded the Distinguished Flying Cross. After the war, he attended the University of California at Los Angeles (UCLA). One of his classmates at UCLA was H. R. Haldeman, with whom he was later associated in the administration of President Richard Nixon. After graduation in 1948, he entered the law school at Stanford University, and he received his law degree in 1951. He returned to Washington State and became a partner in a law firm in Seattle.

Ehrlichman worked in Nixon's losing campaigns in 1960 and 1964 and in his successful campaign for the presidency in 1968. Soon after the 1968 election, he was asked to join the White House staff as counsel to the president and subsequently as Nixon's domestic policy chief, working immediately under Haldeman. His formal title was Director of the White House Domestic Council. As director, Ehrlichman dealt with most of the pressing domestic policy issues that the Nixon administration faced. A major part of his duties was serving as legislative liaison—trying to persuade members of Congress to support the president's policy initiatives. Among the issues with which Ehrlichman was closely concerned were revenue sharing—that is, grants of federal money to state governments—and the president's rejected appointments of Clement Haynesworth and G. Harold Carswell to the United States Supreme Court. He was also heavily involved in the continuing struggle over race and school integration in the South, in which the administration's strategy was to do the legal minimum toward civil rights so as not to alienate southern voters. He was also in

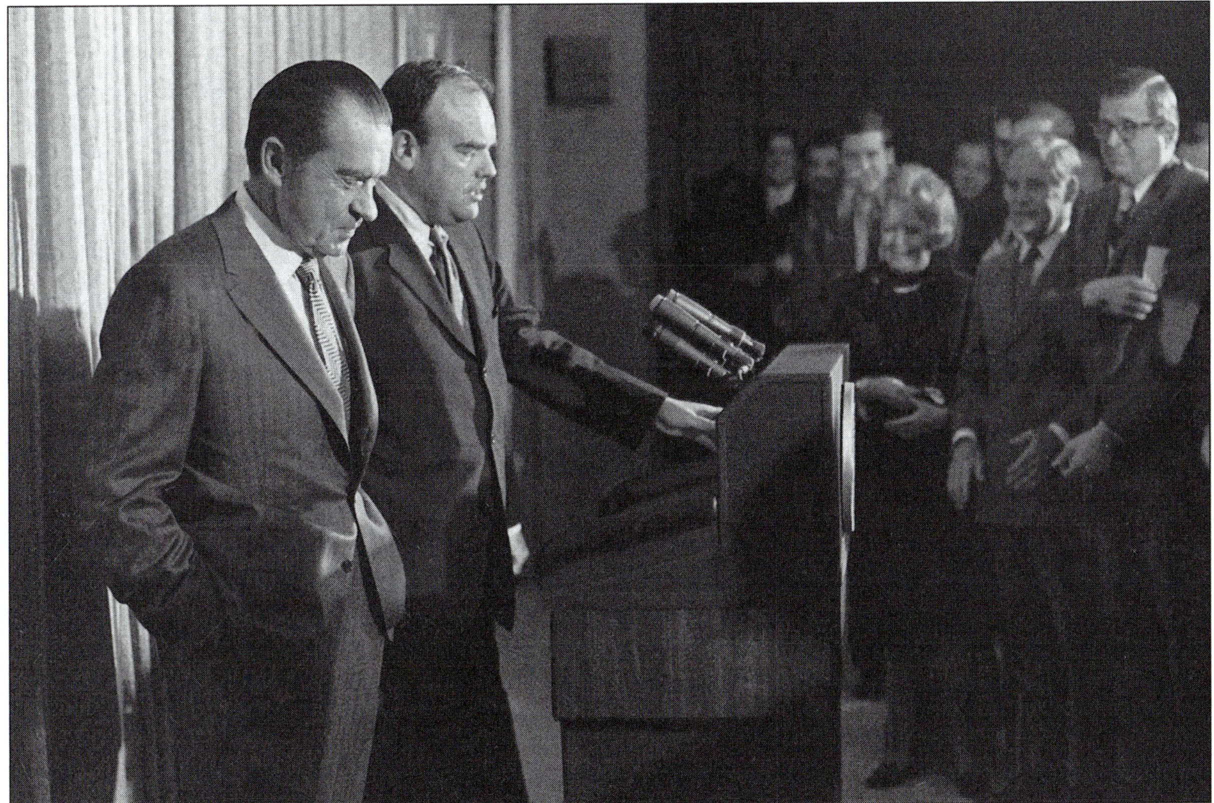

John D. Ehrlichman, at right, with Richard Nixon. (AP/Wide World Photos)

charge of the "plumbers," a group of White House operatives whose function was to discover and prevent the leakage of administration secrets.

Criminal Career

On June 17, 1972, the Watergate break-in took place. Five burglars, later shown to be affiliated with and to have been paid by the Committee to Re-elect the President (CRP), broke into the offices of the Democratic National Committee in the Watergate Hotel. Four of them were former plumbers. Their purpose was to obtain political intelligence by bugging the telephones. They were caught and arrested by the District of Columbia police.

Ehrlichman participated in discussions about the administration's stance toward the burglary the next day. Nixon, Ehrlichman, and John Dean, Nixon's counsel, devised an unlawful cover-up. They attempted to buy the silence of the burglars by secretly funneling campaign funds to them. Simultaneously, they planned that any inquiry by the Federal Bureau of Investigation (FBI) about the matter was to be diverted by getting the Central Intelligence Agency (CIA) to claim that such an investigation would disclose foreign intelligence secrets. Ehrlichman became involved in helping to pass money to the burglars.

During the course of the investigations of Watergate, information about an earlier crime emerged. The White House, with Ehrlichman's knowledge, had sent some of the plumbers to discover what they could about military analyst Daniel Ellsberg. Ellsberg had given the Pentagon Papers—a classified government study of the origins of the war in Vietnam—to *The New York Times*. The White House investigators broke into the office of Ellsberg's psychiatrist in order to find material with which Ellsberg could be discredited.

At the end of April, 1973, as it became clear to the press and public that the conspiracy reached into the heart of the Nixon administration, Erhlichman, along with Dean and Haldeman, was forced to resign. After his dismissal, Ehrlichman testified before the Senate Watergate committee. By concealing his role in the cover-up and by lying to the committee, Ehrlichman committed perjury and obstructed justice. Moreover, his hostile and aggressive stance toward the committee did nothing to dispel the public image of the arrogance and high-handedness of the Nixon administration.

LEGAL ACTION AND OUTCOME

Ehrlichman was convicted of conspiracy for his role in the Ellsberg burglary, as well as obstruction of justice and perjury for his false testimony to the Senate Watergate Investigating Committee and to the grand juries that investigated the crimes. He was sentenced to four to eight years' imprisonment. After serving eighteen months of his sentence at a minimum security federal prison in New Mexico, he was released by the trial judge, John J. Sirica.

IMPACT

The domestic policies of the Nixon administration, most of them promoted by John D. Ehrlichman, were not nearly so conservative as Nixon's critics believed at the time. Revenue sharing in particular became a lasting structural contribution to American government. The manifold illegal activates associated with the Watergate scandal (many not involving Ehrlichman at all) had the long-term effect of reducing public confidence in the government and in the presidency in particular. Ehrlichman's hostile and self-righteous stance toward the Senate Watergate Investigating Committee and the subsequent legal proceedings confirmed and perpetuated the view that the senior members of the Nixon administration were rigid and authoritarian.

FURTHER READING

Ambrose, Stephen. *Nixon*. 3 vols. New York: Simon & Schuster, 1987-1991. This is an illuminating and balanced discussion of Nixon, his personality, career, and presidency. The Watergate material can be found in *Ruin and Recovery*.

Dean, John W. *Blind Ambition: The White House Years*. New York: Simon & Schuster, 1976. Dean recounts his career and his involvement with the Watergate conspiracy and admits his participation in the cover-up.

Ehrlichman, John. *Witness to Power*. New York: Simon & Schuster, 1982. Ehrlichman's own memoir, discussing the domestic achievements of the Nixon administration and Ehrlichman's role in the Watergate scandal.

Safire, William. *Before the Fall: An Inside View of the Pre-Watergate White House*. Garden City, N.Y.: Doubleday, 1975. A laudatory view of the accomplishments of the Nixon administration before Watergate destroyed it.

White, Theodore H. *Breach of Faith: The Fall of Richard Nixon*. New York: Atheneum, 1975. Excellent history of the Watergate affair; Ehrlichman's role is thoroughly discussed.

—Robert Jacobs

SEE ALSO: Charles W. Colson; H. R. Haldeman; E. Howard Hunt; G. Gordon Liddy; James W. McCord, Jr.; John Mitchell; Richard Nixon.

ADOLF EICHMANN

Nazi official in charge of Jewish affairs

BORN: March 19, 1906; Solingen, Germany
DIED: May 31, 1962; Ramle prison, near Tel Aviv, Israel
ALSO KNOWN AS: Ricardo Klement; Karl Adolf Eichmann (full name)
MAJOR OFFENSES: War crimes, namely deporting millions of Jews to extermination camps during the Holocaust
ACTIVE: 1939-1945
LOCALE: Europe
SENTENCE: Death by hanging

EARLY LIFE

Raised in a middle-class Protestant family in Linz, Austria, Adolf Eichmann (AY-dahlf IK-mahn) attended and failed engineering school. He briefly worked as a laborer in his father's mining company, in sales for an electrical construction company, and as a traveling salesman for the Vacuum Oil Company. In 1932 he joined the Austrian Nazi Party, and after he lost his job in 1933 he found work in Bavaria, Germany, with the Nazi-affiliated and exiled Austrian Legion. After fourteen months of military training, he joined the Schutzstaffel (SS) and served as a corporal at the Dachau concentration camp.

Becoming bored, he began work with Reinhard Heydrich's Sicherheitsdienst (SD). As a filing clerk, Eichmann was assigned to collect information on German Jews. Obsessed with Jews and Jewish culture, he visited Jewish neighborhoods, attended Jewish meetings, learned about Zionism, and even studied Hebrew and Yiddish.

His "specialty" was recognized by Hedrich and Heinrich Himmler, who appointed him to lead the SD Scientific Museum of Jewish Affairs in Berlin to investigate "solutions to the Jewish question." Eichmann visited Palestine in 1937 to discuss with Arabs possible Jewish emigration from Nazi Germany to the Middle East, but British authorities ordered him out of the country.

Nazi Career

Sent to Vienna to prepare for the Anschluss, the annexation of Austria by Germany, Eichmann was put in charge of the Central Office for Jewish Emigration. In that role, he had sole authority to issue exit permits for Jews from Austria, Czechoslovakia, and the old German Reich. After extorting their wealth in exchange for safe passage, Eichmann had about 150,000 Jews rounded up and forced them to emigrate. Early in 1939, he began deporting Jews to Poland and by October was made the special adviser on evacuating Jews and Poles.

Transferred to a Gestapo division of the Reich Main Security Office in December, Eichmann took over the office for Jewish affairs and evacuation of Jews from Germany and all occupied countries. He thereby became one of the most powerful men in the Third Reich. His Madagascar Plan of 1940, which would have deported European Jews to the African island of Madagascar, was never realized, but the concentration of Jews continued.

Beginning in Poland, which had the largest Jewish population in Europe, Heydrich and Eichmann implemented the forcible roundup of Jews into ghettos and labor camps, resulting in countless deaths through overcrowding, disease, and starvation. Complying with Adolf Hitler's earlier orders that the German Reich be cleansed of Jews, Eichmann had already been organizing mass deportations of Jews from Germany and Bohemia to the East. With the purported claim by Heydrich that Hitler had ordered the physical extermination of the Jews, the definition of "cleansing" changed for Eichmann from organizing mass deportations to orchestrating mass murders.

Eichmann supervised the mass murder of Jews by SS *Einsatz* groups in occupied areas of the Soviet Union, where more than 300,000 Jews were gathered up, taken to secluded locations, lined up at open pits, shot, and buried. He personally inspected these mass executions but was ordered by Himmler, for reasons of efficiency and secrecy, to devise alternative methods of killing. Jews were then packed into trucks used as mobile gas units, killed by carbon monoxide, and buried. This method was also considered too messy, too inefficient, and too public. Thus, in late 1941 Hermann Göring told Heydrich to prepare for the "final solution" to the Jewish question.

On January 20, 1942, Eichmann helped Heydrich organize the Wannsee Conference near Berlin, where they and other Nazi leaders planned the extermination of the entire Jewish population. Eichmann was authorized by Heydrich to implement the "final solution" by coordinating the deportation of Jews from all over Europe to the gas chambers at Sobibor, Chelmno, Treblinka, and Auschwitz-Birkenau. He took special interest in Auschwitz and visited that site several times, even helping Rudolf Höss select the location of the gas chambers, approving the use of Zyklon-B, and personally witnessing the extermination processes.

While Germany occupied Hungary in 1944, Eichmann and the Gestapo "Special Section Commandos" organized the ghettoization and deportation of Hungary's 750,000 Jews to Auschwitz. Eichmann personally expedited the process, resulting in more than 380,000 Jews "exterminated" at Auschwitz-Birkenau. At the end of 1944, Himmler ordered deportations to cease, but Eichmann ignored the order, rounded up an additional 50,000 Hungarian Jews, and forced them to march for eight days into Austria.

Legal Action and Outcome

Eichmann was captured after World War II but escaped from an American internment camp in 1946 and in 1950 fled to Argentina with the help of the SS underground. He lived near Buenos Aires for ten years under an assumed name, Ricardo Klement, but was eventually tracked down by Israeli Mossad secret agents, captured, and secretly smuggled out of Argentina to Israel. Once in Israel, Eichmann was brought to trial. When he addressed the court he used the defense that he was just obeying orders and that everyone was killing the Jews. On December 2, 1961, Eichmann was sentenced to death for crimes against the Jewish people and against humanity and on May 31, 1962, was executed by hanging.

Impact

Understanding Adolf Eichmann's actions helps define the historical specificity of the Holocaust and genocide in general, which has come to include factors such as the role of systematic bureaucratization in genocides and the necessity to examine the limits of national sovereignties. Notions such as those that reveal that evil can become banal and part of one's routine job function have alerted world society to the ongoing dangers of totalitarianism and extreme ideologies. It is no longer acceptable, post-

Eichmann, to do one's bureaucratic duty without greater awareness of the demands of personal and social responsibilities.

Further Reading

Aharoni, Zvi. *Operation Eichmann: The Truth About the Pursuit, Capture, and Trial*. Translated by Helmut Bögler. New York: John Wiley & Sons, 1997. First-hand account of Eichmann's capture and interrogation in Argentina in 1960 by an Israeli Mossad agent.

Arendt, Hannah. *Eichmann in Jerusalem: A Report on the Banality of Evil*. New York: Viking Press, 1963. Arendt's account of the trial of Eichmann, which first appeared as a series of articles in *The New Yorker* in 1963. It deals with the trial itself, depicting Eichmann as a dutiful participant in the expulsion, concentration, and killing of Jews by German authorities.

Cesarani, David. *Eichmann: His Life and Times*. New York: Vintage Books, 2005. This thoroughly researched biography contests Arendt's thesis of the banality of Eichmann. A key argument is that Eichmann's training in ethnic cleansing in Poland in 1939-1940 prepared him to become a willing and efficient perpetrator of genocide.

—*Jules Simon*

See also: Klaus Barbie; Martin Bormann; Léon Degrelle; Karl Dönitz; Hans Michael Frank; Joseph Goebbels; Magda Goebbels; Hermann Göring; Rudolf Hess; Reinhard Heydrich; Heinrich Himmler; Adolf Hitler; Alfred Jodl; Josef Mengele; Joachim von Ribbentrop; Baldur von Schirach; Otto Skorzeny; Julius Streicher.

Ira Einhorn

American murderer

Born: March 15, 1940; Philadelphia, Pennsylvania
Also known as: Ira Samuel Einhorn (full name); Eugene Mallon; Ben Moore; Unicorn
Major offenses: Murder and bail jumping
Active: September, 1977-January, 1981
Locale: Philadelphia, Pennsylvania
Sentence: Life imprisonment

Early Life

Ira Samuel Einhorn (IN-hohrn) was raised in the north Philadelphia Jewish neighborhood of Mount Airy. He attended the academic magnet Central High School, where he was admitted into the advanced curriculum—select curriculum reserved for high-achieving students. After graduation, he attended the University of Pennsylvania, majoring in English. He also received a fellowship to attend the Kennedy School of Government at Harvard.

Einhorn gained local celebrity in the 1960's in Philadelphia as a peace and ecology activist. However, he possessed a tremendous ego, claiming, for example, undue credit for establishing Earth Day. He also was a political gadfly who ran for mayor of Philadelphia in 1971. Einhorn suffered from a degree of megalomania and paranoia, perhaps from excessive drug use in the 1960's. He adopted the nickname Unicorn (literally, "one horn"), which is a translation of his German surname. He often stated that the Federal Bureau of Investigation (FBI) and Central Intelligence Agency (CIA) were persecuting him because of his political views and activities. Einhorn had permitted little toleration for girlfriends who broke off relationships with him. He allegedly strangled one to the point of unconsciousness and beat another.

Criminal Career

Einhorn's notoriety emerged after the disappearance in 1977 of his girlfriend, Helen "Holly" Maddux, of Texas. Einhorn claimed that Maddux had left him and he never heard from her again. He even called Maddux's father in Texas shortly after she vanished, asking if he had heard from her.

In fact, Maddux had tired of Einhorn's abuse and left for New York, where she began dating another man. On September 9, 1977, when she informed Einhorn that she was leaving him, he demanded that she return to Philadelphia or he would throw her belongings onto the street. She returned immediately to collect her property; no one saw her again after this point.

Maddux's family became concerned since she usually called several times a month. They notified the Philadelphia police, who then questioned Einhorn. He told them that she had gone shopping sometime before and never returned, and he assumed that she had left him because of the problems they were having. Since he was a well-known figure in the community, the officers believed his story.

However, Maddux's family had not trusted Einhorn since a visit he had made to Texas while dating Maddux; his condescending attitude and boorish behavior had offended them. This unkempt "hippie" seemed an odd match for their neat, former-cheerleader daughter and sister. After Maddux's disappearance, therefore, the family was convinced that Einhorn had harmed her. They hired private detectives, who learned from friends of Einhorn that he had wanted to dispose of a trunk, which was still in his apartment. Neighbors also complained about a foul odor emanating from the apartment. The Philadelphia police again became interested in Einhorn and went to his apartment with a search warrant and a camera to record what they might find. They discovered Maddux's mummified body in the trunk.

Legal Action and Outcome

At a bond hearing in which a number of prominent Philadelphia citizens testified on Einhorn's behalf, the judge awarded bail at forty thousand dollars, and Einhorn was released on a 10 percent cash bond. Einhorn's lawyer was Arlen Specter, who later became the mayor of Philadelphia and then a senator from Pennsylvania.

Einhorn jumped bail before trial and fled to Europe, first to Ireland and then to France. There, he married Annika Flodin, a Swedish national. Pennsylvania authorities sought his extradition, but the French authorities were unwilling to extradict Einhorn without a guarantee that he would not be executed; France had abolished capital punishment. In the United States, Maddux's family continued to press for the capture of Einhorn. He was found guilty in absentia in a Philadelphia trial in 1993.

Einhorn assumed the alias Eugene Mallon and managed to escape extradition by hiding. He also relied on a technicality in the French-American extradition treaty. The Maddux case gained national attention, and many thought that the French refusal to extradite Einhorn was a political ploy. Several members of Congress sent a petition to French president Jacques Chirac requesting extradition, but Chirac did not have the power to overturn a judicial decision. The Pennsylvania legislature passed a bill in 1998 permitting Einhorn to have a second trial if he returned. Furthermore, he was not eligible for the death penalty, since the crime had been committed when Pennsylvania had not legalized executions.

In July, 2000, France agreed to Einhorn's extradition on condition that he receive a second trial and not be subject to the death penalty. Einhorn acted as his own attorney at the trial and alleged that agents had murdered Maddux in order to frame him. However, the jury was not convinced, and after only two hours of deliberation, it found him guilty. He was sentenced to life imprisonment and was sent to the state prison in Houtzdale, Pennsylvania.

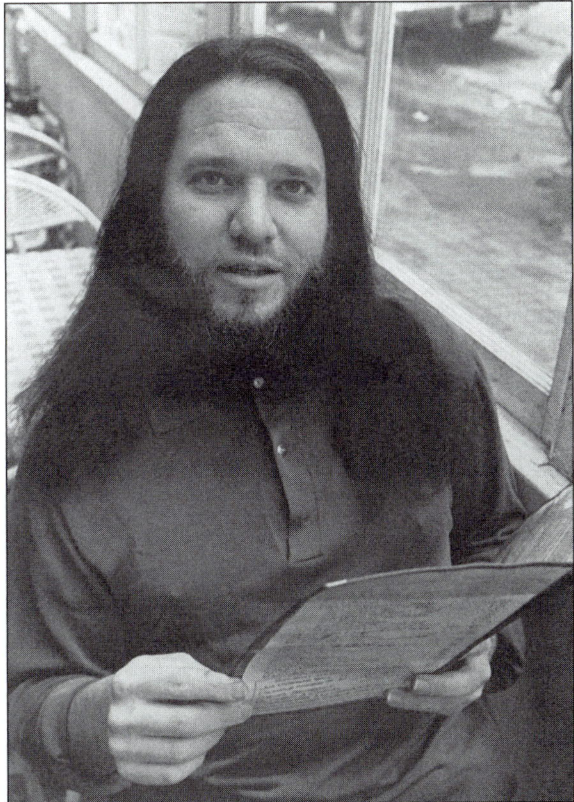

Ira Einhorn. (AP/Wide World Photos)

Impact

The Ira Einhorn case was complicated by judicial intricacies based on the difference between French and American law. The question surrounding Einhorn's extradition spurred legislation and legal wrangling in both countries. The bill passed by the Pennsylvania legislature in 1998, which allowed in-absentia defendants to request another trial, was criticized as unconstitutional by many legal authorities, who noted that a legislature should not be able to overrule a final judgment handed down by a court of law. The notoriety of the Einhorn case also led to several accounts in literature and the media. A documentary was aired by the Arts and Entertainment cable network in 1998, and a fictionalized docudrama titled *The Hunt for the Unicorn Killer* was televised by the National Broadcasting Company (NBC) network in 1999.

Further Reading

Cascio, Michael, Garry Blye, et al. *Peace, Love, and Murder: The Ira Einhorn Story*. New York: A&E Home Video, 1998. A film documentary of the case using interviews of friends, witnesses, the Maddux family, lawyers, and police. The documentary was made before Einhorn's extradition.

Levy, Steven. *The Unicorn's Secret: Murder in the Age of Aquarius—A True Story*. 1988. Reprint. New York: Penguin, 1999. The first written account of the case, which appeared while Einhorn was still in hiding and the story had not completely unfolded.

—*Frederick B. Chary*

See also: Richard Allen Davis; Ruth Ellis; Seventh Earl of Lucan; Scott Peterson; Sam Sheppard; Madeleine Smith; Ruth Snyder; Carolyn Warmus.

Elagabalus

Roman emperor (r. 218-222 c.e.)

Born: 203/204 c.e.; Emesa (now Homs), Syria
Died: March 11, 222 c.e.; Rome (now in Italy)
Also known as: Heliogabalus; Varius Avitus Bassianus (birth name); Varius Avitus Bassianus Marcus Aurelius Antoninus; Elah-Gabal; Varius Avitus Bassus
Cause of notoriety: Elagabalus's promotion of the Syrian sun god Elagabalus, his marriage to the vestal virgin Aquilia Severa, and his supposed sexual excesses led to his overthrow after a four-year reign.
Active: 218-222 c.e.
Locale: Emesa, Syria, and Rome, Italy

Early Life

Elagabalus (ehl-ah-GAB-ah-luhs) was born in late 203 or early 204 c.e. to Sextus Varius Marcellus and Julia Soaemias Bassiana and given the name Varius Avitus Bassianus. He was the nephew of the emperor Marcus Aurelius Severus Antoninus Caracalla (211-217) and grew up among the Roman elite. Through his mother's family he became the hereditary high priest of the Syrian god Emesa, also known as Elagabalus.

Political Career

In 217, Elagabalus's uncle, the emperor Caracalla, was murdered while on campaign in Syria, and Marcus Opellius Severus Macrinus became emperor. His grandmother, Julia Maesa, and his mother designed a plan to take advantage of the Syrian nobility's and Roman army's unhappiness with Macrinus's reign. They claimed that Elagabalus's real father was Caracalla, changing his name to Marcus Aurelius Antoninus to reinforce this connection. On May 16, 218, his mother took Elagabalus to a nearby army camp where the troops proclaimed the fourteen-year-old as emperor. The rebellion quickly spread as the Roman armies in the East joined Elagabalus's revolt. Less than a month later (June 8, 218) at Antioch, Elagabalus defeated the troops loyal to Macrinus and took the name Elagabalus to celebrate his victory.

Elagabalus traveled to Rome in July of 219, bringing with him a large black, conical stone that served as the cult symbol for the god Elagabalus. The stone was housed in a new temple on the Palatine Hill called the Elagaballium. Shortly after his arrival in Rome, Elagabalus married a Roman noblewoman, Julia Cornelia Paula, but divorced her in less than a year. He next married Julia Aquilia Severa, a vestal virgin, as part of a ceremony designed to place the god Elagabalus at the head of the Roman pantheon. Neither the new god nor Elagabalus's marriage to a vestal virgin was well received by the Roman population, and a divorce was arranged in less than a year. According to ancient sources, Romans opposed the worship of the Syrian god Elagabalus. Rumors about the emperor's relationship with the charioteer Hierocles, as well as his sexual excesses, further strained his relations with the Roman population.

Worried about the emperor's declining popularity, Elagabalus's family forced him to adopt his popular younger cousin Bassianus Alexianus as his heir in June of 221. Alexianus soon became a serious rival to Elagabalus and gained the support of their grandmother Julia Maesa, who had been instrumental in helping Elagabalus gain power, and the Praetorian Guard. Public disapproval with his lifestyle, coupled with his choice of men of humble birth to serve as public officials, forced Elagabalus to take a new wife, Annia Faustina, a descendant of Marcus Aurelius (161-180), in an effort to boost public opinion of him. This marriage lasted less than a year, and he soon divorced Faustina and remarried Aquilia Severa. Elagabalus tried unsuccessfully to have Alexianus removed from power or assassinated, but this action caused the Praetorian Guard to murder him and his mother on March 11, 222, and proclaim Alexianus as the emperor Alexander Severus (222-235).

Impact

Due to the stories of his sexual excesses, writers and artists of the late nineteenth century Decadent movement often used Elagabalus as a stock character who reveled in excess. Simeon Solomon, who was fascinated by sadistic and sexual themes, depicted the emperor in his painting *Heliogabalus, High Priest of the Sun* (1886). The most famous painting of Elagabalus, however, is Sir Lawrence Alma-Tadema's *The Roses of Heliogabalus* (1888), a scene depicting a dinner at which Elagabalus supposedly attempted to smother his guests with rose petals dropped from the ceiling. This lack of control is perhaps seen most clearly in Antonin Artaud's *Héliogabale: Ou, L'Anarchiste couronné* (1934; *Heliogabalus: Or, The Anarchist Crowned*, 1976), a novelized biography that portrays Elagabalus's reign as a descent into sexual debauchery and uncontrollable violence.

Further Reading

Ball, Warwick. *Rome in the East: The Transformation of an Empire*. London: Routledge, 2000. An examination of the impact (architectural, religious, social, and political) of the East upon Rome, including a look at the Roman emperors from the eastern provinces.

Grant, Michael. *The Roman Emperors: A Biographical Guide to the Rulers of Imperial Rome, 31 B.C.-A.D. 476*. New York: Barnes and Noble, 1997. A brief examination of the lives of each of the Roman emperors.

Scarre, Chris. *Chronicle of the Roman Emperors: The Reign-by-Reign Record of the Rulers of Imperial Rome*. London: Thames and Hudson, 1995. A chronological examination of the reign of the Roman emperors that provides a brief biography of each ruler.

—*R. Scott Moore*

See also: Caligula; Commodus; Domitian; Fulvia; Galerius; Justin II; Nero; Lucius Cornelius Sulla; Theodora.

Ruth Ellis

English murderer

Born: October 9, 1926; Rhyl, Wales
Died: July 13, 1955; London, England
Also known as: Ruth Hornby (birth name); Ruth Neilson
Major offense: Murder
Active: April 10, 1955
Locale: England, mainly London

Early Life

Ruth Ellis (EHL-ihs), née Hornby, was born in Wales. When she was six, her family moved to London, where she grew into an attractive, easily bored teen. Working as a waitress, Ruth discovered the lure of dancing, men, and peroxide.

At sixteen, Ruth became pregnant by a Canadian soldier. She gave birth to Clare Andrea (Andy) in 1944. Ruth then worked as a dance hostess, which suited her tastes and talents. Although she posed only once for a photographer, newspapers would later refer to her as a model. She married George Ellis, an alcoholic with a violent temper. Pregnant with a daughter, Ellis suffered physical abuse from George; she jealously suspected him of affairs and stalked him. After the birth of their daughter, Georgina, the couple petitioned for divorce.

Criminal Career

Always eager for excitement, Ellis began seeing two members of a motor-racing fraternity. Desmund Cussen, whom the prosecution would later describe as Ellis's "alternative lover," was the only significant man in Ellis's life who was not alcoholic, violent, or sexually unfaithful. David Blakely, by contrast, exhibited all three of those failings. A member of the upper-middle class, Blakely was engaged to a woman his social equal; Ellis remained technically married. Nevertheless, Ellis and Blakely began a stormy affair and continued it intermittently for two years.

Blakely's violence toward Ellis, his dalliances with other women, and Ellis's jealousy increased over time. Blakely occasionally ignored Ellis for weeks on end;

when he did, she occupied her time with Cussen, though remaining intensely possessive toward Blakely. Ellis followed Blakely and spied upon him. On March 28, 1955, Ellis suffered a miscarriage after another of Blakely's violent attacks on her. On April 10, 1955, Good Friday, Blakely abandoned Ellis, although he had promised to spend Easter weekend with her. On Easter Sunday, she tracked Blakely to a pub. When he emerged, she shot him at close range.

Legal Action and Outcome

Because there were witnesses to the shooting, one a policeman, and Ellis made a free confession, her technical guilt was never in question. She exhibited no remorse over Blakely's death or concern for her children; instead she seemed to care more about her hairstyle and clothes for the trial. When asked by the prosecutor, "When you fired that revolver at close range into the body of David Blakely, what did you intend to do?" Ellis replied, "It is obvious that when I shot him I intended to kill him." The jury required only twenty-three minutes to return a verdict of guilty.

Although Ellis's guilt could not be doubted, her story was flawed and incomplete. She obviously had an accomplice whom she shielded, probably Cussen. In Ellis's time, women who committed crimes of passion often could avoid hanging if they appeared remorseful and victimized. Ellis refused to project such an image. Her supporters contended that she was convicted of being an immoral and uncontrolled woman, an affront to prevailing gender and class sensibilities. Many thought Ellis paid too high a price for her crime. Crowds of protesters flocked to Holloway Prison, where Ellis was hanged on July 13, 1955. The executioner received more than the usual number of death threats regarding this case.

Impact

The last woman to be hanged in England, Ruth Ellis was a focus for the arguments against capital punishment. In August, the National Campaign for the Abolition of Capital Punishment was launched, with Ellis's case as a key element in its arsenal. By February, 1956, Parliament debated a bill to abolish the death penalty, but it failed. In 1965 the death penalty was suspended, and in 1969 it was abolished entirely. Many contend that the outrage at the severity of Ellis's punishment helped ensure the abolition of capital punishment in the United Kingdom.

Further Reading

Ballinger, Anette. *Dead Woman Walking: Executed Women in England and Wales, 1900-1955.* Aldershot, England: Ashgate, 2000. Ballinger argues sexist bias against women who kill adult males and uses Ellis extensively as example.

_______. "The Guilt of the Innocent and the Innocence of the Guilty: The Cases of Marie Fahmy and Ruth Ellis." Chapter 1 in *No Angels: Women Who Commit Violence*, edited by Alice Myers and Sarah Wight. New York: Pandora/HarperCollins, 1996. Portrays Ellis as victim of gender and class expectations.

Ellis, Georgie. *A Murder of Passion: A Daughter's Memoir of the Last Woman to Be Hanged.* London: Blake, 2003. Although unscholarly and unobjective, Ellis provides a sympathetic and human picture of her mother.

—*Alex Hunnicutt*

See also: Bambi Bembenek; Richard Allen Davis; Ira Einhorn; Jean Harris; Scott Peterson; Sam Sheppard; Madeleine Smith; Ruth Snyder; Harry Kendall Thaw; Carolyn Warmus.

Werner Erhard

American businessman

Born: September 5, 1935; Philadelphia, Pennsylvania
Also known as: John Paul Rosenberg (birth name); Jack Rosenberg; Werner Hans Erhard; Guru to the Gulag; Werner Spits; The Source
Cause of notoriety: After two decades of teaching people how to transform their lives, the guru of est vanished amid allegations of his running an authoritarian cult, personal tax fraud, and family abuses.
Active: March, 1991
Locale: Worldwide, but mainly the United States

Early Life

Born as John Paul Rosenberg in Philadelphia, Werner Erhard (WUHR-nuhr EHR-hahrd) grew up in a Christianized Jewish family (he was baptized an Episcopalian). His father was a small restaurant operator. Rosenberg graduated from high school in 1952, which was the extent of his formal education, and worked as a supervisor for a construction company. In 1960, when he was twenty-five, married, and the father of four children, he abandoned his family and flew to St. Louis with his mistress. They decided to change their names to make it more difficult for their families to find them. While reading an in-flight magazine article on Germany's economic recovery, Rosenberg decided to change his name to Werner Erhard (inspired by German finance minister Ludwig Erhard and atomic scientist Werner Heisenberg). The fugitive couple soon married and settled briefly in St. Louis, where Erhard worked as a representative for a school that taught operation of construction equipment and sold used automobiles.

The couple moved to San Francisco, and Erhard became a salesman for *Encyclopaedia Britannica*, *Parents* magazine, and the Great Books Foundation. He worked for the Parents Cultural Institute and the Grolier Society, both of which sold encyclopedias door to door, and Erhard hired, trained, and supervised the sales staff.

Foundation of "est"

During this period, Erhard engaged in a wide variety of spiritual and personal growth disciplines, including Scientology, Mind Dynamics, encounter groups, Gestalt therapy, and Zen meditation. In 1971, while driving over the Golden Gate Bridge, Erhard had an epiphany of "self" discovery. After his initial self-realization, Erhard put together an intensive two-weekend course he called "est" (Latin for "it is"). His course was designed both to bring students to a realization similar to his and to be a training program of transformation that was to affect the lives of thousands.

Erhard's course was dynamic, well rehearsed, intensive, and exhausting. The first est seminar was held in October, 1971, at the Jack Tar Hotel in San Francisco with nearly one thousand people in attendance. Many people who attended claimed to have experienced increased vitality and a strong a sense of new personal worth. The early success of est training was bolstered by word-of-mouth advertising by attendees, attracting increasing numbers of new students. The charismatic, voluble Erhard was a master of training people and motivating them to sell—in this case, to sell his own seminars.

During the 1970's, war-weary Americans were beguiled with what came to be known as the human-potential movement, and est quickly became the most publi-

Werner Erhard. (AP/Wide World Photos)

cized and commercially successful of these kinds of growth workshops. The programs were a polished, mass-produced, large-group approach to personal change based on classic techniques of indoctrination and mental conditioning.

The est format consisted of a large group of individuals, usually about 250, who would pay a premium fee to spend two weekends listening to a trainer who instructed, insulted, and shocked them, and then guided them through a number of structured exercises. The training was an eclectic mixture of the spiritual and personal growth techniques that Erhard had studied, with a primary focus on assumption of responsibility. The courses offered a "transforming experience, designed to get rid of old baggage" and provide a fresh perspective on life—a feat described, in est-speak, as training people to get "It," a nebulous New Age concept.

From Erhard's one-man operation, est soon grew to a massive profit-making corporation, Werner Erhard & Associates. He trained a professional staff and a host of volunteers dedicated both to the ideas of est and to him. Between 1971 and 1984, 700,000 people enrolled in est workshops in some twenty American cities. In addition, Erhard established a weekly seminar program concerned with various aspects of life, such as money and commitment, and an intensive communication workshop. All of these enterprises were enormously profitable, and Erhard became the subject of media attention.

As est became a household word and vaulted into the mainstream of American culture, celebrities such as singers Cher and John Denver became devoted followers. The est phrase "thank you for sharing" entered American patois. Erhard became deified by the faithful, who referred to him as "the Source." In addition to his business enterprises, Erhard cofounded a number of independent, nonprofit charitable enterprises, such as the Hunger Project, dedicated to ending worldwide deaths from starvation. In 1988, in recognition of his humanitarian contributions to people and society, Erhard was awarded the Mahatma Gandhi Humanitarian Award.

In 1985, Erhard changed the name of est to the Landmark Forum, a gentler form of training that relied on the Socratic method of inquiry. He also formed a management-consulting firm, Transformational Technologies, that brought est ideas to corporate America, as well as to the Soviet Union, earning Erhard the title Guru to the Gulag.

Not all est alumni were satisfied with the est program. Several sued est in the 1980's, and psychiatrists published criticisms of est tactics. Increasingly, Erhard became the target of allegations and lawsuits pertaining to his personal life and his organization. He was criticized for running an authoritarian cult that humiliated participants, who suffered psychological traumas and personal injury. The most damaging blow of all against Erhard was a 1991 report on television's *60 Minutes* that used detailed testimony from members of Erhard's family, several former est staffers, and a housekeeper who accused him of domestic violence and the abuse of employees. At the same time, Erhard faced tax disputes involving his seventy-million-dollar-a-year business.

In the face of these difficulties, Erhard sold his intellectual properties to Landmark Forum in 1991 and left the United States. He subsequently was reported to have changed his name to Werner Spits and was purported to be living abroad, although no one seemed to know his exact whereabouts.

Impact

Werner Erhard left behind an astounding legacy. Millions of people were influenced by his work through participation in est workshops or by the cultural change that occurred as a result of his ideas. The personal growth industry continued to expand Erhard's original concepts. He was perhaps the most successful American guru, a super-salesman who combined popular philosophies and Eastern religions into an effective way to motivate people. The disappearance of the self-help messiah was disillusioning to many of his followers.

Further Reading

Bartley, W. W., III. *Werner Erhard, the Transformation of a Man: The Founding of Est*. New York: Clarkson N. Potter, 1978. A valuable distillation of the main ideas of the various disciplines Erhard immersed himself in before the creation of est.

Pressman, Steven. *Outrageous Betrayal: The Real Story of Werner Erhard from Est to Exile*. New York: St. Martin's Press, 1993. A San Francisco-based journalist's detailed and critical documentation of Erhard's ascent and fall.

Self, Jane. *"60 Minutes" and the Assassination of Werner Erhard*. Houston: Breakthru, 1992. Details a conspiracy theory about the fall of Erhard, claiming that it resulted from a premeditated plot to discredit Erhard by his former wife and his disgruntled former employees, as well as the Church of Scientology.

—Theodore M. Vestal

See also: L. Ron Hubbard.

Erik XIV

King of Sweden (r. 1560-1568)

Born: December 13, 1533; Stockholm, Sweden
Died: February 26, 1577; Örbyhus, Uppsala, Sweden
Also known as: Erik Vasa
Cause of notoriety: Erik XIV put to death many of the Swedish nobles who opposed him and was eventually killed by poisoning.
Active: 1560-1568
Locale: Sweden

Early Life

Prince Erik (EHR-ihk) was the son of King Gustav Vasa, under whose rule Sweden embraced Lutheranism, thus gaining ecclesiastical independence from the papacy and foreshadowing Sweden's rise as a modern nation. Erik ascended the throne as Erik XIV after his father died in 1560. Sweden's present-day monarchy—today one of the few remaining European monarchies—has always been at ease with modern ideas of civil society. This tradition extends back to Gustav Vasa, who was admired as a human being as well as a leader. Erik, however, quickly gained a reputation as a negative, menacing, and malicious ruler.

Political Career

Whereas the priority of Erik's father had been to defend Sweden against aggression from Catholic Europe, Erik wanted to expand Sweden's territory, which antagonized Protestant neighbors such as Denmark as well as the German barons of Estonia. The new Swedish standing army supported Erik's expansionist plans, but it was opposed by the nobility, which rallied around Gustav Vasa's son by his second marriage, Erik's half brother John. Erik was also opposed by the Sture family, which had supplied many ministers to the royal family over the previous few decades and functioned as the unofficial second family of Sweden.

In 1567, Erik took this rivalry to an unprecedented pitch, trying John for treason and personally strangling one of the Stures, Nils. Killing political opponents was accepted as a fact of political life in Europe of this era, but for the king himself to commit a murder was deemed offensive and sacrilegious.

Meanwhile, the war was not going well for Erik. The Swedish navy cracked the Danish stranglehold on the Baltic Sea, but border warfare in Norway, a Danish possession, was inconclusive, and Erik grew increasingly frustrated. His popularity descended sharply partially because of his reliance on Goran Persson, a low-born adviser whose hold over the king infuriated even those of the Swedish nobility not explicitly affiliated with the Stures. Though educated by some of the leading lights of Protestant theology, Perrson practiced astrology and was thought to have a sinister influence on the king's opinions. Presiding over the Konungens Nämnd (King's Court), Perrson executed many of Erik's opponents.

Erik's behavior became increasingly erratic, and many at the court judged him insane. His personal life, which included involvement with sundry mistresses, also provided fuel for resentment. Erik soon became too unstable to maintain even the semblance of kingship, and, while he was out of touch with affairs, Perrson was imprisoned, and John was released. In 1568, Erik partially recovered, reconciled with John, yet reinstated Perrson. Hatred of Erik had increased among many at court. When Erik married a woman deemed to be of inappropriately low estate, Karin Mansdotter, John rebelled and ousted Erik from the throne in September of 1568.

Erik XIV.

Impact

Erik XIV did not derail Sweden's rise to power in the North in the wake of the Reformation, so his long-term impact was not a decisive one. In the medium term, though, his pugnacious foreign policy did give institutional momentum to Sweden's standing army, which became a military force to be reckoned with in the following century, fortunately under more stable leadership.

Further Reading

Nordstrom, Byron J. *The History of Sweden*. Westport, Conn.: Greenwood Press, 2002. A historical survey that places the reign of Erik XIV in the context of early modern Sweden's political emergence.

Roberts, Michael. *The Early Vasas: A History of Sweden, 1523-1611*. New York: Cambridge University Press, 1986. The leading British historian of Sweden presents an intriguing and meticulous tableau of the period.

Strindberg, August. *The Vasa Trilogy: Master Olof, Gustav Vasa, Erik XIV*. Translated with an introduction by Walter Johnson. Seattle: University of Washington Press, 1966. Sweden's greatest dramatist has often had his historical drama underappreciated in the English-speaking world; here, he dramatizes the reign of Erik XIV in a vivid play that for the past hundred years has been most Swedes' introduction to the story of their demented former king.

—Nicholas Birns

See also: Cesare Borgia; Charles II; Ivan the Terrible.

Pablo Escobar

Colombian drug smuggler and trafficker

Born: January 12, 1949; Medellín, Colombia
Died: December 2, 1993; Medellín, Colombia
Also known as: Pablo Emilio Escobar Gaviria (full name)
Major offenses: Drug trafficking, bribery, murder, and bombings
Active: 1960's-1992
Locale: Colombia
Sentence: Turned himself in to the Colombian government in 1991; was jailed for a mandatory five-year sentence and guaranteed no extradition to the United States; escaped and was killed before he completed his sentence.

Early Life

Pablo Escobar (PAHB-loh ehs-KOH-bahr) grew up in Rionegro, a small town close to Medellín, Colombia. His family was not poor by Colombian standards and eventually moved to Envigado, a suburb of Medellín, where his father worked as a neighborhood watchman and his mother as a schoolteacher. Escobar did well in school, and his parents were well known in the community. However, the early 1960's in Colombia were similar to the counterculture movement in the United States occurring at the same time, and Escobar and his friends began rebelling, showing lack of respect for authority, and doing drugs. In Colombia, marijuana was potent and easily available. Escobar's dope smoking and rebelliousness eventually led him to drop out of school and begin his life of crime as a small-time gangster.

Criminal Career

Escobar's first true criminal activities are somewhat indefinite, but there is no doubt that he was adept at hustling. He entered the narcotics world in the 1960's, dealing marijuana and then moving to cocaine in the 1970's. Eventually, through his ruthless and murderous ways, Escobar would become the head of the notorious Medellín Cartel.

Escobar bribed everyone from police to judges and politicians and assassinated anyone who got in his way. His brutal but effective practice was known as *plata o plomo*, literally "money or lead," which meant that if one did not accept a bribe from Escobar, death by lead bullet was the outcome. Escobar was so influential that he was even voted into Colombia's congress as an alternate. He was responsible for many bombings, including that of Avianca flight 203 in 1989, and was allegedly behind the deaths of presidential candidates and justices of the Colombian Supreme Court in 1985. These callous murders were committed to maintain control of the drug trade and as a defense against his foremost competitors, the Cali Cartel. His methods, and Americans' cocaine habit, made Escobar the most powerful man in Colombia and one of the richest men in the world.

The Brother's View

Pablo Escobar's partner in his cocaine empire was his brother Roberto, nicknamed "El Orsito" (Little Bear). He was in charge of the cartel's finances. In 1992, he surrendered to the police and was in prison when Pablo, on the lam, was killed by Colombian special forces. In 2000, Roberto's book, titled *Mi hermano Pablo* (my brother Pablo), was published; it defended his brother as a loving family man who thought of himself as a Robin Hood, earning money from rich, corrupt North Americans and distributing it in his home region of Medellín.

"Pablo was a good brother to me," Roberto told an interviewer from *De Telegraaf*, a Web news site based in the Netherlands. "He was always kind and friendly. . . . His dream was to become president of Colombia." Roberto cites a specific case of his brother's concern for his compatriots. One day, while being driven in their heavily guarded limousine, the Escobar brothers saw people crowded into tiny huts near a garbage dump in Medellín. Vowing to change things, Pablo bought the area and built Barrio Pablo Escobar for the poor. His generosity endeared him to them.

In his book, Roberto is frank about the brothers' modus operandi. They suborned high-ranking politicians on the island of Aruba and in the nations of Suriname to get Dutch passports so that they could travel freely to establish contacts in the United States and Europe. Their intimidation and bribery of local Colombian officials and politicians are legendary for their extent and ferocity. Roberto even claims that they had connections with the administrations of former presidents Alberto Fujimori in Peru and Manuel Noriega in Panama.

Their use of deception was high-tech and innovative. They had a village built on wheels so that it could be rolled over an airfield to disguise it and the coca-leaf processing factory nearby. They also used submarines and a fleet of aircraft to move large shipments abroad.

Whatever Pablo's self-image as a Robin Hood and political leader, at heart he savored being a powerful gangster. According to his brother, his favorite possession was an antique American car that once belonged to Bonny and Clyde.

Source: Roberto Escobar, *Mi hermano Pablo* (Bogotá, Colombia: Quintero, 2000).

Money and Drugs

At the height of his power, Escobar was said to be the seventh richest man in the world. He owned twenty houses in and around the Medellín area as well as scores of vehicles, boats, planes, and helicopters. Escobar was a multibillionaire and used some of his money to help the poor. He built soccer stadiums, schools, hospitals, and even a whole neighborhood in Medellín—Barrio Pablo Escobar, which consisted of twenty-five hundred houses. It is said that he and his brother, Roberto Escobar, had bank accounts in excess of $24 billion.

This money was the payoff of smuggling cocaine to the United States, said to total roughly 80 tons monthly, using jet airplanes filled with as much as 10 tons of cocaine per flight. Escobar apparently had two remote-controlled submarines that he also used for cocaine transportation. Escobar and the Medellín Cartel had power over 80 percent of the world cocaine market.

Legal Action and Outcome

By the late 1980's, both the Colombian government and the citizenry were tired of violence. The government wanted to put Escobar away but feared the retaliation it would bring. The only way it could stop the violence was to make a deal with Escobar. Fearing extradition to the United States, in 1991, Escobar turned himself over to the Colombian government in an arrangement that had him serving a five-year sentence, in a "prison," La Catedral, which he had built in the hills in Envigado.

La Catedral, however, was no ordinary prison: It had a swimming pool, soccer field, big-screen televisions, and scores of drugs, alcohol, and women. Escobar frequently left La Catedral to visit shops or attend soccer games, nightclubs, and parties. After learning that Escobar was not adhering to the terms of his sentence, the Colombian government tried to move him to another prison, but he escaped.

Escobar became a wanted man. The Colombian and U.S. governments began to cooperate, and the U.S. Delta Force trained a specialized team put together by the Colombian government. The Search Bloc, as it was known, had the task of finding and capturing Escobar. A clandestine Central Intelligence Agency (CIA) surveillance team, known as Centra Spike, which used airborne equipment, also aided the Search Bloc in locating Escobar. However, another group, known as Los Pepes (People Persecuted by Pablo Escobar), were more threatening to Escobar because they were not tied to any government organization. Los Pepes, through their hunt for Escobar, were responsible for the deaths of more than three hundred of Escobar's partners, friends, and relatives, and the destruction of many of Escobar's properties. Although the U.S. and Colombian governments would never claim association with Los Pepes, this group was integral in the Search Bloc's efforts to find Escobar and in his final downfall.

After sixteen months of being on the run, Escobar's outlaw days came to an end on December 2, 1993. The Search Bloc, with help from Centra Spike, located him in a barrio in Medellín, and the ensuing gunfight that broke out on the Medellín rooftops, as Escobar tried to escape, claimed his life.

Impact

Pablo Escobar was not afraid to appear in public, and to some he was a hero. At the same time that he funneled drugs and destruction to a willing market, he also invested heavily in the people and businesses of Medellín, and in return, the people of Medellín kept watch on him and almost never cooperated with authorities about his whereabouts. However, to the Colombian government and U.S. authorities, Escobar was one of the world's greatest outlaws. Many years, many millions of dollars, and many lives were exhausted in the hunt for him.

Further Reading

Bowden, Mark. *Killing Pablo: The Hunt for the World's Greatest Outlaw*. New York: Atlantic Monthly Press, 2001. An account of the ruthless and violent life of Escobar and the story of how Colombia ended the hunt for the world's greatest outlaw.

Dudley, Steven. *Walking Ghosts: Murder and Guerrilla Politics in Colombia*. New York: Routledge, 2004. An account of the complex and bloody conflict that is Colombia's ongoing civil war between guerrillas, the government, and drug lords.

Kirk, Robin. *More Terrible than Death: Massacres, Drugs, and America's War in Colombia*. Cambridge, Mass.: Public Affairs, 2002. Brings to life the most brutal killing place in the Western Hemisphere and recounts the lives of many Colombians, the violence that has been ongoing for half a century, and the United States' sordid relationship to it.

—*Richard D. Hartley*

See also: Joe Colombo; Carmine Galante; Vito Genovese; Sammy Gravano; Manuel Noriega.

Ferdinand Walsin Esterhazy

French army officer and spy for Germany

Born: December 16, 1847; Paris, France
Died: May 21, 1923; Harpenden, Hertfordshire, England
Also known as: Marie-Charles-Ferdinand Walsin Esterhazy (full name)
Cause of notoriety: Esterhazy sold French military secrets to the Germans. Alfred Dreyfus, a Jewish officer in the French army, was falsely accused of Esterhazy's crime, which led to his wrongful conviction and exile and the start of the Dreyfus Affair, a political scandal that divided *fin-de-siècle* France.
Active: 1894-1899
Locale: Paris, France

Early Life

Marie-Charles-Ferdinand Walsin Esterhazy (EHS-tur-hah-zee) was the descendant of a military family that had seen many French-Hungarian marriages. He was a mediocre student and did not manage to qualify for the French military academy as his family had hoped. He took a roundabout route into the French army, volunteering to take part in the guarding of estates abroad and transferring into the French Foreign Legion. After some service in the Franco-Prussian War of 1870-1871, he was temporarily promoted. However, he was then restored to his previous rank, and the demotion left him embittered about the French military establishment.

Esterhazy was an inveterate gambler and womanizer, traits that led him to spend more money than he had. He gambled away his inheritance and tried to amend his fortunes by marriage to an heiress. Legal action on her family's part prevented him from being able to touch the bulk of her wealth and left him financially strapped.

Treasonous Career

Esterhazy decided to improve his financial situation in 1894 by offering to sell French military secrets to the Germans. He made contact with the German legation in Paris, which was instructed by the higher authorities in Berlin to deal with Esterhazy. He argued in subsequent accounts that he was serving as a double agent and that the military secrets he was offering were outdated. No one was able to authenticate his claims.

Information about the deal with the Germans came to the attention of the French intelligence forces, which proceeded to investigate. Suspicion was initially cast on a Jewish officer in the French army, Captain Alfred Dreyfus. Despite his otherwise blameless record and a family history of French patriotism, Dreyfus became the victim both of a general distrust of Jews in French service and of the presence within French intelligence of Hubert Joseph Henry, an old friend of Esterhazy. In what became known as the Dreyfus affair, Dreyfus was convicted, stripped of his military ranking, and exiled to Devil's Island. Esterhazy hoped that the efforts of Henry would keep him uninvolved in the case.

Henry did not, however, succeed to the position of head of French intelligence, and Georges Picquart, who did, rapidly came to the conclusion that Dreyfus was innocent. Various pieces of evidence led to suspicion of Esterhazy, but it seemed for a time that the French military establishment would protect him. Picquart, however, despite being sent abroad for further military service, was able to excite a great deal of public sympathy for Dreyfus, especially with the help of the novelist Émile Zola. Zola's 1898 letter to the French president—titled "J'accuse" ("I Accuse") and appearing on the front page of a Parisian daily—was a masterpiece of polemic. French society argued the rights and wrongs of the case against Dreyfus. After Henry was imprisoned and committed suicide in 1898, Esterhazy fled to England, where he spent the rest of his life and was never charged with the crime of treason.

Esterhazy's public image was further damaged in 1898 by the publication of a passage from a letter in which he spoke contemptuously of the French. Dreyfus was pardoned the next year and was fully exonerated in 1906 and readmitted into the army. Esterhazy continued to publish various accounts of his involvement from abroad. The die-hard anti-Dreyfusards, who had discounted the earlier evidence against Esterhazy, claimed that his confessional writings were the result of his being in the pay of an international Jewish conspiracy.

Impact

The Dreyfus affair was a watershed in French society, pitting conservative against liberal elements. It also gave liberal Jews in Europe cause for concern as the level of anti-Semitism became clearer and thereby spawned the birth of Zionism. Esterhazy himself did not appear to have been anti-Semitic and was perfectly happy interacting with Jews if he felt there was money to be made from it. The enormous consequences of Esterhazy's attempt at treason dwarf his importance on the stage of French history.

Further Reading

Bredin, Jean-Denis. *The Affair: The Case of Alfred Dreyfus*. Translated by Jeffrey Mehlman. New York: George Braziller, 1986. Remains the most complete account in English of the background and details of Esterhazy's story, leaving no doubt about his guilt.

Brennan, James F. *The Reflection of the Dreyfus Affair in the European Press, 1897-1899*. New York: Peter Lang, 1998. Presents thorough documentation of the crucial stages of the change in public opinion in France and elsewhere.

Burns, Michael, ed. *France and the Dreyfus Affair: A Documentary History*. New York: St. Martin's Press, 1999. Gives translations of the crucial documents that created the mystery and subsequently unraveled it.

Derfler, Leslie. *The Dreyfus Affair*. Westport, Conn.: Greenwood Press, 2002. Gives detailed chronology and provides a full account of the Dreyfus affair.

Forth, Christopher E. *The Dreyfus Affair and the Crisis of French Manhood*. Baltimore: Johns Hopkins University Press, 2004. Looks at the way *fin-de-siècle* concerns about degeneracy worked against Dreyfus originally and then against Esterhazy.

—*Thomas Drucker*

See also: Joseph Darnand; Léon Degrelle; Pierre Laval; Philippe Pétain; Vidkun Quisling; Tokyo Rose.

Billie Sol Estes

Texas swindler and con man

Born: January 10, 1925; near Clyde, Texas
Major offenses: Swindling, fraud, interstate transportation of securities taken by fraud, and conspiracy
Active: 1950's-1960's
Locale: West Texas and Washington, D.C.
Sentence: Eight years in prison for swindling, reversed by the U.S. Supreme Court; fifteen years for mail fraud and conspiracy, upheld by the Supreme Court

Early Life

Born in 1925 near Clyde, Texas, Billie Sol Estes (BIHL-ee sahl EHS-teez) grew up on his family farm. His financial genius was revealed at an early age. While still in high school, he borrowed thirty-five hundred dollars from a local bank to buy government surplus grain to sell for profit. After he married in 1946, he moved to his own farm near Pecos, Texas. When electricity costs for irrigation pumps rose excessively, he formed a company providing natural gas-powered pumps to farmers. Then Estes started a business distributing cheap anhydrous ammonia fertilizer. By 1952, he was a millionaire and was named one of the Outstanding Young Men of the Year by the U.S. Junior Chamber of Commerce.

Criminal Career

In the late 1950's, the U.S. Department of Agriculture established allotments and quotas for cotton farmers in order to control production. To offset resulting business losses, Estes turned his fertilizer business into a multimillion-dollar scam. In 1958 he owed $550,000 to Commercial Solvents of New York for fertilizer. Estes made a deal with the firm to defer the debt and lend him $350,000, plus $225,000 to build storage facilities. He used money from fertilizer sales to build grain storage facilities, then collected storage fees under federal price-support programs. He assigned the fees to Commercial Solvents to get more fertilizer for distribution. He undercut the prices of competitors until they went bankrupt, then bought the failed firms' assets cheaply and absorbed their businesses. In 1959-1961, Commercial Solvents collected $7,000,000 in grain storage fees paid to Estes by the federal government.

Estes, however, still owed Commercial Solvents $5,700,000. He devised another scheme involving anhydrous ammonia storage tanks. He persuaded a Texas tank manufacturer to let area farmers buy nonexistent tanks, sign bogus mortgages on them, then lease them to Estes. Estes collected $30 million in loans and storage fees, and used nonexistent storage tanks and fake mortgages as collateral to borrow an addtional $22 million from finance companies in Chicago and New York.

Still in debt in 1960, Estes began yet another scheme using cotton allotments and the eminent domain exception for farmers whose lands were taken by government for public projects. Estes persuaded displaced farmers in Texas, Oklahoma, Alabama, and Georgia to buy Texas farmland from him, transfer their cotton allotments to the new land, and lease the lands and allotments to Estes.

Billie Sol Estes, as depicted on the cover of Time *in 1962.* (Courtesy, Time, Inc.)

The lease default clause virtually ensured that Estes' initial fifty-dollar-per-acre lease payment would effectively transfer ownership of three thousand acres of land and allotments to Estes. He then used nonexistent cotton crops as collateral for bank loans and claimed subsidies from the government for growing and storing the nonexistent cotton. The Agriculture Department finally investigated the deals and found them to be fraudulent. Estes was fined for growing cotton under illegal allotments.

Throughout the 1950's and 1960's, Estes made large contributions to the Democrat Party and to candidates for office, including Vice President Lyndon B. Johnson. It was Estes' defeat in a Pecos school board election that led to the exposure of his massive fraud. A local newspaper, the *Independent*, had opposed Estes' candidacy; to get revenge, Estes established a rival paper. The *Independent* investigated Estes and publicly exposed his storage tank fraud. The finance companies immediately sent investigators to Pecos, as did the Federal Bureau of Investigation (FBI).

Legal Action and Outcome

On March 29, 1961, the FBI arrested Estes on charges of interstate transportation of bogus mortgages. He was released on bond under federal indictment for fraud and state indictment for theft. In March, 1962, the FBI arrested Estes on charges of fraud and theft in a multimillion-dollar swindle involving storage tanks, phony mortgages, and cotton allotments. On April 5, 1962, a federal grand jury indicted Estes and several associates on fifty-seven counts of fraud and conspiracy. Trials were scheduled in Tyler, Texas, for September 24 and in El Paso for December 10, 1962. Estes' trial in Tyler began on October 30, 1962; he was convicted of fraud and sentenced to eight years in prison. The U.S. Supreme Court reversed the conviction on June 7, 1965, because of pretrial publicity.

In the El Paso trial, Estes was charged with twenty-nine counts of mail fraud, interstate transportation of securities taken by fraud, and conspiracy. On December 11, 1962, the judge split the indictment, ordering trial to be held in Pecos on alleged violations that occurred in that jurisdiction. Trial in El Paso was set for March 11, 1963.

On March 28, 1963, the jury found Estes guilty of mail fraud and conspiracy. On April 16, 1963, he was sentenced to fifteen years' imprisonment. After the Supreme Court refused to hear his appeal on January 15, 1965, Estes was committed to the federal penitentiary at Ft. Leavenworth, Kansas, and served seven years. After his release on parole in 1983, Estes and his family settled in Brady, Texas.

Impact

Congressional investigations revealed widespread political complicity in the Billie Sol Estes scandals. The U.S. Department of Agriculture subsidy programs came under intense scrutiny. Three agriculture officials were forced to resign, as was Assistant Secretary of Labor Jerry Holleman. Secretary of Agriculture Orville Freeman, with his own career in jeopardy, created the first Office of Inspector General, which led to legislation in 1978 establishing twelve federal Offices of Inspectors General. The Estes scandals became so embarrassing for Democrats that President John F. Kennedy considered dropping Vice President Johnson from the ticket in 1964 because of his close association with Estes.

Further Reading

Barmash, Isadore. *Great Business Disasters: Swindlers, Burglars, and Frauds in American Industry.* Chicago: Playboy, 1972. Chapter 3 discusses Estes' initial success in agriculture and subsequent turn to illegal activities.

Estes, Pam. *Billie Sol: King of Texas Wheeler-Dealers.* Abilene, Tex.: Noble Craft Books, 1983. A daughter's sympathetic account of Estes' schemes.

Williams, Roger M. *The Super Crooks: A Rogue's Gallery of Famous Hustlers, Swindlers, and Thieves.* Chicago: Playboy Paperbacks, 1974. Places Estes among the foremost scoundrels of the twentieth century.

—Marguerite R. Plummer

See also: Frank W. Abagnale, Jr.; Billy Cannon; Janet Cooke; Tino De Angelis; Susanna Mildred Hill; Megan Louise Ireland; Clifford Irving; Victor Lustig; Arthur Orton; Alexandre Stavisky; Joseph Weil.

Ada Everleigh

American brothel owner

Born: February 15, 1876; near Louisville, Kentucky
Died: January 5, 1960; Roanoke, Virginia
Also known as: Ada Lester (maiden name)
Cause of notoriety: Everleigh amassed significant wealth by owning and operating two successful brothels before she and her sister Minna were put out of business by the Chicago mayor.
Active: 1898-1911
Locale: Omaha, Nebraska, and Chicago, Illinois

Early Life

Ada Everleigh (AYD-uh EHV-ehr-lee) was born Ada Lester near Louisville, Kentucky, in 1876. At the age of twenty-one, Ada left an abusive husband. At the same time, her sister, Minna, also left her husband. Both sisters joined a traveling acting troupe. However, after the death of their father in 1898, the sisters inherited thirty-five thousand dollars. They used this money to open a high-class brothel in Omaha, Nebraska.

Business Career

Once Ada and Minna opened their brothel in Nebraska, they adopted the surname of "Everleigh." This name came from their grandmother's habit of signing letters with "Everly Yours." Their brothel created a luxurious environment that offered food, champagne, and music, along with attractive women for the sisters' gentleman customers.

After two years in business, the sisters had doubled their profits and sold the brothel in Omaha. In 1900, they took over an existing brothel at 2131 Dearborn Street in Chicago, located in the city's red-light district known as the Levee. They transformed the building into separate parlors, each with a different name and theme. The Japanese Throne Room, the Rose Parlor, the Silver Parlor, and the Turkish Room were just some of the different parlors. One room, called the Gold Room, had a gold-leaf piano, gold-rimmed fishbowls, and gilt furniture. Each room had a $650 gold cuspidor and a fountain that sprayed perfumes. Men who demanded privacy could go upstairs to use one of the private rooms.

The clientele of the Everleigh Club consisted of industrialists, politicians, local elite, and occasionally a European noble or royal. Visitors had to have letters of introduction to be admitted and had to be able to afford the exorbitant prices charged by the Everleigh Club. The Everleigh sisters employed *cordon bleu* chefs, who prepared extensive meals for the gentleman customers, such as caviar, oysters, duck, and lobster. The girls employed by the Everleigh Club were chosen for their beauty, intelligence, communication skills, and mastery of the sexual arts. Gentlemen who left without spending at least fifty dollars were advised not to return.

For years, the Everleigh sisters counted on protection from corrupt aldermen, such as John "Bathhouse" Coughlin and Michael "Hinky Dink" Kenna. Over the years, the sisters paid them hundreds of thousands of dollars in bribes to keep their business operating.

Legal Action and Outcome

In 1910, a vice commission was appointed by Chicago's reformist mayor, Carter H. Harrison, Jr.. Because of the brochures circulating all over the Midwest touting the Everleigh Club, Mayor Harrison ordered the club to be shut down. Police Captain Patrick J. Harding ignored the direct order from the mayor, but in 1911, the Everleigh Club was padlocked and business was halted. The Everleigh sisters had amassed a personal fortune of cash, jewelry, stocks, and bonds. Ada and Minna took their

How to Be an Everleigh Girl

The Everleigh sisters provided high-class call girls to wealthy clients in a time when the run-of-the-mill prostitute was a kidnapped teenager, a shop girl, or a factory worker sold into white slavery. According to the Everleigh sisters, their girls had to meet high standards:

- **Eligibility requirements:** "To get in, a girl must have a pretty face and figure, must be in perfect health and must look well in evening clothes."
- **Behavior:** "Be polite and forget what you are here for. Gentlemen are only gentlemen when properly introduced. . . . The Everleigh Club is not for the rough element, the clerk on a holiday or a man without a check book."
- **Leave scruples at the door:** "If it weren't for married men, we couldn't have carried on at all, and if it weren't for cheating married women we could have made another million."

Source: Charles Washburn, *Come into My Parlor: A Biography of the Aristocratic Everleigh Sisters of Chicago* (New York: Bridgehead Books, 1934).

fortune and toured Europe, eventually returning to the United States; they resumed using their maiden name of Lester. The sisters lived briefly in Chicago after returning home and eventually settled in New York City

Impact

The Everleigh Club was one of the most luxurious and notorious houses of ill repute in the country, perhaps the impetus for the vice commission created by Mayor Harrison, which ultimately resulted in the closing of the club. The achievement of Ada and Minna Lester was significant in a time when women were generally considered less capable than men, particularly in running a business. Regardless of the illicit nature of that business, the Everleigh sisters succeeded in identifying a market—rich and socially well-placed men—and packaged a "product" that met the men's needs. Most houses of prostitution were tawdry, cheap, and dirty, catering to a lower class; the Everleigh Club elevated its services to an art and charged accordingly. The two women who headed it became wealthy on a par with their counterparts, the captains of industry in the Gilded Age.

Further Reading

Bukowski, D. *Big Bill Thompson, Chicago and the Politics of Image*. Chicago: University of Illinois Press, 1998. The story of a volatile Chicago leader and the characters who shaped Chicago during his era, including Ada and Minna Everleigh.

Schultz, R. L., and A. Hast. *Women Building Chicago, 1790-1990: A Biographical Dictionary*. Bloomington: Indiana University Press, 2001. This reference book includes individual biographies of the lives of more than four hundred women living in Chicago from 1790 to 1990, and is the result of ten years of research and writing.

Washburn, C. *Come into My Parlor: A Biography of the Aristocratic Everleigh Sisters of Chicago*. New York: Arno Press, 1974. A biography of the Everleigh sisters.

—*Carly M. Hilinski*

See also: Sydney Barrows; Heidi Fleiss.

Julius Evola

Italian right-wing fascist

Born: May 19, 1898; Rome, Italy
Died: June 11, 1974; Rome, Italy
Also known as: Giulio Cesare Andrea Evola (full name); Baron Giulio
Cause of notoriety: A nobleman who had ties to Benito Mussolini's Fascist Party, Evola was a prominent far-right thinker and an advocate of Italian Facsism. He became an important influence on modern fascist and neo-Nazi thinking.
Active: 1920's-1940's
Locale: Europe, mainly Italy

Early Life

Born in Rome to a family from Sicily, Giulio (Julius) Cesare Andrea Evola (EE-voh-lah) began his intellectual career as a member of the European avant-garde. After serving as an artillery officer during World War I, he became a painter associated with the Dada movement. He then became affiliated with the Futurist movement. Under the leadership of Filippo Tommaso Marinetti, the Italian Futurists connected their progressivism in art to an extreme nationalism that was one of the sources of Italian Fascism. In addition to art, Evola was interested in esoteric mystical philosophy. He developed the view that the most positive elements in European society were descendants of a race of people from the north, who had founded the civilization known as Atlantis.

Philosophy Career

Evola never became an active member of any political party, and his defenders have described him as an apolitical traditionalist with a mystical belief in the value of race and ethnicity. However, he did apparently approve of Italian Fascist leader Mussolini: Evola's writings during the 1930's and 1940's seem to have been intended to move fascists toward reverence for the ethnic group.

In 1937, Evola translated the anti-Semitic *Protocols of the Elders of Zion*, a forgery that purported to document a Jewish conspiracy for world domination. When Mussolini fell from power and Italy surrendered to the Allies in 1943, Evola moved to Germany and then to Vienna, Austria, where he worked as a researcher for the German state police, the Schutzstaffel (SS). While in Vienna, Evola was seriously wounded while fighting with the Germans against the invading Russians. For the rest of his life, he was paralyzed from the waist down.

After the war, Evola continued to write on esoteric subjects. In 1951, the Italian state brought charges against him of trying to bring back Fascism, a crime under Italian law. He was acquitted, in part because his activities were limited to writing, and he took no part in active political organizing. He continued to have a small but dedicated following, and his followers laid his ashes into a glacier on Mount Rosa, in the Pennine Alps, after his death.

Impact

Julius Evola—along with American philosopher Francis Parker Yockey, Chilean writer Miguel Serrano, and French-born esotericist Savitri Devi—is often cited as one of the chief sources of an esoteric form of Fascism or Nazism. With the rise of neo-Nazism in Europe and North America during the mid- to late twentieth century, Evola's influence grew among intellectually oriented far-rightists and racial supremacists. He was an influence on the Movimento Sociale Italiano (MSI), an Italian party frequently viewed as the heir to Mussolini's Fascists. Although many of Eviola's writings are obscure, they continued to be in print into the twenty-first century, both in English translation and in several other languages.

Further Reading

Drake, Richard H. "Julius Evola and the Ideological Origins of the Radical Right in Contemporary Italy." In *Political Violence and Terror: Motifs and Motivations*, edited by Peter H. Merkl. Berkeley: University of California Press, 1986. Chapter 2 discusses late twentieth century right-wing tendencies in Italian politics and describes Evola's role as intellectual founder of the extreme right in Italy after World War II.

Goodrick-Clarke, Nicholas. *Black Sun: Aryan Cults, Esoteric Nazism, and the Politics of Identity*. Albany: New York University Press, 2002. Explores the influence of mystical thinking on contemporary neo-Nazism and racist cults. The author considers Evola as one of the sources of fascism.

Griffin, Roger. *The Nature of Fascism*. New York: St. Martin's Press, 1991. A comprehensive work that examines movements throughout history and attempts to arrive at a definition of fascism. Griffin examines Evola as one of the major intellectual influences on the extreme New Right in European politics, which Griffin treats as a modern branch of fascism.

—Carl L. Bankston III

See also: Houston Stewart Chamberlain; Françoise Dior; Savitri Devi.

Judith Campbell Exner

American mistress to President John F. Kennedy

Born: January 11, 1934; New York, New York
Died: September 24, 1999; Duarte, California
Also known as: Judith Katherine Inmoor (birth name); Judith Campbell
Cause of notoriety: Exner was the reported paramour of President Kennedy and mobster Sam Giancana. Her relationships with the men, when revealed later, helped fuel rumors of Kennedy's involvement with the Mafia.
Active: 1960-1999
Locale: Washington, D.C., and California

Early Life

Judith Campbell Exner (EHKS-nuhr) grew up in Pacific Palisades, California. Her father was a German architect, and the family was financially comfortable. Exner's mother nearly died in an automobile accident when the girl was fourteen, which emotionally troubled the teen. She married actor William Campbell when she was eighteen, but the marriage ended in divorce in 1958.

Career

A fixture at Hollywood parties, Exner claimed she met Senator John F. Kennedy in 1960 and began a dating relationship with him. The alleged relationship lasted until 1962 and included a series of meetings between Kennedy and Exner both in the White House and in hotels. In 1960, Exner was introduced by singer Frank Sinatra to Chicago Mafia boss Sam Giancana. Exner's relationship with Giancana fueled speculation that she served as an intermediary between Giancana (and another organized crime figure named Johnny Roselli) and the president. Because of the conflicting stories and Exner's own changing version of events, it is difficult to know the real story.

Exner became widely known in 1975, when she testified before the Church Committee, a Senate select

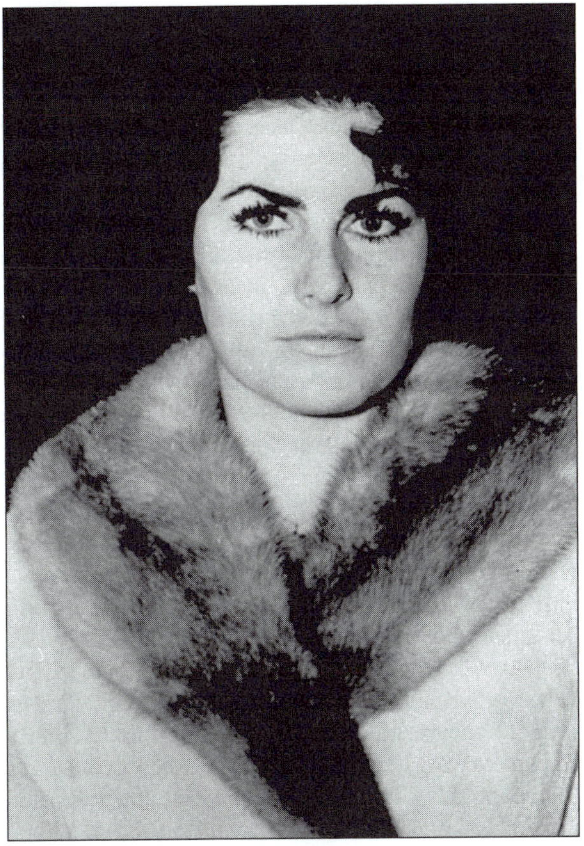

Judith Campbell Exner. (AP/Wide World Photos)

committee that was investigating Central Intelligence Agency assassination attempts. Both at the committee hearings and at a press conference soon after her testimony, Exner denied playing the part of liaison between Kennedy and Giancana. However, in her 1977 autobiography, *My Story*, and again in a 1988 magazine interview, she claimed that she did indeed arrange meetings between the president and the gangster and had engaged in sexual relationships with both men. Exner also claimed that she coordinated contact between Giancana, Roselli, and Kennedy in April, 1961, shortly after the aborted Bay of Pigs invasion. Moreover, Exner said that some of the documents she transported between the president and Giancana were related to a plot to assassinate Cuban leader Fidel Castro. Exner's personal accounts of her relationship to Kennedy also included the claim that she was impregnated by him and that she obtained an abortion. She claimed that shortly after the abortion, she ended her affair with Kennedy.

Exner then married golf professional Dan Exner in 1975 and resided in Orange County, California. In 1977, she published her autobiography, which contrasted both with claims she had made earlier and with those she made in later interviews with other authors. She was diagnosed with cancer in 1978 and died in Duarte, California, in September, 1999. She had one son, David Bohrer.

Impact

Not surprisingly, Kennedy advisers denied any relationship between Exner and the administration. However, Exner's story about her affair with Kennedy seemed to be supported in part by phone logs and her descriptions of White House décor. Her revelations about acting as a courier between Kennedy and the Mafia, as well as claims of transporting documents and cash between the president, Giancana, and Roselli, have been criticized for their lack of supporting evidence beyond her own testimony. Likewise, her claim of having been impregnated by Kennedy remained unsubstantiated.

It is doubtful that the extent of Exner's claims will ever be determined. Just as there is a tendency among some to glorify the mystique of Kennedy's life and his presidency, there are others who are critical of the late president and subscribe to theories that emphasize his darker motives and actions. Kennedy has assumed a larger-than-life meaning for many Americans, and the life of the slain president will always be open to public speculation.

Further Reading

Exner, Judith Campbell. *My Story*. New York: Grove Press, 1977. Exner's autobiography details her life history and her relationships with Giancana and Kennedy. Her story differs from revelations that she made in 1988 about her role as intermediary between the president and the Mafia.

Hersh, Seymour. *The Dark Side of Camelot*. Boston: Little, Brown, 1997. Investigative reporter Hersh publishes a critical account of Kennedy's political and personal life and tends to support Exner's later claims that she did play a role in Kennedy's involvement with the Mafia.

Wills, Garry. *The Kennedy Imprisonment*. Boston: Little, Brown, 1982. Historian Wills analyzes the historical and psychological elements of the Kennedy clan and examines their notions of success, power, and masculinity.

—David R. Champion

See also: Fidel Castro; Sam Giancana; Lee Harvey Oswald; Jack Ruby.

Albert B. Fall

American secretary of the interior (1921-1923)

Born: November 26, 1861; Frankfort, Kentucky
Died: November 30, 1944; El Paso, Texas
Also known as: Albert Bacon Fall (full name)
Major offense: Bribe taking
Active: 1921-1923
Locale: Washington, D.C.
Sentence: One year in prison, nine months served; $100,000 fine, later judicially forgiven

Early Life

After being educated in the rural schools of Franklin County, Kentucky, Albert B. Fall (fahl) studied law, was admitted to the bar in 1891, and began his practice in Las Cruces, New Mexico. He specialized in Mexican law but also developed interests in mining, land development, agriculture, and railroads. His experience in all these fields led him into politics. A Republican, he served in the territorial house of representatives, held several judicial positions, and during the Spanish-American War of 1898 was a captain in the First Territorial Infantry.

When New Mexico became a state in 1912, Fall was elected to the U.S. Senate, where he remained until 1921. He served on the Committee on Expenditures in the Department of Commerce and Labor and on the Committee on Geological Surveys. In each of these assignments, Fall revealed his opposition to government regulation of business and his strong belief in the infinite natural resources of the United States; both of these stances played major roles in his notoriety.

Political Career

In 1920, the Oil and Coal Land Leasing Bill was passed, opening mineral deposits on public land to private mining interests. On March 4, 1921, Warren G. Harding was inaugurated as president of the United States. On the same day, Fall resigned his seat in the Senate and was nominated for the post of secretary of the interior.

On May 10, 1921, Edwin Denby, the secretary of the Navy, was persuaded to transfer control of three Naval oil reserves to the Department of the Interior. The reserves were at Elk Hills and Buena Vista in California and at Teapot Dome, Wyoming. Some private mining would be allowed on the leases, but parts of the reserves would be preserved for naval emergencies. The opportunity for the secretary of the interior to manifest his opposition to government regulation of business was now in place.

In April and again in December of 1922, Secretary Fall secretly leased the reserves at Elk Hills and at Teapot Dome to two old friends, Harry F. Sinclair of the Mammoth Oil Company and Edward L. Doheny of the Pan-American Petroleum and Transport Company. There were no competitive bids for either transaction. Fall soon bought a large ranch in New Mexico. On January 24, 1924, although he had previously denied it, Doheny testified before a Senate committee that on November 30, 1921, he had "loaned" Fall $100,000. The money, in cash, was delivered in a satchel by an intermediary, Edward McLean. Later Senate testimony, in 1928, revealed that Fall had also accepted $233,000 in Liberty bonds from Sinclair delivered to Fall's son-in-law, M. T. Everhart.

The Wall Street Journal reported the Teapot Dome lease to the nation. Rumors of bribery soon swirled around Fall. President Harding, who was never implicated in the scandal, defended Fall, saying that he had approved the lease before it was finalized. Two U.S. senators, Republican Robert La Follette from Wisconsin and Democrat John Kendrick from Wyoming, soon de-

Albert B. Fall. (Library of Congress)

manded a Senate investigation. As a result of the unraveling scandal, Fall and Denby were forced to resign.

On October 15, 1923, hearings began before the Senate Committee on Public Lands and Surveys, led by Democratic senator Thomas Walsh from Montana. In January, 1924, the full Senate passed a resolution declaring that the leases had been obtained under fraudulent and corrupt conditions. In 1927, after years of judicial proceedings, the U.S. Supreme Court voided all oil leases to Sinclair and Doheny.

Legal Action and Outcome

The first criminal trial in the scandal began on November 22, 1926, in the Supreme Court of the District of Columbia. Fall and Doheny were tried for conspiracy to defraud the government but were acquitted on December 16. On March 17, 1927, Sinclair was found guilty only of contempt of Congress for refusing to answer questions.

On October 17, 1927, Fall and Sinclair went on trial for conspiracy. A mistrial was declared upon the revelation that Sinclair had hired a detective agency to keep the jury members under surveillance. This action brought Sinclair another contempt conviction in February, 1928. The second conspiracy trial for Sinclair began on April 9, but Fall was too ill to stand trial. Sinclair was acquitted but began a six-month prison sentence for contempt on May 6, 1929.

On October 7, 1929, Fall stood trial, again in the District of Columbia Supreme Court, for accepting a bribe from Doheny. He was found guilty on October 25, and on November 1 he was fined $100,000 and sentenced to one year in prison. In another bizarre twist, a jury in March, 1930, found Doheny innocent of bribing Fall.

Fall entered New Mexico State Prison on July 20, 1931, and served nine months of his sentence. He was not able to pay the $100,000 fine, and it was judicially forgiven. His last public speech was in April, 1934, at the dedication of the White Sands National Monument near Alamogordo, New Mexico. Fall died in El Paso, Texas, on November 30, 1944.

Impact

Albert B. Fall was the first U.S. cabinet member to be convicted of a felony committed while in office. The entire Teapot Dome episode revealed the constant danger of clashes between public service and the opportunities for personal gain. The phrase "fall guy" originated with Fall.

Further Reading

Davis, Margaret. *The Dark Side of Fortune: Triumph and Scandal in the Life of Oil Tycoon Edward L. Doheny.* Berkeley: University of California Press, 1998. An in-depth examination of the life of Doheny, especially his involvement with Fall and the oil leases. Reveals the dangers of unbridled capitalism in a climate of moral and ethical decline.

Noggle, Burl. *Teapot Dome: Oil and Politics in the 1920's.* Baton Rouge: Louisiana State University Press, 1962. Covers the basic scandal and the larger political and financial events of the time period. Includes photographs of all major figures of Teapot Dome.

Stratton, David. *Tempest over Teapot Dome: The Story of Albert B. Fall.* Norman: University of Oklahoma Press, 1998. Treats Fall as an individual, not as a natural-born crook or even as a typical politician of the era. Includes the role of friendship in paving the way for the scandal. Contains several photos of individuals and events in Fall's career.

—Glenn L. Swygart

See also: Simon Cameron.

Wallace Dodd Fard

Founder of the Nation of Islam

Born: February 25, 1891; New Zealand

Died: After 1934; place unknown

Also known as: Wallace Fard Muhammad; Master Fard Muhammad; Wallace Farad; Wallie D. Ford; Wallace Don Fard; F. Mohammed-Ali; Mohammed F. Ali

Cause of notoriety: Although Fard found trouble with the law throughout his life, he is best known as the founder of the Nation of Islam, a movement that stressed the betterment of African Americans and was criticized by some as a cult.

Active: 1913-1934

Locale: Los Angeles, California, and Detroit, Michigan

Early Life

Although Wallace Dodd Fard (WAHL-ihs dod fahrd) told his early supporters that he was born in Mecca, this lie became part of a lifetime of deception. Fard was actually born on February 25, 1891, in New Zealand. His father was Zared Fard, a New Zealander of East Indian descent. His mother, Beatrice, was white with roots in Britain. Fard likely took his mother's maiden name of Dodd. Scholars know little of his childhood, and while Fard claimed that he attended both Oxford University and the University of Southern California, neither university has records of his attendance.

Fard entered the United States illegally in 1913. He came through Canada and made his way first to the state of Washington and then to Oregon. Fard again lied about his place of birth on immigration documents, as well as about the place of birth of his parents. After his illegal entry into the United States, Fard likely spent several years in menial jobs until he moved to Southern California in 1919. There, Fard met and cohabited with a white woman named Hazel Barton. This relationship produced a son named Wallace Dodd Fard, Jr., with Fard's name on the birth certificate. Barton soon broke off the relationship after learning of his deceptions. Later, she legally changed their son's name to Wallace Max Ford.

Criminal Career

By 1916, Fard had begun using illegal drugs and regularly gambled. These habits later led to a criminal record and prison time during the 1920's and into the 1930's. On November 17, 1918, Los Angeles police arrested Fard and charged him with the beating of a restaurant diner. He was convicted of assault with a deadly weapon and received a suspended sentence. On January 20, 1926, Fard was arrested and charged with four counts of illegally possessing and selling alcohol. A month later, two undercover Los Angeles police officers arrested Fard on drug possession and drug dealing charges.

Nation of Islam

Despite his lengthy criminal career, Fard created the Nation of Islam, a movement that stressed black nationalism and strove to improve the social, economic, and spiritual conditions of African Americans. Fard initially named his organization the Allah Temple of Islam. Moving from California in 1933, Fard arrived in Detroit, Michigan. Variously described as a white man or an East Indian, he initially sold rugs and other products on street corners. Fard was arrested by Detroit police on an unknown charge on May 26, 1933, and he gave them one of his many aliases.

Fard began speaking from street corners in Detroit, denouncing whites and slowly building an audience of curious blacks. Fard claimed he had been born in Mecca and sent to the United States to arouse the long-suffering black masses. Fard was fearless in denouncing whites, and his supporters grew to include several thousand loyalists by 1934. Fard's antiwhite feelings date to sometime around 1916 or even earlier, soon after his arrival in the United States. He often referred to whites as devils and tricksters. Fard admired the Japanese and drew comparisons between Japan and the United States, blaming the latter for colonialism. Blacks in the United States, Fard believed, were often depressed and discriminated against by whites and needed leadership to overcome white racism. He was also critical of the Christian Church, describing the institution as a farce.

Fard's meetings with blacks attracted the attention of the Detroit police again. He was arrested for disturbing the peace, but he waived a jury trial; a municipal judge found him not guilty, saying that Fard had a right to free speech. Although the record does not reveal any additional arrests, local authorities and the Federal Bureau of Investigation (FBI) maintained their watchful vigil over Fard and his activities in Detroit.

Despite being repeatedly harassed by police, Fard witnessed his membership grow rapidly, especially within the working-class community. Perhaps because of the continuing problems with authorities, almost as

FBI File on Fard

An FBI memorandum from Special Agent Edwin O. Raudsep, dated March 8, 1965 (approximately three decades after Fard's death), rehearses the known facts about Fard at that time:

[Wallace] Dodd arrived in the United States from New Zealand in 1913, settled briefly in Portland, Oregon. He married but abandoned his wife and infant son. He lingered in the Seattle Area as Fred Dodd for a few months, then moved to Los Angeles and opened a restaurant at 803 W. Third Street as Wallace D. Ford. He was arrested for bootlegging in January, 1926; served a brief jail sentence (also as Wallace D. Ford)—identified on record as white.

On June 12, 1926, also as Ford, was sentenced to San Quentin for sale of narcotics at his restaurant; got 6-months to 6-years sentence—released from San Quentin May 27, 1929. Prison record lists him as Caucasian.

After release, went to Chicago, then to Detroit as a silk peddler. His customers were mostly Negro and he himself posed as a Negro. He prided himself as a biblical authority and mathematician.

When Elijah Muhammad (Poole) met him, he was passing himself off as a savior and claiming that he was born in Mecca and had arrived in the U.S. on July 4, 1930.

In 1933 there was a scandal revolving about the sect involving a "human sacrifice" which may or may not have been trumped up. At any rate, the leader was arrested May 25, 1933, under the name Fard with 8 other listed aliases (W. D. Farrad, Wallace Farad, Walt Farrad, Prof. Ford, etc.). The official report says Dodd admitted that his teachings were "strictly a racket" and he was "getting all the money out of it he could." He was ordered out of Detroit.

[In a] newspaper article which appeared in the *San Francisco Examiner* and the *Los Angeles Examiner* on July 28, 1963, reporter Ed Montgomery . . . claimed to have contacted Dodd's former common law wife. . . . According to this account, Dodd went to Chicago after leaving Detroit and became a traveling suit salesman for a mail order tailer [*sic*]. In this position he worked himself across the midwest and ultimately arrived in Los Angeles in the spring of 1934 in a new car and wearing flowing white robes. He tried to work out a reconciliation with the woman, but she would not agree to one. . . . He stayed in Los Angeles for two weeks, frequently visiting his son. Then he sold his car and boarded a ship bound for New Zealand where he said he would visit relatives.

On Sunday, February 28, 1965, Ed Montgomery wrote a rehash of the above in which he said the Muslims claim "police and San Quentin Prison records dating back to the early 1920's had been altered and that fingerprints identifying Farad as Dodd had been doctored." Elijah Mohummad [*sic*] said he would have posted $100,000 reward "for any person who could prove Farad and Dodd were one and the same person." Ten days later Muhammad's office in Chicago was advised Farad's common law wife and a blood releative were prepared to establish the truth of Farad's identity. The $100,000 never was placed in escrow and the matter was dropped forthwith.

suddenly as Fard appeared, he turned over the leadership mantle in June, 1934, to Elijah Muhammad, whom Fard had named as Minister of Islam. Reports of Fard's death following this period might not have been true. He allegedly reappeared in California and apparently spent six years there before boarding a ship to a unknown destination in 1940.

Impact

Wallace Dodd Fard laid the foundation for the Nation of Islam. Although he was not in Detroit to witness the growth of the Black Muslims under Elijah Muhammad, Fard nevertheless left an important legacy to the Black Muslims. Muhammad adopted Fard's virulent antiwhite position and maintained it for nearly twenty-five years. Muhammad also used photos and writings by Fard in his speeches as the Nation of Islam took shape.

Thus, despite his criminal background, Fard established a civil rights organization which became a viable alternative to the mainstream movement led by Dr. Martin Luther King, Jr., and others. In the twenty-first century, however, few Black Muslims mention Fard; instead, they credit Elijah Muhammad with founding the Nation of Islam.

Further Reading

Evanzz, Karl. *The Messenger: The Rise and Fall of Elijah Muhammad.* New York: Pantheon Books, 1999. This detailed work makes good use of FBI documents and previously unused sources to unravel the life of Elijah Muhammad. In doing so, it gives insight into the life of Fard and the development of the Nation of Islam.

Lee, Martha F. *Nation of Islam: An American Millenarian Movement.* Syracuse, N.Y.: Syracuse University

Press, 1996. Details the history of the Nation of Islam and the role of Fard.

Lincoln, C. Eric. *The Black Muslims in America*. Trenton, N.J.: Africa World Press, 1961. Lincoln's volume remains one of the most definitive accounts of the rise of the Nation of Islam.

Ogbar, Jeffrey. *Black Power: Radical Politics and African American Identity*. Baltimore: Johns Hopkins University Press, 2004. Ogbar provides a synthesis of previous works on Elijah Muhammad with good insight into his sometimes elusive personality.

—*Jackie R. Booker*

SEE ALSO: Elijah Muhammad; Father Divine.

FATHER DIVINE

African American religious leader and civil rights activist

BORN: c. 1882; Savannah, Georgia, Monkey Run section of Rockville, Maryland, or possibly Providence, Rhode Island

DIED: September 10, 1965; Gladwyne, Pennsylvania

ALSO KNOWN AS: George Baker (probable birth name); the Messenger; Anderson K. Baker; Major Jealous Devine; the Reverend Major Jealous Divine

CAUSE OF NOTORIETY: Father Divine founded a cultlike religion based on himself as a divine savior of humanity and insisted on racial integration at his group's gatherings and at any property that the organization bought.

ACTIVE: 1912-1965

LOCALE: Monkey Run, Rockville, Maryland; Baltimore; Georgia; Sayville, Long Island, New York; Harlem, New York; and Philadelphia, Pennsylvania

EARLY LIFE

The youngest son of a former slave, Father Divine (dih-VIN), then called George Baker, apparently spent his youth in the Deep South before migrating to Baltimore, Maryland, and then to New York City. Little, however, is known about his earliest years. At least one biographer, Jill Watts, believes that he was born and raised in a small town in Maryland.

PREACHING CAREER

After time spent with fellow itinerant preachers, Father Divine went his own way in 1912, gathering followers and declaring himself a god. He began his ministry in the Monkey Run area of Rockville, Maryland. Soon he and his followers founded their own household, or commune, where they shared resources and duties. He later moved to Baltimore and spent time as an itinerant preacher in the South, especially Georgia. After that, Father Divine based his ministry and household in Sayville, Long Island, New York, and then Harlem, New York, and finally settled in the Philadelphia area. At each of these locations in the Northeast, Divine acquired as much property as possible to house and provide jobs for followers.

Father Divine himself did not work outside his commune. Instead, he acted as the group's spiritual leader and used his business acumen to purchase and integrate properties, including hotels. He also used his connections and persuasion to find jobs for members and others who came to him for help. Later, extensions of the Peace Mission movement, as Father Divine's organization was called, sprung up in other parts of the country, as well as in Canada and several European countries. His theology was based on a range of influences, including New Thought, Roman Catholicism, Methodism, African American religious traditions, and "storefront" (small, independent, evangelical) Christianity. A sociologist visiting the group in 1937 reported seeing signs reading "Father Divine is God."

FEEDING THE MULTITUDES

Food played a major role in Father Divine's work and ministry. The primary ritual or liturgy of his group was a banquet, to which all were welcome. This ritual seems to have been designed to reinforce the idea of Father Divine as a Christlike savior. Reportedly six police officers had to be stationed outside Father Divine's headquarters to manage traffic flow during these events. The crowds and noise in 1931 prompted Father Divine's arrest, along with some followers, on a charge of "public nuisance." He was found guilty; a retrial was ordered but never occurred.

Father Divine would bless each banquet item by presenting the first serving. Followers and guests would sing, dance, and testify throughout the meal. When one group

Father Divine. (AP/Wide World Photos)

of diners finished, another group would enter. On Sundays at the height of Father Divine's popularity, there would be continuous seatings from early morning until late at night. During the Depression, these lavish feasts made a strong impression on guests. Father Divine is often credited with prefiguring the 1960's struggle for integration and civil rights. At these banquets, for example, both black and white diners were seated next to one another, breaking a racial taboo of the era.

Later, Father Divine and his followers established a cooperative farm system in Ulster County, New York, and dubbed it the Promised Land. These farms provided jobs for unemployed African Americans and other followers of Father Divine. The produce raised was sold at grocery stores operated by Peace Mission members in the city and served at restaurants, also run by members. Father Divine insisted that these enterprises operate at a very low profit margin so that the food and meals would be affordable even during the Depression. He encouraged followers to launch their own business enterprises, pay off bills, and avoid debt.

In short, the earthly or practical foci of Father Divine's ministry were to provide hope, employment, and economic stability for followers while promoting racial integration. While food held much symbolism for Father Divine and his followers, he did not develop guidelines for restricting or forbidding any food items, as is often the custom with religion. Rather, Father Divine wanted worshipers to enjoy all foods. He did, however, forbid the use of alcohol and tobacco. He also insisted on strict celibacy for members. These guidelines were all part of the International Modest Code, which Father Divine developed and followers were expected to live by.

As Father Divine aged, he became less active in the movement he had created, turning most operations over to his wife, the former Edna Rose Ritchings of Canada. He told followers that she was the reincarnation of his first wife, who had died years before. Both women were known as Mother Divine. Clergy who had formerly shunned Father Divine for his doctrines now sought his advice. Father Divine stopped making public statements in 1963 and died in 1965.

Impact

Father Divine was in many ways a larger-than-life figure, whose flamboyant personality tended to overshadow the positive work he accomplished during the Great Depression on behalf of the poor and oppressed. His controversial ministry and he himself were the targets of sensationalist press coverage throughout his life—which focused variously on his alleged sexual misconduct with young women (never proven), various criminal charges and lawsuits brought against him, and his cultlike following. However, his simple act of providing free or affordable meals for the hungry during the Depression had a profound impact on those directly fed and served as a symbol of hope for others, as did the economic empowerment of jobs and debt reduction. While several scholars and religious leaders have argued that Father Divine took advantage of his followers, many others believe that Father Divine's insistence on full racial integration within his banquets and businesses served as an important model for future civil rights workers.

Further Reading

Harris, Frederick C. *Something Within: Religion in African-American Political Activism*. New York: Oxford University Press, 2001. Examines how other African American leaders turned to religion as a political resource.

Watts, Jill. *God, Harlem, USA: The Father Divine Story*. Berkeley: University of California Press, 1992. Focuses on the theology underpinning Father Divine's work to uplift African Americans socially in the 1920's through 1940's.

Weisbrot, Robert. *Father Divine and the Struggle for Racial Equality*. Urbana: University of Illinois Press, 1983. Offers both basic biographical information and detailed analysis of Father Divine's efforts to further civil rights for African Americans, as well as his relationships with other groups having similar goals.

—*Elizabeth Jarnagin*

See also: Wallace Dodd Fard; Elijah Muhammad.

Orval E. Faubus

Arkansas governor (1955-1967) and segregationist

Born: January 7, 1910; Greasy Creek, Arkansas
Died: December 14, 1994; Conway, Arkansas
Also known as: Orval Eugene Faubus (full name)
Cause of notoriety: Governor of Arkansas during the American Civil Rights movement, Faubus tried to prevent Little Rock schools from being integrated.
Active: 1955-1967
Locale: United States, mainly Arkansas

Early Life

Orval E. Faubus (FAH-bus) was born in rural northwestern Arkansas. His father was an active member of the socialist party in the area. Faubus worked on small farms, taught school, and attended various high schools until the mid-1930's. He was elected to county offices in 1938 and 1940. During World War II he served in the Army overseas, rising to the rank of major. He wrote a column for his hometown paper during his time with General George Patton's Third Army. When he returned home he bought the paper and soon created alliances with the reform wing of the Democratic Party in Arkansas. He was appointed to an important state commission in the late 1940's and served as director of the state highway commission in 1951. In 1952, Faubus's political mentor Governor Sid McMath was defeated for a third term by a conservative east Arkansas judge named Francis Cherry.

Political Career

Faubus sought the Democratic nomination for governor of Arkansas in 1954, campaigning as a moderate. During the campaign he was smeared as communist sympathizer by some opponents but was nonetheless elected to his first two-year term in 1954. During his first term, civil rights issues became prominent throughout the South but were not largely present in Faubus's campaign for reelection in 1956.

Soon after reelection, Faubus faced the issue of integration head-on. A federal plan for desegregation of the Little Rock public schools was set to take effect in September of 1957. Under pressure from arch-segregationists, Faubus tried several tactics to delay the plan's implementation. When a federal judge rejected his means of delay, Faubus called upon the National Guard to prevent nine African American students from entering the Central High School building. On September 2, Faubus addressed the state, saying he feared violence if integration proceeded. The troops remained in Little Rock for three weeks while state and federal officials attempted to reach a compromise. Faubus met with President Dwight D. Eisenhower in an attempt to resolve the crisis, but the two found little upon which to agree. After being rebuffed by the federal courts, Faubus removed the National Guard and left the state for a governors' conference.

On September 23, the so-called Little Rock Nine were admitted to Central High. The following day, Eisenhower federalized the state guard and sent the 101st Airborne Division to Little Rock to maintain order. In 1958, Faubus attempted to close the Little Rock school district rather than have it integrated. A coalition of progressives and pro-business moderates eventually won control of the school board. Integration continued throughout Arkansas at a slow but steady pace through the 1950's and 1960's.

After Central High

After the Central High crisis, Faubus was hailed by some as a hero and castigated by many as a villain. However, he was reelected governor of Arkansas four more times, his being the longest reign in state history. He came closest to defeat in the 1964 general election, when moderate Republican Winthrop Rockefeller received more than 40 percent of the vote. Despite his reputation as a conservative, Faubus supported many populist causes throughout his career, including utility regulation and conservation of natural forestland. Faubus retired from the governor's mansion in 1967. Rockefeller's winning the election that year set the standard for a series of moderate to liberal governors during the following twenty years.

Faubus's life after 1967 was generally not prosperous. Moments of public notoriety came from personal problems and tragedies and attempted political comebacks. He sought—and lost—the nomination for governor in 1970 and 1974. In 1977, when Ernest Green, one of the Little Rock Nine, was named assistant U.S. secretary of labor, Faubus was working as a bank teller in Huntsville, Arkansas. He made a modest return to public life under Republican Governor Frank White when he was named director of the state's Veterans Bureau in 1981. Faubus lived the last years of the life in ill health and obscurity.

The Little Rock Nine

At the center of the political face-off in Little Rock, Arkansas, were nine students entering Central High School. Although not all nine finished school there, they all went on to become educated, influential citizens, in two cases rising high in government positions:

- **Melba Pattillo Beals** earned a master's degree in journalism from Columbia University. She wrote two books about her experience in Little Rock: *Warriors Don't Cry* (1995) and *White Is a State of Mind: A Memoir* (1999).
- **Minnijean Brown-Trickey** involved herself in civil rights efforts. President Bill Clinton appointed her deputy assistant secretary of the Department of the Interior.
- **Elizabeth Eckford** moved to St. Louis and became the first African American to work in a bank as something other than a janitor. She later returned to Little Rock and was a substitute teacher in the public schools.
- **Ernest Green** participated in the Civil Rights movement while at Michigan State University, where he earned a master of arts. He served as director of the Philip Randolph Education Fund and during President Jimmy Carter's administration as assistant secretary of labor.
- **Gloria Ray Karlmark** moved to the Netherlands and worked as an executive in a Dutch company and publisher of a computer magazine distributed throughout Europe.
- **Carlotta Walls Lanier** moved to Colorado and worked in real estate.
- **Thelma Mothershed-Wair** moved to Illinois, where despite a disabling heart condition, she volunteered in a program for abused women.
- **Terrence Roberts** completed a doctorate in psychology at Southern Illinois University and led a management consultant group that helped improve human relations in the workplace. He also served as the official desegregation consultant for the Little Rock school district.
- **Jefferson Thomas** moved to California and became an accountant for the U.S. Department of Defense.

In 1998, the nine received the Congressional Gold Medal, the highest award given by the federal legislative branch. It is awarded to those who perform an exceptional service to the national interest of the United States. The former classmates also sponsor the Little Rock Nine Foundation, which promotes justice and excellence in education for young people of color.

Impact

Orval E. Faubus became a symbol of southern resistance to federally enforced integration. He was named one of the ten most admired men in America in 1958 by a Gallup poll. Whether Faubus was a true believer or simply a political opportunist will never be completely known. He was never the fire-breathing orator other southern demagogues were, nor did he seek a place on the national stage like Alabama governor George Wallace. Indeed, after 1958 Faubus seemed to have no influence outside the state of Arkansas.

Further Reading

Bates, Daisy. *The Long Shadow of Little Rock*. 1962. Reprint. Fayetteville: University of Arkansas Press, 1987. This is the story of the Central High crisis from the perspective of the head of the state's National Association for the Advancement of Colored People.

Donovan, Timothy P., and Willard Gatewood, Jr., eds. *The Governors of Arkansas*. Fayetteville: University of Arkansas Press, 1981. This volume contains short biographies of all of Arkansas's governors to 1981.

Johnson, Ben F., III. *Arkansas in Modern America, 1930-1999*. Fayetteville: University of Arkansas Press, 2000. This volume concentrates on the times that led to the integration crisis and its impact.

Reed, Roy. *Faubus: The Life and Times of an American Prodigal*. Fayetteville: University of Arkansas Press, 1997. This is the definitive full-length biography of Faubus.

—Charles C. Howard

See also: Theodore G. Bilbo; George C. Wallace.

Guy Fawkes

English conspirator

Born: April 15, 1570; Stonegate, York, England
Died: January 31, 1606; Westminster, England
Also known as: Guido Faukes; John Johnson
Major offense: Complicity in the treasonous Gunpowder Plot to blow up the English king and Parliament
Active: November 4-5, 1605
Locale: Westminster Palace, near London, England
Sentence: Death by hanging, drawing, and quartering

Early Life

Born in Stonegate, York, England, in 1570 to Edward Fawkes and his wife Edith Blake, Guy Fawkes (gi fahks) was baptized Anglican and, as a youth, attended St. Peter's School. When he was about sixteen years old, he converted to Roman Catholicism, a religion whose adherents were discriminated against in Elizabethan England. This discrimination led him to leave England for Europe in 1593. He joined the army of the Catholic Spanish, who were fighting against the Calvinist-led Dutch United Provinces. Fawkes returned to England around the time that Queen Elizabeth I died and King James VI of Scotland was crowned James I of England in 1603. Because James had a Catholic mother, many expected him to treat Catholics better than had Elizabeth. By spring of 1604, this misconception had faded, and a plot by a group of Catholics against the king and Protestant Parliament developed.

Criminal Career

The conspirators eventually numbered thirteen and were allegedly encouraged by certain English Jesuit priests. Their plan was to blow up the Parliament building on the day of the State Opening of Parliament, which would find the king, his family, and all of Parliament gathered there together. The next step somehow involved a rising of the Catholic gentry in England and Wales. In March, 1605, the group rented a storeroom beneath the House of Lords' chambers in the Palace of Westminster, part of the Houses of Parliament, which they filled with thirty-six large barrels of gunpowder.

As a military man with much experience in explosives, Fawkes was placed in charge of the detonation. Several days before the opening, one of the plotters sent a letter to Lord Monteagle, warning him to stay away and keep other prominent Catholics from certain death. Monteagle passed the letter on to the secretary of state. The conspirators learned about the letter and had Fawkes check on the gunpowder in late October. The gunpowder was undisturbed, so they determined to stick to their plan. On the night of November 4, hours before the opening, royal soldiers inspected the rooms beneath the palace and discovered the explosives, along with Fawkes, who identified himself as John Johnson. He was arrested and jailed.

Guy Fawkes (center). (Library of Congress)

Fawkes in Rhyme

The British have dozens of traditional ditties for singing around the bonfires on Guy Fawkes Night. Here is one popular example:

Remember, remember, the 5th of November
The Gunpowder Treason and plot;
I know of no reason why Gunpowder Treason
Should ever be forgot.
Guy Fawkes, Guy Fawkes, 'twas his intent.
To blow up the King and the Parliament.
Three score barrels of powder below.
Poor old England to overthrow.
By God's providence he was catch'd,
With a dark lantern and burning match
Holloa boys, Holloa boys, let the bells ring
Holloa boys, Holloa boys, God save the King!
Hip hip Hoorah! Hip hip Hoorah!

Legal Action and Outcome

With royal assent, Fawkes was tortured to reveal the names of his co-conspirators. In a confession dated November 8 he named some of these men, and in a fuller confession dated the following day he named more. All were captured or killed, and the survivors were imprisoned and interrogated further, perhaps under torture, over the following three months in the Tower of London. The trial for treason took place in Westminster Hall on January 27, 1606. All were condemned to death. Fawkes was hanged, drawn, and quartered in the Old Palace yard outside of Westminster Hall on January 31.

Impact

Although discovery of the plot did not lead to an intensification of anti-Catholic policies in England beyond a new and mandatory oath of allegiance, it certainly strengthened anti-Catholic sentiment. The Parliamentary Party in the civil struggles of the seventeenth century used the plot and Guy Fawkes as tools against the relatively pro-Catholic royalists. The anniversary of the capture of Fawkes on November 5 became a national holiday on which the pope, and later Fawkes, is burned in effigy amid displays of fireworks. The word "guy" entered the English language, first as a synonym for a grotesque-appearing man, one who looks like the effigy, and later simply for a man.

Further Reading

Fraser, Antonia. *Faith and Treason: The Story of the Gunpowder Plot*. New York: Anchor, 1997. Though written by a novelist, this work is quite analytical and carefully weighs the testimony about the plot that was derived from the torturing of the participants.

Nicholls, Mark. *Investigating the Gunpowder Plot*. New York: Manchester University Press, 1991. Critical and analytical overview of the plot, the men implicated, and the evidence presented against them.

Travers, James. *Gunpowder: The Players Behind the Plot*. London: National Archives, 2005. Emphasizes the individuals accused of the conspiracy and the reliability of the evidence presented against them.

—Joseph P. Byrne

See also: Titus Oates; Miles Sindercombe.

John Felton

British assassin

Born: c. 1595; Suffolk, England
Died: November 28, 1628; London, England
Major offense: Assassination of George Villiers, first duke of Buckingham
Active: August 23, 1628
Locale: Portsmouth, England
Sentence: Death by hanging

Early Life

John Felton (FEHL-tuhn) was born about 1595 in Suffolk, England, to Thomas Felton and Eleanor (née Wright) Felton, the daughter of William Wright, mayor of Durham. The family, though related to the earl and countess of Arundel, were impoverished gentry. The elder Felton was employed as a hunter of recusants but lost his office after a critical report from a Roman Catholic clerk working under him, Henry Spiller; imprisoned for a debt owed to Spiller, he died in Fleet Prison. His son Edmond accused Spiller of having had Thomas Felton poisoned. Eleanor Felton received a state pension, but the episode was the ruin of the family. As a result, John was obliged to seek a living as a professional soldier. He served in the United Provinces, participated in the failed attack on the Spanish port of Cadiz in 1625, and, after service in Ireland, took part in the unsuccessful attempt to lift the siege of the Isle of Rhe in 1627.

Criminal Career

Felton had sought a captaincy for the expedition to the Isle of Rhe, allegedly telling the campaign's commander, George Villiers, the duke of Buckingham, that he could not live without the position. Buckingham's retort, according to Edward Hyde, the first earl of Clarendon, in *The Lord Clarendon's History of the Grand Rebellion Compleated* (1715), was that he would then have to hang. To add insult to this injury, Buckingham himself owed Felton 180 pounds in back pay.

Felton apparently brooded on his greivances and slights. He had inherited his father's dislike of Catholics, and his Protestant zeal was encouraged by his service against Spain and France. Buckingham, on the other hand, as the royal favorite both of James I and his son Charles I, was popularly regarded as a supporter of the Catholic faction at court, which included members of his own family. Buckingham, as lord admiral, was blamed by the public for the failures at Cadiz and Rhe, which Felton had witnessed at first hand. Finally, he was believed to have been James's lover, and his relationship with Charles was considered suspect at best. There is evidence that Felton's bid for a commission had been thwarted by one of the duke's retainers, Sir Henry Hungate, whom he allegedly assaulted after discovering his homosexuality.

By 1628, Buckingham was not merely Felton's obsession but also that of many politicians. The Parliament of 1626 attempted to impeach him, as did the Parliament of 1628, which called upon Charles to remove him from office. Verse libels circulated widely, linking Buckingham's alleged crypto-Catholicism and homosexuality to charges that he was trying to undermine true religion and the constitutional balance between king and subject in order to erect a Spanish-style tyranny in church and state. The duke's astrologer was attacked in the streets, and predictions of the duke's assassination were freely aired.

In this atmosphere, Felton slowly came to regard himself as a divinely chosen instrument of England's re-

George Villiers.

demption. As Felton told his examiners (according to William Sanderson's *A Compleat History of the Life and Raigne of King Charles*, 1658), after hearing a sermon in which "the preacher spake in justification of every man in a good cause to be judge and executioner of sin," he determined that he had been called upon to do the Lord's work. With money borrowed from his mother, he bought a dagger and set out from London to Portsmouth, where Buckingham was preparing a new expedition to relieve the French Huguenots besieged at La Rochelle. Accosting the duke in the midst of a crowd, Felton stabbed him to death on August 23.

Legal Action and Outcome

Felton intially eluded capture but was taken later that day after revealing himself. He was greeted as a hero by crowds on his way to imprisonment in the Tower of London, and celebratory bonfires were lit in his honor. Arraigned and convicted at the King's Bar on November 27, he was hanged before a large and clearly sympathetic crowd the next day. The earl and countess of Arundel gave him money to pay for a winding-sheet and to make the traditional distribution at his execution.

Impact

John Felton remained a popular hero, and verse encomiums likened him to the tyrannicides of Hebrew and classical antiquity. His name was a byword for popular liberty well into the eighteenth century. Supporters described him as steadfast during his imprisonment and royal apologists as repentant. At his execution, Felton prayed for the reconciliation of king and Parliament but also asked forgiveness of Buckingham's widow. The latter was unmoved, and at her instance his corpse was returned to Portsmouth and hung in chains.

Further Reading

Holstun, James. *Ehud's Dagger: Class Struggle in the English Revolution.* London: Verso, 2000. A work that sets Felton's life and career in terms of a general reading of the resistance to absolutism and the development of class consciousness in early Stuart England.

Lockyer, Roger. *Buckingham: The Life and Political Career of George Villiers, First Duke of Buckingham, 1592-1628.* London: Longman, 1981. The standard modern biography of Felton's victim, which sets Buckingham in the context of his time.

Raylor, Timothy. "Providence and Technology in the English Civil War: Edmond Felton and His Engine." *Renaissance Studies* 7, no. 4 (1993). Contains valuable biographical details on Felton and his family.

—*Robert Zaller*

See also: John Bellingham; Jacques Clément; Charlotte Corday; Guy Fawkes; Balthasar Gérard; Jack Ketch; François Ravaillac; Miles Sindercombe.

Giuseppe Fieschi

Corsican adventurer and criminal

Born: December 3, 1790; Murato, Corsica, France
Died: February 19, 1836; Paris, France
Also known as: Giuseppe Marco Fieschi (full name); Giuseppe Maria Fieschi; Joseph Marie Fieschi
Major offenses: Conspiracy to kill King Louis-Philippe of France, theft, and forgery
Active: July 28, 1835
Locale: France
Sentence: Ten years of imprisonment for theft and forgery; death by guillotine for assassination conspiracy

Early Life

Giuseppe Fieschi (zhyoo-SEHP-eh FYAY-skee) was born in Murato, Corsica, France, and baptized under the name Joseph Marie on December 3, 1790, son of Louis and Marie Fieschi. His birth date is not registered and, like his father, he was a shepherd. From an early age, he became an adventurer. At age eighteen, he joined the army with the Corsican Legion of the Kingdom of Naples and became a royal guard of Joachim Murat (1767-1815), whom the Corsican-born Napoleon Bonaparte had made king of Naples in 1808.

Criminal Career

Fieschi served Murat, who was married to Napoleon's sister Carolina, in the war campaigns of 1812 and 1814. When Murat was deposed, Fieschi followed him, serving as a spy for Ferdinand IV, who had ascended the Bourbon throne. In fact, when Murat tried to land in Pizzo,

In this 1836 political print, King Louis Philippe stands by an overturned chest from which spills a picture of Giuseppe Fieschi along with statements of France's debt. At right are American officers with a chest full of money. (Library of Congress)

Calabria, on September 28, 1815, in order to regain the kingdom, Fieschi had apparently betrayed him. Murat was caught, court-martialed, and shot to death on October 13, 1815. In the meantime, Fieschi and all the French troops were sent back to France and held prisoners at Fort Lamagne in Toulon. After being acquitted, Fieschi was sent back to Corsica, where he engaged in criminal activities such as livestock theft and forgery. He was condemned to ten years of imprisonment for his crimes and served his sentence in the prison of Embrun.

After 1826, Fieschi began an errant life, engaging mostly in criminal activities and sporadic employment. He arrived in Paris after the revolution of 1830 and passed himself as a political victim or refugee by means of forged papers and false documentation; he managed to obtain a pension of five hundred francs. He even had himself hired as a low-ranking officer in a company of veterans working as prison guards in Poissy. He then obtained similar employment in Paris by fraudulent means until he was caught, denounced, tried, and lost everything. Bent on revenge, he took up residency near the Boulevard du Temple, in the heart of the city.

At this time, he began his association with an apothecary named Pierre-Théodore-Florentine Pepin and a saddlemaker named Pierre Morey, both revolutionaries and members of the Société des Droits de l'Homme (Society of the Rights of Men). Fieschi concocted an "infernal machine," which was made of twenty-four gun barrels tied together, placed on a tripedal, and set to be exploded all at the same time. He fired his machine from a window on July 28, 1835, at King Louis-Philippe as the king was passing by with his escort on his way to the Bastille for the commemoration of the July, 1830, revolutionary events. The king, who was accompanied by his three sons and his entourage, was grazed in the head by a bullet but remained miraculously unhurt. However, several horses, including that of the king, and seventeen people were killed. Édouard-Adolphe Mortier (1768-1835), the notable French marshal, also died.

Legal Action and Outcome

Fieschi himself was severely wounded in the attack but managed to escape; he was eventually caught by officers who traced his bloodstains. He received excellent medical treatment so that he could be interrogated and tried. His trial lasted from January 30 to February 15, 1816. During the proceedings, he named his co-conspirators, which included Pepin and Morey, in a move that he felt might grant him a pardon. However, Fieschi was executed with Pepin and Moré on February 19, 1836. It is said that Fieschi was an unrepentant charlatan until the very end.

Impact

Giuseppe Fieschi was not without sympathizers, especially within the ranks of the revolutionaries who were opposed to the monarchy. During the same year that Fieschi carried out his assassination attempt, the police discovered at least seven more plots against the life of King Louis-Philippe. During Fieschi's time, Paris had become a refuge for all kind of exiles from Italy, Poland, Ireland, Germany, and Hungary, and many immigrants were opposed to absolutism. Even though other rulers of Europe labeled Louis-Philippe the "king of the barricades," many exiles and even French citizens advocated for self-determination against absolutism. Thus, the climate was one of potential violence against the rulers.

Further Reading

Du Camp, Maxime. *Les Ancêtres de la Commune: L'Attentat Fieschi*. Paris: Charpentier, 1877. A thorough historical account of the murderous attempt of Fieschi and his accomplices in the light of their criminal history and subversive intent. In French.

Fieschi, Giuseppe Marco. *Procès de Fieschi et de ses complices: Devant la Cour des pairs, précédé des faits préliminaires et de l'acte d'accusation*. Paris: A. E. Bourdin, 1836. The official acts and account of the trial and verdict of Fieschi and his accomplices by the Cour des Pairs (the Court of Peers). In French.

Howarth, T. E. B. *Citizen-King: The Life of Louis-Philippe*. London: Eyre & Spottiswoode, 1961. Provides good historical context for the period in which Fieschi grew up and committed his crimes.

Thureau-Dangin, Paul. *Histore de la monarchie de Juillet*. Paris: E. Noin, 1884-1892. A comprehensive history (seven volumes) of the Restoration period from the July revolution to the abdication of Louis-Philippe. The Fieschi affair is narrated in volume 2, chapter 12, pp. 312-318. In French.

—Giuseppe Di Scipio

See also: John Bellingham; Sante Jeronimo Caserio; Leon Czolgosz; Charles Julius Guiteau; Richard Lawrence.

Albert Fish

American child molester, serial killer, and cannibal

Born: May 19, 1870; Washington, D.C.

Died: January 16, 1936; Sing Sing Correctional Facility, Ossining, New York

Also known as: Hamilton Fish (birth name); Frank Howard; Robert Hayden; Boogey Man; Gray Man; Moon Maniac; Brooklyn Vampire; Werewolf of Wisteria

Major offenses: Murder of eleven-year-old Grace Budd; additional child kidnappings and murders

Active: June 3, 1928-February 11, 1927

Locale: New York City; claimed to have attacked children in twenty-three states

Sentence: Death by electrocution for first-degree murder

Early Life

The father of Hamilton Fish (fihsh), who claimed descent from "Revolutionary stock," was seventy-five years old at Hamilton's birth. When the boy was five, his father died, and his mother sent Albert to St. John's Orphanage, Washington, D.C. There Fish changed his name to Albert; he also began stammering and wetting the bed. Worse, his sadomasochism flowered: "I saw so many boys whipped," he said, "it ruined my mind."

Fish may have been a homosexual prostitute in his teens. At fifteen, he left school to work in a grocery store; soon after, he was apprenticed to a painter and decorator. Fish married an eighteen-year-old woman, Anna, when he was twenty-eight. They had six children, but his wife left him after almost twenty years of marriage in 1917. They were never divorced; Fish raised the children and was a good father. He had three subsequent marriages, short and bigamous, and played quasi-sexual games with a stepdaughter, Mary.

Albert Fish. (AP/Wide World Photos)

were for passing a bad check, embezzling, and continually writing graphic, sadomasochistic letters to women.

His most famous victim was eleven-year-old Grace Budd. Fish presented himself as a wealthy farmer named Frank Howard and received permission to take Grace to a birthday party. When she did not return, all the papers covered her kidnapping. Years later, Fish was caught after he sent a repulsive, detailed letter to Grace's parents, mailed November 11, 1934, and King traced the stationery. Grace's bones were found behind Wisteria Cottage, an abandoned house in Westchester County. Fish then confessed to eating parts of Budd's body as well as to beating, killing, and cannibalizing Billy Gaffney, age four, and to killing Francis McDonnell, age eight.

Legal Action and Outcome

After his arrest, Fish said he no longer cared for life yet subtly appealed to officials and reporters for sympathy. Tried in March, 1935, Fish pleaded not guilty by reason

Criminal Career

The entirety of Fish's crimes may never be known. Detective William King, who tirelessly tracked down Fish, suspected Fish murdered four children in New York City alone; psychiatrist Frederic Wertham believed Fish killed at least five, and the police estimated he killed between eight and fifteen children.

However, Fish attacked perhaps hundreds of children. After Anna left him, he worked around the country; he was never arrested but often driven off by close calls or attention by police or locals. Many of his victims were poor, including African Americans, about whom he said the police were less apt to care. His activities with them, as with himself, involved inflicting pain more than sexual acts, though Fish's gratification was clearly sexual. Influenced by a religious mania, he became obsessed with castrating boys; in St. Louis in 1911, he left one boy bleeding and fled the city. However, Fish's six arrests by 1930, resulting in one prison term and two mental-hospital stays,

A Tell-Tale Letter

Albert Fish was finally caught after he mailed the following anonymous letter to Grace Budd's parents on November 11, 1934, and the authorities traced the stationery:

My dear Mrs. Budd:

In 1894 a friend of mine shipped as a deck hand on the Steamer Tacoma, Capt. John Davis. They sailed from San Francisco for Hong Kong, China. On arriving there he and two others went ashore and got drunk. When they returned the boat was gone. At that time there was famine in China. Meat of any kind was from $1-3 per pound. So great was the suffering among the very poor that all children under 12 were sold for food in order to keep others from starving. A boy or girl under 14 was not safe in the street. You could go in any shop and ask for steak-chops-or stew meat. Part of the naked body of a boy or girl would be brought out and just what you wanted cut from it. A boy or girl's behind which is the sweetest part of the body and sold as veal cutlet brought the highest price. John stayed there so long he acquired a taste for human flesh. On his return to N.Y. he stole two boys, one 7 and one 11. Took them to his home stripped them naked tied them in a closet. Then burned everything they had on. . . . [They were] roasted in the oven . . . boiled, broiled, fried and stewed. . . .

At that time, I was living at 409 E 100 St. near-right side. He told me so often how good human flesh was I made up my mind to taste it. On Sunday June the 3, 1928 I called on you at 406 W 15 St. Brought you pot cheese-strawberries. We had lunch. Grace sat in my lap and kissed me. I made up my mind to eat her. On the pretense of taking her to a party. You said yes she could go. I took her to an empty house in Westchester I had already picked out. . . . How she did kick-bite and scratch. I choked her to death, then cut her in small pieces so I could take my meat to my rooms. Cook and eat it. How sweet and tender her little ass was roasted in the oven. It took me 9 days to eat her entire body. . . .

of insanity. He was convicted; some jurors thought Fish was insane but should be executed anyway. An appeals trial and plea to the governor both failed, and Fish was electrocuted.

Impact

Albert Fish is known primarily for his bizarre and extreme sexual appetite and for breaking the primal taboo against cannibalism. He also represents the transition of American society from one of trust to one in which strangers became feared. His missing victims, who disappeared around the time aviator Charles Lindbergh's baby was kidnapped, fueled widespread fear of kidnapping and hence promoted changes in law enforcement.

Further Reading

"Albert Fish." *World of Criminal Justice*. 2 vols. Farmington Hills, Mich.: Gale Group, 2002. Short, accurate summary of names, dates, and impact of Fish's crimes.

Brottman, Nikita. *Meat Is Murder! An Illustrated Guide to Cannibal Culture*. New York: Creation, 2001. Good exploration of motives for quasi-sexual cannibalism; erroneously implies that Fish had intercourse with Grace Budd.

Martingale, Moira. *Cannibal Killers*. New York: Carroll & Graf, 1994. Slightly inaccurate but provides insight into Fish's crimes and mental abnormalities.

Schechter, Harold. *Deranged*. New York: Pocket Books, 1990. Well-researched coverage of the acts, police investigation, trial, and social context.

Wertham, Frederic. *The Show of Violence*. New York: Doubleday, 1949. A source from which many writers draw, based on interviews with Fish.

—Bernadette Lynn Bosky

See also: Elizabeth Báthory; Kenneth Bianchi; Angelo Buono, Jr.; Richard Allen Davis; John Wayne Gacy; Gilles de Rais.

Jim Fisk

American financier

Born: April 1, 1834; Pownal, near Bennington, Vermont

Died: January 7, 1872; New York, New York

Also known as: James Fisk, Jr. (full name); Big Jim; Diamond Jim; Jubilee Jim; Barnum of Wall Street

Cause of notoriety: Fisk was a major player in stock speculation and manipulation during the mid-nineteenth century. He gained an international reputation for his flamboyant personality and lifestyle.

Active: 1866-1872

Locale: New York, New York

Early Life

The mother of Jim Fisk (fihsk) died when he was an infant, and his father, James Fisk, Sr., remarried, to Love B. Ryan. The family moved to Brattleboro in southern Vermont, where his father was a country peddler. Other than mathematics, Fisk was not interested in obtaining an education. He dropped out of school and became a hotel waiter until assuming his father's profession of peddling wares. The elder Fisk later suffered a nervous breakdown and spent the remainder of his years in a mental institution. As a young man, Fisk joined the circus as an animal trainer and ticket salesman for Isaac Amberg's circus. In 1854, he married Lucy B. Moore of Springfield, Massachusetts. The couple's union lasted seventeen years despite Fisk's repeated infidelity.

Business Career

Fisk and his wife eventually moved to Boston. He became a salesman for a dry goods firm. During the American Civil War (1861-1865), he earned a fortune by managing army contracts for Jordan & Marsh and buying cotton in the occupied South. In 1866, with the help of Daniel Drew (for whom he had been a buyer two years earlier), Fisk started the brokerage house of Fisk and Belden in New York City. He formed a partnership with Drew and Jay Gould in their efforts to get control of the Erie Railroad from Cornelius Vanderbilt by issuing fraudulent stocks. The speculators later compromised with Vanderbilt, and Fisk remained an Erie Railroad official.

Fisk was not adept at management. He almost ran the railway into financial ruin through his repeated attempts at speculation. Fisk oftentimes used funds to bribe public officials through the powerful political machine controlled by William "Boss" Tweed. Fisk also bought an opera house, produced Broadway shows, and paid for an officer rank in the Ninth Regiment of the New York Militia.

The tycoons then tried to corner the gold market by inflating prices. Their actions caused Black Friday, which occurred on September 24, 1869, when one ounce of gold bullion was estimated at twenty dollars, or 30 percent higher than when President Ulysses S. Grant assumed office. Within minutes, the premium price plummeted, and investors were forced to sell. Gould sold his hoarded gold before prices fell, but Fisk lost a great portion of his initial investment. Fisk's reputation with the general public also suffered after Black Friday and the subsequent fall of the infamous Tammany Hall, the Democratic party political machine in New York City.

Fisk was able to recover his assets since he had controlling interests in the Fall River Steamboat on Long Island Sound and a ferry business along the Hudson. It was during this time that Fisk became involved in a love triangle and acrimonious court case. Edward S. Stokes, the secretary of the Brooklyn Refinery Company, was a rival for the affection of Fisk's former mistress, a showgirl named Josie Mansfield. Fisk accused Stokes of embezzling $250,000. Stokes then countered and charged Fisk with malicious prosecution. The courtroom battle between the two men lasted for several months, and the judge decided to reconvene the case on January 6, 1872. On the appointed day, Stokes encountered Fisk on the stairwell and shot him in the abdomen and left arm. Fisk developed peritonitis despite being in robust health; he died the next day.

IMPACT

Jim Fisk's bold business moves matched his boisterous personality. Gould and Fisk were able to form a solid business partnership because each had qualities that the other lacked. Gould maintained incredible business skills but was a quiet man, while Fisk possessed the social affability of a consummate salesman. It is estimated that 100,000 New Yorkers witnessed Fisk's funeral procession. However, Fisk did not leave a vast fortune like his contemporaries. He was a lavish spender who habitually gave his money away to friends or causes. Gould made sure that Fisk's widow remained financially comfortable. However, Fisk's mistress did not fare as well. Josie Mansfield's fame diminished, and she lived in obscurity in South Dakota and later in Paris until her death in 1931. Fisk's murderer, Stokes, went to trial three times. The jury convicted Stokes of manslaughter, and eventually he served four years in Sing Sing Prison for the crime. He lived as social outcast in New York, dying in 1901.

FURTHER READING

Ackerman, Kenneth D. *The Gold Ring: Jim Fisk, Jay Gould, and Black Friday, 1869*. New York: Dodd & Mead, 1988. Recounts the political and economic events as Gould and Fisk attempted to corner the gold market and caused Black Friday.

Gordon, John Steele. *The Scarlet Woman of Wall Street: Jay Gould, Jim Fisk, Cornelius Vanderbilt, the Erie Railway Wars, and the Birth of Wall Street*. New York: Wiedenfeld & Nicolson, 1988. Explains the economic atmosphere of Wall Street and the New York Stock Exchange in the context of nineteenth century capitalism.

Hawes, David S. "Much Ado About John Brougham and Jim Fisk." *Midcontinent American Studies Journal* 8, no. 1 (Spring, 1967): 73-79. Highlights Fisk's ventures with Brougham's Theatre in New York City from 1869 to 1872.

Kirkland, Edward C. "The Robber Barons Revisited." *American Historical Review* 66, no. 1 (October, 1960): 68-73. Addresses revisionist scholarship that focuses on business histories of railroad and oil barons.

Swanberg, W. A. *Jim Fisk: The Career of an Improbable Rascal*. New York: Charles Scribner's Sons, 1959. An unflattering biography of Fisk, portraying him as a man who lacked business and moral scruples.

—*Gayla Koerting*

SEE ALSO: Oakes Ames; Schuyler Colfax; Jay Gould; William Marcy Tweed.

Heidi Fleiss

American madam and panderer

Born: December 30, 1965; Los Angeles, California
Also known as: Heidi Lynne Fleiss (full name); Hollywood Madam
Major offenses: Conspiracy, tax evasion, money laundering, and attempted pandering
Active: 1990-1993
Locale: Los Angeles, California
Sentence: Thirty-seven months in federal prison; concurrent eighteen months for attempted pandering in state prison; served three years

Early Life

Heidi Lynn Fleiss (flis) was born to schoolteacher Elissa Fleiss and Dr. Paul Fleiss, a prominent pediatrician. Her happy childhood included summer camping trips throughout the United States. At thirteen, Fleiss ran a successful neighborhood baby-sitting service which employed twenty babysitters. She dropped out of school in the tenth grade. At nineteen, Fleiss met millionaire financier Bernie Cornfeld, who offered her a job as his secretary. They began dating in spite of a forty-year age difference. Their romantic relationship ended when Fleiss was twenty-three, but Cornfeld remained her close friend and mentor until his death in 1995.

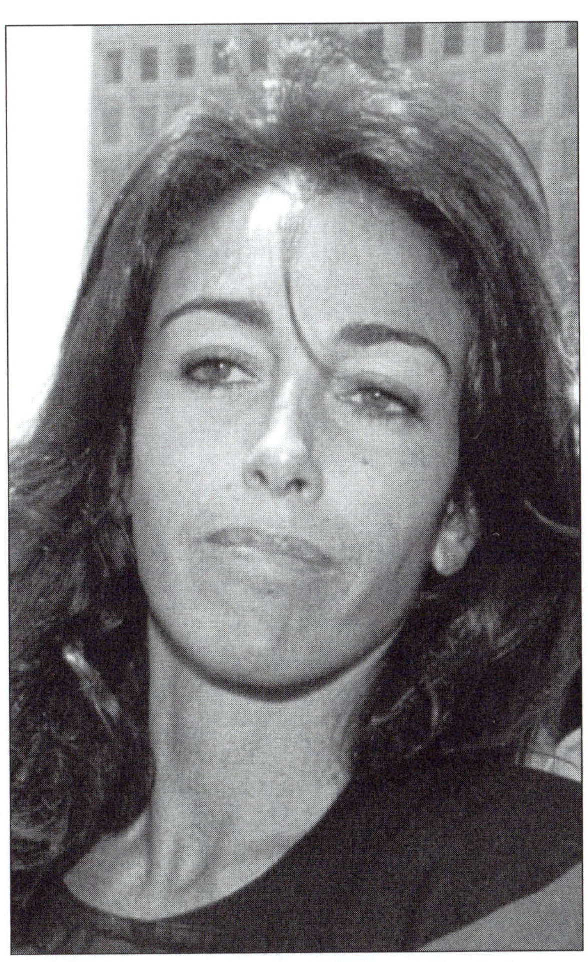

Heidi Fleiss. (Sam Mircovich/Reuters/Landov)

Criminal Career

When Fleiss was twenty-two, she met Madam Alex (Elizabeth Adams), a brothel owner who catered to prominent and wealthy clientele. Madam Alex needed an assistant to help run her business. After working briefly as a prostitute, Fleiss became the assistant madam for Madam Alex. Fleiss restructured the business, hiring new and younger women, including women she had met through Cornfeld. Profits soared, and the business went from $50,000 to $300,000 per month in gross receipts. Clients included actors, producers, royalty, business tycoons, and some of the world's wealthiest men.

Fleiss felt that Madam Alex underpaid her and in 1990 left to launch her own elite prostitution service. Her new business made its first million dollars in five months, and Fleiss became known as the Hollywood Madam. She developed an international reputation and regularly sent her prostitutes to rich and powerful clients in other countries. Her business flourished, with fees ranging from $1,500 to $10,000 or more per customer.

Legal Action and Outcome

In June, 1993, Fleiss was arrested for pandering and selling cocaine. On December 2, 1994, the state grand jury found Fleiss innocent of the narcotics charge but guilty on three of five counts of pandering. On July 28, 1994, a federal grand jury indicted her on fourteen counts of conspiracy, income tax evasion, and money laundering. In August, 1995, a federal jury convicted Fleiss on eight of the fourteen counts.

Fleiss was sentenced to thirty-seven months in a minimum-security federal prison. As part of a plea bargain, she received a concurrent state sentence of eighteen months for attempted pandering. She served three years and was released from the Dublin, California, federal penitentiary in September, 1999.

Impact

Heidi Fleiss became the most famous panderer or madam in history. The revelation of her service for some of the world's wealthiest, most famous, and most powerful men created an international scandal. After her imprisonment, her notoriety continued to grow, as the news media covered her latest projects and relationships. She became a talk-show host, appeared on television interview shows, and opened a boutique in Hollywood. In 2001, Fleiss made a sex tips video with actor Victoria Sellers. Fleiss started her own publishing company, One Hour Entertainment, which published her successful autobiography, *Pandering*, in 2002. In December, 2005, Fleiss solidified plans for opening in Nevada Heidi's Stud Farm, the first legal brothel in the United States featuring male prostitutes who serve a female clientele.

Further Reading

Fleiss, Heidi. *Pandering*. Los Angeles: One Hour Entertainment, 2002. This autobiography uses unique visuals and a bold, nontraditional format to tell Fleiss's story. The pages include court transcripts, newspaper clippings, address books, photographs, personal items, and art.

_______. *The Player's Handbook: The Ultimate Guide on Dating and Relationships*. Los Angeles: One Hour Entertainment, 2004. An entertaining how-to guide covering topics such as developing self-esteem and committed relationships.

Hornberger, Francine. *Mistresses of Mayhem: The Book of Women Criminals*. Indianapolis: Alpa, 2002. Includes a biography of Fleiss. Illustrated. Index and bibliography.

Knappman, Edward. *Sex, Sin, and Mayhem: Notorious Trials of the '90's*. Detroit: Visible Ink Press, 1995. Detailed accounts of sensational court dramas, including Heidi Fleiss's trials, are presented. Illustrated.

—Alice Myers

See also: Sydney Barrows; Ada Everleigh.

Pretty Boy Floyd

American bank robber

Born: February 3, 1904; Bartow County, Georgia
Died: October 22, 1934; near Wellsville, Ohio
Also known as: Charles Arthur Floyd (full name); Chock; James Warren; Mr. Douglas; Jack Hamilton; George Sanders
Major offenses: Bank robbery and murder
Active: 1925-1934
Locale: Midwestern United States
Sentence: Four years in prison for robbery; escaped a subsequent sentence of twelve to fifteen years

Early Life

Pretty Boy Floyd (floyd) was born Charles Floyd on a Georgia farm, the fourth of eight children. His family moved to Oklahoma in 1911, to a farm on the edge of the Cookson Hills. The farm was four hundred square miles of wilderness with few dirt roads, in an agricultural area know for its poverty. By the age of fourteen, Floyd was a harvest laborer, fistfighter, and moonshiner. He hated farming but liked clothes and girls. He married sixteen-year-old Ruby Hargraves in 1924; they had a son the same year.

Criminal Career

In 1925, Floyd left home for the harvests again; this time he teamed up with an experienced robber. The pair held up Kroger stores in St. Louis. Floyd was described by victims as young, with apple cheeks. The nickname of another criminal, Pretty Boy Smith, was applied to Floyd. Floyd was sentenced to four years in prison, and his wife divorced him before his release in 1929. While in prison he made criminal friendships and after parole went to Kansas City to renew them. He met twenty-one-year-old Juanita Ash, who divorced her husband and became his mistress. He alternated between living with her and his with ex-wife until his death.

As an ex-con, Floyd was harassed by police, for which he grew resentful. In 1929 Floyd's father was shot to death in an argument and his killer acquitted; the man disappeared shortly thereafter—presumably murdered by Floyd. Floyd robbed a bank in Ohio in 1930 and was sentenced to twelve to fifteen years in prison. He jumped from the train taking him to the penitentiary and escaped back to the Cookson Hills. In 1931 he and a partner drove back to Ohio, robbed more banks, and had a gunfight with city police in which Floyd's partner was slain.

Pretty Boy Floyd. (Courtesy, F.B.I.)

Floyd killed his first policeman. He again fled to the Cookson Hills.

Floyd went on an Oklahoma bank-robbing spree with a new partner, becoming the most famous bandit in the state. He spent generously to maintain the goodwill of the hill folks among whom he lived. He used his gun more than most professional bank robbers of the era; he also killed for revenge. He was extremely lucky, coming through several shoot-outs unhurt or wounded only superficially. Floyd wore bulletproof vests, sometimes front and back. During his 1931-1932 Oklahoma crime spree, authorities and newspapers blamed him for any large robbery that occurred in the state—which Floyd protested in an interview with a newspaper reporter. Fifty-one bank robberies occurred in Oklahoma in 1931, and Floyd was involved in perhaps half of them.

While home in Oklahoma, Floyd behaved erratically and took odd chances: He visited his mother, robbed a bank in his hometown of Sallisaw, threatened the local sheriff, went to movies, ate lunch in cafés, and attended church. Family members and acquaintances protected him, partly out of loyalty and partly out of fear. In 1932 his partner was killed while robbing a bank without Floyd.

Floyd's final partner was Adam "Eddie" Richetti. In 1933, outlaw Vern Miller contracted Floyd and Richetti to rescue bank robber Frank Nash from being transported to prison by police and the Federal Bureau of Investigation (FBI). The plan went awry as Nash sat inside a police car: The outlaws opened fire with machine guns. Five men, including Nash, died, and two were wounded in what would become known as the Kansas City Massacre. Before Kansas City, Floyd was a regional criminal. Afterward, his name was known nationwide. In 1934, a thousand men raided and searched the Cookson Hills, but Floyd escaped. By August of that year he was the last major outlaw in Oklahoma. He and Richetti, with their girlfriends, drove to Albany, New York, and hid in an apartment.

Several times, Floyd offered to surrender to law enforcement authorities in exchange for life in prison. Oklahoma and the FBI declined the deal. By June, 1934, FBI director J. Edgar Hoover had intensified efforts to find Floyd and ordered him killed on sight. In October, 1934, Floyd and Richetti decided to return to the Cookson Hills. Their car hit a telephone pole in early-morning fog in rural Ohio. Their girlfriends set out for help on foot, while the outlaws hid in the woods. Floyd and Richetti were spotted lying on blankets on the side of a hill, and the police were notified.

Legal Action and Outcome

In a confused firefight, Richetti was captured, and Floyd ran into the woods. FBI chief Melvin Purvis and two dozen agents hunted him with a hundred local police. Around 3:00 P.M., Floyd walked to a farmhouse, bought a meal of pork chops, and asked for a ride to Youngstown. FBI agents and police suddenly appeared in two cars. Floyd ran across a field toward woods two hundred yards away. Police shot him three times. He died fifteen minutes later, with $122 on his person. His body was shipped home after money to do so was raised by Oklahoma neighbors. About twenty thousand people attended his funeral.

Richetti was executed in the gas chamber in 1938, weeping with fear. Widows of the Kansas City Massacre received five thousand dollars apiece from Congress. Floyd's wife, girlfriend, and family were not prosecuted after his death.

Impact

Hoover fired Melvin Purvis for receiving too much newspaper publicity over the death of Pretty Boy Floyd. As a result, Hoover remained the only nationally known personality in the FBI. He stayed on the job until his death in 1972 at the age of seventy-seven. Purvis shot himself in 1960.

Floyd had a significant impact on the public imagination: He was the subject of a ballad by the famous folksinger Woody Guthrie, was mentioned in John Steinbeck's novel *The Grapes of Wrath* (1939), and has been the subject of several films. One, *The Story of Pretty Boy Floyd* (1974), starring Martin Sheen, was introduced by Floyd's mother and included Floyd's younger brother in the cast. Floyd was also the subject of more recent films such as *Public Enemies* (2006), starring Leonardo DiCaprio.

Further Reading

King, Jeffery S. *The Life and Death of Pretty Boy Floyd.* Kent, Ohio: Kent State University Press, 1998. A well-researched biography based on newspaper and magazine interviews.

Stewart, Tony. *Dillinger: The Hidden Truth.* Philadelphia: Xlibris, 2002. Includes a chapter on public enemies, including Floyd.

Wallis, Michael. *Pretty Boy: The Life and Times of Charles Arthur Floyd.* New York: St. Martin's Press, 1992. Describes Floyd in the context of the social conditions of his day and argues that he was not involved in the Kansas City Massacre.

—*Jim Pauff*

See also: Clyde Barrow; John Dillinger; J. Edgar Hoover; Baby Face Nelson; Bonnie Parker.

Jim Folsom

Alabama governor (1947-1951, 1955-1959)

Born: October 9, 1908; Coffee County, Alabama
Died: November 21, 1987; Cullman, Alabama
Also known as: James Elisha Folsom (full name); Big Jim Folsom; Kissing Jim
Cause of notoriety: During his terms as governor, Folsom tolerated corruption by cronies and used state funds for personal benefit. His personal conduct, especially romancing women and drinking, hindered his political power.
Active: 1947-1959
Locale: Alabama

Early Life

As a child, James Elisha Folsom (FOHL-suhm) frequently accompanied his father, Joshua Folsom, a Coffee County tax collector, to the courthouse in Elba, where he learned political strategies. He enrolled at the University of Alabama and then transferred to Howard College in Birmingham but left school without a degree; he joined the merchant marine instead. From 1932 to 1934, Folsom worked as the Marshall County, Alabama, supervisor for the Civil Works Administration.

In 1936, Folsom married Sarah Carnley, whose father, a judge, influenced Folsom's political ambitions. Hired by his brother-in-law at the Emergency Aid Insurance Company, Folsom enhanced his political aspirations because of contacts that he established throughout the state. Folsom served in World War II, returning home when his wife died in 1944. He married Jamelle Moore four years later.

Political Career

In 1933, Folsom, a lifelong Democrat, failed to win a delegate position at the state Prohibition convention. He unsuccessfully ran against incumbent Henry B. Steagall for Alabama's Third District seat in the U.S. Congress in 1936 and 1938. By March, 1942, Folsom announced his gubernatorial candidacy and finished second in the race.

In 1946, Folsom again campaigned for governor, receiving the plurality of primary votes. Preparing for the runoff, Folsom delivered speeches, and his band, the Strawberry Pickers, performed at courthouses throughout Alabama. Folsom good-naturedly displayed a sudsy bucket and mop, vowing to clean out corrupt politicians. His showmanship impressed many rural voters, who liked Folsom's informal manner. Several labor unions endorsed him. On New Year's Day, 1947, the victorious Folsom broadcast, via radio, invitations to all Alabamians to attend his inauguration festivities. He stressed that no one controlled him and that he wanted democracy to thrive in Alabama.

While Folsom was governor, the press suggested that he and political allies had engaged in corrupt activities regarding state agencies. His appointees sometimes abused their powers by accepting money, favors, or political support from people who sought paroles or pardons for crimes. They accepted bribes and interfered with bidding for state projects' contracts. Folsom demanded that corrupt officials resign. However, investigators revealed that Folsom also used state money to purchase gifts for his family, pay personal expenses, and travel in state aircraft.

Prevented by Alabama law to run for a second term in 1950, Folsom sold insurance until he regained the governorship four years later. During his 1954 campaign, Folsom justified any previous corrupt behavior by saying he had acted only to improve Alabama. In 1962, Folsom ran against George Wallace. Wallace's racist rhetoric, as well as media depictions of Folsom as a bumbling drunkard, contributed to Folsom's defeat. He campaigned in four more gubernatorial races but lost.

Impact

Jim Folsom expressed many solid ideas to transform Alabama, but his weaknesses and scandals impaired his political clout. His foes, primarily conservative wealthy Birmingham businessmen long entrenched in Alabama politics, controlled the legislature. Most legislators despised Folsom, impeding his efforts with filibusters or altering his proposed legislation. Legislators unsuccessfully tried to amend the state constitution so they could convene without Folsom's approval. Political enemies denounced Folsom's character, emphasizing his liquor indulgences, a paternity lawsuit filed by a woman claiming she was Folsom's common-law wife, and embarrassing pictures printed in national periodicals.

Further Reading

Baham, Roy, Jamelle Folsom, and E. Jimmy Key. *The Strawberry Pickers*. Nashville, Tenn.: Southern Arts, 2000. Compilation by Folsom's second wife and band members which chronicles Folsom's 1946 gubernatorial campaign. Includes insiders' accounts, family photographs, and contemporary illustrations.

Grafton, Carl, and Anne Permaloff. *Big Mules and Branchheads: James E. Folsom and Political Power in Alabama*. Athens: University of Georgia Press, 1985. Scholarly study of Folsom by professors who had access to Folsom, his family, and associates.

Sims, George E. *The Little Man's Big Friend: James E. Folsom in Alabama Politics, 1946-1958*. Tuscaloosa: University of Alabama Press, 1985. Examines charges of corruption and fraud against Folsom.

Webb, Samuel L., and Margaret E. Armbrester, eds. *Alabama Governors: A Political History of the State*. Foreword by Albert P. Brewer. Tuscaloosa: University of Alabama Press, 2001. Chapter on Folsom succinctly summarizes his political interests, explains his political strategies, and describes how his weaknesses impacted his career.

—*Elizabeth D. Schafer*

See also: Huey Long; George C. Wallace.

Larry C. Ford

American bioterrorist doctor

Born: September 29, 1950; Provo, Utah
Died: March 2, 2000; Irvine, California
Also known as: Larry Creed Ford (full name)
Cause of notoriety: Ford was allegedly involved with biological warfare in South Africa, Angola, and Zimbabwe.
Active: 1970's-1990's
Locale: California, South Africa, Angola, and Zimbabwe

Early Life

Larry C. Ford (fohrd) was born to a Mormon family in 1950. He won first place in the International Science Fair of 1966 for his studies of radiation exposure and received much recognition for that achievement. At the age of eighteen he was invited to work in a government laboratory at an undisclosed location, which started his career with the military and Central Intelligence Agency (CIA). After graduating from Brigham Young University, he married his childhood sweetheart, Diane, and in 1970 began studying to become a physician at the medical school of the University of California, Los Angeles (UCLA). In 1975, he graduated and pursued postgraduate work in biochemistry and gynecology.

Scientific Career

In 1987, Ford moved with his family to Irvine, California. He had three children—two boys and one girl—and was described by his children as a good father. He served as a clinical professor and director of research for the Center for Ovarian Cancer at UCLA. He published more than sixty-five articles in the fields of cancer research, antibiotics, and infectious diseases. An international obstetrcis/gynecological award was named for him.

In 1997, Ford was fired from UCLA after he was found disposing of blood samples improperly. He developed associations with South African officials and was alleged to have a role in biological warfare programs in South Africa that led to hundreds of deaths in South Africa and in the neighboring countries of Angola and Zimbabwe. In the 1980's, he had started a company, Biofem Pharmaceuticals, with an associate, James Patrick Riley. The company's main product was an over-the-counter vaginal suppository contraceptive, Inner Confidence, designed to protect women against HIV/AIDS and other sexually transmitted diseases. The company was waiting for Food and Drug Administration (FDA) approval and never came to the market.

In March, 2000, Riley survived an attempt on his life, a shooting during which the driver of the getaway car, Los Angeles businessman Din D'Saachs, was found to have been a patient of Ford.

Ford was being questioned in connection with the attempted murder when he committed suicide by shooting himself on March 2, 2000, leaving a note behind claiming his innocence. A search of his house found C-4 explosives and other weapons buried in his backyard, along with more than 260 bottles of biological materials such as ricin, salmonella, vibrio cholerae, and botulinum.

His autopsy showed he had six antidepressants in his system at the time of his death. Since Dr. Ford committed suicide even before he could be arrested or a trial conducted, questions about his motives could not be established. His life and findings point toward suspicious criminal activities and involvement in developing agents for biological terror and warfare.

Impact

The sudden suicide of Dr. Larry Ford left many questions unanswered. He had claimed to his colleagues (though not to his family) that he worked for the CIA, and despite being described as friendly, loving to his family, and giving, many also witnessed eccentricities of dress and unusual if not "abnormal" behavior, including his enthusiasm for guns, big-game hunting, and travel. Ford's attorney stated that his client had told him he had worked for the CIA for two decades—including one occasion during South Africa's apartheid days when he parachuted into the country to collect blood samples from dead guerrilla fighters. He had also divulged to colleagues that he worked for the CIA's biological warfare program. Whether these claims were true remains unsubstantiated. However, statements made by CIA agents—as well as Ford's misrepresentations of his credentials (the American College of Obstetricians and Gynecologists, for example, denied his claim to have been a member) and his mysterious suicide—seem to support these claims.

Further Reading

Hardesty, Greg, and Bill Rams. "Doctor's Suicide Uncovers Skeletons That Shock Family Murder Probe; Arsenal in Yard Tarnishes Image." *Times-Picayune*, April 9, 2000, p. A29. A news account of the events following Ford's suicide. Some intriguing facets of his life are discussed.

Humes, Edward. "The Medicine Man: Involvement of Scientist Larry Ford in Subversive Activities." *Los Angeles Magazine* 46 (July, 2001): 94. A detailed account of the investigation of Ford's suicide, his life, and what was found at his home by investigators.

Klein, Peter, Helen E. Purkitt, Trisra L. Sorrells, and Dan Rather. *"Dr. Death" and His Accomplice*. Video (26 minutes). New York: CBS World Wide, 2002. A program, with the transcript available on videocassette, describes the biological weapons used by Ford and elaborates on his associations in South Africa.

Purkitt, Helen, and Stephen Burgess. "South Africa's Chemical and Biological Warfare Programme: A Historical and International Perspective." *Journal of Southern African Studies* 28 (June, 2002): 229-253. This article includes discussion about Ford and his involvement with South Africa's covert chemical and biological warfare (CBW) program, Project Coast.

—*Manoj Sharma*

See also: Linda Burfield Hazzard.

Nathan Bedford Forrest

Confederate cavalry officer and first grand wizard of the Ku Klux Klan

Born: July 13, 1821; Chapel Hill, Tennessee
Died: October 29, 1877; Memphis, Tennessee
Also known as: Wizard of the Saddle; That Devil Forrest
Cause of notoriety: While Forrest's exploits are legion, he is remembered primarily for commanding the massacre against the Union soldiers stationed at Fort Pillow, Tennessee, on April 12, 1864, and for his role as the first grand wizard of the Ku Klux Klan.
Active: 1864-1877
Locale: Tennessee

Early Life

Like most Southern families at that time, the family of Nathan Bedford Forrest (NAY-thuhn BEHD-fuhrd FOHR-ehst) was poor, with the father, William Forrest, attempting to make a living as a blacksmith in the Bedford County town of Chapel Hill, located in Tennessee. Forrest was the oldest of twelve children whose father died when he was seventeen years old. Though he lacked a formal education (he could barely read or write), he became quite wealthy before the Civil War, owning several plantations throughout Mississippi and Tennessee. Although the Southern economy was based on slavery, slave traders themselves were considered "lowly," and were, at best, merely tolerated. Unconcerned about what others thought, Forrest became a slave trader in Memphis and made a fortune; it has been estimated that prior to the firing upon Fort Sumter, Forrest was a millionaire and was considered one of the wealthiest men in the South.

Nathan Bedford Forrest.

Military Career

Considered by many historians to be the finest cavalry commander and one of the greatest tacticians in American history, Forrest was a lieutenant general for the Confederate States of America, earning respect from both sides during the Civil War. During 1861-1865, he killed thirty men in hand-to-hand combat and had twenty-nine horses shot from under him. He faced daunting odds on many occasions but lost no battles until the last days of the war.

In 1862, during the Battle of Fort Donelson, Forrest showed his mettle when he led a cavalry charge against a Union artillery battery and captured it, then led a breakout from a siege by the Union army under Ulysses S. Grant. At the Battle of Shiloh in Tennessee (April 6-7, 1862), a Union infantryman on the ground fired at Forrest, hitting him in the side and lifting him out of his saddle. The ball went through his pelvis and lodged near his spine. Forrest then lifted the shooter up onto his mount and used him as a human shield until threat from gunfire diminished.

While Forrest's exploits are legion, he is primarily remembered for the massacre of the Union soldiers stationed at Fort Pillow, Tennessee, that occurred on April 12, 1864. As he had done before, Forrest demanded unconditional surrender. Instead of acquiescing, the fort decided to fight, resulting in a brutal Confederate attack in which most of their blue-clad opponents were killed. Once the battle was over, reports filtered out that the captured black soldiers were treated inhumanely, including being crucified and burned alive.

Forrest's skill as a guerrilla fighter was unequaled during the war (causing tremendous problems for Grant and General William Tecumseh Sherman). At the Battle of Brice's Crossroads on June 10, 1864, Forrest's 3,500 men defeated the 8,500-man force commanded by Gen-

Forrest on the Ku Klux Klan

Forrest made the following statements in an 1868 interview for the Cincinnati Commercial:

INTERVIEWER: Why, general, we people up north have regarded the Ku-Klux as an organization which existed only in the frightened imagination of a few politicians.

FORREST: Well, sir, there is such an organization, not only in Tennessee, but all over the South, and its numbers have not been exaggerated.

INTERVIEWER: What are its numbers, general?

FORREST: In Tennessee there are over 40,000; in all the Southern states they number about 550,000 men.

INTERVIEWER: What is the character of the organization; May I inquire?

FORREST: Yes, sir. It is a protective political military organization. I am willing to show any man the constitution of the society. The members are sworn to recognize the government of the United States. . . . Its objects originally were protection against Loyal Leagues and the Grand Army of the Republic; but after it became general it was found that political matters and interests could best be promoted within it, and it was then made a political organization, giving its support, of course, to the Democratic party.

INTERVIEWER: But is the organization connected throughout the state?

FORREST: Yes, it is. In each voting precinct there is a captain, who, in addition to his other duties, is required to make out a list of names of men in his precinct, giving all the radicals and all the democrats who are positively known, and showing also the doubtful on both sides and of both colors. This list of names is forwarded to the grand commander of the State, who is thus enabled to know who are our friends and who are not.

INTERVIEWER: Can you, or are you at liberty to give me the name of the commanding officer of this State?

FORREST: No, it would be impolitic.

INTERVIEWER: Do you think, general, that the Ku-Klux have been of any benefit to the State?

FORREST: No doubt of it. Since its organization, the leagues have quit killing and murdering our people. There were some foolish young men who put masks on their faces and rode over the country, frightening negroes, but orders have been issued to stop that, and it has ceased. You may say, further, that three members of the Ku-Klux have been court-martialed and shot for violations of the orders not to disturb or molest people.

INTERVIEWER: Are you a member of the Ku-Klux, general?

FORREST: I am not, but am in sympathy and will co-operate with them. I know that they are charged with many crimes that they are not guilty of. . . .

Source: Nathan Bedford Forrest, interview in *Cincinnati Commercial*, August 28, 1868 (also 40th Congress, House of Representatives, Executive Documents No. 1, Report of the Secretary of War, chapter 10, p. 193).

eral Samuel D. Sturgis, inflicting 2,500 casualties while suffering a mere 492.

Forrest's experience in the Ku Klux Klan (KKK) was a direct result of his military capabilities. The KKK was formed during the latter part of the 1860's as a means for Southern men to resist the Union's attempts at Reconstruction. During the first convention, which took place in 1867, Forrest became the organization's first grand wizard. Under his command, the KKK grew in popularity and notoriety, leading Forrest to state that he could, if needed, quickly bring forty thousand Klansmen together within a five-day period. At that point, the group's mission was not one of keeping former slaves in their place; rather, it was to empty the South of all carpetbaggers. Once the organization became primarily racist, Forrest resigned.

Legal Action and Outcome

After the war, an inquest took place regarding Fort Pillow. Witnesses from both sides claimed that Forrest was not personally involved in the melee and that he attempted to control his men. After the war, an investigation by General Sherman found that Forrest was not liable for the barbaric behavior of the men under his command.

Impact

The twentieth century doctrine of "mobile warfare" was first discussed by Nathan Bedford Forrest during the Civil War. His idea about "get there fustest with the mostest" was always paramount in his thinking, even if it meant riding horses until they fell over dead. During the Battle of Paducah, the twenty-five-hundred-man cavalry led by Forrest rode one hundred miles in just fifty hours. In later years Forrest would be studied for his fast-moving raids and other maneuvers made possible by his early application of guerrilla-style, "hit and run" tactics.

Further Reading

Browning, Robert M. *Forrest: The Confederacy's Relentless Warrior*. Washington, D.C.: Brassey's, 2004. Short but insightful, providing an excellent introduction to Forrest.

Fuchs, Richard L. *An Unerring Fire: The Massacre at Fort Pillow*. Mechanisburg, Pa.: Stackpole Books, 2002. Focuses only on Fort Pillow but offers keen analyses of Forrest and the milieu in which he lived.

Hurst, Jack. *Nathan Bedford Forrest: A Biography*. New York: A. A. Knopf, 1993. Provides detail on Forrest as a man (both before and after the Civil War) and as a first-class soldier.

Wyeth, John A. *That Devil Forrest*. 1899. Reprint. Baton Rouge: Louisiana State University Press, 1989. Written by a member of Forrest's staff. Wyeth knew Forrest professionally and personally and respected him greatly.

—*Cary Stacy Smith*

See also: William Clarke Quantrill; Henry Wirz.

Elisabeth Förster-Nietzsche

Editor of the works of Friedrich Nietzsche

Born: July 10, 1846; Röcken, near Lützen, Prussia (now in Germany)

Died: November 8, 1935; Weimar, Germany

Also known as: Therese Elisabeth Alexandra Nietzsche (birth name)

Cause of notoriety: Förster-Nietzsche made accessible the work and ideas of Friedrich Nietzsche to individuals and groups who used it as the justification of nefarious ends, most notably the Nazis. She also established a racist and anti-Semitic colony in Paraguay with her husband, Bernhard Förster.

Active: 1897-1935

Locale: Germany

Early Life

The second child of the devoted Lutheran minister Carl Ludwig Nietzsche and his wife Franziska, Elisabeth Förster-Nietzsche (FOOR-stehr NEE-tchah) received little in the way of education. Following the death of her father in 1849, Elisabeth and her brother Friedrich—who would become the famous philosopher—became extremely close as Franziska increasingly focused her religious zeal on her two children. Elisabeth kept house for her brother while he was a professor at the University of Basel (1869-1879), since he was often too ill to take care of himself. However, the two siblings split following what Friedrich characterized as Elisabeth's meddling in his relationship with Russian intellectual Lou von Salomé, which led to a severing of the romance.

Prior to this, Elisabeth had become friends with German composer Richard Wagner and his wife and thus began her practice of making important friends. She met Bernhard Förster at Wagner's home in Bayreuth, Germany, in 1870, and the two were married in 1885. It was with Förster that Elisabeth would later found the colony called New Germany in Paraguay, South America.

New Germany was founded on racist, anti-Semitic, and vegetarian principles. Elisabeth's brother Friedrich condemned the move, predicting that it would destroy both of the Försters. He was partially correct. The colony struggled, and in 1889 Bernhard Förster died—most likely by suicide—and Elisabeth fled creditors and the suspicious colonists to return to Germany. She had heard that her brother had gone mad and wanted to see for herself if this rumor was true. In fact, Friedrich had suffered a mental breakdown in 1889.

Literary Career

Elisabeth's literary career really began when her mother died in 1897, leaving Elisabeth in control of her brother's substantial literary estate. She got to work immediately in making the incapacitated Friedrich say and think what she wanted. While she did care for her brother from the onset of his illness until his death in 1900, some maintain it was in order to reap the benefits of Nietzsche's literary output, a bounty that Friedrich was himself far too ill to enjoy.

While at the helm of the Nietzsche Archive, which she founded in Weimar, Elisabeth changed Nietzsche's words to suit her purposes, ignored what contradicted her beliefs, and at times stooped to outright forgery. As Nietzsche's popularity rose, the Nietzsche that Elisabeth brought forth to his fans was a philosopher largely of her own making. Some of the changes she made to his work were minor: She changed Friedrich's words when he mentioned her in order to reflect an ongoing affection for her, when he in fact loathed her after his split with Lou von Salomé.

However, Elisabeth also enacted substantial changes in her brother's work. For example, Nietzsche's long text *Der Wille zur Macht* (1901; *The Will to Power*, 1910) was published by Elisabeth in 1901, a year after her brother's death. This lucrative volume earned Elisabeth a large sum; however, the book was never intended by her brother to be published. The aphorisms that make up *The Will to Power* were actually widely scattered and random scribblings from notebooks and essays abandoned by Nietzsche.

Fascists such as Italian leader Benito Mussolini and German leader Adolf Hitler later adopted Nietzsche's philosophy, or rather, Elisabeth's interpretation and misrepresentation of Nietzsche's thoughts. The Nazis in particular were attracted to Nietzsche's praise of strength, the ideal of the Superman, and Nietzsche's supposed stressing of the martial spirit. Hitler almost certainly never read a word of Nietzsche's writings, however, and merely used Nietzsche's popularity to advance the Nazi cause. The German führer even used Elisabeth's considerable cultural influence as a propaganda tool, making several well-publicized visits to the Nietzsche Archive and being seated at the foot of Elisabeth's casket at her funeral in 1935. By that time, she was one of the most culturally famous women in all of Germany.

Impact

Elisabeth Förster-Nietzsche's deliberate misreading and misrepresentation of her brother's works led to some of the most nefarious twentieth century individuals adopting Friedrich Nietzsche as the inspiration and philosophical justification for the greatest atrocities of that century. Elisabeth distorted her brother's philosophy, with which the Nazis used to justify Aryan supremacy and their ensuing war and mass murder.

Nietzsche's name was sullied in the philosophical community for decades after the end of World War II. Some claimed that the war and the Holocaust would not have been possible were it not for Nietzsche's dangerous writings, regardless of the fact that there is absolutely nothing in Nietzsche's work that would support the Nazi cause. Only after the middle of the twentieth century did serious scholarship of Nietzsche return to the philosophical community.

Elisabeth Förster-Nietzsche.

Further Reading

Cate, Curtis. *Friedrich Nietzsche*. New York: Overlook Press, 2005. A biography of Nietzsche, which provides a better understanding of Förster-Nietzsche, since the two were so close and each played such a crucial role in the fame of the other.

Diethe, Carol. *Nietzsche's Sister and "The Will to Power": A Biography of Elisabeth Förster-Nietzsche*. Urbana: University of Illinois Press, 2003. A biography of Förster-Nietzsche.

Macintyre, Ben. *Forgotten Fatherland: The Search for Elisabeth Nietzsche*. New York: Farrar, Straus, Giroux, 1992. Biography of Förster-Nietzsche with emphasis on the period of New Germany in Paraguay.

Peters, H. F. *Zarathustra's Sister: The Case of Elisabeth and Friedrich Nietzsche*. New York: Crown, 1977. An account of the intertwined lives of Förster-Nietzsche and her brother Friedrich.

—*John F. Gamber, Jr.*

See also: Richard Walther Darré; Adolf Hitler; Benito Mussolini; Winifred Wagner.

Abe Fortas

American attorney and Supreme Court justice (1965-1969)

Born: June 19, 1910; Memphis, Tennessee
Died: April 5, 1982; Washington, D.C.
Also known as: Abraham Fortas (full name)
Cause of notoriety: Fortas was the first nominee for the position of chief justice of the United States to be rejected by a filibuster in the Senate and the first justice of the Supreme Court to resign in the face of public pressure.
Active: 1965-1969
Locale: Washington, D.C.

Early Life

Abraham Fortas (FOHR-tuhs) grew up in Memphis. His parents, Eastern European-born Orthodox Jewish immigrants, ran a furniture factory and later owned a men's clothing and jewelry store. The academically gifted Fortas attended public schools and earned a scholarship to Southwestern College (now Rhodes College), a liberal arts college in Memphis, where he graduated at the top of his class. He attended Yale Law School and became the protégé of future Supreme Court associate justice William O. Douglas, then a professor of law. In 1933, Fortas graduated second in his class and was editor of *The Yale Law Journal*. With the sponsorship of Douglas, Fortas joined the administration of President Franklin D. Roosevelt, working part-time in Washington, D.C., in the Securities and Exchange Commission (SEC) while also teaching at Yale Law School. From 1937 to 1946, he worked at the SEC, the Public Works Administration, and the Department of Interior, where he served as undersecretary.

Judicial Career

In 1946, Fortas entered private practice and started a new law firm, Arnold, Fortas, & Porter, which was to become one of Washington's most successful and prominent firms. It specialized in helping corporations cope with post-New Deal regulation and was active in the defense of government employees charged with disloyalty during the anticommunist Joseph McCarthy era. Fortas's specialty was corporate law, but he also was involved in civil liberties issues. He was an astute legal strategist, a skilled courtroom advocate, and a meticulous craftsman who was considered a "lawyer's lawyer."

In 1948, Fortas adroitly defended the victory of Congressman Lyndon B. Johnson, a Democrat from Texas, in a disputed primary election for a U.S. Senate seat. Thereafter, Johnson considered Fortas the best lawyer he knew. As Senate majority leader in the 1950's and later as U.S. vice president, Johnson regularly called on Fortas, his personal lawyer, for advice. Before the U.S. Supreme Court, Fortas argued and won two landmark pro bono cases: *Durham v. United States* (1954), which modernized the legal definition of insanity; and *Gideon v. Wainwright* (1963), which held that indigent criminal defendants in state felony cases had the right to counsel. After he became U.S. president, Johnson continued to rely on Fortas as an unofficial legal adviser and decided to reward him with appointment to the Supreme Court.

On July 28, 1965, Johnson nominated Fortas to replace Supreme Court justice Arthur J. Goldberg, whom the president had persuaded to retire from the Court. The Senate confirmed Fortas's nomination, and he was sworn in on October 4, 1965. Fortas fit in well with the libertarian and activist Warren Court majority, and he participated in a number of cases that expanded civil liberties

Abe Fortas.

protections. Fortas wrote significant opinions in *In re Gault* (1967), which guaranteed to juveniles the right to counsel and protection against self-incrimination; *Epperson v. Arkansas* (1968), which struck down a law that prohibited the teaching of evolution; and *Tinker v. Des Moines Independent School District* (1969), which upheld as symbolic speech students' rights to wear black armbands in protesting the Vietnam War. In cases involving corporations and mergers, Fortas was more often against government regulation and in favor of business than were his colleagues.

Once on the bench, Fortas was reluctant to confine his interest to the work of the Court alone. Through back channels, he remained a principal adviser to President Johnson, advising him on such matters as the Vietnam War and racial conflicts and even drafting speeches for Johnson.

When Chief Justice Earl Warren resigned in 1968, Johnson nominated Fortas to take his place. Fortas's nomination was opposed by many conservative senators, who accused Johnson (who had already announced that he would not seek reelection in 1968) both of cronyism and of trying to pack the Court as a lame-duck president. In response, Fortas appeared before the Senate Judiciary Committee, the first nominee for chief justice ever to do so. Hostile committee members used the occasion to lambaste Warren Court decisions and raised objections to Fortas's positions on controversial issues. When asked about his continuing relationship with the president and its implied contempt for the doctrine of separation of powers, Fortas was disingenuous.

After the opening round of hearings, the senators learned that Fortas, dissatisfied with his salary on the Court, had accepted fifteen thousand dollars, raised by a former law partner from wealthy clients, for teaching a nine-week course at American University Law School. This financial indiscretion led opponents to claim that Fortas did not have the "sense of propriety" required of a chief justice. On October 1, 1968, Republicans and conservative Democrats launched a filibuster on Fortas's nomination, and Fortas requested that his name be withdrawn from consideration.

Fortas remained on the Court as an associate justice, but he resigned on May 14, 1969, after *Life* magazine revealed that he had accepted twenty thousand dollars in 1966 from the family foundation of an indicted stock manipulator. Fortas admitted that he had engaged in an agreement that would have given him twenty thousand dollars a year for life in return for service to the foundation. Although he had returned the money and terminated the relationship, the damage had been done. Amid clamors for his impeachment or resignation, Fortas resigned, "for the good of the Court," but admitted no wrongdoing.

After his law firm refused to have him back, Fortas opened a two-man corporate law practice in Washington. It flourished, and in March, 1982, he argued and won his first case before the Supreme Court following his resignation. A month later, Fortas died of a heart attack at the age of seventy-one.

Impact

Abe Fortas became the first Supreme Court justice to leave the Court amid public criticism. A moral relativist, Fortas precipitated his downfall through greed and arrogance. Although he was wealthy by most standards, Fortas wanted more money to maintain a lifestyle to which he and his wife had become accustomed. Fortas had the legal acumen, courage, and rhetorical ability to become a great justice, but he lacked the temperament. The filibuster that met Fortas's nomination as chief justice was history-making and set a precedent for congressional objections to presidential nominations to the judiciary. In 2005, for example, both Republicans and Democrats recalled the Fortas filibuster when contemplating their potential response to President George W. Bush's Supreme Court nominees.

Further Reading

Graham, Fred P. "Abe Fortas." In *The Justices of the United States Supreme Court, 1789-1969*, edited by Leon Friedman and Fred Israel. Philadelphia: Chelsea House, 1969. A contemporary review written by a television network reporter and lawyer who covered the Court during Fortas's tenure.

Kalman, Laura. *Abe Fortas: A Biography*. New Haven, Conn.: Yale University Press, 1990. An authorized, full and fair account of Fortas's checkered career written by a historian and a lawyer.

Murphy, Bruce Allen. *Fortas: The Rise and Ruin of a Supreme Court Justice*. New York: W. Morrow, 1988. A political scientist's detailed account of the political maneuvering that led to the forced withdrawal of Fortas's nomination for the chief justiceship.

Rodell, Fred. "The Complexities of Mr. Justice Fortas." *The New York Times Magazine*, July 28, 1968. A personal analysis by a Yale law professor who first knew Fortas during his years in New Haven.

—*Theodore M. Vestal*

See also: Roger Brooke Taney.

Francisco Franco

Spanish dictator (r. 1939-1975)

Born: December 4, 1892; El Ferrol, Galicia, Spain
Died: November 20, 1975; Madrid, Spain
Also known as: Francisco Paulino Hermenegildo Teódulo Franco y Bahamonde Salgado Pardo de Andrate (full name); El Caudillo (The Leader); Generalissimo
Cause of notoriety: Franco's authoritarian administration was considered by many as the lone survivor of the brutal fascist governments of the World War II era.
Active: 1939-1975
Locale: Spain

Early Life

The military and nationalistic fervor of Francisco Franco (FRAHN-koh) was firmly rooted in his family's history. He was born in 1892 in El Ferrol, a small port city in northwestern Spain, to a family with a long tradition of naval service. In 1907, Franco joined the Toledo military academy. His first active service was in the savage Spanish colonial wars in Morocco, where his tenacity, determination, and discipline led to rapid promotion. In 1922, he led Spain's foreign legion, and by 1925 he had achieved the rank of brigadier general. He was named director of a military academy in 1928, but Spain's liberal Republican government closed it in 1931.

During this period, Spain suffered from increasing political turmoil. Spain's monarchy fell in 1931, and elections were held in 1933; a center-right majority won. However, a revolutionary movement erupted in opposition to the new government in the fall of 1934. In the principality of Asturias, where the uprising was particularly violent, Franco was given the task of suppressing the insurgency. His efforts were successful, and he rose to a series of leading military posts.

Political Career

With the narrow victory of the leftist Popular Front in the 1936 Spanish parliamentary elections, Spanish military and nationalist forces rose in revolt. Franco, the youngest but most prestigious of Spain's generals, was soon made both chief general (*generalissimo*) of the nationalist forces and their head of state. During the three years of vicious fighting (in which up to a half million Spaniards died), Franco received assistance from Adolf Hitler's Germany, Benito Mussolini's Italy, and various international and Soviet forces. Franco's nationalists prevailed.

After his victory, Franco continued the harsh repression of vanquished Republican forces with numerous mass executions. Despite a famous meeting between Hitler and Franco in Hedaye, France, on October 23, 1940, Spain remained neutral in World War II. In postwar Spain, Franco's regime turned inward, seeking "traditional" Roman Catholic and Spanish values in a world that Franco found hostile. Dissent was not allowed, and films, as well as much of Spanish social and cultural life, were strictly censored. Franco presided with an iron grip over a one-party state. He dispensed with elections and dreamed of a return to Spain's imperial glory (Morocco, the last of Spain's African colonies, was granted full independence in 1956). In 1947, Franco arranged for a monarchical succession upon his death while assuming dictatorial powers for life.

Francisco Franco. (AP/Wide World Photos)

Franco's Fascism

Excerpts from Francisco Franco's speeches:

- ***July 17, 1936, on the eve of the Spanish Civil War:*** Spaniards! The nation calls to her defense all those of you who hear the holy name of Spain, those in the ranks of the Army and Navy who have made a profession of faith in the service of the Motherland, all those who swore to defend her to the death against her enemies. The situation in Spain grows more critical every day; anarchy reigns in most of the countryside and towns; government-appointed authorities encourage revolts, when they do not actually lead them; murderers use pistols and machine guns to settle their differences and to treacherously assassinate innocent people, while the public authorities fail to impose law and order. Revolutionary strikes of all kinds paralyze the life of the nation, destroying its sources of wealth and creating hunger, forcing working men to the point of desperation.
- ***November 26, 1937:*** I will impose my will by victory and will not enter into discussion. We open our arms to all Spaniards and offer them the opportunity of helping to form the Spain of tomorrow which will be a land of justice, mercy, and fraternity. The war is already won on the battlefields as in the economic, commercial, industrial, and even social spheres. I will only agree to end it militarily. My troops will advance. The choice for the enemy is fight or unconditional surrender, nothing else.
- ***July 18, 1938:*** Our fight is a crusade in which Europe's fate is at stake. . . . Spain was great when she had a State Executive with a missionary character. Her ideals decayed when a serious leader was replaced by assemblies of irresponsible men, adopting foreign thought and manners. The nation needs unity to face modern problems, particularly in Spain after the severest trial of her history. Separatism and class war must be abolished and justice and education must be imposed. The new leaders must be characterized by austerity, morality, and industry. Spaniards must adopt the military and religious virtues of discipline and austerity. All elements of discord must be removed.

Although the Franco regime was ostracized in the immediate aftermath of World War II, the onset of the Cold War found the United States and other Western nations realigning with Spain as a staunch ally against communism. Emblematic of Spain's closer relations with the United States were the four American military bases that Franco permitted on Spanish soil. At the same time, Franco and his ministers were attempting to liberalize Spain's moribund economy with technocratic and industrial reforms. In fact, the 1960's witnessed one of the great periods of development and economic growth in Spain's history, the so-called Spanish Miracle, although this period coincided with increasing terrorism practiced by separatist movements.

In 1969, Franco named the heir to the former Spanish crown, Juan Carlos, as his successor. When Franco died in 1975, General Augusto Pinochet Ugarte of Chile was the only significant head of state to attend his funeral. In the following years, Spain quickly emerged as a constitutional monarchy under King Carlos, with a parliamentary democracy resembling those of other nations of Western Europe.

Impact

Francisco Franco remains one the most significant and divisive figures of the twentieth century. The historical facts are clear. With grim determination, General Franco led the nationalist forces to victory in a vicious civil war, marked by atrocities on both sides. Continuing to war against vanquished Republican prisoners and ideology, Franco remained head of state of Spain for almost forty years, proclaiming himself Caudillo de España por la Gracia de Dios (Leader of Spain by the Grace of God).

However, what is disputed is how to characterize Franco's legacy. To most, especially to those on the Left, Franco was a fascist, an ally of Hitler and Mussolini whose overthrow of a popularly elected republican government and seizure of dictatorial powers was a standing affront to democracy. He remained an unhappy relic of unhappy times, acquiring international acceptance only because of the polarization of the Cold War. In the United States, he was mocked after his death by the American comedy television show *Saturday Night Live*, whose "breaking news" segment often joked that "Generalissimo Francisco Franco is still dead." To others, especially on the Right, Franco—although admittedly a harsh and stern leader—battled fierce forces that threatened to engulf Spain. What cannot be denied is that under the constitutional monarchy that was restored to Spain upon Franco's death, Francoism was rapidly dismantled by Spain's new elected governments.

Further Reading

Hodges, Gabrielle Ashford. *Franco: A Concise Biography*. New York: Thomas Dunne Books, 2002. A psychological biography of Franco, this book traces Franco's legacy of vengeful military tactics and a failed economic regime to his flawed, repressed, and autocratic personality.

Jackson, Gabriel. *The Spanish Republic and the Civil War, 1931-1939*. Princeton, N.J.: Princeton University Press, 1972. Winner of the Hebert Baxter Adams Prize of the American Historical Association, this book is a thorough and sympathetic treatment of the doomed Republican army against what Jackson describes as the forces of imperialism, intolerance, and tyranny.

Payne, Stanley. *The Franco Regime, 1936-1975*. London: Phoenix Press, 1987. Payne, a professor of history, provides a lengthy and comprehensive account of the Franco regime. A scholarly, objective treatment, it portrays an authoritarian but not totalitarian regime and situates Franco's attempts at modernization in the turbulent history of twentieth century Spain.

—Howard Bromberg

See also: Adolf Hitler; Benito Mussolini; Augusto Pinochet Ugarte; António de Oliveira Salazar.

Antoinette Frank

American police officer

Born: January 1, 1970; Opelousas, Louisiana
Major offenses: Murder and robbery
Active: March 4, 1995
Locale: New Orleans, Louisiana
Sentence: Death by lethal injection

Early Life

Antoinette Frank (AN-twah-neht frank) was the second of four children born to Mary Ann and Adam Frank. Though born in Opelousas, Louisiana, she spent most of her childhood in New Orleans. The family moved back to Opelousas in 1987. As a youth, Frank became enamored with the idea of becoming a New Orleans Police Department (NOPD) officer. After graduating from high school, she immediately left Opelousas for New Orleans.

Frank applied to the New Orleans Police Department. However, her application failed to disclose that she had been fired from a job in Opelousas and that her brother was wanted for attempted manslaughter. After scoring poorly on two standardized psychological evaluations, Frank was then evaluated by a board-certified psychiatrist, who concluded that she was unsuitable for the job of police officer.

Depressed over this news, Frank disappeared, leaving a feeble suicide note for her father. Adam filed a NOPD missing persons report on her, only to have her turn up the next day. Frank then received another evaluation from a private psychiatrist, who determined she was suitable to be a police officer. Weeks later, Frank was hired by the NOPD.

Rogers LaCaze was a small-time drug dealer and street thug. Frank met LaCaze while investigating a shooting in which he was injured. They began a romantic relationship and were frequently seen together over the next months.

Criminal Career

On March 4, 1995, around 1:00 A.M., Frank, along with her accomplice, LaCaze, entered the Kim Anh Vietnamese restaurant in eastern New Orleans and shot and killed Ronald Williams and Ha and Cuong Vu during a robbery. Frank had worked off-duty security detail at the restaurant and was aware that the Vu family kept significant amounts of cash around the business. Williams, a young, married father of two, was also employed by the NOPD and worked an off-duty security detail at the restaurant. Ha was the twenty-five-year-old daughter and oldest sibling of the Vu family. She helped run the Kim Anh restaurant with her mother, Bich. Cuong was her seventeen-year-old brother. Cuong played high school football and planned to enter the seminary after graduating. He worked at the restaurant after school.

The criminals left without finding the other two people in the restaurant: Twenty-three-year-old Chau Vu and her eighteen-year-old old brother, Quoc, hid in the restaurant's walk-in cooler when the robbery began. Chau was able to see some of the activity in the front room while she hid. After everything went silent, Quoc called police. Meanwhile, Frank picked up a marked cruiser and drove back to the crime scene and entered it. Chau emerged from the cooler only when she saw uniformed NOPD officers arrive. Detectives arrested Frank at the scene based on Chau's eyewitness report.

Legal Action and Outcome

Frank's trial began in September, 1995. The state took three days to present its case against her. The defense rested without calling a single witness. It took the jury only twenty-two minutes to convict Frank of three counts of first-degree murder, and forty-five minutes to sentence her to death.

One month into Frank's time on death row at St. Gabriel's Louisiana Correctional Institute for Women, a new crime was discovered. In November, 1995, the new family living in the house that Frank had rented in New Orleans East discovered a bone. Police unearthed a human skeleton from under the house; the skull had a bullet wound. Frank's father had not been seen in over a year, and many presumed that the skull was his. This case remained unsettled a decade later.

Impact

Antoinette Frank became the only female on death row in Louisiana and only the second Louisiana woman in one hundred years to be sentenced to death. The sentence's severity, although appropriate for the remorseless Frank, was perhaps more important for the impact it had on the New Orleans Police Department, long considered one of the most corrupt in the nation. As a result of the case, the New Orleans Police Department restructured its recruitment and screening process for hiring new officers, even soliciting the Federal Bureau of Investigation to assist in ethical training. Its officer performance evaluation program was also overhauled.

Further Reading

Hustmyre, Chuck. *Killer with a Badge*. New York: Berkley, 2004. Describes the crime and the backgrounds of the perpetrators and victims. Also provides insight into the culture of New Orleans East and Vietnamese immigrants.

Treadway, Joan, and James Varney. "Coroner: Bones Beneath Home Appear to Be Human." *Times-Picayune*, November 8, 1995, p. A-1. A newspaper account of the discovery of bones under the home in which Frank once lived.

Varney, James. "Cop Turned Killer Gets Death Sentence, Decision Reached Within Forty-Five Minutes." *Times-Picayune*, September 13, 1995, p. A-1. A newspaper feature detailing aspects of Frank's trial.

—*John C. Kilburn, Jr.*

See also: Bambi Bembenek; Eugene de Kock.

Hans Michael Frank

Governor general of Poland during the Nazi occupation

Born: May 23, 1900; Karlsruhe, Germany
Died: October 16, 1946; Nuremberg, Germany
Major offenses: War crimes, specifically ghettoization and exploitation of Jews as slave labor
Active: October 26, 1939-January, 1945
Locale: Warsaw, Poland
Sentence: Death by hanging

Early Life

Hans Michael Frank (hahns MI-kehl frahnk) was the son of a lawyer who had been disbarred and sent to prison for embezzlement. Upon his release, his license to practice law was restored, only to have disbarment proceedings brought against him for a second time. In 1917, Frank enlisted in the German army and fought in World War I. After Germany surrendered to the Allies, he joined the German Workers Party (DAP) in 1919. In 1923, he took part in Adolf Hitler's failed Beer Hall Putsch and then studied law at the University of Munich, after which he was admitted to the bar in 1926. While a student, he joined the anti-Semitic Thule Society, later to state that he had joined because of his relative impoverishment in comparison to wealthy Jews.

In 1927, after becoming a full member of the National Socialist German Workers Party (NSDAP), he became Hitler's personal legal adviser and the party's principal attorney. Subsequently, he defended the NSDAP in twenty-four hundred of the approximately forty thousand lawsuits that were brought against the party, gaining both respect and trust from Hitler for his legal talents.

Political Career

In 1930, Frank was elected to the Reichstag and was made minister of justice for Bavaria in 1933. He headed the National Socialist Jurists Association and was president of the Academy of German Law from 1933 to 1945. In 1934, Frank became the president of the Reichstag and minister of justice in Bavaria. In that position, he complained about extrajudicial killings, objecting to their increasing frequency at Dachau. Frank also complained about the the murders committed during the Night of the Long Knives (1934); he argued strenuously against the proposed execution of 110 members of the Sturmabteilung (SA) without their being tried. Due to his timely intervention, the number of men shot was kept to twenty. Frank, however, lost immense influence with Hitler and the NSDAP hierarchy because of his actions.

On September 1, 1939, Hitler attacked Poland, thus beginning World War II, and on October 26, 1939, Frank became the governor general in the occupied Polish territories—the position that eventually led to his being executed. In essence, he commanded areas not directly incorporated into Germany (equal to approximately 90,000 out of the total 170,000 kilometers Germany had gained). The Shutzstaffel (SS) granted Frank the rank of *Obergruppenführer* (senior group leader). His primary responsibility in Poland was the segregation of Jewish citizens into areas specifically situated for their use (ghettos), as well as using Poles as slave labor.

Frank's authority in Poland was enormous. He received orders to exploit ruthlessly the country's resources in any way he saw fit and was charged with exporting any and all materials important to Germany's war economy. Poland was to operate at a subsistence level, with all educational institutions closed, thus preventing a recrudescence of a Polish intelligentsia. Specifically, Frank was to make Polish citizens the slaves of a "Greater German World Empire."

By 1942, Frank had lost much of his standing with Hitler following a series of speeches he made throughout Germany regarding the war. Moreover, he and Friedrich Wilhelm Kruger, head of the SS and the police in the general government, were locked in a power struggle over control of Poland. Later, at the Nuremberg Trials, Frank claimed to have tendered his resignation fourteen times because he was tired of his job; nonetheless, he said, Hitler would not allow him to quit. After the war, Frank stated that he knew nothing about the "final solution" to the Jewish question, as the entire Holocaust was controlled by Reichsführer Heinrich Himmler. In January, 1945, Frank fled back to Germany as the Soviet army rolled into Poland, thus ending his career as governor general.

Legal Action and Outcome

On May 4, 1945, Frank was captured by American forces. He and the rest of the captured Nazi elite were tried by the Allies from November 20, 1945, to October 1, 1946, at Nuremberg. During the trial, Frank renewed his faith in Roman Catholicism. He surrendered his personal diaries to the Allies, which were then used against him as evidence of his guilt. He confessed to some of the charges and said he viewed his execution as a way to atone for his many sins. He was found guilty of war crimes and crimes against humanity, and on October 1, 1946, was sentenced to death by hanging, as were most of the upper echelon of Nazis. Frank went to his death smiling.

Impact

The use of an international tribunal to try Hans Michael Frank and other Nazi war criminals was a watershed in international law: The trials at Nuremberg marked the first time in modern history that a court representing different nations judged a defeated enemy; thus, it started the practice of international law. In 1998, with Nuremberg as its model, the International Criminal Court was created to ensure that the gravest international crimes, as well as international criminals, received justice. Likewise, Nuremberg initiated international human rights trials, from the prosecution of Serbian leader of Yugoslavia Slobodan Milošević in The Hague to that of Iraqi dictator Saddam Hussein in Baghdad. After Nuremberg, one could not evade responsibility for war crimes by saying that one was only "following orders."

Further Reading

Gilbert, Martin. *The Holocaust: A History of the Jews of Europe During the Second World War*. New York: Owl Books, 2004. An excellent account of the hardships faced by Jews during the Nazi era.

Housden, Martyn. *Hans Frank, Lebensraum, and the Final Solution*. New York: Palgrave Macmillan, 2004. A scholarly study that examines Frank's career as well as emphasizing his complex personality.

Overy, Richard. *Interrogations: The Nazi Elite in Allied Hands*. 1945 Reprint. New York: Penguin, 1995. Discusses how each high-ranking prisoner acted in prison, as well as how each answered questions.

Perisco, Joseph E. *Nuremberg: Infamy on Trial*. New York: Penguin, 1995. The author attempts to re-create Frank's (and each of the rest of the Nazi hierarchy's) psychological state during the trial. Well written.

—*Cary Stacy Smith*

See also: Heinrich Himmler; Adolf Hitler.

Martin Frankel

American financier and fraud

Born: November 21, 1954; Toledo, Ohio
Also known as: David Rosse; Eric Stevens; Mike King; Martin Leon Frankel (full name)
Major offenses: Securities fraud, racketeering, moneylaundering, and (in Germany) carrying a false passport and evading customs taxes
Active: 1985-1999
Locale: Greenwich, Connecticut; Toledo, Ohio; and West Palm Beach, Florida
Sentence: Sixteen years, eight months' imprisonment in the United States; three years' imprisonment in Germany

Early Life

Martin Frankel (fran-KEHL) was born into a well-respected family in Toledo, Ohio. His father, Leon, was an attorney, and his mother, Tillie, worked as a city clerk. Martin was the middle child of three. He was very intelligent but somewhat awkward socially. While Frankel's grades were very good, he had a habit of failing to turn in school assignments, and he experienced a phobia of test-taking. This behavior intensified during his student days at the University of Toledo, where he enrolled in a significant number of courses, yet actually completed and passed very few. He left college with nearly two hundred hours of uncompleted coursework. Soon afterward, he received a license to sell real estate but failed to sell a single property.

Frankel lived with his parents until he was past the age of thirty. He spent many hours reading the financial newspapers and visiting Toledo brokerage houses. In 1985, Frankel entered the brokerage office of John F. Schulte, Inc., and announced that he planned to open an account. Though he never funded the account, he continued to visit and befriend John Schulte's wife, Sonia, who was a partner in the brokerage. After many visits, Frankel talked himself into a job with the firm.

In eight months of employment with Schulte, Frankel had only one significant client. Instead of working, he spent numerous hours explaining his system of amassing great wealth through trading securities but never actually placed trades. Similar to his testing phobia, Frankel claimed to have "trader's block" which stopped him from actually making trades, regardless of how passionately he held an investment idea.

Criminal Career

Frankel later opened a branch office of LaSalle Street Securities, operating it out of his bedroom in his parents' home, with one client he had managed to keep from his previous brokerage job. He created documents that made wild claims about his system of trading commodities, stocks, and bonds for enormous profits. He then teamed up with Douglas Maxwell to recruit investors for the limited partnership Frankel Fund and the Creative Partners Fund. After mismanaging these funds by failing to place trades and using some of the money for his own personal expenses, federal regulators charged Frankel with fraud. He accepted a lifetime ban from the securities industry and was fined $200,000 in 1992.

Frankel maintained a relationship with Sonia Schulte, who eventually divorced John Schulte. Because Sonia alleged abuse in her marital relationship, Frankel offered to provide a safe home for her and her two children. With Sonia's assistance, Frankel set up the Donar Corporation, using friends' names as directors because he was banned from trading by the Securities and Exchange Commission.

Frankel then established the Thunor Trust as a corporation to buy insurance companies. His primary idea was to purchase the insurance companies and then steal the cash reserves that were set aside to pay claims. With the assistance of John Hackney, the Thunor Trust purchased the Tennessee-based Franklin American Insurance Corporation, which then bought numerous other insurance companies throughout the United States.

Frankel moved to Greenwich, Connecticut, and lived in luxury with the cash reserves of the various insurance companies his corporation purchased. He hired a large staff, which assisted him in falsifying financial statements for the various firms he controlled under the name Eric Stevens. Frankel's scheme worked for several years thanks to the complexity of its transactions: numerous corporations frequently transferring large amounts of money from one to another among banks around the world.

By placing and answering ads in special-interest sex-related magazines, Frankel met women seeking sadomasochistic sex. While many of those who responded to his ads became his sexual partners, Frankel offered others employment in his companies. His rationale was that women interested in a sadomasochistic relationship would be obedient employees. In addition to his large house in Greenwich, he rented a neighboring house so that he could house his partners and business associates.

As his appetite to make larger corporate acquisitions

grew, Frankel devised a scheme in which he would acquire insurance companies in the names of charities and claim to give the profits to the charities. Actually, the name of a charity was used to offer a facade of legitimacy to Frankel's fraudulent dealings. He developed the St. Francis of Assisi Foundation with the claim that its funding came from the Vatican. This structure was developed through the nurturing of several politically connected attorneys, business executives, and Father Peter Jacobs.

At this time, several state insurance and banking regulators began to investigate and suspect that Frankel's operations were fraudulent. In May of 1999, Frankel fled to Europe with two women employees and was later arrested in a Hamburg hotel with nine fake passports, 547 diamonds, and an astrological chart drawn up to answer the question "Will I go to prison?"

Legal Action and Outcome

After serving a brief prison sentence in Germany, Frankel was extradited to the United States in May of 2001. All of his assets were seized and sold. While he was officially charged with insurance fraud, money-laundering, and racketeering with $208 million unaccounted for, it is likely that exact figures will never be known. After pleading guilty in a U.S. District Court, Frankel was sentenced to serve sixteen years and eight months in December of 2004.

Impact

Martin Frankel's case drew substantial attention in the popular press because of his deviant lifestyle. However, his actions are not unique among cases of fraudulent accounting. While deregulation of the insurance and securities industry is often considered helpful to modern trade in the global economy, Frankel's actions illustrate the relative ease with which corporate crime may be perpetrated and millions of dollars stolen. Frankel's story is one of many that justify frequent and detailed audits of corporations.

Further Reading

Johnson, J. A., Jr. *Thief: The Bizarre Story of Fugitive Financier Martin Frankel.* New York: Lebhar-Friedman Books, 2000. Provides a journalistic overview of the events that led to Frankel's rapid financial gains and deviant lifestyle.

Pollock, Ellen Joan. *The Pretender: How Martin Frankel Fooled the Financial World and Led the Feds on One of the Most Publicized Manhunts in History.* New York: Simon and Schuster, 2002. A comprehensive work that details Frankel's personal relationships in building his fraudulent empire.

—John C. Kilburn, Jr.

See also: Ivan Boesky; Michael Milken.

Lynette Fromme

American cult member

Born: October 22, 1948; Santa Monica, California
Also known as: Lynette Alice Fromme (full name); Squeaky Fromme; Red
Major offense: Attempt to assassinate the president of the United States
Active: July, 1970-December 23, 1987
Locale: Los Angeles, Sacramento, and Dublin, California
Sentence: Life in a federal correctional institution

Early Life

Lynette Alice Fromme (frohm) was born to William Fromme, an aeronautical engineer, and Helen Benzinger Fromme, homemaker and mother of three. Redheaded Lyn, the eldest child, was a star performer in the Westchester Lariats, a children's dance group that became so popular it performed on *The Lawrence Welk Show* and at the White House. Despite having external social success in her early years, Fromme had a troubled home life during her childhood. She was reared by an emotionally cold, detached father who treated her harshly and who parented through fear and intimidation. Fromme's mother was unable to thwart her father's anger toward the family.

When the family moved to Redondo Beach, California, in 1963, Fromme's academic grades plummeted, and she began drinking and taking drugs. After narrowly graduating from high school in 1966, Fromme moved out of her parents' home and drifted until she met Charles Manson in Venice Beach the following year. Eighteen-year-old Fromme was amazed by Manson, an existential philosopher who did not appear to expect anything of her. Their meeting was so provocative, she left with Manson, never to return home.

Criminal Career

Fromme began living with Manson and his cult of nomadic young people much like her. While with them, she took psychotropic drugs such as LSD and became wholly absorbed with Manson's assertions that racial civil war was imminent and that the Manson family of followers would ultimately rule the world.

Fromme would come to hold a special place in the Manson family hierarchy. After Manson was arrested in 1969, Fromme (called Squeaky within the Manson family) and fellow Manson family member Sandra Good carved *X*'s in their foreheads to show loyalty to Manson. They also carved the letter to protest Manson's impending conviction for grand theft auto and his concurrent arrest for the Sharon Tate and the Leo and Rosemary LaBianca murders in 1969. Fromme later declared, "We have X'ed ourselves out of this world."

Fromme effectively took control of the family in Manson's absence. Soon after his incarceration, she moved to Stockton, California, with Nancy Pitman, Priscilla Copper, Michael Monfort, James Craig, and a couple, James and Lauren (Reni) Willett. In 1972, when the Willetts were found dead within days of each other, the roommates were taken into custody. However, Fromme was released because of a lack of evidence. Leaving Stockton, she moved to Sacramento with Good. Together, they formed the International People's Court of Retribution, an organization intended to frighten corporate executives into believing that they were on a terrorist hit list for environmental degradation. Using his continued influence, Manson encouraged the two women to wear robes and change their names to symbolize their devotion to his new religion, which Manson called the "Order of the Rainbow." He dubbed Lynette "Red" because of her red hair, while giving her the task of protecting all redwood trees. Good he named "Blue" for her blue eyes.

Lynette "Squeaky" Fromme. (AP/Wide World Photos)

For several years, Fromme drifted through a life of poverty and petty crimes until she went to Sacramento's Capitol Park in 1975 to complain to President Gerald R. Ford about the destruction of the environment. The Manson "nun," dressed in her red "habit" and armed with a Colt .45 automatic, shot at Ford from a distance of only two feet. Her weapon had four bullets in the clip, but the chamber was empty.

Legal Action and Outcome

Fromme often claimed she had committed the attempted assassination so that Manson would appear as a witness at her trial and thus give him a worldwide platform from which to talk about his grand vision. However, Judge Thomas J. MacBride refused to give Fromme or Manson a public platform for their views. Serving as her own defense counsel, Fromme boycotted most of the court proceedings. After three days of jury deliberation, she was convicted of attempting to assassinate the president and remanded to the custody of the Federal Bureau of Prisons in Dublin, California.

In 1979, Fromme was convicted and transferred from the Dublin federal prison for striking a fellow inmate in the head with a hammer. After traversing a variety of U.S. federal prisons, she escaped from the Alderson Federal Prison Camp in Alderson, West Virginia, in 1987, in an attempt to meet with Manson, whom she had been told had cancer. She was captured in the nearby woods two days later and sentenced to serve life at the Federal Bureau of Prisons' Carswell Federal Medical Center in Fort Worth, Texas, where she remained in the administrative segregation unit following her arrival in 1998. Although federal law entitled Fromme to a mandatory parole hearing after thirty years, she continued to waive her right to these hearings, and unlike several of Manson's former disciples who remained in prison, she chose not to seek her release. She never renounced Manson.

Impact

When one reflects on the tumultuous 1960's in the United States, the name Squeaky Fromme is synonymous with Charles Manson and his cult family. As the emerging counterculture became a national phenomenon, Fromme and her compatriots espoused liberal ideals and defended the right to commit "political" crimes. As self-proclaimed defenders of the First Amendment, they believed it was their duty to create a new moral and political order. The atmosphere of political and social protest during the period exacerbated their susceptibility to influence by such charismatic criminals as Manson. Indeed, Fromme's crimes, like those of many other Manson followers, were clearly criminal acts masked as political activism.

Further Reading

Bravin, Jess. *Squeaky: The Life and Times of Lynette Alice Fromme*. New York: St. Martin's Griffin, 1998. An account of Fromme's life from her childhood years, her time with Manson, her attempted assassination of President Ford, and her ensuing trial.

Osborne, John. *New Republic* 173, no. 14 (1975): 9-10. A discussion of the effects of Fromme's attempt to assassinate President Ford and on the president's public appearances and security.

Sanders, Ed. *The Family*. New York: Thunder's Mouth Press, 2002. A detailed look at the terror dealt by Manson and his followers with some of the most notorious murders in modern American history.

—*Patricia K. Hendrickson*

See also: Charles Manson.

Klaus Fuchs

German physicist and communist spy

Born: December 29, 1911; Rüsselsheim, Germany
Died: January 28, 1988; East Berlin, East Germany (now Berlin, Germany)
Also known as: Klaus Emil Julius Fuchs (full name)
Major offense: Espionage
Active: 1942-1949
Locale: Birmingham and London, England; New York, New York; Los Alamos, New Mexico; and Boston, Massachusetts
Sentence: Fourteen years in prison; served nine years

Early Life

The childhood and adolescence of Klaus Emil Julius Fuchs (klows ay-MEEL JEW-lyuhs fooks) was dominated by his father, an itinerant Lutheran minister and a dedicated Christian socialist. When Klaus began studying mathematics and physics at the University of Leipzig, he broke with his father, who had become a Quaker, by joining a semimilitary group that believed Nazi thuggery could not be countered pacifistically. In 1930, Klaus moved with his family from Leipzig to Kiel, where he continued his scientific education and anti-Nazi activities. When Adolf Hitler came to power in 1933, Fuchs, who had already been the target of Nazi violence, realized that he would have to leave Germany. Following the advice of Communist Party leaders, he fled via Paris to England.

With financial support, Fuchs was able to complete his studies in physics at Bristol University, receiving his doctorate in 1937. He then became a postdoctoral physicist at the University of Edinburgh in Scotland under Max Born, a prominent German émigré scientist. When World War II broke out in 1939, Fuchs, an enemy alien, was placed in internment camps, first in England, then in Quebec, Canada. Eventually, with the support of Born (who had become a British citizen), Fuchs returned to Edinburgh, but, shortly thereafter, he accepted an offer to work on a secret project in Birmingham, England.

Espionage Career

An ironic confluence of events occurred for Fuchs in 1942. He became a member of the British atomic bomb research project, code-named Tube Alloys, and a citizen of his adopted country. However, after taking the Oath of Allegiance and learning of the nature of his war work, he decided to spy for Russia and initiated contact through a Communist Party member. At the end of 1942, Fuchs was part of a distinguished group of British scientists who traveled to the United States to participate in the Manhattan Project, the American program to develop the atomic bomb. While working at Columbia University in New York City and later at Los Alamos National Laboratory in New Mexico, Fuchs made arrangements to inform the Russians about how the Americans planned to obtain the fissionable isotope uranium-235 for one kind of atomic bomb and how they were developing an improved technique (implosion) for the plutonium-239 atomic bomb. At Los Alamos, Fuchs worked in the theoretical division headed by the German American physicist Hans Albrecht Bethe.

In a series of meetings over the next few years with a Soviet courier code-named "Raymond" (his real name was Harry Gold), Fuchs communicated to Soviet leader Joseph Stalin's spymaster Lavrenty Beria detailed information that Fuchs had acquired by participating in the development of the implosion technique. Beria allowed Igor Vasilyevich Kurchatov, the leader of the Soviet atomic bomb project, to see sizable selections from the massive amount of material that Fuchs was supplying.

Fuchs was present at the Trinity Test of the first atomic bomb, an implosion device nicknamed "Fat Man," at Alamogordo, New Mexico. After the dropping of a uranium-235 bomb on Hiroshima, Japan, and a plutonium-239 bomb on Nagasaki, Japan, brought World War II to an end in 1945, Fuchs remained at Los Alamos, where he participated in the early stages of the development of a fusion or hydrogen bomb. Before returning to England in 1946, Fuchs informed the Soviets of the results of the Trinity Test and Japanese bombs, as well as what he had learned about the hydrogen bomb.

The British had an atomic research facility at Harwell, and Fuchs continued his secret research there, as well as his spying, which was now communicated largely through Alexander Feklisov, a Soviet intelligence agent. Fuchs's lies and deceptions began to be known to the Americans in the late 1940's through the success of the Venona Project, which allowed U.S. officials to decipher Soviet communications during World War II. The Americans alerted the British to Fuchs's spying, and subsequent British investigations confirmed American suspicions. At the end of 1949, a British officer informed Fuchs that he would be charged with spying for the Soviet Union. After repeated denials, Fuchs confessed.

Controlled Schizophrenia

On January 27, 1950, Klaus Fuchs made a statement to the British War Office explaining his espionage, including this discussion of his work in the atomic bomb effort, beginning in England, and his behavior to colleagues:

When I learned about the purpose of the work I decided to inform Russia and I established contact through another member of the Communist Party. Since that time I have had continuous contact with persons who were completely unknown to me, except that I knew that they would hand whatever information I gave them to the Russian authorities. At this time I had complete confidence in Russian policy and I believed that the Western Allies deliberately allowed Russia and Germany to fight each other to the death. I had therefore no hesitation in giving all the information I had, even though occasionally I tried to concentrate mainly on giving information about the results of my own work.

In the course of this work, I began naturally to form bonds of personal friendship and I had to conceal from them my inner thoughts. I used my Marxist philosophy to establish in my mind two separate compartments. One compartment in which I allowed myself to make friendships, to have personal relations, to help people and to be in all personal ways the kind of man I wanted to be and the kind of man which, in a personal way, I had been before with my friends in or near the Communist Party. I could be free and easy and happy with other people without fear of disclosing myself because I knew the other compartment would step in if I approached the danger point. I could forget the other compartment and still rely on it. It appeared to me at the time that I had become a "free man" because I had succeeded in the other compartment to establish myself completely independent of the surrounding forces of society. Looking back at it now the best way of expressing it seems to be to call it a controlled schizophrenia.

Source: "Klaus Fuchs' Statement," January 27, 1950, British War Office.

Legal Action and Outcome

By the time of Fuchs's arrest in February, 1950, the Soviets had surprised the world by testing their own atomic bomb, and Fuchs's trial generated great interest both in the press and in scientific and political communities. Because of his confession and guilty plea, Fuchs's trial at the Old Bailey in London was over in less than ninety minutes. Fuchs expressed regret for having deceived his British colleagues, and he hoped that his confession and cooperation would contribute to atoning for his many betrayals. Fuchs was prosecuted under the United Kingdom's Official Secrets Act, but, since his crimes involved a British ally, he could be given only the maximum sentence of fourteen years in prison. After nine years, he was released on June 24, 1950, for good behavior and permitted to go to East Germany, where he became a citizen. As a committed communist, he received many honors and served as deputy director of the Central Institute for Nuclear Research near Dresden.

Impact

Klaus Fuchs's trial had an immediate impact on his colleagues and family. On one hand, such scientists as Bethe and Richard Feynman, who were his Los Alamos collaborators, felt bewildered and betrayed. On the other hand, Fuchs's father stated that his son's brave actions actually served the good of the British people more than their government did: He saw his son's lawbreaking in terms of previous rebels who followed their consciences and obeyed the "higher law" of true justice.

The revelations surrounding Fuchs's treachery also had an immediate political impact. It had a detrimental effect on British-American nuclear cooperation, since American intelligence officials believed that British security arrangements were lax. Shortly after Fuchs's trial, the Special Committee of the American National Security Council voted to recommend that U.S. president Harry S. Truman order a crash program to develop a hydrogen bomb, advice that he quickly followed. Another immediate consequence of the revelations of Fuchs's spying was the role that it played in the discovery of an American spy ring centered on Julius and Ethel Rosenberg, in which Gold, Fuchs's Soviet courier, was also involved. Even though the information communicated by Julius Rosenberg to the Soviets was far less important than Fuchs's material, the Rosenbergs were executed for their crimes.

During the Cold War, some politicians and scientists tended to exaggerate the damage Fuchs had done to the United States and Great Britain. A congressional committee on atomic energy concluded that Fuchs had compromised the safety of more people than any other spy in history. The nuclear physicist Edward Teller claimed that the information Fuchs supplied to the Soviets saved them ten years of research on the hydrogen bomb. England's lord chief justice and others condemned Fuchs for doing irreprable and incalculable damage to the security of several countries.

When documents became available after the fall of the Soviet Union in the late twentieth century, some scholars took a more modest view of Fuchs's spying. Some believe that Soviet scientists were able to discover much about the atomic bomb on their own, and Fuchs's information simply saved them some time by informing them what lines of research were valueless. However, when the British Security Service released more than

Klaus Fuchs.

twenty files on Fuchs, this material, though heavily censored, convinced certain scholars that Fuchs was indeed the most destructive spy in British history. Estimates of how much time Fuchs's revelations saved Soviet scientists in developing the atomic bomb range from several months to several years.

Further Reading

Feklisov, Alexander. *The Man Behind the Rosenbergs*. New York: Enigma Books, 2004. Feklisov was a professional spy for Stalin, so this memoir has to be read cautiously. Nevertheless, he was Fuchs's handler, and he has much of interest to say about their relationship.

Moss, Norman. *Klaus Fuchs: The Man Who Stole the Atom Bomb*. New York: St. Martin's Press, 1987. This biography is largely based on interviews of people who knew Fuchs. It emphasizes Fuchs's motivations for spying. Illustrated, with an appendix on Fuchs's confession and an index.

Williams, Robert Chadwell. *Klaus Fuchs, Atom Spy*. Cambridge, Mass.: Harvard University Press, 1987. Using archival materials obtained under the Freedom of Information Act, Williams concentrates on Fuchs as a traitor and on the failures of Allied security to detect his crimes. Illustrated, with appendixes on two Fuchs confessions and a Harry Gold statement to the FBI. Selected bibliography and index.

—Robert J. Paradowski

See also: Lavrenty Beria; Anthony Blunt; Christopher John Boyce; Guy Burgess; John Cairncross; Robert Philip Hanssen; Alger Hiss; Daulton Lee; Joseph McCarthy; Donald Duart Maclean; Kim Philby; Ethel Rosenberg; Julius Rosenberg.

Alberto Fujimori

President of Peru (1990-2000)

Born: July 28, 1938; Lima, Peru

Also known as: Alberto Ken'ya Fujimori (full name); Alberto Keinya Fujimori; El Chino

Cause of notoriety: Despite demonstrable improvements in the Peruvian economy, Fujimori's terms as president of Peru were marked by scandal and accusations of corruption and crimes against humanity. He exiled himself to Japan in 2001, only to return to Latin America in 2005 to make another bid for the Peruvian presidency.

Active: 1990-present

Locale: Peru

Early Life

Alberto Ken'ya Fujimori (few-jee-moh-ree) was born to Naoichi Fujimori and Mutsue Fujimori, Japanese nationals who emigrated to Peru in 1934. He received his degree in agriculture engineering in 1961 from the National Agrarian University in La Molina; he became a lecturer in mathematics in the same institution in 1962. In 1964, he studied physics in France, and in 1969 he received his master's degree in mathematics from the University of Wisconsin in the United States. From 1984 to 1989, he was the rector of the National Agrarian University, his alma mater, and was selected as the president of the National Commission of Peruvian University Rectors in 1987.

Political Career

At the head of his new party, Cambio 90, Fujimori won the 1990 presidential elections in Peru, beating novelist Mario Vargas Llosa. Utilizing far-reaching agrarian and infrastructural reforms suggested by the International Monetary Fund (IMF), Fujimori stabilized Peru's economy. He privatized state-owned service enterprises and changed the national laws to encourage foreign investments in the country's gas, oil, and mining resources.

On April 5, 1992, Fujimori conducted a coup against his own party in order to reorganize the structure of the Peruvian government, to increase his power, and to make the government more efficient. He dissolved the congress to form a new governing body, the Democratic Constitutional Congress, which drafted a new constitution in 1993. Two weeks after this coup, the United States officially recognized him as Peru's legitimate leader, primarily because Fujimori had embarked on a campaign to eradicate the insurgent movements known as the Sendero Luminoso (Shining Path) and Túpac Amaru Revolutionary Movement (MRTA).

In the 1992 presidential elections, Fujimori's party received a majority in the new congress; however, some opposition parties did not participate in the electoral process. His authority was legitimized when a majority of Peruvians approved the 1993 constitution. A failed military coup in November of 1992 forced him to seek refuge in the Japanese embassy. In 1994, Susana Higuchi, his former wife, publicly denounced his government as corrupt, alleging that he and his family had misappropriated money donated to the country by the Japanese embassy.

In the 1995 presidential elections, Fujimori was again reelected by a landslide majority, beating his political opponent, Javier Pérez de Cuéllar. Fujimori's second term as president was marked by the signing of a peace accord between Peru and Ecuador, which paved the way for the two countries to receive international financial aid and develop their common border. During his second presidential tenure, Fujimori also granted amnesty to all participants of the Peruvian army who had been accused of human rights abuses between 1985 and 1995. It is also during this second term that Peruvians began to criticize Fujimori's control of the free press and his alliance with Vladimiro Montesinos Torres, his chief of the National Intelligence Service.

Fujimori was reelected for a third, unprecedented term on May 28, 2000. The opposition, led principally by Alejandro Toledo Manrique, wanted the elections annulled because of allegations of fraud and voting irregularities. A scandal involving Montesinos and his bribery of a congressman who had opposed Fujimori compromised Fujimori's credibility and compelled him to announce a new election on September 16 in which he would not participate. The Peruvian congress approved Fujimori's request to hold presidential elections on April 8, 2001. On November 13, Fujimori left to attend the Asia-Pacific Conference in Brunei, and he exiled himself to Tokyo on November 17, after Valentín Paniagua Corazao was selected as president of the congress, following a vote of no confidence against Fujimori. His resignation, sent from Tokyo, was followed by the bloc resignation of all his ministers on November 19. On November 21, 2000, Paniagua became interim president of Peru with authority to oversee the upcoming presidential elections.

President Toledo, elected in 2001, made many attempts to extradite Fujimori to Peru to face trial for many alleged crimes, including murder, kidnapping, arms-smuggling, and crimes against humanity. In October, 2005, Fujimori declared, from Tokyo, that he would run in the April, 2006, presidential elections in Peru, despite a ten-year ban barring him from public office. Nonetheless, he created a new political party, Sí Cumple. On November 6, 2005, Fujimori arrived in Santiago, Chile, where he was detained. At that time, the government of Peru began its attempt to extradite Fujimori back to Peru. Elections were held on April 9, 2006, and two candidates emerged for a runoff election in June; Fujimori was not one of them.

Impact

Alberto Fujimori became an important and controversial personality in the political environment of Peru, mainly because of his persistence in trying to remain in the public, political sphere. Fujimori has been credited with eradicating the terrorist groups Shining Path and the MRTA and with arresting the leaders of both groups, notably Abimael Guzmán Reynoso, leader of the Shining Path.

Despite the controversy surrounding Fujimori and his administration, he brought stability to the country and economic improvement, making it possible for Peru to participate in the global economic system and to attract foreign investment. Peru's currency reserves also increased to ten billion dollars by the end of Fujimori's presidency in 2000, and there was a marked improvement of infrastructural services brought about by the privatization of state-owned facilities such as telephone services.

Fujimori also left a much smaller state bureaucracy and smaller government expenses, as well as a large number of new schools throughout the country and a great number of highways. These legacies have all contributed to the current expansion and revival of Peru's industries, such as tourism and agriculture.

Further Reading

Cameron, Maxwell A. *Democracy and Authoritarianism in Peru*. New York: St. Martin's Press, 1994. An account of the democratic system in Peru and of the political forces that have shaped this kind of democracy, as well as a description of why and how Fujimori was able to use this blend of politics and authoritarianism to become president of Peru.

Kimura, Rei. *Alberto Fujimori of Peru: The President Who Dared to Dream*. New York: Beekman, 1998. A description of Fujimori, depicting his early life, his formative educational years, and his rise to the presidency of Peru.

Wianda, Howard J., and Harvey F. Kline. *Latin American Politics and Development*. Boulder, Colo.: Westview Press, 2000. An overview of politics and its development in Latin America, particularly in Peru. Describes how politics works together with infrastructural developments in Latin America, focusing on Fujimori and demonstrating how he was able to blend politics with development to rise to the presidency in this country.

—*Víctor Manuel Durán*

See also: Juan Perón.

FULVIA

Roman matrona and revolutionary

BORN: c. 85/80 B.C.E.; place unknown
DIED: 40 B.C.E.; Sicyon, Greece
CAUSE OF NOTORIETY: Fulvia led a military campaign against Octavian Caesar on behalf of her husband Marc Antony.
ACTIVE: 41-40 B.C.E.
LOCALE: Rome, later Perusia
SENTENCE: Exile to Greece

EARLY LIFE

Fulvia (FUHL-vee-ah) was born sometime during the early first century B.C.E. to Marcus Fulvius Flaccus Bambulus and Sempronia, daughter of Gaius Gracchus. Fulvia's first husband was the demagogue Clodius Pulcher. After his death in 52 B.C.E., Fulvia married Scribonius Curio, a tribune who supported Julius Caesar in his rise to power. When Scribonius died, Fulvia wed her third and most famous husband, Marc Antony. According to Plutarch, Fulvia was a woman who was not interested in domestic tasks; she dominated Antony both at home and in his political actions.

POLITICAL CAREER

With Antony, Lepidus and Octavian Caesar formed the second Roman triumvirate in 44 B.C.E. Fulvia offered her daughter Clodia (Fulvia's daughter by Clodius Pulcher) in marriage to Octavian to strengthen the political alliance between Octavian and Antony. A short time later, the triumvirs Octavian (destined to become the first Roman emperor, Augustus), Lepidus, and Antony divided the Roman provinces among them. Octavian took charge of Italy, while Lepidus took the western provinces, and Antony sailed to Egypt. There Antony met the Egyptian queen Cleopatra VII and began an affair with her.

While Antony was in Egypt, Fulvia was representing his political interests in Rome. Octavian was planning to redistribute lands within Italy to the veteran soldiers who had supported him during his rise to power. Fulvia wanted to delay the redistribution of land until Antony returned from Egypt and asked the veterans to support Antony. Octavian divorced Clodia and started a propaganda campaign against Fulvia.

Fulvia eventually decided to take military action against Octavian. She and her brother-in-law Lucius Antonius raised eight legions of Roman troops to support Antony against Octavian's power grab. According to Dio Cassius, Fulvia personally led troops against Octavian's forces in early battles. Her army was able to occupy the city of Rome only for a short time before it was driven out and retreated to the city of Perusia. Octavian laid siege to Perusia during the winter of 41-40 B.C.E. and eventually starved Fulvia and her troops into surrendering.

LEGAL ACTION AND OUTCOME

During Fulvia's campaign against Octavian, Octavian held a gathering of war veterans that turned into a de facto trial, at which Octavian convinced the veterans and his followers that Fulvia and Antony were traitors to Rome. After the siege of Perusia, Fulvia surrendered and was exiled to Sicyon on the Gulf of Corinth, where she fell ill and died while Antony was on his way to meet her.

IMPACT

In a time when women were expected to run the household and raise children, Fulvia was not only able to raise an army; she also was remembered for it. The fact that she is the first nonmythological woman featured on Roman coins speaks of her importance. History considers her a traitor only because she happened to be on the losing side. If Antony and his supporters had carried the day, Fulvia may well have been honored as a heroine by the Romans.

FURTHER READING

Bauman, Richard A. *Women and Politics in Ancient Rome*. New York: Routledge, 1992. A study of women's involvement in and influence over politics and society in antiquity.

Fraschetti, Augusto, ed. *Roman Women*. Translated by Linda Lappin. Chicago: University of Chicago Press, 2001. A collection of essays of influential Roman women.

Hemelrijk, Emily A. *Matrona Docta: Educated Women in the Roman Elite, from Cornelia to Julia Domna*. New York: Routledge, 1999. Explores the opportunities available to upper-class Roman women (including Fulvia) to acquire an education.

Kleiner, Diana E. E., and Susan Matheson, eds. *I, Claudia: Women in Ancient Rome*. New Haven, Conn.: Yale University Art Gallery, 1996. A comprehensive study of women as depicted in Roman art.

Pomeroy, Sarah B., ed. *Women's History and Ancient History*. Chapel Hill: University of North Carolina

Press, 1991. A collection of essays on the roles of women in ancient history, as portrayed by the ancient sources.

—*Caitlin L. Moriarity*

See also: Caligula; Catiline; Cassius Chaerea; Domitian.

Fyodor I

Czar of Russia (r. 1584-1598)

Born: May 31, 1557; Moscow, Russia
Died: January 17, 1598; Moscow, Russia
Also known as: Fyodor the Bellringer; Fedor Ivanovich; Fyodor Ivanovich; Fedor Czarevich
Cause of notoriety: Despite his mental retardation, Fyodor ruled Russia for fourteen years, delegating state business to his trusted adviser Boris Godunov.
Active: 1584-1598
Locale: Moscow, Russia

Early Life

Fyodor (FEE-door) was born the third son of Ivan IV, known as Ivan the Terrible, and his first wife, Anastasia Romanov. Fyodor's oldest brother, Dmitry, had died; his brother Ivan was three years older than he. Although Ivan was healthy, Fyodor soon exhibited signs of Down syndrome: short arms, weak legs, and, as he grew older, a perpetual smile, which led to his being called *durak* ("silly fool") by the Russian people, who nonetheless loved him.

Although he was a czarevitch, son of the czar, the robust health of his brother Ivan meant that few imagined Fyodor would ever become czar. However, in November, 1581, Ivan IV, in a fit of rage, killed Ivan, his oldest son. To the horror of all Russia, Fyodor was now heir to the throne. Knowing that Fyodor was incapable of ruling, Ivan set up a five-man regency council, led by Boris Godunov, a Tatar who had become a favorite of Ivan and who entered the royal family when his sister Irina was married to Fyodor.

Political Career

When Ivan IV died on March 18, 1584, the only credible rival of Fyodor as czar was the maternal family of his infant half brother, Dmitry, the son of Ivan IV and his seventh wife. That family, the Nagoys, hoped to exploit the mental failings of Fyodor in order to control Russia themselves. The council led by Godunov thwarted the Nagoys' plan and ensured Fyodor's continued rule.

The daily activities of Czar Fyodor I were predictable: prayer and morning religious services, naps, entertainment (such as jesters and bear fights), prayer, and then bed. At night when he could not sleep, Fyodor roamed the streets of Moscow, ringing church bells, hence his nickname "the Bellringer." When issues of official business arose, he always referred them to Godunov.

During the latter part of Fyodor's reign, Godunov, to increase his own stature, tried to elevate his sister Irina as ruler in her own right. Fyodor and Irina had only one child, a daughter who died before her second birthday. There was thus no blood heir to Fyodor.

Fyodor's death in 1598 led to the usual false reports that there were other sons of Ivan IV, of his son Ivan, and even of Fyodor. These reports were all discounted. Irina assumed temporary authority, but at that time there was no precedent for a female Russian ruler. A duma (assembly) met to decide the future of the monarchy. After several modest "refusals," Godunov agreed to accept the crown.

Impact

The major impact of Fyodor I on Russia took place at his death, which ended the Russian monarchy that had begun with Rurik in the ninth century and included the Muscovite monarchy, beginning in 1263 with Prince Daniel. The most distinguished member of both lines was Fyodor's great-grandfather, Ivan the Great.

Fyodor's death also set the stage for Russia's Time of Troubles, which followed the death of Godunov in 1605. This period ended in 1613 with the beginning of a new dynasty, the Romanov, which lasted until the Bolshevik Revolution in 1917.

Further Reading

Emerson, Caryl. *Boris Godunov*. Bloomington: Indiana University Press, 1986. A biography of the brother-in-law and successor to Fyodor; includes many details about Fyodor, his marriage, his death, and the possible succession of his wife, Godunov's sister.

Madariaga, Isabel de. *Ivan the Terrible: First Tsar of Russia*. New Haven, Conn.: Yale University Press, 2005. Interwoven through this major biography are details about Ivan's son Fyodor. Includes the tragic account of how Fyodor was left as successor to Ivan. An excellent bibliography and an extensive notes section offer further details about Fyodor.

Pavlov, Andrei, and Maureen Perrie. *Ivan the Terrible*. London: Pearson-Longman, 2003. A shorter biography that includes details of the beginning of Fyodor's reign and the power struggle between different factions of the boyars (nobles). Has dynastic charts of the monarchy before and after Fyodor.

Platonov, S. F. *Boris Godunov: Tsar of Russia*. Gulf Breeze, Fla.: Academic International Press, 1973. Covers the "Tale of 1606" (a fictitious legend about Fyodor), the attitude of the Russian people toward Fyodor, and other details of the czar's life.

—*Glenn L. Swygart*

See also: Ivan the Terrible; Ivan V; Ivan VI.

John Wayne Gacy

American serial killer

Born: March 17, 1942; Chicago, Illinois
Died: May 10, 1994; Stateville Correctional Center, Joliet, Illinois
Also known as: John Wayne Gacy, Jr. (full name); Killer Clown; Pogo the Clown
Major offenses: Sodomy and murder
Active: September, 1968; January, 1972-December, 1978
Locale: Des Plaines and Chicago, Illinois
Sentence: Life imprisonment for twenty-one victims murdered between January, 1972, and June, 1977; death by lethal injection for twelve victims murdered between July, 1977, and December, 1978

Early Life

John Wayne Gacy (GAY-cee), Jr., was born on St. Patrick's Day, 1942, and was raised Roman Catholic by his parents, John Wayne Gacy, Sr., and Marion Gacy. His father, who frequently drank alcohol, was physically and psychologically abusive. At age eleven, Gacy was struck on the head with a playground swing, causing periodic blackouts until doctors discovered and treated a blood clot. After dropping out of high school, Gacy drifted to Las Vegas but eventually returned to Chicago and graduated from business college. At age twenty-two, Gacy married and moved to Waterloo, Iowa, taking a position as manager of a restaurant belonging to his new wife's family.

To the shock and dismay of his family, Gacy was arrested in May, 1968, for coercing a young employee into homosexual acts. He pleaded guilty to sodomy and was sentenced to ten years in prison. After serving only eighteen months of the sentence, Gacy was released on parole. While incarcerated, Gacy's wife divorced him and left with their two children.

Gacy returned to the Chicago area and bought a new home in Norwood Park Township. Shortly thereafter, he established his own business, called PDM Contracting, Inc. Gacy, now a well-respected businessman, held elaborate parties at his home for neighbors and entertained children as "Pogo the Clown." He also held an office in the Democratic Party.

Criminal Career

Gacy's serial crimes began to surface when he was arrested on February 12, 1971, for disorderly conduct and attempted rape. However, Gacy's accuser, a young male, failed to appear in court, and Gacy's charges were subsequently dismissed. According to Gacy's estimate, his first murder victim was a teenage boy whom he picked up at a bus depot in January, 1972. Between January, 1972, and December, 1978, Gacy killed more than thirty young men. Gacy's primary modus operandi was to troll the streets of Chicago for young boys and prostitutes and bring them (through coercion or by force) to his house, where he would sexually assault, torture, and strangle them. He then buried the corpses around his house.

Legal Action and Outcome

In early December, 1978, the Des Plaines police department, investigating the disappearance of Robert Piest, confronted Gacy while executing a search warrant at his home. Gacy denied any knowledge about Piest's disappearance. On December 22, 1978, facing mounting physical evidence against him from subsequent searches

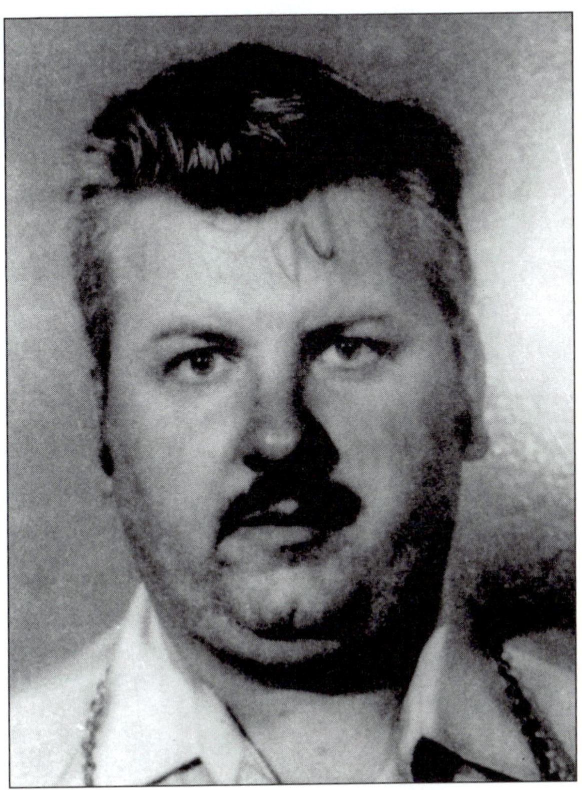

John Wayne Gacy. (AP/Wide World Photos)

of his home, Gacy confessed that he had killed thirty-three young men and boys and buried most on his property. Police summoned the coroner, and when digging was finished on Gacy's property, twenty-eight bodies were unearthed from the crawl space, the garage floor, and the patio. Five additional bodies were later recovered from the Des Plaines River. Of the victims recovered between December, 1978, and April, 1979, nine remained unidentified.

Gacy's trial began on February 6, 1980, in Chicago. Gacy pleaded not guilty by reason of insanity. The defense was ultimately unsuccessful when, on March 13, Gacy was found guilty on all thirty-three counts of murder. Gacy was executed by lethal injection on May 10, 1994, in the Stateville Correctional Center in Joliet, Illinois.

Impact

Dubbed the Killer Clown, John Wayne Gacy lived a double life for years: successful entrepreneur and popular neighbor by day, sexual predator and murderer by night. Gacy's notorious criminal career drew considerable attention. "There's been eleven hardback books on me, thirty-one paperbacks, two screenplays, one movie, one off-Broadway play, five songs, and over five thousand articles," Gacy boasted in one of his last interviews. After his execution in 1994, Gacy's original oil paintings of clowns, made while on death row, were sold at auction to collectors. Author Stephen King reportedly used Gacy as a model for the character of the murderous clown in his novel *It* (1986).

Further Reading

Cahill, Tim. *Buried Dreams: Inside the Mind of a Serial Killer*. New York: Bantam Books, 1986. A thorough examination of Gacy's many mind-sets and personalities—John the politician, the contractor, and the clown, as well as Jack, the sexual predator and killer.

Linedecker, Clifford L. *The Man Who Killed Boys: The John Wayne Gacy, Jr., Story*. New York: St. Martin's Press, 1993. A factual account of Gacy's serial murders and subsequent trial as portrayed in the local media, official police records, and court documents.

Mendenhall, Harlan H. *Fall of the House of Gacy*. West Frankfort, Ill.: New Authors, 1998. Described as the only authorized biography of the infamous serial killer, Mendenhall's psychological study focuses on the early family abuses that shaped Gacy's personality and his subsequent diagnosis as a psychotic schizophrenic.

Sullivan, Terry, and Peter T. Maiken. *Killer Clown: The John Wayne Gacy Murders*. New York: Kensington, 2000. Sullivan, who was involved in the investigation of Gacy, provides an in-depth and comprehensive look at the complexities of the investigation, prosecution, and conviction of Gacy.

—Anthony J. Luongo III

See also: Joe Ball; David Berkowitz; Kenneth Bianchi; Ted Bundy; Angelo Buono, Jr.; Andrei Chikatilo; Andrew Cunanan; Jeffrey Dahmer; Albert DeSalvo; Albert Fish; Ed Gein; Leonard Lake; Charles Ng; Marcel Petiot; Dennis Rader; Gilles de Rais; Aileen Carol Wuornos.

Carmine Galante

American gangster and Mafia boss

Born: February 21, 1910; Castellammare de Golfo, Sicily, Italy
Died: July 12, 1979; Brooklyn, New York
Also known as: The Cigar; Lilo
Major offense: Conspiracy to violate narcotics laws
Active: 1930, 1939-1962, 1972-1979
Locale: New York
Sentence: Twelve and one-half years in prison after a shoot-out with police, served nine years; twenty years in prison, served ten years

Early Life

Regarded by many as one of the more ruthless Mafia bosses in U.S. history, Carmine Galante (CAR-min gah-LAHN-tay), also known as "The Cigar" for the ever-present cigar in the corner of his mouth, was born in Sicily in 1910. In the late 1910's, he relocated with his family to New York and began running with a juvenile street gang in the city's lower East Side at the age of eleven. During the 1920's, Galante made a name for himself by dispatching his Brooklyn-based gang to commit hits (murders), steal liquor, and disrupt legitimate and illegitimate business throughout the city.

Criminal Career

Much of Galante's early criminal activity went undetected by law enforcement authorities. In 1930, however, a New York police officer stumbled across Galante and several others as they were attempting to hijack a truck in the Bronx neighborhood of Williamsburg. A gun battle ensued, leaving the officer and several bystanders injured but still alive. Galante was captured at the scene but refused to reveal the identities of the other men involved in the attempted robbery.

In late 1930, Galante was found guilty of charges stemming from this incident and was sentenced to twelve and one-half years in New York's Sing Sing Prison. After being released on parole in 1939, he began carrying out hits for Vito Genovese, one of New York's most powerful mobsters.

During the 1940's, Galante began working for associates of the Bonanno Mafia family. Starting as a bodyguard for a Bonnano Mafioso named Gaetano Gagliano, Galante was eventually promoted to capo status. By the 1950's, Galante was a well-known and respected member of the Bonanno family and was handpicked by the family godfather, Joe Bonanno, to expand the syndicate's operations into Canada. Galante was quick to establish contacts and firmly put down foundations of the new Bonanno arm in Montreal, Quebec. Throughout the 1950's, Carmine worked tirelessly to globalize the family's narcotics trade and was successful in establishing illegal networks of producers and distributors all across the globe. Galante spent a decade in prison after he was found guilty in 1962 of violating narcotics laws.

Paroled in 1972, he returned to New York and resumed his life of crime. He quickly made his presence felt by blowing the doors off the tomb of Frank Costello, who had died in 1973. Galante was apparently unhappy with Costello for his role in the removal and banishment of his mentor Joe Bonanno.

Galante then set his sights on taking over the Bonanno crime family, whose acting boss, Natale Evola, had recently died. Evola was replaced by Philip "Rusty" Rastelli, but Galante considered this a temporary appointment. Galante soon bullied Rastelli into turning over the leadership of the Bonanno family to him and pushed the syndicate deeper into the drug trade. Relying on his contacts in Canada, he made Montreal the family's main pipeline for heroin from France. The "French Connection" made Galante and his associates millions.

As the family became more involved in the drug trade, Galante began recruiting young, hard Sicilian immigrants to serve as soldiers and bodyguards. These men, who were referred to as "zips" because of the speed with which they spoke their native language, provided Carmine with the necessary muscle to expand and protect his drug operations. Ironically, the zips may have played a critical role in Galante's death. On Thursday, July 12, 1979, while eating lunch with two of his zips, Carmine was approached by several gunmen and was blasted out of his seat. He died with a cigar still clenched in his teeth. Amazingly, both of his bodyguards escaped without a scratch. It is rumored the murder was arranged by Philip Rastelli, who returned to his position as boss of the Bonanno family after Galante's death.

Legal Action and Outcome

In 1958, Galante was indicted along with several other Mafiosi, including Genovese, on charges stemming from his involvement in an international narcotics syndication that smuggled cocaine and heroin into the United States from Cuba, Puerto Rico, and Mexico. In 1962, after some time on the run, Galante was found guilty of conspiracy to violate narcotics laws and was sentenced to twenty years in prison. He served his sentence in the federal penitentiary at Lewisburg, Pennsylvania, and kept himself busy by working in the prison's greenhouse and looking after his pet cats.

While incarcerated, he also enjoyed several other luxuries not normally afforded to inmates, such as choice cuts of meat from the prison butcher. As he did on the street, Galante demanded and received great respect behind prison walls. Prisoners and guards alike abided by Galante's informal rules of conduct. In 1972, Galante was paroled after serving ten years of his sentence.

Impact

Carmine Galante's biggest influence on American organized crime may have been his role in globalizing drug trafficking and establishing the Canadian branch of the Bonanno crime family. The Bonanno family was able to avoid many of the indictments and convictions that have crippled other crime families. The family continued to maintain close ties with the zips, and some believe that the family continued its international drug trafficking into the twenty-first century.

Further Reading

Abadinsky, Howard. *Organized Crime*. 7th ed. Belmont, Calif.: Wadsworth/Thomson Learning, 2003. This text provides a detailed analysis of organized crime in New York and Chicago and examines several emerging international groups.

Capeci, Jerry. *The Complete Idiot's Guide to the Mafia*. 2d ed. Indianapolis, Ind.: Alpha Books, 2002. Capeci provides a comprehensive introduction to Italian organized crime.

Lyman, Michael D., and Gary W. Potter. *Organized Crime*. Upper Saddle River, N.J.: Pearson/Prentice Hall, 2004. A comprehensive textbook that covers the essentials of organized crime theory and practice.

—*James C. Roberts and Thomas E. Baker*

See also: Joe Adonis; Albert Anastasia; Vincent Coll; Joe Colombo; Frank Costello; Pablo Escobar; Carlo Gambino; Vito Genovese; Sam Giancana; John Gotti; Sammy Gravano; Henry Hill; Richard Kuklinski; Meyer Lansky; Salvatore Maranzano; Carlos Marcello.

Galerius

Roman emperor (r. 305-311 c.e.)

Born: c. 250 c.e.; near Serdica, Dacia (now in Romania)
Died: May, 311; Serdica, Thrace (now Sofia, Bulgaria)
Also known as: Gaius Galerius Valerius Maximianus (full name)
Cause of notoriety: Galerius is remembered for his hatred and persecution of Christians.
Active: 303-311 c.e.
Locale: Roman Empire

Early Life

Little is known of the early life of Galerius (gal-AYR-ee-uhs) in the Roman province of Dacia, now Romania. His mother, Romula, was a pagan priestess. Galerius, a herdsman, enlisted in the Roman army and was rapidly promoted during the external and civil wars of the late third century c.e.

Political Career

Galerius was given the rank of caesar (junior emperor) in the First Tetrarchy (293-305), a political junta of two Augusti (senior emperors) and two caesars, devised by

Galerius, as shown on a coin minted c. 311 c.e.

The Great Persecution

The early church author Lactantius (240-c. 320 C.E.), a contemporary of the emperor Diocletian and his caesar Galerius, describes their role in the persecution of Christians in Rome, beginning in 303 C.E.:

[Galerius was] worse than all the bad princes of former days. In this wild beast there dwelt a native barbarity and a savageness foreign to Roman blood; and no wonder, for his mother was born beyond the Danube, and it was an inroad of the Carpi that obliged her to cross over and take refuge in New Dacia. The form of Galerius corresponded with his manners. Of stature tall, full of flesh, and swollen to a horrible bulk of corpulency; by his speech, gestures, and looks, he made himself a terror to all that came near him. . . .

[The emperor] Diocletian and Galerius held councils together, at which no one else assisted; and it was the universal opinion that their conferences respected the most momentous affairs of the empire. The old man long opposed the fury of Galerius, and showed how pernicious it would be to raise disturbances throughout the world and to shed so much blood; that the Christians were wont with eagerness to meet death; and that it would be enough for him to exclude persons of that religion from the court and the army. Yet he could not restrain the madness of that obstinate man. . . .

A fit and auspicious day was sought out for the accomplishment of this undertaking; and the festival of the god Terminus, celebrated on the sevens of the kalends of March, was chosen, in preference to all others, to terminate, as it were, the Christian religion.

"That day, the harbinger of death, arose/ First cause of ill, and long enduring woes;" of woes which befell not only the Christians, but the whole earth. When that day dawned, in the eighth consulship of Diocletian and seventh of Maximian [Galerius], suddenly, while it was yet hardly light, the prefect, together with chief commanders, tribunes, and officers of the treasury, came to the church in Nicomedia, and the gates having been forced open, they searched everywhere for an image of the Divinity. The books of the Holy Scriptures were found, and they were committed to the flames; the utensils and furniture of the church were abandoned to pillage: all was rapine, confusion, tumult. That church, situated on rising ground, was within view of the palace; and Diocletian and Galerius stood, as if on a watch-tower, disputing long whether it ought to be set on fire. The sentiment of Diocletian prevailed, who dreaded lest, so great a fire being once kindled, some part of the city might he burnt; for there were many and large buildings that surrounded the church. Then the Pretorian Guards came in battle array, with axes and other iron instruments, and having been let loose everywhere, they in a few hours levelled that very lofty edifice with the ground.

Next day an edict was published, depriving the Christians of all honours and dignities; ordaining also that, without any distinction of rank or degree, they should be subjected to tortures, and that every suit at law should be received against them. . . .

Source: Lactantius, *Of the Manner in Which the Persecutors Died*, in *The Works of Lactantius* (Edinburgh: T. & T. Clark, 1867-1873).

the emperor Diocletian (284-305). The caesars were expected to succeed to the Augusti, who would retire. The other Augustus was Maximian (285-305), and the other caesar was Constantius I, the father of Constantine the Great. Diocletian and Galerius were based in the East, Maximian and Constantius in the West. Galerius married Diocletian's daughter Valeria.

The role of the caesar was military. Galerius campaigned against the Persians in Mesopotamia and was defeated somewhere between Callinicum and Carrhae in 297. At first angry, Diocletian gave Galerius another chance; Galerius successfully attacked the Persians through Armenia and northern Mesopotamia, capturing Ctesiphon, a major Persian city, in 298. This conquest returned Mesopotamia to Roman rule. Galerius then campaigned against the Sarmatians and Carpi on the Danube. Galerius, a fanatical pagan, allegedly pressured Diocletian to persecute the Christians. The Christian author Lactantius depicts Galerius as hating the Christians, while Diocletian was more moderate. The "Great Persecution" (303-311) had four edicts: first, destruction of churches, with confiscation and destruction of Scriptures; second, arrest of the clergy; third, an amnesty releasing clergy who offered sacrifice to the pagan gods; and fourth, in early 304, an empire-wide order to sacrifice to the gods. After the first edict, a fire broke out in Diocletian's palace in Nicomedia; Lactantius claims that Galerius engineered it as an excuse to persecute more severely. Probably most victims of the Great Persecution incurred martyrdom because of their intransigence.

Diocletian fell seriously ill in 303-304, and Galerius is alleged to have increasingly dominated him, forcing him and Maximian to abdicate in favor of Galerius and Constantius in 305. Galerius also imposed his own choice of caesars, Maximinus (his nephew) and Severus, on Diocletian. Other sources than Lactantius suggest that Diocletian controlled the Tetrarchic succession.

The Second Tetrarchy was short-lived. Constantius died in 306, and his son Constantine was acclaimed Augustus at York in Britain. Galerius reluctantly accepted Constantine as caesar; however, Maximian's son Maxentius revolted, causing a civil war from which Galerius was forced to retreat. At Carnuntum, Austria, in 308 Galerius summoned the present and former Tetrarchs to a meeting, begging Diocletian to resume imperial rule. Diocletian refused, and Galerius appointed a new senior emperor, Licinius.

Galerius fell ill from either intestinal cancer or an infected wound (accounts differ) and died in great pain, infested by worms; the Christian authors emphasize his agony. On April 30, 311, he issued the Edict of Toleration ending the persecution, allegedly in a spirit of repentance, and died soon after. The edict states that though the emperors intended to restore traditional Roman religion, it was worse that the Christians neither revered these gods nor could worship their own deity.

Impact

Galerius is represented by the Christian authors Lactantius and Eusebius as a cruel and barbarous tyrant, the archetype of a persecutor. His "death by worms" echoes that of other tyrants in antiquity, including Antiochus IV Epiphanes, the dictator Lucius Cornelius Sulla, and Herod the Great. The Great Persecution, however, was unsuccessful in eliminating Christianity.

Further Reading

Africa, Thomas. "Worms and the Death of Kings: A Cautionary Note on Disease and History." *Classical Antiquity* 1 (1982): 1-17. Examines ancient stereotypes of the deaths of tyrants, including Galerius.

Corcoran, Simon. *The Empire of the Tetrarchs: Imperial Pronouncements and Government, A.D. 284-324.* New York: Oxford University Press, 1996. This scholarly work analyzes sources for this period.

Eusebius. *The History of the Church.* New York: Penguin Books, 1989. Translated by G. A. Williamson, edited by Andrew Loeth. Primary source. The Church historian Eusebius was a contemporary of Constantine the Great (306-337) and describes the Great Persecution in books 8 and 9.

Grant, Michael. *The Collapse and Recovery of the Roman Empire.* New York: Routledge, 1999. A history of this period for the general reader.

Lactantius. *De mortibus persecutorum.* Oxford, England: Clarendon Press, 1984. Edited and translated by J. L. Creed. Primary source. The contemporary Christian rhetorician Lactantius (writing after 312) describes the policies, personalities, and demises of the persecutors.

—Sara Elise Phang

See also: Caligula; Commodus; Domitian; Elagabalus; Fulvia; Justin II; Nero; Lucius Cornelius Sulla; Theodora.

Joe Gallo

American gangster

Born: April 7, 1929; Brooklyn, New York
Died: April 7, 1972; New York, New York
Also known as: Crazy Joe; Joey Gallo
Major offense: Extortion
Active: 1961
Locale: New York, New York
Sentence: Ten years in prison

Early Life

Joe Gallo (GA-loh) was born in Brooklyn and became involved in organized crime at a young age. When he was seventeen he was arrested for burglary, assault, and kidnapping. He became a "made" soldier for the Profaci Mafia family while still a teenager.

Criminal Career

Gallo supposedly earned the name "Crazy Joe" for his his ruthless and violent behavior as well as his nontraditional ideas about working with African American criminals in Mafia operations—he saw that there was money to be made in neighborhoods like Harlem, and he wanted the Mafia to get some of that money. He may have further cultivated his "crazy" image to assist him in shaking down his extortion victims.

Joe Gallo. (AP/Wide World Photos)

Gallo, along with his brothers Larry and Albert, reportedly served as a gunner for Mafia boss Joseph Profaci and then Joe Colombo. Profaci was an unpopular boss, greedy even by Mafia standards, who dipped heavily into the profits of his "soldiers" for his "tribute." The Gallo brothers rebelled against Profaci, who died of natural causes in 1962. The war waged by the Gallos continued when Joe Colombo took over the family.

Joe Gallo was convicted of extortion in 1961 and sentenced to ten years in prison. Soon after he was freed in 1971, Colombo was shot and subsequently slipped into a coma. Gallo was immediately suspected in the assassination attempt, especially because the shooter was an African American man (who was killed at the scene). Gallo was not tried, however, because of lack of evidence.

Gallo was not a typical gangster. He cultivated relationsips among the New York theater crowd and became friendly with actor Jerry Orbach, who comically depicted Gallo in James Goldstone's 1971 film *The Gang That Couldn't Shoot Straight*. After Colombo's death, Gallo continued to operate, moving between high society circles and criminal circles. On April 7, 1972, Gallo, after celebrating his birthday with guests that included the Orbachs, ended his evening at Umberto's Clam House. He was shot and killed by an unknown assailant while seated at the restaurant with his bodyguard and four women friends.

Legal Action and Outcome

Gallo was not convicted of his most serious offenses. In 1961, however, he received a ten-year prison sentence for extortion.

Impact

Besides helping to inspire Jimmy Breslin's novel *The Gang That Couldn't Shoot Straight* (1969) and its film adaptation, Joe Gallo was memorialized in the song *Joey* by Bob Dylan and Jacques Levy. Gallo's forward-thinking, albeit criminal, views on crossing racial lines in business enterprise and his intellectual aspirations also make him an important and compelling figure in the study of the American Mafia.

Further Reading

Capeci, Jerry. *Jerry Capeci's Gang Land*. New York: Alpha Books, 2003. A compilation of journalist and Mafia expert Capeci's columns in the *New York Daily News* covering organized crime activity in New York City from 1989 through 1995.

Raab, Selwyn. *Five Families: The Rise, Decline, and Resurgence of America's Most Powerful Mafia Empires*. New York: St. Martin's Press, 2005. Recounts the history of the New York crime families; spotlights major figures and events of organized crime in New York.

Talese, Gay. *Honor Thy Father*. New York: World, 1971. Traces Joe Bonanno's career as Mafia boss.

—*David R. Champion*

See also: Joe Adonis; Albert Anastasia; Vincent Coll; Joe Colombo; Carmine Galante; Carlo Gambino; Sam Giancana; Vincent Gigante; John Gotti; Sammy Gravano; Henry Hill; Richard Kuklinski; Meyer Lansky; Salvatore Maranzano; Carlos Marcello; Joseph Profaci.

Leopoldo Galtieri

Argentine military dictator (1981-1982)

Born: July 15, 1926; Caseros, Argentina
Died: January 12, 2003; Buenos Aires, Argentina
Also known as: Leopoldo Fortunato Galtieri Castelli (birth name)
Major offense: Military incompetence
Active: 1981-1982
Locale: Argentina
Sentence: Five years' imprisonment

Early Life

Leopoldo Galtieri (lay-oh-POHL-doh gal-tee-EHR-ee) was the son of working-class Italian immigrants. He studied as an engineer and spent the balance of his career in the Argentine army's engineering corps, becoming its head by 1975. He thus held a prominent place in the army when it seized political power in a 1976 coup. Slowly but steadily Galtieri would increase his power within the new government.

Political Career

Observers at first regarded the new Argentine military government as a typical Latin American dictatorship. The regime, which called itself the National Reconciliation Process, soon revealed itself to be both ambitious and menacing. It waged the *guerra sucia* (dirty war) against political dissidents, some of whom were kidnapped and drugged and then brutally murdered. Ten thousand or more people thought inconvenient to the regime vanished and were termed *desaparecidos* ("disappeared"). Argentine Jews were subjected to particular persecution.

By the time Jorge Rafael Videla, who spearheaded the coup, was succeeded by Roberto Viola in 1981, Galtieri had become chief of the army. In December of that year, Galtieri, along with the navy's Jorge Isaac Anaya and the air force's Basilio Lami Dozo, seized power as a three-man junta.

The rapid turnover of the Argentine military leadership in less than a year—from Videla to Viola to Galtieri—begs some explanation. Galtieri had traveled to the United States in 1981 and had been acclaimed by right-wing elements within and outside the Reagan ad-

National Commission on the Disappearance of Persons

Commission member Ernesto Sabato captures the horror of the junta's "dirty war" in his prologue to Nunca más (Never Again), *the 1984 report:*

During the 1970's, Argentina was torn by terror from both the extreme right and the far left. . . . The armed forces responded to the terrorists' crimes with a terrorism far worse than the one they were combating, and after 24 March 1976 they could count on the power and impunity of an absolute state, which they misused to abduct, torture and kill thousands of human beings.

Our Commission was set up not to sit in judgment, because that is the task of the constitutionally appointed judges, but to investigate the fate of the people who disappeared during those ill-omened years of our nation's life. However, after collecting several thousand statements and testimonies, verifying or establishing the existence of hundreds of secret detention centres, and compiling over 50,000 pages of documentation, we are convinced that the recent military dictatorship brought about the greatest and most savage tragedy in the history of Argentina. Although it must be justice which has the final word, we cannot remain silent in the face of all that we have heard, read and recorded. This went far beyond what might be considered criminal offences, and takes us into the shadowy realm of crimes against humanity. Through the technique of disappearance and its consequences, all the ethical principles which the great religions and the noblest philosophies have evolved through centuries of suffering and calamity have been trampled underfoot, barbarously ignored.

From the moment of their abduction, the victims lost all rights. Deprived of all communication with the outside world, held in unknown places, subjected to barbaric tortures, kept ignorant of their immediate or ultimate fate, they risked being either thrown into a river or the sea; weighed down with blocks of cement, or burned to ashes. . . .

We have discovered close to 9,000 of these unfortunate people who were abandoned by the world. We have reason to believe that the true figure is much higher. Many families were reluctant to report a disappearance for fear of reprisals. Some still hesitate, fearing a resurgence of these evil forces. . . .

Only with democracy will we be certain that NEVER AGAIN will events such as these, which have made Argentina so sadly infamous throughout the world, be repeated in our nation.

Source: Comisión Nacional Sobre la Desaparición de Personas, *Nunca más* (London: Faber and Faber, 1984; *Nunca más = Never Again: A Report*, London: Faber and Faber, 1986).

ministration, so perhaps U.S. support, real or imagined, helped expedite Galtieri's rise.

The Falkland Islands (called the Islas Malvinas by Argentina) are a British dependency in the South Atlantic Ocean populated by two thousand or so people of largely British descent. The Falklands had long been claimed as Argentine territory. Taking advantage of a dispute over sanitation pickup on the outlying British island of South Georgia, Galtieri, on April 2, 1982, ordered the invasion of the Falklands. The army, under General Mario Benjamin Menendez, captured the islands easily, and Galtieri assumed that Britain and the rest of the world would accept the occupation as a fait accompli. Galtieri relied on the anticolonial trend in world politics and assumed that most developing nations would applaud his move as a blow against European hegemony. Although U.S. government officials surely thought of Central America, not the Falklands, when they encouraged Argentina to raise its hemispheric military profile, Galtieri must have assumed U.S. passivity at the very least.

In this he was proved wrong. Many nations saw the seizure as a violation of international law and of self-determination for the islanders, who wished to remain under British rule. The United Nations, in Resolution 502, upheld this principle. In addition, the Argentine government's domestic atrocities did not predispose people who generally sympathized with anticolonial rhetoric to support the seizure.

The United States was disconcerted and surprised by the invasion, but, after a brief debate, the Reagan administration rallied to Britain's side. Britain, under Prime Minister Margaret Thatcher, was determined to regain the islands and sent a large task force to the South Atlantic. Neighbors such as Chile and Brazil were unsympathetic to Argentina. Though Lami Dozo's air force fought well, the Argentine army on the Falklands surrendered to British forces on June 14, 1982. Three days later, Galtieri resigned, humiliated and disgraced.

Legal Action and Outcome

In 1985, Galtieri was arraigned on human rights abuses, for which no judgment was ever rendered. The following year, Galtieri, along with the other junta leaders, was tried for his alleged incompetence in the war. He was sentenced to five years in prison and stripped of his military rank. In 2002, Galtieri was put under house arrest, being exempted from prison because of his diagnosis of pancreatic cancer. He died of a heart attack in January, 2003.

Impact

As the trial of Leopoldo Galtieri showed, the military's defeat in the Falklands, far more than its massive human rights violations, invalidated the junta's rule. Galtieri, more than his brutal predecessor Videla, became the face of the military dictatorship and the dirty war it unleashed against its own people. Though afterward Argentina made a quick transition to democracy, continuing political and economic instability as well as myriad shattered lives were the legacy of the military regime in which Galtieri played so zealous a role.

Further Reading

Freedman, Lawrence. *The Official History of the Falklands Campaign*. New York: Routledge, 2005. Emphasizes the British perspective but gives crucial insight into Galtieri's command decisions.

Jaroslavsky, Andrés. *The Future of Memory: Children of the Dictatorship in Argentina*. London: Latin America Bureau, 2003. Jaroslavsky relates how the youngest victims of the dictatorship, as adults, grapple with their past experience and provides an occasion for a general reflection on the trauma of the period of the military dictatorship.

Mignone, Emilio. *Witness to the Truth: The Complicity of Church and Dictatorship in Argentina, 1976-1983*. Translated by Phillip Berryman. Maryknoll, N.Y.: Orbis Books, 1988. Carefully considers the degree of support offered by the Catholic Church to the military junta.

Osiel, Mark. *Mass Atrocity, Ordinary Evil, and Hannah Arendt: Criminal Consciousness in Argentina's Dirty War*. New Haven, Conn.: Yale University Press, 2001. Compares the authoritarianism and torture of the Argentine regime to earlier models of twentieth century oppression and to previous instances of mass criminality.

Rock, David. *Argentina, 1516-1987: From Spanish Colonization to Falklands War and Alfonsin*. London: I. B. Tauris, 1997. Survey history that places the 1976-1982 military government in the context of Argentine political instability.

—Nicholas Birns

See also: Fidel Castro; François Duvalier; Jean-Claude Duvalier; Eva Perón; Juan Perón; Augusto Pinochet Ugarte; Efraín Ríos Montt; Anastasio Somoza García; Alfredo Stroessner; Rafael Trujillo; Getúlio Vargas; Jorge Rafael Videla.

Carlo Gambino

Italian American organized crime boss

Born: August 24, 1902; Palermo, Italy
Died: October 15, 1976; Massapequa, Long Island, New York
Also known as: Don Carlo; Capo di Tutti Capi; Boss of Bosses
Cause of notoriety: Gambino, who worked his way up the chain of command of the American Mafia over several decades, eventually secured the title of Boss of Bosses and ran the notorious Gambino crime family.
Active: 1921-1976
Locale: New York, New York

Early Life

Carlo Gambino (gam-BEE-noh) was born in Palermo, Italy, the birthplace of Italian organized crime. Young Gambino needed to go no further than his own well-connected Mafia family to form his early identification with organized crime. Gambino dropped out of high school and started working for the Mafia. He earned the respect of his boss by demonstrating his efficient and brutal service to his crime family.

The Italian government's purge of Mafia members forced many young Mafiosi to flee from certain death by using a secret escape route. They eventually found their future destination from various points of entry into Little Italy in New York City. In late 1921, the "secret society" provided an escape route for the nineteen-year-old Gambino; his first destination was Norfolk, Virginia. Eventually, family members smuggled Gambino to New York.

Criminal Career

Once settled in New York, Gambino, an opportunist, organized illegal truck deliveries of alcohol during Prohibition in the 1930's. During World War II, he became a millionaire in the black market of ration stamps. His criminal endeavors later turned to the New York waterfront and garment industry, as well as labor racketeering and legitimate business fronts.

Gambino always managed to be on the "right side" in Mafia wars, such as the so-called Castellammarese War in 1930-1931, a bloody power struggle between two factions of the Mafia. Eventually, Gambino would rise to power alongside Lucky Luciano. Gambino joined the Mangano crime family, which, by the 1950's, was controlled by Albert Anastasia (also known as the Lord High Executioner). Gambino had earned the rank of *capo*, or captain, while working under the authority of Vincent Mangano. When Anastasia assumed command of the family, he promoted Gambino to *sottocapo*, or underboss. However, in 1957, Anastasia was murdered in a hotel, presumably from a hit ordered by Gambino; he took over the family and renamed it for himself.

Gambino earned the title Boss of Bosses for his murder of Anastasia. His position as the Mafia's top leader was further secured when Vito Genovese, a leading Mafia figure, died in prison in 1969. Despite being the Boss of Bosses, Gambino maintained a low profile, and his crime family became the first family of organized crime. In 1971, Gambino was suspected of ordering the murder of Joe Colombo, the head of the Colombo crime family. Wounded by several bullets, Colombo remained in a vegetative state until he finally died in 1978.

Carlo Gambino. (AP/Wide World Photos)

Legal Action and Outcome

The courts failed to convict Gambino despite sixteen arrests over the course of his Mafia career. He followed the principle of the "lion and the fox": He used force as brutally as a lion and was crafty like a fox when it came to his survival and avoiding arrest. His only successful conviction was for a 1939 liquor tax evasion charge. He received a twenty-month sentence; however, the conviction was reversed on appeal because of unconstitutional wiretapping procedures. Gambino was never convicted or deported for illegal immigration.

Gambino did not attend his racketeering trial in the 1970's because of deteriorating health. During the initial days of the trial, a television reporter tried to interview him, but the old man stood mute: He had learned the benefits of remaining silent. Gambino, the master criminal, once again avoided conviction by hiring competent attorneys. Gambino died in 1976 of a heart attack in his Long Island home while watching a ball game and still facing illegal racketeering and immigration charges.

Impact

The Gambino family missed Carlo Gambino's leadership and quiet demeanor. The death of the most commanding Mafia leader left a power vacuum: His cousin, who was also his brother-in-law, Paul Castellano, whom Gambino left in charge of the family, failed to command the same respect. John Gotti resented Castellano's appointment and eventually ordered the murder of Castellano in 1985, thereby becoming the new boss of the Gambino crime family.

Further Reading

Abadinsky, Howard. *Organized Crime*. 7th ed. Belmont, Calif.: Wadsworth/Thomson Learning, 2003. The text is an in-depth analysis of organized crime from a historical and theoretical perspective.

Davis, John. *The Rise and Fall of the Gambino Crime Family*. New York: HarperTorch, 1994. This popular analysis of the Gambino family examines integrated and complex crime and social relationships of America's first family of organized crime.

Lyman, Michael D., and Gary W. Potter. *Organized Crime*. 2d ed. Upper Saddle River, N.J.: Pearson/Prentice Hall, 2000. A comprehensive textbook, covering the essentials of organized crime theory and practice.

—*Thomas E. Baker and James C. Roberts*

See also: Albert Anastasia; Paul Castellano; Joe Colombo; Vito Genovese; John Gotti; Sammy Gravano; Lucky Luciano.

Gilbert Gauthe

American priest and pedophile

Born: 1945; Napoleonville, Louisiana

Major offenses: Eleven counts of aggravated crimes against nature; eleven counts of committing sexually immoral acts; eleven counts of taking pornographic photographs of juveniles; and a single count of aggravated rape, sodomizing a child under the age of twelve

Active: 1971-1983

Locale: Broussard, New Iberia, Abbeville, and Henry, Louisiana

Sentence: Twenty years in prison; served ten years

Early Life

Born in 1945, Gilbert Gauthe (GO-tay) grew up near Napoleonville, Louisiana. He attended the University of Southwestern Louisiana in Lafayette (now known as the University of Louisiana, Lafayette) before attending Immaculate Junior Seminary for one year. He transferred to Notre Dame Seminary in New Orleans, where he completed his theological studies. While a seminarian, he was active with various youth organizations, including the Boy Scouts of America, and was well liked by the families of children with whom he worked. Gauthe was ordained by the Roman Catholic Church in 1971. He served several churches within the Diocese of Lafayette, where he was popular with both children and adult parishioners.

Criminal Career

Gauthe's career as a pedophile spans that of his entire priesthood. He admitted that he began having sexual contact with children in 1971, the year of his ordination. While serving as an associate pastor in Broussard, Louisiana, from 1971 to 1973, he molested at least four boys.

He was confronted by parents of those boys and, consequently, sought psychiatric help. He received approximately eight sessions of therapy before being transferred in late 1973 to a church in New Iberia, Louisiana, where he admitted to molesting sixteen boys. In 1976 he was once again transferred to another church—this time in Abbeville, Louisiana—where he served until 1977. Gauthe admitted to molesting boys at this church before receiving his final transfer to a church in Henry, Louisiana, where he admitted to molesting twenty-two boys before being suspended from pastoral duties in 1983. Gauthe, unsure of his final victim count, readily admitted to at least three dozen; other estimates place this number closer to one hundred.

Legal Action and Outcome

Gauthe entered a plea of guilty to thirty-four counts of contributing to the delinquency of a minor and possession of child pornography. At least twenty-five civil lawsuits were filed against the Diocese of Lafayette, claiming that it failed to protect the public. In response, the diocese opted to thwart Gauthe's actions by moving his first-floor bedroom to the second floor of the rectory, so boys could not climb in and out of windows, and instructed Gauthe to make confession and pray. More than twenty-two million dollars were paid to plaintiffs.

Impact

Gilbert Gauthe's trial marked the first time in U.S. history that the details of a priest's alleged sexual abuse of children were made widely public. His trial served as a test case for prosecuting pedophiliac priests. After his conviction, dozens of other priests in Louisiana and around the United States were accused of child molestation, and various dioceses were sued for alleged cover-ups and gross negligence in handling decades of abuse allegations. In 1986, Gauthe's attorney, along with two priests, drafted a document informing the Roman Catholic Church how best to address allegations of sexual abuse by clergy and estimating its prevalence and potential monetary damage. This document was presented to the U.S. Conference of Church Bishops in 1986 but was not taken up by Church authorities until 2002.

Further Reading

Berry, Jason. *Lead Us Not into Temptation: Catholic Priests and the Sexual Abuse of Children*. New York: Doubleday Press, 1992. An authoritative examination of both the Gauthe case and church policy on celibacy and homosexuality.

Investigative Staff of the *Boston Globe* newspaper. *Betrayal: The Crisis in the Catholic Church*. Boston: Little, Brown, 2002. A chronicle of the events that led up to an international crisis of pedophiliac priests and church officials who were accused of ignoring complaints about sexual predators.

Jenkins, Phillip. *Pedophiles and Priests: Anatomy of a Contemporary Crisis*. New York: Oxford University Press, 1996. An academic and dispassionate review of sex scandals within the Roman Catholic Church and other religious institutions. This book reviews the role of the media in influencing public perceptions about crises.

—*Rachel Kate Bandy*

See also: James Porter.

Ed Gein

U.S. murderer and necrophiliac

Born: August 27, 1906; La Crosse, Wisconsin
Died: July 26, 1984; Madison, Wisconsin
Also known as: Edward Theodore Gein (full name); Mad Butcher of Plainfield; Plainfield Head Collector; Shy Ghoul; Ghastly Gein
Major offenses: Murder and grave robbing
Active: December 8, 1954-November 16, 1957
Locale: Plainfield, Wisconsin
Sentence: Convicted of one count of first-degree murder; judged not guilty by reason of insanity and committed to Central State Hospital for the Criminally Insane in Waupun; later transferred to the Mendota Mental Health Institute in Madison, where he remained until his death.

Early Life

The father of Edward Gein (geen) was an alcoholic and both verbally and physically abusive to Gein and his brother. However, Gein's fanatically religious mother, Augusta Gein, dominated his early life by teaching him that sex was evil and a contaminating influence to be avoided. In 1914, the Geins moved to a farm near Plainfield. Gein's father died in 1940. His brother died in 1944 while fighting a fire near their home. Some investigators have speculated that Gein killed his brother in the fire, but no one has proven this assertion. Augusta's death in 1945 left Gein alone and appears to be the catalyst that drove his descent into full-blown psychopathic behavior.

Criminal Career

Mary Hogan, believed to be Gein's first victim, was found dead on December 8, 1954. Although evidence discovered later would implicate Gein in grave-robbing and other crimes, Gein's neighbors suspected nothing, considering him harmless, if eccentric. When police investigated the disappearance of Bernice Worden on November 16, 1957, they discovered her body hanging in a shed on Gein's property, decapitated and disemboweled, with sexual organs removed. Police found her head inside the house, along with the preserved remains of fifteen women. Gein had made a skull into a soup bowl, and he had crafted human face "masks" by carefully peeling the skin away from the skulls of several victims. A "woman suit"—a vest of preserved female flesh, breasts and sexual organs attached—was also found. Police discovered other body parts, including sex organs, noses, and lips, as well as chairs upholstered with skin, all carefully preserved. Gein claimed to have committed more than forty grave robberies beginning in 1947 and admitted using the corpses for sexual gratification but denied having sex with the corpses or engaging in cannibalism.

Legal Action and Outcome

Initially considered incompetent to stand trial, Gein was committed to the Central State Hospital for the Criminally Insane in Waupun, Wisconsin, on January 6, 1958. A decade later, he was judged fit to stand trial. While convicted of first-degree murder in the death of Worden, during the penalty phase of the trial, he was declared not guilty by reason of insanity and returned to Central State. He was later transferred to the Mendota Mental Health Institute in Madison, a minimum-security facility, where he died on July 26, 1984, of respiratory failure at age seventy-seven.

Impact

The story of Ed Gein's crimes created intense media exposure—reporters from around the world descended on the small town in Wisconsin to cover the story. The public and professionals from the field of psychology were fascinated by a case that combined necrophilia, fetishism, and transvestism. Gein has had an important impact on popular culture: Elements of his story have appeared in films such as *Psycho* (1960), *The Texas Chainsaw Massacre* (1974), *The Silence of the Lambs* (1991), and, most significant, *Deranged* (1974) and *Ed Gein* (2001). A short film, *Ed Gein: American Maniac* (1993), is a graphic, straightforward documentary about Gein's life and crimes.

Further Reading

Frasier, David K. *Murder Cases of the Twentieth Century: Biographies and Bibliographies of 280 Convicted or Accused Killers*. Jefferson, N.C.: McFarland, 1996. Contains substantial information on its criminal subjects.

Schecter, Harold. *Deviant: The Shocking True Story of the Original Psycho*. New York: Pocket Books, 1989. A somewhat sensationalized recounting of the facts; contains a relatively tame photograph section.

Seltzer, Mark. *Serial Killers: Death and Life in America's Wound Culture*. New York: Routledge: 1998. Briefly but intelligently discusses Gein as an example of "The Face System" within "the Techno-Primitive" culture.

Woods, Paul Anthony. *Ed Gein: Psycho*. New York: St. Martin's Press, 1995. A slightly sensational book which contains explicit crime-scene photographs and an account of Gein's influence on popular culture.

—*Charles Avinger*

See also: Joe Ball; Elizabeth Báthory; John Reginald Halliday Christie; Jeffrey Dahmer; Albert Fish; Jack the Ripper; Dennis Rader; Gilles de Rais; Sweeney Todd.

Genghis Khan

Khan of the Mongol Empire (r. 1206-1227)

Born: Between 1155 and 1162; Delyun Boldog, near the Gobi Desert (now in Mongolia)
Died: August 18, 1227; Ordos area in northern China
Also known as: Temüjin (birth name); Temuchin (alternate birth name); Chinggis Khan; Jenghiz Khan; Khan of Khans; King of the Earth
Cause of notoriety: In his drive to unite the clans and tribes of people later collectively known as the Mongols, Genghis Khan left in his wake cruelty, atrocities, mass executions, and total destruction of cities and irrigation systems in order to prevent possible repopulation.
Active: 1206-1227
Locale: Mongol Empire

Early Life

Temüjin, known to history as Genghis Khan (GEHN-ghihs kahn), was thirteen years old when his father, Yesügei, a minor Mongolian chieftain, was poisoned by the Tatars. His mother, Oyelun, and his three brothers, his sister, and his father's other wife with her two children were expelled from the clan and thus condemned to certain death. Contrary to all expectations, however, the family survived thanks to the tremendous efforts of Temüjin's mother, who was a person of great strength and determination. In accordance with an old nomadic custom, Temüjin learned to ride and hunt at a very early age and was able to support and protect his family. During one of many disagreements with his half brother, Temüjin became so enraged that, with the help of his brother Khasar, he killed him. At fifteen, the age at which young Mongols were regarded as reaching their maturity, he was ready to marry his childhood fiancé Börte. Later, Temüjin was captured by rival tribes and held as a slave for almost ten years.

Military Career

Until 1196, Temüjin expanded his family with four sons (Jochi, Chagatai, Ogatai, and Tolui) and established his leadership position as the khan of a small group consisting of his family, friends, and outcasts of the steppes (prairies). In 1202, he defeated the Tatars and gained control over central Mongolia. In 1206, he was proclaimed Genghis Khan, a universal leader of all the Mongol tribes, and began to expand his territory and, eventually, conquer his known world.

In 1211, Genghis Khan attacked China and moved to Manchuria; in 1215, he overran the city of Beijing.

Genghis Khan.

In 1218, Genghis continued from China to Iran, and by 1220 he had reached Bukhara and marched into Samarqand (both cities now in Uzbekistan). By 1225, the entire region of Turkistan was part of the Mongol Empire.

During the next several years, Genghis Khan fought in Afghanistan and returned to Pakistan, where he was forced to retreat. On his way back to Mongolia, his army had to cross the Caucasus Mountains, battling the Georgian and Ukrainian forces. At the Kalka River in 1222, Genghis Khan, with the help of the Tatars, achieved victory over the Russian princes. It is recorded that eighteen thousand Mongols, with the help of five thousand Brodniki (Polish) collaborators, slaughtered an army of forty thousand solders, including sixty princes and seventy nobles.

Genghis Khan's last successful campaign was in 1226 against the Tangut Empire (known as Xi-Xia in Chinese, Tangyud in Mongolian). During the campaign, Genghis Khan became ill, and after several months, he died. No one knows for certain what was the cause of his death; some speculations include malaria or an old injury from a hunting accident. Because Genghis Khan's illness occurred in the middle of the combat operations, his commanders decided to keep silent about his death until the final victory. When the Tanguts were defeated, the entire population and all animals were massacred.

According to some records, Genghis Khan's body was placed on a cart and carried back to Mongolia. He was buried in an unmarked grave. In addition, to preserve secrecy of the burial place, all who participated in or encountered the funeral procession were eliminated. In 1229, his son Ogatai was named the next khan.

Great Granddad Genghis

In 2003, a twenty-two-member science team revealed evidence that Genghis Khan may be the ancestor of sixteen million men living in the modern era. Their report concluded:

The Y chromosome of a single individual has spread rapidly and is now found in 8% of the males throughout a large part of Asia. Indeed, if our sample is representative, this chromosome will be present in about 16 million men, 0.5% of the world's total. The available evidence suggests that it was carried by Genghis Khan. His Y chromosome would obviously have had ancestors. . . . The historically documented events accompanying the establishment of the Mongol empire would have contributed directly to the spread of this lineage by Genghis Khan and his relatives, but perhaps as important was the establishment of a long-lasting male dynasty. . . . Our findings nevertheless demonstrate a novel form of selection in human populations on the basis of social prestige. A founder effect of this magnitude will have influenced allele frequencies elsewhere in the genome: mitochondrial DNA lineages will not be affected, since males do not transmit their mitochondrial DNA, but, in the simplest models, the founder male will have been the ancestor of each autosomal sequence in 4% of the population and X-chromosomal sequence in 2.7%, with implications for the medical genetics of the region. Large-scale changes to patterns of human genetic variation can occur very quickly. Although local influences of this kind may have been common in human populations, it is, perhaps, fortunate that events of this magnitude have been rare.

Military historian Martin Van Creveld provides a bit of supporting evidence in The Transformation of War *(1991):*

Legend has it that Genghis Khan on one occasion was asked to name the one thing most enjoyable in life. His answer was that it consisted of pressing the wives and daughters of the defeated enemy to one's breast; by which he surely did not mean to say that he was short of women to take to bed.

Sources: Tatian Zerjal et al., "The Genetic Legacy of the Mongols," *American Journal of Human Genetics* 72 (2003): 717-723. Martin Van Creveld, *The Transformation of War* (New York: Free Press, 1991).

Impact

Genghis Khan ruled the largest empire ever established by one ruler, stretching from the Caspian Sea to the Pacific Ocean. His strategic genius created the most efficient and effective military force in the history of warfare. Notorious for his lack of mercy, he wiped out urban areas and entire populations to create pastures needed for his large cavalry. On the other hand, he is considered the father of the modern state of Mongolia. He introduced a system of writing, developed highly sophisticated administration, and was tolerant of various religions. In addition, he contributed to the cultural exchange between East and West. Present-day Mongols honor him as a national hero and the founding father of their state.

Further Reading

Gabriel, Richard. *Subotai the Valiant, Genghis Khan's Greatest General*. Westport, Conn.: Praeger, 2004. In this study of Genghis Khan's famous general, there are many passages on combat strategies, with discussion of particular battles fought under the leadership of Genghis Khan. It offers an extensive description of the Mongol war-machine.

Lane, George. *Genghis Khan and Mongol Rule*. Westport, Conn.: Greenwood Press, 2004. An overall positive study of the legacy of Genghis Khan with an emphasis of his cultural achievements. A bibliography and a selection of translated primary documents are included.

Roux, Jean-Paul. *Genghis Khan and the Mongol Empire*. New York: Harry N. Abrams, 2003. A brief and well-illustrated general survey of the Mongol Empire with an excellent selection of documents at the end of the book.

Turnbull, Stephen. *Genghis Khan and the Mongol Conquests: 1190-1400*. New York: Routledge, 2004. Another brief, well-documented survey with maps and contemporary photographs of sites and artworks mentioned in the text.

Weatherford, Jack. *Genghis Khan and the Making of the Modern World*. New York: Crown, 2004. A comprehensive study regarding all aspects of Genghis Khan's reign, with a list of primary and secondary sources and selected bibliography.

—*Rozmeri Basic*

See also: Nadir Shah; Theodora.

Vito Genovese

Italian American mob boss

Born: November 27 1897; Rosiglino, Italy
Died: February 14, 1969; U.S. Medical Center for Federal Prisoners, Springfield, Missouri
Also known as: Don Genovese; Don Genovesene
Major offense: Conspiracy to violate narcotics laws
Active: 1917-1959
Locale: New York
Sentence: Fifteen years in prison; served ten years

Early Life

Vito Genovese (VEE-toh jihn-oh-VEE-zee), the man described by many as the most powerful organized crime figure in American history, was born in Rosiglino, Italy, in 1897. In 1912, Genovese relocated with his family to the United States and settled in Queens, New York. While his father was busy operating a small contracting firm in Queens, the young Genovese enjoyed the activity and excitement of lower Manhattan. He soon moved to Little Italy to live with relatives and began associating with several multiethnic gangs.

Criminal Career

In 1917, Genovese was arrested for carrying a gun and spent sixty days in jail. During Prohibition, he worked his way up the ranks of organized crime, graduating from street gang member to professional killer. It was during this time that Genovese became acquainted with Lucky Luciano. By 1930, Genovese and Luciano were working closely with Joe Masseria. Many believe that Genovese helped Luciano arrange the murder of Masseria, who, on April 15, 1931, was surprised and gunned down by several unknown assailants after a lengthy dinner with Genovese. With Genovese at his side, Luciano took over Masseria's operations, eventually expanding them to reach every corner of the country.

In 1937, Genovese fled the United States after being named as a suspect in the murder of a Mafia gangster named Ferdinand "The Shadow" Boccia, a crime that had taken place three years earlier. Genovese settled in Naples, Italy, and quickly established himself as a major narcotics trafficker in the area. When American forces invaded Sicily in 1944 during World War II, Genovese was quick to offer his services as a translator. He also helped American military authorities rid the area of crime and black-market rings for illegal goods. Military authorities did not realize, however, that as drugs and weapons dealers were arrested, Genovese was replacing them with his own men. His plan was thwarted when a military police investigator realized that the helpful Italian was a wanted felon in the United States. Genovese was arrested and sent back to the United States to face charges stemming from the murder of Boccia. He was acquitted, however, when the only witness in the Boccia case was found dead.

After the war, Genovese became heavily involved in

drug trafficking and began setting up deals with growers in India, Pakistan, and Afghanistan. Mafia leaders, including Luciano, urged Genovese to get out of the drug business. Genovese, however, would not give up the activities that produced most of his income. He soon set his sights on taking over the Luciano crime family. Since Genovese had been away, Luciano had been deported and was no longer the true boss of his family. The only person standing in Genovese's way was the family's acting boss, Frank Costello.

On May 2, 1957, Genovese sent his soldier, Vincent Gigante, to murder Costello in his home. Miraculously, Costello survived the gunshot wound to the head. (He later retired, leaving the syndicate under Genovese's control.) Next on Genovese's list was the removal of Albert Anastasia, boss of the Carlo Gambino crime family. On October 25, 1957, Anastasia was shot and killed by two assailants while sitting in a chair in a Manhattan barbershop.

Vito Genovese. (AP/Wide World Photos)

Legal Action and Outcome

Eager to establish himself as a leader on the national scene and expecting to be named "boss of bosses," Genovese arranged the ill-fated meeting of U.S. Mafia bosses in Apalachin, New York, on November 17, 1957. The meeting had barely started when several in attendance spotted a police officer outside the home and began to flee. Sixty-three men were apprehended, including Genovese. Charges against the men were later dropped after it was determined that they were taken into custody, detained, and searched without probable cause that a crime had been or was being committed. The Apalachin fiasco, however, was a great embarrassment for the American Mafia and may have cost Genovese his coveted boss-of-bosses title.

On April 17, 1959, Genovese was convicted of conspiracy to violate narcotics laws and was sentenced to fifteen years in prison. However, he continued to control the activities of his crime family through his underlings from his prison cell in Atlanta. Genovese died of a heart attack on February 14, 1969, at the U.S. Medical Center for Federal Prisoners in Springfield, Missouri.

Impact

More so than any other individual, Vito Genovese can be credited with keeping the Mafia in the narcotics business, a move that many other Mafiosi of his time opposed. Genovese is also responsible for organizing the disastrous meeting of Mafia bosses in Apalachin, New York, which propelled American organized crime groups into the national spotlight. Before this meeting and the subsequent arrests, Federal Bureau of Investigation director J. Edgar Hoover had boldly stated that there was no such thing as "organized crime." In modern times, the Genovese family is considered one of the richest and most powerful crime families in New York, with an estimated membership of more than 250 "soldiers." It has been reported that, by the twenty-first century, the family had moved into more sophisticated crimes, including computer fraud, stock and securities fraud, and health care fraud.

Further Reading

Dickie, John. *Cosa Nostra: A History of the Sicilian Mafia*. New York: Palgrave Macmillan, 2004. Dickie provides a comprehensive history of Italian organized crime in the United States.

Hanna, David. *Vito Genovese: The Godfather Series.*

New York: Belmont Tower Books, 1974. Hanna provides an intimate portrait of one of most powerful organized crime figures in American history.

Raab, Selwyn. *Five Families: The Rise, Decline, and Resurgence of America's Most Powerful Mafia Families*. New York: Thomas Dunne Books, 2005. Provides an in-depth analysis of the Bonanno, Colombo, Gambino, Genovese, and Lucchese crime families.

—*James C. Roberts and Thomas E. Baker*

SEE ALSO: Albert Anastasia; Frank Costello; Vincent Gigante; Lucky Luciano; Joe Masseria.

BALTHASAR GÉRARD

French Catholic assassin

BORN: 1557; Vuillafans, France

DIED: July 24, 1584; Delft, Holland, United Provinces (now in the Netherlands)

ALSO KNOWN AS: Balthasar Gérards or Gérardts

MAJOR OFFENSE: Assassination of rebellion leader William the Silent

ACTIVE: July 10, 1584

LOCALE: Prinsenhof (home of William the Silent), Delft, Holland

SENTENCE: Death by quartering, disembowelment, heart extraction, and decapitation

EARLY LIFE

Balthasar Gérard (bahl-tah-zahr jay-rar) was born in Vuillafans, France, into a Roman Catholic family. He was one of eleven children. He studied law at the University of Dole. He greatly admired the king of Spain, Philip II. He also harbored an extreme dislike for William the Silent, who had been in the service of the Spanish court and the Catholic Church and then became the major leader of the Dutch rebellion against Spain. William the Silent was also a strong advocate of religious freedom and an ardent Calvinist who stood against Catholic suppression of religious freedom in the Lowlands. While a law student at Dole, Gérard often voiced his desire to sink a knife into William's heart.

CRIMINAL CAREER

Philip II, intent upon ridding himself of William the Silent, declared him an outlaw and offered a reward of twenty-five thousand crowns to whoever would kill him. Upon hearing of this ban in 1581, Gérard determined to go to Delft, Holland, and assassinate William. As part of his first plan, he joined the army of Peter, count of Mansfelt and governor of Luxembourg. However, his service in the army did not result in his having access to William, and he left the army in 1584. Next, he went to Treves, where he presented his plan to the Jesuits. They advised him to seek the support of the duke of Parma. Gérard then sought advice from Father Gery of Tournay. At first, the duke of Parma was uninterested in his plan; however, after consulting with his advisers, he decided to put Gérard in contact with Christoffel d'Assonville to implement the plan. In April, 1584, Gérard gave a document to d'Assonville detailing his plan.

In May of 1584, presenting himself as a French nobleman and fervent Calvinist whose father had died for the faith, Gérard obtained an audience with William. At this time, he gave William the seal of the count of Mansfelt, which would be of use to William in the forgery of messages. Thus, Gérard gained access to William on a somewhat regular basis. In July, he returned to Delft, arranged an appointment with William supposedly for a passport, and gained entrance to his house. As William was crossing from the dining room to his private apartments, Gérard fired three bullets into his chest. William died shortly thereafter. Gérard attempted to escape but stumbled and was captured by household servants.

LEGAL ACTION AND OUTCOME

Gérard underwent a brief interrogation at William's house and was then imprisoned. He endured three days of brutal torture before his trial on July 13, 1584. He was sentenced to death by the magistrates. The sentence ordered that he be quartered and disemboweled, have his heart removed, and be decapitated. The execution was carried out in the market square. Throughout the ordeal, Gérard reportedly remained calm. In lieu of the twenty-five thousand crowns, Philip II gave Gérard's parents three estates in the Franche Comté and elevated the family to the peerage.

IMPACT

Although Balthasar Gérard's assassination of William had little effect on the outcome of the Spanish/Dutch conflict, it is significant as an example of the intensity of the religious conflict that swept Europe during the sixteenth century and its close connection to the politics of the time. By assassinating William and declaring that he did it for Philip II, Gérard contributed to the reputation of Philip II as the foremost Catholic sovereign of the time.

Immediately after William the Silent's death, grief, fear, and despair overwhelmed the Dutch provinces. William had been considered the main defense against Spanish and Roman Catholic domination. Spain immediately set in motion diplomatic and military operations to regain the territories. However, under the leadership of Holland, the provinces continued to resist Spain. William's second son, Maurice, was called to head a state council and to continue his father's work.

Further Reading

Blom, J. C. H., and E. Lamberts, eds. *History of the Low Countries*. Translated by James C. Kennedy. New York: Berghahn Books, 1999. Treats both the political and religious history of the Dutch republic. Chapter 3, "The Formation of a Political Union: 1300-1600," deals with the contributions of William the Silent.

Kamen, Henry. *Philip, King of Spain*. New Haven, Conn.: Yale University Press, 1997. Biography of Philip II places his reign in the social, political, and religious atmosphere of the time and gives insights into why the assassination occurred. The chapters "The World of Philip" and "War in the West: 1580-1586" are most useful.

Lindberg, Carter. *The European Reformations*. Cambridge, Mass.: Blackwell Press, 1996. Thorough discussion of the reformations throughout Europe and their relationship to the political situation. Chapter 12 deals with the rise of Calvinism in the Netherlands and the Spanish reaction.

—*Shawncey Webb*

See also: John Bellingham; Jacques Clément; Charlotte Corday; Guy Fawkes; Jack Ketch; François Ravaillac; Miles Sindercombe.

Sam Giancana

Mafia leader

Born: June 15, 1908; Chicago, Illinois

Died: June 19, 1975; Oak Park, Illinois

Also known as: Salvatore Gilormo Giancana (full name); Mo; Momo; Mooney

Major offenses: Murder, extortion, burglary, producing and selling illegal alcohol, operation of illegal gambling, racketeering, and automobile theft

Active: 1925-1975

Locale: Chicago, Illinois

Sentence: Three years in prison for burglary; four years in prison for alcohol violations

Early Life

Sam Giancana (gee-ahn-KAH-nah) was born in Chicago's Little Italy section to a poor family. His mother died when he was two years old, and his father beat him regularly. At the age of ten, Sam was expelled from elementary school for misconduct and sent to a reformatory school. He eventually dropped out of school altogether and at the age of fifteen was living on the streets of Chicago's west side. He joined a violent street gang called the 42 Gang. The 42 Gang got its name from the children's story "Ali Baba and the Forty Thieves." Giancana gained the nickname "Mooney," a slang word for "crazy."

Criminal Career

Giancana developed a reputation for violence and unpredictability, and he was noticed by such Mafia members as Frank "The Enforcer" Nitti, Paul Ricca, and Tony Accardo, for whom he performed robberies and murders. Giancana was also considered an excellent getaway driver and became the "wheel man," or chauffeur, for Accardo, who was a major player on the Chicago crime scene.

While serving time for alcohol violations, Giancana became acquainted with an African American man by the name of Edward Jones from the South Side of Chicago. Jones told Giancana about a lucrative gambling operation, "running numbers." After his release from prison in 1942, Giancana kidnapped Jones and held him for ransom, thus taking over Jones's numbers running with the support of Accardo. In this way Giancana and Accardo gained control of the numbers racket in Chicago.

Giancana gradually gained control of a sizable portion of the labor racketeering, prostitution, and loan-sharking business in Chicago. In 1957, Accardo appointed Giancana to be a Mafia boss. At this time, Giancana moved his wife, Angeline, and his two daughters to Oak Park, a wealthy suburb of Chicago. Giancana eventually became the most senior Mafia figure in Chicago, with all organized crime activity approved solely by him.

Legal Action and Outcome

Law enforcement authorities were familiar with Giancana from the time he was young. At seventeen, Giancana was arrested for automobile theft and served thirty days in jail. At the age of eighteen, he was arrested twice for murder, although both charges were dropped. After another arrest, Giancana was released because a key witness for the prosecution was murdered. At the age of twenty-one, he served a three-year sentence in a Joliet prison for burglary and theft.

After his release from prison in 1931, Giancana joined his associates from the 42 Gang and began to produce and sell illegal alcohol. In 1939, he was again arrested on several alcohol violations and sentenced to four years in prison.

Sam Giancana, with singer Phyllis McGuire. (AP/Wide World Photos)

Because of constant harassment from the federal government, Giancana spent the last years of his life, from 1966 to 1975, in Mexico, paying Mexican officials for his protection. Eventually, Giancana was brought back to the United States and forced to testify before a grand jury about mob-related activities. Soon thereafter, on June 19, 1975, Giancana was murdered in his home at Oak Park when an assailant shot him seven times. Apparently, the organized crime leaders in Chicago feared that Giancana would provide damaging information to the grand jury in exchange for immunity.

Impact

Sam Giancana's reach extended beyond the mob. During the 1960 presidential election campaign, he struck a deal with Joseph Kennedy to deliver the state of Illinois for his son, John F. Kennedy, by controlling the Chicago wards and labor votes. In exchange, Joseph Kennedy promised Giancana that the federal government would curtail investigations into organized crime and that Giancana would be able to call on the White House for assistance. Some evidence also suggests that Giancana and fellow mobster Johnny Roselli worked with the Central Intelligence Agency during the Kennedy years on a plan to assassinate Cuban leader Fidel Castro.

The removal of Castro would have served both the interests of the U.S. government and the Mafia, who wanted to reopen the casinos in Havana, Cuba. Interestingly, Giancana and John F. Kennedy allegedly shared a girlfriend, Judith Campbell Exner; and J. Edgar Hoover, director of the Federal Bureau of Investigation, apparently used that information as leverage against Kennedy. U.S. attorney general Robert Kennedy, serving in his brother's administration, refused to stop the government's investigation of organized crime, thus angering Giancana, who felt double-crossed by the Kennedys.

Conspiracy theorists have argued that John Kennedy's affair with Giancana's mistress, as well as the federal government's harassment of Giancana, may have caused the Mafia to play a part in the assassinations of John F. Kennedy in 1963 and Robert Kennedy in 1968.

In 1978, the House Select Committee on Assassinations concluded that President Kennedy was probably assassinated as a result of a conspiracy and pointed to organized crime as having the means, motive, and opportunity to carry out the murder. In short, although the theory remains unsubstantiated, Giancana may have played a role in the election and assassination of a U.S. president.

Further Reading

Brashler, William. *The Don: The Life and Death of Sam Giancana*. New York: Harper & Row, 1977. Brashler focuses upon the rise and fall of Sam Giancana as a Mafia figure, but he also provides a history of organized crime in general.

Giancana, Antoinette, John R. Hughes, and Thomas H. Jobe. *JFK and Sam: The Connection Between the Giancana and Kennedy Assassinations*. Nashville, Tenn.: Cumberland House, 2005. The daughter of Sam Giancana documents the tale of two murders: the assassination of President John F. Kennedy ordered by Giancana and the assassination of Giancana by the Central Intelligence Agency to prevent him from testifying before a congressional committee about the role of the CIA in the plot to assassinate Fidel Castro.

Giancana, Antoinette, and Thomas C. Renner. *Mafia Princess: Growing Up in Sam Giancana's Family*. New York: Morrow, 1984. The daughter of Mafia chief Sam Giancana documents her life growing up in a family whose father controlled the city of Chicago in the 1950's and 1960's.

Giancana, Sam, and Chuck Giancana. *Double Cross: The Explosive, Inside Story of the Mobster Who Controlled America*. New York: Warner Books, 1993. The brother of Sam Giancana, Chuck Giancana, and his nephew Sam provide a profile of Sam Giancana's rise from a low-level hood to a Mafia leader with international influence who may have had a role in the assassination of President Kennedy.

—Scott P. Johnson

See also: Joe Adonis; Albert Anastasia; Paul Castellano; Vincent Coll; Joe Colombo; Judith Campbell Exner; Carmine Galante; Carlo Gambino; Vincent Gigante; John Gotti; Sammy Gravano; Henry Hill; J. Edgar Hoover; Richard Kuklinski; Meyer Lansky; Salvatore Maranzano; Carlos Marcello; Joe Masseria; Bugs Moran; Joseph Profaci; Arnold Rothstein; Dutch Schultz; Bugsy Siegel.

Vincent Gigante

American Mafia boss

Born: March 29, 1928; New York, New York
Died: December 19, 2005; Springfield, Missouri
Also known as: The Chin; the Oddfather; Gigs; Enigma in a Bathrobe
Major offenses: Narcotics trafficking, racketeering, and conspiracy to commit murder
Active: c. 1946-1997
Locale: New York, New York
Sentence: Seven years in prison for narcotics trafficking, of which he served five; twelve years in prison for conspiracy to commit murder, extortion, and racketeering

Early Life

Vincent Gigante (jih-GAN-tee) was born in 1928 in New York City to Salvatore and Yolanda Gigante, a watchmaker and a seamstress. His parents were Neapolitan by birth, and Vincent had four brothers. His nickname "the Chin" came from a shortened version of Cincenzo, an affectionate version of Vincent used by his mother. Gigante attended Manhattan's Textile High School but quit in ninth grade and became affiliated with crime boss Vito Genovese. He also boxed during this time period, winning twenty-one of his twenty-five bouts. Gigante eventually hung up his gloves and became a full-time member of Genovese's crew around 1946.

Criminal Career

Gigante was arrested several times as a young man but was convicted only of a gambling charge that resulted in a fine. His early notoriety stems from his alleged involvement in the attempted assassination of rival gangster Frank Costello in 1957. Genovese had ordered Costello's slaying to further his own power, and many observers believe that it was the three-hundred-pound Chin who followed the targeted victim to his apartment building and called out "This is for you, Frank," before firing at Costello's head. It might have been Gigante's words that saved Costello's life, causing him to turn his head enough so that the bullet grazed his head rather than delivering a killing shot. Gigante fled the scene, and Costello stuck to Omerta ("conspiracy of silence"), refusing to identify his assailant. Gigante was identified by another witness and tried for attempted murder, but the case against him fell apart when Gigante appeared in court—after a dramatic weight-loss campaign upstate—svelte and trim, nothing like the huge man originally sought for the murder attempt. Given the confusion over the Chin's physique and Costello's refusal to cooperate with the prosecution, Gigante was acquitted.

Gigante continued his work with the Genovese family and in 1959 found himself the target of a narcotics arrest, reportedly a frame-up engineered by rival gangsters Carlo Gambino, Costello, Lucky Luciano, and Meyer Lansky. Gigante and his boss, Genovese, were arrested after their enemies bribed a narcotics dealer to testify against them. Gigante received a seven-year sentence but was paroled after five years' imprisonment. Soon after his release he was promoted to capo, heading a crew in Greenwich Village.

The Oddfather

In 1966, when Gigante was being investigated for bribery charges, he began to develop his strategy of feigning mental illness to escape the law. He began a three-decade practice of checking himself into psychiatric treatment centers and thereby avoiding prosecution by being declared mentally incompetent for trial. He produced doctors at his 1969 bribery trial to testify that he was schizophrenic, psychotic, and afflicted with numerous other mental defects. The defense worked, hence Gigante's moniker "the Oddfather." Reports of his demented behavior abounded, even as the power of the Genovese family grew.

Authorities tried to prosecute Gigante for years, but the Chin proved to be an elusive target. In 1987, Gigante was named acting boss of the Genovese family after Fat Tony Salerno was convicted. By then Gigante was wandering the Greenwich Village streets in a bathrobe and muttering incoherently, bolstering his reputation for mental illness. Mentally competent or not, Gigante led the Genovese family to dominate the New York organized crime scene by the 1990's.

Legal Action and Outcome

Gigante was convicted of narcotics trafficking in 1959 and was sentenced to seven years; he was paroled after five years' imprisonment. He was indicted for racketeering and murder in both 1990 and 1993, both times avoiding trial because he was declared incompetent. Finally in 1997, prosecutors overcame Gigante's tactics, and he was convicted of conspiracy to commit murder, extortion, and racketeering. Convicted on fourteen counts of murder conspiracy and racketeering, he was sentenced to twelve years in federal prison, where some believe he continued to direct the Genovese criminal enterprises. Gigante died in prison in December, 2005.

Impact

The fact that Vincent Gigante succeeded in evading prosecution for so long made him a compelling figure and the object of public speculation. Gigante's tactics of feigning insanity not only marked him as a colorful character but also highlighted legal issues surrounding the insanity defense. One episode of the television crime-drama series *Law and Order* featured a character based on Gigante. The issues of competence to stand trial and the insanity defense continue to resonate within the criminal justice and public sectors. In 2003, Gigante himself stated in court that his insanity was a ruse, but his attorneys refused to concede the point.

Further Reading

Capeci, Jerry. *Jerry Capeci's Gang Land*. New York: Alpha Books, 2003. A compilation of *New York Daily News* columns by journalist and Mafia expert Capeci covering organized crime activity in New York City from 1989 through 1995.

Raab, Selwyn. *Five Families: The Rise, Decline, and Resurgence of America's Most Powerful Mafia Empires*. New York: St. Martin's Press, 2005. Recounts the history of the New York crime families; spotlights major figures and events of organized crime in New York.

Talese, Gay. *Honor Thy Father*. New York: World, 1971. Covers reign of Mafia boss Joe Bonanno.

—David R. Champion

See also: Joe Adonis; Albert Anastasia; Vincent Coll; Joe Colombo; Frank Costello; Carmine Galante; Carlo Gambino; Vito Genovese; Sam Giancana; John Gotti; Sammy Gravano; Henry Hill; Richard Kuklinski; Meyer Lansky; Lucky Luciano; Salvatore Maranzano.

Mildred Gillars

American broadcaster and propagandist

Born: November 29, 1900; Portland, Maine
Died: June 25, 1988; Columbus, Ohio
Also known as: Axis Sally; Mildred Elizabeth Sisk (birth name)
Major offense: Treason
Active: May 18, 1943
Locale: Paris
Sentence: Ten to thirty years' imprisonment; served twelve years

Early Life

Mildred Gillars (GIHL-lahrz) was born to Mary and Vincent Sisk in Portland, Maine. She may have been physically abused by her birth father. After a divorce, her mother married Robert Gillars, and the family moved to Conneaut, Ohio. Mildred Gillars briefly attended Ohio Wesleyan University. She also attended Hunter College, where she met Max Otto Koischwitz, a professor of German literature. They began an affair. Unknown to Gillars, he was married at the time.

Radio Career

Gillars was an aspiring actress. Her career from 1926 (when she dropped out of college) to 1940 (when she began working for Radio Berlin) was both colorful and dismal. She auditioned for parts in New York; she made an unsuccessful film, also in New York; she was arrested twice while attempting to promote the film; and she traveled to Algiers with a male friend who was attempting to convince his rich aunt that he was not gay. In North Africa, she worked as a columnist. Moving between the United States and Algiers in the 1930's, she performed in plays and returned to her family in tough times.

In the 1930's she moved between Paris and Berlin, perhaps in an attempt to continue her relationship with Koischwitz. By 1940 he had become a major participant in the German radio propaganda network called the Radiorundfunk. In 1940, Gillars moved to Berlin and accepted a position with Radio Berlin, broadcasting American music and expatriate news. As "Midge at the Mike," she aired Nazi propaganda. During 1940 the American embassy seized her passport, and in 1941 she signed an oath of allegiance to Germany. Whether this was done freely or under duress is a matter of debate.

At Radio Berlin, Gillars worked with the leading members of the propaganda effort for Hitler's Germany. These included Koischwitz, William Joyce (known as Lord Haw Haw), Fred Kaltenbach, and later Robert Best. With each escalation of the war, Midge added new features to her programming. To her news reports and popular tunes, she added "free interviews" with American prisoners of war. To get these interviews, she posed falsely as a Red Cross representative. During the 1940's she was reviewed by the American press as a mix of Mae West and Marlene Dietrich. At the same time, however, German intelligence felt that her sultry voice was recognized by nine out of ten American soldiers in the European theater, who dubbed her "Axis Sally."

The Invasion Broadcast

After a 1943 visit to the German fortifications in Normandy, France, Gillars began work on a project to show

Mildred Gillars. (AP/Wide World Photos)

American military personnel a vision of the outcome of an invasion. At her trial, she would claim that her goal was to delay the invasion until the internal collapse of Germany became apparent to the Allies. However, this broadcast, written by Koischwitz and produced by Horst Cleinow, and like the earlier programs of "Midge at the Mike," called for American troops to lay down their arms and go home. The broadcast, in which Gillars played a mother who dreamed the bloody death of her son on the beaches of Normandy, was an unusually powerful piece of World War II propaganda. It was broadcast from the Nazi studios in Paris and replayed frequently in Europe, Britain, and the United States.

Legal Action and Outcome

In July of 1943, a U.S. federal grand jury indicted in absentia a number of Radio Berlin personalities charged with treason. Gillars was not among those so charged. Captured in Berlin, she was moved to Frankfurt and then to the United States to stand trial.

After being held without charges for two and a half years, Gillars was charged in the summer of 1948 with giving aid and comfort to the enemy. Tried on eight counts of treason, she was found guilty of only one, the 1943 broadcast of the mother's dream piece. Sentenced to ten to thirty years in prison, Gillars was paroled after twelve years. Whereas German propagandist announcer William Joyce was hanged in his native Britain for treason after the war, Gillars died of natural causes at the age of eighty-seven.

Impact

Adolf Hilter's radio propaganda was extremely successful. The work of Radio Berlin and other Reichsrundfunk bureaus aided the Nazi cause, and Nazi propaganda was perceived by Britain and the United States as a key ingredient in the collapse of France. This success impelled the Allies to follow suit. Both Britain and the United States established clandestine radio identities which, for the following forty years, broadcast throughout Europe, South America, Africa, and Asia. In 1941, this effort began in the United States as the Office of Foreign Information Services. It continued as the Voice of America.

Further Reading

Doherty, M. A. *Nazi Wireless Propaganda: Lord Haw-Haw and British Public Opinion in the Second World War.* Edinburgh: Edinburgh University Press, 2000. A scholarly study of the range and extent of Nazi radio propaganda against the United Kingdom as well as its response in Britain. The book contains a CD of twenty-four broadcasts from Germany to Britain.

Edwards, John Carver. *Berlin Calling: American Broadcasters in Service to the Third Reich.* New York: Praeger, 1991. A study of characters who served in the Nazi U.S.A. Zone. Gillars is not specifically examined; however, the lengthy chapter dedicated to Koischwitz includes much information about Gillars's work for Radio Berlin. In his epilogue, author Edwards questions the motives behind the U.S. prosecution of Americans broadcasting from Hitler's Germany.

Fuller, M. Williams. *Axis Sally: The Most Listened-to Woman of World War II.* Santa Barbara, Calif.: Paradise West, 2004. A fictionalized account of the life and career of Mildred Gillars. Readable and dramatic, the book presents a version of the events which is difficult to assess. Fuller appears to defend Gillars, accepting arguments made at her trial that she was "mesmerized" by her lover Koischwitz and coerced into working for Radio Berlin.

Soley, Lawrence C. *Radio Warfare: OSS and CIA Subversive Propaganda.* New York: Praeger, 1989. Soley examines the initiation and development of U.S. propaganda using airwaves from the period of World War II though the Cold War.

—Jean Owens Schaefer

See also: Adolf Hitler; William Joyce; Tokyo Rose.

Gary Gilmore

American murderer

Born: December 4, 1940; McCamey, Texas
Died: January 17, 1977; Utah State Prison, Salt Lake City, Utah
Also known as: Faye Robert Coffman; Gary Mark Gilmore (full name)
Major offenses: Robbery and murder
Active: July, 1976
Locale: Provo, Utah
Sentence: Death

Early Life

When one considers the childhood of Gary Gilmore (GIHL-mohr), it is not surprising that he was to become a career criminal and a remorseless, violent murderer. His father, Frank Gilmore, Sr., was an alcoholic and petty con man who routinely abused young Gary and his siblings and ran from the law for most of their childhood. He forced the family to live under a fabricated surname, Coffman, and routinely shuffled them from town to town throughout the American West, often only a step ahead of the authorities.

By the time he was fifteen, family turmoil had taken its toll on Gilmore. He dropped out of school and within a year was an experienced car thief. His rowdiness and lack of respect for authority eventually landed him in Oregon's MacLaren Reform School for Boys. A second robbery charge shortly thereafter resulted in a conviction and imprisonment in the Oregon State Penitentiary.

Criminal Career

By age thirty-five, Gilmore had spent more than half of his life behind bars. Released from his first prison stay in 1962, he promptly committed another robbery and returned to prison. Notoriously uncooperative with staff and belligerent toward other inmates, Gilmore spent much of the next ten years in solitary confinement. He was even treated with Prolixin, a strong antipsychotic drug intended to curb his antisocial tendencies. However, Gilmore claimed that the drug caused him to be depressed and suicidal, and treatment was halted. His time in solitary confinement, however, allowed him ample opportunity to develop his high IQ and cultivate a talent for art. These steps toward rehabilitation earned him early release in 1972 on the provision that he enroll in community college and live in a halfway house in Provo, Utah. Gilmore obtained work in an uncle's shoe shop and a few occasional construction jobs. His family thought this would keep Gilmore out of trouble, but he remained unusually agitated and compulsive.

Despite his family's efforts to help Gilmore readjust to life outside prison, his inherent restlessness and disdain for the law led to tragic consequences in the summer of 1976. Gilmore bought an expensive pickup truck on an impulse, but he could not afford the payments. Then, after his breakup with girlfriend Nicole Barrett, an emotionally distraught Gilmore proceeded to rob a Provo gas station in a convoluted attempt to get the money both to pay off his truck and to lash out at Barrett. The robbery resulted in the point-blank shooting and murder of attendant Max Jensen.

The next morning, Gilmore was still on the run but was having mechanical problems with his truck, which he dropped off at a garage. He robbed the nearby City Center Motel while waiting for the repairs to be finished. During the robbery, he shot and killed motel manager Ben Bushnell and accidentally shot himself in the hand while fleeing. He returned to the garage for his truck, and the mechanic, noticing his suspicious wound, reported Gilmore's license number to local police. Gilmore was quickly apprehended and charged with both murders.

Legal Action and Outcome

Gilmore's trial lasted only two days. A mountain of physical evidence and the testimony of witnesses linking him directly to the killings prompted jurors to convict Gilmore of first-degree murder after only an hour and a half of deliberation. During the penalty phase of the trial, state prosecutor Noall Wootton sought the death penalty, claiming that the gruesome and arbitrary nature of the killings, combined with Gilmore's extensive criminal record, rendered him incapable of rehabilitation. Gilmore refused to testify on his own behalf during the trial or demonstrate remorse for the crimes during the penalty phase. He was sentenced to death.

Utah had not executed anyone since 1958. In fact, the state's laws regarding the practice remained unusually archaic. One particularly outmoded provision allowed the condemned a choice of execution method—hanging or firing squad. However, Utah had disassembled its gallows and possessed no facility in which an execution by firing squad could officially be conducted. Since Gilmore chose the firing squad, his original execution date of November 15, 1976, was postponed. In the interim, a number of entities, including the American Civil Liberties Union, offered to appeal on his behalf. Gilmore adamantly refused all attempts to prolong his ordeal and was shot to death in a converted cannery at the Utah State Prison on January 17, 1977.

Impact

Gilmore's execution—the first death sentence to be carried out after the Supreme Court's four-year moratorium on capital punishment—is generally regarded to have ushered in a return to the legitimization of capital punishment in the United States. In 1972's landmark case *Furman v. Georgia*, the U.S. Supreme Court declared unconstitutional capital punishment as then administered in the United States. A series of later revisions to state laws related to execution, however, paved the way for a lift on the ban in 1976. Gilmore made worldwide headlines by refusing all appeals and demanding that his sentence be carried out as soon as possible.

Gilmore and the Golden Gloves Girl

"I'm not a nice person. I don't want to cause any more harm. I've harmed too many people and by doing so I've harmed my own soul," Gary Gilmore wrote in 1976 to Amber Edwina Hunt, nicknamed Amber Jim. The eleven-year-old girl had written him to find out why he insisted upon being executed. She thought he might be lonely, and this touched Gilmore. Through the next two months, the two exchanged more letters; their friendship deepened.

Amber Jim was a fifth-grader living in Murray, Utah, the daughter of a janitor. She was a tough girl, too—a sixty-five-pound Golden Gloves boxer who regularly beat boys her own age. When Gilmore learned that she was a boxer, he offered to sponsor her. He sent her two hundred dollars and had a relative of his buy her an eight-millimeter movie camera so that she could film her bouts. His favorite fighter was Rocky Marciano, hers Muhammad Ali, they told each other. She asked about his favorite animal, and he wrote back (quoting William Blake's famous poem), "Tiger, tiger burning bright/ In the forests of the night. . . ." He told her of his favorite musicians—Hank Williams and Johnny Cash—and that he felt close to Native Americans: "Indians like me."

Their friendship was strictly via letters. Prison authorities refused Amber Jim's request to visit Gilmore. He sent her a morose poem of his own about his approaching death, but for the most part his letters contained encouragements: "Amber Jim I believe you are a natural-born winner. You're unique"; "you're the most fantastic little girl I've ever heard of. You have the makings, the heart of a true champion." He had a bank account set up for her and altogether gave some twelve hundred dollars in money and gifts, including a bicycle and a book about Ali. "I will always love you honey. You're a beautiful little girl. . . . Knock 'em all out. For me. Hugs and kisses," he wrote two days before he died. When Amber Jim learned of his execution, she wept.

Source: Time magazine, January 31, 1977.

Further Reading

Gilmore, Mikal. *Shot in the Heart*. New York: Doubleday, 1994. Written by Gilmore's younger brother, this nonfiction work not only focuses on many of the same events as Mailer's book but also seeks to probe into the psychological legacy that contributed to the misfortunes of Gilmore and other family members.

Mailer, Norman. *The Executioner's Song*. Boston: Little, Brown, 1979. A "nonfiction novel" recounting of the events leading up to Gilmore's conviction and execution for capital murder, constructed from interviews and documents relevant to the case. Won the 1980 Pulitzer Prize for fiction.

Philips, Tom. "The Revival of the American Death Penalty." In *Death Penalty*, edited by Hayley R. Mitchell. San Diego: Greenhaven Press, 2001. Discusses the influence of Gilmore's execution in fostering the growing use of capital punishment in the United States.

—*Gregory D. Horn*

See also: Velma Margie Barfield; Andrew Cunanan; Ruth Ellis; Karla Faye Tucker.

TAKOMA PARK MD LIBRARY
3 9803 10037282 2